# Economic Growth
## and the Ending of the
# Transatlantic
# Slave Trade

David Eltis

# Economic Growth and the Ending of the Transatlantic Slave Trade

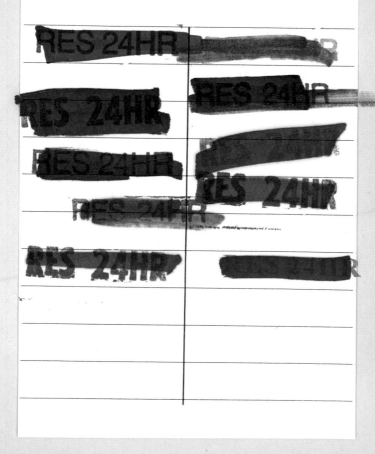

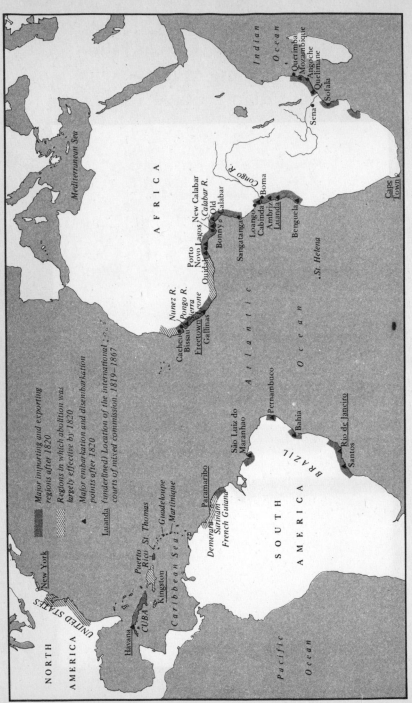

Regions Involved in the Transatlantic Slave Trade After 1820

# Economic Growth and the Ending of the Transatlantic Slave Trade

David Eltis

OXFORD UNIVERSITY PRESS
New York      Oxford

Oxford University Press

Oxford   New York   Toronto
Delhi   Bombay   Calcutta   Madras   Karachi
Petaling Jaya   Singapore   Hong Kong   Tokyo
Nairobi   Dar es Salaam   Cape Town
Melbourne   Auckland

and associated companies in
Berlin   Ibadan

Library of Congress Cataloging-in-Publication Data

Eltis, David, 1940-
Economic growth and the ending of the transatlantic
slave trade.

Bibliography: p.
Includes index.
1. Slave-trade—Great Britain.   2. Slave-trade—
Africa.   3. Slave-trade—America.   4. Slavery in Great Britain—Anti-slavery move-
ments.   I. Title.
HT1162.E48   1987      382′.44      86-8338
ISBN 0-19-504135-6
ISBN 0-19-504563-7 (PBK.)

2   4   6   8   10   9   7   5   3   1

Printed in the United States of America

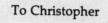
To Christopher

# Acknowledgments

The preparation of this work was greatly assisted by five separate research grants from the Social Sciences and Humanities Research Council and the Canada Council. The Economic History Association and the University of Rochester also contributed grants-in-aid. The Henry E. Huntington Library, San Marino, California, provided a fellowship that made possible an extended visit to this institution. The completion of the volume was facilitated by a Social Sciences and Humanities Research Council research-time stipend and a period of sabbatical leave from Algonquin College.

Any work that attempts to cover long-run economic and ideological developments on four continents is inevitably dependent on others more expert than the author. Among those who have given me the benefit of their ideas and corrected errors of fact and interpretation are Luiz-Felipe de Alencastro, the late Roger T. Anstey, Gervaise Clarence-Smith, Philip D. Curtin, Serge Daget, Seymour Drescher, Robert Goheen, Barry W. Higman, Lawrence C. Jennings, Marion Johnson, Paul E. Lovejoy, Patrick Manning, Phyllis Martin, Joseph C. Miller, David R. Murray, Stuart Schwarz, and Mary Turner, all of whom read parts of this work in typescript. Seymour Drescher read the complete manuscript and provided lively and detailed commentary. Mary Turner bears the major responsibility for first turning my thoughts toward this topic. Philip D. Curtin, Serge Daget, Adam Jones, Herbert S. Klein, Joseph C. Miller and David Northrup generously supplied data—some ready for processing—that saved months of work. An exchange of commentary and references with Robert Paquette, stretching back to graduate-school days, has proved particularly valuable. The latter's knowledge of nineteenth-century Cuba has proved a constant source of comfort. Special mention must be made of Stanley L. Engerman. It has become increasingly difficult in the last decade to pick up a work on U.S. economic history or slavery in the Americas without seeing his name singled out in the acknowledgments for special thanks. Whatever is new in the present volume, omission of this step cannot be counted as part of it. As a fund of references and a source of rapid and constructive criticism, Stanley L. Engerman has already become a legend among scholars of all viewpoints. He read the current work in its original, unwieldy entirety, and his painstaking comments strengthened both the thrust of the argument and the supporting detail. This was in addition to the hospitality which he and his wife, Judy, provided on innumerable occasions.

Sections of this work were presented at the Mathematical Social Science Board conference on the economic history of the slave trade at Colby College, Maine, in 1975; the symposium on the slave trade at Aarhus University, Denmark, in 1978; the African Studies Association meetings in Baltimore in 1978 and Bloomington, Indiana, in 1981; the Economic History Association meetings in Washington, D.C., in 1984; the Colloque International on the slave trade in Nantes, France, in 1985; the Organization of American Historians meetings in New York and the Economic History Workshop at the University of the West Indies in Mona, Jamaica, both in 1986. I am grateful to Henry A. Gemery, Jan S. Hogendorn, Svend E. Green-Pedersen, Serge Daget and Barry W. Higman for giving me access to the international gatherings at Colby, Aarhus, Nantes and Mona, Jamaica.

Among the librarians who made this work possible, I would particularly like to mention Brad Smith at the University of Rochester and Femmy Birks and Madeleine Jennings at Algonquin College. Other librarians who assisted greatly include those at the Bodleian and Rhodes House libraries in Oxford; the British Museum; the British Public Record Office; Carleton University; the Henry E. Huntington Library, San Marino, California; the Institute of Historical Research, London; the Library of Parliament, Ottawa; the Liverpool Public Library; the National Library of Canada; the Schomburg Center for Research in Black Culture in Harlem, New York; the University of Alberta, Edmonton; and the University of Waterloo. Visits to the British institutions in this list were greatly assisted through the hospitality provided by Gordon and Marietta Dodds, Paul King, St. Antony's College, University of Oxford (through the auspices of Patrick O'Brien) and Mary Turner. The programming skills of Terry O'Brien and the remarkable word-processing abilities of Lenore Buness and Angela Romeo were no less important. Charles Reid assisted with some of the figures. Finally, there is my family, particularly my wife, Suzan, whose support, both practical and emotional, was the foundation of this project.

Parts of chapter 9 and appendix E of this work first appeared in this author's Ph.D. dissertation, "The Transatlantic Slave Trade, 1821–43" (University of Rochester, 1979). Some paragraphs in chapter 8 appeared in David Eltis and James Walvin (eds.), *The Abolition of the Atlantic Slave Trade* (University of Wisconsin Press, Madison, Wis., 1981). Tables A.1 to A.4 and part of table A.8 first appeared in *The Hispanic American Historical Review*, vol. 66 (Jan 1987), published by Duke University Press. I wish to thank the publishers for permission to reprint this material.

# Contents

# Tables

# Figures

# I

# Antislavery in the Context of British Expansion and Industrialization

# 1

# Capitalism and Abolition in Britain: Some Scenarios

In the course of the last half century, the relationship between coercion and economic growth has become one of the more explored themes in Western historiography. Its significance goes far beyond the examination of the process of economic growth. It has generated major new work in areas as diverse as intellectual history and historical demography, as well as on questions of class relations, European expansion, exchanges between the developed and less developed world and interracial tensions within those societies. It is the importance of these broad themes that accounts for the controversy that has surrounded the publication of major new statements on the central issue. At the root of many of the debates and the powerful new insights that have emerged from them have been differing conceptions of the role of economics and of ideology. The main subject of the following pages is the role of the slave trade in the nineteenth-century Atlantic economy, but no adequate assessment can ignore the systems of beliefs with which the economic environment inevitably interacts. As the British were in the forefront of economic development, it is natural to begin the study with an examination of their experience with this traffic. But the underlying questions in most of this work are how important was the nineteenth-century slave trade and why did it come to an end.

In 1788 the British Parliament had yet to vote on the issue of abolition of the slave trade, the great petitioning campaign against such traffic was just beginning and the volume of slaves carried by British ships was approaching an all-time high. In that year a British member of Parliament published, or rather reissued, a pamphlet justifying the traffic as well as Negro slavery, not least on economic grounds. Among the reviews it received was a brief notice by Arthur Young in the *Annals of Agriculture:* "To offer any remarks on such [a] position in this kingdom, and towards the close of the eighteenth century, would be paying a very poor compliment to the understanding of my readers." For thousands of years slavery and the slave trade had been not only univer-

3

sally accepted but regarded as compatible with economic progress. Yet the editor of a journal devoted to agricultural improvement in an economically advanced country could assume that his readership would make just the opposite associations. Among practicing Christians there were analogous developments as Christianity and even the Bible came to be viewed as incompatible with coerced labor, despite the long accommodation that all Christian churches had made with the institution of slavery.[1]

Britain was the most successful nation in the modern world in establishing slave-labor colonies overseas. It was also the first to industrialize as well as the first of the major powers to renounce coerced labor in principle and practice. These two developments, industrialization and abolition, evolved more or less simultaneously in the late eighteenth century. But this was only after a century during which the exploitation of Africans in the New World had become the foundation stone of the British Atlantic economy. Indeed the British about face on the issue of coerced labor could be almost described as instantaneous in historic terms. By the early nineteenth century they had become so convinced of its immorality and economic inefficiency that they were running an expensive one-nation campaign to suppress the international slave trade. They went on to free three quarters of a million of their own slaves. Throughout this process their economy underwent major structural change and, of course, continued to expand strongly.

Attempts to make sense of these events and explore what (if any) connection there was between them have preoccupied scholars from a wide range of disciplines and interests since the publication of the work of two West Indians, C. L. R. James and Eric Williams, almost half a century ago.[2] For such writers, in particular future prime minister Williams of Trinidad and Tobago, the connection was unequivocal. The slave trade and the slave colonies, especially the British West Indies, provided a significant share of the markets as well as the capital that made British economic development possible. By the late eighteenth century, however, the British slave system was in decline. Soil exhaustion, competition from the French West Indies and the interruption of the trade in staples—stemming from the independence of most of the British North American colonies—all severely reduced the importance of the English-speaking Caribbean to the British economy. At the same time the British manufacturing sector had grown to the point where it required more markets than the slave colonies could provide and, in addition, was no longer dependent on profits from the slave system for its capital needs. The British attack on coerced labor could thus be seen as the first stage of an assault on the trade barriers that reserved the British sugar markets for British plantations and restricted trade with the rest of the world. "The capitalists had first encouraged West Indian slavery and then helped to destroy it" in Williams's succinct and oft-quoted phrase. The West Indies had become a hurdle between the British manufacturer and world markets. Abolition was as vital an aid to the removal of that hurdle as the slave system had once been to the creation and support of British manufacturing.

This is not the place to review the debates on this position. In the Third World, however, this view has become part of the orthodox interpretation of *triangular trade*

the rise of Western economic power. The quantitative underpinnings of Williams's view are insecure, nevertheless. For Britain, as indeed for all European countries, the domestic market and domestic factor inputs probably outweighed external influences over economic development. Recent work suggests that neither overseas nor domestic demand alone can be given major roles in the expansion process. And on the supply side, capital deepening encouraged by profit inflows from overseas does not seem by itself to have been of the requisite large magnitude. Increased factor productivity is the focus of current research into the origin of the industrialization process, but it is unlikely that overseas possessions could have had an impact here.[3] The initial crops of such regions, sugar, tobacco and coffee, were not raw materials for industry, though sugar did require some processing. Moreover, it now appears that the British slave system was not in permanent decline in the late eighteenth century. The Caribbean islands certainly experienced lower returns during and after the American War of Independence, and the increased incidence of destructive hurricanes in these decades also lowered returns. But the long-run economic data testify to the continuing vitality of the British West Indies well into the nineteenth century. Such a conclusion holds whether the measurement is for the value of the West Indies in absolute terms or their value relative to the overall British economy. For, as Seymour Drescher shows, the value of the slave trade and the slave colonies to Britain had never been greater, neither had the prospects for their future growth been brighter when the British Parliament severed the umbilical link with Africa in 1807.[4]

By the first decade of the nineteenth century, revolution in St. Domingue (later Haiti), military conquests and naval control of the world's trade routes had put the British in control of regions that produced over half of the world's plantation exports. Jamaica had much unsettled land, some of which was brought into cultivation when the drive for black freedom greatly reduced the contribution of St. Domingue to world markets. More important, there were huge additions to the British West Indian possessions during the French wars. Patrick Colquhoun's inventory indicates that unoccupied arable areas of Trinidad and Demerara (later British Guiana, then Guyana) were more extensive than all the existing cultivated land in the rest of the British West Indies put together. To George Canning in 1802, Trinidad's potential alone was only slightly below that of Jamaica and this was at a time when their slave populations were 10,000 and 307,000, respectively. With only a small part of its available land developed, Demerara had already become the major source of raw cotton for British industry within a few years of falling into British hands. Cotton, moreover, was a commodity that few of the older British colonies produced in significant quantities. The new areas lacked only labor at the outset of the nineteenth century. But with over 50 percent of the slave trade in British hands and with little prospect of these territories being returned, this was surely a need that would not remain long unfilled.[5]

Figure 1 charts the position of the British at the pinnacle of plantation power and the gradual erosion of that position. In the first decade of the nineteenth century, regions under British control produced at various times 60 percent of the world's sugar exports and probably 50 percent of all coffee. In addition, in

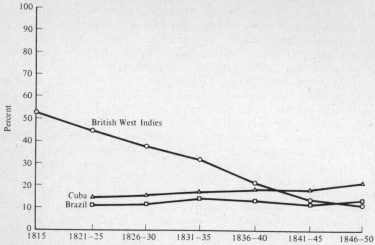

**Figure 1.** Distribution of world sugar exports by region of production: Five-year means, 1815–50.

*Note:* The Brazilian data are for exports of mainly white clayed sugar and have been increased by 20 percent to allow for Brazilian domestic consumption. The British data are for imports into Great Britain from the British West Indies and are mainly muscovado sugar. The Cuban and world data are estimates of production of white clayed sugar. For the reconciliation of the British and Cuban data, see n. 17. It should be noted that world shares of sugar production from all British regions (including Mauritius and East India) fell more slowly than the British West Indies share.

*Sources:* Calculated from Seymour Drescher, *Econocide: British Slavery in the Era of Abolition* (Pittsburgh, Pa., 1977), p. 177; PP, 1856, 55:589; and 1863, 47:299; Manuel Moreno Fraginals, *El ingenio, complejo económico social cubano del azúcar,* 3 vols. (Havana, 1978), 3:35–36; Instituto Brasileiro de geografia e estatística, *Anuário estatístico do Brasil,* Ano V–1939–40, p. 1374.

1796–1800 these same areas produced almost 40 percent of the raw cotton imported into Britain. It is very likely that similarly dominant proportions held for the minor plantation crops. Not until the demise of British slavery itself (not the British slave trade) did either Cuba or Brazil threaten the British leadership in the production of sugar and coffee.[6] Revolution and war between 1789 and 1815 thus helped the British to dominate the world's plantation regions to a greater extent than had happened before or was to happen again. Indeed the world's proportion of plantation produce in British hands almost certainly exceeded the British share of world-manufactured output half a century later when the industrial gap between Britain and the rest of the world was at its greatest. In 1800, if one were to argue in terms of economic self-interest, the British should have been actively encouraging the slave trade and slave settlements throughout the world. Such a policy would have been highly effective in achieving national goals as laid down by the amalgam of London merchants and landed gentry who dominated the British government at this time. It would also have best served the material aims of manufacturers and wage earners alike.

I

From the viewpoint of economic self-interest, British antislavery policy appears wrongheaded enough to qualify for inclusion in Barbara Tuchman's catalog of folly in government.[7] It is certainly worth asking whether or not British suppression of the slave trade was inevitable. For many historians, viewing events against the backdrop of an increasingly popular antislavery ideology, perhaps it was. But from the standpoint of those living at the time, there was no such certainty. The British government might have adopted a wide variety of policy options even after the point at which they abolished their own slave trade. British antislave-trade policy comprised a range of legislation and directives, of which the 1807 act is simply the best known. Among the long list of additional and separate steps were the regulations on the traffic in slaves between their own possessions in the Caribbean and the pursuit of non-British slave traders sailing to foreign territories. Policies on these issues were not generally forged in the arena of public debate and appear to have lacked any irresistible economic imperatives. To highlight the set of decisions that the British implemented, it might be useful to explore the probable consequences of some alternative strategies that they could have adopted toward the issue of forced labor in the early nineteenth century. Instead of espousing a comprehensive policy of abolition of the slave trade, there were at least three other scenarios that, from the economic and diplomatic viewpoints, would have been easier and more rewarding. We shall examine in turn the likely results of a British laissez-faire attitude to first the foreign slave trade, second their own intercolonial trade and third the British transatlantic slave trade.

### The Campaign Against the Foreign Slave Trade

In 1831, shortly after assuming office as part of the new Whig government, the head of the Admiralty asked his counterpart at the Foreign Office, "Wherein consists the necessity of a squadron on this [West African] station? The prevention of the Slave Trade is its only employment; and does it effect its object? it does not." The squadron and the accompanying diplomatic campaign were, of course, retained even though both were directed exclusively against non-British participation in the slave trade. Questioning of the British campaign, nevertheless, continued both inside and outside official circles and rose to a peak in the 1840s when a motion to recall the cruisers narrowly failed to pass the House of Commons. At least some of the benefits of thus abandoning the international campaign against the slave traffic were clear to contemporaries. The potential rewards for never undertaking the campaign in the first place would have been even more considerable. Between 1816 and 1862 British expenditures on the cruiser squadron, treaty payments to foreign governments, compensations for wrongful arrest, the courts of mixed commission and other elements of the antislave-trade structure were very high. Few historians have tried to assess the economic significance of antislave-trade expenditures particularly for the years when the framework of this structure was being established.

The gains from suspension of the British pursuit of the foreign slave trade do not stop here, however. Without these expenditures the volume of slaves carried across the Atlantic would have been greater if we exclude the naval campaign, and greater again if we exclude diplomatic efforts as well. In the absence of suppression, prices of slaves would have been significantly lower.[8]

Cheaper slaves in foreign plantations would have meant little for British consumers of plantation produce. Given the protected British market, it seems likely that foreign sugar would have driven British sugar out of Continental markets somewhat before it did in 1832. Produce prices in England would have been slightly lower. For British export industries the gains would have been more significant. A larger demand from Brazil and Cuba for British goods would have been likely, with part of this demand being for trading cargoes to be exchanged for slaves in Africa. The merchant and manufacturer support for the anticoercionist movement of the 1840s amply demonstrates this last point. Other benefits would have accrued to sugar refiners and palm oil traders among others. Although the sum total of such gains in national income terms would not have been large,[9] the direction of the effect is clear and the costs of achieving these gains however calculated, negligible. Indeed in the absence of cruisers operating on the fringe of international law, British foreign policy would have been much easier to conduct. The international prestige that the British garnered from suppressing their own trade would not have been affected by such a hands-off policy.

## The Suppression of the Intercolonial Trade

In the larger plantation societies in the Americas, where unsettled land existed as the Atlantic slave trade ended, a large internal traffic in slaves quickly developed. In the United States between 1810 and 1860, nearly nine hundred thousand slaves were sold from the old to the new South. In Brazil in the thirty years after final suppression of the Atlantic trade, the annual rate of slave migration into the south and south-center of that country was the same as in the United States.[10] Within the British Caribbean at the start of the century, Trinidad and Demerara were the equivalents of Mississippi and Alabama in the United States and the Upper Paraíba Valley in Brazil. The British government—and we might add British planters, too—were fully aware of the potential of the frontier colonies. There was a strong desire on the part of owners in the long-settled areas to move to the newly acquired regions. In fact, the British suppressed the inter-island trade almost as effectively as they suppressed their own transatlantic traffic.[11] Between 1807 and emancipation in 1834 the annual rate of slaves traded between the British islands was only one-ninth the equivalent rate in the United States and Brazil. It would have been much easier, in fact, for the British to permit the full development of an intercolonial trade than it was to prevent it.

The probable consequences of such a laissez-faire policy seem clear in the light of the subsequent U.S. and Brazilian experience. The British would have facilitated a major population shift to the land-abundant regions of Trinidad and Demerara. It is, moreover, unlikely that such action would have produced any of the moral opprobrium, at least on the international scene, that would have been incurred by a full-scale reopening of the slave traffic to Africa. In the 1820s output per slave was three or four times greater in Demerara and Trinidad than in Barbados, Dominica or Jamaica, and slave price differentials were rather similar.[12] These differences are most striking and point to the effective segmentation of the intercolonial market for slaves after 1807. A free market in slaves between 1807 and 1833 would have seen slave owners in the low-productivity colonies sell their slaves or, more likely, move with their slaves to the more productive regions. The effect of this would have been to move both output-per-slave-ratios and prices closer to equality.[13] Eventually differences in slave prices among the colonies would have primarily reflected the costs of moving from one colony to the other.[14] Aggregate production of plantation produce in the British West Indies would have increased substantially as slaves from the Bahamas, Bermuda, Anguilla, Dominica, Barbados and probably Jamaica, too, shifted south. Sugar production would have increased by perhaps fifty thousand tons of sugar per year, an increase of 24 percent over the actual annual output in the years 1824–33.[15] It is quite probable that slaves moving to Trinidad and Demerara would have increased output by an even greater amount than this.[16]

A 24 percent increment may not appear to be a massive increase. Given the dominant position of the British plantation system, however, it constitutes no less than 60 percent of the average annual output of Cuba between 1824 and 1833.[17] A more realistic assessment of the impact of the intra-Caribbean population shift would probably generate a figure in excess of Cuban output. Thus at virtually no additional cost in either economic or (by then-contemporary international standards) moral terms, the British could have captured for their own possessions all of the gains made by the Cuban producers after 1807. Cuban output would not, of course, have stagnated, particularly if we assume an open African slave trade to Cuba at this time. But the British share of the world's plantation-produce exports would have been largely protected at least until the abolition of slavery itself. The additional output would probably have been sold on the European mainland rather than in Britain, where sugar prices would have been affected only marginally. It is reasonable to conclude, however, that total British exports of finished goods as well as the British West Indian share of total British trade would have increased, though in national income terms, the impact would still have been minor. Nevertheless, of all the British abolitionist moves, the strangulation of the intercolonial traffic is the hardest to explain in terms of direct economic gains.

### The Abolition of the British Slave Trade

The potential benefits for Britain of a laissez-faire approach to the intercolonial and foreign slave trades are clear. They were, nevertheless, much smaller than the gains that might have been obtained from reopening the African slave trade to the British Americas. Of the three policy options discussed, this is the most difficult to visualize if only because contemporaries never considered it as a possibility. As illustration we might note that Liverpool, the last great center of the British slave trade down to 1807, in 1814 generated a huge petition in favor of international suppression of the traffic. Yet for some merchants and planters, the adverse economic implications of abolition of the British trade were obvious. As long as the French wars lasted, British control of the seas ensured that French and Cuban planters could not get easy access to Africa. As John Gladstone, a West Indian merchant and father of the future prime minister, pointed out, however, the ending of the wars combined with the ban on imports into the British Caribbean would quickly undermine British plantation dominance.[18] In the years after 1815 the surge in the African slave trade to non-British territories proved Gladstone correct. As a consequence British planters in the frontier colonies faced labor costs that were at least double (perhaps triple) those faced by their Cuban counterparts; labor costs in Cuba made up at least one third of the total costs of producing sugar on a large scale.[19] Moreover, there seems to have been little difference in labor productivity between Cuba and the frontier British sugar colonies.[20] It thus seems extremely likely that both Cuban and British planters could have obtained all the slaves they needed for prices only slightly in excess of the then-contemporary Cuban cost.

Grounds for speculation on the impact of such prices for slave labor in post-1807 Trinidad and Demerara are fairly secure. Initially the British consumer of sugar would have derived only minor benefit. Before 1846 almost 50 percent of the price of sugar in Britain was taken up with duty. It would thus have required a massive reduction in production costs to change the final selling price significantly. After 1832 and up to 1850, however, the rather large divergence in price that opened up between British and foreign-grown sugar would surely not have happened.[21] Consumers of cotton and coffee may have derived larger benefits. Coffee duties were reduced somewhat in 1808 and cut in half in 1825; British cotton was admitted duty free from 1821. From the British point of view, of course, national income would have been raised more certainly if the U.S. South itself had had free access to the African traffic. Discounting this as not being within British power, the next best alternative for British cotton manufacturers and consumers would have been a free trade in African slaves for British Guiana. That colony's cotton boom began when both regions could import slaves and ended when additional slaves became scarce and expensive. The intriguing question is just how temporary the boom would have been if the British had not terminated the link with Africa. Northern Brazil, which did have access to Africa until 1850, reached peak cotton exports in 1830, and the decline thereafter coincided with increasing restrictions on slave imports.[22]

For sugar and coffee producers at least, British tariff policy meant that the major market opportunities existed outside Britain in the first half of the nineteenth century. It was on the continents of Europe and, to a lesser extent, North America that the strangling of the British plantation sector first became manifest. Access to Africa would have allowed the British to maintain their domination of world plantation produce acquired in the 1790s. Prices in non-British markets would have been lower and the Cuban and Brazilian share of those markets would have been smaller. From the position of the British exporter of manufactured goods, the British shares of the market mattered less than the fact that the total market for produce would have been larger. To the extra opportunities for British manufactures on plantation economies may be added new markets for trade goods to be exchanged for slaves on the African littoral. Just to maintain the slave population of the British Americas at the level it had reached on the eve of abolition of the slave traffic would have necessitated imports of between six and seven thousand per year between 1807 and 1833.[23] In the four decades after 1805, the frontier colonies in the British Caribbean could have gone through the explosive development experienced in previous centuries by Barbados, Jamaica and St. Domingue.

Indeed what might have happened was what, in fact, did happen after emancipation. Between 1834 and 1865 at least 126,000 and 52,000 immigrants entered British Guiana and Trinidad, respectively, compared to about 8,000 and 7,000 in the generation after the 1805 ordinance—and the flow continued unabated to the end of the century.[24] Acreage under cane in British Guiana almost doubled in the forty years after 1846 and population density more than doubled. Trinidad experienced similar expansion. A massive influx of immigrants occurred despite both improvements in labor productivity in the second half of the century and sugar prices that were 50 percent or more below what they had been in the years of the restricted colonial trade. With a free African slave trade, an inflow into the two colonies of far more than 178,000 in the period 1805–33 would seem to have been most likely. In the decades 1811–20 and 1821–30, 534,000 and 595,000 slaves, respectively, were actually imported into the Americas. With an open British slave trade additional decadal imports of 100,000 to 150,000 may be conservatively estimated. Volumes would thus have remained somewhat below the peak levels of just under 800,000 in the 1780s and 1790s.[25]

The three alternatives to the historical reality discussed do not, of course, exhaust the possibilities. Both supplies of raw materials and markets for British goods would have increased by even greater amounts if, in addition to the removal of protection and active British participation in the slave trade, the North American continent had also been open to slave traffic. In national income terms a much more effective way of using the African squadron would have been to station it off the Texas coast to generate and protect an illicit slave trade from Cuba to the U.S. South—and later to recognize and protect the Confederacy in 1862. On these assumptions we might conclude that the flow of coerced labor from Africa to the Americas would surely have continued to exceed that of free labor from Europe until well into the second half of the nineteenth century.[26] The all-time highs in the volume of slaves—attained in the late eighteenth century—would no doubt have been surpassed. None of these developments would have inhibited the growth of trade with the new markets for British goods in Asia and the Far East.

## II

Against the backdrop of these alternatives, we can now see more clearly the consequences of an aggressive antislave-trade policy. As well as destroying the relative world position of the British plantation sector, it was initially the most important factor responsible for its absolute decline. The only factor more important in the latter process was the abolition of slavery itself, which was implemented fully in 1838 when apprenticeship ended. The antislavery movement was initially more effective within British territory than without, so that one effect of antislavery was to foster the development of the slave-based economies of Brazil and Cuba. The distribution of British trade was significantly changed. The British West Indian proportion, of course, fell, but non-British slave regions in the Iberian Americas took up much of the slack. Despite British suppression policy, the Americas as a whole were still accounting for nearly 40 percent of combined British exports and imports in 1850, a figure not much changed since 1800.[27] Within Britain, just as the inception of slave colonies added something to national income in the seventeenth and eighteenth centuries—though not sufficient to induce industrialization—abolition of coerced labor and the system that supplied it reduced British incomes. Prices of foodstuffs were increased, employment was lowered and domestic social tensions were exacerbated by reduced exploitation of Africans in the New World. This, moreover, was at a time when class tensions were closer to the revolutionary flash point than at any time in modern British history.[28] From the broadest perspective of British development, abolition coupled with the continuation of the protective system to midcentury slowed down the shift to an international division of labor in which Britain became the workshop of the world.

If, as seems clear, the real interests of most groups in Britain before 1850 would have been best served by policies that encouraged the use of coerced labor in lightly populated transoceanic regions, why was an antislave-trade policy launched? Some insights into this question are taken up in chapter 2. There is, however, a related and ultimately more important question: To what extent did British or, more generally, antislavery intervention bring about the ending of the slave trade? Whatever attitudes in Britain might have been, that country created only a part of the world demand for plantation produce. It controlled not much more than half of its supply even in 1800. Although it was the most powerful maritime nation in the world throughout the nineteenth century, it was not the only one. Other nations had navies and, more important, rights before international law that the British in other circumstances found it politic to recognize and foster. Except in wartime the British could not legally interfere with slave trading on the high seas or in foreign territory. As they quickly discovered, they could not even stop and search the shipping of other countries without the formal permission of the government whose flag was displayed on the masthead of the suspected ship. In addition, even if the British had possessed these powers, the South Atlantic basin is vast and quite possibly beyond the technological power of any nineteenth-century navy's effective control. The mechanics of suppression thus comprised knotty problems that the British fleet was never really capable of unraveling on its own in peacetime. The resulting frustrations tempted abolitionists and government officials alike to make questionable interpretations of both domestic and international law.

In the last eighty years of its existence, then, the slave trade was subject to intensely conflicting pressures. On the one hand, economic growth exerted increased demand for plantation produce and the labor that produced it. This pressure was alleviated to some extent by the technological revolution that allowed all forms of labor, including slave, to become more productive. On the other hand, there was the campaign against the traffic led by the British, which was perhaps certain to fail unless the British ignored international law or unless they received help from other maritime nations as well as importing countries. Antislave-trade attitudes did eventually become generalized, and all countries on both sides of the Atlantic at length united against the traffic. But the pressure was applied gradually and was uneven in its effect. Given the constraints, it is not obvious at first sight that the trade was forcibly suppressed and, if so, how important the various components of suppression were.

These competing influences had no parallels in earlier periods of the trade. The exigencies of war in the eighteenth century were temporary and usually affected only one or two national branches of the traffic at a time. By the mid-nineteenth-century conditions generally—shipboard mortality in particular—were reputed to be the worst experienced in the history of the slave trade and the most severe of any contemporary traffic involving the transport of large numbers of people. There was a strong popular image of slave traders, hounded by cruisers, packing slaves into suffocatingly small holds and dispatching them without adequate provisions. The slave ships were pictured as tiny clippers, fast, maneuverable and capable of running across the Atlantic several times a year. The profits from the human misery inflicted were held to be immense. The nineteenth-century world unleashed contradictory pressures against the slave trade. Much of what follows will attempt to evaluate that world's impact on the trade itself. Did naval action on the high seas simply make life too difficult for the slave trader?

## III

But the question of why the slave trade and indeed slavery ended cannot be answered without extensive study of the phenomenon of coerced labor in both Africa, which supplied the labor, and the Americas, where most of the plantations were located. Slaves entering the transatlantic trade were the products of a sophisticated African supply network. Some came from societies whose very existence was threatened by continued population loss imposed by the trade. Many traveled for weeks and passed through the hands of several owners before reaching the African coast. Their owners frequently put them to work for a time on a variety of tasks, among which might be the cultivation of crops for export. Almost all slaves had lost their freedom long before they first came into contact with the transatlantic trader and the slave ship. On the American side there was an equally sophisticated demand structure that was subject to the vagaries of the tastes and incomes of European consumers, the availability of substitutes for plantation crops, such as beet sugar, and the supply of forms of labor other than slave. There was, thus, a wide range of potential factors apart from those of abolition and suppression that could have put an end to both the slave trade and slavery.

On the demand side the slave trade to the non British areas that dominated the midcentury traffic could have died a natural death in at least two senses. One possibility was that creole slaves or alternative forms of labor became available in the Americas in such quantities that it was no longer worth trans-shipping Africans to the New World. A variant of this stresses the increasing technological sophistication of work in the nineteenth-century Americas, even on plantations, and argues that slaves could not perform such tasks efficiently. From this standpoint attempts to suppress the trade might have raised the price of the slave in the Americas somewhat, but economic progress in the form of technology decreed that the slave trade and indeed slavery could not endure. Alternatively the slave trade might have continued until land/labor ratios had fallen to the point where wage rates declined and free labor became cheaper than slave. Most of these lines of reasoning may be grouped under the natural-limits thesis that suffused much of Eric William's work.

On the supply side there is the possibility that developments in Africa brought the slave trade to a close. Again there are at least two not necessarily incompatible interpretations that have some prima facie plausibility. For some African regions demographic pressures were such that exports could not con-tinue at the level they had attained in the 1780s—the peak export decade in the history of the slave trade—without the population completely disappear-ing. Even though aggregate departures declined somewhat in the nineteenth century, the cumulative effect of millions of exports and traffic-induced deaths might have seriously reduced the African population and contributed to the ending of the trade. Slaves were carried across the Atlantic for over four hundred years but, of the grand total, more than 40 percent made the voyage in the ninety years prior to final suppression in 1867.[29] It was precisely at this time that Africa began to export a range of cultivated commodities that in some regions quickly came to surpass the slave trade in value. For some writ-ers, particularly contemporaries, a commodity traffic of sufficient volume would guarantee an end to the traffic in slaves. It was at least possible that labor demands for the production of these commodities and the alternative profit-making prospects they offered for foreign traders were significant. The com-modity traffic thus might have ensured the gradual subordination of the slaving business to the legitimate trade, as the former was called.

In fact, as will be seen, none of these versions of the ending of the traffic is plausible. In the Americas the pattern outlined for the British colonies was repeated in much of the rest of North and South America. The demand for plantation produce climbed steadily throughout the nineteenth century. Except at times in the United States, slave populations grew much more slowly than the demand for their labor, and in many plantation societies, those populations declined once the link with Africa was severed. If there was a natural limit to slavery, it was certainly not in view at any point in the nineteenth century. Migration of free labor was never sufficient to displace slave labor before the trade was abolished, and it generally stayed well away from plantation zones before slavery was abolished. Free labor never evinced any willingness to work in sugar production until technological change altered the nature of the work in the aftermath of slavery. Land/labor ratios in the Americas certainly fell steadily during the nineteenth century, but the implications of this for the future of slavery and the slave trade are unclear. If the closing of the land fron-tier in the United States at the end of the century was not followed by wage declines for free labor, why, if slavery had continued, would it have reduced the prices of slaves?[30] The price of slaves in all parts of the Americas rose steadily with some interruptions as long as slavery appeared likely to endure. Although chiefly used in field labor, slaves were employed in a wide range of occupations, including many that required skills. When the slave trade was abolished, the effect was to concentrate slaves in activities where they were most productive. In no sense was the slave traffic displaced by free-migrant flows and nowhere had it become an economic irrelevancy prior to its disappearance. In the long run, production of plantation produce was seriously disrupted by suppression, though not as much as by the ending of slavery itself.

In Africa, too, it is hard to discern pressures that contributed to the ending of the traffic. Interpretations of pre–nineteenth-century African demographic trends vary widely because of the great scarcity of hard data on vital rates. The issue is taken up more fully later, but it seems fairly clear that African suppliers of slaves were sensitive to price changes. Moreover, the price of slaves on the African littoral did not rise in the course of the nineteenth century. This would indicate that a shortage of slaves on the African side was not primarily responsible for the ending of the trade. The same reasoning can be extended to the debate on the role of the commodity trade in the suppression process. Annual data for both slave exports and several different commodities are available for the nineteenth century, and there is little to suggest that these were in competition. If they had been, slave prices would again have increased—or at least held steady—as commodity production claimed significantly greater shares of the domestic labor force. For Africa, certainly at the continentwide level, a case might be made that suppression of the slave trade was not a decisive event.

There can, therefore, be no doubt that the slave trade was of critical economic importance to the nineteenth-century Atlantic basin as long as it lasted. The only part of the basin where this was not the case was Africa, which in view of the historiography is particularly ironic. For the Atlantic region as for the British Empire, the slave trade did not expire naturally. Rather, it was killed when its significance to the Americas and to a lesser extent to Europe was greater than at any point in its history. For the Americas as well as for Britain at the outset of industrialization, there was a profound incompatibility between economic self-interest and antislavery policy. A full exploration of this tension would require a worldwide study of coerced labor systems and their relationships with the advanced economies of the Western Hemisphere. The incompatibility might indeed be generalized in that gains in measured income are not as consistent with freedom of choice as an earlier generation assumed. This is not, however, the place to pursue such an investigation, at least on the broad front. Instead we shall focus on the last century or so of the Atlantic slave trade and attempt to uncover the layered relationship between forced labor and economic progress by a study of one institution only.

We begin in chapter 2 by pursuing the implications for antislavery of the British road to economic development. Chapter 3 examines the impact of early British industrialization on the non-British plantation Americas and chapter 4 takes up the slave trade itself and the adjustments to British and U.S. withdrawal. Chapter 5 reviews the African slave-supply response at the time of abolition and the initial impact of the British decision on that response. The next two chapters describe the tensions generated by official and unofficial British antislave-trade policy. Part 4, chapters 8 through 11, examines the business of slave trading under prohibition, including trends in profits, costs and the continued British links with the traffic. Chapters 10 and 11 assess the response of Africa and the American plantation regions, respectively, to attempts to suppress the trade. The final two chapters attempt to explain the effective suppression of the traffic and to catalog the rather unexpected consequences of that long-awaited event.

# 2

# Antislavery and the Labor Problem: Origin and Impact

In early 1831, well before the cabinet took up the emancipation issue, the British government decided to free all slaves under the direct control of the crown. In response to Lord Goderich's circular dispatch, which went out from Downing Street, the governors' councils in the colonies prevaricated. The result was a prompt renewal of the order, this time supported by an extraordinary criticism of the whole concept of slave labor and directed to Trinidad. Goderich argued:

> The practical question which presents itself, is whether the general interests of the colony would be more advanced by the manumission of those Slaves or by their continued detention in slavery. Were I to regard that interest as confined to the single question of profit and loss, I still entertain a strong belief that it would be best promoted by the enfranchisement of the Slaves. The Council in their Minute, have taken the question entirely for granted and assume as incontrovertible that the labour exacted of these persons could not be performed with equal economy, if free labourers were employed at wages fairly representing the value of their services.

He then went on to list the expenses of owning slaves and concluded:

> A calculation which should fairly embrace them all, would, I believe allow that the employment of Slaves in any labour which does not impose the most extreme fatigue, is, even to private individuals, and when viewed only in the narrowest commercial light much less advantageous than is usually supposed; and that the momentary savings in wages is, in the course of a very few years more than compensated for by losses and liabilities which the Council in framing their Minute forgot to estimate.[1]

The logic of the dispatch was that coerced labor was necessarily uneconomic. Trinidad at that time had abundant unsettled land and had signally failed to attract any free labor in the twenty-five years since slave imports had been effectively halted. As an official statement of a slaveholding power that the slaveholders did not know what they were about, the dispatch was unprecedented. When the planters who formed the governor's council read it, they must have realized that their system was doomed. Arguments in the face of such distortions of Caribbean reality were clearly useless.

The tiny political elite responsible for British policy throughout this period fully shared Goderich's attitudes and were, in fact, as hostile to slavery and the slave trade as any abolitionist agitator. The author of the Emancipation Act and future Tory prime minister, Lord Stanley—scarcely the favorite politician of the humanitarians—toured the United States in 1824–25. His views on slavery, recorded in his journal, strikingly anticipate those of de Tocqueville writing nearly a decade later—even to the famous comparison between free-labor Ohio and slave-labor Kentucky.[2] Lord Howick, Lord Aberdeen, Sir James Stephen, Viscount Palmerston, and Lord John Russell are a few other examples of statesmen and officials whose abhorrence of coerced labor was not so much wanting as controlled by the realities of power and a gradually dawning awareness of the importance of population densities in creating a free-labor market in the colonies. It is noteworthy that the Tory opposition in the House of Commons offered virtually no support to the West Indians during the debate on the emancipation bill.[3]

As we have seen, the actual and potential benefits of plantation regions to the nineteenth-century British economy were considerable, and the lack of an alternative to slave labor, at least before 1850, almost complete. The total absence of any British statesman or non-West Indian interest group willing to support coerced labor—much less the African slave traffic—is thus remarkable. A closer examination of this paradox is essential to an understanding of what happened to the slave trade and, eventually, slavery during the nineteenth century. If there was no likelihood of economic gain from attacking either of these institutions, then some exploration of the ideological imperatives of the leading antislavery nation of the age becomes necessary. Such an explanation does not, however, lead away from economic considerations. Indeed attempts to make sense of the paradox of econocide must begin with trends within the domestic British economy.

The rise and fall of slavery and the trade that supplied it spanned a period when the relationship between capital and labor within Britain was undergoing profound change. Much of the existing literature has tended to see this change as the application of laissez-faire principles to the labor market, as demonstrated by the shift from the Speenhamland system of poor relief to the New Poor Law of 1834.[4] Workers now had the choice between starving or working forced on them more starkly than ever before. Yet if a completely free labor market is to be consistent with economic growth, it must also be the case that workers are prepared to work beyond the level necessary to secure merely subsistence incomes. It is of particular interest here to explore the connection between abolition, on the one hand, and the growing importance of domestic consumers, high wages and labor productivity, on the other.

## I

From the standpoint of the capitalist, the wage payment may be viewed as a cost (a measure of the worker's productivity) and the essential foundation of a market for the goods and services that the worker produces. A wage level that might reward increased worker output and create a high demand for goods and services might at the same time increase the costs of the employer to prohibitive levels. The potential conflict here is obvious. In seventeenth- and early eighteenth-century England, a preoccupation with exports ensured that the cost element was seen to be of greater importance. Compared to the late eighteenth and early nineteenth centuries, capital/labor ratios were lower and labor costs as a proportion of total costs correspondingly higher. Productivity changes, moreover, occurred only gradually, for some industries perhaps not at all. At the same time, for that part of the economy that produced for the market, exports probably loomed disproportionately large in importance by later standards. The income of domestic consumers would thus not be of prime concern. An even stronger reason for holding wages down, however, was the widespread conviction that higher wages would allow laborers to work less rather than induce them to offer more labor input to the prospective employer.[5]

In preindustrial England "freemen were freeholders."[6] Freedom meant self-employment or at least the avoidance of wage labor, a concept that survived in the Chartist land movement of the 1840s and developed independently on the other side of the Atlantic in the republican ideology of the U.S. urban working class.[7] This concept of freedom suggests that in the English case, workers were possibly prepared to forego income in the interests of achieving more control over their lives and perhaps, too, to avoid undesirable working conditions. Any increase in wages beyond subsistence levels would allow a worker to indulge his nonpecuniary aspirations and work less. Given the perceived importance of exports, it is not difficult to understand that of the two aspects of the wage payment mentioned, it was the cost aspect that preoccupied pamphlet writers of the early mercantilist period. Low wages, draconian vagrancy laws and fewer owner-occupied smallholdings encouraged adequate supplies of low-cost labor input and, competitively priced exports. This almost certainly resulted in higher market output (though not necessarily higher total output or welfare) and an augmented national strength, the main mercantilist goal.[8]

It seems unnecessary to dwell on the implications of these developments for slavery. Quite apart from the difficulties of attracting free labor into tropical plantations, the idea of forcing blacks to leave Africa and work in the Caribbean was, in a sense, domestic labor policy carried to a logical conclusion not possible at home for a variety of reasons. At the very least, ownership of an individual could be seen as one end of a spectrum of servitude, the beginning of which was wage labor. By the second half of the eighteenth century, the impulses that drove British consumers to demand ever-increasing volumes of plantation produce, and thus sustain African slavery, were at the same time comprehensively reshaping the domestic relationship between labor and capital. Improvement in labor productivity was a present reality in some industries and a future prospect in others, and a substantial home market had come into existence.[9]

This is not the place to review either the instruments of this change or the exact mix of compulsion and voluntary response that created it. It is worth noting, however, that slave-grown products such as sugar, coffee, tobacco and even cotton generally did nothing to fill biological or subsistence needs. Such goods were not necessary for the clothing, shelter or nutrition of the industrial work force nor, except for cotton, as raw material inputs to the new machines. Rather, they were quintessentially social and cultural products that formed part of the widened range of goods and services to which a significant section of early industrializing society aspired. They may be seen as forerunners of the great mass of products in modern high-income societies that are purchased in the expectation that they will satisfy nonsubsistence or psychological needs. The effect of such consumer aspirations, given unequal distribution of land and capital, was to guarantee a supply of labor on the domestic scene every bit as effectively as did the removal of Africans to the Caribbean for its colonial counterpart. The process was encouraged by the secular decline in the prices of all plantation produce after 1650. Thus tropical produce was the product of one system of labor and helped form the incentives on which another was based.

Want creation and slavery might thus seem alternative methods of ensuring that labor would work for owners of land and capital,[10] though want creation might serve this function only if there was little alternative to wage labor, as in England. This suggests that the important aspects of the relationship between capitalism and abolition that Eric Williams was searching for were, first, that British employers had less need for coercion by the second half of the eighteenth century and that, second, both draconian vagrancy laws at home and predial slavery in the colonies were examples of coercion. In the light of a system that relied on voluntary labor to satisfy individual wants going beyond subsistence needs, forced labor appeared not only inappropriate but counterproductive.

After 1750 increasing numbers of writers such as Josiah Tucker, Benjamin Franklin, Malachy Postlethwayt, James Steuart and, of course, Adam Smith were stressing that high wages "did not necessarily mean high labor costs" and that "an increased availability of the comforts . . . of life could operate as a powerful stimulus to industry."[11] This was consistent with the conviction that society existed for the benefit of all and that, for Smith and the utilitarians, the means of guaranteeing this outcome was clear enough. A free market would limit the power of all groups in society and ensure an optimum level of consumption, with that balance between the extremes of luxury and poverty most appropriate for development. For owners of capital, a population responsive to market forces was a basic prerequisite to such a system, and if that population had no other means of supporting consumption than through wages, so much the better. Once this was achieved, then the last great push to destroy the remnants of paternalistic economic controls and institute laissez-faire could begin, a centerpiece of which was a free-labor market. The strict utilitarian drawing inspiration from Adam Smith and Jeremy Bentham would have no sympathy for the interventionism of Evangelicals and agricultural paternalists.[12] Few utilitarians could support the Speenhamland system of outdoor relief of the poor, the good works of the Quakers or even the Society for the Suppression of Vice. A case could, nevertheless, be made for abolition as simply an extension to Africa and the colonies of utilitarian principles. But the common ground between the Benthamites and evangelicals was far more important than their differences: All could agree, in particular, on the importance of incentives, or the fear of starving, as a motivation for labor. The ideal of both Evangelicals and utilitarians was the maximization of output on the basis of a sober, industrious labor force made prosperous by its own efforts. Both advocated, in effect, government intervention to set up and maintain a system based on laissez-faire principles. The 1807 and 1833 abolition acts were intended to lead naturally to a free-wage relationship between master and slave: The first, by cutting off fresh supplies of coerced labor; the second, more directly, by making coercion itself illegal.

Although some abolitionists were prepared to consider smallholding options in a post-emancipation society, this was seen as a supplement to the plantation system and a way of keeping the planters honest in their labor-market dealings with the ex-slave.[13] The basic point was that the bondsman would be more industrious working for wages or for himself. As Zachary Macaulay wrote to Henry Brougham on the eve of the emancipation bill, "The influence of want and wages is infallible with every human being; and even negro indolence . . . would feel the irresistible force. . . . I have much to say upon it and particularly as respects the vain fear of what is called squatting." From inside the Colonial Office, Sir James Stephen, the younger, had a more realistic view of squatting but considered it, nevertheless, axiomatic that "the dread of starving" should be substituted for "the dread of being flogged." The aggregate labor supply, output per person and the volume of West Indian export crops were all expected to increase in the long run.[14] The emancipation bill originally provided for a twelve-year postslavery apprenticeship period for field hands during which the ex-slaves were to work under close regulation but without pay for their former masters. Although the main intention of the government appears to have been to propitiate the West Indian interest, an earlier generation of abolitionists might have approved such a scheme as a useful preparation for freedom.[15] In 1833, however, the opposition was intense; as a consequence, the twelve years were reduced to six. Four years into the term of apprenticeship and after further pressure, a new act abruptly brought the system to an end. For the leaders of antislavery it was not simply justice for the slave that motivated their opposition to apprenticeship but also a conviction that any delay in the introduction of a free-labor market was unnecessary. The abolitionist leader Sir Thomas Fowell Buxton, was prepared to support severe vagrancy laws and a strong police force as transitional measures but not a system that tied a laborer to a particular employer or diluted the "influence of want."[16]

That the spirit and the ultimate goal of the abolition acts were much closer ɔ the New Poor Law than Speenhamland is well illustrated by an examination ⸍ the parliamentary division lists on the 1833 abolition measure, the New ɔr Law (1834) and the bill renewing the powers of the Poor Law commission

(1841). None of the leading antislavery figures opposed either the principle or any of the significant clauses of the two latter measures, and all would have agreed with the American William Ellery Channing: "Self motion ... that is what our nature hungers and thirsts for as its true element and life ... [To] be deprived of that freedom of action which consists with others' freedom ... this is to be wounded not only in the dearest earthly interests but in the very life of the soul." The tension was not missed by contemporaries. Part of the sustained attack of *The Times* (London) against the New Poor Law consisted of quoting Channing at length, comparing the new workhouses with barracoons on the African coast, and asking how the abolitionists could see the latter as the epitome of evil and at the same time ignore the former.[17]

Although a coalition of utilitarians and the later core of antislavery MPs never actually came about, by the 1830s most leading abolitionists were, in fact, Whigs with the kind of liberal inclinations most sympathetic to utilitarian-inspired reforms. Buxton's chief lieutenant, Stephen Lushington, figured largely in the measures that brought the Church of England and the legal system into the nineteenth century. Daniel O'Connell's activities in the area of political and economic reform are well known. Outside Parliament, the interests of George Thompson and Joseph Sturge, a younger version of William Allen, would have satisfied the most doctrinaire Benthamite. By 1833 those abolitionists who demanded the immediate and unconditional emancipation of the slave had come to predominate over the gradualists. The former "put [their] faith in the innate moral capacities of the individual" rather than "a system of external discipline."[18] At this stage antislavery appeared entirely consistent with laissez-faire principles, and it is hard to view abolitionist espousal of the latter as merely a tactical device aimed at garnering support for their cause.

Abolition was thus more than an application to overseas societies of a formula that had worked well in England. It was also an experiment in social engineering conducted in both the colonies and at home at the same time. If not all societies had attained British levels of civilization, they might get there with help from those that had. The antecedents of the Palmerstonian belief in a world "commercial advance and liberal awakening" based on collaboration between the British merchants and "progressive" elements in peripheral economies may be seen in the African development plans of the 1780s.[19] There was disagreement on the most effective way of achieving this development. Some abolitionists argued for European-managed agricultural projects and others, notably Mungo Park, Wilberforce, James Stephen the elder, Allen and the African Institution, favored African proprietorship encouraged by extensive European trading contacts. But all could agree that first "indolence is a disease which it is the business of civilization to cure. The motives and means of industry must be supplied. ... " The *Edinburgh Review* clarified the last point in its comment that "the multiplication of wants, and consequently ideas, is the commencement of civilization." The wants, of course, had to be of the individual variety. More than one observer deplored the sharing of goods and hence destruction of initiative that local African custom encouraged.[20]

Perhaps the economic factor that preoccupied observers most was the v reservoir of labor available in the tropics, as manifested in the leisure enjoyed by the inhabitants. Africans as well as preindustrial Englishmen regarded wage labor as slavery and in Africa tropical luxury appeared to guarantee a subsistence income with a minimum of effort. In a comment that anticipates Marshall Sahlins's modern anthropological studies, the explorer Richard Lander stated that "the male population . . . seemed to have no employment or occupation whatever, spending the whole of their time in lounging or loitering about their native villages." The corollary of this was a lack of understanding of the importance of time. James McQueen wrote at length about an African who traveled six months to barter a basket of cola nuts for "salt and other trifling necessities."[21] The potential of such a labor force working for itself or others when brought up to British standards of work discipline was enormous, and the consumer behavior of African and West Indian populations was a central concern of the serious literature of the age as well as various official inquiries. If slavery and the slave trade were seen as both inefficient and immoral, then abolition and the inculcation of British consumer habits would lead to the spread of Christianity, civilization and increased prosperity for liberated and liberator alike.

## II

The emergence and achievements of antislavery occurred at a time when many Christians, at least those living in Britain, could interpret their nation's steady rise in international stature as both the workings of Providence and an opportunity to bring civilization to the rest of the world. Exchange or commerce would induce mutual dependence and peace and facilitate the spread of Christian enlightenment. Industrious habits would yield the necessary trading goods. For Evangelicals, in particular, "benevolence performed by one nation for the benefit of other nations initiated a providential reflex action which worked to the benefit of the benefactor."[22] One did not, however, have to be an Evangelical to appreciate the large output gains made by both the domestic British economy and British international trade after 1750. As Howard Temperley has stressed, it was natural to conclude from this, as indeed many non-British did, that the British economic system, a salient feature of which was a free-labor market, was a model that the rest of the world would do well to follow.[23]

As already noted, the same economic expansion that supported and made possible such cultural imperialism on the part of the British also brought the latter into ever-increasing contact with the land-abundant non-European areas of the world. Though Asia and West Africa were exceptions, most of the new non-European markets acquired after 1600 were resource abundant, sparsely populated regions with relatively frangible indigenous cultures. Settlement of free migrants in these areas remained small, partly because high transportation costs discouraged mass movements from Europe and partly because plantation regimes developed here that free labor could choose to avoid. Slaves, indentured servants or self-employment were the only options for most owners of land. Thus, before the nineteenth century, the wealthiest and most dynamic regions of the Americas, including the United States, were those that relied on coerced labor. The labor situation was eventually eased by a combination of phenomenal rates of natural population increase and massive European migration. But the net migration of free migrants across the Atlantic did not exceed the flow of slaves until the 1840s, despite the fact that by then the slave trade remained open only to Brazil and Cuba. Coerced labor was thus the only practical way of maximizing the contribution of lightly populated transoceanic lands to the European economies in the first half of the nineteenth century, just as it had been in the preceding 250 years.[24]

The British fascination with their own economic success as well as the underemployment of labor they perceived in the tropics prevented them from fully appreciating the significance of relative land abundance. Edward Gibbon Wakefield's promotional activities, which stressed the necessity of preventing easy immigrant access to land, reached an influential audience. But there were few who would argue that, as a method of guaranteeing a labor supply, slavery was a more effective alternative to restricting free land. Indeed, except in the limited sense of British domestic reliance on free labor and wage incentive, laissez-faire and abolition were not natural partners in the European-centered part of the early nineteenth-century world economy. The British slave trade, of course, was one of the clearest manifestations of successful free enterprise, and abolition was a similarly striking example of its suppression. But, more fundamentally, as Herman Merivale, the elder James Stephen, and the body of later classical economists in general came to recognize, free markets and free labor could not coexist in many parts of the world.[25] As the abolitionists eventually recognized in the 1840s, a comprehensive policy of laissez-faire toward the international economy would have expanded the coerced labor systems of the Americas rather than destroyed them. It required a considerable increase in the population of such areas as well as severe restrictions on the institution of slavery before free trade became consistent with free labor. The invisible hand of competition and self-interest, which was permitted greater play on the domestic scene than either before or since, would, if allowed, have expanded the plantation systems of the New World, British and non-British alike, to unprecedented levels. The strong link between slavery, industrial capitalism and free trade during the nineteenth century was given its clearest expression in the affinity between Britain and the Confederacy after 1861, though the significance of this link was obscured by contemporary abolitionists.[26]

The British government was not insensitive to this fundamental tension. It attempted to implement Wakefield's schemes in Australia, and there were parallel policies designated to extract "voluntary" labor in Ceylon in the 1840s and in several parts of Africa later. In the British West Indies, the Colonial Office was convinced of the superiority of free labor. But it was also acutely aware of the variations in land/labor ratios and, therefore, the different opportunities for the ex-slave to leave the plantation labor force and exercise the squatting option. Despite Lord Goderich's dispatch to the governor of Trinidad, the Colonial Office expended considerable time and ingenuity between 1832 and 1833 on the problem of ensuring a continued labor supply for the post-emancipation plantation.[27] Here at least there seemed to be a conviction that in terms of the above discussion, preindustrial attitudes to labor existed in the West Indies. However, with the possible exception of James Stephen, the elder, the abolitionists behaved as though the factory and plantation worker had identical goals. If the high population densities of Antigua and Barbados had been typical of the British West Indies, then the abolitionists' interpretation might never have been questioned. Jamaica, Trinidad and British Guiana were not Lancashire, however, though whether it was land availability or the laborer that was different is not clear.

The basic truth was that at the very time the British ability to employ coerced labor in the transoceanic world was growing, there was less and less room in their own system of beliefs for the concept of coerced labor. The process of economic growth, as experienced by the British, fed both developments. It is, therefore, not surprising that abolitionist expectations in the capacity of British influence—including emancipation—to generate increased prosperity for all were repeatedly blunted. In Africa individual British initiatives—from the Sierra Leone experiment beginning in 1783 to the Niger scheme of sixty years later—failed to yield the expected advances. Only the palm oil trade, which relied on African proprietorship, produced a commodity export to rival slaves, but it seems likely that this complemented the slave traffic rather than threatened to supplant it.[28] The epidemiological environment made West Africa one of the most dangerous areas of the world for newcomers and discouraged the European management option. More important was the tendency of British observers to hopelessly underestimate the resilience of the indigenous cultures. That the expectations persisted so long can be explained partly by the persistence of the slave trade, which could be blamed for all failures: Why should man abandon indolence when exile is imminent?[29]

In the West Indies these excuses did not apply, but the crucial test could not come until emancipation of the slave labor force. Not until after 1838 was the liberal solution tried and found wanting, but even then its failure could be attributed to hurricanes, planter recalcitrance and equalization of the sugar duties that allowed slave-trade-supported sugar to compete with the free-labor variety.[30] A final assessment might be delayed until the 1850s, but whenever it was made, the effect of allowing the plantation labor force to choose its own combination of goods consumption, leisure and avoidance of unpleasant working conditions can only be described as catastrophic by the standards of those who pushed for abolition. In common with most societies that have undergone emancipation, both the labor-force participation rate and labor productivity dropped and a shift occurred from marketable to nonmarketable or internally marketed output that substantially reduced exports from the British West Indies. Exports of sugar from Jamaica did not regain preabolition levels until the twentieth century.[31] To return to the question posed above: Was the West Indian worker aspiring to different (and preindustrial) goals compared to his British contemporary or were the goals similar, but there was simply more land available in Jamaica than in Lancashire? Antigua and Barbados, where there was no labor shortage and also no spare land, would suggest the latter.[32] Whatever the answer, as far as the abolitionist was concerned the effect was the same. Freedom of choice was apparently not as consistent with maximizing exportable output in the West Indies as it was in Britain, the northern United States and the post-emancipation southern United States.

The tension between expectations and reality was intense. It undermined the broad agreement among the British elite on the nature of the labor problem and strained the belief that freedom of choice would provide a solution. The remarkable unity of purpose that distinguished British antislavery from its American counterpart was destroyed. The utilitarian element represented by the British Garrisonians pursued the laissez-faire element of abolitionist thought to its logical conclusion. For them responsibility for the welfare of the laborer ceased with the implementation of abolition, and they devoted far more attention to slavery in the rest of the world than to its aftermath in the West Indies. In the 1830s and 1840s, developing a familiar theme from James Cropper's pamphlets of twenty years earlier, the Garrisonians held that slavery in the Americas would be destroyed by the development of free-labor operations in India and that all remaining protective duties should be removed immediately. Then if the West Indies could not compete, the resources employed should relocate or switch into other crops. "The West India interest is doomed; it cannot survive; it must die to live again," proclaimed George Thompson.[33] However, the mainstream movement (e.g., the British and Foreign Anti-Slavery Society), carried on the Evangelical tradition and never lost interest in the ex-slave. They argued for the continuation of protective sugar duties and safeguards on immigration, which would have greatly reduced the inflow of indentured laborers. They also put much of the blame for export declines on planter refusal to allow the free-labor market to function properly. Yet it was not entirely a case of being faced with an uncomfortable choice between principle and humanity and selecting the latter. The abolitionists never quite gave up linking exports with civilization and were never able to contemplate state aid to ex-slaves, which might have eased the transition from preabolition to postabolition societies. This was the natural corollary of William Ellery Channing's comment before emancipation, "We have bound ourselves to resist [the slave's] own efforts for emancipation. We suffer him to do nothing for himself. The more should be done for him." By the mid-1860s private reservations on the ex-slaves' allocation of their daily time had become public warnings.[34]

The persistence of the slave trade throughout this period contributed to antislavery frustration. The abolitionists had viewed eradication of the slave trade as a vital building block in the creation of a new order in both Africa and the West Indies. Abolition was a part of almost every African development plan of the 1780s, and as the trade refused to wither over time, it became less a first step than an end in itself. For the British West Indies, removal of the slave trade was intended to force the planter to so improve the living conditions of the existing slaves that the slave population would increase or at least become self-sustaining. Once the planter perceived the advantages of this approach, he would improve treatment even further and move eventually, through emancipation, to the full implementation of a labor market.[35] As the efficiencies of such a system would be obvious to all, planters in the foreign colonies would quickly follow suit.

By the 1840s more abolitionists had dropped the argument that the superior efficiency of free labor would destroy the slave trade. And they were condemning the latter as a crime, thus efficiency and profitability were irrelevant.[36] Once the slave trade was dismissed in this fashion, the abolitionist position bore some semblance to reality. British sugar producers held their own until the 1820s; even in the 1830s, they were receiving the same price for their sugar as their foreign counterparts. It could be argued that the subsequent price decline for foreign-grown sugar and, after the 1846 equalization of duties, for British sugar, too, was due to the huge supplies of cheap labor made available by the slave trade. At the same time the ability of Barbados and later British Guiana and Trinidad to retain their share of the British market, despite Cuban competition, could be cited as proof of the potential of free labor if only the slave trade could be stopped. Such a position, of course, conveniently ignored the fact that the original abolitionist critique pointed to the demise of the slave trade as a result of free-labor competition. It also skated over the question of how "free" were the indentured labor supplies of British Guiana and Trinidad as well as the fact that such labor was necessary because of the refusal of ex-slaves to work on plantations.

Though forcible suppression was never intended as the only way of eradicating the slave trade, before the 1830s few abolitionists doubted that naval intervention would be effective.[37] Such expectations were reasonable during wartime when the British Navy was at maximum strength and the strictures of international law could be ignored. But even then the abolitionists forgot the huge Portuguese South Atlantic trade with which, because Portugal was a British ally, the navy would not interfere. After 1815, as we have seen, the traffic increased steadily once more to near eighteenth-century levels, despite major efforts by abolitionists and government alike to get the slave trade declared illegal at the subsequent peace negotiations and despite the peacetime naval patrols. Once more the very economic developments that contributed to the evolution of abolition also prevented the rapid realization of abolitionist hopes. British economic power triggered both envy and suspicion of British motives on the part of other nations with whom the British sought agreement on this issue.

On the slave-trade issue, the fragmentation of British attitudes to coerced labor went even further than it had on the post-emancipation labor problem. During the 1840s many of the most forceful exponents of free trade, both in and out of Parliament, launched a prolonged attack on the government's efforts to suppress the slave trade. A trade so profitable, they argued, could not be suppressed by force, and naval interference was simply exacerbating the horrors of the middle passage by encouraging overcrowding and the use of inadequate vessels. It was having no serious impact on the numbers carried. If the trade were left alone, conditions would improve, demand for slaves would quickly become satiated as Cuban and Brazilian planters increasingly realized the dangers of building their economy on black captives and the trade would die a natural death.[38] Strong abolitionist opposition to this position came from Edward Noel Buxton, the son of the old leader of the cause; George Stephen, Stephen Lushington, Sir Robert Inglis and a few other survivors of the emancipation campaign, most of whom were fervent supporters of free trade in other contexts, also supported forcible suppression.

These older abolitionists no longer had major influence on the movement. Many antislavery activists, like Joseph Sturge and the British and Foreign Anti-Slavery Society, now held pacifist beliefs that made coercion out of the question; others, like George Thompson and fellow British Garrisonians, were convinced that the slave trade would survive as long as slavery existed. For them the solution to the slave trade lay in India. The cruisers could never suppress a trade so profitable and would simply increase mortality rates. For this group, in what was perhaps the ultimate irony in the antislavery story, the free-market element of abolitionism had developed to the point where suppression of the slave trade separate from the suppression of slavery no longer appeared possible. Some who shared this approach came back to support naval intervention after the final suppression of the Brazilian trade.[39] But abolitionist support for the policy was weakest in the late 1840s at the very time that the free-trader attack on the cruiser squadron was at its strongest.

Thus the set of beliefs that branded slavery and the slave trade as evil prevented the continued incorporation of the slave trade and slavery into the British and indeed the world economic system at a time when the British economy had greatest need of such institutions. It is attempts to cope with these contradictions in the execution of antislave trade policy with which parts 3 and 4 of this work are concerned. Both government and private antislave-trade groups came close to violating their own ideological norms in the pursuit of suppression. Eventually, of course, the basic tenets of Palmerstonian liberalism itself were called into question. Richard Burton's comment, "I see no objection to render liberated labour forcible until the African race is educated for wages, and such habits are not learned in a day," suggests that the full circle had almost been completed by 1864. It was a small step to increasing racism within English society and demands for direct intervention in Africa without.[40]

# II

# The Atlantic Slave System, 1760–1830

# 3

# The Atlantic Market
# for Slaves at the Close
# of the Legal Slave Trade

Before the late eighteenth century in most parts of the world and long after in many areas, slaves were purchased and used wherever people could afford them. In the Americas an abundance of land relative to labor encouraged a particularly widespread use of slave labor. Quakers and the short-lived Georgia experiment notwithstanding, the issue of to buy or not to buy was decided by economic, not moral, factors. These included the production methods for the crop or activity for which the labor was required, the price of the end product and the cost of alternative forms of labor. Behind the latter, of course, lay the relative costs of bringing slaves from Africa and indentured labor from Europe. As already noted, activities that embodied significant economies of scale and unpleasant working conditions usually required slave labor because, unlike slaves, indentured servants could exercise some choice on the region of their employment. Some early American societies such as Barbados and Virginia began with an exclusive reliance on free or indentured labor and then, as the crop mix and the relative prices of free and indentured labor changed, switched just as completely to slave labor. Other societies such as Mexico, Peru and indeed large parts of Central America began with slave labor, both Indian and African, in mining activities. As mining was replaced by mixed farming for local markets, or subsistence agriculture, these areas gradually developed an almost exclusive reliance on free labor, again mainly non-European in origin. There were even some regions such as parts of northeastern Brazil and Cuba that produced sugar with slave labor at an early date, switched to leaf tobacco and largely free labor and then, in the nineteenth century, returned to sugar and slaves.[1]

The impact of economic and demographic growth in Europe on the Americas in an era predating the transatlantic free-migrant flow was to make plantation slavery feasible in regions where it had been previously of marginal importance or unknown and to raise the price of slaves. Paradoxically the development of the American Northwest illustrates the point. The middle and northern colonies of British North America had few slaves on account of their distance from Africa, their ability to attract indentured servants and their lack of an internationally marketable crop with major economies of scale. They could simply not compete in the slave market with the plantation zones further south. By the first half of the nineteenth century, however, transportation costs had fallen, the market for indentured servants had dried up, and North American wheat and lumber began to sell in Europe. Territories in the Midwest had some element of choice, at least on strictly economic grounds, between free and slave labor, and as late as 1818 Illinois would have preferred to enter the Union as a slave state. That it did not do so was, in part, an indication of how far antislavery sentiment had penetrated the North American consciousness and, in part, of the very high price for slaves induced by developments in the cotton South. A continuation of mid–eighteenth-century attitudes into the following century and an open slave trade with Africa that would have followed from this would surely have seen many family farmers in the nineteenth-century Midwest assisted by slaves rather than hired hands.[2]

In the 1760s as European demand pressures began to build, almost all supplies of plantation produce came from regions controlled by five separate political powers—six if we anticipate the independence of most of British North America. In addition to what became the United States, there were the British Caribbean, the Dutch and French West Indies and the colonies of the two Iberian powers. Although natural endowments dictated some specialization, national rivalries and the prevailing political philosophy in Europe ensured that each system pursued imperial self-sufficiency: Each national grouping of tropical colonies attempted to produce a wide range of products. By the mid-eighteenth century, the British and the French were the most successful, with the latter becoming the major supplier of Continental European markets. In the British case, first Barbados and then Jamaica became the biggest single source of sugar in the world. Before American independence the British system produced significant percentages of the world's marketed tobacco; indigo and rice were also important crops. After 1783 and the loss of the major growing areas for tobacco, indigo and rice, output in the sugar colonies became more diversified. Whereas 90 percent of Jamaican exports were sugar products in 1770, the equivalent figure in 1790 was 75 percent; in the late 1820s it was 67 percent. Coffee became a significant crop for the first time. The French, though consuming little sugar domestically, became the preeminent sugar producer in the eighteenth century. Yet a similar pattern of diversification is apparent in the French West Indies with nearly 40 percent of the exports of St. Domingue in 1767 and over 50 percent in 1775 composed of nonsugar crops such as indigo, coffee and cotton. St. Domingue, nevertheless, remained the largest sugar-producing region in the world. In Surinam, the largest of the Dutch possessions, increasing diversification of exports was also very marked after 1750.[3]

The Iberian Americas were the least developed of all the American regions in the mid-eighteenth century. This was despite the fact that the output of the old established sugar plantations of Bahia and Pernambuco together with the newer units of the Campos region rivaled that of Jamaica. In addition, Bahian roll tobacco was sold throughout the world. The major Brazilian export in 1750, however, was still gold from the Minas Gerais: In the middle decades of the eighteenth century, the slave-labor force of this region contributed the major portion of the world's gold supply. The size of the Portuguese domestic market was such that most Brazilian produce was sold in third markets. Although roll tobacco survived because its properties were difficult to reproduce elsewhere, sugar producers of northern Brazil found it increasingly difficult to cope with the secular fall in sugar prices that continued to the 1730s. Brazilian sugar output changed little between 1650 and 1750, except for periods when war removed either British or French supplies from the European market. By 1750, moreover, gold production in the Minas Gerais had passed its peak.[4] Of the Spanish Americas, Cuba produced hides, tobacco and a small amount of sugar, though only the latter product came from plantations. Only Venezuela, with cocoa and tobacco, produced exportable quantities of plantation products. But without major state initiatives—in the form of the financing of monopoly trading companies—it is unlikely that any Cuban sugar or Venezuelan cocoa would have been produced for export.[5]

The Iberian regions and products were thus very much on the fringe of the developments that expanded plantation cultivation in the Americas. Moreover, the factors that seemed to have generated the rapid development of the British and French plantation systems were not about to end. France and Britain continued as the dominant European powers. The land frontiers of their possessions and their ability to acquire more appeared almost limitless. The supply of coerced labor in addition was subject to no restrictions either from without or within the African continent. Yet a hundred years later, the major features of the eighteenth-century plantation systems had largely disappeared. Three dominant plantation regions had emerged by the mid-nineteenth century: Cuba, southern Brazil and the U.S. South. Not only had none of these been of more than minor importance in the previous century, but neither France nor Britain held sovereignty over them. Indeed Cuba and southern Brazil were controlled or had recently become independent of two of the most economically backward of European countries. The product mix of the new regions, moreover, exhibited a degree of specialization unknown since the early days of the old sugar colonies. By midcentury, between 80 and 90 percent of the exports of Cuba, southern Brazil and the U.S. South were comprised of sugar, coffee and cotton, respectively. Brazil and the United States produced over half the world's output of coffee and cotton, and Cuba was responsible for one third of all sugar production. None of these products had been of much importance in these regions in 1760. The explanation of these shifts in the locus, control and product mix of the major plantation economies falls into three stages, divided chronologically by the St. Domingue revolution and the abolition of the British and U.S. slave trades in 1807. But the whole of these developments were determined to a greater or lesser degree by the structure of European economic growth.

I

*1760–91*

In the generation after 1760, most plantation regions experienced prosperity. Although the British colonies expanded their output, their position relative to St. Domingue slipped. Partly, of course, this is explained by the destructive hurricanes and independence of the mainland colonies that put U.S. supplies and provisions out of legal reach of the West Indian planter. But a more important reason was the phenomenal development of the north and west plains of St. Domingue. The largest French West Indian colony had already overtaken Jamaica in sugar output in the 1730s and established a similar position in other produce thereafter. Yet the most spectacular expansion was yet to come. In the 1780s the slave population of St. Domingue almost doubled and slave imports averaged thirty thousand per annum in the last years of the decade. The French colony had come to overshadow Jamaica in the production of all types of plantation produce, just as the latter's sugar production had overtaken that of Barbados earlier in the century.[6] Aggregate slave imports into the Americas reached an all-time decadal high between 1781 and 1790. Yet the central fact of the period 1770–91 was that despite massive expansion of output in most plantation regions, peacetime prices of sugar, cotton, indigo and tobacco continued to rise. Clearly the increase in demand exceeded the increase in supply, and demand pressures previously felt by non-British and non-French areas only in time of war, now became steady and permanent.[7]

In the case of Portuguese Brazil, expansion was less dramatic than elsewhere in the Americas. Sugar output fluctuated according to the vicissitudes of war and peace, with only a slight upward trend at the time of the French wars.[8] In addition, gold output continued to decline and smuggling in the Spanish Río de la Plata region was curtailed in the 1770s. The importance of gold and sugar was such that total Brazilian exports actually declined after 1760 and did not again achieve 1760 levels until after the Napoleonic wars. Yet development of the minor plantation staples occurred even as total values declined. Indigo was established with major government assistance as part of an attempt to diversify the output of the Brazilian plantation system and to strengthen imperial ties. Aided by the collapse of U.S. production after independence, Brazilian exports grew rapidly from the mid-1770s, with England as the biggest market. Indigo never accounted for more than a small part of Brazilian exports and declined quickly with the revival of production in India during the first decade of the nineteenth century; but long before production peaked, indigo had become part of an agricultural renaissance. The export of rice, which had begun in the 1760s, was stimulated by the drop in supplies to Portugal from South Carolina during the War of American Independence. U.S. rice returned to the market in the 1780s, though in small quantities. Prices remained well above prewar levels, however, reflecting the secular increase in demand that was occurring.[9]

Whereas indigo was a southern crop and rice was produced in several Brazilian coastal regions, the initial effects of the revival were felt mainly in the north. Bahian tobacco exports, making up about 10 percent of Brazilian exports by the 1790s, increased steadily after midcentury in response to increased demand from both Europe and Africa. The lower grades of roll tobacco were sold in West Africa, and the 1780s saw the West African slave trade attaining record levels. Regular production of leaf tobacco, where lay the mass market of the future, began in 1774, though the rolled product remained dominant until well into the nineteenth century. The Minas Gerais and all the coastal centers in the north outside Amazonia, particularly Maranhão, quickly responded to the demand for cotton that began in the 1760s. This demand came not just from England, though Brazil's share of this rapidly growing market did increase, but from France and Portugal, too. The French bought more Brazilian cotton than the English before 1785 and after 1800, and the Portuguese cotton textile industry grew to the point where one third of Brazilian imports from Portugal in the 1790s were cotton goods manufactured in Portugal with Brazilian cotton. Prices for raw cotton increased steadily down to the early 1800s. The effect of the output growth of cotton and the other minor staples on the aggregate export trend was not felt until 1783, mainly because of falling gold output and the lethargic response of the still-dominant sugar sector to rising demand from Europe. There was, nevertheless, a considerable diversification within the Brazilian economy and a reallocation of resources from mining to agriculture.[10].

In the Spanish Americas the leading export to Europe throughout this period remained precious metals.[11] Nevertheless, whereas Brazil diversified and moved away from sugar, Cuba moved into more emphasis on sugar production, though coffee also developed rapidly. Underlying such contrasting responses to increased European demand were the political constraints on Cuban development. For Portuguese Brazil, apart from the running down of gold deposits, the problem was a lack of markets, which the pickup in European demand helped solve. Brazil had direct access to a very price-responsive supply of African labor. In the context of eighteenth-century mercantilism, market opportunities for Cuban produce were inevitably less than those for, say, English or French produce. The major barriers to Cuban development, however, were institutional limitations on access to slave labor and private land tenure. Security of landholdings, Spanish slave stations on the African coast (in other words, with no Treaty of Tordesillas) and a Spanish policy of taxing produce exports from Cuba instead of slave imports into the island would have speeded development. Perhaps the great central plains of Cuba would have provided the basis for a St. Domingue-type development in the seventeenth or early eighteenth centuries. Instead Cuba remained a sparsely populated island that produced a range of products that included sugar, but over which tobacco predominated. Of all the commercial tobacco-growing regions of the Americas, Cuba relied most heavily on free labor.[12] Slaves could be supplied legally only by *asentistas,* or contractors, to the Spanish crown down to the 1790s. As the object of the *asiento* was to create monopoly profits and as royal taxes were levied in addition, the price differential between the Spanish and non-Spanish Americas was considerable. In 1714–19 and 1733 *asiento* slaves sold in Havana at an average price of £56, whereas prices in nearby Jamaica were in the £20 to £25 range. Even in 1768 when the *asiento* contracts were no longer exclusive, the differential was still £20 and, in addition, credit facilities in

Havana were very limited.[13] Smuggling from Jamaica and St. Domingue was an obvious supplementary source, but the fact remains that after over 250 years of legal and illegal imports, the 1774 census counted only 44,333 slaves. The vast majority of this number were no doubt born on the island or arrived during the short British occupation. While the English held the *asiento* between 1713 and 1739, Cuban slave imports averaged well under 1,000 a year, even after allowing for illegal arrivals, and the British almost certainly supplied more than had their predecessors.[14]

After declining at the end of the seventeenth century, Cuban sugar exports expanded slowly down to 1750. Both tobacco and sugar output grew strongly in the 1750s, however, and by the time of the English occupation in 1763, sugar exports had doubled from the beginning of the century. Thereafter, given few alternative uses for slaves on the island, sugar production depended on the vicissitudes not of war and peace as in the case of Brazil, but on Spanish policies toward slave imports and the import of foreign technology. Restrictions on slave imports were gradually eased from the 1760s on as part of a general Spanish shift to commercial liberalization and administrative reform.[15] Initially the exclusivity of the *asiento* was revoked. In 1773 the *asentistas* were allowed to ship slaves from non-Spanish Caribbean regions, which meant Jamaica and St. Thomas, and in the war period of 1779–83, neutral ships were allowed to import slaves. The administered price of the slave sold in Havana did not at first decrease, however, and perhaps in response to this, the size of the *asiento* contracts were steadily increased down to the late 1780s. Up to this point mercantile restrictions had largely insulated Cuba from the effects of European economic and demographic growth. The rising sugar prices of the 1780s, however, appear to have elicited a response as increased numbers of illicit imports entered Cuba toward the end of the decade, many as an offshoot of the St. Domingue trade. The breakthrough, which the Cuban planters had sought for years, came at last in the form of two royal *cédulas* in 1789 and 1791. The first was probably stimulated by a concern that the British were about to abolish their own slave trade. Thus the initial impact of the British agitation for abolition was to precipitate the development of the biggest sugar island of them all. The *cédulas* abolished fixed or administered pricing and import duties and allowed much fuller foreign participation.[16] Not all restrictions were removed, but the effect was to integrate Cuba into the Caribbean slave markets and reduce the price differential for Cuban and non-Cuban slaves. In the quarter century before the 1789 *cédula,* annual slave imports had probably tripled and sugar exports increased by a like amount.[17] In the 1790s growth of both slave imports and sugar exports would probably have been much greater than this but for the wars in Europe.

The region that responded most to the European demand pressures was in the French rather than the Iberian Americas. The rapid growth of St. Domingue in the early part of the century was surpassed by the acceleration of the 1780s. While maintaining a level of sugar output 80 percent greater than that of Jamaica, the French planters took full advantage of the variety of the terrain and soil and built up an even greater dominance in the production of the minor staples of coffee and cotton. By 1790 the slave population of the

French Empire was 50 percent greater than that of the British.[18] The speed ar. strength of the French colonial response may well have precipitated the rebellion. There had always been tensions between the *colons* of St. Domingue and the French administration over the ban on direct trade between the colony and foreign territories. All French plantation regions needed access to the provisions and lumber that in the British case came from the North American colonies. With no French equivalents of these, smuggling was extensive and increased output inevitably exacerbated the problem. By the 1780s the concern of the French metropolitan authorities had come to focus on how to keep St. Domingue within the empire rather than how to enforce trade restrictions. The French Revolution was thus seen by many of the *colons* as an opportunity to establish colonial autonomy, and it was this that formed the first step in the social and economic disintegration of the French Caribbean colonies.[19]

Two more specific and explosive results of the 1780s boom may be discerned. Imports of slaves in the years before the revolution were such that the African component of both the slave and the total population of St. Domingue was among the greatest of any major American colony. Although Creoles came to lead and shape the St. Domingue revolution, here as in most other important slave revolts, it was among African slaves that the initial rebellious impulse germinated.[20] A second and more important consequence, at least in determining the fate of the rebellion was the expansion of minor plantation crops in the 1780s. The production of cotton, indigo, coffee and pimento was characterized by much smaller production units than was the production of sugar. It was in just this activity that many free coloreds, as a group always less wealthy than the *grands blancs,* established themselves. By 1790 the two groups were comparable in numbers. The free coloreds, though experiencing considerable legal disabilities, owned perhaps one fifth of the land and a slightly smaller proportion of the slaves. It was this plus the unusually large number of *petits blancs* on the island that gave the St. Domingue revolution its complexity. More specifically, the racial divisions among the slave-owning class and the hostility of the *petits blancs* to the propertied free coloreds generated a fertile environment for slave rebellion. Rebel leaders were able to play off their opponents against one another once it had begun.[21] One might argue that the French Revolution notwithstanding, a slower rate of growth that put a premium on monoculture would have greatly reduced the rebellion's chances of success. There was, thus, much in the impact of European economic growth on the plantation periphery that made the St. Domingue events probable.

## 1791–1805

For the British, Portuguese and Spanish colonies, the French colonial collapse meant a huge boost in demand for produce and probably, too, a lower African price for slaves. The demise of the French slave trade was mainly responsible for the lower slave prices and this was due mainly to the war with Britain that began in 1793. But there can be no doubt that the expansion of the non-French areas in the 1790s was due in the main to the same European developments that had triggered their earlier growth. The British, Portuguese and Spanish ho had produced, respectively, 36.7, 6.6 and 6.3 percent of the sugar imported by the North Atlantic countries in 1787 increased their market share steadily thereafter. British colonial and Brazilian shares of the raw cotton market jumped by 50 percent between 1786–87 and 1796–1800, and the redistribution of coffee production was only slightly less dramatic.[22] A more important point is that the markets that were thus redistributed were growing at an unprecedented rate. In the twenty years down to 1805, British sugar consumption rose 80 percent and cotton imports quadrupled despite prices that increased in real terms. Even without the St. Domingue rebellion, the 1790s would have been a prosperous decade for non-French plantations in the Americas.[23]

In Brazil there are few signs at this stage of the international specialization that developed in the first half of the nineteenth century. The Brazilian sugar industry expanded as rapidly as its Cuban counterpart in the 1790s. Sugar once more became the leading Brazilian export before the end of the decade as exports doubled between 1790 and 1807. But on the basis of growing markets in both Britain and France, it was cotton production that grew most explosively. Cotton exports from Maranhão, already well established by the 1780s, quadrupled in the next twenty years. In the first quarter of the nineteenth century, cotton and sugar alternated as the leading Brazilian export. Coffee, at first a northeastern crop, was grown along the major roads leading out of Rio de Janeiro from the 1770s. Cultivation spread slowly at first, with more rapid acceleration from a small base coming after 1798.[24] This slow response was, in part, a result of the fact that St. Domingue coffee did not decline as much as sugar output. Even as late as 1800 exports were holding steady at 50 percent of prerevolutionary levels. More to the point, coffee was not an important element among the retained imports of the world's most dynamic economy. It was the United States rather than the British consumer who was to provide the basis of the later coffee boom. Initially the crop was sold to the Brazilian domestic and Portuguese market, and coffee did not make up more than 10 percent of total Brazilian exports until after 1810. The British West Indies exported more coffee than did southern Brazil in every year until the mid-1820s.[25]

Perhaps the major Brazilian impact of the increased demand pressures of the 1790s was on the regional distribution of economic activity. Sugar and tobacco production in Bahia increased significantly. Nevertheless, the relative position of both this region and Minas Gerais, the major centers of eighteenth-century economic activity, declined as nearly 80 percent of the cotton exported between 1796 and 1805 came from Pernambuco and Maranhão. Furthermore, much of the additional sugar produced came from the captaincies of Rio de Janeiro and São Paulo. One center near Parati in Rio de Janeiro specialized in *aguardente,* a sugar-based liquor, for the African market, and by the turn of the century, Rio de Janeiro was exporting more sugar than was Bahia. Trends in the production of the minor staples such as cacao from Amazonia, rice from Rio de Janeiro and hides from Rio Grande do Sul also contributed to the relative decline of the older plantation regions.[26]

In two other major plantation regions, the structure of British demand dictated a much greater degree of specialization. In Cuba an actual reallocation of resources occurred—from hides and tobacco to sugar production. The weight and bulk of sugar products ensured the importance of the transportation factor in the location of plantations. Although a large area of Cuba was suitable for sugar growing, the existing roads and the lands already cleared of forest made the tobacco regions attractive to prospective sugar producers. Relative sugar and tobacco prices and, in many instances, the small tobacco growers' questionable legal title to this land meant that sugar cultivation expanded first in the tobacco regions in the vicinity of Havana, Güines and the road joining the two. The process was accompanied by a steady rise in land prices and, as tobacco shifted to more remote areas, a decline in tobacco output.[27] What tobacco and ranching could not provide in large numbers was slaves, and the prices for them continued at close to pre-1789 levels in real terms despite the greatly reduced import restrictions and lower prices in Africa. Of course, sugar and coffee prices increased in the 1790s, but Cuban producers were competing for slaves with their counterparts on the British islands and with an unprecedented demand for Africans from North American cotton plantations. Coffee output went from insignificant amounts in the 1780s to nearly 2 million pounds per year in 1805 and 1806, largely aided by an influx of St. Domingue refugees, but this was still only one tenth of Jamaican output. Coffee production actually expanded more rapidly than sugar output in Cuba in the first twenty years of the nineteenth century, though it probably never displaced sugar as the most valuable export. Sugar predominated in the island from an early date. Annual exports from Havana from 1804 to 1808 were nearly 150 percent greater than the annual average between 1786 to 1790. This growth was, nevertheless, no more rapid than that of the southern Brazilian sugar industry. The freer traffic in Cuban slave imports at this time was matched in Brazil by the availability of slaves from the declining gold economy of Minas Gerais as well as by easier Brazilian access to Africa.[28]

In the U.S. South, the connection between industrialization and an expanding slave system was unequivocal. A thriving cultivation of the long-stapled sea-island variety of cotton dates from the 1780s. Given the light weight and high volume of the crop, expansion inland first to the Carolina and Georgia uplands and later to the cotton belt and the alluvial plains was a simple function of rising British demand—at least once the cotton gin had resolved the problem of separating seed from fiber for the inland varieties. As long as the slave trade remained open, American cotton expansion made no discernible inroads into the production of other U.S. slave staples. The lands pulled into cotton production had never been used and were not suitable for the cultivation of tobacco and rice. But from an early date, American cotton had a profound effect on the production of cotton beyond U.S. borders. In 1788 British imports were drawn from four continents and the U.S. South was only one of a dozen regions involved. By 1803 the American share had risen to 45 percent. In the face of a secular decline in price that lasted to the Civil War, this share rose eventually to 75 percent as production in other regions grew slowly, stagnated or disappeared completely.[29]

The diversity and strength of plantation development in Brazil, Cuba and the United States was impressive. Nevertheless, it should not obscure the fact that by 1800 it was the British colonies which had gained the most from industrialization in Britain and chaos in St. Domingue. Moreover, as we have seen, British prospects for future gains after the acquisition of Demerara and Trinidad were brighter than at any point in the eighteenth century. At the beginning of the nineteenth century, the British West Indies were producing over half the sugar imported by countries bordering the North Atlantic, a figure that was at least double the combined total for the Portuguese and all the Spanish colonies. As for coffee, Jamaica was exporting five times as much as Cuba and Rio de Janeiro put together. Only in cotton production were the British West Indies losing out, in relative terms, to another plantation polity; even here production had tripled since the 1780s. Moreover, the newly acquired colony of Demerara was the only supplier other than the United States to increase its share of the British market in the early years of the century.[30]

That labor costs (the price of slaves) rose steadily under these circumstances is scarcely surprising. After adjusting for inflation, prices rose slightly from 1761–70 to 1781–90 and more strongly after the 1780s.[31] There are two explanations for this latter increase in the face of the demise of a major American market. One was the continuing and underlying increase in demand for plantation produce; the other was the outbreak of a European war. On the high seas this meant higher shipping costs and an increased spread between the African and American prices of the slave. But prices did not merely increase, differentials between major American markets became smaller. For a brief period at the beginning of the nineteenth century, there came into existence a transatlantic market for slaves that, despite the war, was largely unfettered by mercantilist trade restrictions and attempts to abolish the traffic.[32] It was the closest that the transatlantic slave trade ever came to free trade. Down to 1791 it was the Spanish Americas that were denied free or direct access to Africa; various other nations restricted the ports at which trading occurred: After 1805, restrictions on the British areas and shipping began to build. For most of the years in between there had been war, which tended to affect Brazil less than the Caribbean and North America. Yet the war also meant British conquests in the Caribbean, and the turn of the century saw the slave-trade market straddling the Atlantic as integrated as it ever became. In 1804 prices at Havana and in the British Windward and Leeward islands were very similar.[33] It was perhaps the only period in the history of the trade that all plantation areas, except perhaps the French, competed with each other on equal terms with the major differentials in labor costs being explained by geographic distances from Africa.

### 1805–30

Beginning in 1805 first British and then U.S. abolition of the slave trade destroyed the homogeneity. British and American plantations inevitably faced higher labor costs in the wake of abolition, given the expansion of demand for plantation produce. But in the American case a very high rate of natural increase in the slave population, beginning early in the previous century, greatly mitigated the economic impact of abolition. Indeed if the same rate of natural decrease that existed for Caribbean slave populations had held for U.S. slaves, then nineteenth-century slave trade to the United States would have had to have matched the free-migrant flow from Europe for the slave population to have reached the level it did in 1860.[34] The Caribbean epidemiological environment and the sex and age structure of the British slave population ensured that the slave populations of areas that had imported heavily in the years preceding abolition would decline. These same factors also ensured that when slave populations did begin to increase, they would do so slowly. In the generation after slave-trade abolition, when the American slave population doubled, its British counterpart declined by at least 10 percent and by even more in the colonies with the greatest potential for increased output. British planters showed considerable ingenuity in the deployment and organization of their labor forces, so that production levels, at least for sugar, were maintained or increased slightly. But British producers were now in a straitjacket. The slave price differential between the Spanish Caribbean, on the one hand, and the British and American plantation areas, on the other, that had existed in the eighteenth century reappeared, but this time to the advantage of the Spanish producers.[35]

The new differential in slave prices between British and Iberian plantation regions might be divided into two parts. One is explained by the expanding demand for produce after 1807 that British suppliers could not fill on account of their inability to gain access to a labor supply. The other stemmed from the fall in prices of slaves in Africa for Iberian producers that occurred when the British and Americans pulled out of the African market. Although the African cost component of the American selling price of a slave was not large (perhaps 25 percent at this time), the impact of abolition was perceptible. The British and U.S. traders had been responsible for almost two thirds of the transatlantic slave exports from Africa in the period 1791 to 1805, about double the proportion of the trade held by the French in the 1780s. The sudden disappearance of these traders from the coast in 1808 and the simultaneous closing of perhaps 50 to 60 percent of all transatlantic plantations to new African slaves meant an increased supply of slaves to those plantations in the Americas still open to the slave traffic. On the African coast slave prices fell by a little more than half and remained generally below the pre-1807 price for as long as the traffic lasted.[36]

In Brazil slaves were used in a wider range of occupations than anywhere else in the Americas. There were very few regions or activities in that country with any connection to world markets that did not depend on slave labor. As late as the 1840s British officials at the Rio de Janeiro Court of mixed commission on the slave trade used slave labor and later apprenticed *bozales* to staff their households. When forbidden to do so by the Foreign Office, the same officials complained at length of the difficulty and cost of switching to free labor. Despite the widespread incidence of subsistence agriculture, most estimates of the early nineteenth-century Brazilian population suggest that black slaves outnumbered the white population by two to one.[37] At this time there were more slaves in Brazil than in the United States or indeed in any polity in e Americas. Slaves were basic to the sugar, cotton, rice and indigo areas near

the coast, but they were the mainstay of the labor force in the interior also.[38]
Slaves were rare only on subsistence farms.[39] The broad diffusion of early nineteenth-century Brazilian slavery across region and product is explained, in
part, by the lack of a dominant crop and, in part, by the ready access that Brazil
maintained with Africa. Not only was Brazil geographically closer to Africa
than any other American slave society but the disruptions of war and revolu-
tions after 1792 had less effect on trade relations between the two than on any
other major transatlantic trade route. War and revolution to the north, combined with European economic growth and the restrictions on the British
planter after 1805, nevertheless had profound long-run effects. The withdrawal
of the British and U.S. slave traders from Africa exerted a downward pressure
on slave prices. Yet increased Brazilian demand for slaves meant that between
1766 and 1821 slave prices in Rio de Janeiro actually rose substantially in real
terms. Though reliable data for the intervening years are scarce, it is likely that
some of the increase occurred after 1800.[40] The gradual concentration of Brazilian slaves in sugar and coffee production (see chapter 11) probably began
early in the century.

The inability of British planters to expand their output in response to burgeoning world markets has already been discussed. It was due not so much to
higher labor costs as to the complete unavailability of free labor at a price at
which a plantation could operate profitably. Markets that might have been
filled by British producers were now open to the Brazilians and Cubans. British
sugar consumption increased at a mean annual rate of just under 1.5 percent
between 1805 and 1825. As this was the slowest secular growth in the British
market between 1650 and 1900, it seems likely that the rest of the North Atlantic market was growing more quickly at this time. British West Indian sugar
production was growing at only 0.5 percent per year on average between 1801–
5 and 1821–25, though its rate of growth throughout the 1820s allowed it to
keep pace with consumption in Britain at least. Brazilian and Cuban producers
filled much of the resulting gap in non-British markets as their output
expanded at from double to quadruple the British rates between 1805 and
1830. The different degrees of processing in sugar exports make comparisons
difficult but, by any reasonable measurement, it is clear that the British sugar
colonies continued to produce more sugar than both Brazil and Cuba together
until the final abolition of British slavery itself in 1833. The pattern in coffee
was similar. Exports of coffee from Cuba grew at the phenomenal rate of 13
percent per year in the first two decades of the century, and at a yearly average
of nearly 15 percent during the 1820s. Production surpassed that of the British
West Indies, which changed little in the same period. The strongest growth
came after British abolition of the slave trade rather than before, even though
the shift of growers from St. Domingue to Cuba had already taken place by
1808. Brazilian competition, which eventually contributed to the decline of the
Cuban industry, became significant only after 1810. Although Brazilian output
expanded even faster than its Cuban counterpart, it did not exceed British and
Cuban production until the mid-1820s.[41]

The natural advantages of Cuba and southern Brazil in the production of
sugar and coffee may have outweighed those of Demerara, Jamaica and Trinidad, but there were few signs of it before 1807 or for several years after. As v

have seen, the remarkably flexible response of British planters and slaves meant that as late as the 1820s the British were selling sugar profitably in the same markets as the Cubans despite having higher labor costs. Yet even in the absence of the 1833 Emancipation Act, this situation might not have continued. In the long run Iberian access to Africa meant that after 1805 the Iberian and British planter simply did not compete on equal terms. At the very least, planters in the Iberian Americas could have asked for nothing better from the British government (except perhaps to leave their own slave trade untouched) than to abolish first the slave trade and then slavery in the British colonies.

## II

We can now review the impact of these events on the volume of African slave arrivals in the Americas between 1781 and 1830. The slave import trends into Brazil reflect the major points just discussed. Figure 2 gives the time profile of slave imports into three different regions of Brazil from the earliest point in the eighteenth century when a continuous reliable annual time series becomes possible to the approximate point in the nineteenth century when the British began an active policy of suppression of the Brazilian traffic. For reasons explained later, this occurred at different times for different branches of the trade. The annual import data underlying this figure are presented in appendix A.

It seems likely that arrivals in Rio de Janeiro in the early 1780s were considerably below those in the mid-eighteenth century.[42] The timing of the acceleration thereafter reflects the southern Brazilian agricultural renaissance rather than the events in St. Domingue. The new sugar exports and the strong growth of the minor staples predated the 1790s, whereas the effects of these on slave imports were offset, in part, by the continuing fall in gold output. The major phase in the growth of slave imports begins with the abolition of the British

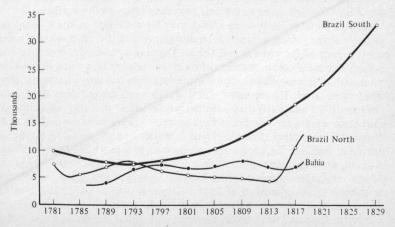

**Figure 2.** Time profile of annual slave imports into Brazil, 1781–1830.

slave trade and was concentrated in south-central Brazil: Between 1796–1800 and 1826–30 slave imports in the south grew at 4.6 percent per annum, with the rate averaging 5.7 percent in the twenty years after 1810. Although data on coffee exports are scarce in the pre-1821 period, production may not have been large enough to influence slave imports significantly until after the rapid acceleration of slave imports began.[43] On the other hand, none of the other crops, nor the trade in re-exports to La Plata seem capable of explaining changes of this magnitude in slave arrivals. Growth rates of slave imports to other Brazilian regions that specialized in sugar and cotton were much more modest.[44] There remains the impact of trade-liberalization measures introduced with the arrival of the Portuguese royal court at Rio de Janeiro in 1808.[45] For Brazilians these meant freedom to trade with any part of the world rather than with Portuguese ports only. The plantation owner could now buy slaves from any part of Africa and from traders of any nationality, and he could ship his produce direct to world markets. For the coffee producer this meant northern Europe and United States markets. Parallels with the Spanish *cédulas* of 1789 and 1791 come to mind. In fact, the Portuguese restrictions on slave imports, which were removed in 1808, had been effectively far less stringent. Moreover, sugar and cotton from northern Brazil benefited to the same extent without slave imports to these regions jumping as much as they did in southern Brazil. Perhaps all these factors contributed, with the delayed response in coffee exports from Rio being a simple function of the long maturation period of the coffee bush.

Import trends into Bahia and northern Brazilian ports are more easily accounted for. As we might expect for regions specializing in crops produced by St. Domingue, the 1790s brought a sharp increase in slave imports. American and British abolition had a much smaller impact on Bahia than on southern Brazil and apparently no impact at all on northeastern Brazil. This latter is explained, in part, by the increasing dominance of the U.S. South among cotton-producing regions. By the 1820s and probably earlier, Brazilian cotton exports, produced mainly in the northeast, had stabilized in volume and were declining in value as prices fell. Their share of the world market share was also declining. This left sugar as the only growth industry in the northeast.[46]

Similar patterns, slightly modified, may be discerned in the Cuban slave imports series shown in figure 3. Higher imports in the 1790s were a natural consequence of the *cédulas* and the St. Domingue rebellion. Yet it is worth noting that the absolute numbers of slaves introduced into Cuba in the 1790s, even with generous allowances for smuggling, was not large in comparison to what came after. Furthermore, more slaves were carried into Bahia alone between 1790 and 1810 than into the whole island of Cuba. Of course, the European wars were significant here as their effects were felt largely in the North Atlantic rather than the South Atlantic. Imports to Cuba in 1802 (in March of that year the Treaty of Amiens restored a short-lived peace to North Atlantic sea-lanes) were nearly triple the average for the 1790–1810 period. Moreover, Cuban importers relied heavily on British and American carriers,[47] as the low levels of arrivals of 1807–9 attest. British and U.S. abolition provided more opportunities for the Portuguese slave trader who had always dominated the Brazilian slave trade. However, the initial impact on Cuba of these events together with the British Orders in Council interdicting neutral trad

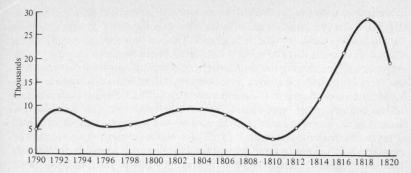

**Figure 3.** Time profile of annual slave imports into Cuba, 1790–1820.

was to cut back the slave trade substantially. The full expansive effect of British and U.S. abolition—larger markets for Cuban producers, cheaper prices for slaves and higher costs for British and U.S. plantation owners—did not come until 1814. As figure 3 shows, it was after 1814 that slave imports expanded dramatically. Thus slave imports doubled between 1806–10 and 1811–15 and tripled again in the next five years. In this last period there was an additional temporary stimulus to slave imports provided by the 1817 treaty between Spain and England that set 1820 as the last year for legal imports. But the treaty probably had a small effect relative to these long-term underlying factors.

Aggregate slave-trade trends do not at first sight reflect events in London, St. Domingue and Washington. Exports of slaves from Africa to the Americas fell from the all-time peak of the previous decade by only 8 percent in the 1790s. They fell by a further one fifth between the 1790s and 1801 to 1810, but between 1811 and 1820 the slave trade was still functioning at two thirds of its record levels of thirty years earlier. This, moreover, was in spite of the fact that the British Caribbean, St. Domingue and the United States were no longer accepting slaves. The relevant question, of course, is how many slaves would have been shipped in the absence of abolition and rebellion. In the face of the accelerating output of plantation produce reviewed earlier, aggregate slave imports would have risen substantially in the absence of supply constraints. As discussed in chapter 11, plantation output per slave increased during the nineteenth century, and this may have restrained the flow somewhat. But it is hard to believe that slave arrivals would have been less than the record numbers in the 1780s. If we assume, first, that a 1 percent increase in plantation sugar output would have induced a 1 percent increase in the demand for slaves and, second, that the supply conditions of the 1780s continued throughout the period, then the decadal volume of the slave traffic would have been at least double its 1780s level by 1830.[48]

Slave prices responded predictably with large differentials opening up, not just between British and Cuban markets but between all regions according to whether or not the region had access to the transatlantic slave trade. During the 1820s recently arrived African males were selling for less than $200 in Brazil and just over $300 in Cuba. In Trinidad and the U.S. South prices were double this; however, as there were no newly disembarked Africans in these regions, exact comparisons are difficult.[49] Prices also tended to vary over time as abolition measures were anticipated. Thus as the formal ending of the Cuban slave trade in 1820 became imminent, prices began to rise, only to fall again when the ineffectiveness of proscription became apparent. In some British West Indian colonies, slave prices began to fall after the campaign to emancipate the slaves began in the mother country in 1823. By the second decade of the century, there were already major differences between systems—and indeed in the British case within the system—on account of the strict limitations on the intercolonial traffic.[50] In the nineteenth century the Americas experienced a wider range of slave prices than ever before. The major differentials, moreover, could no longer be explained as they had in the past by distance, mercantilist policies or the requirements of different crops. Rather it was a question of institutional barriers on the supply of slaves and, it should be added, the continuing shortage of alternative forms of labor.[51] Even when slave prices rose to the very high levels attained in midcentury Cuba and the U.S. South, there was still no question of a significant influx of free labor to the plantations except in Brazilian cotton-growing regions. By then rising incomes for free labor in other parts of the North Atlantic basin had made the plantation option even less attractive.

The structure of the American plantation systems and their relationship with Africa was thus profoundly altered in the generation before 1810. Of the six major systems of the 1780s, only one, the Spanish, did not have free access to African-born labor. Thirty years later the biggest of these systems, the French, had been reduced to fragments of territory and slave imports of a few thousand a year smuggled in during the decade after the Napoleonic wars. A second system, the Dutch, had been partially absorbed by a third, the British, and neither system was allowed even illicitly introduced slaves after 1807. Indeed in the Dutch case few Africans were introduced after 1795.[52] A fourth, that of the United States, had also instituted abolition and although demographic trends provided a natural substitute, product specialization quickly ensured little direct competition between this system and the two others that were relatively free of restrictions on their supply of labor. Of the six systems, therefore, only two, the Spanish and the Portuguese, had free access to Africa in 1810, and this access did not remain completely free for very long. Treaties between England and first Portugal, then Spain and next Brazil had the effect of making illegal the traffic to Bahia and north Brazil in 1815, the Cuban trade in 1820 and the trade to southern Brazil ten years later. But the Africans continued to arrive. There are, thus, two underlying causes of the rapid expansion of the slave systems of the Iberian Americas in the nineteenth century. One was obviously the accelerating demand for produce, behind which lay the economic and demographic growth of the North Atlantic littoral, in particular Great Britain. The other was the destruction or shackling of the non-Iberian systems that, without such restraints, would have claimed much larger shares of the world produce market than they, in fact, did. Because antislavery was responsible for these restraints and was itself linked to the ideological ramifications of economic growth, industrialization gave a double stimulus to slavery in Cuba and Braz̄

# 4

# The Restructuring of the
# Slave Trade, 1780s to 1820s

The paradox posed in the preceding chapters of increased demands for slaves, on the one hand, and the suppression of slavery and the slave trade, on the other, does not fully describe the complex relationship between economic development and coerced labor. As well as increasing the demand for slave labor in the tropical Americas, industrialization also reduced the cost of getting that labor, and it reduced it most for the countries in the vanguard of development. There was, thus, a strong supply-side impact on the transatlantic slave market (still to be discussed), which predated and was quite separate from serious British efforts to suppress the Iberian slave trade. The price of goods exchanged for slaves fell drastically in the early nineteenth century, capital mobilization and transportation facilities improved and there were probably economies of scale in both the American distribution and the African factoring of slaves.[1] At the same time countries in which many of these developments originated prohibited the direct participation of their citizens in the trade. The result was a gradual restructuring of the traffic, one that allowed, indeed depended on, the indirect involvement of the British and the Americans.

Initially the transatlantic slave trade had been a European-based commerce: Ships were owned at, fitted out at, cleared from and returned to European ports. A triangular trade existed, or at least a triangular journey.[2] By the closing years of the traffic, it had become almost entirely based in the Americas, with no direct European participation. There was a temporary and relatively minor revival of the Nantes-based traffic to the Caribbean with the return of peace in 1814. Nevertheless the switch from Europe to the Americas occurred mainly between 1790 and 1810. Before this period 70 percent of the traffic was European; after 1820 over 90 percent was based in the Americas.[3] Of the four major national carriers (British, French, Portuguese and American) in the 1780s, only one, the Portuguese, survived past the first decade of the new century. Yet at the same time the goods and credit used in the trade became more European—

in particular, British—than ever before. An understanding of the nature and significance of these changes requires a brief review of the salient features of the late eighteenth-century slave trade.

Almost all the slaves shipped across the Atlantic in the 1780s were carried in vessels owned by the four major national carriers. For some of these carriers, there were advantages, both natural and institutional, that were not fully available to the others. The Portuguese case is perhaps the simplest to explain. Portuguese slavers rarely ventured into the Caribbean or any American markets north of the equator. Indeed the system was really Brazilian as relatively few of the ships involved had connections of any sort with Europe.[4] Although the other national carriers competed fiercely with each other to the north, the South Atlantic traffic remained largely self-contained. Its insulation was such that throughout the eighteenth century, Brazilian slave supplies were the least affected of those of any plantation region by European wars. At the root of this relative isolation lay the ridge of high pressure that dominates the South Atlantic and determines a wind system, reinforced by ocean currents, that ensures that ships sailing from Europe to southwest Africa have to travel very close to Brazil. Distance and traveling time therefore ensured that Brazilian-based merchants trading between Brazil and Portuguese Angola would have an advantage over European-based rivals, and as early as 1644 the Portuguese crown authorized direct trade between Bahia and Africa. Nor were there convenient nearby colonial bases from which rivals could conduct smuggling operations into Brazil: The nearest north European possession was thousands of miles distant. Indeed in the part of the Brazilian empire that was closest to such possessions—Amazonia—some non-Portuguese trafficking did occur. Europeans could not easily move their operations to Brazilian ports. The mercantilist regulations embodied in the 1758 and 1761 decrees confirmed that only Portuguese citizens could trade in slaves and designated those ports from which trading could take place.[5] Thus the British and American traders who had taken over such a large part of the traffic to the non–Anglo-Saxon Caribbean were excluded from the Portuguese Americas. Had the Portuguese court and trade liberalization come to Rio de Janeiro in 1798 instead of 1808, then the Americans and British would no doubt have taken up residence and broken into the South Atlantic trade. As it was, for branches of the slave trade terminating at Rio de Janeiro natural and institutional barriers to entry combined to ensure Portuguese predominance.

Distance was also important in providing protection for the Portuguese slave traders of northeastern Brazil. Bahia, Pernambuco and Maranhão were the closest to Africa of all the ports of entry to the Americas, and they were among the farthest away from Europe. Thus, unless the European based merchant had considerable advantages in terms of goods and credit, a three-stage slaving venture originating in Europe could not compete with operations located in Brazil. In fact, in the South Atlantic, any advantages with trade goods lay with the Brazilians rather than the Europeans. Africans in several regions, in particular in the Bight of Benin, developed a strong taste for both *aguardente* and *cachaça*, sugar-based liquors made in both the Guanabara Bay region and northeastern Brazil, and roll tobacco of Bahia. Strong economic and cultural ties developed between Bahia, Brazil, and Yorubaland in Africa, with the former sending almost as much tobacco to the Benin ports as it did to Portugal. Though of minor importance in Angola, tobacco made up the greater part of the Bahian cargoes exchanged for slaves in the Bight of Benin. Brazilian produce could be (and was) bought by slave traders of all nations on the African coast and indeed the Dutch allowed the Brazilians access to their West African ports for the sole purpose of gaining access to that commodity. But generally, mercantilist regulations ensured some additional cost for the non-Portuguese. In the late eighteenth century southern Brazil paid for slaves largely with gold as well as produce, and the precious metal was used by Angolan merchants to purchase textiles direct from India.[6] For the most part, then, the eighteenth-century Brazilian slave trade was conducted independently of Europe.

The French traffic of the eighteenth century was also a protected trade.[7] Despite a long and partially successful campaign by French planters throughout the century, only French ships were legally permitted to supply slaves to French St. Domingue. In the French Windwards discriminatory duties were levied on all slaves who arrived in foreign ships. Moreover, before 1784 French slave traders could claim *Acquits de Guinée,* or exemption from the colonial export duty on sugar—based on the number of slaves disembarked by the ship that loaded the sugar. Despite such aid, French metropolitan merchants proved incapable of meeting the demand for slaves in their own colonies. In the 1760s and 1770s about one fifth of the slaves imported into St. Domingue arrived in non-French ships—in particular those of the British—whereas landings by French ships in the British or Iberian Americas were rare. With the revival of the French trade in 1783 after the war years, the French share of imports into St. Domingue increased at the same time that the total volume of the traffic also climbed. The increase in the total volume of imports was, of course, a function of the dramatic development of St. Domingue already discussed, but the reason for the increase in the French ratio of the trade is less obvious. It may have reflected improved French competitiveness, but it is more likely a result of a new subsidy system that in 1784 replaced the *Acquits de Guinée* with payments per measured ton of the slave ship. Although the intention of the French government was to reduce the effective contribution of the taxpayer to the slave trade, there is evidence that abuses of the system resulted in even greater subsidies than had been previously paid. In addition, a substantial bounty per slave was paid to French slave traders who delivered their cargoes to Tobago, St. Lucia, Martinique, Guadeloupe and the southern side of St. Domingue. As slave prices in the French colonies in the 1780s were already high by English standards, it is not surprising that many British merchants sent their ships to French ports to hoist new colors or in some cases moved their business to France. It is certain then that some of the new "French" slave-trading shipping was British; the large Liverpool house of Mason and Bourne, for example, traded only under the French flag. Thus, although French participation in the traffic no doubt increased in the 1780s, it is likely that the apparent superior efficiency of the British was no less than it had been.[8]

For the British, Americans, and we might add, the Dutch, there was little of either government-induced or natural protection. The Dutch government was prepared to countenance the decline of their own slaving fleet in absolute terms when it could no longer survive competition with the French and British for third markets.[9] The British and Americans were rather more successful, though the U.S. share of the total traffic, while increasing steadily in the second half of the eighteenth century was never above and was usually much less than 15 percent. In the fifteen years before 1807, perhaps 95 percent of the traffic outside the South Atlantic was conducted by these two carriers.[10] The withdrawal of the French and the Dutch was, of course, partly responsible for this domination. Yet for many years before 1793 the Anglo-American carriers had been the most profitable of the national participants, though profits, it should be noted, were within the range of normal returns.[11] Evaluation of the reasons for successful participation in any highly competitive business is often just as difficult to make on a *post facto* basis as from an *ex ante* perspective. Competitive markets for goods and factors of production ensured similar long-run costs and returns for all, and there was probably less potential for economic rent in the slave trade than in almost any other eighteenth-century business activity.[12] Nevertheless, a cursory examination of the basis of Anglo-American success is very pertinent to the theme of economic development and coerced labor.

In the context of the above discussion, it is not likely that British and U.S. success lay in the ability to purchase and sell slaves at prices different from the going rate. Africans were traded for goods. But given the range of product type and the number of producers, the mere production of those goods that the African desired would not in itself confer an advantage. For earlier writers British manufactured goods, New England rum and Bahian roll tobacco explained much of the national character of the trade. Yet British textiles did not replace Indian cloth in the trade until the nineteenth century, and the Portuguese and French had just as free an access to the latter as the British. The package of goods exchanged for a slave in West Africa was actually drawn from all over the world.[13] Asian textiles; German linen; Swedish bar iron; British guns, gunpowder, beads, and so on; tobacco and alcohol from North and South America, and cowries from the Indian Ocean were all important. A trading cargo that excluded any one of these was handicapped, and by the second half of the eighteenth century, trading for slaves in West Africa was often preceded by trading among slave traders—none of whom was able to bring to the coast the full range of required goods for the appropriate mix of goods to be exchanged for slaves.[14] But even if all these goods had been produced in one country, say Britain, the cost of buying and bringing them to West Africa should not have been much different for the British slave trader as for anyone else and in itself would not explain British dominance of the traffic. Thus we might expect that situations where the English undersold the French at Sierra Leone in 1790 and the New Englanders did the same to the English on the Gold Coast in 1774 would not be permanent.[15]

For the same reason shipping-cost differences among major carriers are not likely to have been very great. There was little difference between European carriers in some of the key shipping variables such as size of ship, slaves per ton carried, tons per crew member and average time spent on the voyage or or the African coast.[16] "The French do not want [for] ships to carry on this Trade," the Privy Council Committee reported. "They have many fine ships already in it and Ships are at present as cheap as in France."[17] Major differences do appear when the comparison is broadened to include the ships and shipping practices of American slave traders. The latter had smaller ships, carried fewer slaves and crew members per ton and spent less time on the African coast,[18] but the fact that both the Americans and the British were relatively successful slave traders would suggest that such differences in equipment and trading practices were adjustments to relative rather than absolute cost differentials. Both interest rates and wages were higher in the United States than in Britain; however, for capital at least, higher interest was partially offset by cheaper building materials. Smaller ships, crews and faster African turnaround times, made possible by small cargoes, would seem to have been a rational response to transatlantic factor cost differentials.[19]

There were, nevertheless, cost differences among Europeans. Of all the major branches of European long-distance trade, the slave trade was perhaps the most vulnerable to delayed returns and the most reliant on credit.[20] From the assembly of a highly assorted trading cargo to the advancing of goods to African traders on the coast to the sale of the slaves in the Americas involved both an inordinate time and a network of credit transactions. By the end of the eighteenth century, capital mobilization and the financial intermediaries on which it depends were nowhere more advanced than in Great Britain. For the French slave trader at least, there was no equivalent of the London commission agent who matched the liquidity requirements of the slave merchant with the planters' needs for long credit.[21] French slave traders frequently received produce in return for their slaves or bills drawn on the planters themselves.[22] The discount rate for bills of exchange was generally lower and the maturity term shorter for the British trader. "The Circumstance which commands the Whole" (of the British slave traders' superiority) was in the opinion of the Privy Council Committee "the great advantage we have in capital".[23] Nor was this advantage readily available to the non-British. In striking contrast to later periods, in the eighteenth century it was easier for goods than for capital to cross international boundaries. Although Rhode Island traders sought and often obtained bills drawn on London merchants or planters' bills guaranteed by London commission agents, these were not easily available outside the Anglo-Saxon Americas.[24] In Cuba and the French Caribbean foreign slave traders usually required cash in return for slaves rather than accept the foreign debt instruments that were available. This lack of credit restricted the number of slaves that could be sold. British investment in these areas, unlike the Dutch Americas, was minimal and mercantilist regulations and the risk of war ensured that the Spanish and French gained little access to even short-term British credit.[25]

A good part of the British success in slave trading thus stemmed from the sophisticated commercial and financial organization associated with the economic growth process. Indeed it was probably when the British advantage was at its peak that the abolitionist assault got underway. As the British slave trader unceasingly pointed out in the years before 1807, the slave trade was one of the best examples of successful capitalism, the product of the "enterprising genius of the people" at a time when the British constitution put more emphasis on the rights of property and the right to sell anywhere that "offered an advantageous market" than ever before.[26] In fact, the British slave trader might have made his case even stronger. His success in the 1790s and early 1800s occurred not only without state aid but in the face of increasingly restrictive state regulations to which none of his foreign competitors were subject. In 1788 Dolben's Act restricted British slave ships to only five slaves per three tons, up to 200 tons and then one slave per ton thereafter. In 1799 a further act linked carrying capacity to the physical dimensions of ships and thus reduced authorized capacity by a further third from that year. This was at a time when ratios of 2 to 3 slaves per ton in other European national trades were common. It was perhaps fortunate for the British slave merchant that war eliminated the French competition shortly after the institution of these regulations. Though the regulations were likely harder to enforce in trade to non-British regions, it is probable that they contributed to the rapid growth of the U.S. slave trade in this period by increasing the costs of the British.[27]

If the Americans took advantage of these restrictions on the British slave merchants, the Spanish and the Portuguese clearly did not, at least not before 1808. The Portuguese traffic continued to be confined to Brazil, in particular the South Atlantic. The Spanish made many attempts to enter the slave trade to Africa before the Cuban traffic was thrown open. In the 1780s the Philippine Company employed an agent in London to fit out slave ships for the African coast and arranged to have Spaniards on board to learn the business. In addition, merchants from Cadiz and planters from Cuba visited London and then Liverpool to study the outfit of voyages at firsthand. The Spanish government, after failing to get Spanish merchants to take up the *asiento,* offered those merchants a subsidy for slaves delivered to Havana. It also gave citizens of Spain the exclusive right to import into Santiago de Cuba as part of the 1789 liberalization decree. None of these incentives yielded significant results. In the year of the liberalization decree, John Dawson, a British holder of the *asiento,* told a committee of the British Privy Council that "Spaniards did not carry on this Trade at all themselves."[28] Between 1790 and 1794 shipping lists show that 23 percent of the slave ships arriving in Havana flew the Spanish flag, but the very small mean-cargo size of the latter indicates that the vast majority had sailed not from Africa but from other Caribbean markets. Even this inter-island trade did not survive intact, however. The Spanish flag accounted for less than 10 percent of slave imports in the 1795–1804 period, mainly because, after the Spanish declaration of war on England in October 1796, Spanish ships became liable to capture.[29]

Flags, of course, were not infallible guides to the nationality of the ownership, especially in the slave trade, and Spaniards and Cubans no doubt invested in foreign enterprises, entered partnerships with foreign traders or assumed non-Spanish flags. On balance, however, it is more likely that the English, French, Americans, and Danes assumed *pro forma* Spanish ownership than vice versa.[30] Indeed British colonies accounted for perhaps only one third of the slaves shipped in British slave ships after 1800, and Cuba was a major non-British market.[31] Rhode Island slavers, easily the most important of th

U.S. dealers, delivered to Cuba over half the slaves they carried between 1783 and 1807, and the involvement of the French in the early years of Spanish liberalization is also well documented. What was left after these major carriers had taken their share was largely in the hands of Danish nationals resident at St. Thomas and St. Croix.[32] After making allowances for each of these groups of traders and comparing their contribution with the estimates of Havana and Cuban imports, it is hard to see how there could have been more than a handful of Spanish or Cuban expeditions to Africa before 1807. The first successful Cuban-based African speculation may have been 1792, but there were relatively few others before the major carriers had all permanently withdrawn from the traffic.[33]

After 1807 the Havana shipping lists chronicle the disappearance of British and American flags, and a major increase in the use of Iberian flags. The intra-Caribbean trade, moreover, dried up as Denmark and Britain, controllers of the major West Indian markets, prohibited the export of slaves. As the mean-cargo trends clearly indicate, after 1807 Cuba drew the vast majority of its *bozal* slaves direct from Africa.[34] The Napoleonic takeover in Spain meant that the Spanish flag was still liable to British capture at the time of British and U.S. abolition. This no doubt explains the 1808 decision of Portugal, an ally of Britain and thus somewhat more secure from British interference, to issue royal letters permitting "Portuguese subjects to traffic in slaves to the Havannah and Spanish Dominions." Increasing numbers of Portuguese slave ships now appeared in Cuban ports.[35] As the Napoleonic power in Spain crumbled, the latter once more became a British ally. Though some British harassment of Spanish slavers continued, the Admiralty judge, Sir William Scott, could write privately in 1814 that he could see "no restriction arising either from treaty with Spain or from any principle of law which this country has asserted that prevents the subjects of that crown from carrying on this trade (evil as it may be) from any country where they can purchase to any country where they are permitted to sell."[36] British naval officers reported that the Spanish and Portuguese flags had comprehensively replaced all others on the African coast by 1810.[37]

But were the owners of these ships Iberian? The contacts with Brazilian and Cuban ports are clear enough. Of 444 slaving voyages in the slave ship data set for the years 1808 to 1815, all but a dozen either cleared from or touched at such ports before proceeding to the African coast for slaves. For ships carrying slaves into Brazilian ports no doubt ownership remained, as it had been, overwhelmingly Portuguese,[38] but in the Cuban case, Spanish replaced British and U.S. enterprise only gradually. Indeed, as we shall see, in some ways both major branches of the post-1807 slave trade came to rely more heavily on the British and Americans as the century progressed. Moreno Fraginals has published data on slaves shipped by Cuban and Spanish expeditions. A comparison of these with total slave imports into Cuba suggests that Hispanic voyages accounted for about half of all slave arrivals between 1810 and 1814, and almost all arrivals thereafter.[39] Yet the Spanish takeover was probably slower than these figures indicate as British and U.S. capital, principals and ships hid behind ostensibly Spanish firms, or at least papers. Of the fifty or so Cuban-bound slave ships captured by the British Navy between 1808 and 1817, all but two came from British or American ports or had fraudulent Spanish papers covering British or U.S. equity. In addition to these, many others heading for Brazil or an unidentified port when captured had *pro forma* Spanish or Portuguese papers or had cleared from British or American ports.[39] In the federal courts of the United States, nine ships from Rhode Island ports alone were condemned for slave trading activities between 1817 and 1820.[40] Both U.S. and British abolitionists knew of many other slavers owned or fitted out in their ports, but the evidence was regarded as insufficient to sustain legal proceedings. Zachary Macaulay listed thirty-six suspected slavers that had sailed from Liverpool in the seventeen months after December 31, 1807, against most of which no court action was taken. Moreover, after the conclusion of hostilities in 1815 French- and Danish-owned slavers appeared off the coast flying Spanish flags.[41]

The major initial impact of U.S. and British abolition effective on January 1, 1808, was on the flow of slaves into British and American territory rather than on British and U.S. participation in the slave trade. There can be no doubt that the total number of British and American expeditions dropped substantially after 1807. Even if we assume that all Cuban imports were carried in such ships, the absence of major foreign penetration into the Brazilian traffic meant that there could not have been more than three hundred British and U.S. ventures in the seven years after 1807, compared to well over one thousand in the same period before abolition.[42] The greater part of the British slave-trade fleet quickly found alternative non-slaving employment.[43] But it is obvious from the above figures that if only a small proportion of the British and American traders had chosen to remain in the trade they would have dominated the Cuban traffic.

There are indications that some British and U.S. citizens took up residence in foreign countries to avoid slave-trade proscription.[44] But the commonest forms of continued involvement after 1807 were, first, the fitting out of expeditions owned by foreign nationals and, second, the dispatch of wholly or partly owned expeditions under a falsely assumed Spanish or Portuguese flag. For a few years after 1807 that minor part of the Brazilian traffic that had used Lisbon as a base seems to have made extensive use of the expertise and cargo assortments available in Liverpool and London. This practice was extensive enough in 1810 for the Portuguese consul in Liverpool to publish a warning that Portuguese nationals could expect no official support if they fell foul of British law.[45] The abolitionists faced enormous difficulties in proving intent— only one of these ships was ever condemned prior to reaching the coast. Despite this, however, the foreign traders use of British ports did decline markedly after 1811 and the major type of continuing British and American participation assumed the form of direct ownership rather than fitting out foreign ships. As we have seen British slave traders had often used foreign flags in the past. Now however such flags were covering an activity which infringed British laws.[46]

The British- and American-owned vessels usually began their voyages, or at least took on cargo, at the ports at which their owners resided. Almost all the ships in the British sample of Cuban-bound ships described earlier sailed from English and American ports, with Charleston, S.C., leading the list. The historian of the Rhode Island trade has noted that the increase in ship departures to the West Indies after abolition almost exactly matched the decline in clearances to Africa in the same period. Normally such ships went to a Cuban or Brazilian port to get the necessary papers before proceeding to the African coast. In anticipation of sixty years of sham shipping sales in the business, ships were transferred to Portuguese and Spanish nationals of little property, often clerks in the houses to which the ship was consigned. Santiago (São Tiago) in the Cape Verde Islands, Santa Cruz de Tenerife in the Canaries and Matanzas in Cuba were frequently the sites of such transfers, presumably because there were fewer prying British and U.S. consular officials here than in the major ports of Lisbon, Cadiz and Havana. In Bahia, however, the U.S. consul who certified the sale of the *Amelia* was a partner of the house to which the ship was consigned.[47]

Such ships would leave their home ports with the more incriminating equipment concealed or to be picked up along with the false papers. Once at sea their carpenters would commence building a slave deck, convert casks into slop containers and widen or uncover gratings. Bulkheads, trading cargo and a Spanish flag—"the Spanish arms being made in England and şewn into the flag previous to their sailing," according to one naval officer—were normally in place before departure.[48] Commissioners sent to the coast in 1810 reported that "very few real Spanish ships are employed, the great masses of vessels under the Spanish flag . . . are actually Americans; several are supposed to belong to British merchants."[49] The assessment of the relative importance of British and Americans in the Spanish trade contained in the above quote is reinforced by the distribution of ownership in the sample of ships from the British records. U.S.-owned ships outnumbered their British counterparts by almost two to one. Almost all slavers in the sample owned by British residents, moreover, sailed before 1814. It seems likely that British enthusiasm for such speculations was dampened by the 1811 felony act discussed later, which, though seriously flawed, added transportation to the financial penalties of the 1807 act. Withdrawal was facilitated by the fact that even before 1807 slave trading had never been the major part of the activities of the big Liverpool firms.[50] In the United States a similar effect was produced by the 1820 piracy act.

Spanish participation, which had always been crucial in the reception and distribution of the slaves, increasingly moved into the shipping end of the business during the second decade of the century. Occasional Spanish-owned ventures, dating back to 1792, became more numerous and some planter capital was attracted to the traffic.[51] By the time the trade to Cuba became illegal at the end of 1820, both Cuban and British sources indicate that non-Spanish involvement in the trade had become very much the exception, at least in Havana and Matanzas.[52] It is clear that some Americans moved their operations to Cuba, especially the outports, and to the islands of St. Thomas and St. Eustatius. Moreover, peace between the United States and Britain in 1814 brought an influx of heavily armed American privateers into the traffic, just as a few years later the end of the Spanish-American wars of independence saw the entry of Spanish privateers into the business.[53] In general, however, the British and the North Americans greatly reduced their direct involvement in the course of the second decade of the century. The order of withdrawal, first by the British and then by the Americans, probably reflects the chronology of the British felony act of 1811 and its American counterpart that made slave trading a capital offence nine years later. In naval and court reports of the 1820s, there is little evidence of British or U.S. involvement in any aspect of the business of actually shipping slaves.

As the English-speaking traders withdrew however, the French reentered the business in force. Though Spanish capital remained preeminent from at least 1820 to the end of the traffic, ships from both France and the French Caribbean came to dominate the traffic to the southern part of Cuba and also to participate in the expansion of the Havana trade. By the mid-1820s the only foreign capital left in the Havana trade was French.[54] New entrants were greatly encouraged by a rapidly expanding Cuban market. Between 1816 and 1820 slave imports were more than triple those in the first half of the decade due to the market's response to both the return of peace and the approach of official Spanish abolition of the trade.[55] Clearly there was much room for both new French and new Spanish participation. By the early 1820s the Havana traffic was largely Spanish with some French involvement; the much smaller trade to the outports, on the other hand, was largely French with some American and Spanish participation. Moreover, over two thirds of the ships bringing slaves to Cuba between 1821 and 1825 began their voyages in Cuban ports. Less than a third of the ships in the British sample from a decade earlier had left or touched at Cuban ports before proceeding to Africa.[56] In less than ten years there had been almost a complete turnover in the ownership of firms carrying slaves to Cuba as well as shifts in the geographic structure of the trade. The major force for change was the legislative enactments of Britain and the United States. Indeed in the 1820s the African trade was the only international traffic in any commodity from Cuba where Spanish ships and the Spanish flag survived.[57]

On the African coast, techniques and personnel changed more slowly. The procurement, bulking and warehousing of slaves prior to embarkation was called factoring. Three categories of factoring operations may be discerned in the eighteenth and nineteenth centuries. One was carried out by resident and independent European and mulatto dealers of varying importance and, although likely to be found almost anywhere, was most common in Angola and the Windward coast. A second type was performed by the African political authority who in the Bight of Biafra and the Gambia dealt directly with a ship's captain and frequently combined the activities of factoring with the supply of slaves. A third type was represented by the agents of the large European and American trading companies, often resident in forts and tiny settlements, whose main function (at least initially) was to assemble cargoes for ships of the company for which they worked. Such operations were to be found mainly on the Gold Coast. Although slaver captains had the option of carrying on their own factoring activities, most did not. However, there is evidence that a small part of the Liverpool trade was made up of captains who went out to the African coast to act as intermediaries between African supplier and transatlantic shipper. In any event, by the end of the eighteenth century the British trading presence on the coast north of Portuguese Angola was proportionately greater than the British share of all slaves landed in the Americas. Both U.S. and French shippers bought heavily from British suppliers before the Napoleonic wars.[58]

The 1807 abolition legislation brought a sharp reduction in fort trade and a reduced formal European presence on the Gold Coast in particular. The third type of factoring activity described thus became less important, though this was (as we shall see) to be temporary. Some of the resultant slack on the Gold and Slave coasts at least was taken up by the Africans themselves. The nineteenth-century trading networks of Francisco Feliz de Souza and Domingo Martins referred to later were very much an extension of, and dependent on, the power of Dahomey.[59] The establishments of such men (and women, too,) had none of the European political ties of an earlier generation of forts in the Ouidah vicinity. Outside the Bight of Biafra and Portuguese Angola where British abolition had little impact on trading practices, it was the independent factor who did most to fill the gap left by the demise of the fort trade. Most such factors were indeed English and American, or their African relatives prior to 1820. Some were strong enough to fight off naval efforts to suppress their activities, as in the Rio Pongo, north of Sierra Leone, in 1813.[60] Others from the Gallinas and Sherbro rivers to the south were captured, put on trial at Sierra Leone, convicted and then released in England because the 1811 felony act was found to be based on a statute that had been repealed.[61] The majority survived to trade without interference in both produce and slaves for many years.[62] The first Spanish factor on the coast is reported in 1811, and Spaniards or Cubans took up residence at the Gallinas in 1817 and were in Lagos by 1821, the two latter ports being major embarkation points for Cuban slavers in the 1820s and 1830s.[63]

The basic point is that no slave ship could come to the coast north of Angola in the decade after 1807 without using the trading infrastructure that the British had put together over the preceding century and a half. Even if direct trade with English factors could be avoided, rice for the slaves on the return voyage, canoes for those ships intending to embark from the beaches in the Bight of Benin and adjustments of cargoes to achieve the proper assortment for trading were most conveniently available from British merchants in the Gambia, Sierra Leone or the remnants of the British forts on the Gold Coast. In 1843 a London-based Spanish merchant was unsuccessfully prosecuted for supplying goods to slave traders. The comment of the prosecution counsel in that trial— "If merchants in this country would not accept bills drawn by slave traders . . . the trade could not be carried on at all"—was perhaps already true a generation earlier. And if the slave ship itself was not an old English Guineaman, there was a chance it would be insured in England.[64] In several cases it was only the fact that the foreign trader had availed himself of such services that provided grounds for conviction of his property in the British Vice Admiralty courts; these convictions were often subsequently reversed on appeal.

If most such services were gradually dismantled or reduced under the pres-

...re of the British Navy and courts, the most important of them, the supply of British goods and credit, proved to be beyond the power of the law to control. In the same decades that the abolitionists were enforcing restrictions on the traffic, there were two critical developments that both reduced the cost of slave trading substantially for everyone and ensured increasing British ties to the business. First, there was the rapid decline in the cost of manufacturing goods, which began about 1780 but was particularly striking in the early decades of the nineteenth century. Thomas Tobin, a Liverpool palm oil merchant who began his career in the slave trade, was asked in 1848 about the prices of slaves he purchased in the old days. After quoting a range of £17 to £20 in merchandise on the west coast of Africa, he added "But then goods . . . were 300 percent dearer than they are now."[65] One attempt to chart this process with more precision suggests a decrease of 25 percent in the price of Senegambian imports between 1780s and the mid-1820s as well as a further 50 percent decrease in the next twenty years. There was an even greater decline in prices of specific imports such as bar iron and cotton gray goods that were manufactured in England.[66]

The second important development was the shift to trade liberalization and political independence in the Iberian Americas. Trade liberalization and abolition of coerced labor were somewhat contradictory manifestations of nineteenth-century economic growth. It is noteworthy that the first half-century of industrialization saw every national participant in the traffic either withdrawing from the trade or reducing mercantilist regulations. But those who adopted the second, but not the first, of these two steps found that an irresistible pull into the network of British trade and credit went together with a rapid expansion in the volume of their portion of the slave trade. In Cuba the 1789 cédula, which opened up the slave trade to the island, attracted foreign slave ships. Initially, at least, it did not attract the foreign merchants whose commercial connections would have actually facilitated the creation of an indigenous slave trade. By the time the permanent nature of the new regulations and therefore a climate favorable to foreign commercial links was established, Cuba had become enemy territory for British merchants at least. Even the smaller intra-Caribbean shipments of slaves that arrived from St. Thomas down to 1807 were shipped by merchants in St. Thomas rather than in Havana, and a large proportion of the transatlantic shipments were in the hands of the British and Americans resident outside Cuba.[67] A U.S. presence in Cuba was stimulated by rapid growth in U.S.-Cuban produce trade in the early 1790s as well as the U.S. slave trade to Cuba both before and after U.S. abolition. But the full integration of Cuba into the Atlantic trade network was delayed by the Napoleonic wars. There is no evidence in the early years of the century of the large foreign merchant community resident in the Havana of the 1820s.

The same process in Brazil is more clearly demarcated. The shift of the Portuguese royal court to Rio de Janeiro in 1808 and the opening up of Brazilian ports to ships and trade from all nations was followed by a decade of reforms that partially dismembered the old mercantilist economic structure.[68] One of the centerpieces of new policy was the Anglo-Portuguese commercial treaty that gave British imports into Brazil a preference even over goods coming from

Portugal. It was in this period that the Portuguese share of transatlantic shipping entering Brazilian ports fell from nine tenths to less than one third, with most of the remainder being in the slave trade, an activity forbidden to much foreign shipping.[69] It was also the period during which Brazil's share of British trade to Latin America increased to 75 percent, a small part of which represented the rerouting of British goods that had formerly been shipped direct to Africa. Stimulated, in part, by the American nonimportation acts and the continental system that closed off alternative markets, seventy-five British merchant houses had representatives in Rio de Janeiro alone within three years of the arrival of Dom João and his court.[70] By the 1820s a new Atlantic trade configuration had emerged, with the United States and Europe taking Brazilian coffee in sufficient volumes to stimulate a rapid increase in slave imports to Rio de Janeiro. The supply of credit and manufactured goods in this system came largely from the British.

The lack of indigenous or metropolitan financial intermediaries and the strong response to external demand pressures made foreign credit perhaps more important at this time in Brazil and Cuba than at any subsequent period. Certainly Latin America markets were almost inseparable from British credit. The main function of the British mercantile houses, more important even than knowledge of local markets, was the ability to wait for payment,[71] and this in turn derived from their partners in Glasgow, Liverpool and London. Such houses were both importers and exporters, advancing manufactured goods to native merchants and cash to planters, often well before receiving the plantation produce that they returned to Europe. Up to two years elapsed between the time that the British firm bought the goods from the manufacturer and the produce was sold or the bills of exchánge were returned in payment.[72] The Brazilian coastal and interior trade as well as the slave trade depended on British credit. After nearly forty years as British consul in Maranhão and Rio, Robert Hesketh told a House of Lords committee in 1849 that the British were financing half of Brazilian internal trade. This may well be conservative in the light of the high proportion of British goods used in the slave traffic and the official correspondence of British officials during the 1820s and 1830s.[73]

The impact of falling prices for manufactured goods, a buoyant slave trade and the opening of Cuban and Brazilian ports to foreign trade was to increase both the volume and the total value of British merchandise sold in Africa. Measured in terms of constant pounds, the total value of merchandise and specie exchanged for slaves entering the transatlantic market amounted to £13.5 million in the 1780s.[74] About 34.9 percent of this, or £4.7 million, comprised British goods, the greater part of which were carried out to the African coast from England in British ships. A generation later abolition had ensured the contraction of the market for slaves and the merchandise exchanged for them from £13.5 to £8.9 million, a decline of 35 percent. Yet the proportion of British manufactured goods used in the traffic had increased so much that the total value of those goods rose to £5.3 million, an increase of 12.8 percent between the 1780s and 1820s. The produce of the Americas such as tobacco and alcoholic beverages also claimed an increased share of the market in the later period, and most of that produce was now from South America rather than from the Caribbean and the United States. This reflects the shift in the center of gravity of the trade southwards and the relocation of its organizational centers to the Americas and away from Europe. The British component had gained at the expense of other European manufactured goods and, in particular, at the expense of East Indian goods. In the vanguard of the British advance was, of course, textiles, the greater part of which arrived on the African coast via entrepôts in the Americas.

Thus the loss of African markets consequent to abolition was an illusion. Although a significant commodity trade with Africa took two decades or more to develop, that continent did, in fact, absorb increasing quantities of British goods, though they no longer arrived in such volume direct from Europe. Some might be tempted to conclude that abolition of the largest of the transatlantic slave trades was a costless exercise, at least in terms of an African-induced demand for British goods, shipping services and capital. Others might regard an outcome so benign to British capital as one more immutable imperative of relations between capital and labor in Britain and, in particular, the expansion of that capital overseas. In the absence of abolition, however, it seems beyond dispute that, first, the demand for slaves would have increased substantially[75] and, second, that the market for British goods would have expanded at a rate considerably faster than that for slaves. Without British abolition, Africa would have been much more important to the British economy of the 1820s than it was. Compared to the 1780s, that continent would have absorbed not 13 percent more goods, but perhaps double the volume sold in that decade. As noted, Brazilian and Cuban markets would also have absorbed more British goods, and the popular hostility toward Britain and things British in American slave-importing regions, the first manifestation of which appeared in Bahia in 1812, might never have occurred.[76]

The withdrawal of the English-speaking world from the slave trade was thus not only less than complete, in some respects the British at least became even more deeply involved in the traffic. Yet to conclude from this that if abolition had not occurred, the British and Americans would have developed a near monopoly of the nineteenth-century traffic would be to seriously misunderstand the nature of economic growth at this period. The British dominance of the slave trade in the 1790s was based to some extent on the exigencies of war. With the return of peace the expansion of the British trade network and the gradual reduction of trade restrictions in slave-importing countries would have ensured lower costs for all. The advantages enjoyed by the British slave trader in the eighteenth century would have been thrown open to all in the following century. To reformulate slightly an argument made earlier, it was not the British ability to put together a widely assorted cargo or to finance an expedition and its remittances that gave the British an edge over the major slave-trading nations before 1807. Rather, it was the failure of other nations to dismantle barriers to trade and capital flows that prevented their merchants from using British facilities. On the eve of the introduction of steamships, a combination of cheaper trading cargoes, easier credit, improved life expectancy for Europeans on the African coast, small ships and increased security on the high seas would have ensured easier entry to the slave-trading business than ever before

The Portuguese would have continued to play a major role and the Spanish may well have broken into the traffic even without Anglo-Saxon withdrawal.

We can conclude, therefore, that the early nineteenth century witnessed not only a major increase in demand for slaves but also, from the perspective of the market in the Americas, a potential increase in supply that only abolition and British suppressive policies prevented from becoming a reality. This assessment, of course, is based on the assumption that the slaves would have been available for export from Africa, and to this issue we now turn.

# 5

# Africa and the Initial Impact of Abolition

## I

Two broadly countervailing forces affected slave exports from Africa after 1790. Economic growth in Europe and the Americas stimulated demand. The St. Domingue rebellion and attempts to suppress the trade reduced demand. The volume figures reflect the struggle between the two. For Africa as a whole, exports declined nearly 8 percent between the 1780s and the 1790s as first the St. Domingue rebellion and then war forced the French to withdraw from the trade. That the decline was not greater is testimony to the speed with which the British and Americans took over the French role as well as to the burgeoning demand for plantation produce. The next decade brought a further and much larger fall of 22 percent, however, as British and U.S. abolition took effect and the difficulties in supplying French and Spanish territories increased during wartime. The fact that prices of most plantation produce rose to record levels in the same period indicates that the underlying demand for slaves remained very high. The ending of the Napoleonic war in the middle of the next decade ensured that the volume of traffic, though declining on a decadal basis, actually recovered strongly after 1814. Thus, although the traffic declined by one third between 1781–90 and 1811–20, more slaves left the Atlantic littoral for the Americas in both the 1820s and the 1830s than in any other decade in the history of the trade prior to 1780.

A clearer impression of the aggregate impact of British and U.S. abolition may be gained from the annual data. Exports averaged forty thousands slaves a year between 1811 and 1814 and, though we have not carried the annual export series back before these years, data for major import regions indicate that annual departures were even lower during 1808–10. The decadal estimate for 1801–10 implies annual exports of close to eighty thousand slaves between 1801 and 1807 and perhaps even higher levels in the two or three years immediately preceding 1808. British and U.S. abolition thus had the temporary effect of halving the trade in the years down to 1814, with much of the remaining traffic being in the South Atlantic. As the latter was largely removed from British scrutiny, it is not difficult to understand the sanguine expectations of the British abolitionists that the trade was about to come to an end. Between 1816 and 1820, however, exports returned to earlier levels of close to eighty thousand slaves per year.

The temporary decline in the volume of the traffic was not distributed equally across major African regions, however. A comparison of the distribution assembled by Lovejoy[1] with appendix A indicates that the relative decline on the nineteenth-century west coast of Africa was accentuated by the advent, for the first time, of significant departures from southeast Africa. Within the west coast area, the Senegambia, Gold Coast and Congo North regions experienced the major declines. The relatively small Senegambian traffic fell off sharply after 1790. Bissau and Cacheu, the most southerly ports of this region, continued to ship slaves until the 1840s, but decadal export volumes for the region as a whole in the nineteenth century probably never approached the levels of the 1790s, much less those of the peak decade after 1780. On the Gold Coast, annual export volumes of five thousand to ten thousand slaves a year in the generation before 1807 fell to a few hundred a year thereafter and continued at this level intermittently down to the late 1830s. The Congo North decline, though much bigger than that of other regions in absolute terms, was only in the order of 50 percent. The decline here was concentrated in the Loango area and can be attributed to the French withdrawal of the early 1790s and, to a lesser extent, British abolition. For both the Gold and Loango coasts, however, it is likely that some redirection of slave departures occurred with Bight of Benin, Congo and Angolan ports shipping slaves that might previously have left the former regions. The Bight of Benin and Angola, with the basis of the demand for their slaves in the Portuguese Americas, were least affected by the events of the generation after 1780. With the exception of the surge in the 1780s, which saw exports at 40 percent above the trend for 1771–1820 (probably due to French activities), export volumes from the Bight of Benin fluctuated only slightly. It is difficult to disaggregate an Angolan export series from the figures for west-central Africa prior to 1810, but it seems that here too fluctuations were much less than elsewhere. Both Upper Guinea and the Bight of Biafra traffics, on the other hand, were dominated by the British before 1807. As a consequence both regions experienced all-time peaks in the 1790s, with probably continued high annual volumes occurring down to 1807. Though the decline thereafter was sharp, the volume during the 1810s was still within 5 percent and 27 percent (in Upper Guinea and the Bight of Biafra, respectively) of the levels of the two decades before 1790: Here Cuban and French slavers who tended to concentrate on regions north of the line quickly filled the gaps left by the British. The Windward coast exported a tiny proportion of aggregate deportees; given problems of disaggregating the eighteenth-century data, it is hard to comment on trends. It is unlikely, however, that the thinly populated hinterland of this region ever made a significant contribution. Finally in southeast Africa we should note that alone of major export zones transatlantic exports probably increased between the 1780s and 1810s, though the numbers remained well below the levels of major west coast regions. In summary, abolition by the British and Americans caused a temporary and fairly sharp drop in west coast exports from north of Portuguese Angola. Within a decade, however, the traffic was once more approaching preabolition levels in the bights and had substantially recovered in Congo North. Only on the Gold Coast, the northern Loango coast and Senegambia (part of the Upper Guinea region) were the effects permanent, and the decline in the latter two regions was already underway well before 1807.[2]

## II

Ignoring for the moment the wider question of what might have happened if the British and Americans had continued to encourage the traffic, it appears unlikely that the initial impact of European abolition on Africa was significant. Nevertheless, any discussion of the impact of the abolition of the transatlantic slave trade on Africa must necessarily begin with the contentious issue of the impact of the slave trade itself on that continent. Although the broader political, economic and cultural effects of forced African migration have been warmly debated, it is the demographic issue that has lurked behind many of the conflicting positions of these topics. The question of the extent of the depopulation and social disruption in Africa induced by the slave trade goes back only to the beginning of abolitionism.[3] Before the late eighteenth century, slave traders, who had a major personal interest in African population trends, did not take up the issue at length.[4] The discussion here begins with the aggregate demographic implications of the traffic before moving to the same issue in the local context. The bulk of this chapter, however, evaluates the impact on African provenance zones of the initial decline in the slave trade after 1790 and examines the implications of this for African income.

The complexities of the issue stem from the fact that the slave trade was merely one aspect of the European seaborne contact with Africa, which began in the late fifteenth century. Given the European, initially the Iberian, impulse to expand and to enslave, the basic parameter in the exchange was the epidemiological factor. This ensured that the planter and indeed white settlement should occur predominantly on the American rather than the African littoral. It was not only the slave trade that followed from this but also a movement of new crops, in particular maize and manioc, from the Americas to Africa. In one of the more striking paradoxes of the transatlantic exchange, the slave trade developed in harness with the spread of new higher-yield crops and the wider population base that they made possible. The decline in traffic before 1790 and its suppression in the 1860s occurred before the new plants had reached all parts of the continent.[5]

There are few demographers who posit a rapid rate of natural increase in the African population either before or during the Atlantic slave trade. However, the actual rates of change and the fertility and mortality patterns that produced them remain firmly in the speculative arena, with opinions depending on analogy rather than observation. The present discussion is scarcely an exception, but a little extra light is available from data on recaptive slaves disembarked by British cruisers at Sierra Leone and registered by the courts of mixed commission there.[6] Inferences may be derived for three of the key factors determining fertility among the Yoruba, the largest single ethnic group involved in nineteenth-century West African traffic. The first of these is age of mothers at first birth. There are indications that for this group there was a mean age at first birth of at least twenty and that, in addition, Yoruba women began to bear children close to the earliest possible age. At the very least, the delay between fecundity and first birth was much shorter in Yorubaland than the 2.6 to 4.1 years estimated for slave women in the U.S. South.[7] The second key factor is the interval between children. Women in many modern rural African societies—in particular, Yoruba societies—typically experience an interval between births of 3 years with prolonged lactation and sexual abstinence cited as the mechanisms.[8] Early nineteenth-century sources indicate that prolonged lactation is not of recent origin.[9] The third factor is the timing of the closing of the fertility cycle. Indications in Yorubaland of terminal sexual abstinence by women on becoming grandmothers as well as of low nutritional intakes (discussed later), suggest that there was unlikely to have been extensive fertility beyond the late thirties[10] The weight of the evidence on fertility among early nineteenth-century Yoruba peoples thus suggests a child bearing range from about twenty to thirty-eight or thirty-nine years of age, a child spacing interval of not less than 3 years and a resultant average of live births per women of between five and six. Given the institution of polygyny, few women remained childless. This is consistent with a crude birthrate of 40 to 45 per thousand, given a stable population.[11] This would put the crude birthrate at a slightly lower level than modern Nigerian rural rates of 45 to 50 per thousand. Such a rate was high by early nineteenth-century European standards as well as in comparison to rates experienced by Jamaican slaves. On the other hand, it is lower than the 55 per thousand recorded on then-contemporary U.S. plantations.[12]

The mortality picture is less clear. In recent years three factors influencing mortality have constantly surfaced in the literature on precolonial African demography: the disease environment, nutrition and political disturbances. On the first of these the favorable environment for disease vectors, in particular those carrying malaria and yellow fever puts the sub-Saharan rain forests among the environments in the world most hostile to man. Although the indigenous populations developed defences against pathogens, both genetic and partly acquired, the environment still contributes to the extremely high infant-mortality rates of over two hundred per thousand in parts of modern rural Africa. In addition, the prevalence of the tsetse fly ensured a shortage of both animal protein and draught animals, which in turn interacted with nutrition. Poor nutrition reduced resistance to disease; diseases ensured poor nutrition.[13]

On the nutrition issue it might be argued that the nutritional impact of the spread of cassava, maize and Asian rice, which has proceeded right down to the present century, has probably not been very great on a per capita basis. The Sierra Leone recaptives discussed earlier had their heights as well as their age and sex recorded, and final heights are a good indicator of nutritional well-being. After standardizing for age and ethnicity, these measurements indicate two important conclusions. First, Africans in Africa were shorter in the early nineteenth century than first-generation Creole bondsmen in the British Caribbean. Second, and more important in the present context, final heights for early nineteenth-century West Africans were very similar to those of their rural counterparts in the second half of the twentieth century. Distributions of large samples from several African regions indicate that taller Africans were not more likely to be sold into the Atlantic slave trade than their shorter brethren. It seems reasonable to postulate from this that the nutritional and work environment have changed little over the last century and a half despite the spread of cassava along the coast and interior of West Africa in this period.[14] Thus the chief effect of nutritional improvements since 1820—and by implication before this date—seems to have been on population densities rather than on long-run improvements of nutritional status. This is strongly suggestive of the kind of Malthusian interpretation that has been the subject of intense debate in recent years.[15] Mortality rates in the precolonial period probably fluctuated in the 38 to 50 per thousand range, depending on the phase of the Malthusian cycle reached.[16]

The thrust of the argument is that neither long-run fertility nor mortality rates have changed substantially in rural West Africa. The basic pattern over several centuries was most likely one of relatively high and constant fertility rates not quite matched by mortality rates that were susceptible to sharp short-run fluctuation. The nutritional evidence suggests that before the last hundred years, mortality probably increased after any temporary abatement permitted by crop innovations. Each plateau of relative demographic stability would have occurred at a higher level than the last. Although generalizations from a single society are not permissible, it is suggestive that this is the pattern to emerge from the one pre–nineteenth century community for which hard data exist.[17] We might infer first that the balance between population and food supplies was a delicate one both before and after the beginning of the modern era.[18] A second inference is that while the premodern population of the sub-Saharan forest was much smaller than it is now, much of the growth that has occurred came before the population increase of the last century.

On the basis of this discussion of the demographic parameters, we can now turn to the question of the demographic impact of the slave trade. There are really two broad questions here. First, were Africans removed at a rate faster than the rate of natural increase? Second, what would have been the population of Africa in the absence of the slave trade? At the aggregate level it is difficult to see how we can give an affirmative answer to the first of these questions unless the disruptive effects of slave raiding were very severe indeed. Slave departures from Senegambia to the Bight of Biafra inclusive averaged between twenty-five thousand and forty thousand a year for most of the period from 1700 to 1850 except for the two peak decades after 1780, when the flow increased to 47,000 or so. For those departures to have represented a drain of half of 1 percent a year the West African population would have had to have been only 8 million strong.[19] A population decline thus appears possible if two assumptions are made. The first is that the African population was very small;[20] the second that intrinsic rates of population growth could not have attained or exceeded half of 1 percent a year. The evidence discussed earlier throws doubt on both assumptions. Much of the population growth in Africa probably occurred before 1850 and was linked to the spread of new crops. This makes a small early nineteenth-century population unlikely. On the second assumption, intrinsic growth of half of 1 percent per annum is high in historical terms, but the evidence of a Malthusian pattern in African demographic trends makes such a rate feasible in the face of population loss through forced migration. Growth probably occurred through variations in mortality rather than fertility. The same procedure carried through for west-central Africa suggests that this region was somewhat more vulnerable to the demographic pressures of the slave trade. Between 1700 and 1850 departures averaged twenty-three thousand a year from the west coast south of Cape Lopez. The population would have to have amounted to 4.6 million for this annual drain to have represented half of 1 percent a year. While the actual population was likely higher than this, both population and population densities were certainly much lower than in West Africa.[21]

That significant depopulation was unlikely may be demonstrated by some intercontinental comparisons. Part A of table 1 shows emigration from a range of countries in Europe and Asia over a period of eighty-six years expressed as

**Table 1.** Overseas Emigrants from Various Countries, 1781–1932

| Country or Region of Emigration | Number of Emigrants (millions) | Emigrants as Percentage of Population[a] |
|---|---|---|
| Part A: 1846–1932 | | |
| British Isles | 18.0 | 43.3 |
| Portugal | 1.8 | 33.3 |
| Italy | 10.1 | 31.1 |
| Spain | 4.7 | 25.3 |
| Sweden | 1.2 | 23.5 |
| India | 27.7 | 9.4 |
| Russia | 2.3 | 1.8 |
| Part B: 1781–1867 | | |
| (a) West Africa (Senegal to Cameroons) | 2.25 | 8.0 |
| (b) Western half of Africa | 4.70 | 20.1 |
| (c) Western half of Africa | 4.70 | 27.5 |

*Notes:* [a]Percentages are calculated from populations in 1900 except in Part B for West Africa where (a) assumes an 1850 population of 28 million in Africa from the Cameroons to Senegal inclusive based on Fage (see Sources). Rows (b) and (c) are taken from Manning's estimates of the population of the western half of the continent, which formed the catchment zone for the slave trade in 1820 (see Sources). Row (b) is based on the low end and row (c) on the upper limit of Manning's range.

*Sources:* Part A: Kingsley Davis, *The Population of India and Pakistan* (Princeton, N.J., 1951), p. 98. Part B: Export totals for 1781 to 1810 are taken from table A.7, adjusted for the ratio of regional departures calculated from Paul E. Lovejoy, "The Volume of the Atlantic Slave Trade: A Synthesis," *Journal of African History,* 23 (1982): 485, 490. These are added to the appropriate regional exports for 1811 to 1867 from table A.9. For population estimates, see John Fage, "The Effect of the Export Slave Trade on African Populations," in R. P. Moss and R. J. A. R. Rathbone (eds.), *The Population Factor in African Studies* (London, 1975), pp. 17–18; Patrick Manning, "The Impact of Slave Exports on the Population of the Western Coast of Africa, 1700–1850," table 5. Paper presented at the Nantes International Colloquium on the Slave Trade, 1985.

a percentage of the populations of those countries. Part B shows equivalent figures for West Africa and the western half of Africa for the last eighty-seven years of the traffic—years that included all but three of the nine highest-volume decades in the history of the trade. Because of the uncertainty about how many people lived in West Africa, a ratio of departures to population is provided for several population estimates, among which the actual poulation almost certainly fell.[22] Return flows of migrants to some of the countries listed, particularly India, were, of course, very high, whereas returns to West Africa were insignificant. But even on a net basis, West Africa did not experience a relatively large population loss. With the single exception of India, which lost almost exclusively males, the female proportion of Africans was not high relative to other migrant streams. It might be argued that West Africa was at a different stage of development to most of the countries in table 1 and, moreover, that it had already experienced more than 250 years of population loss, albeit at lower levels, before 1781. Yet these characteristics were not unique to West Africa. English and Portuguese emigration began early in the seventeenth century and neither then nor later was Portugal in the forefront of world economic development. Although the flow of Europeans to the Americas before 1820 was only a third or a quarter of that of Africans, the geographic concentration of the former was such that Portugal and England lost a larger proportion of their inhabitants overseas than did West Africa in two of the three centuries between 1600 and 1900.[23] Both regions also experienced a secular rate of population increase over the same period, as did every other country shown in table 1. Thus, as with long-distance trade in commodities, it seems that long-distance population movements generally had weak impacts on established societies in the old world, including Africa, before the mid-nineteenth century.[24]

Nevertheless, as Joseph Inikori has pointed out recently, the relevant question is not how much the population declined, but how much it would have grown in the absence of the traffic.[25] The problem, of course, is to come up with a set of realistic assumptions for African demographic trends in the absence of the slave trade, and it is natural to look at African societies outside Africa for guidance. Unfortunately the range of rates of population change experienced by overseas descendants of Africans was very wide. The relatively few who went to the United States increased rapidly from an early date. On the other hand, of the many who went to the Middle East or—to choose an example in the Americas—the Argentine, no trace remains today. For the Americas as a whole it is clear that by 1820, just before the demise of the slave trade, the black population of all the Americas was less than cumulative black arrivals up to that date. If we take this as the relevant experience, we might hypothesize that in the absence of the slave trade, the West African population by 1820 would have been about 3 million more than it actually was.[26] In fact, as emigrants of all races to the Caribbean and the temperate Americas discovered, vital rates in the Old World were no guide at all to those in the New World. On the more realistic assumption that those remaining in Africa in the absence of the slave trade would have experienced a secular rate of natural increase of two per thousand, then the population of West Africa in 1850 might have been several million more than it actually was.[27]

But the implicit assumption in these types of estimates—namely, that eighteenth-century Africa could have supported the same population as the late nineteenth century or early twentieth century—may not be realistic. It assumes, in particular, that the spread of higher-yield crops, which continued throughout the region down to the twentieth century, could have been considerably accelerated by population pressures. Despite the work of Ester Boserup and others, this smacks a little of the heroic in the light of the West African secular trends in stature discussed earlier.[28] The balance of the evidence thus favors a relatively small increment to the aggregate African population in the absence of the slave trade. It follows that the drop in Atlantic exports of about one third between the 1780s and the 1810s, which constituted the initial impact of European abolition, was probably of only limited demographic significance for the total number of people living in West Africa and west-central Africa.

At the local and perhaps even the regional level, however, the demographic implications of abolition were more important. Quite apart from the obvious point that departures of only a few thousand a year could quickly eradicate a community of even large size, there were major differentials in the age and sex composition of deportees both between regions and over time. Such differences moreover were far more significant than variations between points of embarkation within regions. As regions tended to be dominated by one or two ethnic groups, the ethnic basis of these differentials appears to be fairly clear. The proportion of both women and females as a whole among departures was higher in West Africa than in west-central Africa in the nineteenth century. Within West Africa, the proportion of females in the trade varied directly with exports over time and perhaps also with the price of slaves on the coast.[29] Though plantation owners in the Americas preferred males, the New World sex price differential was never high enough to explain the large male preponderance in the trade. This and the evidence of the age and sex composition of the traffic taken up later suggests that the basic explanation for the latter must lie in African preferences. It seems most likely that demand pressures and a higher price for women would induce those societies responsible for enslavement to sell additional females into the Atlantic trade, and the absence of this tendency in the Congo North and Angola trades suggests that women were more highly valued in west-central Africa than in West Africa.[30]

Differences, however, were not confined to the sex ratio. In the nineteenth century, major differences in the proportion of children embarked and in the sex of those children are apparent between regions, with west-central and southeast Africa embarking particularly high proportions of children under fifteen years of age.[31] In addition, in all regions, girls made up a higher proportion of the females than did boys of the males, though the earlier maturation of females could have biassed the data against girls. Fluctuations over time within these regions are much less dramatic, however; in particular, there does not appear to be any systematic relationship with the volume of exports to parallel Galenson's conclusions on price and child ratios in the earlier traffic to Barbados.[32] The only possible exception to this assessment was the Bight of Benin ports. There demand pressures may have resulted in a higher proportion of adult females entering the trade: 28 percent of deportees were adult females in 1826–30. For the Bight of Benin, as for other African regions, generally less

..an 15 percent of the slaves entering the transatlantic trade in the nineteenth century were women between the ages of fifteen and thirty. If the ratio for 1826–30 had held in the 1780s, then the decadal totals of mature females leaving the Bight of Benin in both absolute and relative terms must have been greater than for any other region or decade in African history.[33] But the region with potentially the most demographically damaging age/sex structure of deportees was the Bight of Biafra in the 1790s. Here there were high volumes of exports, high female ratios, a high proportion of female children and, in addition, very high shipboard mortality rates.

Were these age and sex structures likely to have had a significant regional impact? A simulation model developed by Patrick Manning projects a 15 percent loss in the coastal population over a century as a result of the slave trade—this as opposed to the interior population. Volume data and probable age/sex ratios for the Benin and Biafra bights in the 1780s and 1790s may be substituted in this model.[34] The male ratios were likely lower and the age structures younger than those assumed by Manning. Not surprisingly, therefore, the projected population loss over a century comes to at least 30 percent or more, depending on the hinterland population estimate one wishes to use. The important point, however, is that the conditions observed in the bights of Benin and Biafra in the 1780s, 1790s and the late 1820s, did not last for the entire century. Within the bights, the peak levels of exports in the late eighteenth century were between 50 and 60 percent greater than the decadal means for the century 1741 to 1840. Only in the Bight of Benin were there high export levels in the early decades of the eighteenth century as well as in later decades, and it is here that the strongest case for long-run regional depopulation can be made. In the nineteenth century male ratios in both bights averaged 66 percent. In all other major regions the male ratio was higher still—over 70 percent in west-central Africa.[35] Substituting the ratios for all Africa in the nineteenth century in the Manning model including its assumptions on the ratio of exports to population, yields a projected decline of about one third less for the coastal populations than Manning estimated.[36] Thus even if we leave to one side the Malthusian tendencies discussed earlier, it seems likely that in the nineteenth century and probably, too, in the late eighteenth century, the age/sex ratios of the type that might have induced prolonged regional population decline existed for only short periods. Certainly, the ethnographic map of West Africa displays impressive continuities, and the disappearance of one group or another was surely an inevitable consequence of even a small net population decline if it persisted over several decades.[37]

In the last analysis the mortality trends discussed later, together with the data on the age/sex structure and the volume of deportees serve to reinforce two broad conclusions on the demographic issue. First, some of the conditions put forward in the literature that might have produced a large impact existed in most regions. These included large outflows of slaves relative to population densities from west-central Africa, significantly more females leaving the bights of Benin and Biafra and heavy mortality among captives in the Bight of Biafra. Yet in every case, with the possible exception of the Bight of Benin, there were offsetting characteristics. West-central African male ratios were the highest in the transatlantic trade, very high export volumes were restricted to the 1780s and 1790s, the catchment area was very large and mortality in most years was below the mean. Though the Bight of Biafra combined large export volumes with high mortality and low male ratios, population densities in the Niger Delta were among the highest in Africa. Large-scale exports from these ports, moreover, were restricted to the century 1741 to 1840, the shortest period of significant exports of any major region of export. The other region that combined large outflows with low male ratios, the Bight of Benin, experienced very low mortality among captives, though this may not have been enough to prevent population decline.

Major demographic impact could thus occur only if departures were concentrated in relatively small parts of the broad regions discussed here. This, in fact, did occur in the Bight of Benin to the Adja peoples of the eighteenth century and perhaps too in the Accra region on the Gold Coast. The decadal level of exports from the Bight of Benin before 1740 was considerably greater than after, and from the Gold Coast, departures at midcentury nearly matched those of later decades. Although data on the age/sex composition has not yet come to light for these years, it seems clear that the major source of slaves were the coastal peoples inhabiting the immediate hinterlands and that the level of departures relative to the size of these societies was such that almost any combination of age and sex would have reduced the population. In the Bight of Benin even after 1740 and down to the 1810s, the Adja continued to supply the greater portion of deportees from the Bight of Benin ports.[38]

The second broad conclusion is that without abolition in the first half of the nineteenth century, there would have been a widespread and permanent increase in the demand for slaves that could well have had a major and sustained demographic impact. The impact of economic growth in Europe and the Americas would undoubtedly have produced decadal levels of transatlantic exports in excess of the 1780s peak. Had the proportion of females exported from the Bight of Benin in that decade—and the Bight of Biafra ten years later—increased or even continued, population decline would have been much more likely. West-central Africa would have been similarly affected. Here the proportion of males exported was higher, but a sharply higher demand could have increased pressures on other key demographic parameters such as population densities and mortality in transit. Indeed, it is possible that few regions in Africa would have escaped population decline in the nineteenth century in the face of industrialization in the West. The experience of the Adja peoples in the eighteenth century would have been repeated on a larger scale.

# III

The income and welfare implications of abolition were not very different from the demographic impact. Although trade across national boundaries became significant at a relatively early date in many parts of Europe and Africa, the great bulk of this trade was with neighboring societies and nations.[39] Except for newly settled regions of the world specifically organized to generate exports—such as the plantation Americas—long-distance trade remained confined to

..ned to exotic products. It accounted for only tiny fractions of national income before the second half of the nineteenth century. Indeed, though much harder to measure than exports and imports, production for domestic exchange was normally greatly in excess of production for export markets of all kinds.

That Africa was no exception is suggested by some crude but reliable ratios of imports to domestic consumption. The peak of the Atlantic slave trade came in the 1780s when about 48,000 people a year were taken from the coasts of West Africa north of Cape Lopez and about 42,000 from the southern ports. As this was also the decade in which slave prices reached a peak, it is safe to conclude that the value of merchandise imports into Africa was greater between 1781 and 1790 than at any point before the second half of the nineteenth century, though it must be acknowledged that the rapid fall in the price of manufactured goods after 1800 could have meant a greater volume of European exports to Africa in the 1830s and 1840s. Multiplying the slave export figures by average slave prices, yields imports of £1.3 million in West Africa and £0.8 million for west-central Africa.[40] Compared to the United States and Britain of this period, both with populations much smaller than occupied either West Africa or west-central Africa, imports of this magnitude can only be described as small. They were clearly smaller again in earlier decades when both prices and slave-trade volumes were lower. This assessment is not altered if a generous increment of, say, 50 percent is made to the West African figures to accommodate merchandise entering the region via the trans-Saharan traffic as well as imports purchased with the proceeds of nonslave overseas exports.

The relevant comparison, of course, is between African imports and African domestic production. Gemery and Hogendorn have suggested that £0.8 to £1.10 was the range of subsistence cost per person of food, housing and clothing in eighteenth-century Africa.[41] No West African community relied solely on subsistence crops or lacked a surplus for gifts, tribute and trade.[42] But on the assumption that the improbably low figure of 15 million people lived in West Africa at subsistence income levels, then imports from Atlantic trade may be taken at about 9 percent of West African incomes in the 1780s. With assumptions that are more in accord with reality (i.e. a population of 25 million or more and domestic production in excess of subsistence), then imports decline in importance to well below 5 percent. For other decades in the century when both slave prices and exports were lower, imports would have been much less significant. For west-central Africa, population densities were much lower but import/income ratios could not have been much greater.

Such aggregated estimates, of course, ignore the impact of trade on individual states. Geography and the absence of beasts of burden in the forest regions ensured that the coastal states took a disproportionate share of the oceanic trade. The Adja regions, one of the areas which bore the brunt of the demographic impact, also received the largest per capita quantities of European goods. Patrick Manning's work suggests that eighteenth-century Dahomey contained only 5 percent of the West African population but accounted for 20 percent of the traffic. In this particular region the ratio of exports to total output was probably in excess of 15 percent during the early eighteenth century and may well have averaged 15 percent from the late seventeenth century on.[43]

Both the aggregate data discussed earlier and the comments of contemporaries indicate that the experience of the Adja peoples, in particular those of Dahomey, was not only exceptional but probably defines the upper limit of the impact of the slave trade on any coastal societies of importance. Even in Dahomey, moreover, although the "export of slaves [cannot] be dismissed as lacking real impact [neither] can it be taken as Dahomey's primary economic activity."[44] It would seem that even more than most European nations at this time, Africans could feed, clothe and house themselves as well as perform the saving and investment that such activities required without having recourse to goods and markets from other countries.[45] It would seem possible that the abolition of the slave trade was of greater economic importance to Africa than it was to Europe. In neither continent, however, was it of great economic significance.

## IV

The political impact of British and U.S. abolition was probably no greater than its economic and demographic effects. It is certainly more difficult to define. The disruptions and upheavals of kidnapping and war were responsible for the majority of the slaves who entered the traffic, though in the Niger Delta area, wars and slave raids were much more common far to the north than among the coastal communities.[46] It is thus possible that an overseas trade that formed such a minor part of the complex precolonial West African economy and contributed a small share of West African incomes, could have had a political impact out of proportion to its size. The steady buildup of slave exports in the seventeenth and eighteenth centuries may have altered the West African power structure, facilitating state building and perhaps inducing a greater degree of social stratification.[47] On the other hand, of the four largest states in West Africa at the end of the eighteenth century, Asante (Ashanti), Benin, Dahomey and Oyo, the external position and internal structure of the first two were apparently little affected by the traffic and the direction of possible effects on the remaining two is obscure.

The kingdom of Benin had never been a major participant in the transatlantic trade. The royal monopoly on male slaves that existed in the eighteenth century may or may not have continued, but the volume of departures continued at very low levels. Between 1816 and 1839, only fifteen expeditions, or about one tenth of the number leaving Lagos, are recorded as shipping or intending to ship slaves from the Benin River. This was probably not very different from the preceding thirty years.[48] In the Asante case, slave exports fell precipitously after 1807, which was about the time the Asante, who had previously sold to Fanti middlemen, broke through to the coast. The revival after 1814 was both temporary and relatively small. There is evidence of a continued flow of slaves southward to the British protectorates where the importation of unfree labor was not banned until after the 1873–74 British-Asante war. More important, Asante developed a large trade to the north in kola nuts, which was associated with the beverage needs of an expanding Islam.[49] This ʳade was facilitated by the revenue from the trans-Saharan traffic, of which slaves were an important part. But the ratio of any plausible estimate of the level of exports, either before or after 1807, to any plausible population estimates of Asante suggests that the slave trade can never have been important. Although the position of the war party in Kumasi counsels may have been undermined by abolition, the threat to Asante power in the nineteenth century came from the British, not from neighboring states.[50] Clearly the continuance of Asante dominance to 1874 was not due to the slave trade. Information on prices and volume levels make it unlikely that even in peak years did the total value of slaves leaving any individual West African port exceed £200,000, and net government revenues, even if a state monopoly existed, must have been a small fraction of this.[51] Perhaps the most that can be argued is that abolition on the Gold Coast affected the small coastal states more than Asante and reduced the ability of the former to resist Asante aggression and thereby "hindered the peace necessary for trade and economic change."[52]

In the case of Dahomey and Oyo, there may be a stronger basis for linking political power with the slave trade, although there is no consensus on this among African historians. The origins of Oyo's power lay in the commerce and agriculture of the savanna rather than in coastal trade. Dahomey, created according to one interpretation as a reaction against the slave trade,[53] quickly succumbed to Oyo suzerainty and, with its own Atlantic outlets, assumed a major middleman role in the trade—as indeed had Oyo in midcentury. Unlike Asante and Oyo, Dahomey appears to have drawn, in part at least, from its own human resources to supply the trade. The centralized bureaucracy of Dahomey was not typical of West Africa and was certainly different from Oyo government structures.[54] The appearance of parallels in the kingdom of Benin, however, suggests that the slave trade was not responsible for the difference. In decline, Dahomey continued both to exist as a viable polity and to export slaves, even after its military position had been undermined by the Egba state of Abeokuta. Indeed exports from the main Dahomey outlet of Ouidah, with its strong affiliations with Bahia, continued largely unaffected by either military losses or abolition initiatives, right down to 1850 and sporadically thereafter to the early 1860s.[55] In Oyo internal dissension between the Alafin and the chiefs in both capital and provinces may well have been precipitated by the shrinkage in revenues resulting from the nearly 60 percent decline in exports from the Bight of Benin ports between the 1780s and 1790s. Although Clapperton saw the slave trade as responsible for Oyo collapse, it is never absolutely clear from his comments whether it was its continuance or its decline that caused the problem.[56] It is at least difficult to link in any consistent way internecine Yoruba warfare and the Fulani jihad that became a part of it with the Bight of Benin slave trade. Except possibly for the 1826–30 period, slave departures were always well below levels of the previous century. Lack of centralized power structure was not confined to Oyo—peoples in the Bight of Biafra hinterlands experienced both the expansion and decline of the slave trade with no large-scale political organization.

If there was a political organizational structure in West Africa that can be associated with the Atlantic trade, it was the small but centralized coastal trading state. The Gold Coast of the seventeenth century, Lagos in the nineteenth century and, in particular, the Bight of Biafra were states characterized by local monopoly, extreme specialization and failure to extend either political or economic control into the hinterland or to other parts of the coast.[57] However, even in this case, there were major differences in that warfare and an associated military infrastructure was more prevalent in the Gold Coast. In the Bight of Biafra, by contrast, the vibrancy of these states through the era of "legitimate" trade after abolition suggests that their characteristics derived from trading, not particularly from trafficking in slaves. The fortunes of the Aro trading network among the Ibo and Ibibio rose and subsided with the slave trade, but this was scarcely a political organization. And in the important slaving center of the Gallinas, a quite different structure existed. A confederation of chiefs developed during the height of the slave traffic with the leading chief, King Siaka, able to do little more than call together the other heads who collectively controlled territory extending no more than fifty miles inland.[58] There is no obvious general lesson to be learned from any relationship between fluctuations of the slave trade and the rise and fall of political authority or indeed from political institutions in West Africa. It is tempting to conclude that the lack of a pattern was due to the relative lack of importance of the oceanic slave trade to polities in the interior.

The same lack of a clear cut pattern is apparent in west-central Africa. The vast expansion of the slave trade from the coast north of the Congo in the seventeenth and eighteenth centuries has been linked with the decline of the large Vili Kingdom of Loango. Decentralization of internal political authority occurred both here and in the smaller kingdoms of related peoples, called Kacongo and Ngoyo, which lay between Loango and the mouth of the Congo. In both cases slave-trade brokers gained at the expense of the traditional rulers.[59] Transatlantic slave departures from this broad region probably fell by more than half between the 1780s and 1810s and by a further half in the next two decades. However, the impact of abolition was most uneven within the region. British Foreign Office representatives in the Americas reported no slave arrivals from Mayumba in the 1811–20 decade and only a single arrival in the following decade. In the same period only 3 ships were reported from Loango Bay and the 103 assigned to Malemba (north of Cabinda) were all in the 1821–30 decade—most, in reality, visited Bight of Benin ports rather than Malemba.[60] After 1830 when the Portuguese transatlantic trade was abolished without regard to geographic limits and there was less need for deception, there were only 35 ships (in total) recorded as sailing to or from the Vili and Mayumba regions from that year down to the close of the trade. Cabinda, on the other hand, is recorded as supplying over 350 ships in the 1811–30 period, most of them actually trading there.[61] With only 37 ships identified as from the Congo (Zaire) River in this period, it is clear that Cabinda and later Kacongo were the major outlets for slaves from the supply routes that converged on the Congo. After 1830 embarkation points in the Cabinda and Congo River regions continued to supply over 90 percent of the slaves that left the Congo-River-to-Cape-Lopez region of Africa.[62]

Although these port-based shipping data are clearly more incomplete than the regional slave export series for Congo North shown in appendix A, the slave trade north of Kacongo no doubt declined after 1800.[63] The Vili traders had lost their role as a major link between the Europeans and the slave-supply zones both north and south of the Congo. The important points here are: first, that the trend toward political fragmentation was already established well before the slave trade reached its peak; second, that the trend intensified during the half century of decline in transatlantic exports and, third, that it continued after 1840 when both the slave trade and the produce trade expanded dramatically once more. Moreover, the trend was common to both Loango, where the slave trade had virtually stopped, and in the Kacongo and Ngoyo polities to the south, where a large slave traffic continued.[64]

The region south of the Congo River was least affected by British abolition. Although the British left the region after 1807 and departures from Ambriz, Ambrizete and neighboring points fell off sharply, Portuguese vessels hitherto restricted to Luanda and Benguela began to trade further north. At the same time the demand for slaves in southern Brazil began to accelerate, with the result that the estimated Angolan total for 1811–20 of 147,000 is unlikely to have been much different from total departures in each of the previous two decades. The Portuguese may have regained their share of the Mbundu and Kongo slave trades from the interior that they had lost in the eighteenth century. Their dependence on supplies from the south and east, in particular from the Lunda Empire, may have temporarily lessened before the trade expanded again after 1820. But the major impact of abolition was to come later.[65]

In southeast Africa in this same period, the direct effect of European economic growth was also rather more important than the abolitionist initiatives. Expanding demand for labor in St. Domingue and the Mascarene Islands (the latter in the Indian Ocean) saw slaves displace ivory as the main item of trade in the late eighteenth century. The St. Domingue revolution and the European wars removed the Caribbean as a major market and the wars also reduced the demand from the Mascarene Islands. Nonetheless the labor requirements of the Brazilian south ensured that the lull would be temporary.[66] Moreover, the British takeover in the Indian Ocean of the Ile de France (renamed Mauritius) and the Seychelles in 1810 brought security to both the sugar and the slave trades in the region. The British treated the newly conquered French planters with great circumspection: In particular, the abolition of the slave trade to Mauritius was not proclaimed there until 1813, and it went largely unenforced until the mid-1820s. It is apparent that the British presence intially stimulated rather than suppressed the demand for slaves from southeast Africa.[67] It was thus European war rather than European abolition that may have temporarily slowed the slave trade in the late 1790s and early 1800s. Internal political developments such as the Afro-Portuguese warfare in Macuana and the temporary revival of the prazo system (Portuguese quasifeudal estates) had much to do with the initial expansion of the slave trade in the 1780s, but these were probably less important than external influences in accounting for the relatively minor fluctuations in volumes of exports of the subsequent two decades.[68]

In the absence of both large indigenous states and a continuous pre–nineteenth-century demand for slaves from Arab regions, the political consequences of the transatlantic slave trade may well have been greater in southeast Africa than elsewhere. Yet the general implications of the low value of the trade relative to domestic production and local trade seem to hold for this as for other areas of Africa. If European slave trading did remove the underpinnings of traditional authority in Africa, the mechanism of the process differed markedly among regions. African political structures show no pattern remotely consistent with the volume of the slave trade, either across regions or over time. In Congo North and the Bight of Biafra, European authority stopped at the shoreline—at least until the middle of the nineteenth century. Furthermore, wars played a minor role in the relations between states and no political units to match Asante or Dahomey either broke through to the coast or extended their power inland. Of course, given the sharp differences in social structures among African societies, major differences in the impact of the slave trade are to be expected. As Walter Rodney has pointed out, Kongo society was more hierarchical than most Upper Guinea social groupings.[69] Perhaps John Fage's assessment that the slave trade "tended to integrate, strengthen and develop unitary, territorial political authority, but to weaken or destroy more segmentary societies" is correct. Unfortunately the sources for African history are often such that one feels the definition of a segmentary society is one that broke up.[70] An alternative explanation is simply that the slave trade for most regions and periods was not a critically important influence over the course of African history. At the very least, those who would place the slave trade as central to West African and west-central African history should be able to point to stronger common threads, if not themes, across African regions than have so far come to light.

# III

# The Abolitionist Assault
# on Slave Traffic, 1820–50

# 6

# The Direction and Scope of
# the Attack on the Slave Trade

*Drescher – non-action of Brits*

Attempts to suppress the slave trade could have focused on any part of the international network that took men, women and children from Africa and delivered sugar and coffee and cotton to Europe. Consuming countries could have imposed taxes on tropical produce equal to the extra cost of producing without newly imported Africans or even without any form of slave labor. At the other end of the network, suppressive action might have aimed at raising costs of slave trading within Africa until it was no longer worthwhile to capture slaves and supply them to the Atlantic dealers. The British government, the Niger expedition notwithstanding, attempted neither of these options. The first required an improbable degree of cooperation among consuming nations at a time when each suspected the abolitionist motives of the other. Action by one nation alone, even a country as important as Great Britain, would have simply raised prices within that country while having little impact on the income of plantation owners. Such a policy would also have been an obvious contradiction of the drive for cheaper foodstuffs that was increasingly preoccupying industrializing countries. It would have constituted as well an overt recognition of the superior efficiency of slave over free labor—no mean ideological feat in the early years of the nineteenth century at least. Thus it was that the British actually reduced duties on plantation produce from Cuba and Brazil at a critical juncture in the fight against the traffic. The second option demanded an ability to interfere in the affairs of African politics in the interior; this was not attained until near the end of the century. Instead of targeting the beginning or the end of the network, Great Britain and (later) other countries attempted to sever the labor-supply link at its center. Naval action was aimed at raising the costs of shipping slaves across the Atlantic and thereby increasing the spread between the price paid by the plantation owner and the price received by the African dealer. The success of this strategy hinged on raising the former to a point where noncoerced labor would have been a cheaper substitute. Alternatively the strategy would have achieved its goal if it had forced down the price on the African coast to the point where the dealer's costs were no longer covered. Neither of these effects appeared to be within the power of the British Navy.

In 1850 after almost half a century's effort against the slave trade, the British Admiralty surveyed a group of senior officers, all with experience in the South Atlantic, on the navy's attempts to end the traffic. This internal review came at the end of fifteen years in which the traffic in Africans had come to rival that of the eighteenth century in both volume and the scale of British capital involved. Supplies of coerced labor and the denial of these supplies to other parts of the Americas formed the basis of the unprecedented prosperity attained by Brazil and Cuba. The conclusions of the survey, reached just a few months before the sudden and rather unexpected demise of the traffic's major branch, was unequivocally pessimistic. Much of it indeed would have been acceptable to the pacifist executive of the British and Foreign Anti-Slavery Society. The traffic would continue as long as slavery survived in the importing countries or at least until the local and national governments of those countries decided to suppress it. The naval cruisers moreover exacerbated the trade's cruelties. The naval officers believed that the squadron should not be withdrawn (although some implied even this), but operations should be scaled down until such time as penalties against slaver captains and crews could be exacted.[1]

Naval despondency and the better-known efforts of free traders and some abolitionists to call off the squadron are not explained just by the resilience of the traffic. Not even the escalating African mortality, which accompanied efforts to eradicate the trade, and the vast reserves of unoccupied land in major plantation regions can account wholly for the pessimism. More important from the viewpoint of those inside the government and directly involved in suppression was the scale of the resources unavailingly committed to the struggle. On the one side there were the near-record volumes of slaves traded and the involvement of British merchants in facilitating that trade, on the other there were masses of domestic legislation, treaties with almost every power whose flag or ports could be used by slave ships and a very expensive superstructure of courts, ships and payments to foreign governments. It is hardly surprising to find that when the government defended its policy it stressed what would happen without the cruisers rather than more tangible facts such as ships and slaves actually captured. The relevant question, argued Palmerston, was not how many slaves were shipped but how many would have been shipped in the absence of British efforts.[2] Here we will address the issue of the scale of these efforts, their effectiveness in terms of captured ships and freed Africans as well as the related matters of British involvement in the traffic and the broader implications of the treaty network.

A characteristic of the nineteenth-century trade was that most governments could put an end to the involvement of their own nationals in the traffic or at least reduce it to nominal levels if they really wished to do so. Ironically the nation who had the most difficulty in this was Britain, although in this case the force of the irony is reduced if we view both the ubiquity of British capital and the prevalence of abolitionist attitudes as a function of advanced capitalism. Between 1806 and 1824, Parliament passed no less than fifteen acts on the slave trade. The deficiencies of the legislation governing direct involvement are discussed in chapter 7, but the problem of controlling the flow of British capital into the trade, or indirect involvement, was even greater.

In the year before abolishing the British slave trade, Parliament prohibited British involvement in the foreign slave trade, penalizing specifically the advancing of credit in the form of goods or cash to foreign slave traders. A further clause that banned the sale of goods if the seller knew that they were destined for the slave trade applied only to transactions on British territory.[3] In 1815 Joseph Barham, a member in the West Indian interest, introduced a bill that prohibited the lending of money on the security of land in any territory where the slave trade continued.[4] The bill passed the Commons, but was narrowly lost in the Lords. The 1806 provisions thus remained untouched until the Slave Trade Laws Consolidation Act of 1824 removed geographic limitations and made any infraction a felony with the penalty of transportation.[5] There remained the problem of British owners of slaves in foreign territories. The 1833 and 1838 acts that abolished slavery in the British Empire ignored the subject, and it was only in 1843 that Parliament prohibited British subjects from owning or dealing in slaves anywhere in the world.[6] In summary, down to 1824 there was nothing to stop a British subject selling goods or equipment to a slave trader outside British territory; after 1824 such activities were illegal only if the seller had prior knowledge of the purposes for which the goods were intended. Furthermore, until 1843 British companies and individuals were free to hold slaves outside British territory and, of course, at no time were British loans on the security of nonslave property restricted.

As long as the slave trade existed anywhere and as long as the British remained dedicated to the goals of laissez-faire and civilizing the world through trade, it was impossible to prevent British involvement. Their merchants freighted goods to slave barracoons on the African littoral,[7] recycled slave ships condemned and sold by the Courts of Mixed Commission back to the slave traders,[8] and supplied the greater portion of the goods and credit used by the Brazilian and Cuban slave trader.[9] The availability and cost of credit to the nineteenth-century slave trader was mainly a function of the capture risk to the latter's slave ships. Through most of this period the risk was slight enough that debts on trade goods were paid "at the conclusion of the speculation they were employed in."[10] The formal abolition of the complete Brazilian trade and the 1839 Palmerston Act dismayed the British merchant communities in Brazil and contributed to the parliamentary anti-coercionist movements of the 1840s. And in Havana the failure of a leading slave trader threatened the solvency of British merchants there, one of whom was Charles Tolmé, a former British consul.[11]

The Foreign Office did its best to prosecute. Palmerston, in particular, followed up evidence of British involvement that came to his attention.[12] Urged by Lord Glenelg, son of one of the Clapham Saints, at the Colonial Office, he sent reports from the British commissioners at the Rio de Janeiro Court of Mixed Commission to the Queen's Advocate; when the latter requested more evidence,[13] he attempted without success to obtain it. In the case of a Glasgow merchant who was in partnership with a Havana slave trader, Palmerston instigated a detailed investigation in which the Lord Advocate of Scotland had the merchant questioned and his books examined. Though the evidence, the law officer concluded, was insufficient to sustain prosecution, he was in no doubt that the case "was only one amongst many in which the prohibited traffic in slaves is carried on by means of British capital and enterprises."[14] Though Palmerston was still following leads as late as 1848, neither he nor any other member of the British government was able to bring a case involving the sale of goods on credit to slave traders into court. There was one private prosecution, by George Stephen against a Spanish merchant in London, which resulted in a verdict of not guilty.[15]

The obstacle to a conviction in all cases from the surreptitious fitting out of foreign slave ships in Liverpool after 1807 to the activities of Havana and Rio de Janeiro merchants was the need to prove guilty knowledge. Clause 10 of the 1824 Slave Trade Laws Consolidating Act that listed the proscribed commercial practices included the word "knowingly," and thereby gave the prosecution the almost impossible task of proving criminal intent. The British could have removed the word "knowingly," adopted Barham's bill or at least banned trading at certain locations on the African coast. But this would have run counter to their beliefs in the moral effects of honest trade and would have caused widespread loss of markets as merchants and manufacturers pulled back from any transactions that might conceivably have resulted in merchandise ending up in the slave trade. British credit thus remained a mainstay of the transatlantic trade to the end despite the deliberations of a select committee that considered the subject, the pleas of naval officers and the subsequent erratic efforts of former Lord Chancellor Brougham to change the law.[16]

If the process of squeezing British capital out of the trade was protracted and largely unsuccessful, British slave ships at least, even under foreign flags, had mostly disappeared within a few years of the 1807 act. For foreign slave ships, of course, the navy faced a half century of frustration with the coming of peace in 1815. The commodore of the squadron was perhaps correct when he wrote, "Let me have their Lordships orders to capture every vessel carrying slaves or fitted for the carrying of slaves without any regard to country or flag and I will answer with my commission that in three years there shall be no slave vessels to be found on this Coast"[17]—if as a minimum he could have treated the slavers as pirates. His position, however, was of strictly academic significance. The recently concluded Anglo-American war had been motivated, in part, precisely by differing conceptions of freedom on the high seas. There was little doubt that the sympathies of the other maritime nations lay with the United States despite the British attempt to separate the right of visit, which they argued all maritime police possessed, from the right of search. Indeed Aberdeen himself admitted privately that the British claim of a right to visit foreign ships (to establish the right of a ship to the flag it used) was without "the authority of writers in Publick Law." He could argue only that "our situation is entirely new, and the trade being condemned by all nations, gives us rights which otherwise would not exist."[18]

Unlike robbery and murder, the traffic in slaves was not and never became classed as piracy. Britain, the U.S. and some other countries declared the trade to be piratical, but this was not enough to make the activity a breach of international law and therefore punishable by the laws of any country within whose power a pirate was brought. As with the present-day narcotics traffic, there was nothing in customary international law to make slave trading illegal. Indeed it had been carried on for centuries by almost every maritime nation, and a change in customary international law would require the agreement of all nations.[19] Ironically the British government was not keen to see this happen despite the frequent references in the pamphlet literature and in Parliament that the declaration of slaving as piracy was the solution to the problem. The Foreign Office feared that innocent British traders might run foul of foreign tribunals.[20] Moreover, if slave trading was not against international law, it followed that there could be no justification for the right of search or even the right of visit of suspected slavers on the high seas. Together British hesitation on the piracy issue, on the one hand, and the need to obtain right of search privileges, on the other, ensured the creation of an elaborate treaty system. British pressure on various countries to stiffen their penalties against the traffic had the same origin.

Unfortunately the very strength of the Royal Navy and the penal sanctions against direct British involvement actually reduced the effectiveness of this network. By the 1820s the only active slave traders were foreign ones, albeit assisted by British merchants. This tended to produce two effects. First, it encouraged a sense of moral superiority that developed easily into arrogance when the British dealt with the Iberian governments. The self-congratulatory tone that frequently emerged from the Parliamentary discussions of the slave trade issue in the two decades after 1807[21] gradually hardened into chauvinism. "The Portuguese" wrote Palmerston as prime minister, "are . . . the lowest in the moral scale and the Brazilians are degenerate Portuguese, demoralized by slavery and slave trade, and all the degrading and corrupting influences connected with both."[22] The British felt they had atoned for past behavior and were not about to concede that if it had been Iberian governments that controlled the biggest navy in the world and the Iberian ruling class that first absorbed the free-labor ethic, British slave traders would have been as dominant in the nineteenth century as in earlier years. Such attitudes were not likely to induce cooperation. Second, the absence of British slave traders reduced to absurdity the reciprocity that the British offered in negotiations over slave-trade conventions. The Portuguese and Spanish navies might be granted the right to detain British ships and take them before the courts of mixed commission. But everyone knew that the treaties were in practice a license for the British Navy to capture and the joint courts to condemn the ships of other nations. There was some inconsistency between the British wish to foster the liberal ideal of a world of free, independent nation-states and their unhappiness with French and U.S. refusal to sign such treaties.

These preliminary considerations help explain much of the structure of the treaty network. By the 1850s, four types of treaties had developed between Britain and most of the powers whose flags or ports might be used in the traffic.[23] The first and the one most favored by the British provided for a mutual right of search over the shipping of the contracting parties. Where incriminating evidence was discovered specially constituted joint courts (courts of mixed commission) were to adjudicate the detained property, but not the persons of those associated with it. Each party appointed one judge and one arbitrator and when disagreement between the two judges occurred, lots were drawn to choose one arbitrator who was to give the deciding vote. There was no appeal from this decision. Located before 1842 only at Sierra Leone, Rio de Janeiro, Havana and Paramaribo, these courts eventually ringed the Atlantic basin from New York in the north to Capetown in the south, though the one at Rio de Janeiro closed in 1845.[24] Despite such ubiquity, however, over 80 percent of the slaves and ships captured under this type of treaty were adjudicated at Sierra Leone. The success of this approach to suppression depended on the nature of the incriminating evidence that the courts could recognize. Under the original conventions signed with Spain, Portugal and the Netherlands in 1817 and 1818, ships actually had to have slaves on board before the courts could decree forfeiture. In addition, in the case of the Portuguese, the slave ship had to be trading north of the equator. The shortcomings of these treaties quickly became obvious as the slave trader modified shipping practices. In the course of the next four decades, the British sought to widen the grounds of condemnation, to have the slaver destroyed after conviction, and to bring more countries into the network "[so] that the slave traders when they are driven from the shelter of one flag may not take refuge under the fraudulent assumption of another."[25]

The British strategy was only partially successful. Additional articles or new treaties were signed with the Netherlands in 1822; Sweden and Norway in 1824 and 1835, respectively; Brazil in 1826; and most important, Spain in 1835 (after years of prevarication on one side and pressure on the other), Portugal in 1842 and the United States in 1862. In addition, five South American countries, the Argentine, Uruguay, Bolivia, Chile and Ecuador were recruited between 1839 and 1841.[26] In all cases ships carrying specific equipment such as a slave deck in the form of spare plank, more bulkheads than normal, hatches with gratings attached, boiler tubs, excessive water casks, mess tubs or shackles would be liable to condemnation even if no slaves were on board. Condemnation also meant that the ship would be broken up. The long delay in reaching agreement on these issues with Portugal, Spain, the United States and, of course, France (who never assented to these terms), meant that at different times in the century the respective flags of these nations each dominated the traffic. Moreover, even when detained, slaver captains still could hope for the possibility of a disagreement among the judges that would result in the drawing of a friendly arbitrator and the restoration of their vessel. And, of course, at no time were the persons of officer, crew or owner at risk. Clearly these international courts were no substitute for the domestic criminal courts of any nation that was determined to put an end to the traffic.

But the shortcomings of the second type of treaty were even greater. In 1831 and 1833, France and Britain signed two conventions, the effect of which w⁻ to grant a mutual right of search but without the complementary superstr ture of mixed commission courts. Instead, the cruisers would hand over suspected ships to the respective domestic tribunals of the parties to the agreement. Denmark, Sardinia, the Hanse towns, Tuscany, the Two Sicilies and Haiti all became parties to these Anglo-French conventions. In addition Venezuela, Texas, Mexico, Belgium, Austria, Prussia and Russia signed separate but similar agreements before 1850—Austria, Prussia, and Russia under the Quintuple Agreement of 1841, which France also signed but did not ratify.[27] If all these countries had had the same legislation and, more important, the same public attitudes toward the slave trade as the British, this second type of treaty would have been more effective than the first. As far as France was concerned, this was, in fact, the case. Both significant French involvement in the traffic and the fraudulent use of the French flag ended in 1831, though this was only after a decade when every slaver north of the equator seemed to have a set of French colors on board.[28] Countries that depended heavily on their merchant marine were less accommodating. The Sardinian flag, in particular, was often used by slavers outbound from Bahia in the later 1840s and by cargo ships carrying slave-trading supplies and equipment. The U.S. flag and ships had the same role in the Rio de Janeiro and later the Cuban trade; Hanse towns' shipping was also involved. When the British captured these vessels and took them to Genoa or Bremen, they were almost invariably released. In all cases it seemed that slaves had to be found on board to obtain a conviction, and the slave traders always ensured that flags and papers were switched before Africans were embarked.[29]

Two countries refused to grant a mutual right of search to the British except for limited time periods and signed yet a third type of slave-trade convention with the British. As a consequence of Anglo-French rivalry in North Africa and incidents between French merchant ships and the British antislave-trade squadron, French pressure resulted in the replacement of the 1831 and 1833 treaties with the 1845 convention. Instead of a right of search, there would now be a mutual obligation to maintain squadrons on the coast of Africa of approximately equal strength, which for the French meant a massive increase in their West-African naval forces. Three years earlier, Article 8 of the Webster-Ashburton Treaty had elicited a similar though smaller commitment from the United States to maintain a permanent eighty-gun squadron off West Africa. Under neither treaty could squadrons capture the ships belonging to the other nation, so that the question of international tribunals did not arise.[30] These treaties resulted in an impressive multinational array of warships off Africa in the mid-1840s. A combined operational total of nearly sixty British, French and U.S. cruisers was the norm in these years. In addition, the Portuguese Angolan squadron comprising four to six ships was actively engaged in antislave-trade duties after 1843. Slave traders faced more firepower in these years than either before or after.

Yet the power these fleets represented was largely illusory. The French, Portuguese and American cruisers could detain only their own vessels outside territorial waters, and only the Portuguese had as yet claims to significant parts of the African coast. British negotiators of the 1845 convention had expected that the French squadron would at the very least capture ships without colors,

increasing numbers of which appeared after 1845. Indeed it was for this reason
that the British were able to countenance the loss of the right to search French
ships in that convention. In fact, the French higher courts restored any ship
taken without the French flag as long as it was not engaged in piracy, with the
result that the massive French squadron was grossly underemployed and by
the early 1850s greatly reduced in size.[31] As the American and Portuguese
squadrons were small, frequently absent or incapacitated and as no slave ships
used the French flag in the last thirty years of the trade, only the British had
any real powers on the issue, and some of these were illegally assumed.

The fourth and final category of treaties comprised those between Britain
and a wide range of African powers. As we shall see, Africans were being forced
into an increasingly subservient role in the formal or diplomatic aspect of Afro-
European relationship. But this did little to facilitate the suppression of the
slave trade. The first treaties with African potentates containing antislave-trade
provisions were signed on the east coast, with the king of eastern Madagascar,
the sultan of Zanzibar and the imam of Muscat.[32] In April 1838, before
Thomas Fowell Buxton published his plan for the Niger expedition, the Foreign Office circulated a confidential print urging the extension of this policy to
the west coast of the continent and in the same month instructed the Admiralty
to begin negotiations through the agency of naval officers.[33] Initially treaties
were intended not only to commit African rulers to end the slave trade but also
to ensure a most-favored-nation status for British commerce, freedom of religion, protection for British property and freedom to trade with any individual
or group within the African territory.[34] These were sweeping provisions that
reflected the broader cultural goals of British policy. But the resistance of Africans to such broad terms, particularly the last, meant that the standard slave-
trade treaty quickly came to encompass only the first two of the above
provisions.[35]

It is thus not surprising that the early British approaches to African states
were rebuffed. At Cape Mount (south of the Gallinas), Old Calibar and the
Cameroons, the naval officers could obtain only treaties of amity and commerce. The first slave-trade treaty was signed with the Gallinas chiefs in
November 1840 under the guns of Captain Joseph Denman's force and was
subsequently repudiated by the Africans for this reason. Treaties signed under
similar circumstances in Cabinda and Ambriz met similar fates though the
British insisted that these agreements were valid. Ratified agreements followed
elsewhere, beginning in the Cameroons in May 1841, but the treaties came
close to covering all the provenance zones of the transatlantic trade only in the
1860s. The largest single slaving power, Dahomey, signed late and was able to
break the treaty with little fear of retribution.[36] The British might have been
more successful if they had relied less on force and promises and more on hard
cash. British expectations of the commercial benefits of abolition made the latter unnecessary in their own view and the African rulers were offered the prospect of legitimate trade but only token gifts. When Captain William Tucker
drew a bill for $10,000 as the first of five annual payments to the Bonny chiefs
in 1841, the Foreign Office quickly canceled the agreement on which it was
based. Two years later a similar convention with Dahomey that involved pay-

ments of only one-third this amount was also canceled.[37] Yet by 1857 the network consisted of forty-five slave trade treaties on the west coast. These at least gave the navy a justification for forcible suppression within the territories of African powers if the latter did not live up to their treaty obligations. On the basis of the Gallinas treaty, for example, cruisers under Captain Blount destroyed reestablished slave factories in 1842, and in 1849–50 the navy maintained a total blockade that finally put an end to the transatlantic traffic in that region.[38]

The treaty network was supplemented and reinforced with two pieces of domestic legislation that applied to certain foreign slave ships. In 1839 British frustration with Portuguese reluctance to extend the 1817 treaty led to the passage of Lord Palmerston's Act.[39] As noted, Portugal had agreed only to abolish the slave trade north of the equator. But, as she had also agreed to restrict the slave trade to her own possessions, Palmerston and others argued that Brazilian independence made any transatlantic slave trade under the Portuguese flag illegal. In 1839, however, the foreign secretary had a bill drafted that empowered the navy to search Portuguese ships as well as ships claiming no nationality on the high seas. Such vessels were to be taken before British admiralty courts if they contained slaves or specified articles of slave-trading equipment. The courts could free slaves found on board and order the break up of the ships and confiscation of goods and stores. As a peacetime assault on the flag of an independent nation, this bill, as the Duke of Wellington noted, was unprecedented. Indeed opposition in the Lords led by Wellington meant that the bill had to be resubmitted before it entered the statute book in a simplified form. The act was largely responsible for coercing the Portuguese into accepting British terms embodied in the 1842 Anglo-Portuguese treaty.[40] With the signing of the latter, the part of the act that applied to Portuguese shipping was repealed.

The second act, passed in 1845 and often called Lord Aberdeen's Act, was virtually identical to its predecessor except that it was directed against ships sailing under the Brazilian flag and was marginally less offensive in international law. Most of the Anglo-Brazilian slave-trade treaty of 1826 was of indefinite duration. However, that part of it that provided for mutual right of search and created the Anglo-Brazilian courts of mixed commission was based on the 1817 Anglo-Portuguese convention, that had a twenty-eight-year term. From March 1845 British cruisers would not be able to interfere with Brazilian slave ships.[41] Moreover, even with the right of search in force there had always been considerable doubt as to whether the mixed courts could condemn Brazilian slave ships with no slaves on board. An additional article covering these cases had been signed by Brazil and Britain in July 1835, but the former had never ratified it. In practice the court at Sierra Leone condemned all such ships, whereas the Rio de Janeiro court condemned or restored them, depending on which country's arbitrator drew the lot to cast the deciding judgment.[42] Brazilian reluctance to renew the right-of-search clause and to ratify the equipment article induced Aberdeen to duplicate the measure already used against Portugal. Because the first article of the 1826 treaty declared the trade to be piracy for British and Brazilian subjects and was subject to no time constraint, the British were able to claim that the act merely enforced existing treaty provisions.[43] As Aberdeen himself admitted, however, "The law was certainly a great stretch of power and open to many objections on principle."[44] Unlike the Portuguese act, moreover, this one remained in force for a quarter century and the first clause of the 1826 treaty on which it was founded was not abrogated until 1921: After 1845 Brazil never again agreed to mutual right of search and a revival of the mixed courts.

The international superstructure of proscriptions against the slave trade was as close as it ever came to being complete in 1862 with the signing of the last African treaties and the Anglo-U.S. convention providing for right of search and courts of mixed commission. It then included the vast majority of countries that had a coastline on the Atlantic and Indian oceans and many nations such as Russia, Austria and Ecuador, that did not. The only major country excluded was France: Since 1856 she had had no formal engagements with any power on this issue but she maintained a significant naval presence in the South Atlantic. The system had two striking features that distinguished it from other structures designed to control international crime. First, few of those involved in the traffic and subjected to court proceedings ever suffered imprisonment much less loss of life for their crimes. None of the courts set up by the treaties provided any penalties beyond confiscation of property. Persons on board suspected ships at the time of capture might be handed over to the appropriate national law-enforcement agency for trial. Although the occasional Britain, Frenchman or American was jailed (in one case executed), citizens of Iberian countries and Brazil, comprising the bulk of those involved, were rarely prosecuted. Unlike modern organized international crime, the main culprits, shipowners and creditors (many of the latter British) were never subject to penalties. The British eventually claimed the right to treat Brazilian subjects as pirates under the first article of the 1826 Anglo-Brazilian treaty but, in fact, never exercised the power. Indeed British courts refused even to convict the Brazilian and Portuguese slave ship sailors who murdered an entire British prize crew assigned to conduct them and their vessel to Sierra Leone. A court of appeal ruled that the 1839 and 1845 acts, under one of which these individuals had been captured, did not extend British jurisdiction over foreigners or foreign ships.[45]

Yet the major distinguishing feature of the international antislave-trade system was that it was always centered on only one country. Britain was more than the center of the network. No country in the world in this era signed a treaty containing antislave provisions to which Britain was not also a party. Possessing what was effectively the only navy with power over other countries' ships, not all of it consistent with international law, Britain alone provided the executive muscle that the international antislave-trade system could exercise. We now turn to a brief evaluation of the largely British enforcement arm of the treaty network.

Though the British Admiralty was perhaps less enthusiastic than the Foreign Office in putting slave-trade suppression in the forefront of national objectives,[46] the Royal Navy's commitment to the task was large. Until the 1839 and 1845 acts were passed, the navy could interfere with ships of other countries only if the detaining officers possessed a warrant signed by an appropriate minister of the country to which the suspected ship belonged. Warships assigned to Brazil, the Cape of Good Hope and the Caribbean as well as to West African stations were normally provided with these warrants, so that between one third and one half of all ships on active service were authorized to visit and detain suspected slave ships.[47] In fact, a much smaller proprortion of these vessels were involved in slave-trade suppression at any one time. The question is what proportion. Despite occasional redeployment of cruisers from West Africa to Brazil and the Caribbean, the center of suppression was always on the west coast of Africa. Ships on other stations, including the Cape of Good Hope, were assigned these duties only when circumstances permitted. In the late 1840s, for example, the squadron stationed off Brazil was wholly deployed in sustaining British intervention in the Río de la Plata where the slave trade was non-existent at that time. The Brazilian coast was thus left without an antislave-trade patrol for extended periods. Even off West Africa there were duties unconnected with the slave trade such as the Ashanti War in 1824 and the protection of British trade, which extended occasionally to debt collection. However, the Admiralty made it clear that without the slave trade there would be need for only a single cruiser off West Africa.[48] There was also the question of replacement vessels. Given distances from England and sailing times, there was usually 10 to 20 percent of the normal operating strength of the squadron in transit.[49]

One key assumption facilitates the development of an estimate of the naval antislave-trade effort. One warship was needed for nonslave-trade duties in West Africa; if we add to this cruisers in transit to and from the West African squadron, we would have a figure just about equal the number of ships primarily concerned with slave-trade suppression on all other stations combined. Thus the total number of ships assigned to the west coast of Africa at any point in a given year would be a proxy for the effective strength of the navy committed to the suppression of the transatlantic slave trade. Table 2 shows the ships, manpower and an estimate of the cost of the British force off West Africa. Pre-1816 data are omitted on account of the irregularity of patrols off West Africa, the existence of an undetermined number of schooners commissioned by the governor of Sierra Leone for antislave-trade duties and the inflated size of the wartime navy.

Table 2 requires some preliminary discussion. The ships deployed in the squadron shown in column (1) were generally smaller than the average British warship: Ships of the line were not normally assigned such duties.[50] On the other hand, because of the need to supply prize crews to captured vessels, cruisers off West Africa normally had a very full complement of men (table 2, col. [3]). Slavers were not the only crowded ships off West Africa at this time. Various cost estimates are possible and indeed were offered by contemporaries, particularly during the parliamentary debates and select committee inquiries of the late 1840s when the utility of the squadron was questioned. It was common to include in these costs the wages and victualing costs for the crew as well as the costs of rigging, masts and stores along with a depreciation allowance for the hulls[51]—and these are included in column (4). They are not, however, the fully allocated costs of the squadron that might, more properly, be

**Table 2.** Annual Estimates of British Resources Committed to the Suppression of the Transatlantic Slave Trade, 1816–65

| | (1) Ships Assigned to West Africa | (2) Manpower of West African Ships | (3) Percent of Total Naval Manpower Assigned to West Africa | (4) Cost of West African Force[a] | (5) Total Direct Costs of Suppression[a] |
|---|---|---|---|---|---|
| 1816 | 3 | 475 | 1.6% | £31.2 | £573.9 |
| 1817 | 3 | 600 | 3.1 | 31.2 | 78.5 |
| 1818 | 3 | 600 | 3.1 | 31.2 | 592.6 |
| 1819 | 7 | 765 | 3.9 | 76.6 | 238.0 |
| 1820 | 6 | 655 | 3.2 | 40.1 | 220.2 |
| 1821 | 7 | 900 | 4.3 | 63.6 | 192.7 |
| 1822 | 9 | 975 | 4.9 | 84.8 | 172.8 |
| 1823 | 9 | 916 | 4.1 | 63.0 | 138.2 |
| 1824 | 9 | 1,366 | 5.3 | 107.6 | 154.2 |
| 1825 | 9 | 1,062 | 4.0 | 68.8 | 123.4 |
| 1826 | 8 | 940 | 3.4 | 63.7 | 129.4 |
| 1827 | 10 | 1,330 | 4.8 | 94.2 | 176.7 |
| 1828 | 8 | 955 | 3.6 | 67.4 | 136.1 |
| 1829 | 8 | 1,142 | 4.2 | 89.3 | 174.5 |
| 1830 | 9 | 1,279 | 4.9 | 112.3 | 229.8 |
| 1831 | 7 | 840 | 3.4 | 53.9 | 113.4 |
| 1832 | 9 | 929 | 4.0 | 81.8 | 135.6 |
| 1833 | 10 | 1,013 | 4.3 | 94.2 | 149.5 |
| 1834 | 13 | 1,098 | 4.6 | 83.2 | 141.6 |
| 1835 | 12 | 710 | 3.2 | 42.4 | 127.7 |
| 1836 | 15 | 1,170 | 4.6 | 101.2 | 170.8 |
| 1837 | 17 | 1,159 | 4.4 | 69.2 | 148.3 |
| 1838 | 17 | 1,536 | 5.7 | 95.3 | 150.5 |
| 1839 | 19 | 1,384 | 4.8 | 75.4 | 150.0 |
| 1840 | 13 | 964 | 3.0 | 62.2 | 125.0 |
| 1841 | 18 | 1,618 | 4.6 | 82.3 | 177.2 |
| 1842 | 15 | 1,476 | 4.1 | 92.5 | 159.8 |
| 1843 | 12 | 1,125[b] | 3.3 | 110.7 | 233.7 |
| 1844 | 21 | 3,254 | 9.8 | 268.2 | 373.0 |
| 1845 | 36[c] | 4,445 | 13.1 | 373.0 | 490.5 |
| 1846 | 33 | 4,004 | 10.9 | 332.0 | 417.6 |
| 1847 | 36 | 4,024 | 10.3 | 312.4 | 421.0 |
| 1848 | 32 | 3,384 | 8.7 | 338.1 | 493.3 |
| 1849 | 31 | 3,101 | 9.4 | 362.4 | 505.9 |
| 1850 | 29 | 2,977 | 9.5 | 341.0 | 530.1 |
| 1851 | 31 | 3,444 | 10.4 | 360.5 | 439.6 |
| 1852 | 28 | 2,914 | 8.8 | 315.0 | 383.6 |
| 1853 | 20[d] | 1,652 | 5.0 | 188.9 | 228.5 |
| 1854 | 16[c] | 1,323 | 3.5 | 135.4 | 165.5 |
| 1855 | 16[c] | 1,443 | 2.8 | 133.6 | 162.8 |
| 1856 | 16[c] | 1,629 | 2.6 | 156.7 | 184.8 |
| 1857 | 20[c] | 1,899 | 4.6 | 181.4 | 255.6 |
| 1858 | 25 | 2,438 | 5.5 | 260.5 | 344.8 |
| 1859 | 19 | 2,399 | 5.3 | 187.6 | 251.9 |

| | (1)<br>Ships<br>Assigned to<br>West Africa | (2)<br>Manpower<br>of West<br>African<br>Ships | (3)<br>Percent of Total<br>Naval<br>Manpower<br>Assigned to<br>West Africa | (4)<br>Cost of West<br>African<br>Force[a] | (5)<br>Total Direct<br>Costs of<br>Suppression[a] |
|---|---|---|---|---|---|
| 1860 | 20 | 2,141 | 3.3 | 179.0 | 234.3 |
| 1861 | 18 | 1,938 | 2.9 | 167.9 | 233.2 |
| 1862 | 21 | 2,346 | 4.1 | 187.9 | 258.5 |
| 1863 | 22 | 1,875 | 3.9 | 195.1 | 225.7 |
| 1864 | 20 | 1,635 | 3.2 | 180.5 | 214.5 |
| 1865 | 22 | 2,316 | 4.9 | 202.0 | 230.5 |
| **Total: 1816–65** | | | | | 12,395.3 |

*Notes:*
[a] In thousands of constant pounds sterling (1821−25 = 100).
[b] Mean crew 1841–42 × 12.
[c] Ships deployed on July 1 with one third added for ships in transit.
[d] For the year July 1852 to July 1853.

*Sources:*
Columns (1) and (2): PP, 1830 (57), 21:94–95; 1842 (561), 44:2–4; 1852–53 (920), 39:216–22; 1857–58 (454), 61:2; 1867–68, 44:637–40; (158), 64:2–7.
Column (3): Ratio of column (2) to total complement of ships deployed on all stations. For the latter, see PP, 1860 (168), 42:548–49, 552–57; 1867–68 (167), 45:637–40.
Column (5): The sum of the cost of the African squadron, treaty payments, bounties on slaves and tonnages of slave ships paid to captors, mixed commission courts (inc. pensions), the parliamentary grant for liberated Africans and compensation payments for wrongful arrests are all converted here to constant pounds sterling with the Rostow, Gayer, and Schwarz, and the Rousseaux price indexes (B. R. Mitchell and Phyllis Deane, *Abstract of British Historical Statistics* [Cambridge, 1962], pp. 471–73). See PP, 1842 (426), 44; (561), 44; 1843 (363), 63; 1845 (73), 49; (471) 49; 1847 (653), 67; 1847–48, 23: pt. 3, app. 1, 10–11; 1852–53 (920), 39: 215–22; 1854 (401), 42; 1861 (250), 64; 1865 (412), 5:467; 1867 (374), 73; 1867–68 (158), 64.
Pensions for mixed court personnel have been set at £4,000 per annum for 1836–65.
Tonnage bounties for 1848–54 are estimated from the tonnage of ships captured without slaves and the tonnage bounty of £4 per ton.
The Parliamentary grant for liberated Africans is set at £15,000 on the basis of information in Christopher Fyfe, *A History of Sierra Leone*, (London, 1962), pp. 110, 141, 165–66; J. J. Crooks, *A History of the Colony of Sierra Leone* (London, 1903), pp. 107–8; and PP, 1830 (661), 10:120–21, 135–36. This would have been reduced during the 1840s, at least for Sierra Leone, but landings elsewhere, notably St. Helena, continued until the 1860s and the total grant for all liberated African centers would not have declined much until the very last years of the traffic.

taken as the proportion of the total naval budget absorbed by the West African cruisers. An alternative series, not shown here, might be defined as the product of column (3) and the total naval estimates for each year. This yields figures double those in column (4) that, in effect, include only operating costs plus depreciation.[52] Column (5) of table 2 provides the sum of all payments, as far as can be determined, made by the British government for the purposes of suppressing the slave trade. It includes treaty payments, the costs of the mixed commissions, the liberated African departments, bounties on slaves and ships, compensation for wrongful arrests and, of course, the cost of the navy from column (4).

Table 2 suggests, as might be expected, that the antislave-trade commitment usually absorbed a small proportion of British naval strength and was sensitive, first, to competing demands on naval resources and, second, to the possibilities of success as determined by the treaties and legislation under which the navy operated. Immediately after 1815 when the British had lost the wartime right to search vessels and before the 1817 conventions with Spain and Portugal came into effect, the West African squadron was close to the size necessary to protect British trade, and no more. It was doubled in the year the courts of mixed commission were opened and increased a further 50 percent with the formal abolition of the Cuban trade. Thereafter it changed little until the Anglo-French conventions of 1831 and 1833 and the concomitant formal abolition of the Brazilian trade. These measures effectively opened up the traffic south of the equator to British interference. Further reinforcements coincided with the equipment treaty signed with Spain that went into effect in 1836, the 1839 Palmerston Act and the Anglo-French convention of 1845. The ending of the Brazilian traffic in 1851 saw a diminution of the squadron's strength. But the major weakening of the force occurred in response to armed conflict elsewhere. The sharp drop in 1840 occurred at the time the first naval expedition in the Opium War was being assembled as well as the period of strained relations with France. The Crimean War is also clearly apparent in columns (1) and (2) of table 2 for the years 1854 to 1856. At the peak of the British antislave-trade effort, in the mid-1840s, about 15 percent of British warships in commission and nearly 10 percent of total naval manpower were assigned to the task of interrupting the flow of coerced labor to the Americas.

The British had the biggest but not the only African squadron. Before drawing further conclusions from table 2, some assessment of the non-British effort is necessary to complete the picture of naval suppression. As we have already seen, other African squadrons generally could not interfere with vessels flying flags different from their own except, of course, pirates. For this reason they tended to be small and to patrol only intermittently. The second largest squadron on the coast was that of the French. Prior to 1842 it ranged in size from two to six ships after which the number of cruisers was increased to fourteen, but in response to British interference with French merchant ships rather than antislave-trade duties. It was doubled to twenty-eight as a consequence of the Anglo-French convention of 1845 and at this point was absorbing one fifth of French naval resources. As the powerlessness of the French squadron against non-French vessels became quickly apparent, the force was reduced to its pre-1842 levels by the 1850s. Measured in terms of slave-ship captures as opposed to maintenance of a strong French presence in the face of the ubiquitous British, the squadron was chiefly effective in the years 1825 to 1831. By the end of this period, there were very few French slaving expeditions attempted and very little for the French fleet to do.

U.S. warships learned a similar lesson in the early 1820s (after the 1819 Slave Trade Act was passed) when five of them visited West Africa at different times in a two-year period and captured at least eleven slavers. Unfortunately one was Spanish and the others were French, and the latter were restored with damages.[53] Thereafter only an occasional cruiser was sent to the coast until the Webster-Ashburton Treaty of 1842, though the commander of one of these cruisers did initiate a useful joint cruising arrangement with the British commodore, which was subsequently repudiated by the U.S. government. From 1843 to 1861 more regular cruises were undertaken with the size of the squadron varying from three to eight ships. As the location of the main base was quite far away in the Cape Verde Islands until 1859, often many months and even years would go by without any U.S. presence off the major points of embarkation.[54] Moreover, the cruisers were often too big for the task and therefore easily spotted by illicit traders. In addition, like the French cruisers, they had no authority over vessels without a discernible country of registration. Even with ships that were clearly American, however, the uncertainty of the law was such that most ships taken by the squadron without slaves on board were released by the U.S. courts.[55]

The Portuguese African squadron participated in suppression only in the 1840s. In 1845 it comprised 9 ships, 84 guns and 750 men; over two thirds of the squadron was stationed at Luanda and Benguela.[56] Although not all of the ships were seaworthy, they had the enormous advantage of territorial rights over the Angolan and Mozambique coasts and could thus interfere with ships of all nations within three miles of shore. Indeed the British Foreign Office in the prepartition era was prepared to countenance an expansion of Portuguese territorial claims to expedite suppression. Between 1844 and 1847 a formal agreement existed between the governor general of Angola and the British commodore by which the Angolan coast was assigned to Portuguese patrols to free British cruisers for other regions.[57] The effectiveness of the Portuguese squadron was severely hampered by a diminishing colonial tax base, however. In Angola, slave trading was the major economic activity. As the warships were financed out of customs revenues, the more captures they made, the less stores they received and the larger were arrears of backpay.[58] In addition, there was a suggestion that the cruisers were used selectively, depending on which of the two major Luanda slave-trading groups had the ear of the governor. The goal was thus not to suppress the slave trade, but to eliminate the competition. In any event complaints by the Brazilian government of attacks on its shipping resulted in less rigorous Portuguese enforcement in 1848. The British commodore thereupon assumed full control of the coast once more. British cruisers, nevertheless, respected Portuguese sovereignty and where they discovered shore-based slaving establishments, they called on Portuguese forces to carry out the destruction or, as in southeast Africa, acted themselves, but only with prior and formal Portuguese approval.

The other naval forces were of little significance. Neither Spain nor Brazil had any presence off Africa. In the Americas (except briefly in 1857) Spanish warships became a threat only in 1865.[60] In Brazil cruisers made occasional captures in the two decades after formal abolition, particularly in 1834–35. Most of the sixty-seven ships in the Brazilian navy of the mid-1840s were very small and all were kept busy in maintaining the authority of the central government both within and without the borders of the empire, notably on the Río de la Plata. The British Navy never relied on the cooperation of the force until the 1850s—after the traffic ended.[61] There were no other naval forces involved in significant antislave-trade activities.

The direct costs of suppression were even more unevenly distributed than the naval forces. The French and U.S. navies had bounty systems based on the British model and ten countries had the right to maintain commissioners at the various mixed courts. Nevertheless, over 90 percent of the total direct costs of suppression were borne by the British. As the latter had more treaty powers than any other nation, they naturally captured more slaves, paid more bounties and had to arrange for the settlement of more newly liberated Africans. Unlike their treaty partners, the British also ensured that almost all the offices to which they were entitled were kept filled; at high-mortality locations such as Sierra Leone and Luanda this involved large salaries.[62] However, the major item, next to the cost of the naval squadron, was treaty payments made, in part, for wrongful arrests and, in part, as inducement to other countries to give up the slave trade. Between 1815 and 1823 these averaged £181,000 per annum and greatly exceeded the cost of the naval force. Despite the growing reluctance of foreign governments to push for full compensation where the victim of the wrongful arrest was clearly an illicit slave trader, these payments continued into the 1850s.

Column (4) of table 2 attempts to account for all naval, diplomatic and legal costs discussed earlier. It is, nevertheless, subject to downward bias, first, because some payments are missing and, second, because the naval costs are at most half what they should be. The indirect costs of suppression such as the higher costs of plantation produce are taken up elsewhere.[63] It might also be noted that the British government received no direct revenue from the hundreds of captured ships. Even before the breaking-up clauses were added to the international agreements under which captured ships were destroyed, proceeds from auctions of condemned property were always split between the two parties to the agreement, and the British share was handed over to the captors.[64] For half a century suppression cost the British taxpayer a minimum of £250,000 a year in terms of 1821–25 prices. How significant was this amount? The total annual naval estimates in peacetime rose from £4.8 million in 1818 to £9.8 million in 1858 (again in constant pounds), so that suppression cost the equivalent of from 2 to 6 percent of the naval budget.[65] These ratios would rise by about two thirds if we included the fully allocated cost of the African squadron and by even more if we could discover all the compensation awards against the squadron. As defined here, however, suppression costs amounted to the equivalent of just under one twentieth of 1 percent of the National Product in 1841, the midyear of the 1816–65 period.[66]

A clearer perspective of these costs may be obtained by comparing them with the direct benefits that the slave trade brought to Britain in the half-century before abolition when the traffic was at its peak. In the forty-seven years from 1761 to 1807, just under a million tons of British shipping carried slaves to Africa. Roger Anstey's work on the eighteenth-century trade has suggested an outset cost figure per ton that has yet to be questioned by participants in the debate on the profitability of the slave trade.[67] This outset cost figure and the tonnage data provide us with a rough estimate of the capital committed to the British slave trade. Returns on this capital invested in the business of slave trading is a more controversial topic. Joseph Inikori, who probably knows the documentary evidence of British slave trading as well as any historian, has suggested that the less than 10 percent annual return calculated by Anstey and Richardson is too low. Inikori's own sample of twenty-four voyages returned 26.7 percent. It is improbable that this latter rate would hold for the legal trade as a whole over a long period of time, and indeed Inikori himself suggested that only a few large firms, accounting for less than half the voyages dispatched, could have achieved this or higher rates of return.[68] Nevertheless, if we accept Inikori's figure as the upper limit on what returns might have attained in the 1761–1807 period and assume, too, that his is an annual profit rate, we can derive a total profit accruing to British investors in the slave trade of £13.8 million in terms of 1821–25 prices.[69]

Table 2, on the other hand, suggests that a lower-bound estimate of the direct costs of suppression in a similar period after 1815 is £11.7 million. It would thus appear that in absolute terms the British spent almost as much attempting to suppress the trade in the forty-seven years, 1816–62, as they received in profits over the same length of time leading up to 1807. And by any more reasonable assessment of profits and direct costs, the nineteenth-century costs of suppression were certainly bigger than the eighteenth-century benefits. Of course, in relative terms a different picture emerges in that £13.7 million constituted a minute but still much larger part of British National Income in the 1761–1807 period than did £11.7 million of its mid–nineteenth-century counterpart. Nevertheless, it is worth noting that between 1816 and 1821, when the British were absorbing the start-up costs of the antislave-trade system in the form of treaty payments, the cost of suppression did not constitute that much smaller a share of National Income than did British slaving profits between, say, 1796 and 1801. The two may, in fact, have been roughly the same if we allow for the bias in the calculation of these ratios.[70]

We can now turn to an evaluation of what the system of suppression achieved in terms of captures. Between 1808 and 1867 about 7,750 transatlantic slave ships were sent to the coast of Africa. The international effort against the slave trade resulted in 1,635 ships being condemned or treated in such a way by authorities as to incur loss to their owners. Of these, 823 were condemned and in the vast majority of cases destroyed by the British Vice Admiralty courts under the 1839 and 1845 acts. A further 572 ships were condemned or divested of their slave cargoes by the courts of mixed commission, mainly between 1819 and 1845. In the French courts Serge Daget has found evidence of sixty-five condemnations. There were, in addition fifty-eight detentions by U.S. authorities, thirty-five by the Portuguese, twenty-eight by the Spanish and twenty-six by the Brazilians. In addition, the British took to foreign courts 6 vessels that were not restored with full compensation, and they drove on shore or detained 22 vessels for which no court proceedings can be found. All these have been included in the 1,635 figure. On the other hand, the 50 ships proceeded against in French courts for infractions of slave-trade laws and for which no court decisions have survived have not been included. There were also 114 ships prosecuted in various courts that were subsequently restored to their owners, and neither have these been included in the 1,635 ships.[71] Although less than 1 percent of these ships sailed from or through British territorial waters and almost none were British, over 85 percent of them were detained on British orders. No other statistic can illustrate so clearly the relative fervency of the British as well, perhaps, as their disregard of international law on this issue. Almost half of all slave ships detained in the nineteenth century were adjudicated in British Vice Admiralty courts, and most of these were taken under the authority of the Palmerston and Aberdeen acts, which had no precedent in international relations.

Table 3 shows the distribution of most of these captures by region of embarkation and disembarkation. Table 4 shows the breakdown of these captures over time. The figure for recaptive Africans in these tables is less complete than that for ships because twenty-six full slavers disembarked unknown numbers of slaves.[72] Allowance for these suggests that just over 160,000 Africans were freed from the holds of transatlantic slave ships in the nineteenth century. As these slaves were distributed over only 602 of the 1,635 ships detained between 1808 and 1867, it is clear that the majority of slave ships were captured either before taking slaves on board or immediately after disembarking them.

**Table 3.** Transatlantic Slave Ships Detained and Slaves Disembarked ('000) as a Result of Suppressive Measures, 1811–67

| Country or Region of Embarkation | Country or Region of Debarkation | | | | | | | |
|---|---|---|---|---|---|---|---|---|
| | Cuba | French Americas | Brazil North | Bahia | Brazil South | Other | Not Known | Total |
| Upper Guinea | 115 | 6 | 3 | 2 | 8 | 6 | 31 | **171** |
| | 9.1 | 0.6 | 0.4 | 0.0 | 0.7 | 0.7 | 0.8 | **12.3** |
| Windward Coast | 24 | 1 | 0 | 1 | 3 | 2 | 8 | **39** |
| | 1.7 | 0.1 | 0.0 | 0.1 | 0.0 | 0.0 | 0.2 | **2.0** |
| Bight of Benin | 90 | 0 | 6 | 169 | 20 | 1 | 43 | **329** |
| | 17.2 | 0.0 | 0.4 | 17.2 | 4.1 | 0.2 | 4.0 | **43.2** |
| Bight of Biafra | 134 | 6 | 8 | 13 | 18 | 7 | 11 | **197** |
| | 24.8 | 0.8 | 0.5 | 1.9 | 2.8 | 1.0 | 0.6 | **32.4** |
| Congo North | 151 | 0 | 3 | 4 | 78 | 3 | 50 | **289** |
| | 17.1 | 0.0 | 0.1 | 0.1 | 5.5 | 1.1 | 0.9 | **24.8** |
| Angola | 22 | 0 | 14 | 12 | 156 | 2 | 76 | **282** |
| | 2.2 | 0.0 | 1.7 | 1.4 | 12.9 | 0.0 | 4.2 | **22.4** |
| Southeast Africa | 12 | 0 | 2 | 1 | 35 | 0 | 24 | **74** |
| | 0.7 | 0.0 | 0.4 | 0.1 | 2.9 | 0.0 | 1.0 | **5.2** |
| Not Known | 45 | 2 | 2 | 17 | 55 | 0 | 86 | **207** |
| | 2.9 | 0.3 | 0.0 | 0.3 | 1.4 | 0.0 | 5.4 | **10.3** |
| | 593 | 15 | 38 | 219 | 373 | 21 | 329 | **1,588** |
| **Total** | **75.9** | **1.7** | **3.6** | **21.0** | **30.3** | **3.1** | **17.0** | **152.6** |

*Notes:* The first row in each region of embarkation is the number of ships detained. The second row is the number of slaves disembarked (in thousands). Row and column totals may not add up because of rounding. These data exclude slaves taken from shore barracoons after naval raids and exclude also ships and slaves traded to offshore islands such as São Tomé and Reunion.

*Source:* Slave-ship data set.

**Table 4.** Five-year Totals of Ships Detained and Slaves Disembarked After Capture in the Transatlantic Slave Trade, 1811–67

|  | Ships with Slaves | Ships Without Slaves | Slaves ('000) |
|---|---|---|---|
| 1808–15 | 80 | 44 | 8.3 |
| 1816–20 | 36 | 16 | 4.5 |
| 1821–25 | 45 | 15 | 8.4 |
| 1826–30 | 84 | 40 | 18.4 |
| 1831–35 | 68 | 6 | 19.7 |
| 1836–40 | 95 | 158 | 27.9 |
| 1841–45 | 47 | 222 | 16.1 |
| 1846–50 | 68 | 329 | 24.7 |
| 1851–55 | 8 | 32 | 2.6 |
| 1856–60 | 28 | 95 | 13.3 |
| 1861–67 | 17 | 55 | 8.7 |
| **1808–67** | **576** | **1012** | **152.6** |

*Source:* Slave-ship data set.

Enforcement agencies thus intercepted 1 in 5 ships involved in the traffic but only 1 in 16 of the slaves embarked. A comparison of the distribution of captures with the tables of slave imports and exports in appendix A suggests that ships and slaves from embarkation regions north of the equator are overrepresented. Such regions accounted for over one-half the ships and two-thirds the slaves captured, but only 38 percent of all slaves exported. Among receiving zones Cuba is similarly overrepresented, but not to the same degree. Of course, the trade to Cuba lasted longer than the others, but tables 3 and 4 reflect the treaty limitations and the deployment of British cruisers. Before 1831 the Brazilian traffic south of the equator was legal and between 1831 and 1839 the Royal Navy's coverage of west-central and southeast Africa and southern Brazil was only one fifth of the more northerly branches of the traffic. Only in the last quarter of the century was naval suppression applied evenly throughout the trading zones. Moreover, given the relatively early demise of the traffic in the Bight of Biafra and Upper Guinea, only one embarkation region, the Bight of Benin, and one receiving zone, Cuba, were subject to continuous British interference throughout this period.

These considerations must influence any assessment of the impact of suppression based on ratios of captures to total numbers of ships and slaves involved in the traffic. The crude 1:5 and 1:16 ratios already calculated for ships and slaves, respectively, need refining to reflect the politically determined geography of suppression as well as the fact that many captured ships were empty not only of slaves but also of trading cargoes.[73] In these cases losses to the investors resulting from capture would be far less than the full cost of the venture. Figure 4 shows the annual ratios of captured ships to total number of ventures launched for the three major branches of the nineteenth-century slave trade.[74] It also shows an estimated annual loss ratio for the same regions and years. The losses series is an attempt to cope with the empty ship problem.

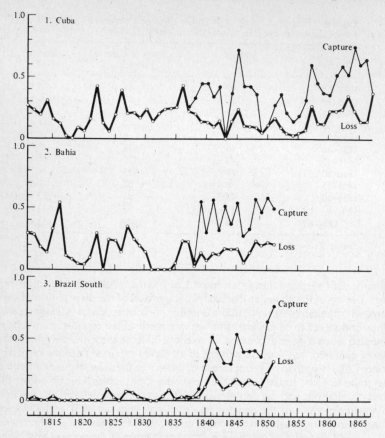

**Figure 4.** Capture and loss ratios in the transatlantic slave trade.

Any ship captured with either slaves who were subsequently liberated or with a full trading cargo would represent a total loss to the investor or to the insurers.[75] If the ship were empty of slaves or cargo, the loss would be a small fraction of the capital invested—perhaps 20 percent if the capture occurred off Africa where inventory costs for the slaves left behind would be significant; 10 percent or less if the ship disembarked slaves in the Americas prior to capture. Over 85 percent of all captured ships were detained off Africa. Moreover, over 95 percent of the empty ships taken were detained in the Cuban traffic after the 1835 equipment treaty went into effect and in the Brazilian trade after the passage of Palmerston's Act. Before these provisions went into force, almost all detained ships had slaves on board or in a few cases trading cargoes. After they went into force, slave traders began to send trading cargoes to the coast in a separate ship—safe from British interference—so that detained ships rarely had on board either slaves or trading cargoes. The loss ratio is thus a weighted capture ratio, with the captures adjusted according to whether or not the ship was taken empty.[76] The annual sum of these weighted captures is then expressed as a ratio of all ventures launched for each year, from 1811 to 1867. Although the loss ratio might be questioned, it is, nevertheless, a better guide than the capture ratio to the impact of suppression on the individuals responsible for slave-trading voyages.

Figure 4 indicates clearly the treaty and legislative pattern just described. Capture ratios in excess of 20 percent occurred throughout the period in the Cuban and Bahian traffic, but appear in the Brazil South trade only after 1839. The Anglo-Spanish equipment treaty of 1835 and the illegal British initiatives against the Bahian traffic of 1811–12 and 1815–16 as well as all the Brazilian traffic in 1850 and 1851 are also reflected in the capture series. In several of the years of greatest pressure, over half the ships sent to the African coast were captured. Yet a close study of the loss ratio series points at a less dramatic impact and hints at the ultimate ineffectiveness of a navy lacking full sovereign powers over the slave traders. For the Cuban trade the loss ratio exceeded 25 percent in only seven of the fifty-seven years surveyed; for the Bahia and Brazil South trades the equivalent figure is even smaller. Moreover, in all cases higher loss figures were temporary, ratios of 20 percent or less quickly reestablishing themselves within a year or two of these higher rates appearing. This pattern suggests that an interactive relationship existed between the British Foreign Office and Navy, on the one hand, and the slave traders, on the other. Each new ploy by the former, which was not struck down by the British courts or law officers, had a temporary effect that elicited a quick adjustment in tactics on the part of the latter. Costs, of course, were increased, but given the demand for slaves in the Americas, the traffic itself continued and likely would have continued indefinitely in the absence of the cooperation of political authorities in the exporting and importing regions. Even at the close of the traffic, loss ratios, as opposed to capture ratios, do not seem high. The significance of this is explored later as is the slave-trader's response to suppression initiatives. But the major point to be noted here is that the hundreds of ships and thousands of slaves captured are not indicative of effective action against the trade.

We can now summarize the effect of the complex of legislation and treaties and the resources that the British at least put behind them. Interdictions of the slave trade were chiefly effective when a government passed and rigorously enforced legislation on their own nationals. In the sense that no further slave trading occurred on their territory and few of their nationals were directly involved in the business anywhere, the American, Brazilian, British, French and Spanish governments all eradicated the trade within a few years of their decision to take firm action. International treaties were neither a guarantee of nor a substitute for this decision. The massive British commitment was thus chiefly effective against British subjects, but even here success did not extend to the exclusion of British capital from the slave traffic. Against the slave trade of other nations, even after doing violence to international law, the British could expect to detain at best one out of perhaps every three ships sent to Africa. In terms of capital invested, they could induce a loss of only one venture in five in any long-run period.

# 7

# The Ambivalence of Suppression

The campaign against the slave trade was fought on two not always compatible levels. There was the physical or naval confrontation (discussed in chapter 6), and, more important, there was the ideological struggle. As we have seen, domestic, social and economic developments led the British to a new worldview. Integral parts of this were attitudes to work, freedom and the rule of law, which the British expected societies in Africa and the plantation Americas to adopt. Many of these societies proved reluctant or unable to behave as the British wished them to. At the same time, closer to home, British law appeared unable to sever ties between the United Kingdom's economy and the slave trade. These situations threw up two related and fundamental questions for abolitionists. The first was whether to use extralegal means where legal means had failed; the second was how to impose British conceptions of freedom on others. In many situations the abolitionists could be successful only if they contemplated force or clandestine operations. There was a very real dilemma in using illiberal means to achieve liberal ends. As dramatist Robert Bolt has written, when all laws are cut down in pursuit of evil, where does one hide from evil. The strength of the point is not diminished if the pursuit occurs in another country or on the high seas.[1]

In the international context there was the related and larger issue of whether one society could force freedom on another. Freedom of choice cannot logically coexist with expectations that a specific type of behavior will subsequently manifest itself. It is, however, a characteristic of Western thought since Locke that liberty, however qualified, has been linked with a definite and essentially benevolent view of human nature. The willingness to work beyond the point of satisfaction of immediate wants and a respect for property rights were considered vital preconditions of freedom. But the British experience of wage labor in the course of the eighteenth century meant that freedom, wage labor and the desire to substitute goods for leisure, which perhaps is the essential meaning of the term *modernization,* were regarded as mutually reinforcing. In the early nineteenth century the British faced the question of how to extend these concepts to the rest of the world; in addition, there was the issue in land-abundant regions that although modernization might imply freedom, did freedom if granted first, induce modernization. As we have seen in chapter 2, the recipients of freedom did not always behave in the way the donors expected.

British abolitionists experienced some difficulty in staying within the ideological boundaries of antislavery and that route to the modern Western economy that has been termed *possessive individualism.* There were always elements of the movement both within and without the government that operated at and sometimes beyond the limits prescribed by both law and the conventions that ensured freedom or, at the very least, civil liberties. Such elements were involved in supplementing the regular channels of law enforcement, gaining access to and using the official sources of information normally barred to the private citizen, bribery, spying, breaking international law and even sponsoring activities that could only undermine the social structure of foreign slave societies. Not only were such activities probably inevitable, given the nature of the conflict between "progressive" and "backward" societies, but they provide an interesting window onto the links between antislavery thought and laissez-faire ideology.

For the abolitionists who dominated the early phases of the movement, the Evangelicals and the Quakers, the difference between the position of the most downtrodden Englishman and the best-treated slave was enormous. Actions that might impinge slightly on the liberties of the former were of trivial significance compared to the status of the latter. Moreover, the Evangelical preoccupation with liberty—defined as freedom from sin[2]—was likely to mean a less than fastidious concern with a more secular perception of the concept. Thus on the domestic front, William Wilberforce gave general support to the younger William Pitt's suppression of political dissent and, with other Evangelicals, he formed the Proclamation Society about the time that the campaign to abolish the slave trade got underway. Its function and that of its better known and more broadly based successor, the Society for the Suppression of Vice, was to prosecute licentious, blasphemous and seditious behavior. In the process, its critics argued, it endangered the liberty of the press and usurped the functions of the state prosecutors.[3] The Evangelical adaptation of the eighteenth-century ethic of benevolence ensured that such activities were carried on at the same time as efforts to relieve misery. Domestically this meant a general sympathy for the Speenhamland poor relief system and a host of legislative reforms. But on all these issues Evangelical initiatives depended heavily for success on the support of non-Evangelicals. If the law courts, especially juries, and the legal and ecclesiastical establishment were not supportive, such initiatives would likely fail.

On the slave trade issue, particularly after 1807, the abolitionists faced no opposition. Within Britain at least they had fewer scruples and their actions were subject to no checks or controls. Moreover, as C. Duncan Rice has pointed out, evangelicalism could lead to an intensity of feeling on issues that might lead to the inhumane, at least in attitudes toward those responsible for the slave trade. Zachary Macaulay wanted the French government to flog those of its citizens who ignored French restrictions on the traffic in the 1820s.[4] Benevolent intentions, passionate commitment, a less than rigorous observation of the legal niceties and recalcitrant foreigners produced consequences disastrous alike for the internal consistency as well as the cause of the abolitionist.

For most of the twelve years between the passage of the Abolition Act and the creation of a special slave-trade department within the Foreign Office, the British government had no special structure for handling the issue of the slave traffic. The latter, however, was quite unlike any other diplomatic issue. Although the British saw abolition as in the national and indeed international interest, it was not a matter of national survival and honor, nor was it even likely to result in any short-run gain for the country. The ultimate goal was not the winning of territory or trade concessions, but rather the imposition of a conception of freedom, specifically a system of labor that had proved highly successful in England and that, it was believed, would prove even more so if the rest of the world could be persuaded to follow suit.[5] The traditional methods of negotiation backed by force were necessary, but by themselves they might be counterproductive. To bring about the modern goal of making other parts of the world ideologically compatible with the dominant culture—and the antislavery campaign might be viewed as an early example of this—required constant persuasion and a constant demonstration of the benefits of an alternative system. In the end, however, it also required both some force and subversive activity, which quite contradicted as well as risked undermining the original goals. Basic to all initiatives was an information network that could keep up the pressure and transmit evidence of change. In Palmerston's hands this is what the slave-trade department became, but in the early days before 1815 there were no precedents for such activity. Embroiled in what turned out to be a traditional war and failing (as many did) to comprehend the novelty of the task, the government turned to the abolitionists—or rather defaulted in favor of them.

By 1807 the abolitionists, in particular, James Stephen, the elder, had already had considerable influence over British policy toward the slave trade and the newly conquered Caribbean possessions.[6] That year saw not only the abolition of the British traffic but the inception of the orders in council that authorized British seizures of neutral shipping trading with enemy colonies. Stephen was as responsible for this policy as any individual in England and saw it literally as a god-given opportunity for the British to shut down the slave trade to the Americas. Ironically, in the light of future international incidents, he told Prime Minister Spencer Perceval that this could be achieved "without violating [even] one of those sacred principles which ought to govern the conduct of nations."[7] The fact that Portugal and Spain were or quickly became British allies and that their shipping therefore was not subject to British interference made such expectations hopelessly optimistic. Of greater long-term significance in the ideological struggle was the formation of the African Institution, also in 1807.

Ostensibly the African Institution was the abolitionists' attempt to foster the commercial and educational development of Africa and to act as watchdog over the suppression of the slave trade, but from an early date, it became almost a de facto slave-trade department of the Foreign Office. "I have no doubt," wrote its secretary, Zachary Macaulay, just after it was formed, " that the government will be disposed to adopt almost any plan which we may propose to them with respect to Africa, provided we will but save them the trouble of thinking."[8] There was little hyperbole in this. Macaulay and James Stephen, the elder, wrote many memoranda of advice before the Privy Council approved the administrative foundation of the British antislave-trade effort in March 1808. As a result, a vice admiralty court was established at Sierra Leone, bounties on captured slaves and their disposal were provided for, directions were sent to the Admiralty and overseas customs officers were required to watch the slave trade and enforce the new legislation.[9] Orders that the Admiralty sent to Captain Parker of the *Derwent* were apparently taken from a letter Macaulay sent to the Admiralty in May 1808.[10] The secretary of state, Castlereagh, routinely passed on dispatches from Sierra Leone to William Wilberforce and Henry Thornton and took their advice on issues to do with the new colony. In return the group sent much information to the Admiralty about slave ships, suspected and actual, most of which was dutifully passed along to the naval commanders at sea.[11] Offices in Sierra Leone were filled with the nominees of the group.[12] Customs officers searched numerous ships in response to intelligence supplied by Thomas Clarkson, Zachary Macaulay and others; if these officers refused to act, then the group appealed to higher authorities, even to Prime Minister Spencer Perceval. They could also get access to the records of the Custom House, which were normally highly confidential.[13] On the slave trade and Sierra Leone there was no obvious dividing line between government officers and the Clapham Sect.

The abolitionists organized a number of committees and individual correspondents to collect and check information on the illicit traffic. In the summer of 1809, Clarkson made another of his many visits to Liverpool and set up a committee to report on infractions of the abolition laws in that port. William Roscoe, former mayor of the city and one of the few Liverpool merchants wholly free of connections with the slave trade in the preabolition days, became local organizer. Other committees followed in London and Bristol, though the latter must have had little to do. Finally information was culled from overseas. Macaulay received news from contacts throughout the Atlantic area, particularly Rio de Janeiro, the Canary Islands, and Sierra Leone, This served to provide a check on the suspicions of the committees in the English ports. Often the abolitionists knew the routes of slave ships for which they did not have enough evidence to detain in England and that also avoided capture at sea.[14] On the basis of this they attempted to initiate criminal prosecutions on both sides of the Atlantic when governments were reluctant to act.[15] Their activities not only predated those of the Foreign Office's Slave Trade Department, they were strikingly parallel to those of the Society for the Suppression of Vice. Yet the same blurring of lines between state and private action stirred up virtually no protest when the issue was the slave trade.

As we have seen earlier, such activities were not particularly successful. Although the volume of the traffic temporarily contracted, it remained at a high level and, what was worse, British ships, ports and merchants continued to occupy vital positions in the traffic. The abolitionists were quickly convinced that stronger initiatives were necessary and it was then that their actions, which had hitherto scarcely been of the type to strengthen civil liberties, became definitely illegal. After exploring some very ambitious alternative plans, the abolitionists settled for new legislation on the domestic front. For the Portuguese slave trade they relied on a clause in the Anglo-Portuguese treaty of 1810 that put geographic limits on Portuguese slaving. In the case of the Spanish traffic, the abolitionists simply assumed that is was in reality British. Each of these are considered in turn.[16]

As early as 1809 Clarkson and Macaulay had planned new legislation to cope with the British traffic. In late 1810 the content of a new bill was considered by the Liverpool and Bristol committees and by Wilberforce, Lord Holland and other African Institution members in London. Henry Brougham's act for rendering more effectual the 1807 act, passed in June 1811, was the outcome: British subjects who engaged in the slave trade were now liable to fourteen years transportation. Brilliant as Brougham was, his knowledge of the law was not all one would expect of a prospective lord chancellor. Perhaps if this had been a government measure subject to careful vetting by the law officers of the Crown, it would not have been based, in part, on a repealed statute. As passed, however, it was virtually inoperative in British possessions overseas until amending legislation was passed in 1819.[17] A more serious question, however, as we shall see, is how the abolitionists used the act while it was still believed to be sound.

The slave trade clause in the 1810 Anglo-Portuguese treaty was of similarly dubious value. Ever since 1806 the British government, prompted by the abolitionists, had attempted to ensure that at the very least the Portuguese would not fill the gaps left by British abolition of the slave traffic. The cession of Bissau and Cacheu, the major slave-trading ports north of Sierra Leone, was pursued from 1808, and the 1810 treaty contained a secret article ceding these territories on conditions that were never fulfilled. In 1809 an Order in Council was passed that provided for British right of search of Portuguese vessels in apparent contradiction of the 1654 Anglo-Portuguese treaty. The slave-trade clause in the 1810 treaty was simply a further increase in British pressure.[18] Yet the treaty itself reflected in full the ideological dilemma of early nineteenth-century British expansion. It effectively pulled Brazil into the world economy, in particular the British-centered part of it, by removing the restrictions that had kept Brazil a preserve of the Portuguese. At the same time the pressure against the slave trade threatened to undermine the basis of that Brazilian prosperity, which the commercial part of the treaty did much to encourage.[19] To the British, at least on one level, clauses providing for free trade and the limitation of the slave trade sat naturally together. Yet given land/labor ratios in the Americas and the lack of alternative sources of labor, there can be no doubt that abolition was not in the best economic interest of Brazil, Britain or Portugal.

It was perhaps the tension in British goals just as much as Portuguese reluctance to give up the traffic that explains the obscure wording of this clause restricting the traffic. Taken at face value, it restricted the Portuguese slave trade to Portuguese possessions, but it contained no commitment by the Portuguese government to pass domestic legislation and gave the British no right of access to Portuguese property or persons. In fact, it was not clear what if anything it did provide. The most eminent of all the British Admiralty judges wrote privately to the Admiralty, "It is quite impossible for me to furnish any explanations of the Portuguese treaty involved as it is by its own obscure and equivocal Phraseology, and by its application to the geography of a coast very superficially known here and to Portuguese claims of sovereignty, not at all understood."[20] Although the abolitionists were aware of the ambiguities in the clause and were very unhappy with the British negotiator, they were determined not only to use it but indeed viewed it as the beginning of the end of the foreign slave trade.[21]

For the trade conducted under the Spanish flag, the abolitionists had a simpler solution. Spain, unlike Portugal, had never been significantly involved in the African traffic. Imports into Cuba, the chief Spanish slave colony in the New World, were a few thousand a year in the immediate aftermath of British and American abolition, only one-tenth the level of the Portuguese traffic. The relatively small scale of the trade and the delicate internal Spanish political situation meant that the British government did not pursue Spain as hard as it might have done immediately after 1807. But a negotiated end to the Spanish slave trade seemed less urgent for another reason. The abolitionists were convinced, not without some justification, that there was no bona fide Spanish traffic. They were also convinced that the British Navy and courts could detain and condemn foreign slave ships if there was any evidence of British ownership or contact with a British port or merchant. On both issues they were wrong.[22]

In suppressing the slave trade, the British faced two problems that persisted through most of the century. First, individuals on foreign territory or the high seas were not subject to British laws: Foreign ships could not be interfered with in peacetime without the express permission of the foreign government. Second, even within British jurisdiction, participation in the slave trade or the intent to participate, had to be proved to the satisfaction of a court of law. The existence and independence of nation-states and the rule of law were elements even more fundamental to the system that Britain was attempting to spread to the rest of the world than was the abolition of slavery. Most early Victorian ideologues from Thomas Babington Macaulay to Thomas Carlyle believed that such phenomena separated the civilized from the barbarian peoples of the world.[23] The issue was what to do when civilized nations refused to behave as they should. As for the difficulties of proving intent on the part of the hundreds of British ships and merchants involved directly and indirectly in the trade, these were such as to make the law a dead letter. The *Commercio de Rio* was a fully equipped slave ship that lay in the port of London for several weeks in 1809 and was eventually seized not for slave-trade law infractions (the authorities felt the evidence of four hundred pairs of fetters on board was insufficient to prove intent), but for not having a license to export gunpowder. In fact, there was not a single instance of a ship arrested in a port in Britain and successfully prosecuted for contravening the slave trade laws.[24]

The trade unfortunately could be seriously damaged only if the law was ignored or at least stretched. Armed with the new felony statute and naval assistance, Governor Charles Maxwell and Chief Justice Robert Thorpe, the Sierra Leone agents of the Evangelicals, arrested several European slave factors in the vicinity of Sierra Leone. The problem was that not all those arrested were British and those that were had not been operating on British soil. Though an attempt was made to declare retroactively that the factors were subject to British law, in no real sense (as Thorpe himself later pointed out) were any of these slave traders within British jurisdiction or arrested with the permission of the African authorities. The sentences of transportation that the factors received would have been quashed by the higher courts even if the 1811 act had permitted the proper trial in Sierra Leone of those arrested.[25]

Similarly, the abolitionists led by Zachary Macaulay gave the slave-trade article of the 1810 treaty a meaning both broader and more precise than the Crown's legal advisers could later sustain. Although the British Navy until 1814 assumed the wartime right of a belligerent to board and search vessels of all neutral and hostile nations on the high seas, it could not detain and condemn ships of an ally without the sanction of that country. The *Fortune* and *Amedie* cases—both involving U.S. slavers taken by British cruisers off Africa—extended British prize law to neutral shipping involved in activities that had been declared contrary to the law of nations by the power to which the prize belonged. Slave ships of nations such as the United States, which had abolished the trade, were thus liable to condemnation in British prize courts.[26] Ever since the 1654 Anglo-Portuguese convention, however, Portugal had been treated as an ally, not as a neutral in time of war. The 1809 Order in Council changed this, without Portuguese consent needless to say, and the Admiralty then ordered the detention of Portuguese ships that were slave trading outside the regions specified in the treaty. The Admiralty also circulated a large body of law reports, legal opinions and even instructions among the officers of the African squadron—all prepared and printed at African Institution expense. The Admiralty, in fact, accepted the abolitionists' interpretation of the 1810 treaty as its own, including a very narrow definition of Portuguese territorial claims in Africa.[27]

As a consequence of this interpretation, the Royal Navy, captured and the Sierra Leone Vice Admiralty Court (staffed with Clapham Sect nominees) condemned at least twenty-four ships taken under the Portuguese flag between 1810 and 1812. Many of these were authentically Portuguese or Brazilian. Portuguese animosity aroused by these actions induced Castlereagh to warn off the navy from Portuguese ships, with the result that only four were captured in 1813 and two in 1814, and some of these were only nominally Portuguese.[28] The damage to the antislave-trade cause was already considerable, however. The Portuguese refused to consider further the cession of Bissau and Cacheu and the British had to agree to the payment of £300,000 compensation for wrongful arrest before Portugal would agree to a further treaty, a treaty involving separate and additional British financial commitments.[29]

Abolitionist influence, nevertheless, continued, as unfortunately did the disastrous consequences. In the 1815 Anglo-Portuguese treaty, the Portuguese undertook to confine their flag to the Brazilian slave trade and to give up all slave trading north of the equator. In return Britain forgave the balance of a £600,000 wartime loan made to the Portuguese, of which about three quarters remained outstanding. The right of search was scarcely mentioned. British rights had lapsed with hostilities and, because of the 1654 treaty, had perhaps never existed as far as Portuguese shipping was concerned. The only reference to the issue was in a clause acknowledging that the Cromwellian exemption from search in time of war was at an end. On the basis of this new treaty, the British government renewed its instructions to the squadron to capture Portuguese slave ships, this time anywhere north of the equator.[30] Abolitionist influence in this decision may be surmised, but it is less easy to document than in the orders issued after the 1810 treaty. But the parallel action taken by the Sierra Leone governor was more clearly abolitionist inspired. In January 1816 Governor MacCarthy commissioned a colonial schooner to sail against the slave trade. During the following twenty months, British cruisers took a further thirty-four ships under the Portuguese flag, almost all of them entitled to that flag. Acting not under the 1815 treaty, but under an extraordinary clause in the 1811 felony act, the colonial vessels, *Prince Regent* and *Princess Charlotte* under Lt. Hagan accounted for a large proportion of these. The government finally acknowledged in July 1816 that in peacetime the navy could not interfere with ships of other nations even if they had agreed to abolish the trade. Yet the Sierra Leone government still commissioned ships to detain foreign slavers. The *San Juan Nepomuceno* was taken by Hagan in December 1817 on the order of the Sierra Leone authorities. "There exists . . . at Sierra Leone," wrote Stephen Lushington after reviewing the case for the government, "a great misapprehension as to the state of the existing law upon this subject, and a lamentable ignorance of the principles that govern the rights of nations in amity with each other."[31]

Attitudes toward the Spanish were even more cavalier. At no point prior to 1817 did the Spanish agree to give up or limit their slave trade to their own possessions. Yet between 1809, when the first ship under a Spanish flag appeared in a British court, and 1819 when a mixed commission court opened at Sierra Leone, at least forty-three slave ships claiming the Spanish flag were detained by British cruisers and condemned in British courts. As with Portuguese ships, any contact with a British port, investor, insurer or even the purchase of canoes at the British Gold Coast forts was deemed sufficient for such actions.[32] Quite illegally, the British assumed the right to search Spanish vessels both before and after the end of the war. Bona fide Iberian ventures were certainly caught in the British net. The response of both Evangelicals and the government to Spanish complaints was to ignore the right of search issue, at least at first, and to stress that if redress was justified it could be obtained in the British courts. This, given the quick sale of prizes and the time restrictions on appeals to London, was in practical terms untrue.[33]

In 1817, the judgment in the *Le Louis* case confirmed what the government had come to realize the previous year. *Le Louis,* a French ship taken by the

*Princess Charlotte,* was restored with damages: The right to search foreign shipping would have to be negotiated. By this time yet another Portuguese as well as Spanish and Dutch treaties had been signed granting mutual right of search and setting up the mixed commission courts. Under the ninth article of the new Anglo-Portuguese convention, Britain granted full indemnification for wrongful detentions and took part in a joint commission to assess damages. This lasted until 1823 and cost the British a further £225,000.[34] The owners of Spanish ships received nothing. The British refused to consider any payments until Spain agreed to abolish the trade. The £400,000 handed over in the 1817 treaty was compensation for Spanish assent to abolition within three years as well as for wrongful arrest of Spanish ships. The money went not to Cuba nor to the aggrieved shipowners, but to the Spanish government, which spent it immediately on the purchase of warships from Russia.[35] Thus almost every slave ship captured in the ten years after 1807 (and there were well over a hundred) was detained under instructions that were, as Stephen Lushington pointed out, "from the beginning to the end illegal . . . [and] in violation of every principle of the law of nations." Perhaps only half of these wrongful captures were compensated.

The point here is not that the abolitionists consciously broke the law, either domestic or international, in their quest for suppression—though it is hard to conclude that this never happened. Rather, it is that for the Evangelicals the eradication of sin was ultimately more important than individual rights and the rights of nations. Of course, as slavery was a sin they would never admit that there could be a conflict between the two. On British domestic issues Evangelical influence was muted by the plural nature of support for and opposition to the Evangelical viewpoint. But on the slave-trade issue the moral authority and the official connections of the group ensured that their policy became official policy. Only on this issue were the implications of evangelicalism (and perhaps any theocratic philosophy) for civil and international rights laid bare. Brougham was not one of the Clapham Sect, but in 1810 he probably voiced their concern when he wondered why force could be used to obtain new colonies and extend the slave trade (in the past) but not to bring the slave traffic to a close (in the present). "It was on the single subject of abolition" that he had heard anyone question the right to interfere with foreign shipping. "On all [other] measures . . . we were ready enough to intrigue, to fight, to pay."[37] Both James Stephen, the elder, and Wilberforce held back on the occasion of this speech from supporting its explicit justification of force, and its implicit criticism of the government. But their reluctance was due to their close association with government policy and the precarious internal situation in Spain rather than to disagreement with the basic argument. In 1816 James Stephen published a pamphlet that presented similar sentiments in much more detail.[38] Indeed on the issue of the slave trade, the providential element in evangelicism appeared to move in a theocratic direction.

And it was not only sin and crime that became merged in the Evangelical world view. The long-run economic gains from the adoption of free labor were beyond question at both the national and individual levels. Although there can be no doubt that Macaulay, Stephen and the other Evangelicals would have sacrificed all in the pursuit of abolition, Providence had ensured that the choice did not arise. As a result of the policy that Macaulay and Stephen had largely created, the Sierra Leone economy and business in the prize courts received considerable stimulus. Macaulay acted as agent for many captors of the wrongfully arrested ships and received a percentage of the prize money that the British government paid out. None of this money was recovered by the Treasury after the illegality of the captures was clearly established. [39] To note that the Macaulay fortune was based (and perhaps lost, too)[40] on the suppression of the slave trade is to make an important ideological point rather than to be cynical.

The abolitionists were undoubtedly correct. Suppression and a rigorous regard for personal and international rights were incompatible. The slave trade in the Rio Pongo could not have been set back without an attack on neutral territory. Portuguese and Spanish slave ships could not be interfered with except illegally. It was, nevertheless, unfortunate that by the time the abolitionists began their big international effort to influence the Concert of Europe in the aftermath of war, their standing in the eyes of the ministers was less than it had been in 1807. Perhaps without these mistakes the antislavery leaders would have had more influence over the British delegations in the postwar negotiations.[41]

By 1818, after the Congress of Aix-la-Chapelle, it was apparent that with or without the aid of the "autocrat of all the Russias" joint international action on the slave trade would not go beyond empty declarations.[42] In addition, the new treaties between Britain and Portugal, Spain and the Netherlands established for the first time a permanent antislave-trade bureaucracy in the form of courts of mixed commission. These and earlier treaties with Scandinavian countries laid the foundation of the enormous nineteenth-century slave–trade-treaty system centered on Britain from which few people in the world found themselves exempt. By 1819 the Foreign Office had decided that the task of imposing the British view of progress on the rest of the world was at once too difficult, too important and too long run to be left to the instincts of other "civilized" nations or to the private and what had turned out to be amateurish activities of abolitionists. In this year was created its Slave Trade Department. Initially perceived as temporary, by 1841 it was part of the permanent establishment of the Foreign Office. With four clerks and a superintendent, it formed one of six divisions between which the business of the premier British Department of State was divided. Charged at the outset with the supervision of the slave-trade treaties and the mixed commission courts, it quickly developed into a hub of an information-gathering system, with contacts wherever there was a British consul. Several consulates such as those in the Cape Verde Islands (1825) and Puerto Rico (1840) were created expressly to watch over the slave trade.[43] Every British diplomatic and consular representative was expected to report on the slave trade, and eventually slavery, and maintain pressure both formal and informal for its abolition.

As most of the world either depended on or controlled areas that depended on coerced labor and as British officials were required to write separately to the Slave Trade Department on these matters, the records of the department came to number in the thousands of volumes. The annual publication in the parliamentary blue books of vast excerpts of this material together with the policy directives and official commentary was itself an instrument of policy. The facts of the system as interpreted by British representatives as well as the equivocation of recalcitrant and ideologically backward governments were there for all to see. Indeed the parliamentary slave-trade papers came to be as eagerly read in Rio de Janeiro, Madrid and Havana as in London. Parts of the slave-trade estimates that they contained were even republished as official Brazilian government information.[44]

The institutionalization of antislavery—its absorption into the "official mind"—did nothing, however, to resolve the tensions inherent in forcing others toward a conception of progress based, in part, on freedom of choice. Despite the network of officials, treaties, courts and cruisers centered on the most powerful nation in the world, the slave trade and slave society in the Americas entered what was probably the most expansionary phase in their existence after 1820. Given European industrial expansion, it could hardly have been otherwise. Both within and outside the Slave Trade Department, there developed a realization that suppression of the slave trade and traditional diplomatic and law-enforcement methods were incompatible. But this was not merely a matter of relearning what the saints in politics had already discovered. Whereas the first generation of parliamentary abolitionists were Tory and were concerned above all with the suppression of sin, the new generation were overwhelmingly Whig or Liberal and drew more from Adam Smith and Bentham than had their predecessors. For such men, regard for the law whether domestic or international was paramount. One of their leaders, Stephen Lushington, was an authority on international law who devoted one of his first speeches on his return to the Commons after a twelve-year absence to ridiculing the mistakes that the Wilberforce generation had made on the slave trade. His objections—ironic in view of his later contribution to the Palmerston and Aberdeen acts—were primarily to the illegal nature of the instructions sent out to the naval commanders. On other occasions he used similar arguments to condemn the methods employed by the Society for the Suppression of Vice.[45]

For Lushington, George Stephen, the later Macaulays, David Turnbull, Richard Madden and indeed Palmerston and the Foreign Office staff, a different accommodation to the tensions in their belief was necessary. In an echo of one abolitionist approach in the United States, first the slave trade and then slavery itself became accepted as evidence of barbarous behavior that was sufficient to place those nations involved beyond the law of nations. Such a position justified almost any action that would achieve the goal of abolition. At root there was the ideologues' familiar conviction that people did not know their own best interest. Laissez-faire would work if only barbaric practices were first cleared out of the way.[46] If the constituted authorities—be they the president of the United States, the captain-general of Cuba or the Brazilian cabinet—would not respond appropriately, then direct action was necessary. By the end of the 1830s, the slaughter in St. Domingue after 1791 had been counterbalanced by the peaceful transition from slavery in the British West Indies, and it was almost inconceivable that such action could lead to chaos.

The equivalent of American abolitionist support for, first, disunion and, then, civil war was, among British abolitionists, backing for the laws permitting the destruction of slave ships of friendly powers on the high seas. Lushington, the critic of the Clapham Sect and the expert on international law, was involved in both the conception and formulation of such proposals before they reached Parliament.[47] Justified also was the adoption of a plan to free slaves illegally imported into Cuba and Brazil, a plan that could scarcely have been implemented in accordance with Quaker principles of nonviolence and that (in the opinion of the Crown's law officers) the British government had no legal right to pursue.[48] The clandestine organization of antislavery groups in slave societies was also fostered. In 1839 the British and Foreign Anti-Slavery Society drew up secret instructions for George and Charlotte Pilkington to take up residence in Brazil and to seek an official position with the Brazilian government. With or without the position, they were to collect information on the illicit slave trade and British mining companies and to establish antislavery societies and an antislavery press. In the course of 1840 the Pilkingtons achieved most of their mandate while keeping their connection with the British abolition movement concealed.[49] None of this was behavior that the abolitionists would have tolerated in their own societies if they rather than the slaveholder had been the target.

The Foreign Office and Admiralty had major roles in these tensions. The British had slight legal precedent for visiting foreign shipping on the high seas in peacetime despite their assertions to the contrary. On the west African coast where cruisers regularly inspected the papers of ships of nontreaty powers, the Admiralty tolerated rather than encouraged the practice. When the Foreign Office cautioned the navy, the First Lord wrote privately to Palmerston that the caution was "too restrictive for practice, tho' correct in law. . . . The practice is that every suspected vessel whatever colours she may have hoisted is brought to and if necessary an officer is sent on board who judges from what he sees and hears whether he may risk her search or detention. We need not order them to do this, but I think we should not say anything implying that they must discontinue the practice as it has always prevailed."[50] But the full logical extension to the treatment of slave traders and their governments as barbarians went far beyond merely stretching the law. Anyone who reads Palmerston's trenchant minutes in the records of the Slave Trade Department must recognize that blockades of Havana and Rio de Janeiro were never far from the foreign secretary's mind. It was precisely this policy that was implemented against several African states, the most well known being the attack on Lagos in 1851. The ending of the Brazilian trade was of course prefaced by British naval incursions into Brazilian territorial waters. On one occasion the Foreign Office even approved the hiring of a former slaver captain to take a fully equipped slave-ship decoy under American colors to the African coast. Usually, however, Palmerston, Aberdeen and Russell had the pragmatism that the Maddens and the Turnbulls lacked. There was first of all a fear of U.S. reaction to such initiatives, at least in the Caribbean. "Which is the greater evil, the continuance of the slave trade or a rupture with the United States? I think a rupture," wrote the British minister in Washington to the Havana commissioner.[51]

But a more important limitation was the point that although force could win territory and trade concessions, too much force would usually ensure failure if the target was ideological. A less direct approach was likely to prove more successful and every British secretary of state for foreign affairs authorized liberal use of the Secret Service Fund to further the cause. Regular payments out of this fund to informants on the illegal traffic began in the 1830s in Rio de Janiero and Pernambuco and a few years later in Cuba when the illegal trade there became less open. By the 1840s the commander of the British cruisers could write, "No slave vessel could arrive or leave any Port of Brazil within 230 . . . miles North and also South of Rio de Janeiro without my knowing it."[52] The most spectacular single example, however, is the Cuban shipbroker, Manuel Fortunat. Based in New York, he communicated in cipher and through third and fourth parties supplied the British consul in New York with voluminous information on slaver departures and arrivals in the late 1850s and early 1860s. He received in return thousands of dollars, none of it recorded in the "Annual Accounts Current" returned to the Treasury.[53] Any disaffected seaman or even principal in the slave trade with a penchant for risk could turn to the local British representative for a sympathetic hearing. The consulates in both Havana and Rio de Janiero had permanent agents in the outports. Those informants who were discovered and roughly treated by their former colleagues and the local authorities were assured of British compensation when retribution fell short of murder.[54] The twentieth century has yielded very considerable evidence that the gains from spying are not always clear: At the very least, double agents can provide misinformation. Several of the British consuls were, in fact, merchants who dealt with slave traders on a regular basis. Their attitude was not necessarily that of the metropolitan abolitionists. In one blatant example the two Portuguese commissioners at the Luanda Court of Mixed Commission in the 1840s—who corresponded with the Foreign Office for nineteen months after the death of the last British official there—turned out to be major slave factors on the northern Angolan coast. They must have alternated daily between Foreign Office and slave business correspondence.[55]

The British would usually stop short of supporting insurrection in slave societies. But Foreign Office representatives overseas did not always share in the restraint of the London office. Apart from the activities of David Turnbull and Francis Cocking in Cuba (discussed later), it is worth noting a chilling letter from the British chargé d'affaires in Brazil in 1848 that argues, in effect, for a slave revolt. Responding to Palmerston's enquiry on the potential outcome of a blockade of Brazilian ports, James Hudson urged the navy to begin with Bahia because the slaves there had "attempted on more than one occasion to throw off their yoke and establish themselves in freedom. If that port is blockaded," he went on, "and a position of which I shall speak later near it is occupied, it is almost certain that the negroes will not let such an occasion of securing their freedom escape." Rebellion here would mean " . . . the existence of slavery itself in other portions of Brazil would be vitally affected."[56]

The Foreign Office (for reasons explored later) preferred more subtle forms of influencing the internal affairs (and compromising the independence) of polities in which slavery flourished. The British had considerable direct ideological influence in the mid-nineteenth century and were emulated by local elites in many parts of the Americas. "When I enter the Chamber [of Deputies] I am entirely under the influence of English liberalism,"[57] said one Brazilian legislator. Some of his colleagues might have added English cash too. When the first major British offensive on the Rio de Janeiro slave traffic opened in 1839, the Brazilian foreign minister, Caetano Mario Lopez Gama, was receiving a regular stipend out of the Secret Service Fund. This individual was also a long-time senator, member of the Council of State and, on one occasion, a Brazilian plenipotentiary in abortive treaty negotiations with Britain. He was described by James Hudson, Palmerston's man in Rio, as "one of the few respectable men in this country," without, one must assume, intentional irony.[58] As early as 1842 the British minister had noted the intense hatred of England generated by the press and had argued that the only remedy was to finance a newspaper better disposed to English interests. Although large-scale purchasing of a favorable press came later, Hudson paid some debts of the newspaper of Leopoldo Muniz Barreto, the vice-president of the Chamber of Deputies in 1848, and discussed the possibility of contributing financially to a free-labor cotton plantation in Minas Novas that Muniz Barreto was planning. The following year he contemplated funding the leaders of the Santa Luzia, the Brazilian opposition party (one of whom was Muniz Barreto), when it adopted suppression of the slave trade as a policy plank. As Hudson was not convinced that the new policy would survive the party's accession to office and as there were signs that their opponents, now in power, were susceptible to pressure, he decided against. At least one of the leading members of Santa Luzia, however, Leopoldo de Câmara, the mulatto captain of the port of Rio de Janeiro, was on the British payroll by 1848.[59]

Leopoldo de Câmara was a leading member of the antislave-trade society and with Hudson's aid, approved in advance by Palmerston, he established and edited *O Philantropo* as the society's newspaper. In 1849 at least £400 came out of the Secret Service Fund to finance the society and its newspaper. The policy of creating a friendly press urged by the British minister now commenced in earnest. By 1849 a major Rio de Janeiro newspaper, the *Correio Mercantil*—which supported abolition of the slave trade throughout the critical events of 1850—was receiving a regular stipend. The *Correio Mercantil* published material supplied by the British legation, and Hudson was ordered to send published excerpts to Palmerston for publication in the London press as evidence of the success of British policy. Such a strategy was a response to the attacks of the British anticoercionists on Palmerston and the whole cruiser policy. The two major Rio papers that supported the slave trade, the *O Brasil* and *Correio da Tarde,* switched camps in August 1850: The editor of the former, "the cleverest paper in this country," was also on Hudson's payroll. The anti-slave-trade newspapers started at this time in Bahia (the *O Seculo*), Minas *'Tamandica)* and Santos *(Revista Commercio)* may also have had British aid.[60]

But the most ambitious and expensive of the British clandestine operations in Brazil was the proposal made by Hudson and approved by Palmerston early in 1850. To improve the effectiveness of the anticipated naval operations in Brazilian territorial waters and to ensure the slave trade would not revive after this action, Hudson proposed to hire "officers in the Brazilian service," "pilots" and "men of independent means" up and down the three hundred miles of the southern Brazilian importation zone. The amount, £5,000 to £7,000 per annum was in addition to the payments already discussed and was again to come out of the Secret Service Fund. The head of this operation though unnamed in the letter was certainly Leopoldo da Câmara. He was described in an earlier letter as having considerable influence over "the greater part of the mulattos of Rio, and as most of the subordinate Custom House Officers are filled with people of colour, he has great power in this Port." The cost of the scheme was probably close to the annual cost of the regular operations of both the British consulate and legation in Rio de Janeiro. It was justified by the fact that "some of the Brazilian Justices of the Peace, officers of custom and pilots . . . are accustomed to receive considerable bribes from the slave dealer."[61]

Neither the morality issue nor the delicate question of dealing with the mulattos as a separate group in a slave society were ever raised in the Palmerston-Hudson correspondence. This was, however, an unorthodox method of tackling corruption, though one consistent with the free-market system that Britain was proselytizing. It was in principle no different to paying ministers and judges a salary high enough to guarantee their impartiality. But apart from the fact that the payments came from a foreign power the question remained of whether morality, which Palmerston equated with moral behavior, can be purchased. If the perpetrators had been pushed, they might have justified their actions in terms of the barbarous-practices argument. There was a clear implication that if a facsimile of the British system could only be created—the means were unimportant—then the ends of morality (and prosperity) would have been served. The issue of how effective this action was in ending the Brazilian slave trade is discussed later. The major and more profound (though scarcely novel) point to be noted here is that quite apart from the unavailability of free labor in midcentury Brazil, it is questionable whether a "free" system could have been established with deception and external interference.

British intervention or imagined intervention in Cuba attained a much greater level of notoriety, yet at the official level it was never as serious as its Brazilian equivalent. The British began to pay for information in the 1840s and although the system became very expensive in the 1850s, there is no record of subsidies to either publications or members of the opposition.[62] In Spain, British consuls were ordered to induce shipbuilders to petition against the transfer of foreign-built vessels to the Spanish flag, but in Cuba opposition was not permitted. There were no representative institutions, and publicizing anti-slave-trade views often presaged banishment. There was as a result little for the British to subsidize. Moreover, encouraging opposition in an autocratically governed colony was tantamount to undermining constituted authority Finally though the Monroe Doctrine covered both territories, that doctrine ha its very origins in the U.S. concerns over the future of Cuba. U.S. suspicions of British motives were far more likely to be aroused over an island ninety miles from the mainland than over a country on another continent.

The British ideological pressure was, nevertheless, real enough. The Spanish economic reforms of Charles III were influenced by *The Wealth of Nations*, and in Cuba the writings and activities of Francisco de Arango y Parreño added to these reforms and helped ensure the free trade that the Cuban plantation system needed to develop. After 1808, in Cuba as in Brazil, the Smithian prescription (or at least that part of it advocating the dismantling of mercantilist restrictions) seemed the certain route to colonial prosperity. Initially it was not widely recognized that in the Americas free trade, property rights, individual initiative and laissez-faire might mean thriving slave-labor rather than free-labor systems. The cohesiveness of the liberal ideology was such that it could not be sampled in portions, however. Liberalism meant appropriate political institutions as well as free labor, and the flood of slave imports and Spanish repression made for uneasiness among Creole intellectuals and even planters. Arango saw the slave trade as a stopgap for European immigration and turned against the former late in life. There were no counterparts to George Fitzhugh, Thomas Roderick Dew and William Harper in Cuba and Brazil.[63] As Cuban and U.S. slavery entered their most prosperous and (if slave prices are guides) most sanguine era, the secretary of the British and Foreign Anti-Slavery Society went to Paris to interview a number of Cuban plantation owners of various political persuasions who were visiting there. "Without an exception," he wrote, "they confessed they regarded the system as bad" for all involved, but they were concerned, not surprisingly, at the prospects of getting the requisite labor any other way. The antislave-trade writings of Cubans—such as del Monte, Saco and Arango y Parreño (in his later years)—had little of the humanitarianism of the British abolitionist and no interest whatsoever in "civilizing" Africa. They shared in full, however, the British conviction in the superior efficiency of free over slave labor. Reliance on slave labor was regarded as a temporary expedient.[64] Although it was understandable that British liberals with scant experience of land-abundant tropical regions and large racial minorities might keep a tenacious grip on such opinions, it was remarkable that the intelligentsia of Cuba and Brazil should follow suit.

Perhaps self-doubts in the face of pressure from the source of liberal ideology help explain the Cuban hysteria evoked by the British government's controversial appointments to Havana in the late 1830s and early 1840s. All British officials in Cuba, with the possible exceptions of the first consuls appointed to Havana and Santiago de Cuba, shared the Foreign Office attitude to the slave trade and were, therefore, in more senses than one alien elements in Cuban society. The British commissioner at the Havana Mixed Commission Court for thirteen years, James Kennedy, had been one of the few members of the British Parliament to vote against compensation for the West Indian planters when the 1833 Emancipation Act was passed. Richard Madden, appointed to the post of superintendent of liberated Africans in 1837, had an established record of hostility to planter interests and was an impassioned advocate of black rights. Though appointed by a Colonial Office whose head and permanent undersecretary were intimates of the old evangelical group,[65] neither the Madden nor the Kennedy appointment was intended as a provocation to the Cuban plantocracy. Madden, in particular, cultivated contacts among progressive Creoles, though the exchange did not move beyond ideas and information. By the time Madden and Kennedy arrived, however, the Spanish government's refusal to allow Cubans to participate in the 1836 constitution had fused a link between aspirations of Cuban independence and slave-trade abolition. Madden's very presence, even without his contacts, brought apprehension among the Spanish authorities and the large slaveholders until his departure in 1839.[66]

The appointment of David Turnbull to the Havana consulship as well as to Madden's old position was less ingenuous. After a visit to the West Indies, including Cuba, in 1838, Turnbull had written a book, *Travels in the West,* which included a plan for liberating all Africans brought into Cuba in violation of the slave-trade treaties: The Havana Mixed Commission Court was to be given the authority to sort out postabolition from preabolition arrivals. Turnbull aggressively sold his scheme to both the British and Foreign Anti-Slavery Society and the British government, and the latter submitted a modified version to the Madrid government in the form of a draft treaty.[67] Turnbull pushed not only the plan, which would have emancipated the majority of the Cuban slave population, but also his own qualifications for the Havana consulship. By 1840 Palmerston was having some success with an aggressive policy against the Portuguese traffic, at the same time the Spanish trade to Cuba had just reached record levels despite the 1835 convention. There is little doubt that Palmerston's selection of Turnbull to fill the Havana positions was both a calculated response to Spanish intransigence and an escalation of British pressure. As Turnbull was not a merchant, the appointment entailed a sevenfold increase in the salary attached to the position.[68]

Yet there is also no doubt that neither Palmerston nor Aberdeen, who replaced him during Turnbull's stay in Havana, ever intended to encourage rebellion. In the course of a dramatic stay lasting almost two years, Turnbull and his clerk, Francis Cocking, not only exchanged ideas and information with Creoles and free blacks but also became aware of, indeed involved in, plans for an insurrection by these groups. The goal, wrote Cocking, was that of "giving independence to the Island of Cuba and thereby insure to the Slave Population their immediate emancipation from bondage." However, from Cocking's later confession to the Foreign Office, it is obvious that the Cuban Creoles involved were chiefly interested in the first part. News of these plans did not reach the Foreign Office until Turnbull's successor, Joseph Crawford, took up his post. Both Crawford and the London officials were appalled when they learned of them.[69]

The main difference between the actions of Palmerston in Brazil, at least before 1850, and Turnbull and Cocking in Cuba was the physical force which the latter pair encouraged. But from the standpoint of the liberalism that the British were trying to inculcate, the difference between bribery and force was slight. The experience of Turnbull and Madden in the British West Indies du ing apprenticeship had convinced them that the abolition of slavery could be brought about without the long-term violence of the St. Domingue revolution. Similarly, when Hudson advocated British support of insurrection at Bahia, he was thinking how "advanced" the Bahian Yoruba people were. "Most . . . are Mahomedans; they possess great intelligence and have formed Benefit Societies and Savings Banks."[70] In other words, they were ready to enter the British conception of the modern world. Though Cuban and the Brazilian whites could be forgiven for missing the distinction, the object of Hudson, Turnbull and Cocking was not to foster another Haitian revolution but to create a government and society amenable to liberal pressure. In Cuba, as in Brazil, or indeed in the U.S. South, this was not likely to happen without force and corruption. Moreover, even if Cuban independence had come about at this stage, the attitudes of Saco, del Monte and other Creoles suggest that the policy of the new government to slavery, if not the slave trade, might not have met the approval of British abolitionists. Similarly, a breakup of the Brazilian Empire might well have entrenched slavery as certainly as would a Confederate victory in the American Civil War.

The same basic dilemma plagued British attitudes and policies toward Africa. Given European industralization, the extension of laissez-faire to the whole Atlantic basin would have meant a vast slave trade and thriving American plantation systems. British intervention reduced this impact but at considerable ideological and financial cost. Moreover, slave systems of production within Africa tended to thrive to the extent that British intervention was successful, particularly as European survival rates in Africa began to improve. Like the Americas, the dark continent did not meet British expectations in the first half of the nineteenth century. Within the framework of the stages theory, popular among the eighteenth-century moral philosophers, Africa was widely regarded as having reached the second, or agricultural, stage of development. Progress through this and later stages would be greatly facilitated by British assistance. Indeed abolitionists and merchants alike assumed that the interests of Africa and Britain were one. Buxton's government-sponsored expedition up the Niger of 1841 was premised on the expectation that British "sovereignty of a few hundred square miles in Benin or Eboe" would, through demonstration and example, result in "bringing forward into the world millions of consumers." The methods to be employed—explored in numerous publications from the 1790s on, including the early African Institution reports—amounted to acculturation, specifically the inculcation of British habits of industry and consumption.[71] Wilberforce and the early abolitionists favored trade and African proprietorship, though the first ten years of crown government in Sierra Leone saw Governor Maxwell and the Macaulays using "apprenticed" liberated Africans in plantation-type conditions. Buxton and later mainstream abolitionists favored temporary reliance on European-managed enterprises. Although these were to use only free labor, there was a clear implication in the plans of the Niger expedition that the "millions of consumers" created by the scheme would probably be African slaves employed by African proprietors, at least until the British example had made its impression. For both the post-emancipation West Indies and precolonial Africa, the mainstream abolitionists believed by the second quarter of the nineteenth century that a little compulsion was necessary to bring liberalism into "backward" areas.[72]

Stronger British initiatives both against the slave trade and in the African interior were inhibited by disease and a long-standing recognition that African polities were entitled to the full rights of nation-states. In 1816 James Stephen, the elder, made an ingenious attempt to harness Grotius, Vattel and other major international law authorities in support of an aggressive antislave-trade policy.[73] But both the theory and practice of international relations, at least since Vattel's time, pointed in the opposite direction. "Men derive the right of punishment solely from their right to provide for their own safety; and consequently, they cannot claim it except against those by whom they have been injured," argued Vattel. Thus, he concluded it was not right for a nation "to compel any one to receive a kindness."[74] And later, James Stephen's son, as legal counsel and then undersecretary to the Colonial Office, took a strong stand in favor of African sovereignty. Yet in Africa as in the Americas and on the high seas, in the struggle to suppress the slave trade, these precepts were subject to increasing de facto modification by the middle of the century. The increase in naval strength off Africa during the 1830s made it possible for the British to institute blockades of selected West African slave embarkation points. These blockades applied only to slave ships under the flags of signators of slave-trade treaties and were, of course, subject to all the loopholes in those treaties. This and the practice in some regions of moving slaves over land to new embarkation points seriously impaired the effectiveness of the navy. The propriety of any interdiction of commerce—even in slaves—in the absence of the formal consent of the African powers concerned was doubtful. Slave-trader tactics pushed frustrated naval officers and the Foreign Office into responses which were clearly inconsistent with accepted international practice.

Ever since the navy had begun to send regular patrols to Africa, cruisers had occasionally attacked shore-based slave-trading establishments, usually after provocation.[75] In the early 1840s, however, the number and severity of these incidents increased and the strict justification for them appeared ever more slight. Commodore Tucker's destruction in November 1840 of the town of Corisco included a great quantity of merchandise and the capturing of Miguel Pons, a Spanish slave factor. It was perhaps an excessive, if understandable, response to Pons's opening fire on the boats of a cruiser. But it pales in comparison to the destruction simultaneously wrought at the other end of the West African coast by Captain Joseph Denman in the Gallinas. The occasion of Denman's attack was the reenslavement of two recaptive Africans from Sierra Leone who were, in fact, returned the day after Denman entered the river. The recaptives were returned before the attack and before most of the factories were destroyed and nine hundred slaves removed to Sierra Leone. A few months later, similar action was taken in the Sherbro in response to the detention and beating of two Kroomen working for the cruisers, and in the Rio Pongo a large slave-trading establishment filled with trade goods belonging to perhaps the most enduring of all slave factors, Mrs. Lightburn, was completely destroyed. In only the first of these incidents had the initial provocation involved loss life, and in none had British property been endangered.[76] Casus belli in three of the cases were no more than insults to the British flag and might more accurately be described as pretexts rather than justifications.

When news of the Denman and Tucker attacks reached London, Palmerston's reaction was enthusiastic. He recommended "that similar operations should be executed against all the Piratical Slave Trade Establishments which may be met with on parts of the coast not belonging to any civilized Power." On this occasion he qualified his instructions by stating that officers should "endeavour to obtain the formal permission of the native chiefs for the destruction of the slave factories within their territories"[77] as indeed Denman had done. A few weeks later, however, he was instructing the Admiralty that "if such an agreement should in any case be found impossible, the Commanding Officer . . . should be perfectly justified in considering European Slave Dealers established in the Territory of a native chief as Persons engaged in a piratical undertaking."[78] A year later the Foreign Office, now under Aberdeen, reversed this policy after a referral to the law officers and once more required the navy to obtain African permission.[79] But this does not alter the importance of the attacks as a watershed in official relations between European and African powers. Aberdeen switched policy not out of a concern for African rights but rather because the destruction or theft of property (i.e., trade goods) in the factories belonging to factors claiming European or American citizenship could provoke a diplomatic incident. Unless the British got the approval of the sovereign power in whose territories destruction occurred, they would have no legal grounds for resisting claims for compensation from the owner of the property.[80] Indeed, as a result of a misunderstanding between the law officers and the Foreign Office, the government believed from 1842 to 1848 that even with the permission of the African powers, property found in barracoons could not be damaged.[81] The large-scale destruction of African property, nevertheless, continued from time to time, even during these years—noticeably in the Gallinas in early 1845. As with the Denman raid, the ostensible cause—the enslavement of a few British subjects, some of whom had no wish to leave when located—appears out of proportion to the British response.[82] The Palmerston instructions of July 1841 thus represented not just a subjugation of international law but a step toward the subjugation of the African.

In the 1850s the progression was clear. Immediately after a renewed blockade in the Gallinas in 1849–50 came to a successful conclusion, Palmerston asked the Admiralty to institute similar measures against Lagos. For the head of the Admiralty and for most conversant with international law, the cases were quite different. "In the Gallinas," Baring pointed out, "we had a Treaty which had been broken—and we blockaded the coast because we had a right of war from their having neglected to carry out their treaty agreements." There was no counterpart with King Kosoko of Lagos. Thus, he continued, "I doubt that we have a right to make war against him or to depose him if he carries on the slave trade." A few months later Baring repeated the argument and added that the slave trade had never been considered piracy by the law of natio.,s and "that we ourselves traded in slaves in 1806."[83] The former commodore of the ,uadron, Sir Charles Hotham, had similar scruples. Palmerston's response summarized the dilemma of nineteenth-century slave-trade suppression as well as the British resolution of that dilemma. It is worth quoting at length:

> I cannot subscribe to the fundamental Doctrine upon which he [Hotham] rests his objections to any interference at Lagos, namely that the African Chiefs have a right to do as they like with their own, and that we have no right to prevent from slave trading. I wonder that with such an opinion the worthy commodore accepted the command from which he has lately returned or how he stood for the three years the constant pinching of his conscience. . . . It is limited power and not limited right that has made us act generally speaking, by persuasion and treaty in regard to other countries rather than by summary force. We have just as good a right to say to the Chief of Lagos . . . you shall not capture and sell your fellow creatures as we have to say the same thing to the malays and Dyahs of the Indian seas.[84]

The attack on Lagos went ahead, although as a sop to tender consciences it was represented as a move to restore the rightful King Akitoye, who had been driven out by Kosoko in 1845 and who was prepared to sign a slave-trade treaty.[85] Similar policies toward Dahomey were thwarted only by the difficulty of reaching the inland capital of Abomey. But both here and in the Congo during the 1850s, total blockades were enforced because the African authorities refused to sign treaties, not because they had signed and then refused to enforce them.[86] If even these measures were not sufficient, then the logic of Palmerston's position pointed to annexation. At the very least it would seem that in the official mind the legal and moral barriers to the European partition of Africa were cleared away in the twenty years after 1840 and ironically that the suppression of the slave trade was an important catalyst in that process.[87] By midcentury, even more than in the Americas, the British were prepared to displace properly constituted authorities in order to move closer to the goal of suppression. And having made the move and suppressed the trade, they found that the long-term goal of encouraging the development of British values was even farther away. Buxton's expectation that African slave systems would be first encouraged and then given up in response to British moves was only half right. The second part had to await formal European annexation and even then it was scarcely a voluntary process. It might even be suggested that if the price of slave-trade suppression was a world dominated by the British, or any single power, then perhaps the price was too high. The acceptance of British claims to search or visit shipping, British covert activities in Latin America and their occupation of large stretches of the African littoral would probably have ended the slave trade quickly. Such action would also have meant an Atlantic basin both policed and adjudicated by the British, and it would have put an end to any possibility of a plural solution to major problems arising in the region. Henry Wise, the U.S. minister at Rio de Janeiro in 1844, asked why did the British not sweep the slave trader from the seas. Those modern historians who echo the question should ponder the inevitable augmentation in British power that would have been necessary to do it.

# IV

## The Mechanics of the Illegal Slave Trade: Economic and Political Aspects, 1820–70

# 8

# The Impact of Suppression
# on the Middle Passage

If the British commitment to abolition was both massive and often of dubious legality, what was its impact? For the British anticoercionists of the 1840s as well as for most observers in Brazil and Cuba, attempts to suppress the trade resulted in tiny, overcrowded, ill-equipped slave vessels; inadequate provisions; hurried embarkations and disembarkations, often in remote locations; and violent clashes between cruisers and slavers on the high seas. Misery and mortality among the forced migrants could only have increased. Some supporters of forcible suppression, including naval officers, conceded these points.[1] The coercionist counterargument stressed the number of slaves saved from slavery in the Americas by the actions of the cruisers. "To judge the merits of our preventive efforts," argued Palmerston, "we must compare the number of slaves now clandestinely carried over ... with the number that would be so carried if no obstruction were offered to the trade." Indeed the true comparison according to Palmerston was between the "demand for slaves now arising from Cuba and the Brazils ... [and] the Demand which would have existed if all the Colonies of Great Britain, France, Holland, Denmark had also continued to import annually an unlimited supply of slaves."[2] Every year the slave-trade volume of the Parliamentary Papers reported new examples of appalling conditions that were used by coercionists and anitcoercionists alike. For the former, they were further evidence of a depraved business that must be eliminated as soon as possible. For the latter, such incidents would not have occurred but for naval intervention. The two central questions in the debate are, in fact, still of major interest. What did the slaves experience and how significant was the movement to suppress the traffic for both actual and potential deportees?

One might attempt to answer these questions through the eyes of the Africans themselves. There are several memoirs written by or taken down from individuals who actually underwent a voyage in a nineteenth-century slave ship.[3] Although these are invaluable human records, they are few in number.

Moreover, their authors would have little hard data on the environment in which they found themselves to enable them to make comparisons. For non-Africans, particularly in Europe, the situation was not much better. Hard information did not enter the policy debates on the slave trade as frequently as it had in earlier discussions over the living conditions of British slaves, for example. The debate on coercion, nevertheless, helped shape a definite image of the trade. As we have seen, the various policing authorities, mainly British, detained and usually destroyed an average of more than one slave ship every two weeks throughout the last half-century of the trade. Few doubted the effect of British cruisers on the behavior of slave traders. According to the press on both sides of the Atlantic, captains of slave ships filled their holds to the point of suffocation, threw slaves overboard when pursued by cruisers and frequently took on board inadequate provisions, including water, in the rush of an illicit embarkation. The contemporary literature—from the solidly researched works of Buxton, Turnbull and Blake to the memoirs of naval officers and travelers—projected a picture of small, fast, cheaply outfitted, overcrowded ships earning record profits from quick trips to the coast and, of course, experiencing high mortality in the process. Such an image also emerges from the evidence given to the several British parliamentary committees of the 1840s, and it is thus not surprising to see it reproduced in the standard modern works on the subject.[4]

The "average" experience is hard to pin down from the literary evidence and the isolated cases cited in the policy discussions of the 1840s. Three examples illustrate this point. In 1842, the *Minerva* was intercepted on its way from Ambriz to Bahia while carrying 126 children. The ship was thirty-six-and-a-half feet long, ten feet four inches at its widest point and had a hold with a maximum depth of five feet seven inches. After stowing fifteen water casks and provisions, there were fourteen inches of space left below decks into which half the children were fitted. The remainder occupied every foot available on deck. There were six slaves for every measured ton of the vessel. Seven years later five crew of a captured slave ship stole the official boat of the Sierra Leone Mixed Commission Court, rowed it into the Rio Pongo, "kidnapped or purchased five or six slaves" and successfully navigated to Brazil where the slaves were sold. The boat was twenty-eight-feet long and was without decking or cover of any kind. A third, and quite different case, was the 453-ton bark *Orion*. Like many slave ships operating in the proximity of cruisers, this vessel took on only part of her intended cargo and left Cabinda in 1859 with ample provisions. According to her captor, the slave deck was "eight feet in height, clear fore and aft, thoroughly well ventilated." The opinions of experienced naval officers whom Buxton consulted as he was preparing *The Atlantic Slave Trade* ranged from that of Captain L. T. Jones who "does not think there is great cruelty on middle passage . . . independent of the cruelty of packing so many into a small vessel" to that of Commodore Kellett who took off slaves from Bolama Island barracoons, "heavily ironed [and] given the least possible quantity of provisions . . . though provisions on the island were abundant."[5]

Conflicting testimony is, of course, the bane of juries and historians alike. The days when such conflict could be summarily settled by referring to quantitative material have long gone. But this is not a reason for ignoring the rich data available for the nineteenth-century slave trade. These allow us to assess trends in the size of ship used in the trade, voyage lengths and certain key ratios such as tons per crew member, slaves carried per ton and mortality. In particular, three kinds of comparisons appear called for. One is between the slave trade of the nineteenth century and that of earlier periods. The second is between the slave traffic of the nineteenth century, on the one hand, and other long distance traffic of the same period, on the other. Finally we need to consider trends in ship size, tons per crew, and so on in the slave trade in relation to the shifts in British suppression strategy. We turn first to the issue of ship size.

Part A in table 5 presents samples of tonnages from the last years of the legal trade and part B gives some equivalent data for the illegal trade. The figures are all in British measured tons of the years 1786–1835. Before drawing comparisons between the legal and illegal traffic some preliminary comments on slave-ship tonnage patterns are required. First, the English data for the 1790s must be used with care. From 1788, legislation restricted the slaves carried per ton and likely increased the size of the British slave ship of these years beyond what it had been.[6] Second, in both the eighteenth and nineteenth centuries, the smaller slaving ports such as those in Rhode Island, Puerto Rico and the French Caribbean tended to operate smaller ships than did the major centers of Bahia, Rio de Janeiro and Havana.[7] Third, the site of the trading location on the African coast had little influence over the size of the ship used. The only exception to this was that ships trading around the Cape of Good Hope to south east Africa tended to be much larger than their west coast counterparts.

With these comments in mind, we can now examine the underlying trends contained in table 5. This table shows first some remarkable similarities between major branches of the slave trade in the size of ship used during the late eighteenth and the first half of the nineteenth centuries. There was a sharp increase in tonnage after 1850 and indications of smaller ships on the Cuba-West African route in the 1830s and 1840s; both trends are discussed later with the aid of more refined data. But it would be very hard to argue that formal abolition of the trade had any impact on the size of the typical slave ship. Only the mean tonnages of Nantes ships show a decrease between the late eighteenth and early nineteenth centuries, but it is not clear whether this difference is statistically significant. Even if such a difference did exist, however, it might be noted that effective prosecution by the French authorities did not begin until the late 1820s. As French ships were largely protected from the British Navy by their flag, the difference can scarcely be attributed to abolition.

But did abolition prevent an upward trend in ship size from developing? Herbert Klein, after examining trends in tonnages of both English slave ships and Nantes slavers, has commented that by the end of the eighteenth century

an optimal size ship had . . . come to dominate the trade with 54 percent of the ships (landing slaves in Jamaica) being in the 100–199 ton range. It would thus appear that a much more specialized vessel had emerged in the English slave trade than a century earlier. This would mean that a vessel in the 100–199 ton range made the ideal transport for slaves across the Atlantic. That the British could have employed larger tonnage is obvious when we look at both the Royal African Com-

**Table 5.** Tonnages of Slave Ships in Selected Branches of the Slave Trade, 1790–1867 (British Tonnage, 1786–1835)

| | Mean | SD | Number of Ships |
|---|---|---|---|
| **Part A: Eighteenth-Century Traffic** | | | |
| Leaving English ports | | | |
| 1790–97[a] | 190.6 | — | 512 |
| Luanda to Rio de Janeiro | | | |
| 1795–1811[b] | 152–212 | — | na |
| Leaving Rhode Island ports | | | |
| 1791–1807[c] | 105.1* | 51.5 | 317 |
| **Part B: Nineteenth-Century Traffic** | | | |
| Cuba-West Africa | | | |
| 1811–30 | 189.3 | 121.7 | 75 |
| 1831–50 | 150.6* | 76.6 | 220 |
| 1851–67 | 273.2* | 159.8 | 180 |
| French Caribbean/Puerto Rico-West Africa | | | |
| 1811–30 | 131.8* | 59.0 | 63 |
| 1831–50 | 103.3* | 44.2 | 14 |
| Brazil North/Bahia-West Africa | | | |
| 1811–30 | 157.4 | 65.1 | 110 |
| 1831–50 | 170.4 | 103.3 | 216 |
| Brazil South-West Africa | | | |
| 1830–50 | 176.0 | 89.3 | 434 |
| Brazil South-Southeast Africa | | | |
| 1830–50 | 261.2* | 103.0 | 77 |
| Cuba-Southeast Africa | | | |
| 1851–67 | 468.5* | 200.3 | 13 |
| Cleared from Nantes | | | |
| 1814–33[d] | 145.0 | — | 337 |

*Significantly different from the Brazil South-West Africa mean at the 5% level. (Significance tests for the data used in rows 1, 2 and 14 were not possible.)

*Notes:*

Tonnages are in the British measured ton used in the period 1786 to 1835. Most of the observations in the table entered the historical record in tons different from this standard.

*Sources:* All data not specifically attributed are from the slave-ship data set. [a]D. P. Lamb, "Volume and Tonnage of the Liverpool Slave Trade, 1722–1807," in Roger T. Anstey and P.E.H. Hair (eds.), *Liverpool, the African Slave Trade, and Abolition: Essays to Illustrate Current Knowledge and Research* (Liverpool, 1976). [b]Herbert S. Klein, *The Middle Passage* (Princeton, 1978), pp. 31, 181. [c]Calculated from Jay Coughtry, *The Notorious Triangle: Rhode Island and the African Slave Trade, 1700–1807* (Philadelphia, 1981), pp. 264–85. [d]Serge Daget, "Long cours et négrier nantais du trafic illégal, 1814–1833," *Revue française d'histoire d'outre-mer*, 62 (1975): 113.

pany ships of a century before and the contemporaneous West Indiamen, whic. averaged at least 100 tons more per vessel than the slavers. That the British did not employ this larger tonnage, at least prior to 1800, would seem to suggest that coastal and upriver African trading required the use of smaller ships."[8]

Klein is writing of pre-1786 tonnages, which because of changes in measuring practices, should be increased by 54.2 percent for this size ship when comparisons are made with post-1786 tonnages. Klein's optimal range thus emerges as 154 to 230 post-1786 tons, and the figures for the major branches of pre-1850 slave trade in table 5 are comfortably within this range, with the exception of the Nantes data. Thus there is no need to look elsewhere for explanations of the relatively small ship used in the slave trade in this period. It has been suggested that a premium on the ability to use shallow creeks and bays for concealment from naval cruisers as well as a need to spread the risk of capture induced shipowners to use ships much below the average oceangoing tonnage of the period.[9] But it is more likely that the optimal size for slave trading before 1850 was also close to the optimal size for escaping the navy's clutches or, alternatively, that tonnages would have been the same without any attempt to suppress the trade. As for risk aversion, the widespread use of joint stock companies in this period made the use of small ships for this purpose unnecessary.

Change over time, nevertheless, did occur. But before exploring this we should note that the typical unit employed in most branches of oceangoing shipping increased in size steadily from the late eighteenth century on. As a result the gap between the average slave ship and other oceangoing vessels increased considerably in the century before 1850. Douglass C. North has attributed the general rise in ship size (and the improved efficiency associated with it) to the suppression of piracy and the growth of markets and market organization that reduced the number of voyages made in ballast. Figure 5 shows time profiles for three major branches of the nineteenth-century slave traffic where the data are adequate, together with a series for ships not involved in the slave trade. Apart from the small size of the slave ship relative to the nonslaver, the dominating feature of figure 5 is the secular increase in the size of the typical slave ship, which began in the late 1840s in all branches of the trade. In the Cuba-West African case the typical slave ships of the 1860s were more than double the size of their early 1840s predecessors. Thus the slave-ship trend in this major branch of the slave trade moved belatedly with the trend in general shipping. There would seem to be two explanations for the increasing size of slave ships, both of which are linked somewhat indirectly to efforts to suppress the trade.

First, there was the increasing spread between slave prices in Africa and the Americas that tended to make slave cargoes more valuable. From the early nineteenth century it became feasible to carry high-value freight and passengers in clipper-type sailing vessels. And from midcentury increasingly larger versions of the clipper as well as the steamship became available.[10] Both the new clipper and the steamship tended to be larger than the typical slave ship. But neither of these vessel types came to dominate the slave trade. Right to the end

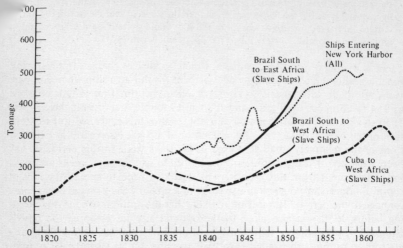

**Figure 5.** Time profiles of mean annual tonnage of ships in major branches of the transatlantic slave trade and ships entering New York harbor, 1811–64.

a surprising variety of hulls and riggings were used. As noted later, voyage time, though faster than in previous centuries, was only moderately reduced during the nineteenth century.[11]

A second factor contributing to increasing ship size was improvements in market organization. In three centuries of transatlantic slave trading, the size of the average cargo varied very little. Even when larger ships appeared in both the French and English trade in the late eighteenth century, the mean number of slaves embarked scarcely changed.[12] The controlling factor was almost certainly the time taken to assemble a cargo; behind this lay constraints of market organization in Africa and perhaps ultimately demographic restraints. Even on the Gold Coast where large European forts and barracoons existed, ships took on average more than four months to acquire a full cargo.[13] For most African regions abolition was eventually imposed in the sense that ships that had previously come from the Americas for slaves, first came in fewer numbers and then stopped altogether. Slave exports tapered off first in Upper Guinea and the Bight of Biafra in the early 1840s, then in all regions after 1850 before ceasing altogether in 1867. During this last thirty years, but particularly after 1850, the supply of slaves was such that it was easier than before to assemble large number of Africans for quick embarkation.[14] As long as the cruisers did not interfere significantly with shore-based operations, abolition paradoxically meant improved market organization for those ships that did get through: Such ships could expect to procure a very large cargo in a short time. Naval reports contain many references to large ships embarking hundreds of slaves from crowded barracoons in this period.[15] Even in 1860, however, the average slave ship remained much smaller than its counterpart in other branches of long-distance commerce: The mean tonnage of ships entering New York harbor in that year was still almost double that of the typical West African slave ship.

Clearly, as in the eighteenth century, much larger ships could have been used if market conditions in the slave business had permitted.

It would thus appear that the process of trying to enforce abolition eventually increased the size of the ship used in the trade rather than reduced it. Yet the popular image of the illicit trade was not without foundation. As figure 6 shows, at the time that Buxton and Turnbull were writing their books and the Parliamentary committees of the 1840s were active, slave ships were smaller than both what they had been and were to become. Indeed in the late 1830s in the Cuban traffic and the early 1840s in the Brazilian trade, the typical vessel was probably smaller than its seventeenth-and eighteenth-century predecessors. It is curious that these were the years when the British squadron was at its most effective. Captures per ventures launched rose to the highest annual levels ever attained in the Cuban trade after the 1835 Anglo-Spanish equipment treaty. The same peak in the Brazilian case came after the 1839 act giving British courts jurisdiction over Portuguese slavers. Moreover, trends in both tonnage and capture ratios were temporary. It is thus possible that the short-run impact of British cruiser activity ran counter to its long-term effects. To this issue we shall return after examining trends in other shipping variables.

Slaves required supervision and control. Apart from the slave deck, the most obvious difference between a regular merchant ship and a slaver was the enormous crew carried by the latter. The nineteenth century was no exception. But here, too, attempts to suppress the traffic had unexpected effects. Figure 6 shows time profiles for tons per crew on ships trading from Cuba, Bahia and other Brazil North ports grouped together as well as Rio de Janeiro and its adjacent ports. Equivalent eighteenth-century rates such as the 7.5 tons per crew member recorded for English slave ships at Jamaica, 1782–86, and the 4.5 for Nantes slavers, 1763–77, were quite similar to those shown in figure 6 for the 1820s for all major slaving ports.[16] As with ship size, tons-per-crew ratios in the general shipping industry were much larger than those in the slave trade in the eighteenth century, and the gap between the two had widened by the early 1830s before closing slightly after 1850. The point is illustrated by the comment of the Portuguese consul in Havana in 1838 that slave ships "were manned at a rate of fifteen men for every ton as opposed to six for normal trading vessels."[17] Much of the nineteenth-century movement in tons per crew is, of course, explained by the increase in ship size. Larger ships could allocate more tons per man, and the rise in the ratio from the late 1840s is particularly marked. However, there is also a rising trend in the 1830s when the slave ships were actually declining in size. This trend was probably related to two factors. One was the security issue described by North in the general shipping business. Armaments carried on slave ships fell between the 1820s and 1840s, a tendency mirrored in the decline of violent clashes between the cruiser squadron and slave trader. The illicit trader increasingly depended more on subterfuge to escape the squadron, and, paradoxically, on the British squadron to keep pirates in check. Attempts to suppress the trade thus led to improved labor productivity, though it should be noted that as general maritime security was improving everywhere at this time, some rise in tons per crew might have occurred in the absence of the antislave-trade squadron.

A second possible factor pushing up the tons-per-crew ratio was the increas-

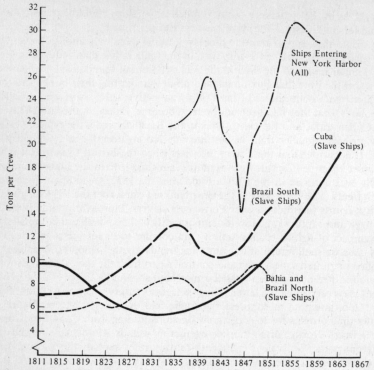

**Figure 6.** Time profiles of mean annual tons per crew, major branches of the transatlantic slave trade and ships entering New York harbor, 1811–66.

ing number of children entering the trade. Children likely made up a greater share of nineteenth-century cargoes than those of earlier periods; in addition, the child ratio steadily increased after 1810. After 1850 children made up 40 percent of cargoes and adult women a further 15 percent.[18] Fewer crew members would, of course, be required to control a young cargo. The higher child ratios should also be reflected in fewer slave uprisings. Although it is difficult to test statistically, it seems likely that slave risings were more common before 1810 than after. Of the 602 slave ships taken with slaves on board, no instances of rebellion on the voyage prior to capture were reported, though admittedly many were taken within a few days of departure. Among other slavers only a half dozen recorded cases of revolt have been uncovered.[19] Shackles were carried but naval officers commented more often on their lack of use than their use.[20] Of course, if mortality and presumably morbidity were higher in the nineteenth century than in earlier times, this in itself should have made slaves easier to control. Slave traders however appear to have had more problems in their land-based establishments than on board ship. But even here the reported incidents are not numerous.[21] The standard accounts of earlier phases of the trade give slave uprising rather more prominence than could be justified from the nineteenth-century evidence.[22]

Fewer shipboard rebellions might also be explained, in part, by the shorter voyage. In general Africans spent less time on the middle passage after 1810 than they had in earlier centuries. Indeed given the change in embarkation procedures, they spent much less time in the hold of the slave ship. There is little doubt that unlike the general oceangoing freight and passenger business, travel time between Africa and the Americas declined between the eighteenth and first half of the nineteenth centuries. Prerevolutionary French ships averaged over sixty days on the middle passage, whereas the smaller Rhode Island ships were still averaging seventy days from the Gold Coast to Charleston, S.C., in the last years of the legal trade.[23] Table 6 shows times for some equivalent routes in the nineteenth century together with Klein's figure for Jamaican-bound slavers from the 1790s. The data suggest a decline of 25 percent, or from eight weeks' duration to six, for a typical slave-ship voyage.

**Table 6.** Voyage Time from Africa to the Americas in Major Branches of the Slave Trade, 1791–1863 (in days)

|  |  | Mean | SD | Number |
|---|---|---|---|---|
| (1) Lower Guinea[a] to Jamaica | 1791–98 | 66.6 | — | 74 |
| (2) Bights of Benin and Biafra to the Caribbean | 1811–40 | 50.9 | 14.2 | 8 |
|  | 1841–63 | 46.9 | 11.7 | 11 |
|  | 1811–63 | 48.6 | 12.6 | 19 |
| (3) Bights of Benin and Biafra to Bahia | 1811–15 | 41.1* | 12.3 | 70 |
|  | 1821–30 | 30.2 | 7.4 | 34 |
|  | 1836–40 | 34.1 | 9.4 | 10 |
|  | 1841–45 | 32.0 | 7.6 | 13 |
|  | 1846–51 | 27.8 | 6.7 | 14 |

*Significantly different from the 1836–40 mean at the 10 percent level.

| (4) West-central Africa to Brazil South | 1821–25 | 37.3 | 7.3 | 35 |
|---|---|---|---|---|
|  | 1826–30 | 33.7* | 8.0 | 334 |
|  | 1836–40 | 36.9 | 13.1 | 48 |
|  | 1841–50 | 31.5 | 9.0 | 7 |

*Significantly different from 1821–25 mean at the 10 percent level.

| (5) Southeast Africa to Brazil South | 1821–25 | 70.8* | 16.7 | 28 |
|---|---|---|---|---|
|  | 1826–30 | 61.4 | 12.3 | 84 |
|  | 1836–51 | 64.5 | 13.4 | 13 |

*Significantly different from the 1826–30 mean at the 10 percent level.

Note: [a]Lower Guinea is defined as Gold Coast, Bight of Benin and Bight of Biafra.

Sources: Slave ship data set except for Lower Guinea to Jamaica where data are calculated from Herbert ?. Klein, The Middle Passage (Princeton, N.J. 1978), p. 157.

Within the nineteenth century, on the other hand, passage times did not change much. Where change is apparent it correlates not at all with suppression and thus the actual data provide little grounding for the popular image of the trade. For the Bahian as well as both branches of the Rio de Janeiro traffic, minor declines occurred in the 1811–20 and 1821–30 decades. For Bahia this trend was established after British cruiser activity began; in the two Rio cases this trend preceded effective British action by several years. Only the drop in the Bahia figure can be described as anything but modest, and indeed it is in the Bahian branch of the traffic that the most sophisticated sailing vessels were reported.[24] Ships in the last two decades of the traffic, though swifter than the slavers in earlier centuries, were not traveling much faster than their pre-suppression nineteenth-century counterparts. Quantitative evidence on hull design is scarce, but naval reports suggest that the rounded, deep, slow-sailing British merchantman design encouraged by pre-1854 ship-measurement rules was replaced early in the nineteenth century by the finer lines of early clipper-type ships. Even in the 1820s most ships in the Cuban traffic and a little later in the Bahian traffic were being constructed specially for the slave trade in the United States and in the Iberian peninsula.[25] Steamers appeared briefly in the Rio trade in the late 1840s and between the Bight of Benin and Cuba in the 1860s. But in neither branch were there sufficient numbers to affect mean voyage lengths very much.[26] In neither the Cuban nor Brazil South traffic did the specialized feluccas of the Bahia trade, built in Oporto, come to dominate.[27] The basic point remains that differences between the eighteenth- and nineteenth-century traffic are more important than those between slavers sailing before and after the British Navy began to intervene. For high-value perishable cargoes, improved sailing times were possible from the beginning of the nineteenth century and this development would have occurred even in the absence of the British cruisers.

But traveling took up a relatively small part of the total time spent on a slaving expedition. Acquisition of slaves in all periods could normally take longer than two crossings of the Atlantic, and this was probably a factor controlling the size of ship used. In the eighteenth-century, round-trip voyage times for Rhode Island slave ships were in the nine- to twelve-month range, which after adjusting for a longer homeward voyage was comparable to those reported for French and English traders.[28] For such expeditions time spent on the African coast must have accounted for over half of total trip time. Table 7 shows round-trip voyage time for various branches of the nineteenth-century traffic. After making an allowance for the shorter nineteenth-century passage times, it is clear that ships in the 1820s and early 1830s spent as much time on the coast trading for slaves as their eighteenth-century predecessors. Significant reductions in turnaround time began for Bahia ships in the 1820s, and for ships based in Cuba and Brazil South about a decade later. By the early 1840s slave ships were returning to Cuba with cargoes in less than six months and to Brazilian ports in less than four months on average.

It is unlikely that conditions in Africa as a whole can explain this trend, though local variations in supply would certainly affect the time taken to assemble a cargo. Rather, the explanation seems to lie in the improved organization of the slave traders. Not only did the larger Cuban- and Brazilian

**Table 7.**  Duration of Round Trip Slaving Expeditions in Major Branches of the Slave Trade to West Africa, 1791–1861 (in days)

| Port of Clearing | | Mean in Days | SD | Number of Expeditions |
|---|---|---|---|---|
| English ports[a] | 1791–98 | 260.0 | — | 187 |
| Havana | 1821–25 | 208.7 | 59.1 | 33 |
| | 1826–30 | 220.4 | 65.1 | 87 |
| | 1831–35 | 216.3 | 58.6 | 125 |
| | 1836–40[b] | 224.9 | 76.0 | 69 |
| | 1841–45 | 178.2* | 70.8 | 9 |
| | 1846–61 | 151.2* | 45.2 | 23 |

*Significantly different from the 1831–35 mean at the 10 percent level.

| | | | | |
|---|---|---|---|---|
| Bahia | 1821–22 | 231.4* | 52.5 | 30 |
| | 1829–30 | 128.2 | 39.2 | 27 |
| | 1841–50 | 92.2* | 32.5 | 15 |

*Significantly different from the 1829–30 mean at the 10 percent level.

| | | | | |
|---|---|---|---|---|
| Brazil South ports | 1837–38 | 229.7 | 57.8 | 27 |
| | 1839–40 | 190.5* | 46.8 | 18 |
| | 1846–50 | 106.8* | 20.1 | 5 |

*Significantly different from the 1837–38 mean at the 10 percent level.

*Notes:* [a]Includes only the journey from England to Jamaica via the African coast. [b]May include some voyages to Southeast Africa.

*Sources:* Slave-ship data set except for row 1 where data are from Herbert S. Klein, *The Middle Passage* (Princeton, N.J. 1978), p. 157; and row 8 where data are from Pierre Verger, *Flux et reflux de la traite des nègres entre le golfe de Bénin et Bahia de Todos os Santos* (Paris, 1968), pp. 660–61.

based traders begin to operate their own factories on the coast in the later 1830s but they also began to supply these establishments with trade goods freighted by ships other than slavers. These cargo ships often sailed under flags less susceptible to British interference.[29] Some traders developed sufficiently sophisticated operations to permit slave ships to leave the Americas only when the slave cargo was expected to be ready. The cost of transporting the trading cargo was of course increased enormously, but lower slave-ship costs and reduced ship captures obviously made it worthwhile. What this meant for the slave was more time spent in the barracoon than in earlier phases of the traffic. This was certainly preferable to confinement in a three- or four foot high slave deck, but the epidemiological environment and, therefore, the mortality rate was probably little different. These trends were probably the clearest consequence of British intervention, but they became general only thirty years after suppression began.

But what of the space available for each slave that traditionally has been measured by the slave-per-ton ratio trends? Pre-1830 nineteenth-century slaver-per-ton ratios were not much different from those in the eighteenth-century French and British trades, though variations around the mean were probably greater in the later period.[30] Neither were there significant differences between exporting or between importing regions. Ratios of 2.0–2.5 commonly appear in all branches of the trade and for all periods. Sharp and temporary increases

‿ the 3.0–3.5 ratio range occurred in the 1830s for the bights of Benin and Biafra and in 1841–45 in west-central Africa. But as the former supplied mainly Cuba at this time and the latter the Brazil South region, the increase was no doubt associated with increased British pressure and the temporary move to smaller ships already noted for these importing regions. In the last twenty years of the trade, slave-per-ton ratios returned to their previous levels, though the ships were by then larger.

An alternative and more vivid indicator of space is provided by the actual dimensions of the few prize ships that the British navy measured when it could not get the captured ship into port for adjudication. From 1839 to 1852, there were 104 such ships—most captured without slaves—that measured on average 82.9 feet in length, 21.6 feet across at the broadest point and 11.8 feet in depth. Because cargoes averaged 350 to 400 slaves, deck space per slave must have been close to 4 square feet. The depth of these vessels further suggests that the height of the slave deck must have been less than the 5.5 feet required for North Atlantic free-migrant shipping by the weakest of the nineteenth-century Passenger Acts. The act of 1799, which regulated the British slave trade until its abolition eight years later, specified 5.0 feet as the minimum height. After 1852 a small sample of 23 ships yields dimensions of 97.0 feet in length, 23.2 feet in width and 12.3 in depth, though it might be noted that the tonnage data for the post-1852 period (based on a larger sample) suggest a somewhat larger mean size. However, the mean cargo also increased, which meant that deck space per slave increased only slightly if at all. These areas probably differed little from those in earlier phases of the traffic except for the last years of the British trade after the passage of Dolben's Act.[31]

It is hard to find any parallels to such conditions in the history of long-distance transportation, particularly when we note that about 10 percent of all slave ships dispensed with a slave deck altogether and stowed slaves directly on water casks covered with hides or mats.[32] The contemporary North Atlantic immigrant ship was required to provide twelve square feet per passenger by British law and fourteen by U.S. regulations. A Boeing 747 passenger aircraft by comparison provides about twelve square feet per person in an economy class configuration. Clearly the occupant of the typical slave ship could neither lie full length nor stand upright for five weeks except for the limited time spent above deck each day. However, the impact of suppression on these conditions was probably fairly limited.

For most observers, nineteenth and twentieth century alike, the most emotive issue on the middle passage was not the space provided, but rather the mortality experienced in that space, although for many the two issues were obviously linked. Table 8 shows mortality adjusted for voyage lengths for selected long-distance routes in both slave and passenger traffics. Three broad points may be made with some certainty. First, slave-trade mortality was as high or higher in the nineteenth century than it had been in earlier centuries. Second, mortality was always higher in the slave trade than in other long-distance traffic, including others in which coercion was involved. Third, the differential between the slave and nonslave traffics increased over time. It is also clear that mortality increased over the course of the nineteenth century and

**Table 8.** Mean Daily Mortality Rates ($\times$ 1,000) on Selected Long-Distance Routes, 1680–1863

| Nationality of Carrier | Route | Years | Daily Mortality Rate (number of voyages) | |
|---|---|---|---|---|
| **Slave Trade** | | | | |
| Holland | West Africa/Caribbean | 1680–1749 | 2.25 | (161) |
| Holland | West Africa/Caribbean | 1740–95 | 2.38 | (119) |
| France | West Africa/Caribbean | 1715–56 | 1.86 | (na) |
| France | West Africa/Caribbean | 1756–? | 1.56 | (na) |
| Britain | West Africa/Caribbean | 1791–97 | 1.01 | (346) |
| Various | West Africa/Americas | 1811–36 | 1.81 | (512) |
| Various | West Africa/Americas | 1837–63 | 3.25 | (136) |
| **Nonslave trade** | | | | |
| Holland | Holland/Cape of Good Hope | 1730s | 0.77 | (73) |
| Holland | Batavia/Holland | 1730s | 0.29 | (11) |
| Britain | England/Australia (convicts) | 1787–1800 | 0.54 | (41) |
| Britain | Calcutta/Caribbean | 1850–61 | 0.40 | (na) |
| Various | Europe/New York | 1836–53 | 0.39 | (1,077) |

*Sources:* Calculated from Raymond L. Cohn, "Comparative Mortality Experiences on Sailing Voyages," unpublished ms., 1982; David Eltis, "Mortality and Voyage Length in the Middle Passage: New Evidence from the Nineteenth Century," *Journal of Economic History,* 44(1984):301–8; Herbert S. Klein and Stanley L. Engerman, "Slave Mortality on British Ships, 1791–1797," in Roger T. Anstey and P.E.H. Hair (eds.), *Liverpool, the African Slave Trade, and Abolition: Essays to Illustrate Current Knowledge and Research* (Liverpool, Eng., 1976), pp. 116, 118; Johannes Postma, "Mortality in the Dutch Slave Trade 1675–1795," in H. A. Gemery and J. S. Hogendorn (eds.), *The Uncommon Market: Essays in the Economic History of the Atlantic Slave Trade* (New York, 1979), p. 251; James C. Riley, "Mortality on Long-Distance Voyages in the Eighteenth Century," *Journal of Economic History,* 41 (1981):652, 655; Robert Louis Stein, "Mortality in the Eighteenth Century French Slave Trade," *Journal of African History,* 21 (1980):35–41; Hugh Tinker, *A New System of Slavery: The Export of Indian Labour Overseas, 1830–1920* (London, 1974), pp. 154, 162.

that there were very marked differences in rates between African regions of embarkation. Explanations for some of these trends are clearer than for others. The variations over time within the slave trade as well as the differences between African regions are probably best explained by the African epidemiological environment. This in turn was strongly influenced by the fluctuations in rainfall and harvesting patterns, both seasonal and over a period of years. It is also possible that related factors might account for some of the large differences between the slave and nonslave trades in all periods. Prior to embarkation African slaves were held in a more epidemiologically hostile and less nutritionally secure environment than other migrant groups represented in Table 8. There might also be a connection between high and rising mortality rates and the high proportion of children carried in the nineteenth-century traffic. Children were particularly susceptible to the diarrheal diseases which accounted for most deaths on board ship and in the coastal barracoons.[33]

There is little in the nineteenth-century evidence to show that changes in the shipboard treatment of slaves explain much of variations in the rate at which slaves died. As in earlier periods, tight packing of slaves—roughly measured by the slave-per-ton ratio—explains little of the variation in daily mortality rates. Moreover, if provisioning the slave ship had been a key determinant of mortality, rates should have been higher on voyages of exceptional length where the route and the slave-per-ton ratios were the same. The evidence of this is at best mixed, whether we use the daily mortality rate or deaths as a percentage of slaves embarked.[34] In addition, we should note that factors controlled by the slave trader or slaver captain cannot explain the very large interregional differentials that are apparent in the nineteenth century. Mortality on ships leaving the Bight of Benin was in some quinquennia not much different from that on nonslave trade routes. Rates from the adjacent Bight of Biafra and from the Congo North region after 1836 were, on the other hand, two or three times higher. Attempts to suppress the trade certainly changed the behavior of slave traders but probably had a small impact on mortality among the slaves. One factor of potential importance that cannot be measured is the probable deleterious consequences of holding slaves in barracoons for long periods. The evidence of rainfall and harvest patterns suggests that British naval disruptions of normal slave shipping schedules could have had a serious effect on the rate at which slaves died.

It is thus apparent that the main physical parameters of the slave trade changed little in the nineteenth century. If Ottabah Cugoano, Oludah Equiano or Zachary Macaulay had made their transatlantic slaving voyage in the 1840s instead of the 1750s and 1790s, they would not have found much that was different. The former two would have spent more time in the coastal barracoons and less on the middle passage and there may have been more children around. Although the ship may have been a better sailer, it would not have been noticeably larger, provided any more deck space nor would the slaves on board have experienced lower mortality. After 1850 ship sizes increased and the crew was proportionately much smaller, but steamships remained uncommon enough not to have fallen within the experience of the typical slave. An eighteenth century slaver captain would have found it much easier to assume command of a nineteenth-century slaver than would his nonslaving counterpart in some other type of oceangoing shipping business.

It follows that the impact of suppression on the observable physical variables, confined as it was to the nineteenth century, cannot have been very great either. The financial implications of these trends as well as others in the slave traders' calculus—for example, wages, insurance and depreciation—are another matter (see app. E). But in the movements surveyed both here and in appendix E, naval intervention brought clear and major disruption to the expected pattern in the case of only two variables: the time the slave ship spent on the African coast and insurance rates. Even then the effect came late. In addition, there were two temporary effects on slaves-per-ton carried, which increased, and perhaps ship size, which decreased. Slave mortality may have also been affected. As the British increased the pressure after 1835, the slave trader temporarily introduced smaller, faster ships and packed more slaves into each ship and sent outbound cargoes to the coast separately. These may be viewed as efforts to offset more numerous captures and the resulting higher insurance rates.

The major effect of the cruisers was, in fact, on profits (treated as a residual in app. E). Even here, it seems that much of the higher profits were due to increased risk arising from the activities of the government authorities in Brzil and Cuba rather than naval activity. Profits in slave trading were at lea. double and at the very end of the traffic were perhaps six or seven times levels calculated from large samples in the eighteenth-century trade. Profits probably exceeded what they would have been in the nineteenth century in the absence of suppressive measures by the same proportion. Before 1850 most of these extra profits can be attributed to the increased risk resulting from naval activities, though in the last ten years of the trade the actions of the Spanish and Cuban governments became the dominant risk-creating factor.

These financial considerations may seem removed from the general experience of the African deportee, but they are crucial to an evaluation of the second major issue raised at the beginning of this chapter. So far we have considered the impact of suppression on those Africans who were unfortunate enough to enter the trade. But what was the impact on those that did not go? In Palmerston's term, how many did suppression save from slavery in the Americas? In chapter 3 we have already attempted a crude estimate down to the 1820s for the broadest of all conceptions of the impact of abolition: How many Africans would have been carried across the Atlantic if all countries had continued to support the trade? There seems little point in continuing such an estimate beyond the 1820s, if only because the imponderables destroy any possibility of precision. In the absence of African demographic constraints, however, it is worth pointing out that the pace of nineteenth-century North Atlantic economic development could only have greatly expanded the slave trade to several times what it actually was. Slaves would have been much cheaper and more intensively used in a wide range of occupations. Brazil, the country closest to Africa and with the lowest cost slaves—at least before 1851—also had the most thoroughgoing slave economy in the Americas, with the possible exception of the plantation islands. Forced African immigration into the Americas would have continued in excess of free European immigration for most of the nineteenth century and perhaps most of the 50 million or so arrivals in the Americas in the century after 1820 would have been African slaves, not free Europeans.

It is somewhat easier to assess the consequences of less sweeping conceptions of abolition and suppression. Given the inception and effective enforcement of abolition of the slave trade to British, French, U.S., Dutch and Danish possessions, what were the likely effects of the naval and diplomatic campaign to suppress the traffic to the remainder of the Americas? As the navy's effect was chiefly on shipping and factor costs and as diplomacy had its major impact on the distribution of slaves in the Americas, the question may be conveniently divided into two parts, both of which may be tackled with the aid of elementary demand-and-supply analysis. Without the navy slave prices in the importing regions of the Americas would have been between 5 and 10 percent lower after 1820 and approximately 213,000 additional slaves would have been carried across the Atlantic. This constitutes a 10 percent increase in total volume. If we confine the analysis to those branches and periods of the traffic over which the navy had jurisdiction, then the naval impact on volume rises to 15 percent. This is not, however, a very large figure relative to the perceptions of contemporary defenders of naval intervention.[35]

Yet, as noted, the impact of the navy was not the same as the impact of abolition. A large part of the increased prices for slaves after 1807 came from higher distribution costs. As these were incurred after disembarkation, they cannot be attributed to the activities of the cruiser squadron. We have attempted earlier to assign responsibility for these higher costs to the moral or ideological effect of abolition operating, in part, through diplomacy. The major components of distribution costs were selling commissions, bribes to officials where imports were illegal and credit charges (the details are taken up in app. E). Distribution costs rose during the nineteenth century, but as other costs also increased, there was little movement in the distribution-cost share of total costs. Bribes tended to increase during the period and depended directly on the attitude of the governing authorities in the importing region. As governments changed so did slave-trade policy; but even when official tolerance of the trade was at its greatest, the importing government's public policy was always hostile to the traffic and de facto cooperation had to be purchased. Naval strategy usually had little impact on fluctuations in policy, but British diplomatic and ideological pressure was of considerable importance.

In Cuba the government of Spain faced the dilemma of "satisfying British demands without prejudicing Cuban planter interest."[36] The Spanish penal law of 1845 constituted the first domestic (as opposed to treaty) proscription of the slave trade, apart from the ineffective royal cédula of 1817. Provided for originally in the 1835 treaty, it was promulgated only after ten years of British reminders and protests. Official Hispanic initiatives against the slave trade in the form of stricter enforcement of the slave-trade treaties by the Cuban captain-general had taken place a few years previously, between 1841 and 1843. But both Captain-General Gerónimo Valdes's activities in this period and the subsequent penal law were responses to the threat of British abolition policy, and it is hard to visualize either taking place in the absence of that pressure.[37] The slave trade, of course, continued for another quarter century after these initiatives. Indeed the 1845 law provided some extra security for the traffic by prohibiting official pursuits of suspected *bozales* onto plantations. The basic point is that government policy increased the price that slave traders paid for official cooperation and thus forced up distribution costs. To a degree, therefore, Spanish attitudes even before the 1841–46 period must have reduced imports, and moves during and after that period reduced them by even more.

In Brazil an antislave trade and anti-Portuguese movement—it was often hard to separate the two—did exist. Liberal ministries included individuals hostile to the slave traders, such as Francisco de Montezuma and Antônio Francisco de Paula e Holanda Cavalcanti. Such governments held power periodically, noticeably in the few years after the entire traffic became illegal in 1830. Criminal sanctions against the trade existed from November 1831 and, though constitutional restrictions on the power of the central government reduced their effect, both these sanctions and the periodic changes in ministries would tend to raise the cost of evading the law.[38] The British influence over distribution costs here was both more direct and more subtle than in colonial Cuba. Increasing the abolitionist inclinations of politicians, newspapers, customs officials and judges with payments out of the Secret Service Fund raised the stakes for the slave trader. But there is also no doubt that the process of ideological emulation so close to the hearts of Palmerston and the British abolitionists did occur to some extent. The issue is taken up in chapters 7 and 12, but clearly it contributed to the firm Brazilian moves to suppress the trade in the early 1850s, and it also had raised the costs of selling newly imported slaves in the twenty preceding years. The intriguing question is how far was it influenced by those payments from the Secret Service Fund. Such influences are difficult to quantify. It seems unlikely, however, that the importation of slaves into either Brazil or Cuba would have been significantly restricted without British diplomatic and ideological pressure, at least before the U.S. Civil War.

Once more we can form an estimate of the effect of this pressure with demand-and-supply analysis. If slave traders had not been forced to risk imprisonment and confiscation of property at the hands of the authorities of the importing region and if they had not been required to pay bribes and disembark slaves at remote areas of the coast, it seems likely that slave prices in the Americas would have been 1 to 2 percent lower before 1850 and probably much lower thereafter. The volume of slaves carried would have been only 5 percent or so greater before 1850 and significantly greater in the last decade of the traffic.[39]

The sum of these two impacts is the total effect on the trade resulting from British attempts to suppress it. For most of the period, then, prices of slaves in the Americas would have been only 8 to 11 percent lower without British naval, ideological and diplomatic pressure. As noted in chapter 1, prices in Cuba in the 1830s would have been only slightly higher than Jamaican prices in the 1790s.[40] The price impact was probably much greater in the last years of the trade. In terms of volume the British effort prevented the shipping of no more than 290,000 Africans between 1807 and 1850. This represents about 19 percent of the volume of slaves carried in that part of the traffic over which the British had some treaty rights, either actual or assumed. The figure constitutes only 12 percent of all slaves carried across the Atlantic between 1807 and 1850. These ratios are not very great in view of the resources employed. As we have seen, the value of the British commitment to suppression in the sixty years after 1807 was comparable to that which had gone into supporting the trade in the same period before that year. In the sixty years after 1750 the British had been responsible for between 40 and 50 percent of the Africans carried to the New World. After 1807 the reduction that the British managed to bring about was only a fraction of this ratio.

Such a comparison is misleading for two reasons. If the British had left the trade in 1750 instead of 1807, it is inconceivable that other carriers would not have taken their place. The volume of the traffic would have been only slightly lower than it actually was. Second, although the Foreign Office struggled unsuccessfully against the trade for much of the nineteenth century, complete suppression, when it was finally effected, must be credited largely to British efforts. Ultimately the British impact on the volume of the trade was extremely high, and, as for prices, much of the sharp increase in slave values that occurred during and after final suppression must also be credited to British antislave-trade policy. Nevertheless, as an indication of the barriers that policy had to surmount, the above estimates have some value.

Finally in the assessment of impacts, we should note that not all British actions after 1807 inhibited the slave trade. The goods and credit that the slave traders used to obtain their slaves were largely British. British credit, in particular, was cheaper than in other countries. If slave traders had been denied access to British goods, their costs would have been increased and the quantity of slaves carried across the Atlantic would have been less. A detailed study of the British contribution to the traffic (as it may be styled) suggests that without it the volume of the traffic would have been a minimum of 5 percent less. The British contribution thus had much less of an impact than their attempts to suppress the trade. But what is ultimately more important than the relative size of these estimates is the differences between British respect for domestic law, on the one hand, and international law, on the other. It was noted earlier that the British found it impossible to prevent their own subjects from indirectly participating in the slave trade without interdicting much of British trade with Africa. At the very least the British might have supported the actions of their naval officers against the most flagrant instances of such behavior. This they refused to do.[41] As chapter 7 indicates, however, they were much less meticulous in their adherence to international law as it related to slave-trade matters.

This argument indeed leads back to a major theme of earlier chapters. The British actions that triggered both final suppression and the changes in slaver tactics that preceded it were highly questionable by the ideological standards of the British themselves. The British, in fact, were at their most effective in tackling the slave trade when their actions were most questionable. In the Bahia trade, the major effective British initiatives came chronologically in 1811–12 when the squadron followed the abolitionists' interpretation of the 1810 and 1815 Anglo-Portuguese conventions and detained large numbers of Bahian ships.[42] The treaties of 1817 and 1826, which are customarily given a major role in ending the Brazilian trade, seem of less significance in the context of the trends in shipping characteristics examined above. This is probably because the 1817 treaty was restricted in application and that of 1826 applied only to the Brazilian flag. A second key initiative, also against the Bahian traffic, came in 1827 when the *Heroina* was condemned at Sierra Leone for sailing north of the equator in breach of a Brazilian passport, which required the ship to trade only to the south. The *Heroina* and most of the thirty-or-so Bahian ships subsequently condemned in the next three years on the strength of this decision had no slaves on board despite the fact that the 1817 treaty made this a prerequisite of condemnation.[43]

The first significant move against the Cuban branch also involved slave ships without a slave cargo. The 1835 Anglo-Spanish convention provided for the condemnation and breakup of ships equipped for the trade as well as those caught with slaves on board. The slave-trader response, apparent by the end of 1836, was to use the Portuguese flag. The counteraction of the Sierra Leone Court of Mixed Commission to this ploy came in 1838 when—at the initiative of British commissary judge H. W. Macaulay (son of Zachary)—the court began to judge the national character of a vessel according to the owner's place of residence rather than the owner's nationality.[44] Thus the Cuban traffic was subjected to a double blow, broadly measured by large increases in court business in the last six months of 1836 and the latter part of 1838. In a lengthy despatch written in October 1836, Charles Tolmé, the British consul in Havana as well as business associate of the slave merchants, accurately predicted developments in the Cuban traffic. The slave traders, he wrote, intend

> (1) to establish more factories on the Coast of Africa and there to have a constant supply of slaves and of articles for . . . equipment, (2) to send out all those articles and whatever may be required for bartering against slaves by foreign, in preference American ships, (3) to send their slave vessels in ballast . . . (4) to send much smaller vessels than heretofore . . . (5) to send three or more [ships] to load in the same place, (6) to avail themselves of the Portuguese flag.[45]

Underwriters, he noted, were still not certain of the success of these devices.

The equivalent to the 1835 treaty for the traffic of Brazil was the 1839 act of parliament that, in effect, applied the terms of that treaty to Brazilian-bound ships. It allowed British cruisers to stop and search Portuguese ships and, if specified slave-trading equipment was found on board, to take the ships before British Vice-Admiralty courts, which courts were empowered to confiscate cargoes and to breakup the ship. Six years later a similar measure was applied to ships using either the Brazilian flag or no flag at all.[46] At the same time naval attacks on shore-based slaving establishments, which had been rare since the disastrous initiatives of the governor of Sierra Leone in the pre-1816 period, temporarily reemerged as a major tactic in the early 1840s. Captain Denman's well-known assault on the eight Gallinas factories in November 1840 was merely the first of half a dozen such attacks on the West African littoral in the next eighteen months.[47]

The effect of all these British moves may be seen in the shipping trends discussed earlier. In the Bahia traffic, round-trip voyages were much shorter in 1827–30 than at the beginning of the decade, and it is significant that this same trend was not apparent in the other branches of the traffic until they, too, felt the impact of naval action in the following decade. Information on the 1811–15 quinquennium is scarcer, but the small ship size and more important the high insurance rates in the Bahia trade of these years are suggestive. In the Cuban traffic the fall in time spent on the coast, changes in insurance rates, ship size and slaves-per-ton carried are all apparent after the equipment clause in the 1835 treaty as well as the shift in the definition of ownership nationality in 1838. For the large traffic to Brazil South, the behavior of these key variables indicates that the period of pressure began as we would expect about five years later. As the Rio de Janeiro trade had always been conducted south of the equator, it was completely untouched by the British initiatives against the Bahian business in 1812, 1816 and 1827. The pre-1826 Anglo-Portuguese conventions applied mainly to trade north of the equator, and it was not until the formal abolition of all the Brazilian trade in 1830 that suppression began to affect the Rio de Janeiro slave traders.

Generally, shipping costs changed much less than the physical variables such as ship displacement, tons per crew, and so on. Extensive establishments on the African coast, the dispatch of outbound trading cargoes in separate ships (often under the cover of the American or Sardinian flag) as well as bribes all increased costs. But the cost increases were limited by slave-trader adjustments to loading ratios and perhaps the use of faster ships. There was also the beneficial but unforeseen side effects of British policy such as increased freedom from piracy. The basic point is that costs could be driven up to the point where the slave trade would cease only if the governments of the importing and exporting regions undertook major suppressive actions of their own. Such actions took effect largely through increasing distribution costs. Here also the British actions, which stimulated effective Cuban and Brazilian intervention against the trade, were mostly illegal. In Cuba the activities of Turnbull and Cocking, though exaggerated by the Cuban authorities, had much to do with the Valdes policy and the eventual passing of the penal law in 1845. Eventually distribution costs, in particular bribes, rose far more than shipping costs. In Brazil British relations with governments and individuals opposed to slave-trader interests were quite simply corrupt. The extent of the corruption increased in the late 1840s and early 1850s, and that it did not show up in large increases in distribution costs in the accounts of the last years of the Brazilian slave trade is explained by its very effectiveness. Within two years of the establishment of Hudson's extended system of bribery and of the British invasion of Brazilian territorial waters, the trade had virtually ended. The British could thus have a serious impact on the slave trade only if they broke or at least stretched the international and maritime law that they themselves had done so much to create. Such law was, of course, an integral part of the economic system that they were attempting to foster and impose on the rest of the world.

Of the British initiatives that changed the behavior of the slave traders after 1807, only the 1835 equipment treaty with Spain could bear close examination in the light of nineteenth-century conceptions of international law and justice. The fiasco of interpreting and enforcing the 1810 treaty has already been explored. Compensation payments and the loss of abolitionist prestige alike were considerable. The treatment of Brazilian passports stemming from the 1827 Sierre Leone decision was approved by the Crown's law officers, but it is hard to see how any strict interpretation of the 1817 treaty could support the condemnation of Portuguese vessels without slaves on board. A Foreign Office memo of 1828 referred to the misgiving of the law officers on the subject, "The Kings' Advocate . . . feels an exceeding difficulty in defending on the terms of the treaty now in force [the 1817 Anglo-Portuguese treaty] the cases of capture which have taken place by Cruizers and of Judgments which have been passed by the commissioners . . . and which are now appealed against by the Brazilian minister."[48] As noted in chapter 6, both the 1839 and 1845 acts giving British cruisers and courts powers over Portuguese and Brazilian shipping were justified in terms of treaty violations that traditionally were casus belli, but these were essentially pretexts. Portugal had never undertaken to abolish the traffic south of the line, which was the target of the 1839 act, and the Brazilian interpretation of the 1826 treaty seems no weaker than the British once we remove the latter from the ideological glare of abolitionism. Thus, whether we measure shipping trends, the price and volume of slaves in the traffic, or, as in chapter 6, the capture of slave ships, we might conclude that whatever damaging effect the British did have on the slave trade after 1807 would have been largely nullified if they had abided by their own laws and their own precedents governing behavior between nations.

# 9

## The Slave-Trading Firm Under Suppression

Early in 1859 a crew of Spaniards and Portuguese, who had traveled the 250 miles from London by rail, took possession of a newly built screw steamer, the *Wilhemina,* in the northeastern port of Hartlepool. They sailed it to Cadiz and then to the west coast of Africa where they acquired a cargo of slaves that was successfully disembarked in Cuba. In the course of the next four years this steamer, renamed the *Noc Daqui,* as well as other British-built steamships made several slaving voyages from Bight of Benin ports. Many of these were owned by a company or association based in Cuba and organized on joint stock principles. Its shares were traded in Havana, and it had professional managers and a chain of agents extending from New York to Quelimane in southeast Africa. Arrangements for embarking and paying for the slaves as well as the transport of management personnel were made with the aid of the fast West African mail-steamer service. The slaves brought to Cuba were sold to owners of *ingenios* who utilized the most sophisticated machinery available both inside and outside the mill. The sugar they produced was sold to countries in the van of economic and social development.[1]

It is indeed the modernity of this operation that constitutes its most striking feature. The world's most advanced industrialized country built the ship, provided the machinery for processing the sugar on which the slaves were employed and bought much of the end product. The slave-importing company was perhaps indistinguishable from its nonslaving counterparts carrying on business in Britain. The British, of course, abhorred the slave trade. In the absense of the abolition laws, many more of the phases of the operation just described might have been British, as indeed they had been over half a century earlier. Further insight into this symbiotic relationship between the slave trade and economic development may be provided by examining who these slave traders of the industrial age were and how different their behavior and outlook was from proprietors of British trading companies. What were the main characteristics of the business and industrial organization of slave-trading firms in the nineteenth century and how were they affected by attempts to suppress the traffic?

With the exception of Spain, every nation that held territory in the New World before 1800 participated in the slave trade, often with the aid of mercantilist restrictions on international competitors. Between two thirds and three quarters of all slave ships began their voyages in European ports. Although the British share of the trade had tended to increase, no nation predominated and the overall structure of the trade was highly competitive.[2] For most British firms slave trading was only one of a number of activities and, like most manufacturing and long-distance trading firms, such businesses generated much of their own investment funds or used credit extended by their suppliers to finance their activities. There were thus many alternative investment opportunities available and few barriers to entry into the industry. Moreover, until the 1780s the traffic had no moral connotations that distinguished it from any other line of business and might have influenced the decision to invest.[3]

At the turn of the eighteenth-century, trade to Brazil and Cuba was liberalized. But for abolition this would have made the Atlantic slave trade even more competitive. By the 1820s legal proscription, diplomatic maneuvers and naval activity had ensured, first, that the traffic was centered in the Americas and, second, that the Brazilian and Cuban trades were dominated by Spanish and Portuguese slave merchants. The port of origin and the intended region of disembarkation are known for fourteen hundred slave voyages that began after 1820. Table 9 indicates that 80 percent of these slave ships began their voyages in the regions where they intended to disembark slaves. Most, in fact, sailed from one of only three ports: Havana, Bahia and Rio de Janeiro or their vicinities. Some ships were built in European ports, particularly after 1830, but Europe collectively did not account for a significant share of total slave-ship clearances. Moreover, trading across the major branches of the traffic—for example, ships clearing from Havana to carry slaves to Brazil South—was unusual. Clearly the movement toward an internationally integrated transatlantic market for slaves (described in chap. 3) had aborted. The mercantilistic straitjacket had been replaced by other—and from the abolitionist viewpoint morally inspired—institutional restrictions. The chief among these by the mid-nineteenth century was not the activity of the British cruisers so much as the difficulties imposed by the authorities of the importing regions on the reception and distribution of the slaves.[4] Adjustments to these, which included bribery, tended to give a premium to the slave trader who resided in the region of importation.

The relocation of the industry left the world view of its major participants largely unaffected. Intellectuals and eventually even planters in Cuba were influenced by the free-labor ideology of Britain and the northern United States, but abolitionism had only a limited impact on Cuba as a whole, at least before 1850. Hostility to the slave trade was often expressed on the racial grounds of fear of Africanization of the island. In Brazil antislave-trade sentiment made greater headway, but its advance in all the slaveholding Americas was slow.

**Table 9.** Regions of Departure of Slave Voyages, 1821–67, by Region of Intended Disembarkation

| Region of Intended Disembarkation | Region of Origin | | | | | | |
|---|---|---|---|---|---|---|---|
| | Cuba | Bahia | South Brazil | Iberian Peninsula | United States | France and French Americas | Other |
| **Cuba** | | | | | | | |
| 1821–30 | 192 | 1 | 0 | 10 | 0 | 33 | 11 |
| 1831–40 | 405 | 8 | 0 | 23 | 0 | 0 | 17 |
| 1841–50 | 55 | 2 | 0 | 1 | 5 | 0 | 5 |
| 1851–67 | 61 | 0 | 0 | 7 | 43 | 0 | 2 |
| **1821–67** | **713** | **11** | **0** | **41** | **48** | **33** | **35** |
| **French Americas** | | | | | | | |
| 1821–30 | 0 | 0 | 0 | 0 | 1 | 28 | 6 |
| **Bahia region** | | | | | | | |
| 1821–30 | 0 | 88 | 2 | 0 | 0 | 1 | 3 |
| 1831–40 | 5 | 27 | 1 | 0 | 0 | 0 | 2 |
| 1841–50 | 0 | 116 | 3 | 1 | 0 | 0 | 1 |
| **1821–50** | **5** | **231** | **6** | **1** | **0** | **1** | **6** |
| **Brazil South** | | | | | | | |
| 1821–30 | 1 | 2 | 10 | 4 | 0 | 0 | 1 |
| 1831–40 | 0 | 0 | 103 | 1 | 0 | 0 | 2 |
| 1841–50 | 1 | 7 | 112 | 4 | 4 | 1 | 11 |
| **1821–50** | **2** | **9** | **225** | **9** | **4** | **1** | **14** |

*Source:* Slave-ship data set.

There were very few merchants, as opposed to politicians and intellectuals, like Leopoldo Muniz Barreto who believed that slavery and the slave trade were both wrong and less profitable than free labor.[5] The correspondence of the slave traders reveals no hint that the writers thought of the business of slave trading as either criminal or immoral. The dealers and their agents were in contact with their captives for a very short time and wrote of them with an impersonality rarely found on plantations. When the navy began to capture this correspondence along with slave cargoes, the writers simply substituted the term *packages* ("*bultos*" or *volumes*) for *slaves*. Sick slaves became *damaged packages*. Although this would not mislead naval officers, it might provide a pretext for acquittal in an appropriately stacked court of law. But the vital point is that such a small change in wording allows the uninitiated to read many pages of these letters without realizing that the main topic is, in fact, human beings.[6] Perhaps the commoditization of labor reached its most complete development in the Atlantic basin rather than in the industrializing cities of the West at this time. Yet the correspondents were in their own view no different from other merchants and acted according to values that they felt the majority of the community shared. It was this that separated the trade from most other trafficking in illicit substances.

Attempts to proscribe the traffic were interpreted as a British strategy to protect the West Indian colonies or to give British shipping a monopoly in African trade. The more obvious evils such as overcrowding and high mortality rates could be attributed to the impact of the cruiser patrols.[7] Thus the outrage at British actions in slave-trading communities stemmed from a clash of values as much as from the losses that the navy inflicted on these communities or on British affronts to Cuban and Brazilian sovereignty.[8] In such circles the ideological influence often flowed toward rather than from the British, as British merchants in Havana, Bahia and Rio tended to adopt the attitudes of the commercial environment. The secretary of the British legation in Rio de Janeiro observed that "long resident British merchants are far from looking on participation in the slave trade with the same feelings it generally excites in England . . . nor is it easy to get information from them."[9] The Brazilian and Cuban slave traders shared the attitudes of their British eighteenth-century predecessors. For Brazilians and Cubans, abolitionist values were not organic in the sense that such values were a product of a British-type industrialization process. Indigenous abolition movements notwithstanding, the ultimate ideological pressure for change came from outside their societies rather than within. For the slave traders, therefore, naval and diplomatic initiatives were nothing more than additional risks to be countered with the reallocation of scarce resources rather than a source of ideological tension or self-questioning.

Abolitionist pressures, nevertheless, had fundamental effects on the organization of the slave-trading business. The nineteenth-century traffic required higher stakes than its predecessors. Capital outlay per slave was always much higher in the nineteenth century than in peacetime in the previous century, and capital risked per slave doubled after 1825.[10] This perhaps helps explain why in all major nineteenth-century slave-importing centers ownership tended to become more concentrated than in the previous century. Before 1821 in Cuba several large family groupings carried on the business; Moreno Fraginals mentions 76 firms and five major groupings of these firms. After 1820 a single firm was usually dominant. Although the identity and owners of that firm changed over time and the firm could have many partners for particular ventures, those involved were normally peninsula Spaniards resident in Havana. Their connections with the pre-1821 importers, moreover, do not appear to have been strong. Creoles did become more important in the last decade, but the Creole domination of mercantile capital noted by David Turnbull in 1840 did not extend to the slave trade.[11] The point is illustrated by the development of the largest firm in the illicit Cuban trade. Definite ownership interests can be tracked down for 140 Cuban slaving voyages between 1821 and 1843, all but 8 in the last sixteen of these years. No less than 60 of these can be attributed to one cluster of companies that evolved from the enterprise established by Don Pedro Martínez of Cadiz. In the 1820s this company was first Campo, Labieneta and Martínez; later Martínez, Martínez and Carballo, with branches in Havana and Cadiz.[12] In the early 1830s one of the captains and later a factor of the firms, Pedro Blanco, formed a most successful independent partnership with Lino Carballo, the third partner of the latter group. At the end of 183_ the Havana and Cadiz Martínezes separated, with the latter becoming le_ involved in slave trading. The Havana branch was reconstituted with Cipriano Lopez Martínez, Pedro Martínez, Francisco Riera and José Raimon Recur as partners.[13] Except for Blanco and Carballo all these firms continued to be known popularly as Pedro Martínez and Co. We do not know the birthplace of all these individuals, though Blanco and Pedro Martínez were Spaniards, but it is clear that the usual place of residence was Cuba. None of them had been leading names in the pre-1821 trade.

The Martínez firm adapted comfortably to the increased naval pressure after the 1835 treaty but apparently found the new domestic restrictions culminating in the 1845 Spanish law more of a threat. It was either these or, more generally, the sharp decline in the volume of the Cuban trade in the eight years after 1844 that persuaded the firm to switch its capital into commodity trade. Twenty-five years earlier dominant firms had responded similarly as traffic volumes fell precipitously after 1820. Pedro Martínez attempted to reestablish the traffic to the Sherbro in 1850 and in the same year was involved in a joint venture with the largest of the Rio de Janeiro importers to bring slaves to Havana from west-central Africa. As the trade revived in the later 1850s, the firm appears as an outfitter of some and owner of other expeditions, including the *C.F.A. Cole,* which was involved in a noted Baltimore trial. But as a slave importer, the firm was overtaken by others. In 1859, Ximenes, Martínez and Lafitte (the first named probably an old Martínez slave factor, Angel Ximenes) was described as a "wealthy Havana firm connected both with Paris and London" and occupied in legitimate trade. Unlike many slave dealers Pedro Martínez moved out of the industry gracefully.[14]

After the Martínez group reduced its involvement, the role of dominant firm was assumed first by Pedro Blanco and then by Pedro Forcade, a Frenchman. The former had dissolved his partnership with Carballo by 1840, and both he and Forcade prospered during the years of steady decline in the volume of the trade from 1838 to 1843. Blanco was responsible for ten out of twenty-eight ventures in 1844 and 1845 for which ownership interest can be traced, with Forcade accounting for a further nine of these ventures. After switching capital into the U.S.-Cuban trade in 1845, Blanco retired to Genoa, leaving two nephews in charge in Havana.[15] The house of Blanco continues to appear in the slave-trade records down to 1851. But Forcade was the dominant firm—indeed perhaps the only firm in the low-volume years 1846–48: It accounted for nine out of twelve ventures for which data exist between 1846 and 1851.[16]

From 1852 on, a multitude of names appear in the sources as owners. But as nominal ownership became common, these were rarely the principals. Capital outlay per slave was in excess of $200 as ships doubled in size and steam power came into use for the first time. Large joint stock companies were the usual owners. The Expedición por Africa Company in 1857 owned twenty-one of twenty-five ships known to the African squadron. Three years later a new company with capitalization of $600,000 owned thirty-seven vessels, all of which did not actually go to the coast for slaves.[17] Julián Zulueta was the largest shareholder in the first company and probably the second as well. Zulueta had arrived in Cuba with few funds in 1832, but by 1845 his returns from the slave rade and an inheritance allowed him to establish one of the largest plantations in Cuba. By 1860 he probably owned more slaves than anyone else in Cuba and, in addition, had established a reputation for honest dealing as a slave merchant. An intimate of captain-generals, he invested in the traffic from the late 1830s to the middle 1860s and filled a wide range of roles in the business. In 1848 he visited Spain to lobby for easier regulations on slave imports. His connections with the government and sugar-estate holdings made him a key figure at a time when the greater share of the selling price of a *bozal* was accounted for by distribution costs and a time when law-enforcement officials were not permitted to search for suspected *bozales* on existing estates. Zulueta's name can be attached to nine out of twenty-three ventures with ownership data between 1858 and 1864. However, after allowing for the fact that many ventures are linked with individuals who were merely nominal owners, it seems likely that only a minority of successful ventures sold their cargo in this period without Zulueta's involvement in some capacity.[18] Other major figures in the closing fifteen years of the traffic such as José Luis Baró, Mariano Borrell and Nicolás Martínez de Valdiviso were also estate owners with good official connections. Indeed after 1845 these two characteristics were prerequisites of a successful importing operation. In this final period individuals who came to prominence after long apprenticeships as factors on the coast or officers of slave ships such as Salvador Castro of Trinidad de Cuba appear to have been the exception.[19]

In Brazil, too, there was a pattern of higher concentration ratios and domination of the industry by Iberian nationals in the illegal phase of the traffic. Although the British chargé d'affaires exaggerated a little when he commented, "There are 30,000 Portuguese in Rio, all it may be said slave dealers," immigrant Portuguese did predominate wherever the slave trade flourished in Brazil, and those identified as Brazilian were frequently naturalized citizens. Many simply stayed on in Brazil after the latter became independent.[20] The firms made up of northern Europeans that flourished in Bahia in the 1840s and the major Spanish enterprise in Rio in the 1840s, stand out as exceptions. Credit lines from Britain to merchants in Brazil became direct after 1808, and Iberian ports, never of central importance to the Brazilian slave trade, participated even less in the nineteenth century as table 9 suggests. Coastal factors did become key figures in the illegal traffic and many more Angolan and West African merchants sent slaves on freight to Brazil (and to Cuba) after 1830, but it is clear that they supplemented rather than threatened the hegemony of the expatriate Portuguese.

Concentration of ownership before 1830 in Brazil was similar to that noted by Anstey in the last years of the English traffic. In the eleven years 1820 to 1830, the British navy brought fifty-eight Bahia-bound ships before the Sierra Leone Mixed Commission Court, mainly for trading north of the line. Of the 38 listed owners, the biggest 4 owned one third of all ships. Verger's work on ship clearances in the Bahian archives confirms the preeminence of 3 of these, António Pedrozo de Albuquerque, Joaquim José de Oliveira and José de Cerqueira Lima, "le grand nom du commerçant de cette époque."[21] For Rio in this period ownership data are scarce, but if we take consignees as a surrogate for ownership, Klein's newspaper lists show a similar pattern. Between 1825 an

1830, 428 slave shipments were consigned to 102 merchants. The biggest 4 merchants accounted for one quarter. As in Cuba, joint stock operations hiding behind nominal ownerships developed in Brazil after 1830. The 27 Bahian slave ships brought before the mixed courts between 1831–41 were owned by no less than 24 different persons, with no single owner holding more than 2 ships.[22] A more accurate picture is provided by Verger's fragmentary ship-clearing data as well as references in British sources to ships other than those taken to Sierra Leone. These indicate that the large firms such as António Pedrozo de Albuquerque, José de Cerqueira Lima and Joaquim and José Alves de Cruz Rios (father and son), carried on their operations after 1830 and were joined by other large operators such as Joaquim Pereira Marinho.[23] In 1842–51, the last decade of the Bahia trade, it is possible to track down ownership of 143 slaving ventures. The largest 4 owners accounted for about half of these, with the Joaquim Pereira Marinho firm alone having an interest in over one fourth of the total.[24] Pedrozo de Albuquerque and Cerqueira Lima were not active in this final period, but there is no indication that anything other than normal attrition explain these changes. The Alves de Cruz Rios firm was the second largest owner in these years, and many of the smaller operators of the 1840s appear on the earlier lists. Slave importers continued to be merchants of substance and stature in Bahia. The terms *freebooter* and *adventurer,* which many writers have used to describe the slave traders of this period, give a misleading impression of the standing of the individuals who were the principals in the traffic.

A similar post-1830 pattern is apparent in the Rio de Janeiro traffic, with perhaps a rather more rapid turnover. The consignee or owner (unfortunately it is not possible to distinguish between the two) is known for 200 slave ships arriving between 1838 and 1844. Only twenty individuals are listed, with the biggest four accounting for 131 (or 60 percent), a level of concentration comparable to the Havana figure. Although most of the names on the postabolition list may be found in the 1825–30 newspaper listings, there is no overlap between the top ten in the two periods: José Bernadino da Sá (the largest single firm of these years), Joaquim Tomas dos Santos and António Guimaraes, among others, rose to dominance after 1830.[25]

In the following, and final, seven years of the trade, the big four concentration ratio for 76 ventures changed only slightly, to 67 percent, but the share of the leading firm rose from 22 to 36 percent. This firm, the well-known Manoel Pinto da Fonseca Company, had been in sixth position in the previous period.[26] Bernadino da Sá and Guimaraes continued as leading traders to the end of the traffic, but a number of smaller traders appeared for the first time in the last two years of the trade. Here also, however, joint stock companies hiding behind nominal owners were not uncommon, and it is not always clear if these new names and indeed the small traders in all years are authentic dealers or fronts for the larger companies. In both Bahia and Rio de Janeiro, however, in the 1840s, there were numerous minor traders called *velantes* who crisscrossed the Atlantic in company with their own goods and slaves, paying freight for both and trading perhaps twenty-five to forty slaves at a time.[27] These are not included in the above assessments. It would thus appear that one of the few reliable comments that José Cliffe, the Brazilian slave merchant, made to the 1847–48 parliamentary committees was that most of the major slave importers of the 1840s had acquired their wealth since 1830.[28]

The two wealthiest traders of the last phase of the Brazilian traffic had been lowly retail store clerks a few years earlier. They were also expelled from Brazil as the trade was suppressed. Such men were, nevertheless, an integral part of Brazilian society. Like their counterparts in the Cuban trade, the major dealers owned large plantations and had close business and family connections with influential members of the government and society going beyond mere bribery. The final landings of slaves in Brazil South were engineered by the great *fazendeiros* "who by the extent of their possessions, the number of their retainers . . . and their turbulent spirit, somewhat resemble the feudal slave chiefs of former times."[29] Unlike Cuba, slave traders had always had a major presence in Brazil though the individuals who led the industry in the 1840s were, in fact, recent entries. Many of their activities have entered the historical record through the contemptuous and outraged prism of English observation: Foreign Office officials in Brazil preferred to view the traders as outcasts or at least parasites.[30]

Like the geographic shift, the trend to larger-scale operations and the attendant increase in concentration ratios were certainly associated with attempts to suppress the traffic. The standard British, French, Hispanic and pre-1820 Portuguese slaving firm had been a family operation, individual proprietorship or partnership. The use of the term *company* or *association* was uncommon, particularly in the Brazilian context.[31] After 1810 risks in the traffic increased, specie was increasingly substituted for goods in the outbound cargoes and, in midcentury, there was some technological change embodied in the use of larger ships and steam. These generated a number of organizational responses that revolved around the need to raise more capital and attract more investors. In Cuba in the 1820s, as in the early European-based trade, partnerships were formed for the duration of individual ventures, often around one or two individuals of established credit, perhaps with experience in the intra-Caribbean trade. A good part of the financing of the slave trade was provided by smaller *accionistas* (shareholders) with "shares as low as $100 . . . eagerly sought for by clerks in public and mercantile houses,"[32] though a more typical share was $1,000 and a more typical small shareholder was a professional man, shopkeeper or planter—and in many cases the slaver captain. But before the end of the 1820s, houses specializing in the business had appeared and the larger ones, although occasionally dividing the interest in a voyage among themselves, no longer made shares available outside their select group.[33] Much of the Martínez correspondence in the 1820s concerns details of share divisions, but by the later 1830s the Martínez company was obviously in control of all or the greater part of the expeditions it dispatched.[34] There were probably some economies of scale, not so much in size of ship as in the number of factor locations and variety of goods maintained at the African end of the voyage. The small shareholders persisted, however. The *Socorro,* which made perhaps the largest single disembarkation in the busy year of 1836, had a dozen shareholders whose stake averaged $2,500 each.[35] Moreover, an exchange was established at the store of

José Abreu at which these and similar shares could be traded. In Bahia, too, a "great part of equipping ... vessels [was] born by casual subscribers whose share of the ventures sometimes does not exceed £20," and by 1850 shares of tiny denominations were being traded.[36] Joint stock companies, as opposed to joint stock voyages, developed first in Brazil. By the mid-1830s they were being established on a permanent footing or for a term of years. Such firms wholly owned and operated ships and distributed profits at regular intervals. Shares were small enough to be purchased by "second class merchants" and the direction of the enterprise was normally vested in one or two of the shareholders.[37] Such organizations, or associations as they were termed, appeared in Cuba in the later 1830s, but not until the 1850s did their ownership become broadly based with fifty or more shareholders. It was only in this last period that U.S. citizens reentered the slave trade as small investors.[38]

As the pressures on the traffic increased, other capital-mobilizing and risk-reducing devices developed. Naval operations on the African coast increased the role of the factor, whose task it was to procure and arrange the shipment of slaves. Success usually hinged on coordinating the assembly of a slave cargo with the arrival of a slave ship in the absence of cruisers. Policy shifts by governments in the importing regions were additional constraints. As a consequence companies sought ways of integrating operations in the Americas and Africa more tightly than ever before. One method was simply to maintain permanent trading bases on the African littoral manned by employees.[39] There had always been individual owners who had alternated between permanent establishments on the two continents. Manoel António da Silva Brandao of Pará, Isidore Powell of Matanzas and several Afro-Brazilians and Afro-Portuguese of Bahia were examples.[40] But, as discussed in chapter 10, the new factories were bigger and part of a larger network. The factors who headed them were at first employees, but they increasingly became full partners, particularly if the firm was not among the biggest companies. Ramón Rovena and Pedro Maniquet were part of a Cuban partnership that had factories at Cabinda, Loango, Black Point and the Congo River; both performed the factor role in the early 1840s.[41] Of the factories in the Congo at the end of the Brazilian trade, two were independent, two were headed by partners of Rio de Janeiro firms and six were operated by agents of other Brazilian companies, including Amaral e Bastos, Pinto da Fonseca, and Bernadino da Sá. Amaral e Bastos, however, stationed one of their partners at Ambriz and Tomás da Costa Ramos had three brothers who alternated between his firm's Brazilian and African coast establishments.[42] Further north in Lagos and Ouidah, it was more common for partners of Bahia firms to conduct business in Africa in person.[43] An alternative but less-used strategy was a joint venture between the firm in the Americas and one of the major independent African slave traders such as de Souza.[44]

After 1850 the elaborate slave establishments remained but were more likely to be operated by the independent African-based slave merchants than by Cuban importers. This was also a function of pressure on the trade. The major export points in these years were on the beaches near Ouidah, in the Congo region, and scattered locations in southeast Africa. For reasons reviewed later,

mainly to do with geography and African sovereignty, the navy could not eliminate the traffic from these zones. Effective demand from Cuba always elicited
a response in these regions, especially as there was no longer any competition
from Brazilian purchasers. Reserves of slaves were usually available and ship
capture ratios did not reach the intimidating levels experienced by some other
exporting regions. In addition, all three zones had a pool of long-established
independent African-based slave merchants. In the Bight of Benin it was the
Afro–Portuguese-speaking community. In the Congo many of those dealers
from Luanda and elsewhere who were not independent when the Brazilian
traffic ended and who were not bankrupted by that event quickly set up on
their own. In southeast Africa there were Portuguese, Arabs and Banyans
(Hindu traders from India) who traded to many locations other than the Americas. The major problem after 1850 was not acquiring and shipping the slaves
so much as distributing them in Cuba. The price of the slave on the African
coast came to comprise less than 5 percent of the selling price in Cuba. Except
in isolated instances in Upper Guinea, importing companies in Cuba no longer
found it necessary to control their own African shore establishment in the last
years of the trade. Steamer packet lines and supercargoes on board fast slave
ships provided adequate enough links between buyers and sellers on opposite
sides of the Atlantic.[45]

Higher risk also generated an increase in the practice of freighting slaves
across the Atlantic. Ships of even the largest firms carried slaves belonging to
others. Sometimes these were owned by the hired factor of the company or the
slaver captain, separate from the company's slaves. Pedro Blanco entered the
entrepreneurial end of the business in this way. But the larger share of freighted
slaves came from other companies and from the already-mentioned Afro-Brazilian and Afro-Portuguese communities in Africa. Several Bahia dealers and
Tomás da Costa Ramos, a major Rio dealer in the late 1840s, entered the business in this fashion. Freighting slaves was not new, both U.S. and Portuguese
ships had offered this service in the preabolition period.[46] The practice was
greatly encouraged by the increasing importance of the African factor and the
African-based trader under the pressures of suppression and the need to spread
risk. The Afro-Portuguese community in the Bight of Benin made particularly
heavy use of the freighting services offered by Bahian dealers. Indeed in Brazil
in the later 1840s it was rare for a house to bring back a full cargo of its own
slaves in its own ship. A naval officer observed of the Rio traffic that since the
1839 act, slave traders previously involved in individual speculations "have
separated themselves from the shipping enterprise . . . The slave factor now in
Africa . . . complete[s] the cargo of one vessel by portions of slaves from all the
factors residing there. They prefer this method of sending their slaves in 5 or
6 trips to that of one venture as . . . insurance."[47] Thus full slave ships captured
in the Bight of Benin or off Angola might have cargoes owned by thirty or more
dealers.[48]

It is also clear that before 1845 in the Cuban trade and before 1850 in the
Brazilian traffic, the shipping of the slave made up a larger proportion of the
slave's selling price in the Americas than ever before. After these dates suppressive measures by authorities in the importing region ensured that distri

ution costs—basically bribery—dominated price patterns. In the 1830s and 1840s shipping costs were close to 50 percent of final selling prices on most Cuban routes and somewhat less on the major west-central Africa to Rio de Janeiro route. By comparison, in the last year of the legal U.S. traffic, the *Tartar* agreed to freight a cargo from the Rio Pongo to Martinique for an average of $30 a head, or about 15 percent of the final selling price.[49] A naval officer made the reason clear when he pointed out that "the slave ship interest . . . separate from the slave factor . . . incurs the most hazard and the most profit . . . nothing is paid if the slaves are captured."[50] Thus against the *Serpente,* a steamer built for the trade in 1849 at a cost of £22,000 that never landed a single slave, must be set the *Andorinha,* which generated revenues from freight of £40,704 and profits of 800 percent from eight return voyages before being captured and destroyed.[51] Both Martínez and Pinto da Fonseca, the biggest dealers of their day in Cuba and Brazil, respectively, shipped more slaves than they themselves owned. Pinto da Fonseca, in particular, had ships that carried only freighted slaves.[52]

Both Manoel Pinto da Fonseca and Bernadino da Sá refined this sytem even further by advancing the funds to minor slave dealers to purchase the trading goods. Both acted as financial intermediaries between the British importing house and the smaller Portuguese merchant whose credit standing would not support direct dealing with the former. Both also freighted the trade goods to Africa. Pinto da Fonseca and da Sá typically charged 1 percent a month on the goods advanced in addition to freight and insurance on the same, with the insurance being arranged with a third party. All these charges were payable whatever the outcome of the voyage. On the return trip, also, freight for the slaves was payable whether or not the vessel arrived safely. Thus any losses from capture would be spread to the minor dealers who, for their part, could expect to land the slaves that made it across the Atlantic for £30 after all charges, and this at a time when the final selling price was rarely less than £50. The British minister felt that the security that da Sá and Pinto da Fonseca received for their advances to the small dealers allowed them to escape unscathed from the naval squadron. Before accepting this assessment, however, we should note that the major slave dealers assumed such Mephistophelean proportions in the eyes of many British observers that they could scarcely put a foot wrong in their pursuit of illegal profits.[53]

A major source of financing in the nineteenth-century slave trade was credit advanced by the merchants (mainly British) who provided the slave dealers with their trade goods. Other shipping costs and (later) distribution costs increased in importance in the half-century after 1810; the relative significance of the trade goods accordingly declined somewhat. Between one third and one half of the capital outlay per slave in a slaving venture was accounted for by trade goods before 1850, less later.[54] Indeed as specie came to be employed instead of goods, particularly in the Cuban traffic, this source of credit became even less important.[55] This did not, however, prevent the value of British goods absorbed by the slave trade actually increasing between the last quarter of the eighteenth century and the second quarter of the nineteenth century. Nevertheless, only the British were able to supply these goods on long credits and, as noted above, the removal of this facility would have reduced the volume of the trade. One of the arguments of the British abolitionists in the 1790s had been that if any nation filled the gap left by British withdrawal from the traffic, that nation would still have to use British goods to exchange for slaves. Credits on goods tended to increase from twelve months in the last years of the British trade to eighteen months or twenty-four months later in the nineteenth century.[56] At the same time, the length of the average return voyage to the coast decreased. There was also pressure on goods' suppliers to take up an equity position in the slaving enterprise by accepting slaves in payment for goods. For British merchants this was clearly in contravention of British law, but there can be little doubt that it happened. It was certainly common in Rio de Janeiro for British houses to advance merchandise in the knowledge that the chief security for payment was the successful exchange of that merchandise for slaves on the African coast.[57] Even after specie became a part of the trading cargo, British funds remained important. Most of the large mining operations in Brazil were British and all employed slave labor. There were, moreover, neither legal nor moral barriers to the extension of British credit to businesses other than those involved in transatlantic slave trading. Slave owners, in particular planters, had unrestricted access to British credit.[58]

A variety of innovative local financial intermediation techniques and specialized services appeared on the scene. A primitive futures market developed when dealers in Pernambuco contracted to deliver slaves at fixed prices before fitting out an expedition. By the late 1830s dealers were issuing bills on the security of future imports. Despite the trend to increased concentration of ownership, smaller firms could find niches in this growing and increasingly sophisticated business. A company in Rio de Janeiro specialized in discounting these slave-trader bills.[59] Other firms operated reception centers on the Brazil South coast as supplements to their own slave-trading activities. Through these passed newly imported Africans belonging to many different owners. There was also a company set up to refit slave ships immediately after they had discharged their cargoes so that the ship would not have to return to one of the ports designated for international trade. Similar speciality firms had developed in Havana by the early 1840s. Indeed the man described in 1850 by J. Kennedy as the "head of slave trading interest here," Joaquín Gómez, apparently avoided ship ownership altogether. He specialized in receiving slaves on consignment or purchasing them in Africa on his own account for transportation in the ships of others. His specialty was the distribution of slaves within Cuba.[60] The flexibility of the slave-traders' response to British and domestic pressure was thus not limited to the choice of a flag.

For the established traders in the Americas, the penultimate adjustment to the pressures of prohibition was to seek new markets. Though table 9 suggests that the major branches of the traffic were relatively self-contained after 1820, some crosstrading did occur. Slavers leaving Cuba bound for the Bight of Benin occasionally called at Bahia to load the roll tobacco which was so popular on the coast.[61] In the wake of Brazilian prohibition of the traffic in 1830, itself a function of the 1826 Anglo-Brazilian convention, several Bahian and Maranhão merchants sent slave cargoes or part cargoes to Havana, often consigned to Juan Zangronis.[62] At the same time the community of small Portuguese-speaking slave merchants in the Bight of Benin redirected a part of their steady supply of small batches of slaves from Bahia to Havana. Joaquim Almeida, who resided at different times in both Brazil and Africa, had thirty-six slaves consigned to José Mazorra of Havana in 1844.[63] In the mid-1840s the actions of Captain-General Gerónimo Valdés, fear of slave conspiracies and the Spanish penal law of 1845 reversed the direction of this crosstrading. By 1844 the Afro-Portuguese were refusing to send consignments to Havana, and in 1845 the Havana dealers were for a time directing all slave cargoes to the Brazils.[64] Within a few years, however, the continuation of these tighter Cuban controls coupled with a strong recovery in the Cuban slave market widened the price differential between slaves in Cuba and Bahia, with much of the difference accounted for by rising Cuban distribution costs.[65] In 1849 and 1850 Havana dealers, led by Pedro Forcade, brought several cargoes of Portuguese-speaking slaves from the province of Bahia. At least one of these shipments was jointly organized and others were planned by Forcade, Manoel Pinto da Fonseca and Bernadino da Sá of Rio de Janeiro.[66] At the same time Bahian slave ships began to return once more to the Havana market.[67] It should be stressed, however, that although the existence of alternative markets gave the firm greater flexibility in the short run, in comparison with the total trade these shipments were of small importance.

A few slave-trading firms exercised the option to move in response to suppressive measures. Perhaps the most successful of this select group was a Spaniard, Francisco Robirosa. Robirosa was an established Havana slave dealer in the early 1840s, became the fourth largest dealer in Rio de Janeiro after the Havana traffic dwindled in mid decade, and then shifted his activities back to Cuba when the Brazilian trade was suppressed.[68] He was, in fact, one of a small group of refugees from the suppressed Brazilian traffic who successfully broke into the Cuban trade after 1850. Most of this group, however, were Portuguese and eventually came to reside mainly in New York. Manuel Fortunat Botelho, his partner Lemus, the principals of Abranches e Almeida Co.—José da Costa Lima Viana, Joaquim Texeira de Miranda, João Alberto Machado and, perhaps the best known, Manoel Basilio da Cunha Reis—were the leading members of this group. Most of these men had been factors on the west-central African coast in the 1840s and Lima Viana and Cunha Reis, in particular, had risen from agents of major Brazilian houses to independent exporters, first shipping their own slaves on freight and later owning their own expeditions.[69]

With the demise of the Brazilian traffic, this group established an important niche in the Cuban trade in time to benefit from the upswing of the traffic from the mid-1850s. By 1855 Lima Viana and Cunha Reis were well established, the latter in partnership with César de la Figanière , the Portuguese consul, and his brother, William. From here they launched ventures of their own such as the *Flying Eagle,* the *Charlotte,* the *Panchita* and *Isla da Cuba* as well as procured ships under U.S. colors for major Havana interests.[70] One of the shipbrokers involved in these transactions, Emilio Sánchez y Dolz, a naturalized American of Cuban origin, was in the pay of the British consul at New York throughout 1859. His reports and other sources suggest that the New York Portuguese never had a distribution network in Cuba separate from the major Havana slave traders. The expeditions they sent out obtained slaves from their own factories in both west-central and East Africa; in the latter region, they were acknowledged as the largest of the transatlantic dealers in the late 1850s.[71] But the sale of the slaves in Cuba at a time when distribution costs made up the largest part of total costs continued under the control of established Cuban firms.[72] Moreover, the Portuguese group never owned more than a minority of the slavers that sailed, even from New York,[73] and in the Cuban traffic as a whole they accounted for a much smaller proportion again. In these final years, as in the post-1820 period generally, the locus of control and the source of the capital for the Cuban trade was Cuba itself.

The activities of the Portuguese Company, as it was known in New York, was part of a general rise in the importance of African-based slave dealers in the final years of the traffic, at least on the west coast. Most did not have operational bases in the Americas. None were able to bypass the distribution system established by the Cuban and (earlier) the Rio de Janeiro dealers, and many indeed were defrauded by the Cuban firms during the 1850s.[74] Before 1850 the biggest dealers operated their own ships, and in Bahia at least employed agents to sell their slaves on a commission basis. Francisco Féliz de Souza had a Bahia agent and an interest in at least eleven slave ships, as opposed to slave cargoes between 1821 and 1841. Interests of members of his extensive family may be traced to four other ventures, and as late as 1847 António Féliz de Souza had a slaver built at Oporto and sailed it on the Ouidah-Bahia route.[75] Another dealer, Domingo José Martins, shipped small batches of slaves on his own account in ships consigned to him by Bahia owners in the early 1840s. He also graduated to full ownership and had a reciprocal relationship with Joaquim Pereira Marinho of Bahia, whereby each acted as the other's agent on the two continents, without apparently any formal partnership being established.[76] In the late 1840s a naval officer observed that in the Bight of Benin there were two classes of slave ship. One was the "regular" slaver, sent direct from Bahia with meticulous planning; the other was "bought up suddenly by the slave dealers for double [its] value, . . . a temptation that few American [ship owners] can resist . . . [such ships] come to the coast expressly for this speculation."[77] The purchasers of this second type were usually Afro-Portuguese from Lagos or Ouidah. Large numbers of minor Afro-Portuguese dealers also took advantage of the freighting facilities offered by Bahia shippers. In the north, a Portuguese national, Caetano José Nosolini, governor of Bissau, also straddled the Atlantic with his slaving business in the 1830s and 1840s. In the first half of 1841 he sent 790 slaves to Cuba and 460 to Maranhão on a consignment basis.[78] To the south, Luanda dealers were probably less successful in establishing independent transatlantic businesses, though Portuguese sources indicate that at least one trader, Donna Anna Joaquina dos Santos Silva, was managing her own transatlantic business in the 1830s and 1840s. As the Brazilian trade died, Angolan dealers sent their own cargoes in small coasting vessels, one of them the twenty-ton *Vinte-cinco de Setembro*.[79] At least some Africans had already tried this latter strategy. In November 1844 the King of the Sherbro, widely known as Henry Tucker, dispatched 348 slaves to Cuba in the *Engador,* a schooner owned and equipped by himself and other Sherbro chiefs.[80]

After 1850 few slavers were owned by African-based traders, but the share of total slave departures dispatched on the account of these traders probably increased nevertheless. A growing palm oil business provided a stronger base from which to conduct slave-trading ventures. The major dealers in the Bight of Benin in 1853 were João José de Lima, formerly of Lagos but now of Lomé, Joaquim Almeida of Agoué, near Anecho, and the Martins brothers, one at Ouidah and the other at Porto Novo. The de Souza family continued in the slave and palm oil business at Ouidah. The Martins brothers and Lima together with Domingo Mustiche of Ouidah sent several large shipments to Cuba in 1853 and 1854. Mustiche, a native of Spain, accompanied the slaves, but this did not prevent the Cuban government from capturing two of the shipments after disembarkation.[81] Losses from these ventures and unhappiness at the treatment they received from the Cuban importers had no long-term effect. Although the Martins at Porto Novo, together with several Ouidah dealers, refused to sell slaves for specie to the *Adams Grey* early in 1857, the reason was simply that they preferred to await an opportunity to freight their slaves on their own account. As late as 1864 João Soares, who was the leading trader in the Afro-Portuguese community after the death of Domingo José Martins, left Lagos for London by mail steamer for the express purpose of obtaining a suitable vessel for a transatlantic venture.[82] Further south Francisco António Flores, a former partner of the Rio de Janeiro firm Amaral e Bastos and a Luanda resident, shipped slaves from Ambriz to Cuba and imported goods from New York and London on his own account as well as acting as agent for Havana companies. He also sent a partner to Havana along with the slaves.[83] The cargo of the *Pierre Soulé,* which embarked 479 Africans near Benguela in December 1855, had no less than forty-eight separate owners, most of them living in the Benguela area. The *Dolores* carried 595 slaves from Ambriz in the same year. The biggest four shippers owned 293 of the slaves, but thirty-seven other shippers, mostly Luanda and Ambriz merchants, shared the remaining 302 slaves and all were sent on consignment to Havana firms.[84] Only on the southeast African coast is there little evidence of local merchants' involvement in slave markets in the Americas. However, even on the west coast, there was never any possibility of African-based dealers dominating the trade. The majority of slaves leaving Africa were owned by large Havana companies.

Finally we should turn briefly to the third major slave carrier of the nineteenth century, the French. The contrast between the French traders and the slave traders of Havana, Bahia and Rio de Janeiro dealers is very striking. Of 751 French ships suspected of participating in the slave trade between 1814 and 1833, over half were in the hands of Nantes merchants.[85] Unlike the shipowners of Havana and Rio de Janeiro, those of Nantes always had a range of alternative employment possibilities for their ships, to which all eventually turned. Only a few firms were clearly specializing in the traffic even at its height. Nantes slave traders tended to be well-established merchant houses with abundant capital and easy access to capital markets. La Société d'assurances de Nantes was a major shareholder of La Banque de Nantes, formed in

1817, and both institutions were controlled by slave-trading merchants. Serge Daget comments, "le commerce maritime nantais s'est protégé par un véritable consortium de négriers habilité à escompter les effets de commerce, appuyé sur ses propres ressources et sur la finance locale . . . et pas sans liens probables avec la banque française."[86] The pressure for financial innovation was clearly not as great as in Spanish and Portuguese America. Concentration of ownership, moreover, was comparable to eighteenth-century figures, with the six biggest slave-ship owners accounting for 92 out of the 190 voyages for which ownership is known. At least ninety-three Nantes merchants are suspected of having invested in the illegal traffic.

Once on the African coast, French ships, protected to a large extent from the British navy, traded in the old manner. This involved calling at several locations and trading with independent factors, African headmen or (at St. Louis and Gorée) their own agents, though there is a suggestion that French ships accepted slaves on freight from Cuban traders in Africa. When the French government determined to suppress the trade after 1827, it did so with relative ease and the impact of abolition was rather to destroy the trade than to modify its practices. As in the British case, most of the direct involvement ceased fairly quickly as ships and firms redeployed in other long-distance trade. Information on the business activities of French West Indian colonial slave traders is scant, but such firms certainly used the credit offered by British merchants at Danish St. Thomas. The Nantes traffic, at least, may be seen as a carryover from the eighteenth century.[87]

In all slaving centers, including those in France, the slave-trading firm's costing and organizational adjustments could not eliminate the high risk that was the basic feature of the nineteenth-century slave trade. As might be expected, profits were high and increased sharply in the last years of the trade. Table 10 compares estimates of profitability in the British eighteenth-century trade with data on the post-1825 Brazilian and Cuban traffic taken from appendix E. The data have not been standardized for voyage length and as the nineteenth-century round-trip was shorter than its predecessors, the annualized returns would show a greater difference between the two centuries than indicated here. The eighteenth-century British trade was probably more remunerative than its contemporary Dutch and French counterparts, yet by most estimates it could not match the nineteenth-century returns to Cuban and Brazilian investors. The rates available to the latter turned clerks of trading houses and petty shopkeepers into wealthy proprietors of sugar and coffee estates within a few years. For Manoel Pinto da Fonseca and José Bernadino da Sá these returns bought titles in the Brazilian nobility in the 1840s and in the Spanish and Portuguese nobility after their expulsion from Rio de Janeiro in 1851. Zulueta was similarly ennobled in Cuba. And, of course, these financial gains fueled the often wildly exaggerated estimates of slave-trading profits made by many contemporary observers.[88]

But high risk also meant severe losses for many investors, including most of those who savored success. The British commissary judge in Havana in 1830 commented on the many shopkeepers in that city who had gone bankrupt on account of their slaving speculations. Twenty years later his successor was able to observe that "there is not a single person in this city who has latterly been

**Table 10.** Estimates of Profit Rates per Venture or per Slave in Selected Branches of the Slave Trade

| Selected Branches of the Slave Trade | Percentage |
|---|---|
| British | |
| 1757–84 | 10.5 |
| 1760–1807 | 9.5 |
| 1770–1806 | 26.7 |
| 1800 | 9.5 |
| Cuban | |
| 1826–35 | 19.6 |
| 1836–45 | 19.2 |
| 1856–65 | 91.3 |
| Brazil South | |
| 1831–40 | 17.8 |
| 1841–50 | 21.8 |

*Sources:* Row 1, Roger T. Anstey, *The Atlantic Slave Trade and British Abolition* (London, 1975), p. 47. Row 2, David Richardson, "Profits in the Liverpool Slave Trade: The Accounts of William Davenport, 1757–1784," in Roger Anstey and P. E. H. Hair (eds.), *Liverpool, the African Slave Trade, and Abolition: Essays to Illustrate Current Knowledge and Research* (Liverpool, Eng., 1976), p. 46. Row 3, Joseph E. Inikori, "Market Structure and the Profits of the British African Trade in the Late Eighteenth Century," *Journal of Economic History*, 61 (1981):772. Row 4, E. Phillip LeVeen, *British Slave Trade Suppression Policies, 1821–1865* (New York, 1977), p. 22. Rows 5 through 9, see app. E.

engaged in the trade who can be pointed out as enriched by it."[89] Although evidence will not support full statistical analysis, an impressive proportion of the major slave traders underwent bankruptcy during their careers. Pedro Blanco's firm was bankrupt by 1848, with liabilities of $500,000, and the principal was living in Genoa by then. Lino Carballo, the partner of first Martínez and then Blanco in the 1830s, committed suicide a year later, leaving behind an insolvent estate. Figanière, Reis and Co., the largest and best known of the Portuguese operations in New York, failed at the end of 1859 despite the Cuban traffic reaching in that year its highest level[90] in two decades. Even the large Havana companies of the same period could not avoid severe losses. The itinerant Francisco Robirosa had to begin again in Lisbon and Havana in the early 1850s after bankruptcy in Rio de Janeiro. Pinto da Fonseca had already experienced very heavy losses in 1849 before the British attacks in Brazilian ports. Both he and Bernadino da Sá subsequently left large amounts of slaves and merchandise on the African coast in 1851 and spent heavily in trying to avoid arrest and expulsion from Brazil.[91] In Africa the largest dealer in Angola was insolvent by 1859, and many of his colleagues experienced a similar fate in naval-induced crises in 1851, 1855 and 1863.[92] Further north the da Souza family fortunes had declined so much by the late 1840s that its head ﬔuld not raise the capital necessary to assume the responsibilities of chacha ⸜the official intermediary with Europeans) to the king of Dahomey.[93]

Successful firms were usually those that either always had other interests or that diversified when the traffic was most profitable. Julián Zulueta's long association with the slave-trading business, for example, became a supplement to his sugar-growing operations, though even he was twice arrested and experienced some financial embarrassment in the 1850s. Juan Aguirre had similar links and like Zulueta and the Borrell brothers gained much of his wealth first from slave trading. José Mazorra and Pedro Forcade moved into large-scale sugar growing and disappeared from the slave trade, the former in the 1840s and the latter in 1853.[94] In Brazil Pinto da Fonseca and his brothers invested in the expanding coffee sector.[95] The Martínez firm did not enter the plantation business and pulled its capital out of the slave trade before the slump of the mid-1840s. Although it reentered the trade, it seems thereafter to have committed no more than a small fraction of its resources to such activities. In Africa the slave-trader survivors adopted a similar strategy. Caetano José Nosolini, the major figure at the northern limits of the trade, moved all his capital into legitimate trade between 1839 and 1842 and died a wealthy man in 1850. The parallel move of Domingo José Martins into the Bight of Benin palm oil business in the late 1840s is well documented.[96] There are few examples in the nineteenth century of individuals on either side of the Atlantic who combined long-run success with exclusive dependence on the business of trafficking slaves across the Atlantic.

For the slave-trading firm, then, abolition came in two stages, both defined by the British. One was British withdrawal from the traffic and the inception of a naval and diplomatic campaign against the foreign slave trade. The other was the enforcement of domestic measures by the governments of the importing region. The first shifted the industry to the Americas, put it into the hands of Spanish and Portuguese merchants and began the trend to greater concentration of ownership. The second probably had the greater influence on risk and the attendant increase in profits and losses. American and British involvement in the trade, though very important, did not take the form of direct ownership of ventures. Most of the capital was raised locally, a significant portion initially from small investors, but the majority portion in all slaving centers was self-generated from earnings. In this, the slave trader was little different from other preindustrial and early industrial enterpreneurs.

Plantation capital was not critical to the industry in either Brazil and Cuba.[97] Two partners of the Martínez firm in the 1830s, Lino Carballo and Simon Perez de Terán, had planter connections, though this did not prevent the bankruptcy of the former.[98] Other planters may have been among the purchasers of venture shares, and in the last years of the trade some capital did come into the business from agriculture. By then, however, a significant minority of the large plantations were owned by old slave traders.[99] The names of the old established families of Cuban nobles and officeholders who came to form the core of the sugar plantocracy do not appear in the slave-trade business.[100] The rapid expansion of Spanish involvement in the transatlantic slave trade actually came before the most explosive growth phase of the sugar industry. For the

Spanish in the generation after 1810, the slave trade was a new and rapidly growing industry and the leading slave traders tended to rise through the ranks, often after immigrating. If they survived long enough, they moved into the plantation sector thereafter. Even among the successful slave dealers, however, many avoided the plantations and put their funds instead into "legitimate" trade, or in one case a candle-manufacturing business. Throughout the period there was a considerable turnover of firms, with very few maintaining continuous links with the industry. This was true of both Brazil during, say, the second quarter of the century and in Cuba from the 1820s to the 1860s. The high profits thus were sufficient to overcome the barriers to entry that in other industries were associated with increasing concentration ratios. It is worth noting that the larger ships of the post-1850 period might have encouraged a trend to larger firms and more highly concentrated ownership even in the absence of abolitionist pressures.

On the evidence here, then, the slave-trading firm could have continued to adapt almost indefinitely to the pressures of abolition, at least in the form of naval and diplomatic intervention. Given the demand for plantation produce and the determination of free labor to avoid plantation work, it seemed impossible for the navy and home governments in the Americas to raise the cost of slave labor to the point where the slave trade would cease. Not until actions against the persons of slave-trading entrepreneurs were instituted would investors begin to move out of the business completely. The characteristics that distinguished the slave-trading firm from its counterparts in other international business activities—the absence of North Americans and northern Europeans, the large profits and losses and the high concentration ratios—were thus largely the results of efforts to suppress the traffic. Without this pressure the slave-trading firm would have continued to thrive along with the plantations they supplied.[101]

# 10

# Suppression and the Supply of Slaves from Africa

Abolition and suppression recast the relationship between Africa and Europe. In the eighteenth century the slave trade had come to dominate ties betwen the two continents as more than 90 percent of the value of intercontinental Atlantic exports from Africa were made up of slaves by the 1790s. The overwhelming cause of changes in the overall volume of this trade was always intra-European wars. In the nineteenth century unprecedented economic growth outside Africa brought a new complexity to exchange between the continents. On the one hand, it meant the slave trade came to be of greater potential importance than ever before as British and eventually Continental European demand for plantation produce accelerated. On the other hand, economic growth was also associated with the evolution of attempts to suppress the trade as chapter 2 has made clear. Without industrialization there would probably have been neither a naval nor a diplomatic campaign to suppress the slave trade. Moreover the growth process meant increasing European demand for African produce. Before 1800 the relative importance of this "legitimate" trade with Africa had shrunk. After 1800 it became increasingly important as palm oil and later, peanuts, entered the stream of European and North American raw material imports. For the first time large quantities of African labor were needed not only by plantation owners in the Americas but also by produce exporters in Africa. Europe continued to be of small importance for the average African, but the tension generated by such influences defined Afro-European relations in the first half of the nineteenth century and beyond.

Thus, abolition notwithstanding, slave departures from Africa showed little signs of diminution before 1850. Although the peaks of the 1780s and 1790s were not again attained, export volumes remained at historically high levels until 1850. Just over 2.5 million Africans left for the New World between 1811 and 1850 compared to just under 3 million in the forty years before 1811. Both these totals are well in excess of those in comparable periods before 1781, and the decadal figures for the 1820s and 1830s are, respectively, the third and fourth largest in the history of the traffic. In the nineteenth century as a whole, 3.4 million slaves left Africa for the Americas, and they continued to depart in greater numbers than European transatlantic emigrants down to the 1840s.[1] The above contradictions also help explain the very uneven regional patterns of exports. As we have seen in chapter 5, the flow of slaves had never been distributed equally either geographically or on a population density basis. Some large and heavily populated areas provided few slaves for the Americas, whereas other local areas may well have experienced varying degrees of depopulation. Few slave ships left Senegambia, the Windward coast, the Gold Coast and the Loango Coast north of Cabinda after 1820. The transatlantic traffic had ceased in the Bight of Biafra north of the Príncipe Island by 1840 and, less certainly, in most of Portuguese Angola by midcentury. In southeast Africa transatlantic export volumes oscillated wildly down to the end of the traffic, reflecting not so much abolition policy as the alternative possibilities of selling slaves in the Indian Ocean and Arab markets. Exports from southeast Africa to all overseas markets combined would have changed much less violently. This region, Upper Guinea, the Bight of Benin and the Congo River were always likely to supply slaves down to the mid-1860s with the Congo claiming the dubious distinction of being the last major source of African labor for the Americas. Overall, two broad distributional trends stand out in the last half-century of the traffic. One is the shift southward in the center of gravity of the trade, a continuation of a trend apparent since 1780. Between 1821 and 1867 almost two thirds of the deportees left from ports south of the equator and after 1855 the ratio rose to over 80 percent. The second is the increasing concentration of departures in certain ports within the above regions. Despite naval blockades, nine ports or their immediate vicinities accounted for 80 percent of all shipments between 1811 and 1867. Centers such as the Gallinas, Ouidah, Bonny, Cabinda, Benguela and Quelimane were tiny settlements compared to the American reception ports, but the hundreds of thousands of slaves who passed through them after 1811 made them bywords among abolitionists.

Why were some African regions more affected by suppression than others? And what was the African response to the changing external economic environment? Clearly the exact mix of suppression and European demand for American-plantation as opposed to African-grown produce varied, and most of this chapter is devoted to an evaluation of these factors at the regional level. Yet above all stands the central fact that throughout this period African markets and African demand for African produce were always more important than any external sources of trade. As we shall see, both here and in chapter 13, any reasonable ratio of export income (from both slaves and produce together) to total income suggests the continued predominance after 1808 of internal influences in the African economy.

## UPPER GUINEA

We begin with Upper Guinea. Here the slave trade became increasingly concentrated in the Gallinas and, to a lesser extent, the Pongo and Sherbro rivers

.d at Bissau.[2] Shipments from other points were always likely, but many took .he form of coastal transfers to the bulking stations of Bissau, the Pongo and the Cape Verde Islands prior to embarkation for Brazil North and Cuba. The largest center however, the Gallinas, drew its slaves from inland. Although all of these ports had participated in the traffic for many years, none had been dominant entrepôts in the presuppression era. Each, in fact, offered some protection against British naval interference. Bissau and the Cape Verde Islands were under the Portuguese flag: At Bissau and neighboring Cacheu the factories were within artillery range of the Portuguese fort, and the largest slave trader north of the Gallinas was Portuguese governor of Bissau for several years. Not until 1843 did the Portuguese stop the sale of slaves into the Atlantic trade from points adjacent to their forts.[3] At the Gallinas, Pongo and Sherbro rivers, the protection was geographic. Innumerable creeks and mangrove swamps as well as shallow waters made policing difficult and unhealthy. Indeed the Lightburn factory at Faringuira, fifteen miles up the Rio Pongo, with its martello tower and nineteen-pound muzzle loaders, was never attacked, and the Curtis factory, also in the Pongo, successfully resisted British assault.[4] The estuaries of the Senegal, Gambia, Scarcies and Rokel rivers all north of Freetown, and the large eighteenth-century bulking centers at Bulama, Gorée and other islands off the coast were simply too exposed to figure in the nineteenth-century trade except as staging posts. By 1822 the Fulbe slave caravans from the Futa Jallon focused on the Rio Nunez, near Cape Verga. Slaves traded there were taken to the new centers together with the local Nalous and Bagas via coastal transportation.[5]

The slave trade petered out in this region before the spectacular rise of slave-grown peanut output, which eventually became many times more valuable than the slave trade had been.[6] Slave prices and slave departures declined together after 1840, suggesting that the fall in demand apparent at the aggregate level operated here also. The immediate factors responsible were mainly political. A temporary decline in demand from Cuba occurred in the early 1840s due largely to Cuban and Spanish initiatives that would likely not have happened without British diplomatic pressure. The decline came immediately after major British attacks in the Gallinas, the slave trade recovery from which was slow despite the law officers' apparent repudiation of the navy's actions in 1842. Although some Brazilian traders moved in to replace the Spanish, declining demand and the Gallinas attack formed the backdrop to a series of anti-slave-trade treaties that the British signed with African coastal powers in the following decade. The British assisted the Liberian government first to buy what was taken to be the sovereignty of the Gallinas and then to enforce abolition in this region and New Cestos.[7] African consent to the British treaties would have been much more difficult to obtain without a flagging demand from the Americas. Once signed, however, the treaties provided the legal justification for British blockades and direct attacks at the end of the decade when Cuban slavers returned to the coast in force.

The role of commodity production in the suppression process does not appear to have been large. There was always a vigorous internal trade between the coast and the interior, centered on the rivers, which continued to thrive

both before and after abolition.[8] The external commodity trade in the pre
groundnut era was greatest in the very rivers from which the slave trade had
disappeared. In the Gallinas, on the other hand, the soil was "wretchedly bad
for more than 20 miles from the sea coast" and there was "no other commerce
but the slave trade".[9] Exportable quantities of produce were to be had in Bissau
and the Pongo and Sherbro rivers, but much less in the latter two regions than,
say, in the Nunez and Sierra Leone rivers. Peanut exports began in the late
1830s and became significant in the next decade. The commodity trade of the
Pongo river, for example, tripled between 1846 and 1851. But this was a case
of filling a vacuum rather than displacing an existing staple. Slave prices, which
had declined in the 1840s, held steady after 1850 despite the continuing pre-
cipitous drop in slave exports.[10] This suggests that the alternative demand for
labor in peanut production had become significant at some price below what
traders to the Americas were normally prepared to pay. Indeed it was probably
the drop in labor costs as well as the increased demand for peanuts from
Europe that was responsible for the rapid rise in peanut exports. Slave trading
and farming for export—mainly peanuts and coffee—nevertheless, existed side
by side in the Gêba, Pongo and Sherbro rivers for some years, but the former
was always the preferred activity when the opportunity arose.[11]

Except for Senegambia (discussed later) there is no sense of slaves becoming
less available in the region as a whole. Slave price and quantities were both
below eighteenth-century levels and prices probably continued to decline
together with the volume of exports down to the 1840s.[12] In contrast to west-
central Africa, the slaving frontier for transatlantic purposes shifted back
toward the coast. The ethnic origins are available for 259 Africans embarked
in 1822 at Bissau, the Pongo River and Grand Bassa in three separate shipments. For the pre-1808 period Barry Higman has drawn a much larger sample
of ethnic origins from the African-born population of the British West Indies.
A comparison of the two groupings suggests that peoples coming from beyond
a line drawn one hundred miles from the coast such as Mandingo, Foulah,
Kissi and Bambara took up a smaller share of the later Sierra Leone sample.[13]
The latter, of course, is very small, but there is much other evidence to support
this conclusion. Curtin's analysis of Koelle's linguistic inventory of the late
1840s Sierra Leone population suggests that the Soso, Temne and other coastal
populations were heavily represented.[14] The same pattern was apparent for
1,180 slaves leaving the Rio Pongo in 1834 in four Spanish vessels. No less
than 1,000 were "from the Scarcies and Melicouri rivers principally of Tim-
manee and Loco Nations."[15] Most of the small contingent of Amistad captives
embarking at the Gallinas in 1839 and subsequently landed in the United
States after a mutiny were Mende from no more than sixty miles inland. Portuguese at Bissau and Cacheu allied themselves with the peoples of Kanyabac,
the largest of the Bissagos Islands (Arquipélago dos Bijagos), and they raided
villages on the rivers over which they claimed sovereignty. The trade in reen-
slaved liberated Africans is well known, many of them passing through the
Gallinas on their way to the Americas. There is abundant testimony that the
majority of Gallinas deportees were obtained from the territory drained by
minor rivers between Cape Mount and Sierra Leone. Local warfare, kidnap-

ᴧing and judicial procedures rather than long-distance caravans were the major source.[16] Mandingo traders traveled from the far interior but were actually more likely to buy slaves on the coast for markets to the north than to sell them.[17]

South of the Gallinas stretched the rest of the Windward coast from which after 1820 only a few hundred slaves per year were taken. Never a major slave-trading region, the lightly populated hinterlands and lack of easy access to more traditional provenance zones in the interior militated against any change in this status in the closing years of the traffic.[18] East of Cape Palmas, the Ivory Coast continued free of the slave trade after 1807, but further east slaves left parts of the Gold Coast down to at least 1839 and, via coastal transfer to Keta and Ouidah, for many years before and after this. The numbers may not have been great, but the catchment area was very wide. The *Ulysses,* a captured Cuban-bound slaver taken to Kingston, Jamaica, embarked 540 "Mandingoes [few], Chambas (northern Asante), Asantees, Fantees, Nagos (Yoruba), and Pohpohs (Adja or Ewe)" west of Accra in 1839. This suggests that the Anlo from whom the Afro-Brazilian slave factors acquired their slaves in this region were purchasing at the great long-distance salt/slave centers of Kratchi (Kete-Krachi) and Salaga over one hundred miles inland. There can be no doubt that European sovereignty claims in the area were the key factor in reducing exports from the Gold Coast, a major provenance zone in the previous century. The last-recorded direct shipments from Dutch Accra were the occasion of British protests and promises of Dutch cooperation.[19] The main African hinterland state, Asante, adjusted successfully to this change without developing an Atlantic commodity substitute for slaves. Although the land-borne cola trade to the north grew rapidly, the total value of Atlantic exports probably did not regain levels reached in the peak years of the slave trade (1780s) until the last third of the nineteenth century.[20] Here at least the Atlantic commodity trade bore no discernible relationship to the Atlantic slave trade.

## BIGHT OF BENIN

In the Bight of Benin the geographic concentration of the trade was as extreme as in Upper Guinea. Despite embarking no slaves after 1851, Lagos was easily the leading slave exporting port in the nineteenth century and together with Ouidah probably accounted for 60 percent of all departures from the region. In that slaves were often embarked at some distance from their barracoons, especially in the case of Ouidah, these figures are to some extent misleading, but the factories themselves may well have been the leading Atlantic slaving centers on the continent.[21] Geography contributed much to such preeminence. All slaving centers in this region were located on the long lagoon system that runs parallel to the ocean and is fronted by a beach with a dangerous surf. Indeed in the early nineteenth century a canoe could travel from the Volta River east to Lagos and beyond on the internal waterway. Slaves were likely to be embarked by canoe through the surf from almost any part of the long beach because the lagoon behind it provided the ideal facility for quick passage to the least-watched section.[22] As a large part of the beach was under the suzerainty, albeit uneven, of the king of Dahomey, there were few political barriers to this operation, and the Dahomean capital, Abomey, was far enough inland to deter a seaborne assault. Lagos was an independent maritime city-state that could be occupied with the aid of the existing African squadron once the British government had resolved to its own satisfaction the moral, political and diplomatic issues involved. Ouidah, on the other hand, was five kilometers from the sea, protected by a swamp and was only one of the potential slave-shipping outlets for Dahomey. In the 1850s the British commodore twice recommended against attacking any part of Dahomey despite the king's violation of the 1852 treaty.[23] Lagos was not assaulted until many years after the buildup of the British African fleet in the 1830s and even then was taken only on the second attempt. It was not just bravado that induced one of the last Afro-Portuguese slave traders in the region to comment to a naval officer in 1867 that "the slave trade is finished for the present so I am going into legal trade; your cruizers have not stopped it, but there is no demand from Cuba."[24]

Ouidah and Lagos were the main outlets for two overlapping supply systems, and the foundations of both were upheavals associated with major states in the area. Dahomey became even stronger under King Ghezo and conducted regular and far-reaching military expeditions documented by many missionaries and naval observers. In the process the king enforced tribute and captured slaves. Bounded on the west by another large state, Asante, Dahomey directed most of these ventures eastward into Yorubaland. Here the collapse of the Oyo Empire, formed the prelude to the internecine Yoruba warfare that fed the stream of deportees heading down the rivers to the Lagos lagoon.[25] In both ports the African ruler and his aristocracy used intermediaries, usually Afro-Portuguese, to deal with the slave ship. In Lagos these individuals might be the factor employees or partners of the slave-trading firm in the Americas. In Ouidah they were more likely to be officials of the Dahomey state, such as the chacha or independent factors, such as Domingo Martins at Porto Novo. The chacha's considerable authority never amounted to a monopoly even over the King's slaves, though both he and other factors had the resources and contacts on occasion to send their own ships to the Americas. Unlike Ghezo, the king of Lagos bought rather than captured slaves. His agents purchased captives from whichever Yoruba warlord was currently victorious.[26] The Ijebu were a common source but no Yoruba group, least of all the Egba whom the British missionaries backed in their struggle against Dahomey eschewed the business.[27] The king of Dahomey sent his own captives through Ouidah and both he and the king of Lagos levied duties on others traded in their respective markets. The British attack on Lagos left Ouidah as the major slave-export funnel for the whole region, but by this time palm oil production was taking a major share of the slaves generated by the political unrest.[28]

The supply of slaves to Bight of Benin ports had two striking characteristics. one was the wide range of ethnic origins represented. Yoruba slaves predominated, but Africans from the Upper Volta eastward through the Hausa and Nupe areas to the Igbo of the lower Niger embarked from Lagos and Ouidah.[29] Late in 1858 as the last great surge of Cuban demand began to peak, a Liverpool palm oil dealer on the Niger River north of Aboh noted the pickup of activity in his diary. "Great numbers of canoes keep passing up the river daily for the purpose of buying slaves, from which I should infer that the slave trade must be carried on to a great extent in the Brass, Bonny and Calabar rivers."[30] His inference was wrong; the slaves were being assembled hundreds of miles away on the lagoon south of Dahomey. The basic point is that the catchment area for Bight of Benin ports was very large, well populated and well organized. The second feature may be found in the age and sex structure of the deportees. The Bight of Benin slave trade had fewer children and more women proportionately than the traffic from other regions. Moreover, the female ratio rose during the years when the volume of the traffic was high and there were no barriers to lactating women entering the traffic. Rising volumes did not have a similar effect on the proportion of children carried off, but this may be explained, in part, by the distances traveled. Children were worth less than adults, were less able to withstand the rigors of travel and, if taken in war, were easier to assimilate and control within the captor's society.[31] A high-enough price increase might well have elicited a responding rise in the child ratio also. A provenance zone of this size and this age-and-sex pattern among its deportees was not likely to be exhausted by the combined demands from the Americas and the domestic palm oil sector at the levels at which they operated in the mid-nineteenth century.

It follows from this that once more the rise of produce exports was not a critical element in the suppression process. Although the quality of the data on the slave and palm oil trades will not support formal analysis, they do support some general comments.[32] The rise in Liverpool palm oil prices during the 1830s no doubt triggered the first Bight of Benin exports to Europe (as opposed to Bahia) in the last years of the decade. The spectacular growth in these exports in the 1840s, however, was accompanied by declining oil prices to 1845 and recovery thereafter. Slave exports showed little diminution in these years and as many scholars have pointed out, the two trades functioned comfortably together, with perhaps the same marketing structures and indeed entrepreneurial personnel. Thus the growth of the palm oil trade after 1840 was not dependent on either the decline of the slave trade or a secular rise in palm oil prices.[33] Whatever the explanation for the output rise, its impact on slave prices is clear enough. In the late 1840s when slave departures were only slightly above their 1836–40 levels, slave prices were 30 percent higher and, in fact, reached their highest point in the nineteenth-century price series. After 1850, with the Brazilian pullout from the trade, slave prices declined significantly, but by nowhere near as much as slave exports. Because palm oil exports continued to expand strongly after 1850, this suggests that the labor requirements of the expanding Dahomean palm oil plantations put a floor under slave prices. In the last years of the traffic, Dahomean slaves, in fact, were twice as expensive as those in the Congo river where commodity exports were very small. Despite these high prices the annual value of slave exports in, say, 1856 and 1857 could not have been much above £75,000, whereas the total value of commodity exports in those years from all Bight of Benin ports averaged nearly £1 million.[34] Those who might interpret this as commodity exports squeezing out the slave trade should remember that after 1850 African slave prices were only 8 to 15 percent of final selling costs in Cuba. It was not the high prices of slaves in Africa that put an end to the trade.[35]

At the factoring level on the coast, there was certainly little tension between the two trades. The great chacha, Francisco Féliz de Souza invited the first Ouidah palm oil agent of the London firm of W. M. Hutton to visit Abomey accompanied by himself. For the slave traders such European firms were an additional source of slaving goods. When de Souza, Martins and the other slave factors broke into the palm oil export business, their profits from the slave trade allowed them on occasion to undercut the "legitimate" traders, a tactic that could only increase produce exports.[36] Rivalries developed but these were within the palm oil business not between palm oil and slaving activites. As in the Rio Pongo, however, there is a clear sense that commodity trade was a second best option.[37] King Ghezo's response to the abortive British blockade of 1852 was an offer to give up the slave trade but only if the cruisers would funnel all the lagoon system's oil exports through the port of Ouidah. He then attempted to establish a monopoly without British aid. The king did not have a monopoly on slave exports from the region, but monopoly profits on palm oil were essential if the royal revenues from the latter were to match those from the former, at least in the early 1850s.[38] In the Bight of Benin then, as in Upper Guinea, both slave and produce exports would have grown in tandem in the absence of the antislave-trade impulse. It is thus clear that attempts to suppress the trade should be given considerable emphasis.

## BIGHT OF BIAFRA

In the Bight of Biafra a different mix of factors determined the end of the trade. Embarkation points here drew slaves from a much smaller geographic zone than the adjacent Bight of Benin. Despite the easy transportation possible along most of the Niger River, there is little evidence of any but Igbo and Ibibio peoples leaving Bonny and Calabar, with the former predominating.[39] There was substantial movement of slaves from Aboh, a major market at the head of the delta, toward embarkation points in the Bight of Benin, probably in response to major price differentials between the slave coast and Niger Delta ports. In addition, there were probably restrictions on the sale of lactating women and their infants that did not hold in Yorubaland. This was, however, probably the most densely populated region of Africa and was able to meet the peak demands of the late 1830s without any adjustment in sex-and-age ratios. There is some evidence of a geographic child-ratio pattern. The proportion of children leaving the most distant provenance zones occupied by the Agbaja and Isuama Igbo was less than the equivalent ratio in the Ibibio Anang and Arochukwu areas closer to the embarkation points. The lower prices in Bonny and Calabar relative to other parts of the African littoral no doubt reflected, in part, the close proximity of these densely populated areas.[40]

The important factors that separate Bight of Biafra ports in the abolition process lie elsewhere. In contrast to the Bight of Benin, embarkation of slaves in the Bight of Biafra took place in the deltas and estuaries of rivers that were readily accessible from the sea. There were many square miles of mangrove forest, but the river channels themselves were deep and their bars often navigable. Bonny and Calabar dominated the slave trade here almost as much as did Lagos and Ouidah in the Bight of Benin, but geographically there were many other potential outlets.[41] Political structures here also differed from the Bight of Benin. Some have seen the Aro network as a state in all but name, but from the standpoint of external powers seeking treaties, political authority in the region was well diffused.[42] The Efik and Ijo traders with whom the Europeans dealt were independent intermediaries with no political and military ties with the suppliers of slaves upriver. In addition, both the Bight of Biafra's severe epidemiological environment and the long slave-trading dominance of the British in the area meant that other European powers had neither forts nor territorial claims on any part of the mainland prior to 1845. In the Bight of Biafra, then, the naval power of the British was always likely to count for more than in most other parts of the African coast.

Measured in terms of losses inflicted per ship embarked the impact of the navy was only slightly greater here than, say in, the Bight of Benin. Most significantly the loss ratio averaged nearly 40 percent per annum in the years 1836–39 when slave exports underwent their final decline. But for the period 1821–39 the annual loss ratio explains only 6 percent of the annual variations in slave exports.[43] And Bight of Benin ports experienced annual loss ratios of almost one third in the same period, without seeing any permanent decline in slave departures. It seems unlikely that ship losses alone brought the traffic to a close. A key event was the signing of the abolition treaties between the British and African rulers in the rivers that began in 1839 and continued into the 1840s. These, in effect, gave belligerent rights to the British if the trading states failed to abide by their terms. As Bonny and Calabar, unlike Dahomey, were well within range of the squadron's guns, a treaty here meant something more than did subsequent conventions in the lagoons of the Slave Coast to the west.

The crucial question becomes why did the Efik and Ijo authorities agree to these treaties. It is here that the palm oil traffic becomes important. The coastal trading states could and did deal in either slaves or palm oil. The years 1833 to 1837 formed the highest volume quinquennia in the nineteenth-century Bight of Biafra slave trade. Assuming a price of £7.6 per slave, total revenue for slaves amounted to nearly £0.9 million. This was almost certainly above the total revenue generated by palm oil sales alone. As annual slave departures plummeted in the late 1830s and oil production increased, the value of produce exports exceeded their human counterparts by many times.[44] This was particularly the case for Bonny and Calabar. They had been the dominant oil and slave ports in the 1820s, but both centers experienced a decline in slave-ship departures relative to other Bight of Biafran ports after 1830. This in itself was not a reason for giving up the trade but, given the above loss ratios, the prospect of the trade reviving would have to be weighed against subsidies that the British were prepared to pay. King Pepple of Bonny, for example, was at one point promised $10,000 a year. He did not, in fact, receive this, as problems in coordinating four major British departments of state (Foreign Office, Treasury, Admiralty, Colonial Office) and Treasury reservations on the size of subsidies meant that the first ratified suppression treaties were not signed until

May 1841. These agreements with kings Acqua and Bell of the Cameroons were followed by others with Eyo of Creek Town and the chiefs of the Old Calabar trading states in December of that year, and two years later King William of Bimbia, near the Cameroons, accepted the same terms. King Pepple of Bonny did not sign a slave-trade treaty that was finally ratified until 1848, though both sides had believed that a treaty was in force at various times from 1839 on.[45] There is no evidence that the slave trade constituted a restraint on the palm oil sector or that the suppression of the slave trade unleashed the renewed growth of the palm oil sector.

Pepple continued to ship a few hundred slaves a year through other branches of the Niger in the early 1840s. The same routes were used by Spanish factors in the Brass River during the mid-1840s and as late as 1857.[46] But the major Cuban market declined and the Brazilians did not fill the vacuum in the Bight of Biafra as they did in the Gallinas. Though it remained a profitable alternative for risk-takers, the slave trade became of very minor significance relative to palm oil. At the Gabon River and Sangatanga, near Cape Lopez, the transatlantic slave traffic continued into the late 1840s and exports to the São Tomé coffee plantations intermittently for some years beyond. The trade survived here because of French reluctance to disturb a lucrative commerce in the first years after asserting a sovereignty claim in the Gabon and also because the creek system at Cape Lopez was reminiscent of the Slave Coast, though on a much smaller scale. Here some commodity trade developed in the 1830s and 1840s but was scarcely an alternative to the slave traffic. For the major Bight of Biafra ports to the north, however, free trade conditions (i.e., no suppression) would have meant increasing palm oil exports and slave departures.[47] The great predominance of oil did, however, mean that the external slave traffic was easier to give up. The navy and a strategic decline in Cuban demand for slaves (itself a result of British pressure) combined to kill off a traffic that was no longer critical to the economic and political survival of the coastal trading states, with the exception of the Mpongwe at Sangatanga and the Orungu at Cape Lopez. And for states higher up the Niger there were always the alternative outlets of Ouidah and Lagos.

## WEST-CENTRAL AFRICA

In Africa south of Cape Lopez both suppression and the rapid expansion of commodity exports occurred much later than north of the equator. The basic feature in the distribution of west-central African slave exports after 1830 was a rise in the relative importance of the Congo River coupled with pronounced cyclical fluctuations. Near record volumes of slave departures in 1826–30, 1845–50 and 1857–60 were followed by dramatic and ultimately permanent declines.[48] The reasons for the pattern lie largely outside Africa. The fluctuations over time were a function of great swings in demand that stemmed from formal abolition of the trade in Brazil in 1830, effective suppression in that country in 1850–51 and finally the decline in the price of Cuban slaves in the 1860s. The geographic shift was induced by European actions against the trade. South of the Congo the Angolan trade was pressured by a series of measures from the Portuguese antislave-trade decree of 1836 up through the active cooperation of the Portuguese-Angolan squadron with the British starting in 1844. The key was Portuguese sovereignty claims that allowed land-based operations against slave depots without the prior permission of African rulers.[49] Such measures had the effect of choking off Luanda and (eventually) Benguela as slave-exporting ports and making it gradually more difficult to ship slaves from adjacent points such as Rio Dande, Quicombo, Lobito and Catumbella.[50] The Ambriz region to the north remained outside effective Portuguese occupation until 1855, and much of the Luanda business was transferred there from the late 1830s.[51] To the north of the Congo the traffic to Mayumba, Loango and Malemba was already in decline before the end of the eighteenth century. Renewed Cuban interest in markets south of the equator revived the Loango trade, and in the 1830s slaves left in both transatlantic and coasting vessels, the latter chiefly to Cabinda. An unusual reef system outside Loango Bay made the port easy to blockade, however, and from 1839 when the British began regular patrols south of the equator, direct shipments declined.[52] Thus although slaves departed from all parts of Angola and Congo North as far south as Cabo de Sta Marta prior to 1851, the focus of the traffic increasingly became the Congo River with its great depots to the north and south, Cabinda, Ambriz and Ambrizete.

What little is known about slave-supply patterns in the interior accords with these shifts on the coast. The west-central African hinterland was geographically far bigger than that of any other major transatlantic exporting region. Population densities were, however, much lower than in West Africa, with the result that many victims of the slave trade traveled more than halfway across the continent before boarding ship. The relative wealth of materials on ethnic origins in West Africa has no parallel here, however. Koelle's Sierra Leone inventory indicates that peoples close to the coast such as the Mboma were well represented. The savanna south of the Congo River was also a significant provenance zone. Some slaves traveled down the tributaries of that river, but before the nineteenth century most came direct to the coast from the Lunda and Ovimbundu states, either via the Cuanza River or overland from Bihe to Benguela.

A second long-distance supply route ran from the Upper Congo and Tio regions that supplied perhaps 40 percent of the slaves at Loango in the 1780s. This ratio probably increased in the nineteenth century as the rising importance of the Congo outlet on the coast was paralleled by the spread downstream of the Bobangi trading network on the Congo River above Malebo Pool and its northern tributaries. West of Malebo Pool the Mussorongo traders completed the network and played the same intermediation role as did the Kasanje and Matamba to the south.[53] The explanation for the rise of the northern routes is not obvious, however. The volume of slave departures cannot have been a major factor. For close to a century before 1850, decadal departures had ranged from 200,000 to 430,000. The figures in the last thirty years of this period fall into the middle of this range, though given cyclical variations some five-year totals may have matched the highest in the history of the traffic.[54] The Cokwe attacks on Lunda were a major factor only after this pattern came to be established and were perhaps a consequence rather than a precursor of the decline of the trade.[55] There is also a puzzle in the high proportion of children in the traffic at a time when internal trade routes were certainly not shortening.[56] Perhaps attempts to suppress the traffic had an influence here. The basic fact, however, is that relatively low prices for slaves was combined with long distances traveled and a level of decadal exports below the peak levels of the late eighteenth century. Long supply lines meant that sudden surges of demand could result in slave ships being kept waiting in the Congo or alternatively the embarkation of domestic slaves from Portuguese settlements. But there is little evidence here of supply crises in the region as a whole.[57]

At the mouth of the Congo European force could achieve little, given British reluctance to recognize Portuguese sovereignty in the region. Ambriz and Cabinda (or rather the towns loosely grouped under these names) had close links with Boma and Puerto de Lenha. The former at the head of the Congo Delta was as far inland as the slave factors were allowed to trade. The latter, between Boma and the open sea, was a deep-water anchorage and factor headquarters.[58] In 1842 before their temporary second thoughts on the legality of the Gallinas assault the British destroyed extensive slave traders' property at Ambriz, Cabinda and Puerto da Lenha in similar attacks. In the Congo itself they maintained a blockade against slave vessels more or less continuously from 1840.[59] In the mid-1840s when the Anglo-French convention was in full operation and the Portuguese Angola squadron was active and again in the late 1850s, there were at times twenty cruisers in the area. Yet the slave-ship loss ratio in this region was never above one third except for isolated years, and the traffic continued for a further quarter century after the strengthening of the naval forces. Indeed if we include French engagés, it reaches its nineteenth-century quinquennial peak in the years 1858 to 1862. Naval action was clearly not of critical importance.

The reason for the durability of the trade was not just a lack of European sovereignty rights, though a residual European respect for the rights of African states did linger on past midcentury. The British sought treaties with African rulers constantly but by 1858 there were only three agreements in existence on the west-central African coast—none of them in the Congo River.[60] The fissiparous nature of coastal political structures were partly to blame. The power of the king of the Kongo over the Congo River communities had dissipated long before. At Boma the factors paid dues to two separate rulers, depending on the location of their buildings, and along the banks of the Congo there were many small semi-independent communities.[61] At Cabinda, Principe Jack signed a treaty in 1853, but it proved so unpopular with his fellow chiefs that he refused to ratify it the following year. Although naval officers were convinced that ordinary Africans (even those in the trading states) wanted the trade to end, the Cabindan chiefs hoped to continue the trade in launches registered under the Portuguese flag. In the right circumstances, however, blockade of one river, albeit the Congo, might have been effective.[62] There were probably two factors that prevented this.

The first was the lack of a significant overseas commodity trade as an alternative to slaves at least in the Congo. Trade from the Congo may have rivaled ₙat of the Niger by the 1880s, but there was no hint of this in the early 1860s. In 1858–62 transatlantic slave departures earned the Congo region well in excess of $500,000 per annum. During the slaving slump of the early 1850s a few slaving factors had tried to establish a trade in orchella gum and palm oil. By 1857, before the last great explosion of slave departures, the value of palm oil, by far the most important export, was averaging less than $100,000 per year and thereafter declined.[63] In Angola an alternative developed earlier. The abolition of the government monopsony on ivory was followed by dramatic increases in the ivory trade. Luanda and Benguela were opened to foreign vessels in 1844. Exports of perfume, urzella, beeswax and orchella began to grow rapidly even before this but not enough to prevent the total value of trade at Luanda (slaves and commodities) dropping 70 percent between 1825 and 1844.[64] This latter trend is to some extent deceptive. Few slaves left Luanda after 1840, but few merchants in that city were unconnected with the slave trade. Slave ships left from points to the north and south, empty slavers regularly called there for supplies and Luanda firms had slaving depots at Ambriz and in the Congo until the late 1850s.[65] The rapid growth of commodity exports in the mid-1840s was from such a small base that no doubt slave trafficking continued to earn more revenue than commodity exports for Luanda and other ports south of the Congo down to 1850.

After a period of stagnation in the early 1850s, commodity trade grew throughout the late 1850s and early 1860s; it encompassed all points of export south of the Congo River to Moçamedes. In 1857 produce valued at $1.1 million (in 1821–25 prices) left Luanda and strong growth occurred in each of the next two years. Ambriz and Ambrizete (the former occupied by Portugal since 1855) exported copper ore, ivory and some palm oil, which was probably worth somewhat less than Luanda exports. The Ovimbundu trade route to the south guaranteed Benguela an increasing trade in ivory and wax. But the value of both this and the trade of the smaller centers such as Moçamedes is unlikely to have exceeded that of Luanda.[66] In the late 1850s, then, commodity exports from Angola and Ambrizete were probably in the range of $2.5 to $3.0 million per annum. This was certainly more than the region had ever earned from slave exports. For Angola and probably for west-central Africa as a whole, it would seem that the overseas commodity trade overtook the slave trade in 1851 as the Brazilian slave trade collapsed. But before that year the slave trade was many times more valuable. In the late 1850s both the slave and commodity trades expanded. The pattern then was that the major branch of the slave trade ended before produce exports became significant, but the evidence of the late 1850s suggests no incompatibility between the two.

The second factor inhibiting suppression was the ease with which blockading cruisers could be avoided. The Congo River was large and swift flowing and right to the end of the trade the occasional slaver escaped by drifting out at night under furled sails.[67] But the vast majority of slaves from the Congo drainage basin who crossed the Atlantic after 1840 did not leave from the river itself but from a range of secluded points on the open coast located on either side of the estuary. They were often conveyed to these places by large launches, built and manned by Cabinda men, and usually by an inland route. Cabinda and

Puerto de Lenha, for example, were linked by a creek. The swift and commodious Cabinda boats were the foundation of factoring operations in these last years of the slave trade in this region. They were more specialized and essential to the Congo system than were the Fanti canoes to shippers in the Bight of Benin. Together with well-beaten trails these boats enabled slave factors to use this coast as though it had the lagoons of the Slave Coast. They were able to move provisions, trading goods, incriminating equipment and, of course, slaves at short notice back and forth anywhere from Mayumba in the north to Luanda in the south.[68] As extensions of foreign territory and in the absence of treaties, the boats were left largely unmolested by the British despite the fact that a flotilla of them could shift the embarkation point of a large slaver by many miles in a single night. "Generally speaking there are no established ports for shipment" wrote the British commodore. With the excusable exaggeration of a man in command of an ineffective fleet of thirty-two fighting ships, he went on, "From Cape Lopez to little Fish Bay, there is not a foot of ground untrod . . . by the slave dealers; the slaves are run from point to point . . . nearly all . . . come from Embomma [Boma]."[69]

West-central Africa thus presents some interesting contrasts with the bights. The traffic continued in west-central Africa not because there was a powerful African state like Dahomey involved, but rather because of the absence of one. Outside Portuguese Angola no European surrogate for such a power existed. European naval might of the strength that Britain was prepared to commit was ineffective in the face of the geography of the river system and the skill of Cabinda men. Also, in contrast to the bights, there was no strong commodity-trade sector. If in the bights such trade could and did develop independently of the slave trade, here its lack probably encouraged slave traders—African and European alike—to persist in the business. One further contrast is in the significance of overseas trade relative to domestic economic activities. In both areas the latter was of far greater importance, but in west-central Africa, by any reasonable per capita measurement, exports were of miniscule significance.[70] For small groups such as the Bobangi boatmen and perhaps the Cokwe, overseas trade may have had a strong impact, but for the vast majority of west-central African peoples, the income effects of Atlantic trade were utterly unnoticeable.

## SOUTHEAST AFRICA

Finally we turn to southeast Africa where most of the Atlantic trade was conducted within territory nominally under Portuguese sovereignty. There were, in fact, three broad, separate sources of overseas demand for slaves in early nineteenth-century East Africa. As well as the Americas, there was the northern rim of the Indian Ocean and, third, the offshore islands—chiefly the Mascarenes but later Zanzibar and Pemba. The first and second were supplied by European and Arab shippers, respectively, the third was supplied by both. The Comoro Islands and Madagascar were frequently used as staging posts where slaves were handed over from Arab to European. This increased complexity, however, does not alter the basic pattern of major trends at the regional level ɔeing determined by factors in the Americas and Europe rather than on the African side of the market. Once more there is the familiar tension between the rising demand for plantation produce and the abolitionist impulse, both of which were rooted in the industrialization process.[71] The general level of slave departures from East Africa did not decline until the last quarter of the nineteenth century. After 1840, however, the traffic to the Americas from this region became steadily less important relative to the other branches of the commerce. The basic explanation for this secular shift as well as the erratic annual fluctuations in absolute volumes lies in the suppression process in Brazil and Cuba. The disappearance of the trade to the Americas in the early 1830s, the cyclical highs in the late 1830s and the 1840s and the drastic fall after 1850 follow Brazilian import trends. After 1850 the Cuban market set the pattern with transatlantic departures lasting almost as long as the Cuban market remained open. For both Brazil and Cuba there was probably a threshold level of costs below which trade with southeast Africa could not be justified. Above this point, however, supplies of slaves to the Americas would be very responsive to price changes. Slaves were drawn from the great lakes regions along the Maravi and Yao trade routes and from petty local traders and the Prazo proprietors of the Zambezi valley. Once on the coast, they were available to buyers from the Persian Gulf, the Red Sea and Zanzibar, as well as the Americas. Indeed, when demand in the Americas died, the external traffic in slaves to the north intensified.[72]

Events within Africa became more important at the subregional level. Low rainfall at times made water transport difficult and cut down supplies south of the Zambezi in particular. Pressure from peoples called Mapezitas or Landins, perhaps Nguni invaders, as well as Boer expansion also disrupted trade routes to the southerly ports of Inhambane and Lourenço Marques. But the major disruptions came from British and Portuguese attempts to suppress the traffic. For most of this period Portuguese authority existed only at the six principal settlements on the thousands of miles of coastline claimed by Lisbon. Before the 1836 decree most of the slaves embarked on transatlantic ships left by only two of these ports, Mozambique and Quelimane, although slaves were taken to these bulking centers from all over the coast.[73] Mozambique was the most important of the two, though the traffic was growing more rapidly at Quelimane. Initially the decree had little effect, mainly because the Portuguese governor omitted to publish it. British ships however began a partial blockade of Mozambique as early as 1837, before equivalent action was begun in west-central Africa. The Portuguese themselves confiscated and condemned three Atlantic slavers at Mozambique in 1840. A new governor, Rodrigo Luciano Abreu de Lima began to replace subordinate officials unwilling to enforce the law, though finding replacements hostile to the trade was not easy. Such actions and a temporary decline in the demand for slaves from the Americas brought the Mozambique trade to an end by the early 1840s. Direct shipments from Quelimane itself also declined, but significant numbers of slaves from the upstream markets of Sena and Tete continued to leave the surrounding Zambezi Delta.[74] Restrictions were increased however by an Anglo-Portuguese agreement in 1843 that allowed the British to destroy slave-trading establishments and pursue slave ships in territorial waters in areas where the Portuguese government had no presence.[75] Thus the British found themselves in a position of potential power over the slave trade that they were only able to attain on the west coast after many years of naval assaults and diplomatic pressure on many small African states. That the traffic in Portuguese southeast Africa did not come to a rapid end was due to the size of the coastline, the very few cruisers available and the involvement of many junior Portuguese officials in the business.

Under British and Portuguese pressure[76] the revived trade to the Americas, nevertheless, assumed new directions. Within the territory claimed by the Portuguese, it moved increasingly to the Querimba Islands, in particular Ibo, though the Zambezi trade route continued to keep the Quelimane area important.[77] The transatlantic traffic also began to draw for the first time on the Iles Angoche, an independent Arab enclave near Mozambique, which had supplied slaves to Zanzibar, the Comoro islands, and western Madagascar for many years.[78] Finally ships from the Americas began to draw much more heavily from north and east of Cape Delgado in the territories of the imam of Muscat. The entrepôts of Ibo, Comoro and western Madagascar were also important provenance zones during the last phase of the Cuban traffic.[79] The British and Portuguese attacked Angoche several times between 1846 and 1851 until its sultan agreed to a treaty. Both here and at Pemba Bay, Portuguese sovereignty could not have been asserted in the absence of British slave-trade policy.[80] British attacks on Banyan slave depots north of Cape Delgado continued into the early 1850s, after the imam signed a treaty in 1845 and a letter in 1850 giving the navy access to the mainland south of Kilwa.[81] But the distances were vast, potential embarkation points numerous and the demand for slaves from all sources increased rapidly after 1845. As late as the early 1860s slaves left for Cuba from places as widely separated as Delagoa Bay, Nos Beh (Nossi Bé) and Zanzibar.[82] Even though the British had the authority to destroy slave traders' property on the whole East African coast by 1850, the suppression of the trade to the Americas at least was beyond their power. As already noted, effective suppression had to await developments in the Americas.

As in most other areas the trade in produce played little role in the abolition process. An Atlantic trade in commodities had predated the slave traffic in Portuguese southeast Africa as in other parts of that continent. It remained relatively more valuable than slaves here for longer than on the west coast. In fact, in East Africa as a whole slaves were probably the dominant export for little more than half a century between the late eighteenth and mid-nineteenth centuries.[83] Before this period, when ivory exports predominated, there was little conflict between the two exports. Ivory and slaves were supplied by different trading networks both on the coast and in the interior; as the ivory was not cultivated, it was not likely to be disrupted by massive slave departures. After midcentury when an exportable labor-intensive product appeared in the form of cloves, the price of slaves in East Africa remained very low compared to prices in the Americas. This suggests that the supply of slaves was sufficiently elastic to meet all the demands of both clove plantations of East Africa and the *ingenios* of Cuba—at least under the conditions that existed in the 1850s. If a free transatlantic trade in slaves had existed in the nineteenth century, then the clove industry and indeed all other commerce might eventually have been seriously affected—but this is a question taken up in chapter 13.[84]

In all the exporting regions examined the traffic shifted away from the few established European settlements. As a consequence slaves began to be shipped covertly under less than ideal conditions. This implies that a new and expanded role for the factor developed. The function of the factor was to procure and detain the slave prior to shipment. In chapter 4, three types of factor were defined: the independent shore-based trader, the African headman and the agent of the slave-importing company who maintainted a permanent establishment on shore. While all three types could be found on the coast, even in the closing years of the illegal trade, one tended to predominate at different times. The first two were dominant north of the line, at least before 1830, and survived the changes in factoring techniques induced by the naval activities. The numerous Portuguese and Spanish ships captured in the bights in 1815 and 1816 usually had a portion of both their inbound and outbound cargoes on board. Many slavers traded at more than one location.[85] This suggests that part of the optimal method of gathering a cargo was small shore establishments and trading at many different places. Under such a system there would clearly be abundant scope for the independent trader.

In the 1830s in response to the slave-trade treaties, the practice developed of keeping the slaves on shore until the complete cargo was collected and then loading all the slaves at once just before the ship sailed.[86] In the 1820s, of the 122 ships with known cargoes taken before the Sierra Leone Court of Mixed Commission, only sixteen had part-slave cargoes on board. Most of these had been taken in the act of loading. Although the factor role was thus expanded, the Americas-based slave trader made no attempt initially to establish a presence on shore. Most of the ships brought before the Sierra Leone courts in this period carried supercargoes, an indication that the owner had no agent on the coast and was prepared to trade his outbound cargo at more than one place. Business letters that have survived instruct the ship's officers to trade at the best available market.[87] At Calabar the cargo was handed over, as before, to Duke Ephraim, the leading Efik trader, but instead of embarking the slaves as they become available, the slavers "unbend their sails and the majority of their spars. . . . [The masters] sweep the vessels about ten or fifteen miles higher up the river and there they leave them in charge of the Mates. The Masters return with 5 or 6 of their crew and take possession of a barracoon . . . or slave house which they hire and there they await the pleasure of the Duke in getting their cargoes." Similar practices occurred in the Bonny and Cameroons. In Angola and Mozambique a Portuguese political presence and the practice of spreading a shipment of slaves over several ships ensured significant shore establishments even before naval pressure. Official Portuguese disapproval of the trade developed in the later 1830s.[88] But there is nothing to suggest that such places were predominantly in the hands of merchants based in the Americas.

It is only after 1830 that firms importing into the Americas significantly expanded their operations in Africa. The Pedro Martínez firm had a permanent base at the Gallinas by 1828, at Lagos in 1838 and at Brass River by 1841. At Brass River, slaves were collected (from King Pepple of the Bonny among others) who previously would have been supplied direct to the slave ship.[89] In the second quarter of the century, a company wishing to buy slaves in Africa normally had to commit substantial resources to the African coast first. Captain Denman found no less than eight factories in the Gallinas in November 1840, all owned by Havana dealers. Further south in Gabon, Loango, the Congo, Cabinda and at the R. Cuanza south of Luanda, both Havana and Rio de Janeiro dealers were maintaining their own barracoons and resident agents by the early 1840s.[90] Very large barracoons existed at Palmarinas Bay (just outside Luanda) and Benguela by 1840, and these became a basic feature of the last quarter century of the slave trade. Near the close of the Brazilian trade, there were fifteen large factories at Ambriz. And on the Cabinda bank of the Congo, there were eleven barracoons—for five thousand slaves—that had been built on a "magnificient scale;" there were also luxurious houses, three boat-building sheds and extensive gardens.[91] By the end of the 1830s the small independent trader and the African ruler, the dominant factor types of the 1820s, were dealing with shore-based agents of the American importer rather than with the slave ship itself. Those smaller importers who did not have their own factors on the coast used the agents of the larger firms. The large African-based traders such as Caetano Nosolini, de Souza and later Domingo Martins survived and indeed thrived in the new conditions because they operated on a scale big enough to collect and maintain large quantities of goods and slaves on shore until the slaves could actually be shipped. As noted in the previous chapter, factors of this type became more numerous after 1850 as Cuban firms resorted to Afro-Portuguese agents once more. But the elaborate shore establishments remained.

The expanded duties of the factor went far beyond buying and holding extra quantities of slaves. He or she first had to acquire land as well as trading and provisioning rights from an African state willing to carry on the traffic.[92] The factory itself had to be located close to a safe and convenient embarkation point but far enough inland and sufficiently concealed to escape the attention of naval landing parties. By the 1840s networks of large barracoons had become standard, all connected by paths and lagoons along which factors could move the slaves in response to the deployment of the cruisers.[93] Warehouses for trading goods and provisions sufficient to purchase and maintain several slave cargoes became essential. The best location for escaping cruisers was not necessarily among the most fertile land. The areas adjacent to Sierra Leone and indeed the British colony itself were well-known sources of provisions for the Gallinas and Sherbro dealers. In the Congo there were extensive provision grounds and Portuguese and Africans who specialized in the business.[94] Factors also had to gather intelligence on the disposition and movement of cruisers, keep up-to-date on policy developments, particularly those of the British, and compete for the favor of African landlords against naval threats and overtures.[95] These information-gathering, provisioning and slave-purchasing networks depended heavily on fleets of locally built launches, canoes, schooners, pilot boats and, on the east coast, dhows, all of which the factor had to maintain.

The factor's duties eventually came to absorb many of the functions of the transatlantic shipper of the slaves. In Upper Guinea and the Congo from the 1840s on, oceangoing ships were commonly concealed in creeks or swamps until needed. This meant dismasting and then refitting the ship when an opportunity for shipment arose.[96] If ships failed to arrive, a factor would occasionally buy a vessel locally, perhaps from a trader in produce or from the various courts that auctioned off condemned slave ships.[97] Factories, therefore, came to hold large quantities of shipping stores as well as trading goods. As equipment clauses came into force, the leaguers (large water barrels) manacles and slave decks, which were grounds for condemnation of a ship whether or not it had slaves on board, came to be manufactured at these shore-based establishments. Iron bars were fashioned into hoops for the leaguers and manacles, and staves and decks were on occasion made from local materials.[98] Indeed there are seventeen cases on record of the transatlantic ship itself being built in Africa, some from prefabricated units sent from Brazil, others constructed from scratch with local woods. At one site in the Congo even the nails were manufactured at the construction site. Théodore Conneau not only built his own 150-ton vessel at Cape Mount, on the Windward Coast, but had it rowed out full of slaves in the low-lying mist of the rainy season, towing its masts aft. When clear of the cruising ground, the masts were reshipped and the schooner successfully completed the voyage to Brazil.[99] Factories thus came to assume some of the modern functions associated with their name. At the very least the slave trade cannot be described in the purely extractive terms used by many observers. It is not difficult to see why the factor himself during much of the illegal phase of the slave trade was often a full partner in the slave-trading firm or an independent dealer.[100]

We can now return to the issue of the African response to attempts to suppress the transatlantic traffic in slaves. The above review of patterns at the regional level and the role of the factor suggests a number of significant conclusions. In all regions examined, major variations in slave exports were caused by changes in demand from the Americas, usually on account of shifts in official attitudes toward the trade in American importing areas. As demand shifted, the price and quantity of slaves traded changed in unison, suggesting that the supply of slaves was strongly price responsive. Higher prices apparently made it worthwhile to divert slaves from alternative uses, to bring slaves from longer distances in the interior or to adjust culturally determined sex-and-child ratios. Indeed for Africa as a whole between 1821 and 1865, it is possible to calculate that a 10 percent rise in price generated slightly more than a 9 percent rise in quantities of slaves sold.[101]

A second conclusion—one that reinforces the findings of earlier chapters—is that the navy was not especially effective, particularly off Africa. Cruiser action shut down the slave trade in the palm oil rivers in 1839–40, in the Gallinas in 1850 and in Lagos in the following year. Similar efforts in the Bight of Benin against Dahomey in 1851–52 and the Congo River after 1840 were just as clearly total failures. Although the geography of the coastline had some influence, generally the navy could not stamp out the slave trade without, first, the cooperation of the sovereign powers in Africa and, second, the commitment of even greater naval resources than were actually sent. In the absence of strong ideological support for abolition in both the importing and exporting regions, slave traders could make effective counters to almost any naval strategy. The key figure in this game was the head of the slave factory in Africa. In the knowledge that they were not likely to suffer penalties against either life or limb, the slave factors could usually bring together a price-responsive supply on the African side with an effective demand for the Americas. Yet it was also true that in the 1840s the price differential between a slave in Africa and a slave in the Americas was many times the cost of transporting that slave across the Atlantic under normal conditions. Effective suppression made the differential even greater. The navy contributed to this wedge but in the main it was the result of the enormous diplomatic and ideological presure that the British exerted against Brazil and Cuba rather than cruiser activity.

A third conclusion is that produce exports accelerated as the slave trade came to an end, so that in Africa as a whole by midcentury nonslave exports were more valuable than slave exports. Nevertheless, the role of the former in the suppression process does not appear to have been large. It is well known that most of the early growth of palm oil was concentrated in southeast Nigeria where slave exports grew almost in step in the 1820s and 1830s before ending rather abruptly.[102] In the Bight of Benin, Congo North and Gold Coast regions, palm oil production grew more slowly. But in the first two, the slave trade continued to the 1860s, and in the latter, it ceased forty years earlier. From all regions, however, there is abundant literary evidence of the preference on the part of most African rulers and traders for the slave traffic. The loading of palm oil cargoes to Europe was invariably given lower priority than the dispatch of slave ships where embarkation points coincided. Furthermore, there is the clear suggestion that in some important slaving regions—for example, Angola and the coast south of Sierra Leone—the slave trade ended without any substantial produce trade either competing with or immediately replacing it. Did suppression of the slave trade provide an opportunity for the produce traffic to grow (as many contemporaries maintained) or did the development of the produce-export sector bid away resources from the export-slaving business.[103] The best answer is that neither of these possibilities appears likely. Rather it would seem that the slave and commodity-export trades together formed such a small percentage of total African economic activity that either could expand without there being any impact on the growth path of the other. Conflicts certainly existed at the local level and probably would have appeared regionally if both had continued to grow rapidly. But in the mid-nineteenth century neither the slave nor the commodity trades were large enough to have to face the problem of inelastic supplies of the factors of production.

The fact that produce exports expanded as the slave trade declined is, nevertheless, of supreme importance in understanding the suppression process, particularly as it affected Africa. One of the major themes of the current volume is that sustained economic growth particularly in Britain was responsible both for the ending of the slave trade and eventually slavery and for the extraordinary growth in long-distance commodity trade. The connection between the first two of these factors was ideological and, given the transmission process between the British and slave-importing governments, diplomatic. At the aggregate level and over the long run, we would, therefore, not expect to find production of African commodities for industrializing economies rising together with slave exports. The pressures driving the former had the same origin as those that suppressed the latter.[104]

# 11

## The Markets for Slaves
## in the Americas

During the generation or so after 1820, the industrializing world subjected the slave-importing regions of the Americas to the same contradictory pressures directed toward Africa. On the one hand, almost no one in the North Atlantic countries would support the slave trade on moral grounds. Those few who could were probably themselves connected to the slave trade. On the other hand, the demand for cotton, sugar, coffee, tobacco and other produce was intensifying as never before. Prior to 1850 the European and North American masses could get access to cheap supplies of sugar, coffee and cotton only if the latter were grown with slave labor. Save for a rise in slave prices, the resolution of this tension varied between one part of the Americas and another. Some regions attempted to switch to indentured labor, others relied on a rapid rate of natural increase of the indigenous slave population, still others smuggled Africans across the Atlantic. All regions adjusted the mix of crops that they produced. It is the response of the Americas to these pressures with which this chapter is concerned.

Brazil, Cuba and U.S. South produced, respectively, the coffee, sugar and cotton that an industrializing Western world needed and that the British plantation colonies could no longer supply. The link between an exploding demand and the development of new areas of the Americas worked by bondsmen seems direct and simple. Yet a closer look reveals many complexities germane to the main theme of the present work. In the first instance Britain, with the most dynamic economy in Europe, was not the direct source of demand for two of the three principal plantation products. In 1820, the British took little sugar from Cuba or coffee from Brazil. By midcentury, despite reducing import duties on foreign-grown sugar and coffee, Britain was taking only a slightly greater share of the produce of the Iberian Americas and was actually absorbing a smaller share of the U.S. cotton crop. In absolute terms Britain was taking much more produce from all regions by 1850.[1] But the point remains that except for cotton, the major sources of demand for the majority of the dynamic plantation areas of the Americas was not Britain.

For both Brazil and Cuba the major foreign produce markets were in the United States and on the continent of Europe. By the mid-1840s the United States was taking almost half of Rio de Janeiro's coffee exports, with most of the remainder going to Hamburg and Antwerp, although re-exports from London were significant. Cuban sugar was also widely distributed. Between 1842 and 1847 about half the annual exports went to north European ports with the rest shared equally between southern Europe and the United States, although, as with Brazilian coffee, much of this crop eventually found its way via re-exports to northern continental Europe. For Cuban coffee, on the other hand, the United States was important in the 1820s, but southern Europe had become the main market by the 1840s, absorbing consistently over half the total exports.[2] Yet as we have seen in chapters 1 and 3, developments in Britain were, nevertheless, of central importance to these new plantation regions. Both Brazilian and Cuban sugar, and to a lesser extent coffee, were taking over markets in continental Europe that British producers had been forced to give up. Labor problems imposed on them by imperial antislavery policy crippled British planters. When these problems were alleviated by the arrival of indentured labor beginning in the 1840s, British Guiana quickly recovered its market share in Britain and successfully competed against Cuban sugar in foreign markets—mainly the United States.[3] Brazil, Cuba, and perhaps the U.S. South, too, would not have been plantation backwaters in the absence of the British abolition, but they would no doubt have experienced a lower rate of growth in the face of continued competition from the massive British plantation sector.

Yet the key developments in the nineteenth century plantation economies, as with their industrializing counterparts, were not on the demand side but rather in the production and marketing of the produce. Prices for all plantation produce registered a secular decline in the first half of the nineteenth century at the same time that the output of these commodities—and for most regions profits, too—steadily increased. In this, the nineteenth century differed rather markedly from the eighteenth century; from the 1730s to the early 1800s, the price of plantation produce increased steadily.[4] Although the effect of the European wars muddies the picture somewhat, before 1800 it would seem that the increased demand for sugar, cotton and coffee exceeded the increase in supply. After 1800, this situation was reversed. Even more remarkably, the latter trend persisted even as the cost of the labor input (slaves) was increasing strongly throughout the Americas. Figure 7 shows the price trends for the products of three different plantation societies and crops together with trends in the price of slaves for the period 1804–60. It was not just in the southern states that slave prices accelerated after 1807. Indeed prices in Brazil and Cuba rose by much more in percentage terms after 1820, though what is not shown in figure 7 is the higher base price for U.S. slaves at the beginning of the century. Effective suppression of the slave trade came to the Iberian Americas much later than to the United States. In all societies where slavery survived past midcentury, however, slave prices grew to at least double what they had been at the beginning of the century.[5] The juxtaposition of declining produce prices and rising

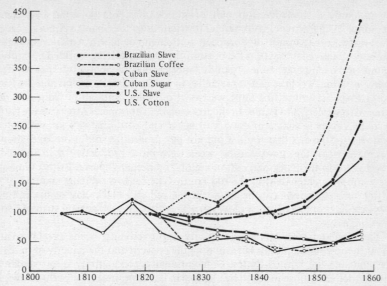

**Figure 7.** Index of mean prices of U.S. cotton and slaves, 1804–60; Cuban sugar and slaves, 1815–60; and Brazilian coffee and slaves, 1821–60 (1804–7 = 100 for the United States; 1815–25 = 100 for Cuba; 1821–25 = 100 for Brazil).

slave prices, which led Ulrich Bonnell Phillips to erroneously hypothesize declining plantation profitability, in fact, was a universal phenomenon in the plantation Americas. It is also now clear that despite these trends both profitability and planter expectations for the future were as high in the major non-U.S. plantation regions as they were in the American South.[6]

The full explanation for these apparently contradictory patterns outside the United States awaits the analysis of the same kinds of plantation records that have been exploited so successfully for the cotton South. It seems likely, however, that any differences between U.S. and non-U.S. regions will be matters of emphasis rather than substance. We can tentatively identify three broad factors that more than offset both the rising price of slaves and the steady increase in demand for plantation produce. They are (1) the exploitation of new land particularly well suited for plantation crops, (2) labor-productivity improvements and (3) economies of scale in marketing crops. The collective impact was to make slaves more productive workers. As a consequence the secular decline in the price of plantation produce was consistent with the maintenance and perhaps improvement of plantation profitability. We shall briefly consider each of these three supply-side influences separately.

Free fertile land had been available to Europeans in the Americas since the sixteenth century. By the mid-eighteenth century the only parts of the Americas, including plantation regions, that had been pulled into the world economy were those that were geographically and politically accessible. Much occupied land, especially in the Iberian Americas, did not produce overseas exports;

overall only a small fraction of the land with export potential had been exploited. The freeing of commercial restrictions in the Spanish Americas and the westward expansion of European settlement in North America brought more productive land within the orbit of the industrializing world. The equivalents in the temperate zone of South America, despite poorer internal natural transportation, were the gaucho societies in the Rio Grande do Sul and the Río de la Plata as well as the shift westward of coffee cultivation from Rio de Janeiro to western São Paulo. In the tropical and subtropical Americas the shift in the geographic center of gravity of sugar and cotton is well known. After allowing for the fact that it often did not pay to fertilize soil in the land-abundant Americas, the newly settled areas were more productive than the old. Crop yields in the black-belt cotton region and perhaps coastal British Guiana were simply greater than in the old South. The sugar-producing counterparts of the former regions can be found in the red and black clay of the rolling western plain of Cuba, much of western Trinidad, and the coastal strip of British Guiana.

The second factor, labor-productivity improvements, needs careful treatment in view of the pitfalls surrounding the concept and the paucity of refined data outside the United States. Conventionally, productivity improvements are divided into those induced by changes in factor proportions (perhaps owing to relative price changes) and, on the other hand, improved technology that raises the efficiency of all factors. The relative importance of these two has been debated in the U.S. case, and the issues raised there are not likely to be clarified by reference to Brazil and Cuba where the pre-1850 data are less abundant. More fertile land would, of course, in itself make labor more productive, but shifts to more fertile land were continuous from the earliest days of the plantation settlement and did not accelerate suddenly in the nineteenth century.[7] It might also be noted that although the extent of improved acreage increased strongly in these years, so also did increments to the labor force brought about by the slave trade. Large gains in labor productivity on this account are unlikely. An improved output per slave is demonstrated for Cuba later, and some of this occurred before the massive increase in slave prices began in the 1840s. The latter, it might be noted, could induce the substitution of capital or land for labor and thus increase output per slave. New plant varieties, transportation improvements and autonomous shifts in the technology of sugar milling all contributed to improved total factor productivity. The role of labor in the actual cultivation process perhaps changed less rapidly than these other influences in the early years of the nineteenth century. The impact in the field of mechanization, for example, occurred well after 1850 rather than before. It is at least clear that improved labor productivity was not a phenomenon exclusive to the manufacturing and agricultural zones of the temperate North Atlantic regions.

The third source of improvements on the supply side of the market for plantation produce may be dealt with more quickly. Credit facilities, transportation from the plantation to the export point and storage and loading at this point became cheaper for all products in the nineteenth century. Transoceanic freight rates and traveling times declined, but probably more important was the economies of scale possible in the bulking and handling of cargoes. The integration of financial markets and the resulting declines in credit costs were also significant, particularly after 1840.[8]

The impact of these developments was felt everywhere in the plantation Americas. Table 11 presents some very crude indexes of physical product per slave for four major plantation regions to give some idea of the magnitude of the gains for three plantation crops. Unhappily none of the series incorporates estimates of hours worked or acres tilled per person and none of them are adjusted for the changes over time either in the age structure of the slave population, the crop mix on plantations or in the location of the land cultivated.[9] There were certainly major shifts in the age structure of the non-U.S. slave populations, but they were all in the direction of reducing the number of prime-age workers rather than increasing them. The known bias in table 11 is toward understating rather than overstating productivity increases. A more refined measure of slave productivity than is possible here—say, output per male-adult-hour worked—would likely show no less an increase over time than the crude data.

The significance of the trends in table 11 can be best appreciated with the aid of some comparisons with equivalent data from contemporary nonslave work forces. A more precise productivity ratio for wheat, corn and cotton in the United States shows that improvements in cotton fell between those in

**Table 11.** Indexes of Physical Output per Slave in the Nineteenth-Century Americas

United States (cotton exported per slave resident on cotton plantations)

| | 1801 | 1811 | 1821 | 1831 | 1835 | 1840 | 1850 |
|---|---|---|---|---|---|---|---|
| | 100 | 150 | 168 | 168 | 167 | 203 | 210 |

British West Indies (sugar exported per slave resident on sugar plantations)

| | 1810 | 1820 | 1830 |
|---|---|---|---|
| Jamaica | 100 | 110 | 100 |
| Barbados | 100 | 138 | 185 |
| British Guiana | 100 | 156 | 337 |
| Trinidad | 100 | 106 | 174 |

Cuba (sugar produced per slave resident on sugar plantations)

| | 1827 | 1841 | 1846 | 1861[a] |
|---|---|---|---|---|
| | 100 | 125 | 168 | 223 |

Brazil (coffee exported per slave resident on coffee plantations)

| | 1854 | 1872 | 1874 | 1884 |
|---|---|---|---|---|
| Rio de Janeiro | | 100 | | 130 |
| São Paulo[b] | | 100 | | 135 |
| São Paulo[b] | 100 | | 133 | |

*Notes:* [a]About 13 percent of the labor force included in the calculation of the 1861 ratio for Cuba was indentured Chinese labor. [b]For an explanation of the two indexes for São Paulo, see table F. 9.

*Source:* Calculated from app. F. Note however that the index in each case is calculated from the original data, not the rounded data presented in the appendix.

corn and wheat, the latter two grown largely with free labor. It is also clear that the pace of improvement in cotton dropped far behind that in other crops after the abolition of slavery.[10] Yet perhaps the most instructive comparison is between the slave economies of Cuba and the United States, on the one hand, and the British economy, on the other. Real values of exports per worker in Britain increased by 75 percent between 1804–6 and 1854–56. This rate of increase, however, fell below the trends shown in table 11 for U.S. and Cuban slave labor over approximately the same period. In the British cotton industry output per man-hour increased at an average annual rate of just under 3 percent a year between 1830 and 1892, compared to 2.5 percent for sugar exports per slave from Cuba between 1827 and 1861.[11] The sources of productivity growth in the factories of Britain and the plantations of the Americas may have been different but the rates of change themselves are similar. Moreover, in the Cuban case the slave trade remained open throughout the period covered in table 11. If, as noted later, many of the gains in output per slave came after the restrictions on the African slave trade were tightened, not all did. Enough came before to suggest that a trend to higher per capita output was not inconsistent with abundant supplies of relatively cheap labor.

Restrictions on slave imports and the higher prices for slaves associated with them came to different American societies at different times. As a consequence wide differentials in the pace and timing of economic development opened up. Yet it is possible to discern a common pattern in the response of the various slave systems. All three of the most dynamic American plantation economies of the era produced a variety of crops as long as the traffic with Africa remained open and importing authorities behaved cooperatively. In the United States this situation ended in 1807. The slave population, which had been widely distributed over plantation crops and occupations, was by midcentury overwhelmingly concentrated in cotton production.[12] In Cuba the production of all produce expanded rapidly in the 1820s and 1830s. Table 12 shows the trend

**Table 12.** Indexes of Cuban Sugar Output and Coffee Exports, Volume and Real Value, 1821–65 (five-year annual means, 1821–25 = 100)

| | Volume | | Value (constant dollars) | |
|---|---|---|---|---|
| | Sugar | Coffee | Sugar | Coffee |
| 1821–25 | 100 | 100 | 100 | 100 |
| 1826–30 | 133 | 197 | 122 | 150 |
| 1831–35 | 160 | 229 | 142 | 155 |
| 1836–40 | 205 | 215 | 165 | 140 |
| 1841–45 | 269 | 153 | 202 | 94 |
| 1846–50 | 401 | 88 | 285 | 42 |
| 1851–55 | 616 | 62 | 379 | 42 |
| 1856–60 | 689 | 42 | 548 | 31 |
| 1861–65 | 793 | 20 | 545 | 18 |

*Source:* Calculated from appendix F. Note that in each case the index is calculated from the original data, not the rounded data given in the appendix.

for the two major crops of sugar and coffee. Sugar output averaged an annual rate of increase of almost 5 percent between 1820 and 1850. The volume of coffee exports grew even more quickly, at 8 percent per annum in the 1820s and somewhat less rapidly to the mid-1830s. Tobacco cultivation, in which only a minority of the labor force was slave, almost doubled between 1811 and 1846. Copper ore exports, mined near Santiago de Cuba by British companies using slave labor and shipped to south Wales, expanded to 43,000 tons a year in 1845 from trivial amounts in the early 1830s.[13] The value of coffee production was close to half that of sugar in the later 1820s, and volume of output grew strongly over the next decade. Yet from the mid-1830s coffee exports declined and *cafetales* almost disappeared from the western department.[14] Traditionally this trend had been attributed to Brazilian competition and a discriminatory U.S. tariff on Spanish coffee imposed in 1835. Net U.S. prices did indeed decline steadily in the 1830s and 1840s, though a strong price recovery in the 1850s elicited little Cuban response. Yet the large decrease in export volume, an 80 percent fall in twenty-five years, 1831–35 to 1856–60, can scarcely be explained by a price trend that actually rose in real terms over the same period. Similarly, the price trend for sugar cannot account for the explosive growth of sugar exports in these same years.

It is the trend in slave prices that is the key to explaining the rise and fall of the two produce sectors.[15] Prices for prime male *bozales* increased from the mid-1830s as sugar production continued to expand and then increased again, by a much larger amount, from the mid-1840s. In a striking parallel to the then-contemporary reallocation of U.S. slaves into cotton, it seems likely that the first increase choked off the expansion of the coffee sector and the second began, or at least accelerated, the well-known shift of the Cuban slave-labor force from coffee to sugar production. In 1827 there was perhaps a quarter of the Cuban slave population in sugar and a third in coffee production. By 1841 there were still more coffee than sugar plantations, but the greater number of slaves were not living on the latter: About 29 percent of the slave population resided on *ingenios,* compared to 21 percent on *cafetales.* As slave prices began their marked rise in the 1840s, the shutting down of coffee plantations accelerated, encouraged no doubt by long droughts and hurricanes in 1844 and 1846. The 1846 census indicates that only 18 percent of the slave population were on *cafetales* compared to 36 percent on *ingenios.*[16] At the start of 1847 the British commissioners reported the "almost entire abandonment" of coffee estates, though residing as they did in Havana, their comment may be taken to exclude the east of the island where much of the coffee was produced.[17] An official inquiry in 1848 reported 38,000 slaves, or over one third of the *cafetales'* population in 1841, had been transferred from coffee to sugar production in the previous two years. The steady recovery in coffee prices in the 1850s was not enough to offset increased labor costs, and the process continued until 49 percent of the slave population was by 1861 on sugar estates and only 9 percent lived on *cafetales.*[18] The slave-labor force was rapidly becoming both more concentrated in sugar production and more productive.

There is less direct evidence of this process in tobacco and copper. Copper ore exports dipped after 1845 before resuming expansion in the 1850s though the number of slaves involved was very small relative to the major staples. On tobacco farms small producers did require labor even though their requirements were relatively modest. The majority of this was free labor, some no doubt from the white immigration, chiefly from the Canary Islands, which was briefly significant in the 1830s. Based on the classic study of Fernando Ortiz, the high proportion of free labor in this sector is usually explained as being due to the delicate skill requirements of tobacco growing. Modern evidence on occupations of slaves in both the Caribbean and the U.S. South suggests that slave status was not incompatible with skill acquisition.[19] Moreover, slaves were used in production of leaf tobacco in both Virginia and Bahia as well as roll tobacco in the latter. Trends in slave imports and prices offer an alternative explanation. There were no significant economies of scale in tobacco growing anywhere in the Americas and, like most employers in the northern United States, proprietors always had difficulty in competing for slaves with sugar and cotton growers. But tobacco farmers in Virginia and Bahia were usually able to buy slaves from Africa for less than their Cuban counterparts.[20] Cuban tobacco producers very likely were not able to afford slaves. For these producers the increased restrictions on slave imports in the 1830s and 1840s thus made the possibility of converting fully to slave labor even more remote and may have induced a switch of coerced labor from tobacco into sugar. The size of the switch was not likely to have been great, however, if only because the number of slaves in tobacco production was small. Tobacco exports actually increased in volume in the late 1850s.

Even if sugar exports had not been expanding in these years, its labor force would have required constant replenishment. As in other parts of the Caribbean at a comparable stage of development, a skewed age-and-sex distribution induced by the slave trade and probably also a high infant-mortality rate meant that the slave population experienced a natural rate of decrease.[21] The *ingenios* must have absorbed almost all of the 250,000 *bozales* that arrived in Cuba in these years, particularly after 1835, as well as many slaves from the coffee and perhaps other sectors. It is not surprising that 57 percent of the population of a large sample of sugar plantations in the years 1856–63 were African born[22] and that in all the reports of the British commissioners, sugar estates are the only productive enterprises mentioned as receiving illegal imports.[23]

Yet the concentration of slaves in the sugar sector is not in itself enough to explain the rapid increase in Cuban produce output after 1844. There was, in addition, a significant increase in the value of output per slave and indentured laborer.[24] Between 1846 and 1861 the population available for plantation work increased by perhaps one quarter. This included not only slaves but also, for the first time, about thirty thousand indentured Chinese laborers and a few hundred Indians from the Yucatán peninsula. In the same period the real value of sugar production and coffee exports doubled. Thus the rise in the physical output per Cuban slave shown in table 11 was actually exceeded by the increases in the value of product per slave in these fifteen years. An insight into the rising value of the slave can be obtained by tracing the real per capita value of coffee and sugar exports over these years. Between 1827 and 1846 the ratio rose from $122.0 per slave to $184.8 per slave, and then it increased even faster over the next fifteen years to $286.7 in 1861.[25] Certainly by the 1860s slaves were performing a wide range of tasks on Cuban sugar plantations.[26] In the mechanization of milling and transportation, it was the 1840s that were the watershed years.[27] "The only check which it [sugar] would receive," wrote the British commissioner in Havana, "would be occasioned by plantation labour not being obtainable on as moderate terms as formerly, but this Planters seek to remedy by the adoption of the most perfect class of machinery."[28] It seems probable that the technological progress noted by contemporary observers arose from both the substitution of capital and perhaps land for an increasingly expensive labor as well as from improvements in total factor productivity. At least part of this process may be attributed to the buildup of Cuban pressure on slave importers described later. Slave prices increased more between the mid-1840s and early 1860s than in any other comparable period in the history of Cuban slavery. The increase, in fact, was greatly in excess of the rise in U.S. slave prices in the same period.

These same factors also provide an insight into the recruitment of indentured Asian workers not just in Cuba but also in the British West Indies. The first Chinese arrived in 1847. There were no further arrivals until 1853, but between that year and the ending of the slave trade 93,000 indentured workers disembarked. The cost to the Junta de Fomento of Havana, which acted as importer, rose from $160 for an eight-year indenture in 1847 to $170 in 1855, $343 in 1861, and $384 as the slave trade drew to a close in 1865. Wages, at $4 per month, and the indenture term appear not to have changed during this period. In the British West Indies the pattern of arrivals over time, as well as costs, were comparable.[29] Cuban slave prices were always higher than indenture contracts; given the permanent nature of slavery and the temporary nature of an indentured contract, this was to be expected. Only when the cost of *bozales* exceeded $600 in the early 1850s did it become worthwhile to recruit indentured workers in large numbers from Amoy, China, 12,000 miles distant. British West Indian planters could not, of course, buy slaves at any price after 1834, nor could they profitably employ indentured Asian labor until the costs of their Brazilian and Cuban competitors had been inflated by restrictions on the Atlantic slave trade.[30] Although fuller data on costs and productivity are necessary, it seems likely that the great flow of indentured labor to Cuba and elsewhere in the second half of the nineteenth century was closely tied to the vagaries of antislave-trade policy.

The slave-price increase and the related trend in slave imports thus had a major impact on the Cuban economy. As well as contributing to technological change and increased productivity, it also slowed the development of nonsugar produce and in the case of coffee helped bring about the virtual collapse of the sector. By midcentury only sugar producers could afford to pay the prices of slaves or the cost of an indentured contract. The orientation of Cuban society shifted inexorably toward the *ingenio*.

In Brazil attempts to suppress the slave trade had a similar impact, though the timing was different and the major crop became coffee rather than sugar. During the 1820s sugar was the leading export, followed by cotton. Coffee was third in importance and, in fact, Brazil produced less coffee than Jamaica for much of this decade. In several years exports of hides and pelts, the fourth leading product, were almost as valuable as coffee shipments to overseas markets. Although coffee exports grew at 8.5 percent a year between 1821 and 1850, for most of this period all four major products were important, accounting for 85 percent of export values. Tobacco, cocoa and even some rubber were also exported.[31] There was, however, considerable geographic specialization, with cotton exported exclusively from the northeastern centers, coffee mainly from Rio de Janeiro and cattle products mainly from the south. Only sugar exports were widely distributed. In the late 1820s Bahia accounted for about half of all sugar leaving Brazil, with the balance evenly divided between Rio de Janeiro and the northeastern ports, mainly Pernambuco. Some Rio de Janeiro shipments were grown as far away as Santos.[32] Nevertheless, regions producing for export markets were no more than isolated pockets in a vast, lightly populated wilderness. Most were situated inland and were connected by river to a single port. Of all African arrivals, 95 percent may have disembarked between Santos in the south and Pernambuco in the north. But even as the slave trade came to an end, the coast between Santos and Rio de Janeiro, Campos and Bahia, and Bahia and Pernambuco was described as "neither thickly settled, nor wealthy, nor possessed [of] good ports".[33]

During the last thirty years of the slave trade, it was the products most dependent on slave labor that expanded the most rapidly. Table 13 shows five-year annual averages of the volume and value of exports in index form for this period.[34] The explosive growth in the volume of sugar and coffee relative to cotton and indeed to tobacco (not shown in table 13) is particularly striking. Trends in cotton production in this period for any region outside the United States are usually explained in terms of competition from the frontier southern states driving down prices. But the trend in cotton prices in these years was not markedly different from those in coffee, sugar and indeed many other commodities where U.S. influence on the supply side was negligible. A fuller expla-

**Table 13.** Indexes of Brazilian Sugar, Coffee, and Cotton Exports, Volume and Real Value, 1821–60 (five-year annual means, 1821–25 = 100)

|         | Volume |        |        | Value (constant pounds) |        |        |
|---------|--------|--------|--------|--------|--------|--------|
|         | Sugar  | Coffee | Cotton | Sugar  | Coffee | Cotton |
| 1821–25 | 100    | 100    | 100    | 100    | 100    | 100    |
| 1826–30 | 133    | 206    | 92     | 143    | 96     | 57     |
| 1831–35 | 170    | 424    | 99     | 144    | 319    | 68     |
| 1836–40 | 199    | 579    | 84     | 134    | 326    | 44     |
| 1841–45 | 217    | 731    | 83     | 154    | 317    | 41     |
| 1846–50 | 287    | 1037   | 97     | 211    | 459    | 59     |
| 1851–55 | 300    | 1245   | 109    | 223    | 689    | 63     |
| 1856–60 | 258    | 1386   | 107    | 233    | 853    | 65     |

*Source:* Calculated from data based used in appendix F. Note that in each case the index is calculated from the original data, not the rounded data given in the appendix.

nation would have to take into account the steady increase in Brazilian labor costs. In Rio de Janeiro slave prices doubled between 1820 and 1850, an increase well in excess of that recorded in the United States in the same period. In response, cotton output contracted slightly, particularly between 1836 and 1845 when prices were at a century low point. Cotton, however, was increasingly produced by free labor on a sharecropping basis. In the Paraíba region by the mid-1840s, seven eighths of the sugar labor force was slave, four fifths of the cotton labor force was free.[35] On the basis of free labor, cotton output in the 1850s was able to regain its earlier levels as prices recovered. Slave imports from Africa into Brazil north of Bahia fell 80 percent between 1821–30 and 1841–50, though this does not include some re-exports from Bahia in the 1840s. In tobacco the accommodation was slightly different. A marked increase in leaf tobacco production occurred, as opposed to the more labor-intensive roll tobacco. There was a shift also to smaller-scale production units using less slaves. As a consequence the volume of tobacco exports was maintained down to midcentury and increased thereafter.[36] Cotton and tobacco thus played the role of reservoirs of slave labor in Brazil, much like urban slavery in the U.S. South. It might be concluded that slaves in coffee and sugar in Brazil, as in cotton in the U.S. South, were more productive than in all other sectors of the two economies.[37]

A comparison of tables 12 and 13 shows that the volume of Brazilian sugar exports increased more rapidly than did Cuban sugar output in the ten years 1821–25 to 1831–35. Most of this expansion took place in the north, especially Bahia where slave imports in the 1820s and 1840s were probably close to historic highs.[38] Commerce of all kinds was stimulated by the discovery of diamonds in the Bahia hinterland in the mid-1840s and slaves were employed in many nonplantation activities. But sugar was clearly at the center of this last boom in Bahian slave arrivals.[39] Thus despite the image in the literature of inefficient debt-ridden sugar estates in the Brazilian northeast,[40] it is apparent that in the first half of the century Brazilian producers were as capable as their Cuban counterparts of capitalizing on British West Indian withdrawal from European Continental markets. Not until the 1840s did the pace of Brazilian sugar expansion lag behind that of Cuba, and not until the 1850s was there an absolute, but also a temporary, decline in output. The latter occurred only after the jump in slave prices attendant on the effective closing of the Atlantic slave trade to Bahia. Total suppression came a decade and a half earlier to Brazil than to Cuba.

As table 13 demonstrates, however, the major Brazilian growth industry was coffee cultivation, which before 1850 meant essentially the province of Rio de Janeiro, the Mata area of Minas Gerais, and the Paraíba Valley in São Paulo. During the period 1821–50 more slaves arrived on a four-hundred-mile stretch of coast around Rio de Janeiro than in the rest of the Americas put together. A few were re-exported, for example, to Rio Grande do Sul where they were employed in preparing jerked beef. Of the vast majority who remained, many were employed in a wide range of tasks apparently not connected directly with the export economy. Many, including new arrivals awaiting resale, were hired out in all Brazilian ports as porters. In the eyes of English observers their ready availability inhibited improvements such as aqueducts, dockside equipment and even wheeled transportation.[41] Close to 80,000 slaves alone lived in the city of Rio de Janeiro as the slave trade ended. It seems likely that in this region, as in Bahia and the noncoffee-growing areas of Minas Gerais, the incidence of slaveholding among the free population was high, although the average number of slaves owned was probably small.[42] Perhaps only 311,000 or perhaps 24 percent of the bondsmen in Brazil were actually growing coffee.[43] But there were extensive linkages extending from the coffee sector to transportation, the production of farinha and other foodstuffs. Coffee exports were the only way of paying for slave imports into Brazil South in these years.[44] It is inconceivable that the concentrated influx of Africans could have occurred without coffee. Coffee was the heart of the south-central Brazilian slave economy.[45]

As in Cuba, slave productivity improved in these years. Both overseas demand for produce and rising output per slave were reflected in the rising slave prices of the pre-1850 years. As Leff has pointed out, the mere fact that scarce resources flowed into the export sector indicates that productivity gains in the latter were greater than elsewhere in the Brazilian economy. The literary evidence of labor-saving techniques in coffee growing is strongest for the post-1850 period but some improvements likely predated the closing of the transatlantic slave traffic.[46]

The concentration of slaves into coffee production began well before 1850, both for the Brazilian economy as a whole and within the province of Rio de Janeiro. As in the north with sugar, the case for a link between this process and the secular rise in the price of African slaves appears persuasive. In Rio de Janeiro province the volume of sugar exports declined almost 60 percent between 1829 and 1847-50. By 1850 coffee had already come to dominate the provincial economy. The 83 percent of total exports from the province accounted for by coffee in 1849-50 was probably close to the historic high,[47] coming as it did before the main part of the westward shift of coffee culture. The slaves moving up the roads from the ports of Rio de Janeiro and Santos to the upper Paraiba Valley in the later 1840s could not all have been *boçals*. At the very time Cuban slaves were switched from coffee to sugar estates, a reverse flow must have been underway in south-central Brazil. In Brazil as a whole, as we have seen, sugar exports continued to increase at this time, but coffee expanded even faster. Between 1821-25 and 1846-50 coffee more than doubled its share of total exports. In the final years of the slave trade, the two major slave export crops, coffee and sugar, were accounting for 69 percent of Brazilian exports by value.[48] Much of the former was produced in the hinterlands of Rio de Janeiro and almost all the latter in the Bahia and Pernambuco regions. It would, thus, seem that increases in both labor costs and North Atlantic commodity demand together pulled land into coffee culture in south-central Brazil and into sugar in northeastern Brazil.

After 1850 the process intensified. Coffee and sugar prices rose 50 percent in ten years but slave prices rose even more. Between 1846-50 and 1856-60 the price of a prime male in both Rio de Janeiro and Bahia more than doubled. The contrast here with Cuba is instructive. Slave prices in the Spanish island did not climb by as much, perhaps because the slave trade and the indentured Chinese traffic remained open. With the African traffic to Brazil cut off, the internal slave trade broadened. One estimate puts the scale of this traffic proportionately on a par with that in the United States.[49] There is debate over the origins of the slaves entering this trade, but not over the fact of the increasing concentration of bondsmen in coffee cultivation. Coffee accounted for almost two thirds of total exports in the years before the abolition of slavery in 1888 (compared to 18 percent in 1821–25), but most of the slaves absorbed by the sector after 1850 came from nonplantation activities rather than the sugar industry in the north.[50] Relative to coffee, sugar exports declined after 1850, but with some help from free labor sugar exports were maintained in absolute terms as long as slavery endured. By 1887 the Brazilian slave-labor force had shifted southward; 89 percent of the slave-labor force in São Paulo and 63 percent in Rio de Janeiro were in coffee cultivation. In the south-central region, only in Minas Gerais was a substantial proportion of the slave population employed in noncoffee activities. In contrast to Cuba twenty years earlier, free immigration became significant as the major export crop became dominant. Although more extensive than the indentured labor flow into Cuba, the free-migration flow was scarcely adequate.[51] The impact of rising slave prices on the two regions remains fundamentally similar. In both cases the development of the least profitable crop was slowed as the export economy shifted toward monoculture. Given the range of raw materials required by the industrializing world, an open slave trade could only have meant more diversified as well as more rapidly expanding slave economies in the Americas.[52]

In both Brazil and Cuba it is the midcentury that emerges as the critical period during which the import, volumes, prices and productivity of coerced labor took decisive shifts. From the mid-1850s the world economy as a whole entered a period of more rapid growth and the link between this and prospering slave economies in the Americas is clear enough—particularly in the U.S. South. Yet for the slave societies that still had access to Africa, the preceding decade was just as important. Major increases in the prices of slaves and decreases in quantity landed occurred not because of purely market forces, but because of new institutional constraints, the ostensible instruments of which were the governing authorities of the importing regions. Having established the broad parameters of the market for Africans in the Americas, in particular, the strong inverse relationship between price and quantity of slaves, we shall now turn to a closer examination of these political factors, in particular, the reaction of the slave importers to them.

As with any other large-scale, long-distance traffic, the slave trade was dependent on highly organized financial markets and supply facilities. The preparation of ships entering the trade, the reception and distribution of their return cargoes, the need for financial services (e.g., credit and insurance) and for legal services to support claims and expedite transfers of assets were the *raison d'être* of ports the world over. Any commercial activity that could not get free access to these services would be more costly to conduct. In the early years of the illegal slave trade, there was little to interfere with slave-trader access to such services in any of the ports of Brazil, Cuba or the French West Indies. For nearly a quarter century after the Spanish government officially abolished the trade, slave ships had virtually free access to the Havana harbor. Much of the financing and insuring of expeditions was carried out at an exchange that in the early 1840s was located in a large store in the city's Government Plaza. Shares were publically traded here, and James Kennedy, the British commissioner, was able to verify the reports on the traffic that he sent to the Foreign Office. The ships themselves were fitted out at Casa Blanca or Regla, away from the main docks, but close to HMS *Romney,* the British hulk that from 1837 to 1845 housed Africans liberated by the mixed commission court. The slave ships or, after the 1835 treaty, their cargo- and equipment-carrying sister ships, took in manufactured trading cargoes from the bonded warehouses in the harbor. Havana for much of this period was the only bonded port in the island. On their return these ships normally disembarked their slaves within easy reach of Havana before returning to port for refitting. After 1826 the naval commander of the port inspected logbooks of returned slavers in compliance with the royal order of January of that year, but no further action was ever taken. The *bozales* were quickly marched or trans-shipped to the capital where they were sold openly at one of the several slave markets located in and around Havana. When J. J. Gurney was there in 1839, he found six large barracoons distributed within two miles of the city for the reception and sale of newly arrived Africans, all of them privately owned auction businesses. Bribes in the 1830s were in the $25-to-$30-a-slave range or in real terms about 10 percent of slave values.[53]

The Cuban government was responsible for only modest increases in the cost of carrying on the slave trade during the two decades following formal abolition. In the early years of illegality slavers did not clear out directly for Africa or, if they did, it was to the Portuguese offshore islands. When they returned to harbor in ballast, they reported other ports in the Americas as their point of departure and some times indeed actually called at these ports for documentation. The Danish island of St. Thomas was a crossroads for the slave trade at this time. Returning slavers called for instructions and outbound ships from Puerto Rico, southern Cuba and the French Antilles bought duty-free goods there. By 1829, however, Spanish complicity in the traffic was such that even these subterfuges were no longer necessary.[54] What cost-raising impediments that did exist were largely the result of naval activity. French and occasionally Dutch papers were purchased in the West Indies to keep British cruisers at arms length. As noted in appendix E and chapter 8, the 1835 Anglo-Spanish treaty and the unilateral British moves of 1837 and 1839 drove up insurance rates and induced a switch, first, to the Portuguese flag and, then, on the outbound voyage at least, the U.S. flag. These slave-trader strategies were not costless, but they were clearly less than what became necessary later to avoid confiscation of cargoes and incarceration.[55] It took domestic pressure, for example, to induce slave traders to burn ships at the end of the voyage or deposit their cargoes temporarily on remote Bahamian islands, not the British navy.

In Brazil there were regional variations in the freedom allowed to slave-trader operations. Authorities at the port of Bahia interfered least with the business, until just before the effective ending of the trade in 1851. Between

1815 and 1830 when Portuguese and Brazilian slave ships were restricted by treaty to Africa south of the equator, Bahian authorities issued passports consistent with the treaty but did nothing to enforce the passport directives. It was general knowledge that Bahian ships rarely deviated from Bight of Benin markets, all north of the line. When in 1827 the Sierra Leone Mixed Commission Court condemned vessels sailing in these latitudes in violation of their passports, the Bahian port captain countered by issuing two passports per ship—one for slaves south of the equator and one for produce to the north.[56] For ten years after 1830, when Brazil formally prohibited all slave imports, slave ships fitted out and cleared from Bahia with regular merchant ship documentation and a licence to return in ballast from Príncipe island in the Bight of Biafra. After the British act of 1839 and for the last decade of the traffic, the same equipment and goods continued to leave Bahia but now in French, Sardinian and U.S. bottoms. The equipment or perhaps the whole ship was then transferred to the Portuguese or Brazilian owners on the coast of Africa if there were no British cruisers in attendance.[57] The slaves themselves were no longer taken directly into the port of Bahia after 1830 but were disembarked at reception centers at islands in the Baía de Todos os Santos or latterly at the mouth of Rio d'Una. The west side of the island of Itaparica was the main depot. From here the Africans were distributed among Creole slaves being shipped in the coastal trade or else taken to the Bahia city slave marts where "they are sold without fear of interruption from the authorities." Only in the late 1840s were any of these operations carried out under cover of darkness, and throughout this period bribes to the Juizes de Paz (magistrates) were about the same as the regular import duty on Africans before 1831. It was African fevers rather than abolitionist sentiment that occasionally induced the police to shut down these markets.[58]

The traffic was not carried on quite so openly in Rio de Janeiro. The city was not only a major slave-trading center but also the capital. Unlike Havana and Bahia, it was the location of the ultimate governing authority as well as a full British legation. From 1831 to 1837 and occasionally thereafter, ministries held power which were not prepared to connive openly at the traffic. Enforcement of the impressive Brazilian antislave-trade law of November 7, 1831, was more likely here than anywhere else in Brazil. At the same time Rio de Janeiro was the hub of both the road system to the coffee-growing regions and the coastal shipping network of Brazil South. Ventures were planned and financed in the capital and most of the slaves that they brought back were ultimately disembarked at one of the great Rio depots at Saco de Jurujuba, (Niteroi) Ponta d'Area, São Clemente or the Ponta de Cajú opposite the Ilha do Governador. In the 1840s there were probably more slaves traded at the Vallongo market in Rio de Janeiro than all the New Orleans markets put together.[59] Yet only a few of the transatlantic slave ships actually left the port fully equipped or entered with slaves on board. From the early 1830s Rio slavers adopted the Portuguese flag, cleared for Angola with a trading cargo and returned with slaves ostensibly for Montevideo but in reality to a small outport with no customs facilities. Campos, Macaé and the island of São Sebastião were the most commonly used, but after 1837 some slavers debarked at points as close as the bay beneath Sugarloaf Mountain. Slavers would then enter the harbor of the capital in ballast, their contact with Brazilian import and exporting authorities having been limited to clearing out with goods and entering in ballast six or seven weeks later. Returned slavers were routinely subjected to police inspection, at least before 1838, and the Brazilian Navy made the occasional capture. Indeed in the first six months of 1836, twenty ships were detained in Rio harbor. In the same period in the following year, the last justice minister of the liberal interlude detained thirty more. All were subsequently released.[60]

At the end of the decade, however, the provincial slave depots became more than just relay stations for the capital city. Slave ships began to load the manufactured component of their trading cargoes at these depots to avoid the reexportation duty payable at bonded warehouses in the capital.[61] Moreover, a fuller role for the outports was part of the slave-trader response to British moves against the trade. The 1839 British act allowed the Royal Navy to detain Portuguese ships equipped for the trade and for a time it seemed that Hanseatic and U.S. ships ferrying out equipment to the African coast could also be taken. In 1845 the Aberdeen Act made Brazilian-registered ships similarly liable. Prior to this the latter, under conditions laid down in the 1826 treaty, could be captured by the British only if they had slaves on board.[62] Part of the slave-trader adjustment to this threat was to avoid Rio de Janeiro, a frequent port of call for British cruisers. The illicit traffickers turned the provincial depots into full slaving ports with complete fitting-out facilities. By 1850 the biggest had forges, rope manufactories, large warehouses at the dockside, auxiliary steamships for towing and communication as well as massive stone barracoons for two thousand slaves with attendant banana and orange groves and acres of mandioca fields for the restoration of new arrivals.[63] As the coffee frontier expanded further into São Paulo and the volume of the slave trade approached fifty thousand per year, these bases became more numerous and more distant from the capital. Before the end of the trade they ranged over five hundred miles of coastline from Espírito Santo to the north to Paranaguá in the south, and slaves increasingly bypassed the Rio market. Santos developed a trade of its own and Paranaguá, too, the latter specializing in the larger ships on the southeast African route.[64] No serious police action against these establishments was taken until 1851, and the price of cooperation on the part of the local authorities does not seem to have been much above the going rate in Bahia despite the relative proximity of the central government. Until the very last year of the trade, the juizes de paz normally received 10 percent of the value of the imported slave, often in bills paid on sight in Rio de Janeiro.[65] But the overall impact of this bribery and relocation on the costs of carrying on the slave trade could not have been major.

Serious domestic, as opposed to British, actions against the slave trade in the Iberian Americas began in early 1842 when the recently arrived Captain-General Gerónimo Valdés ordered the enforcement of regulations against slave importations. In the course of a year the government closed down the six principal Havana markets for *bozales,* seized part cargoes of newly arrived Africans and made it illegal to purchase foreign-made vessels for registration under Spanish colors. In addition, a Spanish naval vessel captured a slave ship on the high seas. These actions "transformed the Cuban slave trade from a thriving business to a persecuted criminal activity." Slave ships now took on the most incriminating equipment at night, beyond the fort at the harbor mouth or at a small outport. Others fitted out at Iberian ports or eventually at remote cays.[66] But no counterparts to the elaborate establishments on quiet stretches of the Brazilian coastline ever developed. The Cuban government wished to keep the trade completely hidden and, in addition, the volume of the Cuban traffic was small in most years after 1842.[67] At the end of a voyage the ship might now for the first time be scuttled, abandoned or head for a foreign port to pick up a legitimate cargo as a cover.[68] Just over 4,000 slaves arrived in 1842 compared to an annual average of over 20,000 in the mid-1830s. As the price of sugar reached an all-time low in that year, one third below the annual means of the mid-1830s, it is unlikely that official actions were alone responsible for this drop in arrivals. Nevertheless, of the 4,100 Africans, 754 were seized by the authorities and the bribes paid on the remainder reached new highs.[69] Valdés left the island on September 16, 1843, and under his successor, Leopoldo O'Donnell, both sugar prices and the traffic revived. But early in 1845 came the first law against the slave trade ever to be passed by a Spanish legislative assembly. It provided for the imprisonment of slave traders and slaver crews and for the destruction of the slaver itself. Unfortunately it also prevented Cuban officials from pursuing suspected *bozales* onto private estates. Henceforth newly arrived *bozales* would be sold not in Havana but from sugar estates near the coast.[70]

In one sense the 1845 penal law gave a new security to the slave importer: Once on the estate his slaves were not going to be seized. Yet the major effect was in quite the opposite direction. After 1845 it was impossible for the authorities to revert to their open tolerance of the traffic practiced in the years 1821 to 1842. Officials in the Cuban government and indeed the Spanish royal family would continue to benefit from the trade—the trade itself would continue for twenty-two more years,[71] but the difference between having domestic sanctions against the traffic as opposed to only the provisions of an unwanted treaty were important.[72] For the slave trader the effect was to increase costs. A temporary recovery in sugar prices in 1846 and 1847 created a demand for labor that the British commissioners thought would induce "the slave dealers and others to run all risks whatever to supply it." Yet to their surprise imports did not respond. Between 1846 and 1850 slave arrivals were the lowest of any quinquennia between the 1780s and 1865.[73] As the flow of indentured Chinese was insignificant before 1853, the reason was simply that the costs of marketing Africans in Cuba had risen beyond the level planters could pay. As James Kennedy put it, the dealers were "not . . . able to afford slaves at such prices as to meet the wants of the planters." The slave importers, he wrote later, "complain especially of the exactions from the authorities of the island, the demands made on them on all sides continually increasing." Slave prices, which had already increased slightly during the 1830s in response to British naval activity, now rose by half during the 1840s, whereas the price of sugar actually fell by one fifth in real terms.[74] The slave price trend was enough to switch slaves from urban areas and coffee estates to sugar cultivation within Cuba. It also set the

⌐nta de Fomento thinking of Chinese indentured laborers. But it was not enough to cover the risks and bribery associated with the mass importations of Africans.

In the following decade rising sugar prices carried the demand for slaves beyond the threshold level at which importers were prepared to operate. Remote cays continued to be the site of the surreptitious fitting out of slavers, though an increasing number of vessels took their chances in U.S. ports as well as more exotic locations such as the Yucatán Peninsula. In the early 1860s slave traders established a base on the southernmost island of Anguilla, unoccupied territory claimed by the British. The American Civil War, however, made European ports popular once more.[75] On their return from Africa, slavers would run directly into secluded coves or transship cargoes to small coasting craft off the north or south coasts, depending on cruiser deployment. As the slave-price rise made the vessels themselves worth only a small fraction of their cargoes, many were subsequently burnt or scuttled. The slaves were dispersed to sugar estates as quickly as possible, often under cover of coastal shipping passports or at night.[76] After midcentury the cost of buying slaves in Africa and transporting them to Cuba probably made up only a third or so of the final selling price. The remainder comprised the costs of keeping the slaves out of the hands of the authorities. The most important of such costs were bribes and payments to the owners of estates where the *bozales* were first lodged. In 1852, for example, one cargo of slaves were hurried to the estate of Mariano Borrell near Trinidad. The owner of the estate "insisted upon keeping as many as he wanted, paying only $425 each for them, instead of the going rate of $590 . . . thus taking what he perhaps considered equivalent to the protection of this estate." Seven years later the price had risen to $900, but a shipment of 650 healthy Africans, which arrived without prior arrangement among the Cayos de las Doce Leguas, was purchased for only $400 each by Julián de Zulueta and taken to his Savanilla estate.[77] Bribes to government officials were no doubt paid on top of the $400 by Zulueta. The Lieutenant-governor of Trinidad received $51,000 for conniving at one shipment in 1860, and this does not include payments to officials at both above and below this level. The evidence suggests, however, that after 1851 the cost of shipping a slave to Cuba, say cif, before the costs of illegal introduction of that slave into the Cuban slave-labor force, was not much above $400.[78]

The volume of the traffic in the later 1850s and the obvious connivance of Cuban officials should not be allowed to obscure the risks involved in bringing African slaves to Cuba. Although all ships carrying slaves did eventually disembark their cargoes somewhere in the island, there were many instances of full slavers being forced to seek alternative landing sites because of the refusal of the local authorities to cooperate.[79] Why else indeed would bribes have been so high? During the short tenures of Valentin Cañedo and Juan de la Pezuela as captains-general in 1852 to 1854, officers invaded estates in search of *bozales*. Of an estimated 11,400 slaves landed in 1854, 3,000 were seized, the Lieutenant-governors of Trinidad and Sancti-Spíritus were superseded and Julián de Zulueta among others was imprisoned, Zulueta for nearly five months. The ratio of slaves seized to slaves landed fell after Pezuela's departure, but a British naval officer asserted in 1858 that any non–Spanish-speaking slave was liable to capture.[80] Senior officials were always liable to be removed from office for accepting bribes in the last years of the trade and arrests and expulsions from Cuba of crew and dealers alike were also constant features of the final period. There were no less than seventeen criminal cases undertaken in 1857 that arose from slave-trading activities. Although many offenders escaped prosecution, and many of those convicted were subsequently pardoned, the costs of obtaining these favors have to be considered a major expense of carrying on business. Any increases in costs, of course, could only result in fewer slaves imported. By 1863 Captain-General Domingo Dulce y Garay was not only removing transgressors from office but sending them to Spain for trial. After the defection and damaging revelations of José Augustín Argüelles, Lieutenant-governor of Colón in 1864, it would seem that official connivance with slave dealers was virtually at an end.[81]

Finally we should note that the process of criminalizing the slave trade introduced many costs other than payoffs to authorities. As in the modern drug subculture, illicit property was likely to be the subject of theft and fraud. In Nuevitas in 1854 bribes paid to the governor of the district were insufficient to prevent the latter seizing part of a shipment. The partners of the expedition thereupon began robbing each other to recoup their losses. Where consignment selling was involved, it was often the African supplier who suffered. The disembarkation and transportation overland of large numbers of slaves was accompanied in several instances by attacks from local residents who either carried off slaves for themselves or in one case demanded $85 for each African allowed to pass on.[82] No such incidents are recorded before the early 1840s. Moreover, a luxuriant crop of informers sprang up in the later period fostered by both British officials and the government. Slave trader attempts to control this involved both cash and violence.[83] As in any criminal activity, rewards in this business could be massive, but it would be a mistake to think that losses were confined to those who were beaten up and murdered.

It would, therefore, be overly pessimistic to label the penal law of 1845 a failure as many historians have done, just as it would be an error to assume that every or even most slave traders and government officials waxed prosperous from the slave-trafficking business. There were clear differences in slave-importing costs between the first and second half of the era of illicit trading. Spanish and Cuban initiatives against the business, albeit at British behest, did not cut off the flow of slaves into the Spanish Antilles, but they did reduce it. Portuguese factors from the Congo River visited Cuba in 1862 and tried, unsuccessfully, to bolster a declining business. They promised cargoes of 800 slaves at $35 per slave at a time when the same slave in Cuba might fetch $700.[84] Given this availability of slaves in Africa, particularly after 1851, there is no doubt that without the efforts of the captains-general and the penal law, the price of *bozales* might well have been half the $1,000-or-so mean of 1856–60, and the volume of slaves carried two or three times greater. This impact is considerably in excess of the most optimistic assessments of the effectiveness of the British Navy.

Spanish moves against the traffic in the post-Valdés years were more effective than any Brazilian measures prior to 1850. The Brazilian law of November 1831 and the additional regulations of April 1832 were much more severe on paper than the Spanish penal law of 1845. The former included the purchasers of slaves, in its definition of slave importers, and subjected them to the same penalties of imprisonment as the captains and owners of slave vessels. More important it contained no restrictions on the pursuit of slaves once landed. The law also declared all newly imported slaves to be emancipated on entering the country, and provided a bounty from public funds for all those informing on slave traders.[85] The Brazilian laws were not enforced, however. As we have seen, in Rio de Janeiro the slave trade had to be at least partially concealed. But compared to the last twenty years of the Cuban trade, the Brazilian government imposed relatively minor additional costs on the slave traders. It was the British naval intervention of 1850 and the government of Brazil's response to this that made the climate for importing slaves similar in Brazil and Cuba. In Brazil, slave prices jumped by 50 percent in five years and 130 percent in a decade, paralleling and indeed exceeding the rapid price rise in Cuba between the 1830s and 1840s.[86]

The market for African slaves in the Americas, as with slavery itself, thus did not fade away in the second half of the nineteenth century, rather it was suppressed. But for the intervention of governments and, in particular, the British, there would have been a thriving demand for and supply of slaves throughout the eastern seaboard of the Americas. Without suppression, prices at well under $1,000 (in real terms) for a prime male seem likely. The key influences over the price in the long run would probably have been African population parameters and perhaps technology, which was steadily increasing the value of labor in the North American countries. Ideology apart, it would seem that there were extensive opportunities for the employment of coerced labor. Institutionally determined price increases prevented the exploitation of these opportunities. From 1803, Denmark, the United States, Britain, Holland, France and eventually Brazil and Spain all imposed barriers against the transatlantic slave trade, which greatly increased the price of slave labor. The result in one American country after another was that slaves gravitated toward the economic activity in which they could be most profitably employed. This meant cotton in the United States, sugar in the Caribbean and, eventually, coffee in Brazil. Activities that could not afford slaves at these higher prices were forced to use free labor, much of it eventually to come from Europe. In the absence of slave-trade suppression, then, the situation in Minas Gerais where slaves were employed in a wide range of occupations prior to 1850 would likely have become the norm for most of the Americas.

# V

# The Midcentury Atlantic Economy and Final Suppression, 1830–70

# 12

## Suppression Effected

There were few plantation societies in the Americas that voluntarily stopped slave imports into their territories. The likelihood of such action was, nevertheless, greater than those same societies spontaneously giving up slavery itself. In several importing regions there were divisions on the suppression issue between prospective slave buyers. In the U.S. South, Virginia and North Carolina came out relatively early in favor of banning the transatlantic traffic. Later there were splits within Georgia and South Carolina between established planters, who were prepared to see an end to the traffic, and frontiersmen, who needed the cheap slaves that only the continuation of the trade could ensure. Generally, however, "the drive to build an empire in the West" won out.[1] In the late ante-bellum period after years of natural population increase among slaves, there was probably a southern consensus against reopening the trade. The very high price of U.S. slaves, relative to the cost of importing Africans, meant that a new slave trade would have brought a stream of low-priced bondsmen to reduce the net worth of existing slave owners. It might also have sparked "an antislavery form of southern 'nativism'."[2] But such a consensus is not to be confused with the phenomenon of slave owners supporting the abolition of the slave trade when transatlantic markets were still open. In the British case economic interest was clearly motivating the planters in the older colonies when they negotiated with the abolitionists for the temporary suspension of the traffic in 1804. Closer examination shows, however, that planter interest in the proposal evaporated when the 1805 Order in Council abolished the African slave trade to the underpopulated and highly productive newly conquered colonies that were the chief rivals of the older British Caribbean in the sugar markets of Europe.[3] Planter support for abolition had clearly hinged on the need to control or suppress an important new source of competition, an aim that the Order in Council helped them achieve without any immediate cost to themselves. But, in general, through one medium or another, suppression of the slave trade was imposed on the importing society from outside.

In one sense, of course, all suppression could be voluntary. The ending of the trade depended on the price of slaves in the Americas falling below the cost of enslaving, transporting and distributing Africans on the west side of the Atlantic. The key division is between those societies where the cost increase was due to attempts to suppress the trade and those societies where it was due simply to normal market forces subject only to some minor mercantilist regulations. The transatlantic market for slaves expanded more or less continuously from its beginnings, and it was the former source that predominated. Earlier chapters indicate that increased cost pressures on the nineteenth-century slave trade came from outside the slave society itself. For the European colonies in the Americas, including those of France, it was the metropolitan power that imposed suppression, and in the U.S. case it came as the result of a constitutional pact between north and south. But in the regions to which the slave trade survived the longest, Brazil and Cuba, there were few metropolitan pressures of the kind that stemmed from the ideological shifts explored in chapters 2 and 6. In Spain the antislave-trade movement before 1867 was barely stronger than in Cuba itself, and it was no match either for the Cuban planter or the broader colonial interest within Spain itself. Brazil after 1822 was an independent power. Here the slave society was not subject to any formal outside controls. At the same time suppression was apparently beyond the powers of the British Navy at least if it was confined to the high seas and if the slave trade was not recognized generally as piracy. The relevant question is, thus, not why did the slave trade endure well into the industrial era, but rather why did Brazil and Cuba so soon take the steps necessary to eliminate the slave trade when so much of their economic success depended on the cheap labor it provided. Rising slave prices had already helped reduce Cuban coffee and Brazilian cotton production and a continuation of the process might eventually do the same for Cuban sugar and Brazilian coffee.

Any explanation that focuses on social or economic change within American slave societies appears questionable in the light of the above discussion and the experience of other slave societies in the Americas. Clearly there was always an abundant demand for slaves at prices that held both before and after effective suppression. Internal resistance to the continuation of the slave trade seems of minor significance. There were real fears of African fevers, in particular yellow fever, which caused temporary interruptions to the traffic, but fatal diseases in the Americas—most spectacularly cholera in Cuba—tended to increase demand and have just the opposite effect: The net epidemiological contribution to the trade was certainly positive.[4] Concerns about the Africanization of Cuba, in particular, fueled a considerable literature despite the fact that slaves accounted for large, but minority shares of the total population of Brazil and Cuba. The African component of the contemporary French American or the pre-emancipation British Caribbean populations was much greater. White intellectuals such as Francisco de Arango y Parreño and Saco in Cuba (the former somewhat belatedly) certainly wished to see their country developed without the aid of the African race. But white migrants to Brazil and Cuba were relatively few in number and always avoided the sugar sector until late in the century. It is, thus, unlikely that the wish for a white labor force, tinged though it was with racism, could ever have outweighed the need for cheap labor.

In the absence of the slaves freeing themselves en masse, there were perhaps two conditions that might have generated the possibility of serious internal action against the trade. The first was the security implications of an over-whelmingly high ratio of recently arrived slaves in the total population such as existed in St. Domingue in 1790—though in St. Domingue itself, it might be noted planters continued to import Africans after the rebellion began. The second was the presence in the importing region of large numbers of free migrants who might see Africans as competition in the labor market. If the law and the price of slaves had been such as to allow northern U.S. employers to buy African slaves in the mid-nineteenth century, one might assume that the Irish would have rioted in favor of rather than against the abolitionists—at least on the slave-trade issue. With slave prices low enough, of course, there might have been far fewer Irish in the Americas in the first instance.[5] There is some evidence of popular antislave-trade feeling in Brazil, but in the main neither of the above two conditions existed in Brazil or Cuba in the 1850s and 1860s.

Although developments within Brazil cannot be ignored, the major pressures for suppression came from outside the importing regions. The most general-ized of these by mid-nineteenth century was the international opprobrium in which the slave trade was held. As the Brazilian foreign minister conceded in 1852, his country could not any longer "resist the pressure of the ideas of the age in which we live."[6] Concrete manifestation of this came with the British attack on shipping in Brazilian ports in 1850, which was obviously casus belli before international law. Despite this, the diplomatic community in Rio de Janeiro made no gesture of support for Brazil at the time of the incidents. Sub-sequent Brazilian approaches to Britain's arch rival, France, elicited the response that on this issue Brazil was alone. It is worth noting that one of the first actions of the Montgomery (Alabama) Constitutional Convention of 1861, as the new confederacy strove for international acceptance, was to prohibit slave importations from any foreign source.[7] For governments of Brazil and Cuba, the public fitting out of slave ships and marketing of Africans had become impossible to tolerate openly.

But the self-appointed instrument of international opinion was clearly the British government, and we should explore briefly the shifts in British policy without which suppression in Brazil and Cuba would not have come when it did. As the British commander of the cruiser squadron in 1831 pointed out, an unfettered navy backed with antipiracy powers could have swept the ocean clear of slave traders. Both the American minister to Brazil, a slave-holding Virginian, and Lewis Tappan, the U.S. abolitionist leader asked the same ques-tion from opposing sides of the slavery divide: Why does not the British gov-ernment suppress the slave trade? For the former it could only be the lucrative markets for British goods created by the slave traders that prevented it.[8] As many British expected much larger markets in Africa to spring up in the wake of suppression, such a consideration was not however a major constraint. Nevertheless as chapter 7 has pointed out, the campaign against the slave trade—and in particular the efforts to force Brazil and Spain on the righteous path—was riddled with moral ambivalence and internal inconsistency. The form and timing of British intervention and the Brazilian and Cuban response was determined to some extent by the ability of the British themselves to come to terms with these tensions.

Before exploring the latter further, it is necessary to note the limits beyond which the British were not prepared to travel on the issue of slave-trade suppression. Although suppression was viewed as leading to tangible material benefits in the form of increased trade in commodities with Africa, there were more immediate national foreign policy goals that always took precedence. The British never contemplated, for example, major increases in the naval estimates for the express purpose of putting down the slave trade. Prime Minister Russell specifically exempted the African squadron from naval cutbacks in the 1840s,[9] but there was a large political difference between this and proposing an increase. Indeed the exceptionally large naval forces off West Africa in the 1840s are explained to some extent by the relative peace, from the British perspective, on most of the rest of the world's sea-lanes. The appearance of issues such as the maintenance of a friendly government in the Río de la Plata, the monitoring of U.S. designs on Cuba and, in the next decade, the Crimean War, always meant some sacrifice in the British commitment to slave-trade suppression. Similarly the British command of the seas did not mean a willingness to push their own conceptions of the right of visit (much less right of search) and piracy on other major powers to the point of a rupture in relations. Eventually they were prepared to risk such a rupture with Portugal and with Brazil, but not with France and the United States. It seems inconceivable, for example, that if the New Orleans slave market had been supplied from Africa instead of from the upper South that the British would have sent their cruisers into U.S. ports to cut out and destroy slave ships as they did in Brazil. If the 1839 act against Portuguese slavers had extended to all nations and the British had, say, doubled their naval commitment, the slave trade might have ended twenty-five years earlier than it did. A major maritime conflict would have been a more likely outcome, however.

Action within these constraints, at least in the form of initiatives involving or risking military intervention, really meant action against Brazil alone. Cuba was the center of a subtle three-handed international card game that precluded serious naval operations. Spain was obsessed with the fear of losing its last major colony in the Americas and saw slavery and the slave trade as helping to bind tight the colonial ties. Some in the United States were just as obsessed with acquiring the island or at least keeping it out of British or African hands. Britain, the third player, wished to see the end of the slave trade and slavery, but above all wished to keep Cuba out of U.S. hands and most logically, therefore, within the Spanish Empire.[10] These incompatible goals had two implications for the Cuban slave trade. The first was that in order to gain British support in the 1840s in the face of the annexationist threat, the Spanish increase the pressure on slave traders with the consequences explored in the chapter 11. It became more expensive to import slaves into Cuba than into Brazil before midcentury. The second was that British naval intervention in Cuba became much less likely—at least in the absence of a U.S. invasion of the island. If the British interfered first, then the United States expanionists would be handed a rallying cry for a full-scale attempt at a takeover. When the British tried something less than a blockade in 1857–58—the dispatch of four small gunboats to Cuban waters to search shipping for slaving equipment—the reaction in the U.S. press dictated a quick policy reversal.[11] Thus, efforts to suppress the slave trade were greater within Cuba than within Brazil in the mid-1840s, but the slave trade persisted longer in the former region. Not until sectional differences in the United States were decided could an externally imposed naval solution have even a slight chance of success.

Yet that the British would initiate unilateral action against the slave trade cannot be taken for granted. During the 1840s the unity of the British abolitionist world shattered over the twin disappointments of failure to suppress the slave trade and the failure of West Indian freedmen to maintain sugar production. Given the importance of antislavery, it was inevitable that these tensions would be felt by all social commentators and not just the minority of the British public active in the abolitionist movement. These tensions were certainly echoed in the British cabinets of the 1840s and 1850s, whose decisions shaped British commercial policy and the British impact on American slave (and ex-slave) societies. Palmerston and Russell usually advocated policies broadly consistent with the position of the old abolitionist leadership of Buxton, Macaulay and the elder Stephen. By the 1840s only Buxton survived, and he was not in Parliament. Their position, however, was maintained in the Commons by Robert Inglis who worked closely with Monckton Milnes on the Commons select committees on the slave trade in the later 1840s. Milnes was regarded as Palmerston's informal representative on these committees.[12] For these men the transatlantic slave trade was such an abomination that the means of suppression were ultimately less important than the fact it should be suppressed. For them there was no tension between the freedom of choice inherent in laissez-faire and forcing other nations to give up the slave trade.

During the 1830s indeed British policy had achieved some success without stepping too far outside the bounds of international law. At the beginning of the decade the Anglo-Brazilian treaty went into operation and the Anglo-French treaties were signed; the equipment treaty of 1835 with Spain followed. Only the 1839 act against Portugal was questionable as the protest of the eight members of the House of Lords indicated. The traffic to the French Americas died completely and the Brazilian traffic, the largest of the surviving branches of the trade, had fallen dramatically in the first half of the decade. When it revived after 1834, the British reaction had focused on Portugal under whose flag this revival occurred. In the 1840s however the continued flow of slaves into Brazil suggested that British policy was less successful. The Aberdeen Act of 1845, unlike its 1839 counterpart against Brazil and despite the arguments of Lushington and Aberdeen, could claim only the most tenuous of links with either earlier treaties or established international practice.[13] Yet for Palmerston, who returned to the Foreign Office in 1846 in the Russell administration, the Aberdeen Act was too weak. It gave jurisdiction to British courts over Brazilian property, but it kept those courts from punishing the slave traders themselves, a situation that Palmerston tried to change in 1848. The problem, in Palmerston's view, was thus one of insufficient coercion and too careful a regard for international law. For both Palmerston and Russell, the failure of the Brazilian and Cuban authorities themselves to halt slave disembarkations justified, and indeed demanded a British blockade of Havana and Rio de Janeiro. Palmerston had held this view since at least 1844.[14]

There was, however, another group in the British cabinet headed by Earl Grey, who as Parliamentary undersecretary to the Colonial Office had been responsible for an abortive slave emancipation scheme in 1833. Grey's antipathy to Palmerston was such that he agreed to serve in the same cabinet only if the government gave priority to free trade.[15] Where Palmerston and Russell shared in the willingness of the Buxton/Macaulay group to overlook strict legal observances in the pursuit of slave-trade suppression, Grey and company had more affinity to the laissez-faire element in British abolitionism identified in chapter 2. Although the makeup of the group is not known with precision, it almost certainly included George Grey, Lord Clarendon and Charles Wood. These were the Whigs most sympathetic to free trade who sided with Earl Grey, now head of the Colonial Office, on most issues. For Earl Grey the slave trade could not be suppressed by the navy and would most likely wither if left alone. Like George Thompson, the abolitionist, he was averse not only to aggressive action against Brazil and Cuba but to the very concept of an anti-slave-trade cruiser squadron. The issue was not, however, important enough to warrant staying out of or resigning from the cabinet even though Brazil and Cuba between them accounted for about half of all British exports to Latin America at midcentury. The antisquadron group within the cabinet also included Lord Campbell, a former attorney general and future lord chancellor. Campbell was neither an ardent free trader nor linked to Grey, and his objections may well have been grounded in the legal implications of an aggressive policy. The support of the Grey faction was important to a government that always had difficulty commanding a majority in either house.[16]

Perhaps because of this situation Palmerston and Russell chose to make a coercionist slave-trade policy a government confidence issue only once, and indeed the subject was never of such central importance to the cabinet as, say, Ireland or free trade. The occasion, however, is instructive. In March 1850 William Hutt, the leader of the anticoercionists in the Commons proposed a further motion calling on the government to withdraw from any treaty that required the use of force to put down the slave trade. Of all the antisquadron motions of the 1840s, this was the one that came closest to winning a majority vote. Before the vote was taken Palmerston and Russell threatened their supporters that they would resign if it passed. The result was that the suppression policy was preserved.[17] The point to note, however, is that the favorable vote was for maintenance of an existing policy, not for new initiatives. As Russell had observed just a few weeks earlier, a "blockade [of] Brazil and Cuba . . . is so violent that altho' I should be prepared to support it I do not think th*

Cabinet or the House of Commons would do so."[18] Indeed at no point during or after the 1840s could they or any other group in tune with the older generation of abolitionists gain support for such action. It was not that the British commitment to abolition was weakening, but rather that abolitionism itself was much less focused than it had been. By midcentury abolitionist principles could be sincerely invoked by those who supported, as well as those who opposed, anti–slave-trade policy.

In a sense the differences over blockading ports in the Iberian Americas was academic. Until 1849 almost the entire South American squadron was continually involved in Río de la Plata affairs. But a united cabinet could no doubt have diverted ships from elsewhere—notably the West African coast—as Palmerston had argued in 1844 when in opposition.[19] British priorities were such that in the later 1840s new British coercionist initiatives could be taken only within three broad parameters. The first was that there should be no major augmentations of naval strength off South America, the second was that no formal blockade should be imposed, and the third was that nothing should disturb the existing balance of power in the Caribbean. Palmerston and Russell operated skillfully within these limits, with some independent help from the Foreign Office and naval personnel on the spot in Brazil. But clearly such limitations ruled out action against Cuba in a period when American annexationist pressure built to a climax. The same factors also delayed action in Brazil until the circumstances were right. The availability of the South American squadron—freed from intervention in the Río de la Plata—during 1849 was one such circumstance. A second arose from local intiatives taken by British naval officers and James Hudson the British chargé d'affaires in Brazil.

As the squadron gradually returned to antislave-trade duties in South America, an increasing number of captures occurred within Brazilian territorial waters. There was actually nothing new in this. British cruisers had captured slave vessels inside domestic limits in the past though never within Brazilian ports. Although the law officers had declared such proceedings illegal under the 1817 and 1826 treaties, the 1839 and 1845 acts allowing the detention of Portuguese and Brazilian slavers had no such territorial restrictions written into them. The British minister in Rio did, in fact, point this out some years before Palmerston decided to take full advantage of the freedom this gave to the navy.[20] The occasional pursuit of slave ships onto the very shores of Brazil, nevertheless, continued. The British government normally offered reparations whenever the navy pursued slave ships into Brazilian waters—at least under Aberdeen. It did not, however, treat the offending British naval officers with any great severity, not at least if we examine the fate of their counterparts who trifled with the U.S. flag off Africa.[21]

What was new about the situation in 1849 and 1850 was the refusal of the Foreign Office to censure its naval officers in the face of Brazilian protests. In April 1850, shortly after the defeat of the latest Hutt motion, Palmerston subtly extended the policy. He notified the Admiralty that the Aberdeen Act permitting British cruisers to capture Brazilian ships "contains no restrictions as to the limits within which the search, detention and capture of slave traders . . . to take place and therefore such proceedings may be made at any place within Brazilian waters as well as on the high seas."[22] There is no record of this interpretation of the 1826 treaty on which Aberdeen based his act ever being referred to the law officers for an opinion. The response of Hudson and Admiral Reynolds in Brazil was to instigate a series of assaults on slave ships in Brazilian harbors beginning in June 1850. These were almost immediately followed by the rapid and strict enforcement of Brazilian laws against the slave trade and, of course, the quick demise of the latter.[23]

The connection between these events has been debated by Brazilian and British historians ever since, but the point is that the British actions did not constitute a blockade and were instituted without major additions to naval strength. Even though they were probably inconsistent with both the 1826 treaty and an emerging law of nations, they received the acquiescence of the British cabinet, not least one suspects because Brazilian slave imports collapsed in their wake.[24] Unlike 1807, 1814 and 1833, neither institutionalized nor popular abolitionism played any role in this process either in Britain or Brazil. For most of the 1840s the British and Foreign Anti-Slavery Society was against force of any kind and earned the full measure of Palmerston's contempt for its position.[25] Yet the same ideological crosscurrents that left the antislavery group as spectators also ensured the timing and direction of British intervention. Given the structure of opinion in the British cabinet after 1846 and the Río de la Plata intervention, this aggressive policy could not have been executed before 1850 and could never have been pursued at all in Cuba. It was not entirely fortuitous that it came just as the Brazilian government was more than usually harassed. As Hudson pointed out to Palmerston, the Praieira revolt in Pernambuco to the north, with the rebels offering to abolish slavery in return for British recognition, was matched to the south by an invasion threat from General Rosas.[26]

But the fact remains that it was the Brazilians not the British that closed down the slave-importing operations. Brazil was arguably the only non–English-speaking region to embrace mass abolitionism and, though the latter was confined mainly to the decade from 1879, no assessment of slave-trade suppression can ignore the shifts in opinion within Brazil. In 1834 one of the special magistrates appointed to enforce the 1831 slave-trade law wrote, "the measures which may be taken, according to our code, cannot in any way be efficient inasmuch as the parties engaged in this contraband . . . [are] . . . by their social position and pecuniary means the influential class. [I]t is from that very class that the Justices of the Peace, municipal officers, members of the chambers, Juries, Public Prosecutors and all other authorities to be elected by the People are to be selected. . . . This class necessarily make use of [the people] profiting by their want of information and by their belief that the cessation of the [slave] commerce will be fatal to Brazil."[27] This observation could probably have been penned at any point in the 1830s or 1840s. Yet by the end of 1850 James Hudson was marveling at "the entire change which has taken place in the opinions . . . of the Brazilian Press." We might assume from this that not all of the press opinion was being orchestrated by the British legation.[28] There is nothing to suggest hyperbole in the Justice Ministry's report of May 13, 185ᵀ when it observed that the new slave-trade law of the previous September ᵇ "met with the powerful support of public opinion." The law itself made importing slaves into Brazil piracy for the first time, provided for significant bounties for informers and established maritime courts with specially appointed judges to try offenders. Passports for ships sailing to Africa and the disposition of captured slaves were both more effectively controlled than under the 1831 law. In the fifteen months from mid-1850, the Brazilian Navy and police raided depots, confiscated ships and even invaded estates in search of newly arrived Africans. Local populations who had often attacked British seamen before 1850 now handed over slave traders to the authorities and welcomed British ships. After trying unsuccessfully to land a cargo of slaves at several locations in 1851, the captain of the *Tentativa* attempted to auction them off to the locals on a beach near Macaé. Despite prices of $10 to $12 there were few takers. Another captain expressed amazement at the extent of the opposition to his attempt to land a cargo and claimed that had he realized it before leaving Africa, he would have sailed for Havana instead.[29]

By 1851 the British were financing antislavery societies in Brazil, subsidizing the majority of newspapers in the province of Rio de Janeiro and were able to use the Brazilian customs department as their own information service. Yet to assign the shift in Brazilian opinion to this pecuniary influence would be to misunderstand it. It is probable that the steady rise in slave prices from the 1820s to the 1840s was accompanied by a reduction in the number of slaveholders in the nation. In Rio de Janeiro at least, the whites and free blacks increased relative to the slave population, and the two former groups took over occupations previously performed by slaves.[30] The potential opposition to slave imports was thus greater in 1850 then it had been in 1830. Leopoldo da Câmara, the captain of the port of Rio de Janeiro with great influence among the Rio free-colored community, was hostile to the slave trade and the Portuguese alike. Moreover, there was an outlet for such opposition. In contrast to Cuba, Brazil did have representative institutions in which the slave-trade issues were freely debated from time to time. In the late 1840s a member of the provincial council of Bahia published in a local newspaper a four-page plan for the gradual abolition of slavery itself—an action which no Cuban government would have tolerated. The popular nativist element in Leopoldo da Câmara's attitude was increasingly apparent by the early 1850s. It manifested itself not against Africans so much as against the Portuguese who dominated the slave-trade business. The tension between Portuguese and Brazilian was a basic element in the history of late colonial and early independent Brazil, and it is striking how in 1850–51 antislave trade merged with anti-Portuguese feeling. Like the Americans in regard to the British at the time of the Revolution and indeed the Cuban Creoles against the Spanish government, it was important that Brazilians could link the slave trade with foreign domination.[31]

The British role was, nevertheless, catalytic. The naval interventions of 1850, especially the incident at Paranaguá, created a huge impression throughout the country. For a few vital weeks it seemed that the reaction could go either way: against the British or against the Portuguese slave trader. If the British had not quickly suspended operations in Brazilian territorial waters and ʲlowed the Brazilian government to take up the cause, a tactic dictated as much by their own cabinet divisions as by the Brazilian situation, the outcome might have been different. As it was, the Brazilian government was faced with unrest in Pernambuco and Rio Grande do Sul and was loathe to risk a head-on confrontation with the British either through physical resistance or the encouragement of anti-British sentiment. The selectivity of the British action (only slave ships were destroyed), the latent hostility toward the Portuguese and the preoccupation of the government with other issues meant that the British got the response they wanted. By August 1850 even *Brasil* and *Correio Mercantil*, the leading pro–slave-trade newspapers in Rio de Janeiro, had abandoned the slave-trader cause. Russell could observe, "Opposition to our proceedings come rather from the Portuguese combination than from public opinion in that country."[32]

Whatever its source the shift in favor of suppression was profound. In 1856 a group of old Brazilian slave traders now involved in the Cuban trade made the last recorded attempt to introduce slaves from Africa into Brazil. Although many of the slaves were Portuguese-speaking and the Brazilian price left an ample margin for bribes, the *Mary E. Smith* made three separate landfalls on the Brazilian coast without effecting a disembarkation. At the third attempt a Brazilian brigantine of war caught up with the expedition and the officers and passengers, including one of the three owners, were imprisoned together with their Brazilian contact.[33] There is a real sense after 1852 that the possibilities of Brazil ever accepting slaves from Africa again were remote. There is no equivalent sense in the case of Cuba in the years after 1867, the year of the last recorded arrival of Africans there. Though Palmerston and Hudson would never admit it and the Aberdeen Act remained on the statute book, further British pressure on Brazil over this issue was unnecessary. Unlike the Cuban situation the expected profit from importing slaves into Brazil now no longer compensated for the risks to property and person.

Yet the strength and speed of the change remain something of a puzzle, and it is easier to pick out factors that clearly did not contribute to the shift in attitudes than it is to account for it fully. The very rapid rise in the price of slaves during 1850 and 1851 suggests that the major purchasers of slaves were completely unsympathetic to the shift. It also suggests that suppression was a sudden event and that there was no significant internal pressure to put an end to the traffic prior to 1850. The coffee sector was as dependent on slave labor in the 1850s, after suppression, as it had been before, as the massive internal slave trade of the later period demonstrated. The conservative Saguarema party was in office throughout the period of final suppression, and it represented the landed interest and the slave trader alike. But in no sense could the government convince either of these groups that on a strict accounting basis their interests would be best served by suppression of the slave trade. Least of all, as Foreign Minister Paulino Soares da Sousa later acknowledged, was there any sudden conversion to humanitarian principles on the part of either group. For each, suppression was an unwelcome event made palatable only by the fact that the alternative appeared to involve war with Britain.[34]

The position of the Brazilian government itself was probably little different to that of the slave traders and the coffee planters. During and after the event of 1850–51 both Foreign Minister Paulino and Justice Minister Eusébio de Queiroz argued that effective measures against the slave trade as embodied in the law of September 4 had always been planned. The project of law on which the legislation was based had been announced as early as January 1850; its subsequent passage and enforcement had, they argued, been made much more difficult by British interference. This had created a backlash against the anti-slave-trade cause. There can be little doubt, however, that the key articles in the Project of Law, which separated it from almost all earlier projects since 1831, were added in a secret session of the lower chamber as a direct consequence of the British attacks on Brazilian ports in late June and early July 1850. Its rapid passage through both houses may be ascribed to the same pressure. The Project of Law that the justice minister had in mind in January 1850 was based on a proposed law of 1837, the Barbacena bill, which would have had the effect of legalizing the traffic. British pressure turned a pro–slave-trade proposal into an effective instrument of suppression.[35]

Yet Eusébio and Paulino were not entirely wrong. They admitted the regular infractions of the law before 1850 but implied that this was the first Brazilian government strong enough to institute suppression. Paulino correctly pointed out the inability of the British Navy to suppress the trade unaided in the twenty years since 1830. The government of which they were members was certainly strong, but it was also conservative, with close ties to the landed and slave-trading interests. It is difficult to believe that it seriously intended at the beginning of 1850 to terminate slave imports. It is reasonable to ponder, however, whether the Brazilian state had the power to enforce suppression much before that year. As Leslie Bethell has pointed out, prior to the late 1840s the central government had neither the administrative structure, nor the revenues nor the naval resources necessary to implement abolition. Reforms in the early 1840s provided the first; the expiry in 1844 of the Anglo-Brazilian commercial treaty that had held down tariffs generated the second; the winding down of the Río de la Plata dispute yielded the third. Added together these factors constituted a necessary prerequisite of suppression, but they clearly were not sufficient in themselves to bring it about.[36] Luiz Felipe de Alencastro has considerably extended this line of reasoning by arguing that after 1838 the coffee frontier had expanded so far inland that the cost of getting coffee to market was as important in the *fazendeiros's* calculus as was the cost of buying slaves. Coffee growers were prepared to accept, indeed promote, a strong central government and suppression of the slave trade in exchange for government support of transportation, in particular railroads, and an aggressive immigration policy. The problem with this approach was that, but for British and international pressure, Brazil would surely have had both publically supported railroads and slaves from Africa. A strong central government did not inevitably imply suppression nor indeed did suppression imply railroad construction: the latter did not pass the one-thousand-mile mark in Brazil until the mid-1870s and much of the capital came from British rather than Brazilian government sources. As for immigration, not until the 1880s, did the five-year annual average of free immigrants approach what slave arrivals had been in the first half f the century.[37]

This extended discussion of the demise of the transatlantic slave traffic to Brazil provides some interesting insights into the implementation of Cuban abolition. In Cuba there was no single event that heralded suppression and the rise in slave prices following upon it was more modest than in Brazil. Paradoxically the process is easier to explain. The rough counterpart in Cuba to the Brazilian Law of September 4 was the Spanish penal law of 1845. In both countries the new law was accompanied (actually in the Cuban case preceded) by energetic action on the part of the enforcement agencies. If the British could have found the cabinet unity and had possessed the strategic freedom to treat the Cubans and the Spanish as they dealt with the Brazilians perhaps slave imports into Cuba might have finished twenty years early. Given the structure of Cuban society and government, it seems unlikely that British intervention would have acted as quite the catalyst that it did in Brazil, but perhaps this would not have mattered in an autocracy. The Spanish government did not want to end the trade completely if such action would weaken its hold on the island. Severe punishment of slave purchasers and the opening up of estates to searches for illegally imported Africans such as occurred in Brazil might, for example, have done both. Thus the market price for *bozales* in Cuba was often sufficient to cover the costs of importing, including bribery. There was accordingly some transatlantic movement of slaves into the island in the decade or so after the penal law.

Slave arrivals accelerated in the late 1850s as a result of rising sugar prices and continued technological progress, which pushed up the value of the slave. There were no major new domestic initiatives against the traffic in these years that might have offset rising slave prices. Thus although it is hard to get accurate figures of the Africans detained by the Cuban authorities after disembarkation, the annual returns of recaptives as a proportion of total arrivals from Africa, do not seem to have varied much during the 1850s and 1860s.[38] There is some evidence of increased zeal on the part of the Spanish governors of the early 1860s, Francisco Serrano y Domínguez and Domingo Dulce y Garay, who saw suppression as a way of perpetuating slavery itself. Both pressured Madrid for stronger sanctions. The number of officials expelled from office for collaborating with slave traders in these years probably increased, and in 1863 the authorities entered two estates and extracted from them a complete cargo. There was also an increase in the Spanish naval force patrolling Cuban waters from 1865 as well as additional British ships from 1863, following the Anglo-American slave-trade treaty of the previous year. On the other hand, in 1858 British free-trade interests once more obstructed the suppression effort, this time by encouraging the government to give up the long-standing British claim to the right to visit foreign merchant ships. The British mercantile marine was now of such magnitude that the British interest lay in emphasizing the rights of neutral shipping. U.S. protests against the activities of British cruisers off Cuba in 1857–58 got a sympathetic response in the British mercantile community.[39]

But the major change that put an end to the traffic in the mid-1860s came from the demand side of the market for slaves in the Americas, not as in Braz' from direct British interference with supply. Sugar prices fell by 26 percent in real terms between 1856–60 and 1866–70.[40] Perhaps more important, the emancipation of the slaves in the United States and the subsequent victory of the north in the Civil War threw a shadow over the future of slavery throughout the Americas. There was also the beginnings of an abolitionist movement in Spain. Cuban slave owners were simply not prepared to pay the prices that had been current in the late 1850s. The price of a prime male *bozal* between 1861 and 1865 fell back below what it had been ten years earlier, though prices recovered somewhat by the end of the decade.[41] Without any effort required from the Cuban authorities other than maintaining existing policies, the slave trade to Cuba died a market death in the sense that the cost of the clandestine introduction of Africans was now no longer covered by the going price for those Africans.

The new and stronger antislave-trade law promulgated in Cuba in September 1867 was thus unnecessary except as a symbol. It increased the costs of importing slaves even further, but in the absence of a massive increase in the price of sugar, these costs were already high enough, and the law was never actually invoked.[42] The same may be said of the 1862 Anglo-American treaty despite the tendency of historians to assign this pact a pivotal role in the ending of the trade. In the early 1860s during the Civil War, the U.S. North wished to curry British support or at least neutrality. Moreover, in 1858 the British had finally given up their fifty-year-long claim to visit foreign ships for the purpose of establishing the right of a ship to the colors displayed at the masthead. The American government now conceded both the right of visit and the right of search to British ships and joined with Britain to set up courts of mixed commission in Sierra Leone, Capetown and New York to adjudicate suspected slave ships.[43] The commissioners tried not a single case before the courts were disbanded in 1870. American capital, as opposed to ships built in the United States, had never been important in the slave trade. Reports of American registers being used to cover the outbound leg of the slaving voyage were rare after the outbreak of the Civil War. Despite the acclaim with which this treaty was greeted, there was actually no reason to believe that it would have been any more effective than its Anglo-Dutch, Anglo-Spanish, and Anglo-Portuguese predecessors on which it was modeled. Slave ships would shift to another flag or use no flag at all, as they did in the last years of the Brazilian trade. Indeed, as much of this work has argued, naval measures without the backing and enforcement of the municipal law of the importing country were almost inevitably ineffective.

The one small success of naval tactics on the high seas as opposed to the invasion of domestic waters was in Puerto Rico. Here the slave trade, which had thrived in the 1820s and 1830s, ended before the Spanish penal law of 1845. Apart from the cargo of the shipwrecked *Majestad* (alias *J. W. Reid*) in 1859, the last slave ship to disembark slaves in Puerto Rico was the *Volador* in 1842 according to the slave-ship data set, though a few imports probably occurred in 1843 or 1844.[44] As long as the slave trade continued, slave prices in the island remained slightly lower than those in Cuba. In the quarter-century after 1840, slave values climbed steeply along with those everywhere else in the Americas, but the price differential between Puerto Rico and Cuba, nevertheless, became more marked.[45] Clearly planters in Puerto Rico could not compete with their Cuban counterparts. It would thus appear that the diplomatic and naval initiatives of the 1835–39 period, which had a relatively small impact on costs, were sufficient to choke off the Puerto Rican traffic. It should be noted, however, that competition for slaves from Brazil and Cuba was also important in this process. The key factor was the ability of the coffee and tobacco sectors of the Puerto Rican economy to thrive on peasant labor. Although precise figures are not yet available, it would seem that the switch of slaves from coffee to sugar in the 1840s was even more dramatic in Puerto Rico than in Cuba.[46]

It would thus appear that Brazilian and Puerto Rican suppression was effected by a rise in the costs of importing slaves imposed by the British and, in the former case, the Brazilian government whereas the demise of the Cuban trade was triggered by a decline in the value of slaves. It is also true, however, that the Cuban traffic would not have ended without the restrictions introduced by Spain in the 1840s, which in turn were largely a response to British pressure. There remains the intriguing question of what might have happened to the trade without British pressure. What was the potential for a self-generated suppression of the slave trade on the part of the last two societies in the Americas to have access to slaves in Africa? An antislave-trade association was formed in Havana in 1865 and slavery itself was an issue in the Ten Years War. Three quarters of the elected Cuban delegates to the Colonial Reform Commission of 1866–67 favored suppression and, as in the earlier British West Indies and U.S. cases, there were planters among the antislave-trade group.[47]

The motives of these planters varied however and three points should be weighed carefully before this is taken as evidence that the slave trade was doomed regardless of the actions of the Spanish and British governments. First, the large estate owners continued to be dependent on coerced labor of one kind or another for a further twenty years. Given international condemnation of the slave trade and the diplomatic complications that this generated for the Spanish, suppression was seen by some slave owners as a way of buying time for slavery itself. Indeed, a few years later Cuban planters saw *formal* abolition of slavery itself as a device for deflating abolitionist pressures for substantive freedom for slaves. In addition, the planters who supported suppression were generally from older Creole families who owned well-established estates. This did not, however, prevent some of these planters from purchasing new Africans for as long as the trade continued.[48] Their counterparts in earlier years might be seen in Virginia in the eighteenth century and the older British West Indies in 1804. Second, suppression of the slave trade had become tied to the quest for independence. Cuban abolitionists were usually Creoles who also wanted political reforms leading to representative government and ultimately independence from Spain. The slave trade and slavery were useful weapons to turn against the Spanish at a time when the *peninsulares* drew much of their support from the newer and more dynamic part of the Cuban sugar sector. Third, as in the 1840s, Cuban opposition to the slave trade was dominated by the desire to develop Cuba with a white labor force hired in a free-labor market. Although fears of Africanization had receded somewhat, there was a widespread belief in the inferiority of nonwhite labor. As the British commissioner in Havana commented in 1867, "Public opinion in this island has undergone a great change within the last three years, and the feeling as to the absolute necessity of putting an end to the Slave Trade is now almost general . . . unfortunately [this] cannot be attributed to the advance of civilization, or to the nobler feelings of philanthropy."[49] Without British pressure on Spain, planters would scarcely have thought in terms of buying time for slavery, and the slave trade would have been a much less effective weapon in the independence struggle. The Africanization fear was not connected to British pressure but, as earlier decades had shown, it was scarcely strong enough to cut off imports by itself. In Brazil, too, the early manifestations of antislavery were linked to the independence movement, reflected a desire for a racially homogeneous society or were simply derivatives of an ideology forged on another continent.[50]

In the first seventy years of the century at least, in neither Brazil or Cuba was there the ideological transformation that turned the British and much of the population of the U.S. North into abolitionist sympathizers. Nor was there a large pool of white labor fed by inflows of poor migrants, potential competitors for slaves, to fuel a nativist drive against slave imports. Suppression of the slave trade was imposed on the Iberian Americas as it had been on the British and French Americas. Brazilian and Cuban attitudes in favor of suppression were derivative and synthetic rather than organic in the sense that they were the product of indigenous social developments. Beneath them lay political and even racist goals rather than the transmutation in attitudes toward labor and wages that nurtured British and U.S. abolitionism. If Cuba had been an independent nation from, say, 1810 and the Portuguese had been of insignificant standing in the Brazilian merchant community, the transatlantic slave trade would have perhaps continued a little longer than it did. But only for a few years. After the U.S. Civil War the slave traffic and slavery itself were, in fact, doomed, but not because of any innate economic shortcomings or on account of the social and racial composition of importing societies. The key factor was the overwhelming ideological impulse from the North Atlantic region. The great Brazilian statement of the abolitionist viewpoint, Joaquim Nabuco's *O Abolicionismo,* is essentially as much a profession of English liberalism as is J. E. Cairnes book, *The Slave Power,* written about the U.S. South twenty years earlier.[51] Both portrayed slavery as economically regressive, but as the author of the former spent his boyhood on a sugar plantation it is the more remarkable of the two. A free-labor Western world would not have tolerated the continuation of a transatlantic slave trade into the present century and enough of the inhabitants of Cuba and Brazil would have absorbed this attitude that suppression would have been self-administered. Once the slave trade was closed slavery itself became more vulnerable. The new urban classes that feature so prominently as a source of abolitionism in the debate on Brazilian emancipation in the 1880s would surely have been much less numerous without the suppression of the slave trade. As noted later, the slave trade had reempted or at least swamped free migration everywhere in the Americas whenever there had been free access to both streams of labor. We might thus conclude that in the long run the spread of the powerful bourgeois idea of the virtues of free labor, backed up as it was by the economic development of the North Atlantic fringe, was the key factor in the suppression process. Neither British naval intervention nor structural change in the Brazilian and Cuban economies were as important in the ending of the slave trade and slavery.

# 13

# The Consequences of Suppression in Africa and the Americas

Those abolitionists who continued to support the forcible suppression of the transatlantic slave trade expected much from its demise. In the Americas suppression would increase the value of the slave and induce owners to improve slave living conditions. If, despite such improvement the Caribbean and Brazilian slave populations continued to decline, then in the long run slavery itself could not survive and free migration would be the only alternative. In any event suppression of the slave trade was the first step in the campaign against slavery itself. In Africa the ending of the traffic would be of particular significance. Populations would increase, the incidence of warfare would fall dramatically and the production of African commodities traded would take a quantum leap forward. The new commodities, moreover, would eventually be produced with free labor when the long-run exposure to nonslave-trading Europeans, properly infused with Christian values, had taken effect. And immediately, of course, the miseries of the middle passage would be no more.

Considering the enormous gap in cultural perceptions between abolitionists and Africans, a surprising number of these expectations came to pass, though cause and effect were not always accurately reflected in the abolitionists' prognosis. Slave values in the Americas did rise, immigration to Brazil did accelerate, African commodity production did increase rapidly and slavery itself did come to an end eventually on both sides of the Atlantic. Yet from the perspective of an abolitionist in the late nineteenth century, it would be very difficult to draw up an accurate balance sheet that showed a clear net benefit arising from suppression of the slave traffic. Before exploring this theme further, it is important to locate suppression and indeed emancipation in the context of developing relations between Africa and American slave societies, on the one hand, and the industrializing economies of the North Atlantic, on the other.

The abolitionists habitually overestimated both the actual and the potential impact of pre-nineteenth-century Europe on societies fringing the rest of the

Atlantic basin. The slave trade dominated relations between Europe and Africa in the eighteenth century, but no reasonable estimate or manipulation of slave exports and population figures can point to this trade being of central importance to either continent. This is true whether we focus on population loss or income generated. These numbers make it unlikely that long-distance trade brought about fundamental change of any kind in African societies except perhaps in select local areas.[1] In the Americas, exports per capita were much larger than in Africa, and plantation societies were closely integrated with the metropolitan country that governed them. But the fact remains that less than half the population of the Americas lived in plantation societies. Many others, mainly in the Iberian Americas, drew little of their income from Atlantic exports and relied on local markets or on what they themselves could grow.[2] Deprived of European trade, societies in the Americas would not have been thrown back to subsistence levels of income in the early nineteenth century. More controversially the same could be argued for the significance of the Americas to Europe. Any reasonable assessment of per capita exports, profits and investment makes it implausible that European industrialization would not have happened in the absence of trade with the Americas, Africa or indeed all long-distance trade combined.[3]

In the course of the nineteenth century and because of the industrialization process, this situation changed. Trade between Europe and the Atlantic basin south of North America grew to a level where it seems possible to look for shifts in the social and economic structures of some of the non-European regions at least. In West Africa, for example, total overseas exports of commodities (excluding slaves) rose from £3.5 million in the early 1850s to about £15 million a half-century later. In per capita terms, annual exports were still extremely modest by world standards—at perhaps £0.5—but for coastal states the figure would be much larger. For example, Manning has estimated double this rate for Dahomey in 1900.[4] For most trading states revenues from commodity trade came to greatly exceed what revenues from the slave trade had been in the preabolition era. Moreover, the terms of trade shifted dramatically in favor of the African producer during the first seventy years of the century as prices of manufactured goods tumbled. Abolition of either the slave trade or slavery had little to do with these changes except insofar as both abolitionism and an exploding long-distance commodity trade stemmed from the same source—dynamic economic growth in northwestern Europe and the United States. Abolitionism, nevertheless, helped direct and shape the response of Africa and the Americas in several fundamental respects. Most important, it determined that the expansion of American agricultural produce would have to take place without the centuries-long link with Africa and eventually without slave labor of any kind. But what was a hindrance to production on the west side of the Atlantic turned out to be a stimulant on the African side. Slaves who could no longer be sent to the Americas could be set to work as slaves in their home continent. The aim of this final chapter is to chart the development of this process and draw some implications on both sides of the Atlantic. We begin with Africa.

Evaluation of the impact of suppression on Africa depends heavily on assessments of the presuppression African economy and slavery. Most studies of African slavery are based on direct observation or oral data from the recent past when slavery on the continent was already in decline. Because of the paucity of evidence, interpretations of African slavery in earlier centuries vary widely. Most recently Paul Lovejoy has argued in a major synthesis that the external demand for slaves, from the Mediterranean and Asia as well as the Americas, transformed African slavery. From a marginal type of dependency centered on lineage or kinship, where slaves were not in the first instance producers, slavery became in West Africa at least primarily a productive system. The transatlantic slave trade was particularly important in this process. As long as the traffic lasted, the major commodity produced was slaves. Power accrued to the commercial and political elite that owned the slaves. The slave export trade died as rising overseas commodity demand developed. Lovejoy argues that little social adjustment was needed for the slave owners to direct their slaves into the production of commodities instead of sending them to the Americas, though in west-central Africa this process was incomplete at the end of the slave-export era.[5] Yet the discussion in chapters 5 and 10 suggest that whatever the origins or nature of structural changes in African slavery, it is unlikely that external influences could have been very great. Lovejoy's impressive survey establishes the very wide incidence of slavery as a productive system, particularly after suppression of the traffic. There is considerable evidence of a substantial increase and change in the orientation of slavery in Africa during the nineteenth century. Nevertheless, the connection between African slavery and external influences prior to the rapid expansion of the North Atlantic commodity demand in the nineteenth century appears weak. Two modifications to this transformation thesis appear called for.

First, much of the extent and nature of slavery in West Africa, particularly in the first half of the nineteenth century, can be attributed directly or indirectly to developments within the region itself. Rejuvenated Islam created a slavery frontier that first spread west across the savanna belt and then east in the course of the century. Sokoto and Hamdallahi were merely among the earliest and best known of a series of jihad states. Moreover, this development was accompanied by a long period free of generalized drought in the savanna region during which the productive base of all savanna societies widened.[6] The expansion of agriculture, manufacturing and trade was built on slave labor, but the markets served were internal to the savanna or in the forest zones rather than outside Africa. Located to the south of the major West African savanna states, Asante had decreasing contact with the Atlantic economy between 1800 and 1875. Increased slave use within the state was based on trade with the north, encouraged no doubt by the drought-free conditions in the area. A second major state, Oyo, was in the throes of a disintegration not obviously triggered by the Atlantic slave trade. The masses of slaves in the region had either a primarily military function or were by-products of war. Plantation slaves in the area produced commodities for the internal market. Only in Dahomey can a clear causal relationship be established between the transatlantic slave market and the extent and nature of domestic holdings of slaves.

The expansion of commodity demand from the Atlantic economy stimuᴧated the production of African commodities before the demise of the transatlantic slave trade in several regions, particularly the Bight of Biafra. The transatlantic slave trade does not appear to have had the major influence over the form of labor used, however. In mid–nineteenth-century southeast Nigeria, there were three distinct economic zones. These radiated inland from the coastal trading states with their reliance on slaves as canoe men and porters, through the palm oil belt with its small-scale producers and a mild form of domestic servitude, to the third and more lightly populated northern and eastern areas with their slave settlements devoted to yam production. Although it is clear that European demand for palm oil caused structural changes after 1820, the differences between these zones are explainable in terms of population densities and the availability of arable land.[7] Variations in the way the three regions modified their social structures to accommodate the external need for slave labor in the previous century seem less plausible in accounting for these differences.

It is, moreover, particularly striking that the labor responsible for the increased output of southeastern Nigeria was organized within the traditional African kinship system even though the latter was subjected to considerable strain.[8] Thus the difference between slave production of yams, maize or kola nuts for markets internal to Africa, on the one hand, and peanuts and palm oil for overseas markets, on the other, seems of little consequence. Nor does the prior existence of a system supplying slaves from the areas producing these commodities seem to have been of critical importance. The relevant question is would the slave mode of production as defined by Lovejoy have been any slower in appearing if such market opportunities had developed before contact with the European or Mediterranean world—if, for example, the drought-free period in the nineteenth-century savanna had occurred much earlier? Widespread production for markets did, of course, exist long before 1800, and there is no reason to think that the flexible response to increased demand in the nineteenth century could not have occurred earlier whatever the source of that demand. We know almost nothing of volume trends in African commodity production away from the coast before the nineteenth century. In any event, demand from outside Africa *was* significant in the extension of slavery as a productive system within Africa, but not before the later nineteenth century. The key element was neither the slave trade nor its suppression per se, but rather the industrial expansion of the North Atlantic economy.[9] If suppression had not come when it did, however, the ability of African economies to respond would have been curtailed by the drain of labor overseas. For there can be little doubt that industrialization without suppression would have meant a mass steamship-borne deportation of Africans to the Americas. Paradoxically an open transatlantic slave trade could have meant less slavery in Africa though more persons enslaved.

This last point leads to the second modification of the transformation thesis, which is its assessment of the impact of suppression of the traffic on African slavery. In Africa south of the savanna, it is argued that suppression had a small effect on slave recruitment. In this view slaves were redirected from the Atlantic trade to the production of commodities from the internal market with little if any slowing in the expansion of the slaving frontier or the intensity of enslavement. This seems unduly pessimistic. It is now certain that the supply of slaves on the African coast was price responsive and that the price of slaves declined during the era of suppression. In the absence of any major increase in the supply of slaves from Africa as a whole (for some reason other than price) the price decline can only have resulted from a fall in demand. We know that demand on the African littoral had two sources. One was within Africa, for all purposes including the growth of produce for export; the other was the plantations in the Americas. Suppression meant the collapse of the latter, whereas North Atlantic industrialization meant the expansion of the former, most of such expansion occurring on the coast rather than the African interior. But because the price of all slaves declined, it seems clear that although domestic demand increased, it did not increase sufficiently to offset the decline in trans-atlantic demand. As a consequence, the number of slaves traded as well as the price of those slaves declined during the century. It is doubtful if the price of slaves in Africa ever again reached the levels of the late eighteenth and early nineteenth centuries; accordingly, suppression must have meant some reduction in the enslavement of Africans.[10] We might conclude that the Atlantic slave trade was only one of several factors contributing to the emergence of slavery as a major African institution in the late eighteenth century. Although the eventual suppression of the trade did have some effect on the incidence of slavery, the strength of the effect lay somewhere between the dramatic impact that the abolitionists expected, and negligible consequences argued for in the transformation thesis.

For most erstwhile slave-exporting regions, the third quarter of the nineteenth century may be taken as the immediate post–slave-trade era. There were perhaps three major and a handful of minor African commodity exports during this period. The major growth crops were peanuts, palm kernels and palm oil taken together, and Senegal gum. Among the minor products were cloves, coconuts, wax and an assortment of dyes and timber. The differences between the two groups were substantial: even in their peak years cloves and coconuts together never approached 20 percent of the value of any of the first three major products. It is worth noting, however, that the most explosive period of growth for two of the major crops, gum and palm oil, came before the demise of the Atlantic slave trade.

After 1840 peanut cultivation spread rapidly in local riverine and coastal areas from the Senegal River to Sierra Leone. By the mid-1860s when peanut prices were close to their nineteenth-century peak, exports from the region as a whole may have been forty thousand tons a year and had a total value of approximately $1.25 million.[11] This was larger than annual revenues derived from selling slaves in the second half of the eighteenth century. In both Senegal and the Gambia the crop was cultivated by small farmers or with migrant wage labor. South of the Gambia in the Casamance, Gêba, Nunez, Pongo and Mela-kori rivers, where perhaps a third of the region's crop was grown, the labor force was almost all enslaved.[12] Slave labor does not appear to have displaced free labor in the south, but rather it became an additional source of labor for growers in Africa as the demand for peanuts became effective and as the slave rade declined. Rice, a traditional crop along the banks of the above river areas, continued to be produced with slave labor, and there was also some slave-grown coffee and ginger produced for export. In any event all crops in these rivers drew on slaves supplied from the Sherbro and the Gallinas south of Sierra Leone. Prices of slaves in these provenance zones were only one-third to one-half those in the peanut-producing areas.[13] The British naval and colonial authorities intercepted many canoes of slaves as they made their way north inshore to the commodity-producing zones. The Soso and Mandingo traders thereupon switched to an inland route that used creeks and rivers to skirt the boundaries of effective colonial authority, though even this was liable to British interference. The flow continued through the boom years from 1846 to 1864. But totals of slaves recaptured from this coastal traffic in the 1850s and 1860s were always small. This and the lower slave prices in the Sherbro and Gallinas from the 1840s suggest that the slaves absorbed by peanut production were less numerous than those absorbed by the oceanic slave trade a few years previously.[14]

A second major product from Africa north of Sierra Leone was Senegal gum. The major Senegambian export during the first half of the century, it had been overtaken in importance by peanuts shortly after midcentury. It, nevertheless, easily maintained second place in the export rankings thereafter. Gum was collected rather than cultivated, and the labor regime was largely slave. Yet the slaves appear to have been drawn from the banks of the Senegal River, a region not much affected by the Atlantic slave trade since the previous century, and it is difficult to include gum collection in any assessment of the impact of suppression.[15] Although local riverine societies may have been profoundly restructured (in particular groups of the Soso), per capita exports from the region cannot have been more than a tiny fraction of per capita income.

There are interesting parallels in the regions growing the third major African transatlantic export crop. By the late 1850s palm oil was accounting for over 80 percent of the value of total exports from the bights of Benin and Biafra, and total revenues for oil alone at approximately $4 million per year were in excess of any sum ever generated by the slave trade. Except for the two exceptional years of 1829 and 1835, slave sales in the two regions combined could not have amounted to half this figure. Despite the rapid growth of palm kernel exports, declining prices meant that gross values increased very slowly thereafter, however.[16] By 1857 combined exports from points scattered between the Benin River west to Agoué were already matching total shipments from the Bight of Biafra, and after the Ibadan-Abeokuta (Egba) wars of the early 1860s, Lagos became the leading point of export. Production and collection methods in the two regions were different, however. In the oil rivers the small-scale producer predominated, though most of the product was channeled through Bonny or Old Calabar under the Efik traders. In the Bight of Benin, Lagos was the most important single port for oil in 1856 and 1857, but the Benin river, Palma (near Lagos), Ouidah, and Porto Novo were not far behind, and Appi Vista, Agoué and Badagry were also significant export points.[17] Production and trade were thus dispersed over a wide area; perhaps, more important, the West

African palm was cultivated here under a variety of labor regimes ranging from peasant to large-scale plantations worked by hundreds of slaves.

The reason for the differences in labor regimes within the Bight of Benin are no clearer than in the peanut-growing areas north of Sierra Leone. Population densities may have been important, but there seems to have been no geographical divisions between small and large-scale production consistent with this pattern. Africans were heavily involved as both laborers and operators in both large- and small-scale operations, and the Portuguese-speaking community in the bights cultivated as well as traded oil. Provision grounds in the neighborhood of slave-embarkation points were pulled into oil production along with much additional land. In the mid-1850s the king of Dahomey became directly involved, and Yoruba warlords had their own slave-worked plantations. But barriers to entry in both the production and marketing of oil and kernels were never very significant in the region as a whole.[18]

Did this expansion of the palm-products sector constitute a revolution in West Africa? To Hopkins it helped commercialize labor and provided new opportunities for the small producers that resulted in a large step toward the creation of a mass market and a revolution of rising expectations. Manning, too, stresses the stimulus to family farms, which produced "most of the palm products exported" and received "major addition[s] to the revenue available from ... the domestic market." Manning also points to the expansion of the slave sector, but for Lovejoy this latter effect was the main result of increased transatlantic commodity trade, the "strengthened slave mode of production" that resulted made slavery "the basis of the political economy in Africa." Others have stressed the large political consequences of the change and pointed to the beginnings of an African merchant class whose later destruction by European trading firms set back African development.[19] It might be argued, however, that none of these interpretations takes into full account the trends in per capita export figures, which remained extremely modest in the immediate post-suppression era of 1850 to 1875 and probably beyond. Manning has estimated per capita export revenue for Dahomey at $2.35 per annum for the 1870s, substantially below the equivalent figures for the mid-eighteenth century. Yet $2.35 per annum was certainly higher than for West Africa as a whole. By the 1870s the population of the subcontinent cannot have been less than 25 million and total exports to Atlantic countries were certainly less than $38 million. Whatever the exact number the per capita export figure was well below the ratio for Great Britain from the seventeenth century on and for any slave society in the Americas. Moreover, it must have constituted less than 5 percent of Dahomean per capita domestic product.[20]

Nor does the case for change appear any stronger at the local level, at least outside certain trading enclaves on the coast. Transportation problems limited the production of palm products to forest areas contiguous to the coast or rivers. Although this production belt was fairly narrow, it extended a great distance east and west along the coast. Export income cannot therefore have been concentrated geographically nor, given the above evidence, in the social sense either. The dispersion of this revenue among the coastal population and cer-

.ainly among the West African population as a whole was such that a major social or economic impact was highly unlikely. Local domestic markets and trade within Africa must have continued to preoccupy the vast majority of Africans, incuding the wealthiest, as it had in the past. It is hard to read Manning's careful description of the Dahomean economy in the 1880s without concluding that Atlantic influences were not of critical import.[21] There is no doubt that the incidence of slavery as a productive system within West Africa increased with exports of palm products. But the absence of economies of scale in the production of the latter and the fall of slave prices strongly suggests that fewer slaves were delivered to the coastal areas after suppression of the transatlantic slave trade than before. The shifting political and social relationships within the coastal trading states, including the buildup in slave numbers, were perhaps a direct result of the increase in overseas commodity trade, but Lagos, Bonny and Old Calabar were not paradigms for Africa.[22]

As the slave trade died the Portuguese slave traders in the Bight of Benin were not the only outsiders to attempt plantation agriculture in Africa. The Dutch and the Danes had tried and failed at the end of the previous century, but this did not inhibit a string of equally doomed British and French initiatives, private and public, culminating in the Niger expedition and the Gabon settlement in the 1840s. As late as 1850 a pamphlet published in London could list half a dozen well-known plans any one of which in the opinion of the author would bring Africa to "quickly yield . . . abundant produce."[23] Perhaps the most sanguine and ingenuous of all were the attempts of the Portuguese liberals, in particular the Marquês de Sa da Bandeira, to generate increased agricultural and mining ouput in Angola in the 1850s with the aid of wage labor. Yet 85 percent by value of Luanda exports in the late 1850s were still ivory and wax, collected rather than cultivated products. By the 1870s only two thousand tons of coffee annually was leaving the port. This was the leading cultivated product, but even some of this was gathered wild. Cotton exports were important briefly during the American Civil War, but much of this was grown by free labor.[24] Coffee cultivation on the islands of Príncipe and São Tomé in the Bight of Biafra was scarcely more successful. Slave supported plantation agriculture had long been practiced here though in 1861 only one tenth of the island was cultivated.[25] Increased demand for produce from Europe and suppression of the transatlantic slave traffic encouraged a small coastal traffic in coerced labor to coffee and cacao farms.[26] This was, however, a very minor development viewed against the backdrop of either the African or Angolan economies, and certainly the world market for coffee. In the early 1870s production of coffee, at about two thousand tons a year did not exceed that of Angola, and both together amounted to about 1 percent of Brazilian exports.[27]

The most successful attempt by non-Africans to establish plantations on the African continent at this time was in Zanzibar. Here the Omani arabs developed widespread clove cultivation from the 1830s using slave labor. Demand came primarily from India rather than the industrializing economies of the North Atlantic and, as Frederick Cooper has pointed out, the factors determining the rapid growth of production are to be found on the supply rather than the demand side.[28] Compared to midcentury values of the major African exports, the dramatic expansion of clove cultivation was not a major development. The peak values of clove exports from Zanzibar, which occurred in the 1860s, comprised about one tenth of contemporary palm oil exports from the bights, less than 15 percent of exports from Zanzibar itself (the island was a major entrepôt) and never matched peak values of slave exports from east Africa even to markets in the Americas alone.[29] These ratios and the perspective they suggest do not change much if we take into account coconut cultivation and the later slave-based commercial agriculture sectors of Malindi and Mombasa. The social impact on these areas was profound, but the areas themselves were relatively small and few in number. They must have absorbed far fewer slaves than did the Atlantic trade from the east coast in the course of the nineteenth century, and only a small fraction of the total Indian Ocean slave traffic. The impact of East African plantations on the continental economy in the abolition era therefore could scarcely have exceeded the limited effects of suppression and the development of overseas commodity exports on the west coast.

The abolitionists tended to view free labor, increased production and civilization as indivisible. For educated Europeans the ties between slave trade suppression and expectations of increased trade with Africa were even tighter than those between emancipation and expectations of increased plantation output in the pre-1840 British West Indies. Increases in palm oil, peanut and clove exports after midcentury were encouraging but fell considerably short of the projected African response. Much of the increased output was made possible only through slave labor. The abolitionist prescription was beginning to look no more promising in Africa than it had proved in the British West Indies. Buxton's willingness to accept coerced labor as a short-term necessity on the Niger expedition provoked surprisingly little opposition. By the 1860s there were probably many who would have agreed with the British naval officer who, after patrolling the inshore slave traffic from the Gallinas to the peanut-growing regions, wrote the following in his diary, "Even if possible, it would be a very doubtful good for the country [Africa] to stop the . . . supply of slaves from a part where the people either cannot or will not grow anything, to a part where the legal trade is now so great and increasing every year."[30]

The ideological momentum was too strong for there to be any real possibility of reversals of abolitionist policies. And when not only the slave trade but slavery itself was abolished, as in the Gold Coast in 1874, it was followed by a variety of measures designed to extract more labor than would have been offered voluntarily in a completely free-labor market (though certainly less than what slaves would have been required to supply). In British Africa the key figure in these strategies was Earl Grey whose emancipation plan conceived during his short stay at the Colonial Office in 1832–33 had been among the most coercive of the schemes under serious consideration. Grey was minister for the colonies for six years from 1846 and espoused the principle of personal taxation of those in tropical climes in order to force participation in the labor

.1arket. Grey's policies, where implemented, were not particularly successful—mainly because British colonial authority was too imperfectly established to ensure effective tax collection. In Ceylon indeed they contributed to rebellion. Similar policies were, however, widely used in British Africa in the colonial period.[31] This is not to suggest that the antislavery lobby supported such strategies but merely to point to the fact that they were a logical extension of the early abolitionist position. The goals of the colonialists of the late nineteenth and early twentieth centuries were not really any different from those of the abolitionists of a century earlier. It was just that the British now had serious rivals in the struggle to dominate African overseas trade.

There were similar tensions between expected and actual outcomes in the Americas. Slave populations, for example, were expected to increase in the aftermath of suppression.[32] Most of the New World societies affected by suppression had experienced heavy immigration in the years before suppression and consequently had population pyramids in which males and older people were heavily overrepresented. Rates of natural population change were thus likely to be negative before and immediately after suppression, but this was largely irrelevant to the long-term viability of the population. Assuming no intra-American migration, the sex ratios could be expected to move closer to equality, and the crude mortality rate to fall as the ending of the slave trade receded into the past. Abolitionist expectations of population increases were based partly on a changing age and sex structure and partly on the improved care with which masters would look after their slaves when the African source for the traffic was no more. In Barbados, for example, where net imports of slaves had been small for many years, the registered slave population was growing strongly in the early nineteenth century.

In the varied pattern of demographic adjustment to suppression some common threads may be discerned. Everywhere in the Americas slave-labor forces became concentrated in the crop in which they were most productive: sugar in the Caribbean and Bahia, coffee in south-central Brazil and cotton in much of the U.S. South. In addition, whatever the change in the treatment of slaves induced by suppression, it now appears unlikely that vital rates were much affected either before or after suppression. Planters simply did not know enough about the epidemiological and nutritional environment to be able to influence key variables, such as the infant-mortality rate. Outside these two general considerations, however, responses varied enormously. In North America the slave population was already experiencing rates of natural increase well before the ending of the slave trade, and the scale of arrivals was never large enough relative to the total black population to have much impact on the age-and-sex structure of the latter.[33] In the British Caribbean the experience was particularly varied. Twenty years after the end of the slave trade, with the intercolonial traffic strictly controlled, the older sugar and nonplantation economies exhibited healthy rates of increase. A second group of sugar colonies, settled in the eighteenth century, demonstrated negative but improving crude rates and a third, Jamaica, the largest of all, experienced a light but deteriorating negative trend. Overall the British West Indian slave population was still declining when slavery was abolished, but the trend was toward a positive rate. Within the British West Indies crop type had an important influence over vital rates with sugar growing accounting for much of the intercolonial variations, particularly in mortality.[34]

In the French Americas, Cuba and Brazil, where the slave trade continued longest, crop type is less likely to explain intra-American differentials in vital rates than those within the British Caribbean. In Cuba by 1860 the decline in the slave population had almost ceased despite the increasing preponderance of sugar cultivation.[35] On the other hand, in the Danish sugar islands and in the French Americas, the sharpness and persistence of the rate of decline suggest a different pattern. Indeed in the former the decline continued long after the abnormal population pyramid caused by the slave trade had worked itself out.[36] The picture is confused further by the high rate of natural increase among slaves on sugar estates in Louisiana. The demographic implications of coffee cultivation are no clearer. In the British Caribbean coffee production was associated with lower mortality than sugar in the years after the ending of the slave trade. But in the biggest coffee exporting nation of all, Brazil, the slave population was still declining more than two decades after the suppression of the Atlantic traffic despite the fact that the population pyramid was almost certainly less skewed here than in the British Caribbean at the beginning of the century.[37]

The impact of suppression on the long-term viability of the slave population of the Americas is thus mixed. Obviously suppression meant fewer peoples of African descent in the Americas than there would have been without suppression. Given the highly elastic demand for slaves explored in chapter 11, free access to Africa and the continuation of slavery could only have resulted in record traffic volumes. Ultimately the limiting factors on the size of the trade would have been the closing of the land frontier and the natural increase in slave populations in the Americas as vital rates in the tropical Americas began to respond to nineteenth-century improvements in nutritional and epidemiological knowledge. Such conditions would have ensured the early emergence of a largely Creole slave population as happened in the United States. As it was, in the middle of the nineteenth century the majority of the slave population of Cuba and a large minority of Brazilian slaves must have been African born. Indeed in Cuba in 1840 the ratio of African born would have been similar to that in St. Domingue in 1791, and in Brazil in 1850 the ratio was probably comparable to the 1807 British West Indian figure.[38]

The implications of suppression for the European and Asian populations of the Americas were perhaps just as significant as for those of African descent. After the sixteenth century the flow of Europeans to the Americas rarely approached the number of African arrivals until after the African trade had been forcibly put down.[39] In the tropical and subtropical Americas, the best land and indeed most of the economic opportunities were dominated by plantation agriculture. Moreover, for most of the nineteenth century the epidemiological environment continued to be significantly more hostile than in areas to the north and south. European migration to the plantation regions had never been large, and British and Spanish attempts to reverse this pattern as slave prices climbed during the nineteenth century produced few results before the

ა80s. As free Africans were no more willing than Europeans to work in a plantation environment, the planters had to look much farther afield. Not until
midcentury did the rising cost of slave labor make it feasible to tap Asian
sources.[40] In parts of India and China income levels and social conditions were
apparently such as to make indentured plantation work in the Americas a viable alternative. The numbers of indentured Asian laborers never approached
the totals entering the African slave trade, but the important point is that without the suppression of the latter there would probably not have been any indentured Asian laborers at all.[41] The Asian population of the Caribbean was as
much a result of the suppression of the slave trade as the African population
was a result of its inception.

Free migrants from Europe chose the more temperate zones of the two
American continents, where for the most part slaves could not be as profitably
employed as in the plantation areas. Plantations and temperate zones did,
however, overlap in two regions—south-central Brazil and the U.S. upper
South. In this U.S. area, the natural increase of the slave population made any
outside source of labor—whether African, European or Asian—unnecessary;
in the Brazilian region, the slave population declined after suppression, but
planters were able to call on a massive intra-Brazilian slave traffic for nearly
forty years after the transatlantic source was cut off. Significant white migration
to Brazil—chiefly from southern Europe—got underway only as this internal
source was brought to an end by the demise of slavery itself.[42] In Montevideo
and Río de la Plata the connection is less direct. The last slave imports
occurred in the 1830s when access to Africa was still relatively easy and prices
of slaves in Brazil, from whence came most of the imports, were still moderate.
At such prices, some jerked beef and hide processors could compete for labor
with the Brazilian coffee and sugar planters. The price rise from 1840 however
eliminated such marginal slave purchasers. The region declined as a market
for slaves and the black population shrank to nothing. Abolition of slavery
itself came gradually between 1813 and 1861 but employers could not attract
Europeans in large numbers until after this.[43] We might, however, question
whether suppression, abolition or mass European immigration could have
occurred when they did anywhere in temperate South America if slave prices
(and access to Africa) had continued at early nineteenth-century levels.

The link between the demise of the slave trade and the pick up in European
and Asian immigration seems weakest in North America. Indeed as the internal movement of the U.S. black population to the northern cities did not get
under way until European immigration was curtailed in the 1920s, it might be
argued that here cause and effect were reversed: The end of European immigration preceded and encouraged black migration—at least within America.
Yet the relevant question is the same for the United States as for South America. How extensive would slave use and abolitionism have been if a prime male
slave in New Orleans had cost on average the Cuban price of $350 in the first
quarter of the nineteenth century instead of the actual price of nearly $700?[44]
The basic point is that at the appropriate price very few merchants and farmers
anywhere, certainly in the eighteenth-century Americas, would have hesitated
to purchase and use slave labor. Slavery in the South aided abolitionism in the

North in the sense that southern competition for slaves precluded northerner. from establishing a broadly based slave society. The oft-quoted comment of Adam Smith that "the late resolution of the Quakers in Pennsylvania to set at liberty all their negro slaves may satisfy us that their number is not very great" is particularly relevant in this context.

Immigration into the nineteenth-century United States was thus white and free rather than black and enslaved for three reasons. First, the technology of production for most northern products had long prevented the northern employer from paying the price for slave labor that his southern planter counterpart could afford. Second, despite the presence of 37,000 slaves in the northern states in 1800, abolitionism had already established a thirty-year history of enshrinement in the law by the time the Atlantic slave trade was abolished. The misplaced belief in the inherent inefficiency of slave labor was almost as widely held in the northern states as in England at the end of the eighteenth century—probably for similar reasons. One of these was the development of an extensive well-organized market for wage labor that had no parallels in the rest of the Americas. Finally, well before large-scale European migration began—indeed as early as the late seventeenth century—white workers were protesting the depressing effect of slaves on wages. The third reason was, thus, the certainty of a white nativist reaction to African slave arrivals on the part of northern wage earners.[45] Of the three, the first preceded and made possible the other two. As antislavery sentiment was already entrenched before the closing of the African slave trade, developments in the absence of suppression may not have been much different—at least in the North. But such an approach does suggest that the whole of North America and not just the U.S. South could have been exploited with slave labor. What prevented it—apart, of course, from the high cost of that labor, made even higher by suppression—was ideological restraints and the vested interests of free workers. These rather than the northern climate or any innate inefficiency in the process of coercion reserved large areas of the continent for free labor.

As long as the land frontier remained open, free immigration was perhaps a second best alternative to the slave trade for most employers in the Americas. That it was not always perceived as such in much of the two continents is a comment on the power and ubiquity of English liberalism in the nineteenth-century world. The implications of this situation for income levels in the Americas is clear. The curtailment of the supply of labor, slave or free, at a time when total factor productivity was rapidly increasing, could only have reduced the pace of economic growth in all slave-importing areas. Relative to the slave provenance areas of Africa, all slave-importing countries had very high levels of per capita exports. In the late 1820s Cuba was exporting $30 per person, whereas the British West Indian figure was more than half as great again in 1830. Even Brazil, with its very large self-sufficient agricultural sector, was exporting $6 of produce per capita in 1850, or triple the equivalent figure for Dahomey, perhaps the most export oriented of the slave-supply states.[46]

Per capita exports is not the same as per capita income, much less do these figures establish the long-term development prospects of slave societies in the Americas. But setting aside the issue of income distribution, it would appear nat slave societies in the Americas were very prosperous. Juan Pérez de la Riva has estimated per capita income in the western region of Cuba at $350 in 1862. This was between two and three times the contemporary figures for the United States and Great Britain. A similar gap probably existed in the eighteenth century, and indeed, a case would be made for this gap increasing rather than diminishing as a consequence of industrialization in the Western world.[47] At the very least, chapter 11 suggests that there is considerable evidence of productivity increases in slave economies in the Americas after 1800. Much of it came after the major increases in slave prices and may be viewed as a result of land and capital being substituted for expensive labor. But it is also clear that the divergence of slave values and product prices was well established before effective suppression of the trade began.[48] All workers in nineteenth-century market economies were becoming more productive regardless of their slave or free status. A shortage of workers in the sectors producing for world markets must have retarded the growth in both total and per capita output.

The actual impact is very hard to measure. Unlike the abolition of slavery itself, which outside Cuba and Barbados had an immediate and depressing effect on plantation output,[49] there was no clearly readable response to suppression of the slave trade. Output was maintained in the wake of the latter and even expanded as new crop strains, improved transportation and other productivity-enhancing changes occurred. The true measure would be the difference between the observed trends and the growth that would have occurred with a more elastic labor supply. From this standpoint the impact was probably least in the United States, where a strong rate of natural population increase ensured a highly elastic supply of labor as long as slavery itself endured. In Brazil and Cuba and the French and British West Indies the impact was much more severe.

Brazil was probably the more seriously affected in the Iberian Americas. Paradoxically, in the thirty years preceding suppression, per capita exports increased little if at all for the Brazilian economy as a whole.[50] This should not, however, be taken as an indication of stagnation in the productivity of the export sector. Rather, it is a reflection of the growth of the self-sufficient Brazilian agricultural sector relative to the latter. As in most of South and Central America, subsistence agriculture was the dominant economic activity prior to the twentieth century and, of course, was largely independent of the international economy. In the absence of navigable rivers which might have linked the interior with world markets, the expansion of this sector in Brazil was based on rapid growth of the free population and abundant land.[51] The vitality of subsistence agriculture ensured that free indigenous labor for the major export crops would be expensive. This same vitality also ensured that although coffee and sugar production grew strongly, per capita exports for the economy as a whole did not. After allowing for the subsistence sector, per capita income trends followed a different path, however. There is no reason to believe that productivity in the subsistence sector fell, and it may in fact have increased slightly as seed varieties and basic cultivation techniques improved. Output per person in the export sector was clearly greater than this, however. Slave prices increased prior to 1850 and the export sector was able to bid away resources from subsistence activities. Despite the poor performance of per ca, ita exports in the second quarter of the century, we might conclude that average per capita income (including nonmarket income of the self-sufficient sector) actually increased during the period.[52]

The suppression of the slave trade at midcentury occurred before the beginning of large scale free immigration as well as in the face of the continued vitality of the nonmarket economy. In spite of the rise in slave prices, the export sector failed to attract free labor. Indeed if unsubsidized free immigration had occurred, it would no doubt have quickly entered the subsistence economy.[53] Although slave labor from the rest of Brazil was shifted to the south-central region, the failure of this traffic to develop before 1850 and the massive increase in slave prices during the 1850s indicates that the internal slave trade was a second-best alternative. The Brazilian export sector's response to booming North Atlantic commodity demand in the third quarter of the century was hindered by the lack of labor. Output per slave certainly increased, but all export crops and the incomes they generated could have increased much more rapidly. It is noteworthy that the explosive growth of Brazilian exports in the generation before 1914 came only when the manpower problem had been solved by free immigration. In terms of measured income at least, the third quarter of the century were years of lost opportunity for the Brazilian economy. Income would have been higher if the slave traffic with Africa had remained open.

In Cuba significant subsidized free migration began later than in Brazil, but the arrival rate per 100,000 of the population was similar to Brazil's in the decade before 1895, when the War of Independence began.[54] The transition to free labor in Cuba was greatly facilitated by buoyant sugar prices, the very gradual disappearance of slavery, the relative shortage of land suitable for smallholdings and technological developments that made possible the reorganization of sugar cultivation into smaller production units. These were worked by free farmers, *colonos,* and fed cane into very large central mills.[55] One additional advantage for the Cuban planter was that Cuba was the last major sugar economy to give up the slave trade and slavery. In contrast to the British West Indies at emancipation, there were no slave owners in other producing areas waiting to benefit from a production shortfall. Emancipation put Cuban planters on the same footing as others. Thus a collapse of sugar production in Cuba was less likely than, say, in the British West Indies. Whatever the relative importance of these factors, there was no diminution in sugar production.

Yet once more it should be stressed that subsidized immigration and reorganization of sugar production around the centrales did not develop until the price of slaves had first increased to several times the levels current when the African slave trade was uninterrupted, or second, slavery itself was abolished.[56] Small-scale cane farming developed alongside plantations worked with free and indentured labor in several parts of the late nineteenth-century world.[57] But it is hard to conceive of any technology that would have permitted free labor to compete with a slave-labor force supplied from Africa at the slave prices that held in the early 1830s. The cost of suppression to the Cuban economy may thus be traced back to the 1820s when interference with the slave ade began. It must take into account not only the sugar production lost because of higher labor costs but also the collapse of nonsugar exports, in particular coffee, that might have been prevented by a more elastic supply of labor. An open slave trade might have meant a much more diversified Cuban economy than actually developed. Although a quantitative estimate of the "lost" production is impossible, it is worth noting that per capita exports, which had jumped in the second quarter of the century, were about the same at the end of the century as they had been in 1850.[58] The domestic economy, of which the subsistence portion was very small, had grown considerably in the interval, and exports as a share of Cuban national income had no doubt declined. Nevertheless, the fall in the export potential of the island must have lowered the potential earnings for the economy as a whole after midcentury.

The consequences of suppression were, nevertheless, more serious in Brazil than in Cuba. In the former, subsistence agriculture was widespread and the response of domestic labor to the market opportunities provided by the export sector was very limited. The best prospect for widening the internal domestic market in Brazil lay with the rapidly growing export sector and the development of an internal transportation network. Certainly output per slave accelerated after 1850, returns from slaveowning were high and coffee production doubled between the late 1840s and early 1880s. Yet the average annual growth rate of both coffee and sugar output was substantially lower in the generation after 1850 than in the thirty years before. The Brazilian share of world coffee output actually declined in these years before recommencing its upward climb when free migration became significant.[59] Thus the ability of the market sector, fueled with slave labor, to overwhelm and absorb nonmarket activities was severely circumscribed by the termination of the African slave trade. The widely recognized poor performance of Brazilian measured income in the nineteenth century might have been improved if Brazil had had continued unfettered access to labor in Africa.

For the typical slave already in the Americas, suppression probably meant little immediately although in many regions it came to be a precursor of the abolition of slavery itself. It is tempting to argue that the increased output per slave following in the wake of suppression was achieved through increased work intensities. This was certainly the case for many younger, older and female slaves pressed into service in the first field gang on British plantations because of the shortage of prime-age males.[60] But in its almost total ban on the intra-American slave traffic, the British Caribbean was rather exceptional and it was this that greatly exacerbated the British slave-supply situation. For most slaves in the Americas, the net impact of productivity improvements is unclear. Many of the improvements occurred off the plantation. Rail transportation, both on and off the estate in Cuba, as well as the increasing mechanization of the milling process reduced the labor input required to a significant degree. It is possible that the impact of machinery on the life of a displaced peasant drafted into a factory was to raise work intensity, whereas the effect on a slave accustomed to working eighteen hours a day in the mill during the crop season might have been in an opposite one.

The social impact of suppression is more clear-cut. It ensured the reasonably quick emergence of a wholly Creole Afro-American society. There was never a significant voluntary African emigration to the Americas apart from several thousand to the British Caribbean after 1840.[61] The cultural implications of this were profound as adaptive Afro-American patterns of family structure, values and conceptions of life without slavery quickly became dominant in all Afro-American societies.[62] The black freedman's aspiration to be an independent smallholder, which was present in all American ex-slave societies, had no parallel in pre-1800 Africa, for example. As Sidney Mintz has pointed out, the postslavery labor force faced increasing pressure from subsidized immigration and indentured labor, as well as planter strategies designed to eliminate all alternatives to plantation work. These were the "two jaws of of Caribbean plantation discipline."[63] Yet some movement from the sugar estates occurred everywhere after emancipation, and there are hints of intriguing similarities to the Chartist land-bank scheme in then-contemporary industrial England and to the goals of the white North American artisan.[64]

But perhaps the most uncomfortable implications of the suppression of the transatlantic traffic are suggested by the secular nutritional trends discussed in chapter 5. A wide range of data from many different European countries has established the connection between industrialization and increases in human stature that can only have been the result of improved nutritional intakes. It is now apparent that a similar process was associated with plantation slavery. Creole slaves in the U.S. South, the British West Indies and probably, too, in Cuba and northern Brazil were significantly taller than their African contemporaries on both sides of the Atlantic.[65] Africans driven to the New World in the nineteenth century clearly experienced some material gains among the exigencies of plantation slavery.[66] Suspension of the trade cut off African access to the material benefits of the Americas though just as clearly Africans in no sense desired such benefits if American slavery was the only way of achieving them. But the fact remains that the descendants of the forced migrants, both enslaved and free, were nutritionally better off than those who escaped the middle passage. Slavery itself was abolished in most regions within a few decades of suppression of the traffic. Yet the return flow of freemen to Africa was of miniscule proportions, especially when comparisons are made with other transcontinental population shifts.

The economic, as opposed to moral gains of putting down the slave traffic are thus not very obvious. Anything that limited the growth of a coercive labor system was, of course, to be welcomed. Clearly the abolitionists and the legislatures that listened to them made a decision that was morally correct by any value system that denies precedence to ends over means. There could be no objections to paying higher prices for tropical produce if that was also the price of ensuring that the massive nineteenth-century transatlantic population shift was composed primarily of free persons rather than slaves. There would still be few objections if the price of suppression was raised to include the retarded growth of the export sectors of Brazil and other parts of the tropical Americas after 1850. But the moral calculus becomes less clear if we take into account the largely extralegal means employed by the British to terminate the trade. It becomes fuzzier again if we contrast the frequent famines of west-central Africa and the Sudan with the relative plenty of most of the Americas. The dilemma is perhaps most intense, however, when we trace the connection between abolitionism, on the one hand, and colonialism and racism, on the other. If, as has been argued here, the influence of Europe on Africa was rather small before the late nineneeth century, what came after was of a different order of magnitude. Much of the latter can be traced to the refusal of Africans to behave as a European elite expected in the wake of suppression. Despite the unexpected collapse of plantation output in the post-emancipation British West Indies, it was in Africa that the abolitionists received their largest disappointments. But abolitionists were not alone in exaggerating the extent of European influence on the African continent. African cultures and values remained obstinately non-European, and trade growth lagged behind the rate of increase in world trade as a whole. Direct European intervention at the end of the century was in a sense one further attempt to bring these culture-bound expectations to reality, but it did, of course, throw up a new set of moral conundrums. Today we know better than the abolitionists, though as Ralph Austen has suggested, it is not at all clear how we would use this knowledge to improve on their decisions.[67]

# APPENDIX A

# Volume of the Transatlantic Slave Trade, 1781–1867

The estimates of slave arrivals in the Americas in tables A.1 to A.8 are extracted from an unpublished paper, and an essay in the *Hispanic American Historical Review*. Sections of these were presented to the 1975 Colby Conference on the Slave Trade and the 1981 African Studies Association meetings at Bloomington, Indiana.[1] For the post-1810 period the annual figures are based largely on the opinions of contemporary observers, many of them attached to the British Foreign Office. Some inferences are employed to fill in missing years, but in most cases it is possible to support both direct observation and inferences with evidence of actual arrivals computed from the slave-ship data set. For the pre-1811 period the estimates are based entirely on the detailed work of others though the fitting together of this work results in new aggregate figures. For the complete 1781–1867 period the estimates here are 23 percent greater than those of Curtin and perhaps 3 percent greater than Lovejoy's revisions of the Curtin estimates.[2] Clearly, whatever is new in tables A.1 to A.8 lies in the annual and geographic breakdowns rather than the aggregate totals.

The export series 1811–67 that are shown in table A.9 are derived mainly from the import series though for many years these also receive support from the counts of embarkations computed from the slave-ship data set. The derivation process depends on this same data set, however. British observers recorded the points of embarkation for many ships arriving in the New World (and many more prevented from arriving by capture). It is possible to obtain relative distributions of departure points for ships arriving at each major port in the Americas—sometimes for each year, but more often for multiyear periods.[3] These distributions are then used to allocate annual imports to broad regions within Africa. To this base may be added an allowance for Africans who died on the crossing—data on shipboard mortality being relatively abundant for the nineteenth century. One further addition is necessary to derive a full export series. Navies from several countries, but mostly the British, captured slave ships and their human cargoes en route to the Americas. These data are presented supra, tables 3 and 4. In most cases it is possible to find out where the slave ship embarked its slaves. The export series is thus the sum of allocated imports, estimated mortality on the crossing and Africans captured (or recaptured) by the naval squadrons for each of the years from 1811 to 1867. The African regions are defined as follows: Upper Guinea is the coast northwest of and including Cape Mount and takes in the Gallinas, Sierra Leone and Senegambia; the Windward Coast here extends from Cape Mount to Cape Three Points (though as very few slaves embarked on the Ivory and Gold coasts in this period, for all practical purposes it constitutes the area between Cape Mount and Cape Palmas); the Bight of Benin ranges from Cape Three Points up to but not including the main outlet of the Niger River (again very few left the Gold Coast); the Rio Nun to Cape Lopez inclusive makes up the Bight of Biafra region, and Cape Lopez to the mouth of the Congo are the limits of the Congo North region. Angola is defined as the remainder of the west coast and excludes the Congo River. South East Africa includes all export points on the east coast, in practice all observations falling between Lourenço Marques and Mombasa. Finally the slave-ship data set makes possible a distribution of ship departures by major export point in Africa. This is shown in table A.10 and gives a good indication of individual as opposed to regional slave-export centers.

For neither import nor export series is any claim made for completeness. It is unlikely, however, that bias in either direction was consistent over time. Given the determination of the British and the scale of the resources they devoted to the task, it seems unlikely that the real totals can be much greater than those developed here.

**Table A.1.** Annual Imports of Slaves into Brazil, 1781–1856 ('000)

| | Brazil South of Bahia | Bahia | Brazil North of Bahia |
|---|---|---|---|
| 1781 | 8.0 | | 7.1 |
| 1782 | 6.8 | | 5.6 |
| 1783 | 6.4 | | 6.3 |
| 1784 | 5.4 | | 4.8 |
| 1785 | 8.2 | | 4.6 |
| **1781–85** | **34.8** | | **28.3** |
| 1786 | 9.4 | 3.9 | 5.0 |
| 1787 | 10.1 | 3.9 | 7.8 |
| 1788 | 10.7 | 3.7 | 8.5 |
| 1789 | 8.9 | 4.2 | 6.1 |
| 1790 | 5.7 | 4.7 | 5.3 |
| **1786–90** | **44.8** | **20.3** | **32.7** |
| 1791 | 7.5 | 6.3 | 7.3 |
| 1792 | 8.5 | 6.3 | 8.2 |
| 1793 | 11.1 | 6.7 | 9.4 |
| 1794 | 10.2 | 8.1 | 9.1 |
| 1795 | 10.3 | 37.1 | 9.1 |
| **1791–95** | **47.6** | **34.3** | **43.1** |
| 1796 | 9.9 | 7.0 | 7.5 |
| 1797 | 9.3 | 7.5 | 6.4 |
| 1798 | 6.8 | 7.0 | 5.2 |
| 1799 | 8.9 | 8.5 | 4.3 |
| 1800 | 10.4 | 6.3 | 4.0 |
| **1796–1800** | **45.1** | **36.2** | **27.4** |
| 1801 | 10.0 | 7.2 | 5.9 |
| 1802 | 11.3 | 6.8 | 5.9 |
| 1803 | 9.7 | 8.3 | 5.9 |
| 1804 | 9.0 | 7.4 | 7.9 |
| 1805 | 9.9 | 6.5 | 5.9 |
| **1801–5** | **50.1** | **36.3** | **31.5** |
| 1806 | 7.1 | 8.6 | 4.6 |
| 1807 | 9.7 | 7.9 | 6.0 |
| 1808 | 9.6 | 7.5 | 6.0 |
| 1809 | 13.2 | 7.5 | 5.0 |
| 1810 | 18.7 | 7.5 | 4.5 |
| **1806–10** | **58.3** | **39.1** | **26.1** |
| 1811 | 17.4 | 5.8 | 5.1 |
| 1812 | 17.2 | 8.8 | 4.0 |
| 1813 | 17.1 | 6.8 | 4.5 |
| 1814 | 12.2 | 8.2 | 5.4 |
| 1815 | 14.8 | 6.8 | 5.3 |
| **1811–15** | **78.7** | **36.4** | **24.3** |
| 1816 | 20.1 | 4.8 | 8.7 |
| 1817 | 18.2 | 6.1 | 11.2 |
| 1818 | 20.1 | 8.7 | 13.0 |
| 1819 | 17.1 | 7.0 | 15.5 |
| 1820 | 20.2 | 7.7 | 9.9 |
| **1816–20** | **95.7** | **34.3** | **58.3** |

**Table A.1.** (*Continued*)

| | Brazil South of Bahia | Bahia | Brazil North of Bahia |
|---|---|---|---|
| 1821 | 20.4 | 6.7 | 10.1 |
| 1822 | 27.8 | 7.1 | 9.4 |
| 1823 | 19.2 | 2.7 | 11.0 |
| 1824 | 26.2 | 3.1 | 4.0 |
| 1825 | 26.5 | 4.1 | 2.9 |
| **1821–25** | **120.1** | **23.7** | **37.4** |
| 1826 | 30.4 | 7.9 | 4.5 |
| 1827 | 27.4 | 10.2 | 5.7 |
| 1828 | 43.4 | 7.8 | 6.9 |
| 1829 | 43.7 | 15.0 | 6.3 |
| 1830 | 31.2 | 7.0 | 2.8 |
| **1826–30** | **176.1** | **47.9** | **26.2** |
| 1831 | 1.0 | 1.0 | 1.5 |
| 1832 | 4.0 | 3.3 | 3.8 |
| 1833 | 9.0 | 3.6 | 4.1 |
| 1834 | 13.8 | 3.6 | 4.1 |
| 1835 | 30.0 | 5.2 | 5.7 |
| **1831–35** | **57.8** | **16.7** | **19.2** |
| 1836 | 46.0 | 2.9 | 2.9 |
| 1837 | 46.0 | 4.0 | 4.0 |
| 1838 | 42.8 | 4.0 | 4.0 |
| 1839 | 46.0 | 2.9 | 5.5 |
| 1840 | 22.0 | 2.0 | 5.6 |
| **1836–40** | **202.8** | **15.8** | **22.0** |
| 1841 | 11.4 | 2.0 | 5.5 |
| 1842 | 13.9 | 3.8 | 2.3 |
| 1843 | 30.0 | 3.1 | 0.9 |
| 1844 | 19.5 | 6.6 | 0.1 |
| 1845 | 16.0 | 5.6 | 0.2 |
| **1841–45** | **90.8** | **21.1** | **9.0** |
| 1846 | 42.5 | 7.4 | 0.5 |
| 1847 | 49.0 | 10.3 | 0.3 |
| 1848 | 52.0 | 7.6 | 0.0 |
| 1849 | 46.0 | 9.8 | 0.5 |
| 1850 | 19.4 | 9.9 | 2.3 |
| **1846–50** | **208.9** | **45.0** | **3.6** |
| 1851 | 2.2 | 1.9 | 0.9 |
| 1852 | 1.1 | 0.0 | 0.0 |
| **1851–55** | **3.3** | **1.9** | **0.9** |
| 1856 | 0.3 | 0.0 | 0.0 |

*Source:* David Eltis, "The Nineteenth-Century Transatlantic Slave Trade: An Annual Time Series of Imports into the Americas Broken down by Region," *Hispanic American Historical Review* (forthcoming); idem, "The Volume of the Transatlantic Slave Trade, 1781–1867," unpublished paper, 1983. Note that columns may not add up because of rounding.

**Table A.2.** Annual Imports of Slaves into Cuba, 1786–1867 ('000)

| | | | | | |
|------|------|---------|-------|---------|------|
| 1786 | 2.3 | 1816 | 23.6 | 1846 | 1.0 |
| 1787 | 2.3 | 1817 | 34.5 | 1847 | 1.7 |
| 1788 | 2.3 | 1818 | 26.5 | 1848 | 2.0 |
| 1789 | 2.3 | 1819 | 20.2 | 1849 | 7.4 |
| 1790 | 3.4 | 1820 | 22.9 | 1850 | 3.3 |
| **1785–90** | **12.6** | **1816–20** | **127.7** | **1846–50** | **15.4** |
| 1791 | 11.3 | 1821 | 4.5 | 1851 | 5.0 |
| 1792 | 11.4 | 1822 | 4.0 | 1852 | 7.0 |
| 1793 | 5.0 | 1823 | 1.9 | 1853 | 12.5 |
| 1794 | 5.6 | 1824 | 7.7 | 1854 | 11.4 |
| 1795 | 7.8 | 1825 | 13.8 | 1855 | 6.4 |
| **1791–95** | **41.1** | **1821–25** | **31.9** | **1851–55** | **42.3** |
| 1796 | 7.6 | 1826 | 4.0 | 1856 | 7.3 |
| 1797 | 6.1 | 1827 | 5.0 | 1857 | 10.4 |
| 1798 | 2.7 | 1828 | 12.9 | 1858 | 15.0 |
| 1799 | 6.6 | 1829 | 14.9 | 1859 | 25.0 |
| 1800 | 5.5 | 1830 | 14.4 | 1860 | 21.0 |
| **1796–1800** | **28.5** | **1826–30** | **51.2** | **1856–60** | **78.7** |
| 1801 | 2.2 | 1831 | 16.1 | 1861 | 13.8 |
| 1802 | 18.4 | 1832 | 13.6 | 1862 | 10.1 |
| 1803 | 12.9 | 1833 | 13.8 | 1863 | 3.8 |
| 1804 | 11.9 | 1834 | 16.7 | 1864 | 2.4 |
| 1805 | 6.7 | 1835 | 25.7 | 1865 | 0.8 |
| **1801–05** | **52.1** | **1831–35** | **85.9** | **1861–65** | **30.9** |
| 1806 | 5.9 | 1836 | 20.2 | 1866 | 0.7 |
| 1807 | 3.4 | 1837 | 20.9 | 1867 | 0.0 |
| 1808 | 2.1 | 1838 | 21.0 | **1866–67** | **0.7** |
| 1809 | 1.5 | 1839 | 19.9 | | |
| 1810 | 8.9 | 1840 | 13.7 | | |
| **1806–10** | **21.8** | **1836–40** | **95.7** | | |
| 1811 | 8.5 | 1841 | 11.6 | | |
| 1812 | 8.1 | 1842 | 4.1 | | |
| 1813 | 6.4 | 1843 | 7.1 | | |
| 1814 | 5.8 | 1844 | 10.0 | | |
| 1815 | 12.1 | 1845 | 2.6 | | |
| **1811–15** | **40.9** | **1841–45** | **35.4** | | |

*Source:* David Eltis, "The Nineteenth-Century Transatlantic Slave Trade: An Annual Time Series of Imports into the Americas Broken Down by Region," *Hispanic American Historical Review* (forthcoming); idem, "The Volume of the Transatlantic Slave Trade, 1781–1867," (unpublished paper, 1983). Note that totals may not add up because of rounding.

**Table A.3.** Annual Imports of Slaves into the French Americas ('000) by Colony, 1811–62

| | Guadeloupe | Martinique | French Guyana | French West Indies |
|---|---|---|---|---|
| 1814 | 0.3 | 0.2 | 0.1 | 0.7 |
| 1815 | 0.7 | 0.5 | 0.3 | 1.5 |
| 1816 | 0.6 | 0.4 | 0.2 | 1.2 |
| 1817 | 0.8 | 0.5 | 0.3 | 1.6 |
| 1818 | 1.4 | 0.9 | 0.5 | 2.8 |
| 1819 | 1.9 | 1.2 | 0.7 | 3.8 |
| 1820 | 3.6 | 2.3 | 1.3 | 7.2 |
| 1821 | 3.1 | 2.0 | 1.2 | 6.3 |
| 1822 | 3.8 | 2.5 | 1.4 | 7.7 |
| 1823 | 2.0 | 1.3 | 0.8 | 4.1 |
| 1824 | 4.2 | 2.7 | 1.6 | 8.5 |
| 1825 | 3.9 | 2.5 | 1.5 | 7.9 |
| 1826 | 2.7 | 1.7 | 1.0 | 5.4 |
| 1827 | 2.7 | 1.7 | 1.0 | 5.4 |
| 1828 | 2.1 | 1.3 | 0.8 | 4.2 |
| 1829 | 2.2 | 1.3 | 0.8 | 4.3 |
| 1830 | 2.0 | 1.3 | 0.8 | 4.1 |
| 1831 | 0.3 | 0.2 | 0.1 | 0.6 |
| **1814–31** | **38.3** | **24.5** | **14.5** | **77.3** |
| 1854 | | | | 0.2 |
| 1855 | | | | 0.3 |
| 1856 | | | | 0.3 |
| 1857 | | | | 1.5 |
| 1858 | | | | 2.0 |
| 1859 | | | | 4.5 |
| 1860 | | | | 3.7 |
| 1861 | | | | 2.7 |
| 1862 | | | | 3.2 |
| **1854–62** | | | | **18.5** |

*Note:* Columns and rows may not add up because of rounding

*Sources:* The years 1814–31 are estimated from shipping data supplied in a personal communication by Serge Daget. I am indebted to Professor Daget for the opportunity to examine his data before the completion of his thèse d'état. A partial list of this data has appeared in H. A. Gemery and J. S. Hogendorn (eds.), *The Uncommon Market* (New York, 1979), pp. 299–301. The estimation procedure may be found in David Eltis, "The Nineteenth Century Transatlantic Slave Trade: An Annual Time Series of Imports into the Americas Broken Down by Region," *Hispanic American Historical Review* (forthcoming). The years 1854–62 are calculated from François Renault, *Libération d'esclaves et nouvelle servitude* (Abidjan, Ivory Coast, 1976), pp. 175–77, 189.

**Table A.4.** Annual Imports of Slaves into the United States, Puerto Rico, Montevideo and British Americas[a] ('000)

| | | | | | | | |
|---|---|---|---|---|---|---|---|
| 1811 | 1.3 | 1821 | 3.1[b] | 1831 | 2.0 | 1841 | 1.4 |
| 1812 | 1.3 | 1822 | 3.0 | 1832 | 2.3 | 1842 | 1.0 |
| 1813 | 1.3 | 1823 | 2.0 | 1833 | 2.1 | 1843 | 1.4 |
| 1814 | 1.3 | 1824 | 2.0 | 1834 | 5.6 | 1844–57 | 0.0 |
| 1815 | 2.2 | 1825 | 2.0 | 1835 | 9.3 | 1858 | 0.3 |
| 1816 | 2.2 | 1826 | 2.0 | 1836 | 3.3 | 1859 | 1.0 |
| 1817 | 2.2 | 1827 | 2.0 | 1837 | 3.6 | | |
| 1818 | 2.2 | 1828 | 2.0 | 1838 | 3.4 | | |
| 1819 | 2.2 | 1829 | 1.9 | 1839 | 1.4 | | |
| 1820 | 3.0 | 1830 | 1.9 | 1840 | 2.6 | | |

*Note:* [a]British Americas category refers mainly to slaves shipwrecked in the Bahamas or captured in the Caribbean by British ships and disembarked in the British Americas. [b]Includes 143 landed at Paramaribo, Surinam.

*Source:* David Eltis, "The Nineteenth Century Transatlantic Slave Trade: An Annual Time Series Broken Down by Region," *Hispanic American Historical Review* (forthcoming).

**Table A.5.** Decadal Imports of Slaves into the Americas by Major Importing Region, 1781–1810 ('000)

| | 1781–90 | 1791–1800 | 1801–10 |
|---|---|---|---|
| United States | 55.8 | 79.0 | 156.3 |
| Cuba | —[a] | 69.5 | 74.0 |
| Rio de la Plata[b] | 2.8 | 2.7 | 6.3 |
| Other Spanish Americas | 39.4 | 5.2 | 5.4 |
| St. Domingue (French) | 319.0 | 65.7 | 0.0 |
| Other French Americas | 38.8 | 16.9 | 17.0 |
| Jamaica | 68.8 | 122.3 | 58.5 |
| Barbados | 3.0 | 3.0 | 1.0 |
| Trinidad and Demerara | —[c] | 40.6 | 26.0 |
| British Leewards | 1.0 | 1.0 | 0.8 |
| Other British Americas | 27.4 | 27.4 | 19.1 |
| Dutch West Indies | 12.3 | 5.3 | 0.0 |
| Danish West Indies | 4.6 | 14.5 | 3.3 |
| Brazil, north of Bahia | 61.0 | 70.4 | 57.6 |
| Bahia | 40.6 | 70.5 | 75.4 |
| Brazil, south of Bahia | 79.6 | 92.7 | 108.3 |
| **Total** | **754.1** | **686.7** | **609.0** |

*Notes:* [a]Included in Other Spanish Americas category. [b]Includes only slaves imported direct from Africa. [c]Included in Dutch West Indies and Other Spanish Americas categories.

*Sources:* Row 1, Robert William Fogel and Stanley L. Engerman, *Time on the Cross: The Economics of American Negro Slavery,* 2 vols. (Boston, 1974), 1:25; 2:30–31. Rows 2, 14, 15, and 16, tables A.1 and A.2. All other rows, see David Eltis, "The Volume of the Transatlantic Slave Trade, 1781–1867," unpublished paper, 1983. (Totals may not add up because of rounding).

**Table A.6.** Decadal Exports of Slaves from Africa to the Americas by Nationality of Slave Ship, 1781–1810 ('000)

|                 | 1781–90 | 1791–1800 | 1801–10 |
|-----------------|---------|-----------|---------|
| Portuguese      | 194.0   | 250.1     | 247.6   |
| French          | 311.5   | 69.8      | 0.0     |
| British         | 360.0   | 447.5     | 250.1   |
| Dutch           | 9.7     | 3.5       | 0.0     |
| United States   | 17.8    | 56.3      | 112.7   |
| Danish          | 14.0    | 8.7       | 2.0     |
| Spanish         | 0.0     | 0.0       | 4.0     |
| **Total**       | **907.0** | **835.9** | **616.4** |

*Sources:* Rows 1, 2, 5 and 7, see David Eltis "The Volume of the Transatlantic Slave Trade, 1781–1867," (unpublished paper, 1983). Row 3, Seymour Drescher, *Econocide: British Slavery in the Era of Abolition* (Pittsburgh, 1977), p. 28. Row 4, Johannes Postma, "The Origin of the African Slave Trade: The Dutch Activities on the Guinea Coast, 1675–1795," in Stanley L. Engerman and Eugene D. Genovese, (eds.) *Race and Slavery in the Western Hemisphere* (Princeton, N.J. 1975), p. 49. Row 6, calculated from Svend E. Green-Pedersen, "The History of the Danish Negro Slave Trade, 1733–1807," *Revue française d'histoire d'outre-mer,* 62 (1975): 200–201.

**Table A.7.** The Volume of the Transatlantic Slave Trade, 1781–1810 ('000)

|                                          | 1781–90 | 1791–1800 | 1801–10 |
|------------------------------------------|---------|-----------|---------|
| Imports from import based series         | 754.1   | 686.1     | 609.0   |
| Exports from shipping based data         | 907.0   | 835.9     | 616.4   |
| $\dfrac{\text{Row 2} - \text{Row 1}}{\text{Row 2}} \times 100$ | 16.9 | 17.9 | 1.2 |
| Weighted mean losses in transit (mortality) | 10.3 | 7.8    | 8.3     |
| Inferred imports (exports less mortality) | 813.6  | 770.7     | 568.9   |
| Preferred import series                  | 813.6   | 770.7     | 609.0   |
| Preferred export series                  | 907.0   | 835.9     | 653.2[a] |

*Note:* [a]Imports plus an allowance for losses in transit shown in row 4.

*Sources:* Row 1, table A.5;
row 2, table A.6;
rows 4 to 7, see David Eltis, "The Volume of the Transatlantic Slave Trade, 1781–1867" (unpublished paper, 1983).

Table A.8. Decadal Imports of Slaves into the Americas, 1781–1867 ('000)

| | 1781–90 | 1791–1800 | 1801–10 | 1811–20 | 1821–30 | 1831–40 | 1841–50 | 1851–60 | 1861–70 |
|---|---|---|---|---|---|---|---|---|---|
| United States | 55.8 | 79.0 | 156.3 | 10.0 | 2.0 | 0.0 | 0.0 | 0.3 | 0.0 |
| Cuba | —[a] | 69.5 | 74.0 | 168.6 | 83.1 | 181.6 | 50.8 | 121.0 | 31.6 |
| Rio de la Plata[b] | 2.8 | 2.7 | 6.3 | 0.0 | 0.0 | 8.7 | 0.0 | 0.0 | 0.0 |
| Other Spanish Americas | 39.4 | 5.2 | 5.4 | 9.2 | 20.4 | 16.7 | 3.8 | 1.0 | 0.0 |
| St. Domingue | 319.0 | 65.7 | 0.0 | 0.0 | 0.0 | 0.0 | 0.0 | 0.0 | 0.0 |
| Other French Americas | 38.8 | 16.9 | 17.0 | 18.8 | 57.9 | 0.6 | 0.0 | 12.5 | 5.9 |
| British Americas | 100.2 | 194.3 | 105.4 | 0.0 | 0.4 | 10.2 | 0.0 | 0.0 | 0.0 |
| Dutch and Danish Americas | 16.9 | 19.8 | 3.3 | 0.0 | 0.1 | 0.0 | 0.0 | 0.0 | 0.0 |
| Brazil, north of Bahia | 61.0 | 70.4 | 57.6 | 82.6 | 63.6 | 41.2 | 12.6 | 0.9 | 0.0 |
| Bahia | 40.6[c] | 70.5 | 75.4 | 70.7 | 71.6 | 32.5 | 66.1 | 1.9 | 0.0 |
| Brazil, south of Bahia | 79.6 | 92.7 | 108.3 | 174.4 | 296.2 | 260.6 | 299.7 | 3.6 | 0.0 |
| Unassignable imports | 59.5 | 84.0 | 0.0 | 0.0 | 0.0 | 0.0 | 0.0 | 0.0 | 0.0 |
| **Total** | **813.6** | **770.7** | **609.0** | **534.3** | **595.3** | **552.1** | **433.0** | **141.2** | **37.5** |

Notes: [a]Included in other Spanish Americas. [b]Includes only slaves from Africa. [c]Arrivals 1781–1785 are assumed equal to those in 1786–90.
Sources: Tables A.1 to A.7.

Table A.9. Annual Transatlantic Exports of Slaves by African Region of Embarkation, 1811–67 ('000)

| | Upper Guinea | Windward Coast | Bight of Benin | Bight of Biafra | Congo North | Angola | Southeast Africa | Africa |
|---|---|---|---|---|---|---|---|---|
| 1811 | 3.7 | 0.8 | 6.0 | 6.1 | 8.9 | 15.6 | 1.0 | 42.1 |
| 1812 | 3.6 | 0.7 | 7.9 | 6.0 | 9.5 | 15.5 | 1.2 | 44.4 |
| 1813 | 3.0 | 0.7 | 6.3 | 5.6 | 10.1 | 12.1 | 1.8 | 39.6 |
| 1814 | 3.5 | 0.6 | 8.8 | 5.2 | 5.3 | 12.6 | 1.1 | 37.1 |
| 1815 | 5.5 | 1.4 | 5.6 | 10.2 | 7.5 | 14.7 | 3.6 | 48.5 |
| **1811–15** | **19.3** | **4.2** | **34.6** | **33.1** | **41.3** | **70.5** | **8.7** | **211.7** |
| 1816 | 8.4 | 1.8 | 8.3 | 11.3 | 10.7 | 17.5 | 11.5 | 69.5 |
| 1817 | 11.9 | 2.1 | 13.2 | 12.1 | 11.7 | 18.4 | 13.9 | 83.5 |
| 1818 | 10.0 | 1.7 | 13.9 | 11.6 | 15.5 | 17.8 | 11.7 | 82.1 |
| 1819 | 8.1 | 1.5 | 11.1 | -11.4 | 9.2 | 21.6 | 10.2 | 73.1 |
| 1820 | 10.0 | 1.9 | 12.7 | 14.2 | 9.8 | 18.9 | 12.3 | 79.7 |
| **1816–20** | **48.4** | **9.0** | **59.2** | **60.6** | **56.9** | **94.2** | **59.6** | **387.9** |
| 1821 | 4.9 | 0.6 | 8.4 | 10.8 | 4.5 | 19.9 | 10.3 | 59.3 |
| 1822 | 4.4 | 1.2 | 10.7 | 12.4 | 7.9 | 23.7 | 8.6 | 68.9 |
| 1823 | 2.9 | 0.4 | 4.5 | 8.0 | 2.8 | 18.8 | 8.5 | 45.8 |
| 1824 | 4.5 | 0.8 | 8.6 | 13.1 | 6.5 | 19.6 | 8.4 | 61.5 |
| 1825 | 6.0 | 1.0 | 12.0 | 16.3 | 5.6 | 19.1 | 7.4 | 67.2 |
| **1821–25** | **22.7** | **4.0** | **44.2** | **60.6** | **27.3** | **101.1** | **43.2** | **302.7** |
| 1826 | 2.9 | 0.8 | 11.6 | 8.7 | 6.4 | 23.6 | 7.4 | 61.4 |
| 1827 | 3.9 | 0.9 | 13.1 | 11.7 | 9.5 | 19.8 | 6.6 | 65.5 |
| 1828 | 5.6 | 0.9 | 13.3 | 15.4 | 15.0 | 25.5 | 14.4 | 90.1 |
| 1829 | 7.1 | 1.0 | 21.0 | 16.7 | 18.5 | 22.1 | 15.5 | 101.8 |
| 1830 | 7.2 | 1.3 | 11.5 | 14.2 | 8.9 | 15.1 | 14.2 | 72.3 |
| **1826–30** | **26.7** | **4.9** | **70.5** | **66.7** | **58.3** | **106.1** | **58.1** | **391.1** |
| 1831 | 4.2 | 0.2 | 4.8 | 11.1 | 1.5 | 4.5 | 0.5 | 26.7 |
| 1832 | 3.4 | 0.2 | 6.5 | 9.7 | 2.0 | 9.8 | 0.4 | 32.0 |
| 1833 | 7.7 | 0.0 | 5.3 | 11.5 | 1.4 | 13.5 | 0.0 | 39.4 |

| Year | | | | | | | | |
|---|---|---|---|---|---|---|---|---|
| 1834 | 4.7 | 0.3 | 9.1 | 15.1 | 3.8 | 20.5 | 0.6 | 54.0 |
| 1835 | 7.4 | 0.4 | 12.0 | 24.5 | 6.2 | 39.6 | 1.5 | 91.6 |
| **1831–35** | **27.4** | **1.1** | **37.7** | **71.9** | **14.9** | **87.9** | **3.0** | **243.7** |
| 1836 | 5.0 | 1.6 | 9.7 | 14.7 | 1.1 | 43.2 | 18.3 | 93.5 |
| 1837 | 5.7 | 0.0 | 12.4 | 12.0 | 1.6 | 41.7 | 22.7 | 96.2 |
| 1838 | 8.8 | 1.7 | 13.2 | 7.4 | 6.8 | 32.9 | 20.2 | 91.0 |
| 1839 | 8.2 | 0.7 | 9.5 | 2.6 | 17.1 | 28.2 | 24.4 | 90.8 |
| 1840 | 7.6 | 1.7 | 5.6 | 4.1 | 9.8 | 11.1 | 13.8 | 53.6 |
| **1836–40** | **35.3** | **5.7** | **50.4** | **40.8** | **36.4** | **157.1** | **99.4** | **425.1** |
| 1841 | 4.7 | 0.6 | 6.5 | 0.8 | 6.4 | 19.8 | 2.4 | 41.2 |
| 1842 | 2.5 | 0.6 | 8.6 | 0.3 | 1.4 | 15.0 | 3.8 | 32.2 |
| 1843 | 4.1 | 0.3 | 9.7 | 1.8 | 8.1 | 20.4 | 6.7 | 51.0 |
| 1844 | 5.2 | 0.3 | 11.3 | 1.3 | 8.9 | 14.1 | 5.1 | 46.2 |
| 1845 | 2.6 | 0.2 | 9.2 | 0.2 | 9.1 | 9.7 | 2.3 | 33.3 |
| **1841–45** | **19.1** | **2.0** | **45.3** | **4.4** | **33.9** | **79.0** | **20.3** | **203.9** |
| 1846 | 2.4 | 0.1 | 8.2 | 0.6 | 17.6 | 24.9 | 8.6 | 62.4 |
| 1847 | 3.0 | 0.1 | 11.8 | 1.0 | 19.1 | 24.2 | 16.5 | 75.7 |
| 1848 | 3.0 | 0.1 | 11.2 | 1.0 | 20.4 | 24.8 | 17.5 | 78.0 |
| 1849 | 4.2 | 0.1 | 11.3 | 3.4 | 18.4 | 24.6 | 16.7 | 78.7 |
| 1850 | 2.1 | 0.3 | 10.9 | 1.7 | 8.5 | 14.5 | 7.4 | 45.4 |
| **1846–50** | **14.7** | **0.7** | **53.4** | **7.7** | **84.0** | **113.0** | **66.7** | **340.2** |
| 1851 | 1.3 | 0.0 | 2.6 | 0.4 | 2.8 | 2.6 | 2.2 | 12.0 |
| 1852 | 1.7 | 0.0 | 1.2 | 0.5 | 2.6 | 1.3 | 2.3 | 9.5 |
| 1853 | 2.9 | 0.0 | 2.1 | 0.8 | 4.0 | 1.5 | 3.4 | 14.7 |
| 1854 | 2.6 | 0.3 | 1.9 | 0.8 | 3.6 | 1.4 | 3.1 | 13.7 |
| 1855 | 1.8 | 0.0 | 1.1 | 0.4 | 2.0 | 0.8 | 1.8 | 7.9 |
| **1851–55** | **10.3** | **0.3** | **8.9** | **2.9** | **15.0** | **7.6** | **12.8** | **57.8** |
| 1856 | 2.0 | 0.0 | 1.2 | 0.5 | 2.3 | 1.2 | 2.0 | 9.2 |
| 1857 | 0.4 | 0.3 | 3.3 | 0.0 | 9.3 | 2.3 | 1.0 | 16.6 |
| 1858 | 0.0 | 0.0 | 1.5 | 0.3 | 18.8 | 0.0 | 0.0 | 20.6 |
| 1859 | 0.0 | 0.0 | 4.5 | 1.7 | 23.3 | 3.4 | 4.7 | 37.6 |

**Table A.9.** (Continued)

| | Upper Guinea | Windward Coast | Bight of Benin | Bight of Biafra | Congo North | Angola | Southeast Africa | Africa |
|---|---|---|---|---|---|---|---|---|
| 1860 | 0.7 | 0.0 | 3.5 | 1.9 | 26.8 | 0.8 | 3.6 | 37.3 |
| **1856-60** | **3.1** | **0.3** | **14.0** | **4.4** | **80.5** | **7.7** | **11.3** | **121.3** |
| 1861 | 2.1 | 0.0 | 0.6 | 0.0 | 16.0 | 1.1 | 2.2 | 22.0 |
| 1862 | 0.4 | 0.0 | 1.4 | 0.0 | 15.1 | 0.5 | 0.0 | 17.4 |
| 1863 | 0.0 | 0.0 | 0.6 | 0.0 | 4.2 | 1.2 | 0.0 | 6.0 |
| 1864 | 0.2 | 0.0 | 0.0 | 0.0 | 1.3 | 0.8 | 0.5 | 2.9 |
| 1865 | 0.0 | 0.0 | 0.0 | 0.0 | 1.0 | 0.0 | 0.0 | 1.0 |
| **1861-65** | **2.7** | **0.0** | **2.6** | **0.0** | **37.6** | **3.6** | **2.7** | **49.1** |
| 1866 | 0.0 | 0.0 | 0.4 | 0.0 | 1.7 | 0.0 | 0.0 | 2.1 |
| 1867 | 0.0 | 0.0 | 0.0 | 0.0 | 1.3 | 0.0 | 0.0 | 1.3 |
| **1811-67** | **229.7** | **31.6** | **421.2** | **353.1** | **489.1** | **827.8** | **385.8** | **2,737.9** |

*Source:* David Eltis, "The Volume of the Transatlantic Slave Trade, 1781-1867," unpublished paper, 1983. Note that columns and rows may not add up because of rounding.

**Table A.10.** Ships Embarking and Intending to Embark Slaves, Major Port of Embarkation by Decade, 1811–67

| | 1811–20 | 1821–30 | 1831–40 | 1841–50 | 1851–60 | 1861–67 | 1811–67 |
|---|---|---|---|---|---|---|---|
| **Upper Guinea** | | | | | | | |
| Bissau | 4 | 10 | 4 | 11 | — | — | 29 |
| Rio Pongo | 8 | 7 | 20 | 10 | 7 | 1 | 53 |
| Sherbo | — | 10 | 13 | 4 | 3 | — | 30 |
| Galinas | 5 | 44 | 49 | 21 | 2 | 1 | 122 |
| Other Upper Guinea | 27 | 24 | 10 | 9 | 1 | 4 | 75 |
| | | | | | | | |
| **Bight of Benin** | | | | | | | |
| Costa da Mina | 58 | 4 | — | 4 | — | — | 66 |
| Popo, Little and Grand | 2 | 6 | 5 | 9 | 6 | — | 28 |
| Ouidah | 17 | 44 | 33 | 35 | 11 | 4 | 144 |
| Porto Novo | 8 | 1 | — | 10 | 2 | — | 21 |
| Lagos | 12 | 54 | 64 | 82 | 3 | — | 215 |
| Other Bight of Benin | 4 | 23 | 5 | 3 | 5 | 2 | 42 |
| | | | | | | | |
| **Bight of Biafra** | | | | | | | |
| Bonny | 6 | 66 | 44 | — | 1 | — | 117 |
| Calabar | 13 | 43 | 14 | — | — | — | 70 |
| Other Bight of Biafra | 13 | 33 | 39 | 21 | 4 | — | 110 |
| | | | | | | | |
| **Congo North** | | | | | | | |
| Loango | 3 | — | 7 | 11 | 5 | — | 26 |
| Malembo | — | 103 | 38 | 3 | 2 | — | 108 |
| Cabinda | 170 | 188 | 38 | 66 | 17 | 10 | 489 |
| Congo River | 13 | 24 | 28 | 32 | 54 | 36 | 187 |
| Other Congo North | — | 16 | 2 | 3 | 11 | 1 | 33 |

**Table A.10.** (*Continued*)

|  | 1811–20 | 1821–30 | 1831–40 | 1841–50 | 1851–60 | 1861–67 | 1811–67 |
|---|---|---|---|---|---|---|---|
| Angola |  |  |  |  |  |  |  |
| Ambriz | 2 | 89 | 24 | 66 | 9 | 2 | 192 |
| Luanda | 3 | 5 | 20 | 11 | — | — | 39 |
| Benguela | 58 | 95 | 47 | 90 | 2 | 4 | 296 |
| Angola | 111 | 198 | 206 | 138 | 5 | 1 | 659 |
| Other Angola | — | — | — | 37 | 1 | — | 38 |
| Southeast Africa |  |  |  |  |  |  |  |
| Mozambique | 47 | 81 | 59 | 15 | 7 | 2 | 211 |
| Quelimane | 9 | 76 | 57 | 43 | 1 | — | 186 |
| Other Southeast Africa | — | 13 | 2 | 14 | 6 | 1 | 36 |

*Source:* David Eltis, "The Volume of the Transatlantic Slave Trade, 1781–1867" (unpublished paper, 1983).

# Age and Sex of Slaves Entering the Transatlantic Slave Trade After 1810

For some slave ships arriving in the Americas and for most ships captured with cargoes on board information on the sex and age categories of the cargo have survived. The age categories are usually "men," "women," "boys" and "girls," with no indication of the cutoff points in terms of years of age. This information is available for 435 voyages, carrying 114,225 slaves in the 1811 to 1863 period. This comprises a sample of about 7 percent of all expeditions that embarked slaves. Though all major routes in the trade are covered, the distribution over time is somewhat uneven. Two thirds of the observations occurred in the years 1821 to 1845 when the nineteenth-century traffic was at its peak for all major importing and exporting regions. The major sources (for two thirds of the set) are mixed commission and Vice Admiralty court records, with the remaining one third of the observations coming from post-disembarkation sources in the Americas such as British consular officials. The captured vessels often yielded information on the port of intended disembarkation.

Tables B.1, B.2 and B.3 provide a preliminary breakdown of these data by regions of embarkation and intended disembarkation. To preserve degrees of freedom the time-series analysis is performed only for the traffic as a whole.[1] The time profiles for the male and child ratios are shown in figure B.1.

**Table B.1.** Mean Age and Sex Ratios of Transatlantic Slave Cargoes by Regions of Embarkation and Intended Disembarkation, 1811–67

| | Male | Men | Women | Child | Boy | Girl | n Slaves (cargoes) (Sex) | n Slaves (cargoes) (Sex/Age) |
|---|---|---|---|---|---|---|---|---|
| **Region of embarkation:** | | | | | | | | |
| Upper Guinea | 0.68 | 0.44 | 0.18 | 0.38 | 0.26 | 0.13 | 11,526 (59) | 8,421 (46) |
| Windward Coast | 0.50 | 0.32 | 0.21 | 0.47 | 0.26 | 0.21 | 4,266 (15) | 919 (8) |
| Bight of Benin | 0.66 | 0.46 | 0.21 | 0.33 | 0.22 | 0.12 | 29,504 (114) | 23,326 (96) |
| Bight of Biafra | 0.66 | 0.46 | 0.16 | 0.39 | 0.20 | 0.19 | 30,871 (133) | 28,070 (126) |
| Congo North | 0.71 | 0.38 | 0.11 | 0.53 | 0.37 | 0.15 | 15,731 (32) | 4,521 (15) |
| Angola | 0.69 | 0.32 | 0.10 | 0.59 | 0.36 | 0.23 | 12,885 (34) | 5,435 (18) |
| Southeast Africa | 0.80 | 0.34 | 0.05 | 0.61 | 0.50 | 0.12 | 2,223 (5) | 2,173 (4) |
| **Intended region of disembarkation:** | | | | | | | | |
| Cuba | 0.69 | 0.46 | 0.15 | 0.39 | 0.24 | 0.15 | 51,577 (182) | 42,552 (158) |
| Brazil North | 0.64 | 0.42 | 0.19 | 0.39 | 0.22 | 0.16 | 1,033 (11) | 1,033 (11) |
| Bahia | 0.64 | 0.44 | 0.23 | 0.33 | 0.20 | 0.13 | 14,235 (61) | 11,491 (53) |
| Brazil South | 0.67 | 0.33 | 0.13 | 0.54 | 0.35 | 0.19 | 12,097 (38) | 8,648 (29) |

*Source:* Age/sex data set.

**Table B.2.** Mean Male and Child Ratios of Transatlantic Slave Cargoes, Major Regions of Disembarkation by Five-Year Periods, 1811–67

| | Male Ratios | | | Child Ratios | | |
|---|---|---|---|---|---|---|
| | Cuba | Bahia | Brazil South | Cuba | Bahia | Brazil South |
| 1811–15 | 0.646 (7)[a] | 0.789 (12) | 0.75 (1) | 0.396 (7) | 0.143 (12) | 0.333 (1) |
| 1816–20 | 0.561 (4) | 0.747 (5) | — | 0.059 (1) | 0.286 (5) | — |
| 1821–25 | 0.684 (9) | 0.641 (14) | 0.666 (4) | 0.363 (9) | 0.375 (8) | 0.333 (4) |
| 1826–30 | 0.650 (35) | 0.534 (20) | 0.541 (7) | 0.379 (31) | 0.380 (20) | 0.564 (6) |
| 1831–35 | 0.727 (57) | 0.505 (2) | 0.662 (3) | 0.398 (55) | 0.781 (2) | 0.749 (3) |
| 1836–40 | 0.680 (49) | 0.687 (4) | 0.727 (13) | 0.406 (42) | 0.388 (4) | 0.547 (12) |
| 1841–45 | 0.788 (6) | 0.545 (3) | 0.637 (5) | 0.341 (5) | 0.419 (2) | 0.416 (1) |
| 1846–50 | 0.656 (1) | 0.885 (1) | 0.753 (5) | — | — | 0.667 (2) |
| 1851–55 | 0.822 (3) | — | — | 0.206 (2) | — | — |
| 1856–60 | 0.750 (12) | — | — | 0.387 (5) | — | — |
| 1861–67 | 0.703 (10) | — | — | 0.504 (4) | — | — |
| 1811–67 | 0.696 (193) | 0.641 (61) | 0.674 (38) | 0.390 (161) | 0.334 (53) | 0.538 (29) |

*Note:* Number of cargoes are in parentheses.

*Source:* Age/sex data set.

257

**Table B.3. Mean Male and Child Ratios of Transatlantic Slave Cargoes, Major Regions of Embarkation by Five-Year Periods, 1811–67**

| | Male Ratios | | | | Child Ratios | | | |
|---|---|---|---|---|---|---|---|---|
| | Upper Guinea | Bight of Benin | Bight of Biafra | Congo North/Angola | Upper Guinea | Bight of Benin | Bight of Biafra | Congo North/Angola |
| 1811–15 | 0.755 ( 9) | 0.759 (13) | 0.704 (11) | 0.656 ( 1) | 0.315 ( 9) | 0.171 (13) | 0.267 (11) | 0.522 ( 1) |
| 1816–20 | 0.618 ( 9) | 0.593 ( 4) | 0.671 ( 3) | — | 0.310 ( 4) | 0.327 ( 3) | 0.246 ( 3) | — |
| 1821–25 | 0.640 ( 5) | 0.721 (19) | 0.657 (17) | — | 0.376 ( 4) | 0.277 (13) | 0.423 (13) | — |
| 1826–30 | 0.664 (12) | 0.585 (35) | 0.606 (38) | 0.0 ( 1) | 0.33 (10) | 0.372 (34) | 0.411 (37) | 1.0 ( 1) |
| 1831–35 | 0.694 ( 5) | 0.712 (13) | 0.712 (35) | 0.741 (11) | 0.343 ( 5) | 0.451 (12) | 0.389 (35) | 0.592 (10) |
| 1836–40 | 0.683 (14) | 0.693 ( 8) | 0.635 (26) | 0.739 (12) | 0.514 (10) | 0.382 (12) | 0.408 (26) | 0.509 (11) |
| 1841–45 | 0.703 ( 4) | 0.665 ( 2) | 0.624 ( 1) | 0.609 ( 4) | 0.515 ( 3) | 0.348 ( 4) | 0.416 ( 1) | 0.640 ( 2) |
| 1846–50 | 0.825 ( 1) | 0.643 ( 2) | 0.673 ( 2) | 0.667 (19) | 0.335 ( 1) | 0.202 ( 2) | — | 1.0 ( 1) |
| 1851–55 | — | 0.754 ( 2) | — | 0.958 ( 1) | — | 0.206 ( 2) | — | — |
| 1856–60 | — | 0.730 ( 3) | — | 0.753 ( 7) | — | 0.222 ( 1) | — | 0.386 ( 3) |
| 1861–67 | — | — | — | 0.703 (10) | — | — | — | 0.504 ( 4) |

*Note:* Number of cargoes are in parentheses.

*Sources:* Age/sex data set.

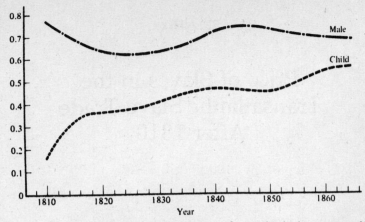

**Figure B.1** Time profiles of male and child ratios of transatlantic slave cargoes, 1811–63.

# APPENDIX C

# Price of Slaves in the Transatlantic Slave Trade After 1810

Although information on prices paid for slaves in nineteenth-century Cuba, Brazil and Africa does not as yet rival the quality of the data on U.S. slave sales, it is, nevertheless relatively abundant. Moreover, as Africans had few skills that the planters could immediately use, data from societies that still received African imports are actually more homogenous than most U.S. data. Yet the major problem remains standardizing the information. Observers tended to cite prices of prime male slaves as the average slave price and were not always specific as to the terms of credit or the degree of seasoning incorporated into that price. There are two series that it would be desirable to extract from the observations. One is for slaves of a specific category, for example, newly imported males in the age range of sixteen to thirty years who were sold for cash. Such standardization is obviously essential to any discussion of price trends. For other purposes, however, particularly assessments of profitability, it would be desirable to have a time series of average prices of all slaves landed. This latter would, of course, be lower than the former, given the large proportion of women and children as well as sick slaves disembarked in the Americas. Moreover, as shown in appendix B, the sex-and-age composition of the series did not remain constant either over time or between regions.

The approach used here is similar to that followed by Bean and Curtin on an earlier period of the traffic.[1] The price observation is first noted as it appeared in the historical record and is then adjusted according to age, sex and condition of the slave as well as the credit involved in the sale, the exchange rate and changes in the general price level. Where the reference is simply to a price of a slave of unspecified age or condition or to slaves in general, the assumption is made that the subject was a prime male unless there is a clear indication that the reported price was an average that included women and children. Prime male was the standard frame of reference used throughout the history of the Atlantic slave trade. As reported prices are not always linked to precise quantities, no attempt is made here to weight prices by the volume of slaves involved in the transaction.[2] Where a range of prices is reported, the midpoint of the range is taken before any further adjustment is made unless there is an implication that the high end of the range was for prime males, in which case the high price is accepted. There are 412 observations for large groups of slaves, often complete cargoes. Also included are a few general comments on slave prices that are not tied to specific quantities. The geographic breakdown of observations is Brazil, 130; Cuba, 117; Bahia, 40; Upper Guinea, 21; Bight of Benin, 44; Bight of Biafra, 8; west-central Africa, 30; Southeast Africa, 22.[3] The number of slaves included in the sample is thus much greater than the number of observations.

The sources are a mixture of primary and secondary, with the former predominating. The Brazil South series incorporates the Stein series for Vassouras, the Dean data for Rio Clara and the Carvalho de Mello series from the *Jornal do Comercio* of Rio de Janeiro. However, here as in other regions in the Americas the British consular reports are a major source. The latter were made in response to specific orders from the Foreign Office and toward the end of the slave trade were submitted every six months from those Brazilian centers with British consular offices. As these estimates were attempts to give the average price prevailing in the period surveyed, other observations by the consular officials have been ignored on the assumption that they had already been incorporated into the mean. However, not all the consular averages have been incorporated into the data. Annual estimates made in 1851 by consul Robert Hesketh for 1832, 1834 and 1836, respectively, have been set aside. These were made in response to a Foreign Office request and are double the levels of the next highest observations. It is possible that Hesketh was indulging the Foreign Office's conviction that formal abolition in 1831 had sent slave prices soaring. For Bahia the major source is the cache of letters written to King Kosoko of Lagos that was captured when the British occupied that place in 1851. Details of twenty different transactions usually involving groups of slaves are available from this source for the years 1848–50. One other source for this period has been set aside. In the 1840s José Estevano Cliffe, a Brazilian doctor, gave evidence to two parliamentary select committees on the slave trade and to another on sugar and coffee planting. As part of his evidence he submitted a paper on slave prices purported to be based on the books of the proprietor of a mine on the coast near Rio de Janeiro. He presented average prices for selected years going back to the mid-1820s, but for most years the prices are well out of line with every other source. In particular, they show newly arrived Africans priced well above their seasoned counterparts in the Stein series. Moreover, a British mining proprietor who knew Cliffe in Brazil wrote to a British MP disputing much of his evidence and indeed his honesty.[4]

Conversion of this data to a properly, standardized price series required careful consideration of the historical evidence of age, sex, credit differentials and exchange-rate trends. A full exposition of the procedures followed may be found in a separate paper.[5] It should, however, be noted that African slave

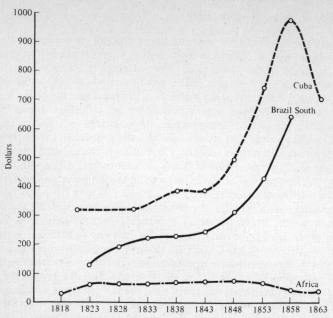

**Figure C.1** Time profiles of price of prime male slaves in the transatlantic slave trade, 1818–63 (in constant dollars, 1821–25 = 100).

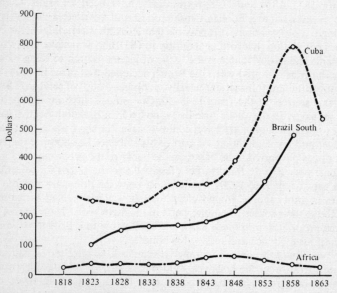

**Figure C.2** Time profiles of price of average slaves sold in the transatlantic slave trade, 1818–63 (in constant dollars, 1821–25 = 100).

**Table C.1.** Price of a Prime Male Bozal Slave in the Transatlantic Slave Trade, 1815–65 (in constant dollars, 1821–25 = 100)

| | Cuba | Bahia | Brazil South | Africa |
|---|---|---|---|---|
| 1815–20 | 317.2 (5) | — | — | 31.6 (5) |
| 1821–25 | | 220.7* (6) | 140.6*** (5) | 40.1 (8) |
| 1826–30 | 342.9 (8) | | 194.8*** (13) | 62.4 (16) |
| 1831–35 | | 249.6* (7) | 187.3*** (8) | 47.2 (5) |
| 1836–40 | 364.5 (28) | | 233.4** (14) | 64.1 (18) |
| 1841–45 | 395.3* (14) | 267.7 (3) | 282.5 (22) | 40.4 (10) |
| 1846–50 | 577.2*** (14) | 326.1 (24) | 284.1 (28) | 84.1 (20) |
| 1851–55 | 661.5*** (18) | 394.0 (1) | 428.3*** (21) | 53.1 (9) |
| 1856–60 | 1,018.0*** (23) | — | 652.1*** (19) | 46.9 (21) |
| 1861–65 | 681.0*** (7) | — | | 47.0 (12) |
| **1815–50** | **408.0 (69)** | **292.5 (40)** | **246.3 (90)** | **60.4 (82)** |

*Notes:* Numbers of observations are in parentheses. Most of the observations included are based on average prices for either complete cargoes or large lots of slaves. See text. Note however that very few slaves entered Brazil after 1850. Brazilian prices for 1851–60 are thus mostly the adjusted prices of slaves born in Brazil, or Africans who had survived the "seasoning" period. For the adjustment process see David Eltis, "Price Trends in the Atlantic Slave Trade after 1810," unpublished paper, 1984. *Significantly different from the Bahia mean, 1846–50 at the 20 percent level. **Significantly different from the Bahia mean, 1846–50 at the 5 percent level. ***Significantly different from the Bahia mean, 1846–50 at the 1 percent level. African prices were not subjected to significance tests.
*Source:* Slave-price data set.

**Table C.2.** Price of an Average Slave in the Transatlantic Slave Trade, 1815–65 (in constant dollars, 1821–25 = 100)

| | Cuba | Bahia | Brazil South | Africa |
|---|---|---|---|---|
| 1815–20 | 266.2 (5) | — | — | 26.2 (5) |
| 1821–25 | | 173.5* (6) | 110.6*** (5) | 33.3 (8) |
| 1826–30 | | | 153.4*** (13) | 51.9 (16) |
| 1831–35 | 281.7 (7) | | 137.9*** (8) | 37.5 (5) |
| 1836–40 | 295.2* (28) | 189.6* (7) | 172.2** (14) | 50.9 (18) |
| 1841–45 | 320.0** (14) | 203.3 (3) | 208.3* (22) | 32.1 (10) |
| 1846–50 | 448.7*** (14) | 247.7 (24) | 209.6* (28) | 66.8 (20) |
| 1851–55 | 535.6*** (18) | 299.0 (1) | 316.0** (21) | 43.2 (9) |
| 1856–60 | 824.3*** (23) | — | 480.8*** (19) | 38.2 (21) |
| 1861–65 | 522.6*** (7) | — | — | 38.2 (12) |
| **1866–70** | **325.1 (69)** | **223.1 (40)** | **183.5 (90)** | **48.6 (82)** |

*Notes:* Numbers of observations are in parentheses. Most of the observations included are based on average prices for either complete cargoes or large lots of slaves. See text. Note however, that very few slaves entered Brazil after 1850. Brazilian prices for 1851–60 are thus mostly the adjusted prices of slaves born in Brazil, or Africans who had survived the "seasoning" period. For the adjustment process see David Eltis, "Price Trends in the Atlantic Slave Trade after 1810," unpublished paper, 1984. *Significantly different from the Bahia mean, 1846–50 at the 20 percent level. **Significantly different from the Bahia mean, 1846–50 at the 5 percent level. ***Significantly different from the Bahia mean, 1846–50 at the 1 percent level. African prices were not subjected to significance tests.
*Source:* Slave-price data set.

**Table C.3.** Price on the African Coast of Prime Male Slaves in the Transatlantic Slave Trade Before and After 1850 (in constant dollars 1821–25 = 100)

| Region of Embarkation | 1821–50 | 1851–65 |
|---|---|---|
| Upper Guinea | 53.9 (17) | 35.9 (2) |
| Bight of Benin | 80.1** (32) | 76.0* (9) |
| Bight of Biafra | 42.9 (7) | 45.7 (1) |
| West-central Africa | 56.5 (12) | 41.7* (17) |
| Southeast Africa | 37.4* (9) | 39.9* (13) |

*Notes:* *Significantly different from the Upper Guinea mean at the 20 percent level. **Significantly different from the Upper Guinea mean at the 1 percent level.
*Source:* Slave-price data set.

prices quoted here and elsewhere in the present volume are in terms of currency or merchandise valued at the slave ship's port of departure, not on the African coast. Occasionally in the text it has been necessary to use a cif value in Africa (or, alternatively, fob for the slave), and in such cases the recorded price has been multiplied by 1.5.

**Table C.4.** Price of Prime Male Slaves Entering the Transatlantic Slave Trade at Bight of Benin Ports, 1816–60 (in constant dollars 1821–25 = 100)

| | |
|---|---|
| 1816–25 | 33.8* (6) |
| 1826–30 | 71.3 (4) |
| 1836–40 | 72.9 (8) |
| 1841–45 | 54.1 (1) |
| 1846–50 | 96.7* (16) |
| 1851–65 | 76.0 (9) |

*Note:* *Significantly different from the 1836–40 mean at the 1 percent level.
*Source:* Slave price data set.

# APPENDIX D

# Mortality in the
# Nineteenth-Century Slave Trade

The slave-ship data set contains records of 1,534 voyages in which the number of slaves embarking or disembarking was noted together with the numbers dying at sea and the region of embarkation. Almost all slave ships after 1820 embarked cargoes immediately prior to departure; all the mortality was experienced during the actual voyage. There was no counterpart to the loading period of earlier centuries when some slaves might spend several weeks on board before sailing. As mortality was tied to the duration of the voyage and as the geographic dispersion of the nineteenth-century trade ensured great variation in voyage length, an analysis of mortality as a percentage of slaves embarked (or disembarked) is not particularly useful. One measurement that takes into account voyage length is the daily mortality rate or the mortality rate per slaves embarked divided by voyage length and multiplied by 1,000. Of the 1,534 records of mortality, 765 also have data on voyage length available. For these the calculation of a daily mortality rate is straightforward and an analysis of the data has appeared elsewhere.[1]

For the 769 ships that lack data on voyage duration, it is possible to infer the length of the voyage and thus estimate a daily mortality rate for all 1,534 ships. For almost all these ships the point of embarkation in Africa and disembarkation in the Americas was recorded. For a large sample of the slave-ship data set (946 ships), including many for which mortality records have not survived, the length of the crossing in days was recorded. It is now clear that daily mortality rates did not vary systematically with voyage length for most African regions, nor was there any significant secular trend in voyage time between 1820 and 1867. It thus appears useful to calculate mean voyage times between the major points of embarkation and disembarkation for the 946 ships and assign, on the basis of these, an inferred voyage length to those ships lacking such information. This procedure yields an enlarged mortality data set from which 1,534 records of daily mortality may be calculated: 765 using the actual voyage time and 769 for which the voyage length is inferred.

The enlarged data set may be used to examine trends over time. Figure D.1 shows time profiles for the daily mortality rates derived from polynomials in the year of embarkation for those branches of the traffic where the data are adequate. For all regions together a fifth-degree polynomnial was used and was significant at the 8 percent level. For Brazil South the polynomial was of the seventh degree and for west-central Africa, of the third degree. Both the latter profiles were significant at the .001 percent level, and in all cases the use of polynomials of a higher order added nothing to the profiles. The trend line for the traffic as a whole shows a pronounced upward movement during this half century, with the steepest increase occurring in the 1830s. The last decade of the traffic saw mortality running at two or three times the level of the 1810s. In the case of both west-central Africa and Brazil South (the latter drawing most heavily on the former), on the other hand, the secular upward trend did not get underway until the late 1820s though the subsequent increase was fairly rapid.

It is also possible to examine the monthly distribution of daily mortality rates on board slave ships. Table D.1 shows the mean monthly rates for six African regions, using the enlarged data base. For all six, the range of monthly mortality is very great, with mortality in the worst months running at double or triple that of the months with the lowest rates. Indeed if the death rates for the best months had held for the rest of the year, Africans on most slave-trade routes would have died at rates much closer to those experienced by contemporary European migrants in the North Atlantic. The best explanation for these

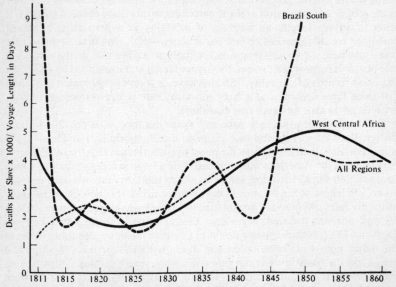

**Figure D.1** Time profiles of daily mortality in the post-1810 transatlantic slave trade: Selected regions of embarkation and disembarkation.

**Table D.1.** Index of Mean Daily Mortality Rates on Board Transatlantic Slave Ships, Month by Major Region of Embarkation, 1811–67 (December = 100)

| Month of Embarkation | Bight of Benin | | Bight of Biafra | | Congo North | | Luanda Region | | Benguela Region | | Southeast Africa | |
|---|---|---|---|---|---|---|---|---|---|---|---|---|
| | Mean | N | Mean | N | Mean | N | Mean | N | Mean | N | Mean | N |
| January | 513** | 15 | 216* | 11 | 148 | 36 | 206* | 16 | 117 | 9 | 131* | 34 |
| February | 289 | 20 | 149 | 10 | 125 | 34 | 261*** | 20 | 186* | 15 | 127 | 19 |
| March | 438** | 20 | 115 | 11 | 130 | 39 | 192* | 37 | 146 | 10 | 105 | 13 |
| April | 443** | 29 | 162 | 14 | 94 | 26 | 163 | 20 | 127 | 7 | 193** | 5 |
| May | 143 | 15 | 206* | 6 | 170* | 17 | 138 | 14 | 113 | 7 | — | |
| June | 319 | 14 | 167 | 10 | 104 | 19 | 169 | 12 | 112 | 8 | 361*** | 2 |
| July | 298 | 17 | 171 | 8 | 116 | 17 | 149 | 18 | 151 | 12 | — | |
| August | 530*** | 18 | 230*** | 11 | 95 | 14 | 193 | 21 | 93 | 7 | — | |
| September | 340* | 15 | 129 | 11 | 91 | 33 | 130 | 17 | 130 | 10 | 94 | 7 |
| October | 191 | 23 | 155 | 15 | 81 | 22 | 168 | 28 | 73 | 12 | 79 | 35 |
| November | 283 | 25 | 85 | 5 | 43* | 24 | 185 | 16 | 73 | 15 | 107 | 34 |
| December | 100 | 12 | 100 | 13 | 100 | 29 | 100 | 18 | 100 | 9 | 100 | 56 |
| Actual rate in base month | 0.47 | | 3.26 | | 1.91 | | 1.55 | | 2.11 | | 2.41 | |

*Notes:* ***Significantly different from the base month at 1 percent level. **Significantly different from the base month mean at 5 percent level. *Significantly different from the base month mean at 20 percent level.

*Source:* Slave-ship data set.

variations seems to lie in the harvest and rainfall patterns of major African provenance zones. The months with highest mortality—statistically significant in all cases at the 7 percent or lower levels—coincide either with the planting period or the period of most intense rain. Indeed although both the historical record and modern medical knowledge make it clear that Europeans did not die for the same reasons as Africans on the African littoral, there was, nevertheless, a very pronounced and rather similar mortality cycle during the year for both races. "African" factors thus do appear to be rather important in explaining mortality differentials between regions as well as over time. Such factors may also play a role in accounting for differences between slave-trade mortality and deaths in other long distance traffic.[3]

APPENDIX E

# Costs and Profits in the Illegal Slave Trade

The costs of carrying on the business of slave trading in the period before abolition have been the subject of extensive discussion.[1] For the years after the British began to exert pressure, however, there are only the sometimes wild estimates of contemporary abolitionists who were usually seeking to magnify profits in an effort to dramatize the evils of the trade. Captured documents and the correspondence of British officials do, however, make possible the reconstruction of slave-trading costs on a more objective basis. Although the details in the reconstructed accounts presented here might be criticized, it should be remembered that the major parameters involved such as slave prices, ship size and cost, cargo size, shipboard mortality, voyage length and bribes are well grounded in documentary evidence.

The breakdown presented was first developed by a contemporary abolitionist, David Turnbull, and was subsequently elaborated by E. Phillip LeVeen in a 1971 thesis.[2] Turnbull pointed out four separate functions in moving a slave from Africa to the Americas: acquisition and transportation to the coast, which he called African cost; bulking at or near the point of embarkation, which he called factor cost; transatlantic transportation, or shipping cost, and marketing in the New World, or distribution cost. As noted in chapter 8, the major parameters in the trade were affected by international efforts to suppress the trade, in particular British efforts. Key initiatives were the 1835 Anglo-Spanish convention, the 1839 and 1845 British Acts of Parliament and the 1845 Spanish penal law, which would probably not have been implemented without British pressure. None of these ended the trade, but all of them induced adjustments in slave-trader tactics. In addition, there were changes in slave prices during the nineteenth century that had as much to do with changing demand for plantation produce as with suppression. Slave prices everywhere in the Western Hemisphere rose strongly after 1855, for example. To accommodate these changes the reconstructed accounts are arranged in ten-year groupings,

though because of the limitations of the data not all years and routes are covered. The Cuban traffic for 1826–35, 1836–65 is represented, and this covers
80 percent of the slaves imported into Cuba after 1820. For the Brazil South
region, accounts for 1831–40 and 1841–50 cover almost all of the traffic carried
on there after formal abolition. The traffic to the French Americas and, more
important, to Bahia and Brazil North is not represented on account of lack of
data on slave prices, though it is worth noting that imports into these areas
collectively comprised only one third of total imports into the Americas after
1820.

African cost may be dealt with quickly. Enslavement and transportation
were the major elements involved in selling an individual to a factory on the
African coast, and if we follow Curtin's analysis, transportation was the more
important of the two.[3] Both together, however, had never formed a major part
of the final selling price in the Americas. That the price fluctuated cannot be
doubted; slaves might be by-products of wars or famine and abolition came
fitfully to different parts of the African littoral. It is unlikely that suppression
would have much effect on the costs of enslavement.

Descriptions of factoring operations in the nineteenth century are not
numerous and are frequently complicated by the question of how far inland
the factor's operations extended. Thus in Senegambia, the factor markup—or
the difference between the price paid by the factor to the African supplier and
that received when he resold the slave to the ship—varied according to where
the initial purchase occurred.[4] The strict definition of the factor function
excludes the transportation operation. Efik traders in the late 1820s typically
had a mark up of 67 percent on prices paid by the ship, but this included more
than mere factoring.[5] Similarly, in the revived French trade in "apprentices"
in the 1840s the Galam Company was buying slaves up the Casamance River
for $30 and selling them at Gorée and Senegal for shipping to the French col-
onies at $60,[6] clearly allowing for some transportation cost. The caravan that
arrived at John Ormond's factory in the Rio Pongo in 1826 received $40 each
for forty slaves of varying quality at a time when the price to slave ships was
$65–$70 according to Conneau. Conneau himself the following year received
26 percent of the ship price for what was to a large extent no more than a
brokerage operation.[7] When firms began to place their own agents on the coast,
a first-rate factor such as Pedro Blanco, before he started his own firm, received
4 percent of the gross sale price in Havana as remuneration, amounting to
about 25 percent of the price on the African coast.[8] Maintenance of the factory
and the wages of subordinate personnel were extra as was the cost of allowing
the factors (in the Brazilian traffic other personnel, also) to place a few slaves
in the firm's ships on their own account. Even so, it is hard to see that commission, profits on a few slaves and wages and maintenance costs combined
totaled more than 40 percent of prices paid by the ship.

There is no doubt that the factor cost proportion of the African price was
higher than it had been in the late eighteenth century: On the basis of the Rogers and Davenport papers, LeVeen suggests a markup of 20 percent fob in the
1790s.[9] But not much of the difference was due to suppression. In the 1790s
much of the factoring function was performed by the slave-ship captain; shor

establishments were limited in scale and some transactions were made directly between African supplier and slave-ship captain, sometimes upriver. Thus the factor cost was not so much lower as it was partially absorbed in shipping costs. In an earlier period, when the great chartered companies were still active, a situation analogous to the 1830s existed, with shore establishments of some size and slave ships restricted to providing, in effect, only a transatlantic transportation service. For the Compagnie des Indes and the Royal African Company in mid–eighteenth-century Senegambia, Curtin found factor costs of around 40 percent.[10]

The major change in factor costs occurred in the later 1830s. The time that slave ships spent on the African coast dropped dramatically from this point, and shortly afterwards the size of the average cargo began to increase steadily and permanently (tables 5 and 7). As described in chapters 8 and 9, factors were now keeping large inventories of slaves on hand at variable locations who had to be embarked quickly at short notice. In Luanda in the 1840s and Lagos in the 1860s, Africans destined for the Americas were often separated into small groups and disguised as domestic slaves in houses around the town to aid concealment.[11] Factors were also often responsible for holding and even manufacturing essential slave-shipping equipment. In the two regions where the slave trade survived the longest, the Bight of Benin and the Congo River, slave prices fob increased in the 1850s, but the price paid to the African supplier either decreased or remained constant. By the end of the traffic, factor cost was certainly amounting to as much as the African cost.[12] The outcome of this discussion is that factor costs are taken as 40 percent of prices in Africa in the decades 1826–35 and 1831–40 and 50 percent in the following decades. African cost accounted for the balance of the price.

Shipping operations, the third and largest of Turnbull's four cost categories, should have been affected most by the suppression policy. As we have seen, the various policing authorities, mainly British, detained and usually destroyed an average of more than one slave ship every two weeks throughout the last half century of the trade. The ship and crew size, the number of slaves embarked and lost during the voyage and the length of both the round-trip and the middle passage are all readily available from the slave-ship data set and have been extensively discussed in chapter 8. Table E.1 arranges both shipping and slave price data into the decadal periods used in the reconstruction of slave-trading accounts. Table E.2 presents the actual accounts themselves—one for each region of disembarkation and decade covered. Most of the data are taken from table E.1, but some require separate discussion. The ship-construction-cost figure is based on an estimate made by the British consul in Baltimore on the instructions of the Foreign Office. Consul McTavish estimated the cost of a clipper in 1840 at $7,000 to $10,000 or from $40 to $60 per ton.[13] In the early years of the illicit trade, slave ships were built primarily in Brazil or the Iberian Peninsula. The Americas became more important as a source in the 1820s. After the 1835 treaty in the Cuban traffic and the 1839 act in the Brazilian trade, U.S.-built ships increasingly displaced Spanish and Portuguese slavers.[14] The reason for this was partly the quality and cost advantages of the U.S. ships, but also significant was the fact that a U.S. register offered protec-

**Table E.1.** Shipping and Cargo Characteristics of the Transatlantic Slave Trade by Selected Decades and Regions of Disembarkation, 1826–65

| | Cuba | | | Brazil South | |
| --- | --- | --- | --- | --- | --- |
| | 1826–35 | 1836–45 | 1856–65 | 1831–40 | 1841–50 |
| Slaves embarked | 350 (110) | 374 (92) | 649 (60) | 537 (333)[a] | 589 (332)[a] |
| Slaves per ton | 2.15 (47) | 2.78 (59) | 2.30 (48) | 3.27(175)[a] | 3.01 (100)[a] |
| Tons per crew | 5.8 (52) | 6.1 (152) | 16.5 (81) | 11.7 (127) | 11.8 (194) |
| Mortality rate | 0.163 (35) | 0.169 (38) | 0.209 (31) | 0.192(14) | 0.182 (24) |
| Tonnage (inferred)[b] | 163 | 135 | 282 | 164 | 196 |
| Crew[c] | 28 | 22 | 17 | 14 | 17 |
| Voyage length (days) | 52 (21) | | 48 (18) | 42 (59) | 35 (11) |
| Round trip (months) | 7.3 (212) | 7.3 (78) | 5.0 (23) | 7.1 (45) | 3.6 (5) |
| $ Price of slave (fob, Africa) | 50.6 (15) | 44.2 (28) | 38.1 (33) | 39.3 (10) | 37.6 (9) |
| $ Price of slave | 281.7 (7) | 303.5 (42) | 753.9 (30) | 159.7 (22) | 209 (50) |
| Loss ratio | 0.219 | 0.236 | 0.228 | 0.067 | 0.184 |

*Notes:* [a]Slaves disembarked with an allowance for losses in transit. [b]Row 1/Row 2. [c]Row 5/Row 3. Numbers of observation are in parentheses.

*Source:* Slave-ship data set; Table C.1.

tion against British interference. Under American law only U.S.-built ships were entitled to U.S. registers. The relative importance of these two factors in the rise of U.S. ships in the slave trade is not clear. In the last twenty years of the trade, a count of 136 ships for which information on place of construction can be found indicates that 64 percent were built in the United States, 13 percent in Spain (mainly Barcelona) and 8 percent each in Brazil and Portugal, mainly in Rio de Janeiro and Oporto, respectively. The predominance of the U.S.-built vessel, though not its monopoly, seems fairly well established and the McTavish range is acceptable. As Baltimore costs were somewhat higher than those in other shipbuilding regions in the United States and as McTavish's counterpart in Oporto was convinced that slave ships could be built in Portugal for less than in the United States, the figure of $40 per ton— the low end of the range—is used for all five of the decades for which calculations are attempted. As with the slave price data, these costs are expressed in terms of 1821–25 prices.[15]

Apart from adjustments for price changes, however, some allowance has to be made for steam-powered slave ships, which were a much more costly proposition. The *Serpente* was built at Rio de Janeiro in 1848 for $110,000 and the Glasgow-built *Ciceron,* which plied the Cuba/Bight of Benin route in the 1860s—and was reputedly capable of sixteen knots—cost $75,000. Such ships appeared late in the trade and were never numerous.[16] The first recorded steam slaver was the *Cacique* captured off Cabinda in September 1845. Capture lists suggest that less than 5 percent of the vessels in the Brazil South trade were steam powered in the late 1840s, and such vessels never made an appearan

**Table E.2.** Slave-Trade Costs, 1826–65 (in constant dollars, 1821–25 = 100)

**(a) Cuba 1826–35**

*Shipping Costs*

Ship: 163 tons at $38.4 per ton ($6,259)

| | |
|---|---:|
| Depreciation at 7 percent per trip | $ 438 |
| Outfit | 7,824 |

*Labor:*

| | |
|---|---:|
| Wages—24 sailors at $37 per month and 4 officers at $74 for 7.3 months | 8,643 |
| Commissions and privileges at 5 percent | 4,127 |

*Other:*

| | |
|---|---:|
| Food for 350 slaves at 5.2¢ per day for 52 days | 946 |
| Food for crew at $87 per month | 638 |
| Mortality at 16.3 percent (57 slaves, $51) | 2,907 |
| Insurance at 28 percent | |
|     Ship and outfit at $14,083 | 3,943 |
|     Cargo and stores at $20,907 | 5,854 |
| Miscellaneous expenses | 1,613 |
| **Total shipping costs** | **36,933** |

*Distribution Costs*

| | |
|---|---:|
| Selling commissions at 7 percent of final sale price | $ 5,778 |
| Bribes at $25 per slave | 7,325 |
| Coastal transportation and maintenance at $5 per slave | 1,465 |
| **Total distribution costs** | **14,568** |
| Shipping cost per slave | $126.1 |
| Distribution cost per slave | 49.7 |
| Capital outlay per slave | |
|     (ship and outfit, cargo and insurance) | 152.9 |
| Capital risked per slave (insurance) | 35.3 |

**(b) Cuba 1836–45**

*Shipping Costs*

Ship: 135 tons at $38.4 per ton ($5,184)

| | |
|---|---:|
| Depreciation at 7 percent per trip | $ 363 |
| Outfit | 6,480 |

*Labor:*

| | |
|---|---:|
| Wages—18 sailors at $37 per month and 4 officers at $74 for 7.3 months | 7,023 |
| Commissions and privileges at 5 percent | 4,719 |

*Other:*

| | |
|---|---:|
| Food for 374 slaves at 7.3¢ per day for 52 days | 1,419 |
| Food for crew at $69 per month | 504 |
| Mortality at 16.9 percent (63 slaves, $44.2) | 2,785 |
| Insurance at 30 percent | |
|     Ship and outfit at $11,664 | 3,499 |
|     Cargo and stores at $20,067 | 6,020 |
| Freight for trading cargo | 6,551 |
| Ship's papers | 1,638 |
| Miscellaneous expenses | 1,613 |
| **Total shipping costs** | **42,614** |

*Distribution Costs*

| | |
|---|---:|
| Selling commissions at 7 percent of final sale price | $6,607 |
| Bribes at $25 per slave | 7,775 |
| Coastal transportation and maintenance at $8 per slave | 2,488 |
| **Total distribution costs** | **16,870** |

**Table E.2.** *(Continued)*

*Distribution Costs*

| | |
|---|---:|
| Shipping cost per slave | $137.0 |
| Distribution cost per slave | 54.2 |
| Capital outlay per slave | |
| (ship and outfit, cargo, insurance, ship's papers and outward freight) | 159.0 |
| Capital risked per slave (insurance, ship's papers, and outward freight) | 56.9 |

**(c) Cuba 1856–65**

*Shipping Costs*

*Ship:* 282 tons at $57.6 per ton ($16,243)

| | |
|---|---:|
| Depreciation at 40 percent per trip | $ 6,497 |
| Outfit | 20,304 |

*Labor:*

| | |
|---|---:|
| Wages—13 sailors at $50 per month and 4 officers at $92 for 5.0 months | 5,090 |
| Commissions and privileges at 5 percent | 17,792 |

*Other:*

| | |
|---|---:|
| Food for 649 slaves at 7.3¢ per day for 48 days | 2,274 |
| Food for crew at $165 per month | 265 |
| Mortality at 20.9 percent (136 slaves, $38.1) | 5,182 |
| Insurance at 29 percent | |
| Ship and outfit at $36,547 | 10,599 |
| Cargo and stores at $28,814 | 8,356 |
| Freight for trading cargo | 9,827 |
| Bribes for clearing out | 5,149 |
| Ship's papers and flag captains | 1,638 |
| Miscellaneous expenses | 1,613 |
| **Total shipping costs** | **94,586** |

*Distribution Costs*

| | |
|---|---:|
| Selling commissions on 472 slaves at 7 percent of final sale price | $24,909 |
| Slaves captured by Cuban authorities (41 at $ 38.1) | 1,562 |
| Bribes at $136 per slave (472 slaves) | 64,192 |
| Coastal transportation and maintenance at $16 per slave (513 slaves) | 8,208 |
| **Total distribution costs** | **98,871** |
| Shipping cost per slave | $ 200.4 |
| Distribution cost per slave | 209.5 |
| Capital outlay per slave | |
| (ship and outfit, cargo, insurance, bribes for clearing out, ship's papers and outbound freight) | 213.8 |
| Capital risked per slave (insurance, ship's papers, outward freight and bribes for clearing out) | 75.4 |

**(d) Brazil South 1831–40**

*Shipping Costs*

*Ship:* 164 tons at $38.5 per ton ($6,314)

| | |
|---|---:|
| Depreciation at 7 percent per trip | $ 442 |
| Outfit | 7,893 |

*Labor:*

| | |
|---|---:|
| Wages—10 sailors at $23 per month and 4 officers at $46 for 7.1 months | 2,939 |
| Commissions and privileges at 5 percent | 3,212 |

*Costs and Profits in the Illegal Slave Trade*

**Other:**

| | |
|---|---:|
| Food for 537 slaves at 5.2¢ per day for 42 days | 1,173 |
| Food for crew at $44 per month | 312 |
| Mortality at 19.2 percent (103 slaves, $39.3) | 4,048 |
| Insurance at 13 percent | |
|     Ship and outfit at $14,207 | 1,847 |
|     Cargo and stores at $25,864 | 3,362 |
| Miscellaneous expenses | 3,275 |
| **Total shipping costs** | **28,503** |

*Distribution Costs*

| | |
|---|---:|
| Selling commissions at 7 percent of final sale price | $ 4,852 |
| Bribes at $15.2 per slave | 6,597 |
| Coastal transportation and maintenance at $5 per slave | 2,170 |
| **Total distribution costs** | **13,619** |
| Shipping cost per slave | $65.7 |
| Distribution cost per slave | 31.4 |
| Capital outlay per slave | |
| (ship and outfit, cargo, insurance and miscellaneous expense) | 104.3 |
| Capital risked per slave (insurance) | 12.0 |

### (e) Brazil South 1841–50

*Shipping Costs*

*Ship:* 196 tons at $42.2 per ton ($8,271)

| | |
|---|---:|
| Depreciation at 7 percent per trip | $ 579 |
| Outfit | 10,339 |

*Labor:*

| | |
|---|---:|
| Wages—13 sailors at $23 per month and 4 officers at $46 for 3.6 months | 1,739 |
| Commissions and privileges at 5 percent | 5,037 |

*Other:*

| | |
|---|---:|
| Food for 589 slaves at 7.3¢ per day for 35 days | 1,505 |
| Food for crew at $53 per month | 191 |
| Mortality at 18.2 percent (107 slaves, $37.6) | 4,023 |
| Insurance at 24 percent | |
|     Ship and outfit at $18,610 | 4,466 |
|     Cargo and stores at $27,117 | 6,508 |
| Freight for trading cargo | 4,376 |
| Miscellaneous expenses | 3,275 |
| **Total shipping costs** | **42,038** |

*Distribution Costs*

| | |
|---|---:|
| Selling commissions at 7 percent of final sale price | $ 7,052 |
| Bribes at $15.2 per slave | 7,326 |
| Coastal transportation and maintenance at $8 per slave | 3,856 |
| **Total distribution costs** | **18,234** |
| Shipping cost per slave | $87.2 |
| Distribution cost per slave | 37.8 |
| Capital outlay per slave | |
| (ship and outfit, cargo, outbound freight and insurance) | 126.7 |
| Capital risked per slave (insurance freight) | 31.8 |

*Sources: Shipping costs.* For tonnages of slave ships, numbers of slaves carried, crew, mortality, price of slaves, voyage lengths and insurance costs see Table E.1. Depreciation and outfitting costs are based on

**Table E. 2.** (*Continued*)

LeVeen's research into the late eighteenth-century trade (E. Phillip LeVeen, *British Slave Trade Suppression Policies, 1821–1865* (New York, 1977) p. 94) except that depreciation has been increased slightly on the assumption that piracy and the navy increased the wear and tear to which the nineteenth-century slaver was subjected. The cost of the outbound cargo is derived from the average number of slaves embarked (slaves disembarked plus deaths in transit) multiplied by prices on the African coast plus the costs of food and miscellaneous expenses, which were paid for out of the cargo. Freight for the trading cargo in parts (b), (c) and (d) is from Admiralty to Palmerston, Sept. 23, 1841 (enc.), FO 84/385; W. G. Ouseley to Palmerston, Mar. 13, 1841, FO 84/364; H. W. Macaulay and R. Doherty to Palmerston, Dec. 15, 1838 (enc.) FO 84/237; Admiralty to Palmerston, June 8, 1841 (enc.), FO 84/384. Miscellaneous expenses included the duty paid to the African ruler, unloading charges in Africa and from the late 1830s the costs of registering the ship in a foreign flag—and in Angola bribes to the Portuguese authorities. For these costs, see W. Macleay to Backhouse, July 21, 1829 (enc.) FO 84/100; H. W. Macaulay, Apr. 26, 1837 (enc.) FO 84/211; J. Campbell and W. W. Lewis to Palmerston, Jan. 6, 1837, FO 84/212; H. Hamilton, Nov. 24, 1842 (sub enc.), FO 84/442. For other costs see text.

*Distribution costs.* In addition to those sources cited in the text, see Col. Off. to Palmerston, Sept. 22, 1836 (enc.), "A few cursory remarks on the present state of the slave trade in the Spanish islands," July 14, 1836, FO 84/209; W. Macleay to Palmerston, Jan. 1, 1831 (enc.) FO 84/118; J. Parkinson to Palmerston, Dec. 10, 1834, FO 84/157; May 29, 1835, FO 84/180; J. Samo and F. Grigg, Jan. 5, 1843, FO 84/453; W. Cole and H. W. Macaulay to Palmerston, June 5, 1835, enc. B. Campbell to Sierra Leone Commissioners, Jan. 5, 1835, FO 84/166. A Puerto Rican official stated under oath in 1838 that Cuban officials were receiving a total of $30 per slave landed (Fernando Ortiz, *Hampa afro cubana: los negros esclavos* [Havana, 1916], p. 162).

in the Bahian traffic where yachtlike vessels, often built in Oporto, tended to predominate in the last decade before suppression.[17] Steamers did not appear in the Cuban traffic until the late 1850s and were common only in the rather minor Bight of Benin traffic where winds tended to be light.[18] An increase in cost per ton of perhaps 10 percent on the Brazil South traffic between 1841–50 and 50 percent in the last decade of the Cuban trade would probably be adequate to reflect the impact of steam power on mean costs of building a slave ship.

There is little hard information on depreciation in the illegal trade. In the last years of the English trade, LeVeen calculated a rate of 4 percent from surviving accounts. Vessels built for speed were often less durable, however, and although ships making half a dozen trips were common, no instances of slavers making twenty or more voyages have been found. It is intuitively reasonable that wear and tear on hulls would be greater under conditions of attempted suppression.[19] A rate of 7 percent is assigned for all accounts except for the final decade of the Cuban trade. In these years owners began to sink or burn vessels that had disembarked slaves in order to conceal evidence of the voyage. After 1855 there are records of 134 vessels that landed slaves and were then reused or resold compared to 25 that were destroyed by the owner after successful completion of the voyage. Those that were destroyed were perhaps less likely to come to the attention of the Foreign Office and, making some allowance for these unknowns as well as normal risks, suggests a figure of 40 percent for this last decade. The final item in ship costs is the outfit, which included sails, rigging, slave decks, bailers and other equipment that for most long-distance trade amounted to 75 percent of hull costs but for the late eighteenth-century English slave trade has been calculated at 125 percent.[20] This ratio has been accepted for the illicit nineteenth-century traffic, though it is possible that the more sophisticated rigging of the clipper ships entailed a higher ratio.

Labor costs were a further major cost to the slave trader. The articles or muster rolls of ten ships in the Cuban traffic between 1820 and 1839 list wages for sailors of $25 to $40 a month, a range supported by considerable court evidence. Data on sixteen ships leaving Bahia and Rio de Janeiro in the 1840s indicate lower wages than in the Cuban trade. In the later years of the traffic, wages were generally higher. Two ships from the small post-1862 traffic (when Nathanial Gordon was executed for slave trading in the United States) paid $50 a month plus performance bonuses.[21] Commission rates for captains were normally 5 percent and when they were lower than this (as occasionally in the Brazilian trade), the masters and other officers were allowed to carry slaves on their own account.[22] As with ship costs, labor costs are expressed in terms of 1821–25 dollars. Crew size and round-trip voyage time, both of which are needed for the calculation of the wage bill, are taken from the slave-ship data set and table E.1.

We turn next to Other Shipping Costs. Provisions for the slaves were purchased on the African coast in the first decades of the illicit traffic. Rice in the Upper Guinea region, yams and cassava flour (termed farinha) in the bights and farinha in west-central and southeast Africa; these were supplemented with calavances (chick-peas) and some salted provisions. Before the 1840s, major provisioning centers existed on the islands off the African coast, at Grand Popo, Nunez and adjacent rivers, some Gold Coast ports and Ambriz. In the 1840s and later, however, slave ships captured on their way to Africa typically carried provisions.[23] These were not specified as grounds for detention under the slave-trade treaties. Yams disappeared from the slave diet as the traffic to the Bight of Biafra fell away, and after the Brazilian traffic closed, farinha, too, was replaced by rice. The carrying of provisions from the Americas was probably dictated by suppressive measures: A slave ship already provisioned before arrival off Africa would have more flexibility on the coast in avoiding cruisers. But there is also the possibility of food scarcity in Africa in these years making provisions harder to obtain; this could have been reflected in the higher shipboard mortality rates discussed earlier. Before 1840, a price of 5¢ a day per slave is set (in 1821–25 prices). This was the provisioning allowance for liberated Africans at Sierra Leone in the late 1820s during the six months they were supported by the British government after disembarking from captured slave ships.[24] After 1840 (1835 for Cuban-bound ships) the tactic of shipping provisions from the Americas is reflected in an increase in this rate to 7¢ per day.[25] Crew provisioning is taken at three times the daily rate of slave provisioning prior to 1840.

The important insurance-rate variable is simply the decadal mean loss ratio derived from figure 5, with the addition of 6 percentage points for hazards that were not associated with the British squadron's activities. Actual observations of insurance rates for Cuban slavers provide support for this approach. Insurance costs during the illegal slave trade varied enormously. In the Cuban traffic between 1821 and 1836, rates were normally 15 to 30 percent of total outset costs. In the later 1830s only ships under the Portuguese flag could get insurance, and rates of up to 40 percent were cited.[26] In the last decade of the traffic there is no evidence of insurance coverage for slave ships on the return voyage as opposed to the outbound leg, but the loss ratio plus 6 percent continues to be included on the grounds that losses would be absorbed by the slave traders themselves. This facilitates comparison of costs between periods without biasing the profit and rate of return calculated below. For the Brazilian traffic in the first decade or so after total abolition, rates were lower—11 percent to 15 percent, though in 1813 and 1816 when the navy was capturing Bahian ships somewhat indiscriminately, rates were temporarily in the 30 percent to 40 percent range. In the later 1830s, however, contracts began to include a variety of different clauses, and rates varied erratically. In some cases, only a portion of the voyage could be insured, in others contracts were written on the ship but not on the cargo. Rates of up to 50 percent were quoted in Rio de Janeiro.[27] Nevertheless, the generally lower rates in Brazil South during the 1830s do receive independent support from contemporary observers. In the accounts presented in table E.2 the insurance rate is applied first to the cost of the ship and outfit and second to the cost of the outbound cargo and stores. The full insurance cost of the venture is the sum of these two. The outbound cargo cost is taken as the product of the number of slaves embarked and the fob African slave price plus the costs of food and miscellaneous expenses in Africa paid for out of the cargo. These latter included the duty paid to the African ruler, unloading charges and, in Angola, bribes to the Portuguese authorities.[28]

The final shipping costs listed here apply only after 1835 in the Cuban traffic and 1840 in the trade to Brazil South. The 1835 Anglo-Spanish treaty and the 1839 British Act of Parliament encouraged a switch to Portuguese and U.S. registers, respectively, which usually cost in excess of $1,000. These measures also began the practice of dispatching the outbound cargo in a separate ship. Freight costs for this cargo thereupon became a separate expense.[29]

Distribution costs, often underestimated in the literature, were a further major expense, especially in Cuba. Selling commissions were always a major item. Although a few traders stocked their own plantations with the slaves they brought over, most *bozales* in Brazil and Cuba of this period were sold alongside Creole slaves in the open market. In Bahia in the late 1840s the normal rate was 5 percent of the final selling price; in the late eighteenth-century British Caribbean rates of 5 percent to 10 percent were common.[30] Hard data on the equivalent rates in Cuba and Rio de Janeiro are lacking, but distribution was always subject to greater interruption by the authorities in these regions, and a rate of 7 percent is adopted for both these importing areas in all the years covered by the accounts. Bribes to the authorities of the importing country varied considerably and eventually became an even more important item than selling commissions. Indeed the amount per slave paid in Cuba in the early 1860s would have almost purchased a slave outright in Rio de Janeiro a generation earlier. In Brazil in the 1830s and 1840s the bribe was about the same as the duty levied before the trade became illegal.[31] Antislave-trade ministries did hold power from time to time in Brazil and not all Cuban captains-general accepted bribes. But in any event, illegally imported slaves were normally landed outside the main ports and the magistrates and local authorities were as important as the central government to the slave trader. Bribes to the local police tended to rise when the central authorities applied pressure so that the accession of an antislave-trade ministry often affected the distribution of bribes rather than their size—at least in the short run.[32] Nevertheless, in Cuba after 1845 the penal law and firmer central government intiatives tripled the going rate. A registration system for all slaves in Cuba was part of further pressure on importers in the 1850s.[33]

Two further distribution costs should be mentioned. The coastal shipping-costs item attempts to allow for the transportation of slaves to main marketing centers from the more remote part of the coast where they were typically deposited by the transatlantic carrier. In Bahia in the late 1840s these costs averaged nearly $8 per slave in 1821–25 prices for ten different groups of slaves.[34] This figure is accepted for Cuba between 1836 and 1845 and for Rio de Janeiro 1841 to 1850. Before 1836 in Cuba and 1841 in Brazil South, Africans were disembarked somewhat closer to the slave markets, whereas after 1855 landings in extremely remote parts of Cuba were common. Coastal transportation costs have thus been reduced by just over one third in the first case and doubled in the second to reflect these changed circumstances. During the final years of the Cuban trade, an additional distribution cost appeared as the Cuban authorities began to detain cargoes, or more often part cargoes, after they had been disembarked. Very occasional captures had been made during the 1840s, but between 1856 and 1865 the Cubans captured an average of 8 percent of newly arrived shipments within a few days of disembarkation.[35] Detainees were often Africans who would have fetched a below average price on the open market—the young, the female and the sick—but the loss is taken here simply as the price of the average slave in Africa. Finally it might be noted that one distribution cost not included here is credit costs, which all transatlantic traders had to face. The explanation is simply that the selling price of the slaves in the Americas taken from appendix C is net of credit costs.

Drawing up hypothetical accounts of an illicit slaving voyage was a popular activity among contemporary observers. Few abolitionist and naval officers who wrote about the slave trade could resist the temptation to publicize the enormous profits of the illicit traffic. Two of the more careful and less publicized estimates of slave traders' outlays lend broad support to the reconstructed accounts in table E.2, at least for Cuba. In 1825 the British commissioner in Havana estimated capital costs at $40,000 for the average expedition, and the Havana merchant that Richard Madden questioned a few years later came up with the same figure.[36] Table E.2 yields capital outlays of 20 percent higher than this, but the variation of the size of expeditions was considerable and in this context it is the similarity of the estimates rather than the difference that is striking.

We can now summarize the above discussion of costs before calculating profits and rates of return. Table E.3 gives costs per slave for each of the four broad categories. The structure of this table as well as the following procedures for deriving profits are taken from LeVeen.[37] Shipping and distribution costs are taken from table E.2 and African and factor costs are simply the price paid by the ship on the coast broken down in the proportions already discussed. The

**Table E.3.** Summary of Supply Cost Data (per Slave) in the Nineteenth Century Slave Trade, Selected Regions and Decades (in constant dollars, 1821–25 = 100)

| Period | Importing Region | African Cost | Factor Cost | Shipping Cost | Distribution Cost | Profit | Market Price |
|--------|-----------------|-------------|-------------|---------------|-------------------|--------|--------------|
| 1826–35 | Cuba | 30.4 | 20.2 | 126.1 | 49.7 | 55.3 | 281.7 |
| 1836–45 | Cuba | 22.1 | 22.1 | 137.0 | 54.2 | 68.1 | 303.5 |
| 1856–65 | Cuba | 19.1 | 19.1 | 200.4 | 209.5 | 305.8 | 753.9 |
| 1831–40 | Brazil South | 19.7 | 19.7 | 65.7 | 31.4 | 23.2 | 159.7 |
| 1841–50 | Brazil South | 18.8 | 18.8 | 87.2 | 37.8 | 46.4 | 209.0 |

*Sources:* See table E.2 and text. Structure adopted from Phillip E. LeVeen, *British Slave Trade Suppression Policies, 1821–1865* (New York, 1977), p. 10.

final column is the price of the slave in the Americas and the data for this as well as slave prices on the African coast are examined in appendix C. Profits are shown in column 5. They are calculated by subtracting the sum of the first four columns from the price of the slave in the Americas. As we can see, shipping costs made up somewhat less than half of the total cost of the slave in the Americas. This ratio receives some independent support from the fact that the standard charge for freighting a slave across the Atlantic in the 1820s and 1830s was 50 percent of the final selling price on the Cuban route and 33.3 percent on the Rio de Janeiro branch.[38]

The profits' residual in table E.3 is for each slave successfully landed, but the profitability of the slave trade like any other activity is determined by the return on capital invested. Table E.4 shows the derivation of this rate. It adjusts the profits per slave data in table E.3 for losses from all sources as indicated by the insurance rate in table E.2, and expresses this adjusted profit as a percentage of capital per slave invested, also taken from table E.2.

Table E.4 indicates that after allowing for losses, profits before 1850 were in the 20 percent range in the two major branches of the illegal slave trade. Although these rates are high compared to contemporary returns on alternative investments, particularly when we remember that the average time period involved was less than a year, they are much below those calculated by nineteenth-century abolitionists. The most influential treatment of the subject published in 1839 contained estimates of 180 percent; and although these figures were severely criticized by Foreign Office observers, nevertheless they became widely accepted.[39] Modern estimates have tended to yield lower figures, mainly because most have recognized that the price of the average slave was below that of the prime male and that selling commissions, mortality and coastal transportation were all significant costs.[40]

There is no doubt that even after allowing for losses inflicted by the navy, the trade was very profitable by the standards of eighteenth-century returns to investors. It is possible that costs in the hypothetical accounts have been underestimated, but it seems more likely that the high returns are explained by the considerable increase in variance in yields from the illegal traffic as opposed to the legal traffic. According to one merchant[41] slave mortality and market fluctuations as well as captures made the Cuban traffic "a species of gambling

**Table E.4.** Summary of Rate-of-Return Data (per Slave) in the Nineteenth-Century Slave Trade Selected Regions and Decades, (in constant dollars, 1821–25 = 100)

| Period | Importing Region | (1) Profit | (2) Capital Outlay | (3) Col. 1 ÷ Col. 2 | (4) Capital Risked | (5) Probability of Loss | (6) Expected Profit | (7) Col. 6 ÷ Col. 2 |
|--------|------------------|-----------|--------------------|--------------------|--------------------|------------------------|---------------------|---------------------|
| 1826–35 | Cuba | $ 55.3 | $152.9 | 36.2% | $35.3 | 28% | $ 29.9 | 19.6% |
| 1836–45 | Cuba | 68.1 | 159.0 | 42.8 | 56.9 | 30 | 30.6 | 19.2 |
| 1856–65 | Cuba | 305.8 | 213.8 | 143.0 | 75.4 | 29 | 195.3 | 91.3 |
| 1831–40 | Brazil South | 23.2 | 104.3 | 22.2 | 12.0 | 13 | 18.6 | 17.8 |
| 1841–50 | Brazil South | 46.4 | 126.7 | 36.6 | 31.8 | 24 | 27.6 | 21.8 |

*Sources:* Column 1: table E.3; Column 2: ship, outfit, insurance, cargo and freight costs per slave are calculated from tables E.2 and E.3; Column 4: insurance costs calculated from table E.2; Column 5: see text; Column 6: col. 6 = (col. 1 × [1 − col. 5]) − (col. 5 × col. 4). Procedures are adopted from Phillip E. LeVeen, *British Slave Trade Suppression Policies, 1821–1865* (New York, 1977), p. 23.

281

that generated instances of great wealth as well as many failures. The *Firme de Cádiz* returned $94,000 on a $40,000 investment in six months. The *Fama de Cádiz,* on the other hand, pirated a total of 980 slaves off the African coast and experienced a smallpox outbreak on the return trip that wiped out over two thirds of the slaves and crew. The owners sold the surviving 300 slaves for less than $100 each.[42] The cruiser squadron obviously contributed to this variance but a further factor was the unreliable attitude of the government authorities of importing regions. In Brazil in the few years after 1830 and in Cuba at times even before the 1845 penal law, the uncertain official attitude toward slave imports certainly increased the perceived variance of returns and thereby increased profits. It is very difficult to separate the impact of the navy on profits from that of the local authorities. However, it is argued elsewhere that local initiatives to suppress the trade, when they occurred, were largely due to British pressure—though diplomatic rather than naval. The whole of the impact on profits might thus be assigned to British abolitionism and the proportion of this due to the navy might be of interest mainly to naval historians.

Profit rates in the last years of the Cuban trade finally did approach the levels imagined since 1807 by the abolitionists. Indeed if we allow for the shorter voyage times after 1855, the increase in profits on an annual basis is even greater than the figures in table E.4 indicate. It might be noted, however, that as the volume of the trade was much lower in these years, gross profits would not have increased in proportion. As losses inflicted by the navy did not change much in this period compared to the pre-1850s, the reason for this increase lies mainly with the local authorities. Increased zeal by the Cuban authorities had two effects. Slave traders experienced increased personal risk as well as increased variance in financial returns. In addition, as total suppression became a real possibility, all slave prices increased, yielding an economic rent to the importer of new slaves. A further factor, unrelated to abolition, was the rather sharp increase in demand for slaves experienced everywhere in the Western world in the late 1850s. The implication of this last point is that a part of the increased profits of the last decade could not have endured. Without the firmer suppressive measures of the early 1860s and the increased uncertainty as to the future of slavery generated by the U.S. Civil War, both of which helped bring the trade to a close, such profits would have attracted more investment in the slave trade in the course of the 1860s. It is not possible to separate precisely the effects of these different non-naval influences, but it is clear that collectively they were important. Given the highly elastic supply of world shipping, it is not possible that shipping costs per se could have increased very much in response to the higher demands for labor from Cuban planters after 1855.

# Plantation Output and Productivity Estimates in the Nineteenth-Century Americas

## VOLUME, PRICE, AND TOTAL VALUE

All historians who have worked with nineteenth-century trade statistics in their original form are acutely aware of their shortcomings.[1] Customs authorities often had erratic recording practices, little idea of the extent of smuggling and usually employed "official" rather than "market" values when converting physical quantities into values. The official values often bore no relationship to prices and remained unchanged for decades. For the first two of these problems we can only take refuge in the assumption that all countries were equally susceptible—at least when it comes to international comparison—and the further assumption that smuggling and recording techniques did not change drastically over time.[2] In addition, the Cuban sugar series below is for total output rather than exports. The third problem, official valuations, may be handled by replacing the official values with price series that are available for major trading centers.[3]

### Cuba

Data on the volume of sugar output are available from Moreno Fraginals' work; these have become the standard source since their publication despite the fact that they start only in 1820 and conflict with data in other sources.[4] To convert these into values and at the same time circumvent the official valuation problem we have the choice of using series for the wholesale price of sugar in London, Rio de Janeiro, New York or Philadelphia. As the United States was the largest single national buyer of Cuban sugar and as the freight component of the New York price would be lower than in any of the other series, it is the New York price series that is used here. The latter is however incomplete, covering as it does only the years 1825–61. To extend it to the period

821–65, regressions were run on the Philadelphia price, which is available for 1821–61 and on the London sugar price available for 1814–65.[5] The price series is then expressed in terms of constant dollars of the period 1821–25 with the aid of the Gayer, Rostow and Schwarz price index before 1850 and the Rousseaux index after. The product of the volume of output and the New York price yields a value of output in real terms. This is not, it should be noted, the value of sugar exports. The volume figures are for total production and the price incorporates shipping costs and tariffs. In Puerto Rico, at least, sugar prices were about half those in New York so that the value of sugar exports might be adjusted accordingly.[6] The trend in the value of exports would not however be much different to the series presented in table F.1.

There are no equivalent volume figures for Cuban coffee production. The series that appears most often in the literature is from Pezuela's *Diccionario . . . de la Isla de Cuba* and is purported to be for exports. At least part of the series, however, is taken from de la Sagra, who presents it as export data for Havana alone.[7] This and the considerable consumption of coffee in Cuba would suggest that this series understates total output by at least a fourth and probably more.[8] Price series are available for Rio de Janeiro, Philadelphia and New York, and again the New York series is selected to convert the volume series into a value series. Once more it covers only the years 1825–61 and must be used in conjunction with the other series to fill out the remaining years.[9] As in the case of sugar, prices are converted into constant dollars (1821–25 = 100) before the value series is derived. The results are presented in table F.2.

## Brazil

For Brazil data for all plantation crops after 1820 are available in the *Anuário estatístico do Brasil,* Ano V, 1939–40. The latter provides not only the volume of produce but also average values, used here as a proxy for price, and sterling

**Table F.1.** Quantity, Price and Total Value of Cuban Sugar Output, 1821–65

|  | Total Quantity in Metric Tons ('000) | Mean Price (constant $ per lb) | Mean Annual Value (millions of constant $) |
|---|---|---|---|
| 1821–25 | 63.2 | 0.088 | 12.6 |
| 1826–30 | 84.2 | 0.083 | 15.3 |
| 1831–35 | 101.3 | 0.079 | 17.9 |
| 1836–40 | 129.8 | 0.075 | 20.8 |
| 1841–45 | 170.3 | 0.068 | 25.4 |
| 1846–50 | 253.5 | 0.065 | 35.8 |
| 1851–55 | 389.5 | 0.056 | 47.6 |
| 1856–60 | 435.3 | 0.072 | 69.0 |
| 1861–65 | 501.4 | 0.055 | 68.5 |

*Source:* Column 1: See text, in particular n. 4; Column 2: See text, in particular n. 5; Column 3: Annual quantity × annual price for each quinquennia ÷ 5.

**Table F.2.** Quantity, Price and Total Value of Coffee Exports from Cuba, 1821–65

| | Total Quantity in Metric Tons ('000) | Mean Price (constant $ per lb) | Mean Annual Value (millions of constant $) |
|---|---|---|---|
| 1821–25 | 10.0 | 0.230 | 4.6 |
| 1826–30 | 19.8 | 0.157 | 6.8 |
| 1831–35 | 23.0 | 0.140 | 7.1 |
| 1836–40 | 21.6 | 0.134 | 6.4 |
| 1841–45 | 15.3 | 0.123 | 4.3 |
| 1846–50 | 8.8 | 0.104 | 1.9 |
| 1851–55 | 6.3 | 0.137 | 1.9 |
| 1856–60 | 4.2 | 0.156 | 1.4 |
| 1861–65 | 2.0 | 0.174 | 0.8 |

*Source:* Column 1: See text, in particular n. 7; Column 2: See text, in particular n. 9; Column 3: Annual quantity × annual price for each quinquennia ÷ 5.

value equivalents. It might be noted, however, that the series does not always agree with data for particular years that may be found scattered in the older literature. For example, Simonsen, from whom Deerr took some of his data, provides data for isolated years that differ from the *Anuário estatístico*. The British parliamentary select committee on the sugar industries for 1878–79 also obtained post-1852 data that differ from the latter. For coffee Luís Amaral has also published a different series that yields annual volumes of export that are generally lower than those of the Instituto brasileiro.[10] The latter are nevertheless the most complete available and are used here. Prices are expressed in terms of 1821–25 pounds sterling. A good price index is now available for Brazil, but all values (slaves and exports) are converted into British pounds at exchange rates current at the time. This establishes purchasing power parity between the two currencies and makes reference to a Brazilian price index unnecessary.[11] Tables F.3 to F.5 present the results.

**Table F.3.** Quantity, Price and Total Value of Brazilian Sugar Exports 1821–65

| | Total Quantity in Metric Tons ('000) | Mean Price (constant $ per ton) | Mean Annual Value (millions of constant $) |
|---|---|---|---|
| 1821–25 | 41.2 | 117 | 4.7 |
| 1826–30 | 54.8 | 124.3 | 6.8 |
| 1831–35 | 69.9 | 95.2 | 6.8 |
| 1836–40 | 82.2 | 77.3 | 6.3 |
| 1841–45 | 89.1 | 81.1 | 7.3 |
| 1846–50 | 118.3 | 84.0 | 10.0 |
| 1851–55 | 123.4 | 85.9 | 10.5 |
| 1856–60 | 196.2 | 102.2 | 11.0 |
| 1861–65 | 126.8 | 85.0 | 10.5 |

*Source:* See text, in particular nn. 9 and 10.

**Table F.4.** Quantity, Price and Total Value of Brazilian Coffee Exports, 1821–65

|  | Total Quantity in Metric Tons ('000) | Mean Price (constant $ per ton) | Mean Annual Value (millions of constant $) |
|---|---|---|---|
| 1821–25 | 12.5 | 309 | 3.6 |
| 1826–30 | 25.7 | 137 | 3.4 |
| 1831–35 | 52.9 | 211 | 11.5 |
| 1836–40 | 72.2 | 167 | 11.8 |
| 1841–45 | 91.2 | 125 | 11.4 |
| 1846–50 | 129.3 | 131 | 16.6 |
| 1851–55 | 155.3 | 162 | 24.8 |
| 1856–60 | 172.8 | 178 | 30.7 |
| 1861–65 | 139.7 | 229 | 31.8 |

*Source:* See text, in particular nn. 9 and 10.

## OUTPUT PER CAPITA

Trade and output data, especially on the physical volume of produce traded are generally much more readily available than data on the size of the work force that produced the crop. On the other hand, the work force was much less liable to sudden changes in size and composition than were crops and trade magnitudes.

Contemporary estimates of the share of the slave population residing on cotton and coffee plantations are available for the U.S. South and parts of post-1850 Brazil, respectively. For mid–nineteenth-century Cuba there are census data for 1841, 1846 and 1861. Unfortunately the 1841 and 1846 censuses provide only a count of residents of *ingenios* without specifying free, slave or indentured status. The 1861 census did provide such a breakdown, and calculation from this suggests that 78.6 percent of *ingenio* residents were slaves. In addition, however, there were Asian and Yucatan Indian laborers in the sugar sector although no precise breakdown of these latter groups was supplied.

**Table F.5.** Quantity, Price and Total Value of Brazilian Cotton Exports, 1821–60

|  | Total Quantity in Metric Tons ('000) | Mean Price (constant $ per ton) | Mean Annual Value (millions of constant $) |
|---|---|---|---|
| 1821–25 | 12.7 | 389 | 5.0 |
| 1826–30 | 11.7 | 254 | 2.8 |
| 1831–35 | 12.6 | 268 | 3.4 |
| 1836–40 | 10.7 | 202 | 2.2 |
| 1841–45 | 10.6 | 196 | 2.1 |
| 1846–50 | 12.3 | 238 | 2.9 |
| 1851–55 | 13.8 | 226 | 3.1 |
| 1856–60 | 13.6 | 245 | 3.2 |

*Source:* See text, in particular nn. 9 and 10.

There were no Asians or Yucatan Indians present before 1847, but in 1861 there was 35,874 in Cuba. Most of these would have been resident on *ingenios*. It seems safe to assume that 90 percent of the residents of *ingenios* were slaves before 1847 and slaves and indentured workers thereafter. Column 2 of table F.8 is thus the product of this ratio and the number of *ingenio* inhabitants reported in the 1841, 1846 and 1861 censuses. The 1861 census also lists 25,942 slaves on *cafetales,* amounting to 77.4 percent of all residents of *cafetales.* Allowing for a few indentured laborers on these estates it seems likely that 80 percent of the residents of *cafetales* were slaves and indentured laborers in 1861. Using this same ratio for 1841 and 1846, it is possible to derive estimates of the slave-labor force in the Cuban coffee sector referred to in chapter 11. Productivity ratios are derived by dividing these work force estimates into the annual average physical exports or total output for five years, centered on the year for which the work force estimate exists. The productivity measurement is thus a simple ratio of the five-year average to the individual member of the work force. No adjustment is made for hours worked, the age-and-sex composition of the work force, the fertility or location of the soil or the intensity of the labor regime. Possible bias from some of these sources is, however, discussed in the text and notes of chapter 11. Tables F.6 to F.9 present the data for the United States, British West Indies, Cuba and Brazil, respectively.

**Table F.6.** Cotton Output and Exports per Plantation Worker in the United States, 1801–50

| | Labor Force[a] (millions) | Exports | | Total Crop | |
|---|---|---|---|---|---|
| | | Millions of Pounds[b] | Exports per Worker (lbs.) | Millions of Pounds[b] | Output per Worker (lbs.) |
| 1801 | 0.10 | 23.6 | 236 | 43.6 | 436 |
| 1811 | 0.14 | 50.8 | 355 | 80.0 | 559 |
| 1821 | 0.33 | 132.0 | 396 | 180.4 | 542 |
| 1831 | 0.75 | 297.4 | 396 | 387.0 | 516 |
| 1835 | 1.00 | 393.0 | 393 | 478.0 | 478 |
| 1840 | 1.20 | 573.8 | 478 | 670.6 | 559 |
| 1850 | 1.82 | 899.2 | 495 | 1,125.4 | 620 |

*Notes:* [a]House Document no. 146 describes the labor force as "Persons employed in growing, and dependent." This would include a few free persons and no attempt has been made to adjust for their presence. [b]Mean annual data for five-year periods centered on listed year.

*Sources:* Column (1): House Document, no. 146, 24–1, p 16; Matthew B. Hammond, *The Cotton Industry: An Essay in American Economic History* (New York, 1897), pp. 59–60. Columns (2) and (4): James L. Watkins, *Production and Price of Cotton for One Hundred Years,* Miscellaneous Bulletin no. 9 (U.S. Department of Agriculture, Division of Statistics, 1895).

**Table F.7.** Sugar Exports per Slave Resident on Sugar Plantations in Selected Parts of the British West Indies, 1810–30

| | Sugar Exports[a] ('000 metric tons) | Slave Population ('000) | Share of Slave Population in Sugar | Sugar/Slave (tons) |
|---|---|---|---|---|
| **Jamaica** | | | | |
| 1810 | 76.3 | 347.0 | 0.52 | 0.42 |
| 1820 | 82.1 | 342.4 | 0.52 | 0.46 |
| 1830 | 70.3 | 319.0 | 0.53 | 0.42 |
| **Barbados** | | | | |
| 1810 | 7.5[b] | 75.0 | 0.77 | 0.13 |
| 1820 | 10.9 | 78.4 | 0.77 | 0.18 |
| 1830 | 15.3 | 82.0 | 0.78 | 0.24 |
| **British Guiana** | | | | |
| 1810 | 13.9[c] | 107.3 | 0.48 | 0.27 |
| 1820 | 27.1[d] | 100.8 | 0.63 | 0.42 |
| 1830 | 58.0 | 88.9 | 0.71 | 0.91 |
| **Trinidad** | | | | |
| 1810 | 7.3 | 26.2 | 0.55 | 0.51 |
| 1820 | 8.1 | 23.4 | 0.65 | 0.54 |
| 1830 | 14.0 | 22.8 | 0.70 | 0.88 |

*Notes:* [a]Mean annual data for five-year periods centered on listed year. [b]Based on two years only. [c]Based on one year only (1812). [d]Imports into Great Britain.

*Sources:* Column (1): Patrick Colquhoun, *A Treatise on the Wealth, Power and Resources of the British Empire,* 2nd. ed. (London, 1815), p. 383; Nöel Deerr, *The History of Sugar,* 2 vols. (London, 1949–50), 1:235–36, 240; PP, 1856, 55:2. Columns (2) and (3): calculated from Barry W. Higman, *Slave Populations of the British Caribbean, 1807–1834* (Baltimore, 1984), pp. 68–71, 417–18. Note that Deerr describes his data as production, but in fact they are exports only.

**Table F.8.** Sugar Output per Slave Resident on Sugar Plantations in Cuba, 1827–61

| | Sugar Output[a] ('000 metric tons) | Slave Population in Sugar ('000) | Sugar per Slave |
|---|---|---|---|
| 1827 | 74.4 | 70.0 | 1.06 |
| 1841[b] | 165.6 | 124.8 | 1.33 |
| 1846[b] | 208.1 | 116.8 | 1.78 |
| 1861 | 466.5 | 197.8 | 2.36 |

*Notes:* [a]Mean annual data for five-year periods centered on listed year. [b]Both 1841 and 1846 census counts are included in the table even though it is unlikely that both can be correct (Kenneth Kiple, *Blacks in Colonial Cuba 1774–1889* (Gainesville, Fla., 1976), pp. 47ff). The true ratio is likely to be between the figures for those years.

*Sources:* Column (1): Manuel Moreno Fraginals, *El ingenio, complejo económico social cubano del azúcar,* 3 vols. (Havana, 1978), 3:35–37. Column (2): 1827: Ramón de la Sagra, *Historia económico politica y estadística de la isla de Cuba* (Havana, 1831); 1841: Cuba, *Cuba, Resúmen del censo de población de la isla de Cuba á fin del año de 1841* (Havana, 1842), pp. 56–57. I would like to thank Robert Paquette for this reference. 1846: Cuba, *Cuadro estadístico de la siempre fiel isla de Cuba correspondiente al año de 1846* (Havana, 1847). 1861: Cuba, *Noticias estadísticas de la Cuba en 1862* (Havana, 1864).

**Table F.9.** Provincial Coffee Exports per Slave Resident on Coffee Plantations in Rio de Janeiro and São Paulo, 1854–84

| | Coffee[a] Exports ('000 metric tons) | Slave Population ('000) | Share of Population in Coffee | Coffee per Slave (tons) |
|---|---|---|---|---|
| **Rio de Janeiro** | | | | |
| 1872 | 106.6* | 292.6† | 0.443* | 0.82 |
| 1883 | 131.6* | | | 1.07‡[c] |
| **São Paulo** | | | | |
| 1874 | 52.5* | 156.6† | 0.285* | 1.18 |
| 1883 | 130.0* | | | 1.59‡[c] |
| **São Paulo** | | | | |
| 1854 | 28.2† | 57.9†[b] | — | 0.49 |
| 1874 | 52.5† | 81.1†[b] | — | 0.65 |

*Notes:* [a]Coffee exports are mean annual averages for the periods 1852–55, 1871–75, 1881–85 as appropriate. [b]Populations for 10 major coffee counties in Sao Paulo. [c]The Laërne estimates for 1883 contain some downward bias. The denominator in the equation which yielded these estimates is the number of slaves present on 44 coffee plantations on January 1, 1883. The numerator is the average crop in the years leading up to and including 1883. The period on which this average is based varies, but in several cases is the decade 1874–83. Coffee output almost certainly increased over these years by more than did the slave population.

*Sources:* *Amilcar Martins Filho and Roberto B. Martins, "Slavery in a Nonexport Economy: Nineteenth-Century Minas Gerais Revisited," *Hispanic American Historical Review,* 63 (1983):545, 547.

†Pedro Carvalho de Mello, "The Economics of Labor in Brazilian Coffee Plantations, 1850–1888." Ph.D. diss., University of Chicago, 1977, pp. 32–33, 74, 76.

‡C. F. Van Delden Laërne, *Brazil and Java: Report on Coffee Culture in America, Asia and Africa* (London, 1885), pp. 325–29, 336, 341, 352.

# APPENDIX G

# Exchange Rates and Price Level Adjustments

Transactions in the nineteenth-century slave trade were carried out in a wide variety of currencies, though the milreis and the Spanish dollar predominated. On the African coast in the years immediately after 1807 slave prices were often quoted in terms of goods bartered for the slave rather than in currency or in African units of equivalency such as the bar, ounce or piece. It has, however, been possible in most cases to convert such prices into Spanish dollars. After 1835, specie quickly came to dominate transactions for slaves in Africa, with the Spanish dollar ousting milreis as the standard unit even before the Brazilian trade died out. The milreis was a unit of account rather than a coin. The African units of equivalency were rarely used after the 1820s, and wherever possible in this work prices in the slave trade are quoted in dollars.

This raises the question of exchange rates. As the Spanish dollar was normally at par with the U.S. dollar, it is possible to use the well-documented exchange rate of British pounds into U.S. dollars for many conversion requirements. The rate used throughout this work is £1 = $4.80. A more refined time series of the rate is readily available, but fluctuations were relatively small and allowing for them would not significantly change the calculations in the text, which in most cases are necessarily rough. For the Brazilian currency, an annual pounds sterling/milreis exchange ratio exists for the years after 1820, and the conversion of the Brazilian milreis into the Spanish dollar is carried out through the pound sterling.[1]

This issue is related to the question of adjusting to changes in the general price level—in other words, converting market or current values into real or constant values. Price indexes, where they exist, are necessarily for a particular country. The slave trade, on the other hand, called on resources which were drawn from almost every country with an Atlantic coastline and even some without. Price indexes for this period exist for Brazil, Britain, the United States and France. As most of the goods used in the traffic were British, and as the ocean freight business was both highly competitive and contained a large British contingent, the price index used here to derive real values is the Gayer, Rostow and Schwarz "Index of Wholesale Prices of Domestic and Imported Commodities." This series ends in 1850, and from 1851 on the Rousseaux combined index[2] is blended with it to provide a continuous index for 1811 to 1867, with the base period of 1821 to 1825. Britain, Cuba and the United States, were linked by a metallic-based standard for their respective currencies for most of this period, and this decision to use a British price index does not inflict excessive damage on the historical reality of long-term price trends. In the Brazilian case, however, inflation persistently exceeded that in Britain, and the currency of the country was effectively linked to neither gold nor silver standards. Fortunately, the annual pounds sterling/milreis exchange ratio series establishes an approximation of purchasing power parity among the currencies.[3]

# Notes

## Chapter 1

1. The pamphlet was Samuel Estwick's *Considerations on the negroe cause* . . . , 3rd ed. (London, 1788); this was an expanded version of a tract that first appeared in 1772: Arthur Young's review appeared in *Annals of Agriculture,* 9 (1788):185–86. Important insights into many of the questions raised in this chapter are to be found in David Brion Davis, *Slavery and Human Progress* (New York, 1984), pp. 107–68.

2. C. L. R. James, *The Black Jacobins, Toussaint L'Ouverture and the San Domingo Revolution* (London, 1938); Eric Williams, *Capitalism and Slavery* (Chapel Hill, N.C., 1944). Elements of the economic interpretation were, in fact, raised earlier in the century by Franz Hochstetter, "Die wirtschaftlichen und politischen Motive für die Abschaffung des britischen Sklavenhandel im Jahre 1806/1807," in G. Schmoller and M. Sering (eds.), *Staats und Sozialwissenschaftliche Forschungen,* 25 (1905), pt. 1, cited in Roger Anstey, "A Re-interpretation of the Abolition of the British Slave Trade, 1806–1807," *English Historical Review,* 87 (1972):320.

3. Paul Bairoch, *Commerce extérieur et développement économique de l'Europe au XIXe siècle* (Paris, 1976); Patrick O'Brien, "European Economic Development: The Contribution of the Periphery," *Economic History Review,* 35 (1982):1–18; R. P. Thomas and D. N. McCloskey, "Overseas Trade and Empire, 1700–1860," in Roderick Floud and Donald N. McCloskey (eds.), *The Economic History of Britain Since 1700,* 2 vols. (Cambridge, 1981), 1:87–102; R. Findley, "Trade and Growth in the Industrial Revolution," in C. P. Kindleberger and G. di Tella (eds.), *Economics in the Long View: Essays in Honor of W. W. Rostow,* 2 vols. (New York, 1982), 1:178–88; Joel Mokyr (ed.), *The Economics of the Industrial Revolution* (Totowa, N.J., 1985), pp. 22–23, 97–118. Assessments of the importance of the West Indies to British economic development have usually stressed the contribution of the former to British income and investment. See Richard B. Sheridan, "The Plantation Revolution and the Industrial Revolution," *Caribbean Studies,* 9 (1969):5–25; idem, "The Wealth of Jamaica in the Eighteenth Century," *Economic History Review,* 18 (1965):292–311. For a recent restatement of this position that uses a variant of general equilibrium analysis, see William A. Darity, "A General Equilib-

rium Model of the Eighteenth Century Atlantic Slave Trade: A Least-likely Test for the Caribbean School," *Research in Economic History,* 7 (1982):287–326. Cf. David Richardson, "The Slave Trade, Sugar and British Economic Growth, 1748–1776," in Stanley L. Engerman and Barbara L. Solow (eds.), *Caribbean Slavery and British Capitalism* (forthcoming, Cambridge Univ. Press); and Barbara L. Solow, "Caribbean Slavery and British Growth: The Eric Williams Hypothesis," *Journal of Development Economics,* 17 (1985):99–115.

4. Seymour Drescher, *Econocide: British Slavery in the Era of Abolition* (Pittsburgh, 1977); Lowell J. Ragatz, *The Fall of the Planter Class in the British Caribbean, 1763–1833* (New York, 1928).

5. Drescher, *Econocide,* pp. 99–108, 142–146; Patrick Colquhoun, *A Treatise on the Wealth, Power and Resources of the British Empire,* 2nd ed. (London, 1815), pp. 382–85; William Cobbett (ed.), *The Parliamentary History of England,* 36:443, Apr. 2, 1802. Canning's actual estimate of the Jamaican slave population was 250,000.

6. See Drescher, *Econocide,* pp. 78, 85, 148, for cotton and sugar figures. The Brazilian data for sugar in figure 1 are for exports of mainly white clayed sugar and have been increased by 20 percent to allow for Brazilian domestic consumption. The British data are for imports into Great Britain from the British West Indies and are for mainly muscovado sugar. The Cuban and world data are estimates of production of white clayed sugar. For the reconciliation of the British and Cuban data see n. 17. It should be noted that world shares of sugar production from all British regions (including Mauritius and East India) fell more slowly than the British West Indies share. There are less data available on global coffee exports than on either sugar or cotton. Average annual coffee imports into the United Kingdom for British plantations (excluding East India) were 13,300 metric tons between 1821 and 1825 (Great Britain, Parliamentary Papers [henceforth PP] 1831–32, 20:946–7) compared to Cuban coffee production of 10,100 tons and Brazilian coffee exports of 12,500 tons (app. F). From 1826 to 1830 the equivalent figures were 12,500, 19,800 and 25,700 for British plantations, Cuba and Brazil, respectively. Hans Scherrer gives the Brazilian share of world coffee output as 18.2 percent in the 1820s, rising to 40 percent in the 1840s (*Die Kaffeevalorisation und Valorisationsversuche in anderen Artikeln des Welthandels* [Jena, 1919], p. 5). As British plantation output did not change much in the first half of the nineteenth century and Brazilian and Cuban production increased rapidly from very low levels in the early nineteenth century, the British plantation share of world output could easily have been 50 percent in the aftermath of the St. Domingue revolution.

7. Barbara Tuchman, *The March of Folly: From Troy to Vietnam* (New York, 1984), chapter 1, "Pursuit of Policy Contrary to Self-Interest."

8. Sir James Graham to Palmerston, Nov. 1, 1831, Great Britain, Public Record Office, Foreign Office, Slave Trade Series (henceforth referred to as FO 84), vol. 124. The observed price of the average slave landed in Cuba between 1826 and 1845 was $300 and in southern Brazil, 1831–50, $194 (in constant dollars). Without British intervention prices in Cuba would have been much closer to the $230 (in constant dollars) paid by Jamaican planters in the 1790s for newly arrived Africans. (See infra, table C.2) For prices in Jamaica see Richard B. Sheridan, "Slave Demography in the British West Indies and the Abolition of the Slave Trade," in David Eltis and James Walvin (eds.), *The Abolition of the Atlantic Slave Trade* (Madison, Wis., 1981), p. 277. For currencies used and adjustments to changes in price levels, see app. G.

9. For estimates see E. Phillip LeVeen, *British Slave Trade Suppression Policies, 1821–1865* (New York, 1977), p. 80; and infra, 139–42. The recent revisions of British

national income figures change neither the ranking nor the order of magnitude of the costs and benefits.

10. Robert William Fogel and Stanley L. Engerman, *Time on the Cross: The Economics of American Negro Slavery*, 2 vols. (Boston, 1974), 1:44–52; Robert W. Slenes, "The Demography and Economics of Brazilian Slavery: 1850–1888." Ph.D. diss., Stanford University, 1976, pp. 120–78.

11. There were probably less than 23,000 slaves traded among the British islands in these years. See Barry W. Higman, *Slave Populations of the British Caribbean, 1807–1834* (Baltimore, 1984), pp. 80–85; and D. Eltis "The Traffic in Slaves Between the British West Indian Colonies, 1807–1883," *Economic History Review*, 25 (1972):55–64, for a fuller discussion of the intercolonial trade and its abolition.

12. Annual average sugar output for 1824–34 in tons per member of the 1830 sugar slave-labor force for Demerara, Trinidad, Dominica, Jamaica and Barbados was 0.88, 0.76, 0.48, 0.41 and 0.23, respectively (calculated from William A. Green, *British Slave Emancipation: The Sugar Colonies and the Great Experiment, 1830–1865* [Oxford, 1976], p. 246; Higman, *Slave Populations*, pp. 70–71). Average prices of slaves over the period 1823–32 for the same regions were £115, £105, £43, £45 and £47, respectively in pounds sterling (PP, 1837–38, 48:329). For a fuller discussion of slave price and output differentials within the British Caribbean, see Stanley L. Engerman, "Economic Adjustments to Emancipation in the United States and the British West Indies," *Journal of Interdisciplinary History*, 13 (1982):195–200.

13. As long as restrictions on the intercolonial movement of slaves existed, then population and output would not be subject to major changes and large price differentials would open up in response to differences in the quantity and quality of land in each colony. With no political interference, the intercolonial market in British slaves, on the other hand, would have resulted in a drop in population and output, a rise in price of slaves in the low-productivity region, and a rise in population and output and a fall in the price of slaves in the high-productivity colonies.

14. See Richard N. Bean, *The British Trans-Atlantic Slave Trade, 1650–1775* (New York, 1975), pp. 175–80, for a discussion of intra-Caribbean transportation costs and their impact on slave prices. In peace time these differentials were less than 5 percent of the final selling price.

15. The increase is estimated by raising the productivity of all the slave populations in the low-productivity British islands (as defined supra, n. 12) up to the average output per slave for the British Caribbean as a whole.

16. Two constraining factors should be noted. First, productivity in the expanding areas would have decreased as their labor force expanded. Second, as life expectancy in the frontier colonies and on major sugar estates generally was lower than elsewhere, the aggregate rate of natural population change in the British West Indies would have been adversely affected. It is hard, for example, to envision the vital rates of the Bahamian slave population—where the major occupation was fishing and some cotton cultivation—remaining unaffected by a move to Demerara. Thus, the slave population of the British colonies as a whole would have fallen more rapidly than it did. Neither factor would have had major effects in the short run and, even as a net estimate, the fifty thousand-ton increase must be regarded as a minimum.

17. Cuban output averaged 82,500 metric tons of white clayed sugar per year, 1824–33 (Manuel Moreno Fraginals, *El ingenio, complejo económico social cubano del azúcar*, 3 vols. [Havana, 1978], 3:35–36). The British output figure is actually imports into Britain from the British West Indies and is for muscovado sugar in part. Allowance for losses in transatlantic transit and domestic consumption in the British West Indies probably requires a 20 percent increase in these data to arrive at a British

West Indian production figure. On the other hand, the conversion of muscovado to white clayed sugar entailed a loss of weight variously estimated at 17 percent to 50 percent (Drescher, *Econocide*, pp. 193–94). The assumption is made here that these adjustments roughly cancel out.

18. Seymour Drescher, "Capitalism and Abolition: Values and Forces in Britain, 1783–1814," in Roger Anstey and P. E. H. Hair (eds.), *Liverpool, the African Slave Trade, and Abolition: Essays to Illustrate Current Knowledge and Research* (Liverpool, 1976), pp. 189–90.

19. Cuban *bozales,* or newly arrived Africans, sold for an average price of $300 between 1826 and 1845. In Trinidad and Demerara in the last years of slavery, the price of Creole slaves was £110 or $528, (£1 = $4.80). Some adjustment must be made for Creole/*bozal* differentials as well as for the depressing effects of anticipated emancipation on post-1823 British slave prices. The former would tend to reduce the spread between the British and Cuban slave prices, whereas without the latter, the Cuban/British difference would have been much greater. Cf. PP, 1830–31, 9:558–60. Of course, an open slave trade would probably have meant that slaves cost more than $300 cif in the Caribbean: British demand was substantial, and the supply elasticity of slaves was certainly less than infinity. We must remember, however, that the British Navy could not have continued its attacks on foreign slave ships if the British traffic had been reopened and that, as a consequence, the relevant price was not $300 but some lower price that would have held in the absence of abolitionist pressures.

20. According to supra, n. 12, slaves on British Guiana sugar estates in 1830 produced a per capita output of 0.88 tons, based on average annual output in 1824–33. If we accept Sagra's figure of seventy thousand slaves on Cuban sugar estates in 1827 (Ramón de la Sagra, *Historia económico-politica, y estadística de la Isla de Cuba* [Havana, 1831] and divide this into average sugar production for Cuba 1821–30 (infra, app. F), we derive a figure of 1.04 tons per head (allowing 1 ton = 1.01 tonnes). The upward bias in the Cuban ratio is substantial, however. The slave trade ensured a rapidly expanding Cuban slave population at this period. The age structure of that slave population must have guaranteed a much greater number of prime-age workers than were available to British planters. Some authorities also feel that Sagra's estimate of slaves in sugar production was low (Hugh Thomas, *Cuba: The Pursuit of Freedom* [London, 1971], p. 168). On the other hand, given the higher value of slaves in British Guiana and assuming similar land and capital costs in British Guiana and Cuba, we would expect factor substitution to increase the productivity of slaves in the British territory. After appropriate adjustments, however, including the standardization of Cuban and British data taken up supra, n. 17, output per able field-worker may well have been similar. For a comparison of labor productivity in Jamaica and Cuba at this time, see Richard B. Sheridan, "'Sweet Malefactor': The Social Costs of Slavery and Sugar in Jamaica and Cuba, 1807–54," *Economic History Review,* 29 (1976):236–57.

21. For sugar prices, see App. F; PP, 1856, 55:2–3; and the discussion in Philip D. Curtin, "The British Sugar Duties and West Indian Prosperity," *Journal of Economic History,* 14 (1954):160–61; W. A. Green, "The Planter Class and British West Indian Sugar Production, before and after Emancipation," *Economic History Review,* 26 (1973):462.

22. For trends in cotton production, see Fogel and Engerman, *Time on the Cross,* 1:86–94; Gavin Wright, *The Political Economy of the Cotton South, Households, Markets and Wealth in the Nineteenth Century* (New York, 1978), in particular pp. 89–127. See also app. F. The strong rate of natural increase by the U.S. slave population was

based, in part, on the latter's normal age distribution and its small African-born component in 1807 as well as the relatively benign epidemiological environment of the U.S. South. That Demerara and Berbice and their slave populations possessed none of these characteristics in 1807 must explain much of the temporary nature of the Guiana cotton boom. If Demerara had been able to get an abundant supply of labor at $300 per head at a time when U.S. prices were rising to between two and three times this level, then it might have been able to compete with the United States in cotton production. For U.S. prices, see Robert Evans, Jr., "The Economics of American Negro Slavery," in Universities National Bureau Committee for Economic Research, *Aspects of Labor Economics* (Princeton, N.J., 1962), p. 216—these prices must be adjusted for differences in life expectancy between newly imported Africans and slaves born in the Americas.

23. The slave population of the British West Indies declined from 753,300 in 1817 to approximately 674,000 in 1832 (PP, 1833, 26:474–77; PP, 1835, 51:289, with some minor allowances for smaller colonial populations that reported dates different from 1832). Allowance for "seasoning" mortality of 15 percent suggests imports of 6,100. However, the rate of population decline was probably greater before 1817. George Hibbert, a West Indian merchant, suggested in 1807 that 7,000 slaves a year would be necessary to maintain existing population levels (*Hansard*, 1st ser., 8:985).

24. G. W. Roberts and J. Byrne, "Summary Statistics on Indenture and Associated Migration Affecting the West Indies, 1834–1918," *Population Studies*, 20 (1966):125–34. It should be noted, however, that much of the indentured labor replaced the ex-slaves who left the plantations in large numbers after emancipation.

25. For estimates of the annual volume of the Atlantic slave traffic after 1780, see app. A.

26. As it was, European migration exceeded African migration for the first time in the 1840s (David Eltis, "Free and Coerced Transatlantic Migrations: Some Comparisons," *American Historical Review*, 88 [1983]:256).

27. The Americas accounted for negligible amounts of British trade in 1650, 16 percent in 1700 and 42 percent in 1800. Calculated from F. J. Fisher, "London's Export Trade in the Early Seventeenth Century," *Economic History Review*, 3 (1950):151–61; Ralph Davis "English Foreign Trade, 1600–1700," *Economic History Review*, 7 (1954):164–65; idem, *The Industrial Revolution and British Overseas Trade* (Leicester, 1979), pp. 88–93. B. R. Mitchell and Phyllis Deane, *Abstract of British Historical Statistics* (Cambridge, 1962), pp. 309–21.

28. There is a parallel here with the argument of A. H. Imlah, that a British policy of free trade carried out in 1800 instead of midcentury would have reduced social tensions within Britain (*Economic Elements in the Pax Britannica* [Cambridge, Mass., 1958], pp. 114–55). As a laissez-faire free trade policy would have encouraged slavery and the slave trade, the argument here is, in fact, very close to Imlah's.

29. Calculated from app. A and Paul E. Lovejoy, "The Volume of the Atlantic Slave Trade: A Synthesis," *Journal of African History*, 23 (1982):497.

30. The question posed in Stanley L. Engerman's "Slavery and Emancipation in Comparative Perspective: A Look at Some Recent Debates," *Journal of Economic History*, 46 (1986):317–39.

## Chapter 2

1. The correspondence was printed in *Papers Relating to Emancipation of Crown Slaves in the Colonies*, PP, 1831, 19:303–15.

2. Edward George Stanley, *Journal of a Tour in America, 1824–5* (Edinburgh, 1930),

pp. 224–28; Alexis de Tocqueville, *Democracy in America*, 2 vols. (New York, 1966), 1:360–65; see also David Brion Davis, *Slavery and Human Progress* (New York, 1984), pp. 251–53.

3. Izhak Gross, "The Abolition of Negro Slavery and British Parliamentary Politics, 1832–3," *Historical Journal*, 23 (1980):78–79.

4. Karl Polanyi, *The Great Transformation* (Boston, 1957), pp. 68–102; Reinhard Bendix, *Work and Authority in Industry: Ideologies of Management in the Course of Industrialization* (New York, 1956), pp. 73–99.

5. Joyce Oldham Appleby, *Economic Thought and Ideology in Seventeenth-Century England* (Princeton, N.J., 1978), pp. 24–72; Stanley L. Engerman, "Coerced and Free Labor: Property Rights and the Development of the Labor Force," *Annales: Economies, sociétés, civilisations* (forthcoming French translation). Cf. Herman Freudenberg and Gaylord Cummings, "Health, Work and Leisure Before the Industrial Revolution," *Explorations in Economic History*, 13 (1976):1–12.

6. Christopher Hill, "Pottage for Freeborn Englishmen: Attitudes to Wage Labour in the Sixteenth and Seventeenth Centuries," in H. Feinstein (ed.), *Socialism, Capitalism and Economic Growth: Essays Presented to Maurice Dobb* (Cambridge, 1967), p. 343.

7. Ibid., p. 350; C. B. Macpherson, *The Political Theory of Possessive Individualism: Hobbes to Locke* (Oxford, 1962), pp. 128–29; Eric Foner, *Free Soil, Free Labor, Free Men: The Ideology of the Republican Party before the Civil War* (New York, 1970), pp. 16–29.

8. Edgar S. Furniss, *The Position of the Laborer in a System of Nationalism* (New York, 1920). Sir William Temple's pamphlets are examples of the contemporary emphasis on low wages (e.g. *An Essay upon the Advancement of Trade in Ireland* [Dublin, 1673]). For the predominance of this development strategy over a nascent laissez-faire approach at the end of the seventeenth century, see Appleby, *Economic Thought and Ideology*, in particular pp. 242–79. For the movement of labor from agriculture to industry—a restatement of an older view of the role of labor in British development, see N. F. R. Crafts, "Income Elasticities of Demand and the Release of Labour by Agriculture During the British Industrial Revolution," *Journal of European Economic History*, 9 (1980):153–68.

9. See W. A. Cole "Factors in Demand, 1700–80," in Roderick Floud and Donald N. McCloskey (eds.), *The Economic History of Britain Since 1700*, 2 vols. (Cambridge, 1981), 1:36–63, and the literature cited.

10. As James Steuart put it, people must be either slaves to others or slaves to want (*Principles of Political Economy*, 2 vols., [London, 1805], 1:52). Cf. the proslavery "Memorial of the Havana Tribunal of Commerce," March 30, 1841: "Between education and perpetual slavery there is no remedy or alternative" (British and Foreign Anti-Slavery Society Papers, G77, Rhodes House, Oxford).

11. A. W. Coats, "Changing Attitudes to Labour in the Mid-Eighteenth Century," *Economic History Review*, 11 (1958–59):46, 49; Nathan Rosenberg "Adam Smith on Profits—Paradox Lost and Regained," in Andrew S. Skinner and Thomas Wilson (eds.), *Essays on Adam Smith* (Oxford, 1975), pp. 377–80. For the contribution of these shifts in attitude to the creation of a modern labor force, see Engerman, "Coerced and Free Labor."

12. For the persistence of paternalistic attitudes, see David Roberts, *Paternalism in Early Victorian England* (New Brunswick, N.J., 1979).

13. One fundamental question here is whether the ex-slaves could have achieved the levels of civilization expected by the abolitionists if they had merely entered a mar-

ket economy (selling the produce of their self-employment) instead of forming a market society (selling their labor as well), as defined by C. B. Macpherson, *Possessive Individualism*, p. 48. Some abolitionists, William Wilberforce and William Knibb among others, appeared to think that only the former was necessary (D. Eltis, "Abolitionist Perceptions of Society after Slavery," in James Walvin [ed.], *Slavery and British Society, 1776–1846* [London, 1982], pp. 198–204).

14. Zachary Macaulay to Henry Brougham, May 13, 1833, MY 426, Macaulay mss.; James Stephen the younger, commentary on Lord Howick's plan, July 6, 1831, Grey Papers, cited in D. B. Davis, *Slavery and Human Progress*, p. 218. See Davis's discussion of this point, ibid., pp. 214–21. From inside the cabinet Lord Holland wrote of the need to ensure the "subordination of the Emancipated" [Abraham D. Kriegel (ed.), *The Holland House Diaries, 1831–40* (London, 1977), p. 56]. By 1841, however, the younger Stephen was defending the flight of the ex-slave from the plantation (T. J. Barron, "James Stephen, the 'Black Race' and British Colonial Administration, 1813–47," *Journal of Imperial and Commonwealth History*, 5, [1977]:142–43). It might be noted that a similar determination to maintain or increase production in the French slave colonies stopped well short of triggering an emancipation of French slaves despite an attitude to labor among the French elite that had much in common with its British counterpart. On this last point, see the discussion of Gustave de Beaumont and Alexis de Tocqueville in Seymour Drescher, *Dilemmas of Democracy: Tocqueville and Modernization* (Pittsburgh, 1968), in particular pp. 61–69, 151–95, as well as Tocqueville's "Report on Abolition," in Drescher, (ed.) *Tocqueville and Beaumont on Social Reform* (New York, 1968), pp. 107–8, 112–15, 121. Indeed, the post-emancipation production trends in the British colonies—keenly observed in France—helped ensure that French slaves would not be freed until a revolutionary government came to power in 1848. See Lawrence C. Jennings, *France and British Slave Emancipation* (forthcoming).

15. For the value of apprenticeship to the planters, see Robert W. Fogel and Stanley L. Engerman, "Philanthropy at Bargain Prices: Notes on the Economics of Gradual Emancipation," *Journal of Legal Studies*, 3 (1974):382–98.

16. Eltis, "Abolitionist Perceptions," p. 202.

17. William Ellery Channing, *Emancipation* (London, 1841); *The Times* (London), Mar. 30 and May 3, 1841; Steven B. Webb, "Saints or Cynics: A Statistical Analysis of Parliament's Decision for Emancipation in 1833," in Robert W. Fogel and Stanley L. Engerman (eds.), *Without Consent or Contract* (forthcoming, W. W. Norton), establishes the greater than average antislavery feeling among those MPs who voted against the various clauses of the New Poor Law in May and June 1834. The relevant question here, however, is the proportion of antislavery supporters who opposed the New Poor Law. A survey of the division lists in *Hansard* (3rd ser., 23:842, 971; 24:330, 351, 433, and 718–19) shows first, the very small number of MPs opposing the measure and, second, the fact that those that did were of three types: Tory squires, radicals and Irish. The last two groups tended to support antislavery measures, but the fact remains that the vast majority of those who voted for emancipation voted in favor or abstained on the New Poor Law divisions. Daniel O'Connell was the only well-known abolitionist who voted against the Poor Law. *The Times* (London) noted the absence of abolitionists opposing a similar bill in 1841. For an argument parallel to the one presented here, see D. B. Davis, *Slavery and Human Progress*, pp. 122–23.

18. David B. Davis, "The Emergence of Immediatism in Anti-Slavery Thought," *Mississippi Valley Historical Review*, 49 (1962–63):229.

19. Ronald Robinson and John Gallagher, *Africa and the Victorians* (London, 1961), pp. 3–5; Anthony J. Barker, *The African Link: British Attitudes to the Negro in the Era of the Atlantic Slave Trade* (London, 1978), pp. 180–81.

20. *Report of the committee of the African Institution read to the general meeting on the 15th July, 1807* (London, 1811), p. 24. For the division between trade-based and agricultural-based strategies, see Philip D. Curtin, *The Image of Africa: British Ideas and Action, 1780–1850* (Madison, Wis., 1964), pp. 117ff. The Sierra Leone Company attempted to establish plantation-type operations, but within a few years of the settlement becoming a Crown Colony, slaves taken by the naval squadron were being put into villages rather than farmed out as apprentices (ibid., pp. 275–76; Christopher Fyfe, *A History of Sierra Leone* [London, 1962] pp. 117–32). The abolitionist defence of this (e.g., Kenneth Macaulay, *The Colony of Sierra Leone Vindicated* [London, 1827])—echoed in the 1840s in the debate over Jamaican free villages—was more than just a rationalization after the fact. See supra, n. 13, and *Edinburgh Review,* 12 (July 1808):375. See also Henry Smeathman, "Substance of two letters Addressed to Dr. Knowles of London on the Productions and Colonization of Africa," (July 21, 1783) in C. B. Wadstrom, *An Essay on Colonization,* 2 vols. (London, 1794–1795), 2:197–207.

21. Richard Lander and John Lander, *Journal of an Expedition to Find the Course and Termination of the Niger,* 3 vols. (London, 1832), 2:133; Barker, *African Link,* pp. 110–12; Marshall Sahlins, *Stone Age Economics* (New York, 1972), pp. 1–36; James McQueen, *A Geographical Survey of Africa* (London, 1840), p. xci. For the association of wage labor and slavery on the part of Africans see J. C. Mitchell, "Wage Labour and African Population Movements in Central Africa," in K. M. Barbour and R. M. Prothero (eds.), *Essays on African Population* (London, 1961), pp. 199–200.

22. Brian Stanley, "'Commerce and Christianity': Providence Theory, the Missionary Movement, and the Imperialism of Free Trade, 1842–1860," *Historical Journal,* 26 (1983):71–76.

23. Howard Temperley, "Capitalism, Slavery and Ideology," *Past and Present,* 75 (1977):94–118; idem, "Anti-Slavery as a Form of Cultural Imperialism" in Christine Bolt and Seymour Drescher (eds.), *Anti-Slavery, Religion and Reform* (Folkestone, 1980), pp. 335–50.

24. Infra, chapters 3 and 11; David Eltis, "Free and Coerced Transatlantic Migration: Some Comparisons," *American Historical Review,* 88 (1983):251–80; David W. Galenson, *White Servitude in Colonial America: An Economic Analysis* (Cambridge, 1981), pp. 97–168. One estimate of per capita wealth (excluding the value of slaves) puts the southern states, Jamaica and the middle colonies (in that order) all ahead of New England in 1770 (Stanley L. Engerman, "Notes on the Patterns of Economic Growth in the British North American Colonies in the Seventeenth, Eighteenth and Nineteenth Centuries," in Paul Bairoch and Maurice Lévy-Leboyer [eds.], *Disparities in Economic Development Since the Industrial Revolution* [New York, 1981], table 4. These estimates are, in part, derived from the work of Alice Hanson Jones, *Wealth of the Colonies on the Eve of the American Revolution* [New York, 1977]; and Richard B. Sheridan, *Sugar and Slavery* [Baltimore, 1973]).

25. Edward Gibbon Wakefield, *England and America* (London, 1833); idem, *Letter from Sydney* (London, 1829). Like the Colonial Office, contemporary economists became increasingly conscious of the difficulty of using free labor on plantations. Jean Baptiste Say and Baron Storch were prepared to argue that free labor was always more productive than slave labor (Adam Hodgson, *A Letter to M. Jean Baptiste Say on the Comparative Expense of Free and Slave Labour* 2 ed. [London

1823], p. 60—includes a letter from J. B. Say to Hodgson, Mar. 25, 1823, on this point; Baron Storch, *Cours d'économie politique,* 5 vols. [Paris, 1823–24], 3:147–56). Later, however, J. R. McCulloch, Herman Merivale and John Stuart Mill conceded that free labor would not work in plantation agriculture but did not disagree with Adam Smith's general contention on the relative performance of free and slave labor when both were working at the same task. See Stanley L. Engerman, *New Palgrave Dictionary of Political Economy* (forthcoming), s.v. "slavery" on this point. The *Quarterly Review* (30:568–76) pointed out as early as 1824 that there had been no example anywhere of free negroes "collectively cultivating cane"—I am indebted to Seymour Drescher for this reference. The *Quarterly Review* however was firmly in the West Indian camp in the 1820s. For the slave trade as an example of free enterprise, see Seymour Drescher, "Capitalism and Abolition: Values and Forces in Britain, 1783–1814," in Roger Anstey and P. E. H. Hair (eds.), *Liverpool, the African Slave Trade, and Abolition: Essays to Illustrate Current Knowledge and Research* (Liverpool, 1976), p. 188.

26. D. B. Davis, *Slavery and Human Progress,* pp. 231–50.

27. See the discussion in Stanley L. Engerman, "Economic Change and Contract Labor in the British Caribbean: The End of Slavery and the Adjustment to Emancipation," *Explorations in Economic History,* 21 (1984):135–36.

28. David Northrup, "The Compatibility of the Slave and Palm Oil Trades in the Bight of Biafra," *Journal of African History,* 17 (1976):353–64; infra, chap. 10; Curtin, *Image of Africa,* pp. 140–76.

29. *Report of the committee of the African Institution . . . July 15, 1807,* p. 30.

30. Perhaps the expectation that abolition would increase output and reduce prices explains the fact that the sugar-refining constituency, Tower Hamlets, in east London was represented in Parliament for most of the first twenty years of its existence by two of the leading abolitionists, Stephen Lushington, 1832–41, and George Thompson, 1847–52.

31. For income estimates for individual colonies see Gisela Eisner, *Jamaica, 1831–1930: A Study in Economic Growth* (Manchester, Eng., 1961), pp. 25–59; and Michael Moohr, "The Economic Impact of Slave Emancipation in British Guiana, 1832–1852," *Economic History Review,* 25 (1972):588–607. For a comparative survey, see Engerman, "Notes on the Patterns of Economic Growth," pp. 46–57. For trends in sugar production in the Americas before and after emancipation, see Stanley L. Engerman, "Economic Adjustments to Emancipation in the United States and British West Indies," *Journal of Interdisciplinary History,* 13 (1982):196, 202; and William A. Green, *British Slave Emancipation: The Sugar Colonies and the Great Experiment, 1830–1865* (Oxford, 1976), p. 246.

32. Stanley L. Engerman, "Economic Change and Contract Labor in the British Caribbean"; Sidney Mintz, "Slavery and the Rise of Peasantries," *Historical Reflections,* 6 (1979):230–36; idem, *Caribbean Transformations* (Chicago, 1974), pp. 180–224; W. Emanuel Riviere, "Labour Shortage in the British West Indies After Emancipation," *Journal of Caribbean History,* 2 (1972):17–24.

33. *Hansard,* 3rd ser., 99:1222, June 26, 1848. See also letters to Maria Weston Chapman, July 11, 1839, and May 24, 1844, in Clare Taylor (ed.) *British and American Abolitionists: An Episode in Transatlantic Understanding* (Edinburgh, 1974), pp. 72, 219, and Thompson's introduction to Angelina E. Grimké, *Slavery in America* (Edinburgh, 1837), p. xii.

34. For Channing's comment, see *Slavery* (Boston, 1835), p. 8. For hardening attitudes, see Lewis Tappan to John Scoble, July 31, 1844, in Annie Heloise Abel and Frank J. Klingberg, "The Correspondence of Lewis Tappan with the British and Foreign

Anti-Slavery Society," *Journal of Negro History,* 12 (1927):317. Douglas Lorimer, *Colour, Class and the Victorians: English Attitudes to the Negro in the Mid-Nineteenth Century* (New York, 1978), pp. 127–28. The *Westminster Review,* which had strongly supported the emancipation campaign and had been edited for many years by Perronet Thompson, a former governor of Sierra Leone, justified slavery in 1850 as a proper transitional step from "barbarism to civilization" (52 [1850]:258, cited in Curtin, *Image of Africa,* p. 453). The first imperially funded development project did not come until 1868 (W. L. Burn, *Emancipation and Apprenticeship in the British West Indies* [London, 1937], p. 379).

35. See for example R. I. Wilberforce and S. Wilberforce, *The Life of William Wilberforce,* 5 vols. (London, 1838), 4:242, and William Wilberforce's speech in *Hansard,* 1st ser., 3:672, Feb. 28, 1805.

36. See Stephen Lushington's speech in *Hansard,* 3rd ser., 58:82–84, May 7, 1841; and his evidence in *Report of the Select Committee of the House of Lords for the . . . Slave Trade,* PP, 1850, 9:75–86.

37. In turn each of the major slave-trade treaties signed between 1815 and 1835 was greeted in Parliament as the ultimate solution to the problem, and their failure to meet such expectations does something to explain the abolitionist disenchantment with coercion in the 1840s.

38. Howard Temperley, *British Antislavery, 1833–1870* (Columbia, S.C., 1972), pp. 176–79; William Law Mathieson, *Great Britain and the Slave Trade, 1839–1865* (London, 1929), pp. 101–14.

39. Temperley, *British Antislavery,* pp. 179–83. David Livingstone was probably the most prominent of the anticoercionists who began supporting naval action in the 1850s. He was also one of the few who had been to Africa (Clarendon to Gabriel and Jackson, Dec. 4, 1856, enc. Dr. David Livingstone to Clarendon, Mar. 19, 1856, FO 84/985).

40. Sir Richard Burton, *A Mission to Gelele, King of Dahome,* 2 vols. (London, 1864), 1:206. On the increasingly unsympathetic British attitudes toward Africa and Africans after midcentury, see Christine Bolt, *Victorian Attitudes Towards Race* (London, 1971).

## Chapter 3

1. For the transition from free to slave labor, see Richard S. Dunn, *Sugar and Slaves: The Rise of the Planter Class in the English West Indies, 1624–1713* (New York, 1972), pp. 68–74; Russell R. Menard, "From Servants to Slaves: The Transformation of the Chesapeake Labor System," *Southern Studies,* 16 (1977):355–90; Ralph Gray and Betty Wood, "The Transition from Indentured to Involuntary Servitude in Colonial Georgia," *Explorations in Economic History,* 13 (1976):353–70; David W. Galenson, *White Servitude in Colonial America: An Economic Analysis* (Cambridge, 1981), pp. 117–82.

2. Duncan J. Macleod, *Slavery, Race and the American Revolution* (Cambridge, 1974), pp. 47–60; Gavin Wright, *The Political Economy of the Cotton South, Households, Markets and Wealth in the Nineteenth Century* (New York, 1978), pp. 11–13; Charlotte Erickson, "Why Did Contract Labour Not Work in the Nineteenth-Century United States?" in Shula Marks and Peter Richardson (eds.), *International Labour Migration: Historical Perspectives* (London, 1984), pp. 34–46. The low-cost rural labor in the Northwest and middle Atlantic regions described in Carville Earle and Ronald Hoffman, "The Foundation of the Modern Economy: Agriculture and the Costs of Labor in the United States and England, 1800–60," *American Historic*

*Review,* 85 (1980):1055–94, would have restrained the use of slave labor in these regions however.

3. Nöel Deerr, *The History of Sugar,* 2 vols. (London, 1949–50), 1:235–36, 240; Robert Stein, "The French Sugar Business in the Eighteenth Century: A Quantitative Study," *Business History,* 22 (1980):4–8; Seymour Drescher, *Econocide: British Slavery in the Era of Abolition* (Pittsburgh, 1977), pp. 46–60; Richard B. Sheridan, *The Development of the Plantations to 1750: An Era of West Indian Prosperity, 1750–1775* (Kingston, Jamaica, 1970), pp. 73–111, Radjnarain M. N. Panday, *Agriculture in Surinam, 1650–1950* (Amsterdam, 1959), pp. 18–21.

4. José Jobson de A. Arruda, *O Brasil no comércio colonial* (São Paulo, 1980), p. 611; Roberto C. Simonsen, *História econômica do Brasil (1500–1820)* 6th ed. (São Paulo, 1969), pp. 269–302, 361–87; Deerr, *History of Sugar,* 2:530; Catherine Lugar, "The Portuguese Tobacco Trade and Tobacco Growers of Bahia in the Late Colonial Period," in Dauril Alden and Warren Dean (eds.), *Essays Concerning the Socioeconomic History of Brazil and Portuguese India* (Gainesville, Fla., 1977), pp. 26–57.

5. Roland D. Hussey, *The Caracas Company, 1728–1784* (Cambridge, Mass., 1934), pp. 52–70, 86–89, 178–81, 207–17, 233–34. For the relatively small importance of slavery in Venezuela and its decline, see John V. Lombardi, *The Decline and Abolition of Negro Slavery in Venezuela, 1820–1854* (Westport, Conn., 1971), pp. 3–9, 95–121.

6. Médéric-Louis-Élie Moreau de Saint-Méry, *Description . . . de la partie française de l'isle de Saint Domingue,* 3 vols. (Paris, 1958; originally published in 1797), 1:28, 118–19; Philip D. Curtin, *The Atlantic Slave Trade: A Census* (Madison, Wis., 1969), pp. 75–79; Drescher, *Econocide,* p. 47.

7. Paul E. Lovejoy, "The Volume of the Atlantic Slave Trade: A Synthesis," *Journal of African History,* 23 (1982):473–501; Nicolaas W. Posthumus, *Inquiry into the History of Prices in Holland,* 2 vols. (Leiden, 1946–64), 1:Table 58; Earl J. Hamilton, *War and Prices in Spain, 1651–1800* (Cambridge, Mass., 1947), pp. 238–41, 246–49, 254–57; Robert Stein, "The French Sugar Business in the Eighteenth Century, p. 14.

8. The available data on sugar exports have been pulled together in Dauril Alden, "Late Colonial Brazil, 1750–1808," in Leslie Bethell (ed.), *The Cambridge History of Latin America,* 8 vols. (Cambridge, 1984), 2:630.

9. Ibid., 626–53; Rudolph W. Bauss, "Rio de Janiero: The Rise of Late Colonial Brazil's Dominant Emporium, 1777–1808," Ph.D. diss., Tulane University, 1977, pp. 52–102; Dauril Alden, "The Growth and Decline of Indigo Production in Colonial Brazil: A Study in Comparative Economic History," *Journal of Economic History,* 25 (1965):35–60; Vitorino Magalhães Godinho, *Prix et monnaies au Portugal, 1750–1850* (Paris, 1955), pp. 56–67, 244–45 and charts at end of the work; Harold B. Johnson, Jr., "A Preliminary Inquiry into Money, Prices, and Wages in Rio de Janeiro, 1763–1823," in Dauril Alden (ed.), *Colonial Roots of Modern Brazil* (Berkeley, Calif., 1973), p. 253. For a series on Brazilian gold production, 1751–94, see *Select Committee Report on the High Price of Gold Bullion,* PP, 1810, 3:173–74. Jean Tarrade, *Le Commerce colonial de la France à la fin de l'ancien régime: L'Evolution du régime de "l'exclusif" de 1763 à 1789,* 2 vols. (Paris, 1972), 2:760–73, has the most convenient survey of price trends of the major plantation products in the 1780s.

10. Arruda, *O Brasil no comércio colonial,* pp. 608–10; Lugar, "Portuguese Tobacco Trade," pp. 41–53; Simonsen, *História econômica do Brasil,* pp. 368–69, 381; Bauss, "Rio de Janeiro," pp. 62–65, 158; Drescher, *Econocide,* pp. 84, 251; Thomas

Ellison, *The Cotton Trade of Great Britain* (London, 1886), pp. 80–89. The spread of cotton cultivation in northeastern Brazil is described in Luís Amaral, *História geral da agricultura brasileira,* 2 vols. (São Paulo, 1958), 2:3–25, and Alden, "Late Colonial Brazil," pp. 631–37.

11. John Fisher, "The Imperial Response to 'Free Trade': Spanish Imports from Spanish America, 1778–1796," *Journal of Latin American Studies,* 17 (1985):35–78.

12. For tobacco, see Fernando Ortiz Fernandez, *Cuban Counterpoint: Tobacco and Sugar,* trans. Harriet de Onis (New York, 1947). For other crops, see Allan Cristelow, "Contraband Trade Between Jamaica and the Spanish Main, and the Free Port Act of 1766," *Hispanic American Historical Review,* 22 (1942):309–43. The royal decrees of Aug. 30, 1815, and July 16, 1819, are usually recognized as making private land tenure in Cuba secure.

13. For the early history of the *asiento,* see Georges Scelle, "The Slave Trade in the Spanish Colonies of America: The Asiento," *American Journal of International Law,* 4 (1910):612–61. For post-1715 developments, see Colin A. Palmer, *Human Cargoes: The British Slave Trade to Spanish America 1700–1739* (Chicago, 1981), pp. 59–82. For prices, see Palmer, *Human Cargoes,* pp. 123–24; Richard N. Bean, *The British Trans-Atlantic Slave Trade, 1650–1775* (New York, 1975), pp. 200–201, 206; David R. Murray, *Odious Commerce: Britain, Spain and the Abolition of the Cuban Slave Trade* (Cambridge, 1980), p. 6.

14. Murray, *Odious Commerce,* pp. 3, 9; Palmer, *Human Cargoes,* pp. 83–111; Kenneth Kiple, *Blacks in Colonial Cuba, 1774–1899* (Gainesville, Fla., 1976), pp. 25–27; José Antonio de Saco, *Colección de papeles históricos, políticos y de otros ramos sobre la isla de Cuba,* 3 vols. (Havana, 1960):1:164;

15. Richard B. Sheridan, *The Development of the Plantations to 1750* (Kingston, Jamaica, 1970), p. 70; C. H. Haring, *The Spanish Empire in the Americas* (New York, 1947), pp. 335–47; Hubert H. S. Aimes, *A History of Slavery in Cuba, 1511 to 1868* (New York, 1907), pp. 20–53; James F. King, "Evolution of the Free Trade Principle in Spanish Colonial Administration," *Hispanic American Historical Review,* 22 (1942):34–56. John Fisher has charted a 400 percent increase in imports into Spain from Spanish America between 1778 and 1782–96, most of it precious metals. European demand pressures no doubt reinforced the impact of trade liberalization on this process (Fisher, "The Imperial Response to 'Free Trade.'").

16. Bibiano Torres Ramirez, *La compañía gaditana de negros* (Seville, 1973), in particular pp. 167–78; Murray, *Odious Commerce,* pp. 4–19. For prices before 1789, see Aimes, *History of Slavery in Cuba,* p. 47n.

17. See app. A for slave imports. For sugar exports see Jacob de la Pezuela, *Diccionario . . . de la Isla de Cuba,* 4 vols. (Madrid, 1863–66), 4:63; and Alexander von Humboldt, *Ensayo político sobre la isla de Cuba* (Havana, 1960), pp. 205–6. A crude comparison of slave prices in Cuba and Jamaica in the 1790s suggests that the differential between the two regions was closed by British prices rising rather than Spanish prices falling. Presumably, in the British case the increase in demand for slaves was greater than the increase in supply, whereas in Cuba the change in demand was matched on the supply side as the measures liberalizing slave imports took effect. For price data, see Richard B. Sheridan, "Slave Demography in the British West Indies and the Abolition of the Slave Trade," in David Eltis and James Walvin (eds.), *The Abolition of the Atlantic Slave Trade* (Madison, Wis., 1981), p. 277; Aimes, *History of Slavery in Cuba,* pp. 267–68; and, in particular, see Roger T. Anstey, *The Atlantic Slave Trade and British Abolition, 1760–1810* (London, 1975), pp. 41, 47.

18. R. Stein, "The French Sugar Business," pp. 4–8; Drescher, *Econocide,* pp. 46–60

Alexander Moreau de Jonnès, *Recherches statistiques sur l'esclavage colonial et sur les moyens de la supprimer* (Paris, 1842), pp. 15–42.

19. Tarrade, *Le Commerce colonial de la France*, in particular 1:146–56; Gabriel Debien, *Les Colons de Saint Domingue et la Révolution* (Paris, 1953), pp. 33–34, 54–78; Thomas O. Ott, *The Haitian Revolution, 1789–1814* (Knoxville, Tenn., 1973), pp. 28–35.

20. Eugene D. Genovese, *From Rebellion to Revolution: Afro-American Slave Revolts in the making of the Modern World* (Baton Rouge, La., 1981), pp. 18–20, 98–102; Gabriel Debien, *Les Esclaves aux Antilles françaises (XVIIe–XVIIIe siècles)* (Basse-Terre, Guadeloupe, 1974), pp. 66–68, notes the rapid Africanization of the St. Domingue slave-labor force. It seems likely, however, that the African proportion was even greater in 1791 than the scattered plantation data (much of it from 1797) suggest. The ratio of imports in the 1780s to the slave population in 1791 in St. Domingue was much greater than the equivalent ratio for Jamaica in the decade 1798–1807 yet the ratio in the 1796–97 St. Domingue sample discussed by Debien is very close to that projected by Barry Higman for Jamaica in 1807 (*Slave Population and Economy in Jamaica, 1807–1834* [Cambridge, 1976], p. 76). David Patrick Geggus, however, has pointed out that the implications for rebellion of a large African-born ratio are not entirely clear (*Slavery, War and Revolution: The British Occupation of Saint Domingue 1793–1798* [Oxford, 1982], pp. 23–24).

21. For the *petits blancs* see Moreau de Saint-Méry, *Description . . . de Saint Domingue*, 2:1105; Charles Frostin, *Les Révoltes blanches à Saint Domingue au XVIIe et XVIIIe siècles* (Paris, 1975), pp. 68–69. For the free coloreds, see Robert Stein, "The Free Men of Colour and the Revolution in Saint Domingue, 1789–1792," *Histoire sociale*, 14 (1981):7–28, in particular 14; and Michel-Rolph Trouillot, "Motion in the System: Coffee, Color, and Slavery in Eighteenth-Century Saint Domingue," *Review*, 5 (1982):349–63.

22. Market shares are from Drescher, *Econocide*, pp. 77–78. It should be noted, however, that estimates of Cuban sugar exports at this time vary.

23. Supra, chap 1.

24. Arruda, *O Brasil no comércio colonial*, pp. 351–54; Alden, "Late Colonial Brazil," pp. 630–31, 643–46; Drescher, *Econocide*, pp. 199–201; Stanley J. Stein, *Vassouras, a Brazilian Coffee County, 1850–1900* (Cambridge, Mass., 1957), pp. 7–10; Amaral, *História geral de agricultura*, 2:24; Afonso de Escragnolle Taunay, *Pequena história do café no Brasil (1727–1937)* (São Paulo, 1945), pp. 35–47; Instituto brasileiro de geografia e estatística, *Anuário estatístico do Brasil*, Ano V–1939–40, pp. 1374, 1376. On the relative importance of sugar and gold, see Bauss, "Rio de Janeiro," pp. 282–84, the assessment of which is accepted here over Simonsen, *História econômica do Brasil*, p. 380. The latter shows that sugar remained the major export down to 1820.

25. *Anuário estatístico*, Ano V, p. 1374; PP, 1831–32, 20:946–47.

26. Arruda, *O Brasil no comércio colonial*, pp. 179, 204; Alden, "Late Colonial Brazil," 630–31; idem "Manoel Luis Vieira: An Entrepeneur in Rio de Janeiro During Brazil's Eighteenth-Century Agricultural Renaissance," *Hispanic American Historical Review*, 39 (1959):536–37; Bauss, "Rio de Janeiro," pp. 60–69, 96–100, 157–59, 177–80, 369.

27. Manuel Moreno Fraginals, *The Sugarmill: The Socioeconomic Complex of Sugar in Cuba, 1760–1860*, trans. Cedric Belfrage (New York, 1976), pp. 20–25, 41–42. The takeover of tobacco by sugar is a central part of Moreno Fraginals's thesis.

28. For the development of coffee, see Francisco Pérez de la Riva y Pons, *El café: Historia de su cultivo y explotación en Cuba* (Havana, 1944), but the basic data source

for exports is Pezuela, *Diccionario . . . de la isla de Cuba,* 1:225. For sugar exports, see Ramón de la Sagra, *Historia económico—politica y estadística de la Isla de Cuba* (Havana, 1831), p. 172; Aimes, *History of Slavery in Cuba,* p. 267; Richard Robert Madden, *The Island of Cuba* (London, 1849), p. 28.

29. Lewis C. Gray, *History of Agriculture in the Southern United States to 1860* 2 vols. (Washington, 1933), 2:673–90; Drescher, *Econocide,* pp. 84–85; Robert William Fogel and Stanley L. Engerman, *Time on the Cross: The Economics of American Negro Slavery,* 2 vols. (Boston, 1974), 1:90–93; Ellison, *The Cotton Trade,* pp. 80–105.

30. Drescher, *Econocide,* pp. 16–112; supra, pp. 10–11.

31. Anstey, *Atlantic Slave Trade,* p. 47; Sheridan, "Slave Demography in the British West Indies," p. 277.

32. For Dutch restrictions, see "Petition from Planters of Essequibo and Demerary, 6th Feb., 1788, to the States General of United Provinces," in PP, 1789, 26:(646a). The slave trade was not, of course, completely unfettered even in 1800. From 1788 British traders were subjected to restrictions on numbers of slaves carried; the Portuguese and other traders could ship from and to designated ports only. In addition, various U.S. states closed their ports to the transatlantic trade prior to 1807. The basic point however stands.

33. The mean price of 914 African male adults recruited for the British Army's Windward and Leeward Islands Command was £71 (Roger Norman Buckley, *Slaves in Red Coats: The British West India Regiments, 1795–1815* [New Haven, Conn., 1979], p. 55). Over a period of three months in the same year, the *Enterprise* sold 180 African male adults in Havana for £70.8 (Account Book of the *Enterprise,* Liverpool Public Library).

34. See Fogel and Engerman, *Time on the Cross,* 1:20–29; C. Vann Woodward, *American Counterpoint: Slavery and Racism in the North-South Dialogue* (Boston, 1964), pp. 78–91; and Stanley L. Engerman, "Some Economic and Demographic Comparisons of Slavery in the United States and the British West Indies," *Economic History Review,* 29 (1976):258–75 for discussions of American slave demographic trends in a comparative context. A rate of natural population change of −1.0 percent per year and a "seasoning" mortality of 10 percent suggests that imports between 1807 and 1860 would have had to have been 3.6 million to produce a slave population of 4.0 million in 1860.

35. Higman, *Slave Population and Economy,* pp. 60–66, 201–5, 215–24; D. Eltis, "The Traffic in Slaves Between the British West Indian Colonies, *1807–1833," Economic History Review,* 25 (1972):59. Higman, *Slave Populations of the British Caribbean, 1807–1834* (Baltimore, 1984), chaps. 4, 6; Richard B. Sheridan, "'Sweet Malefactor': The Social Costs of Slavery and Sugar in Jamaica and Cuba, 1807–1854," *Economic History Review,* 29 (1976):239–49. Stanley L. Engerman, "Economic Adjustments to Emancipation in the United States and the British West Indies," *Journal of Interdisciplinary History,* 13 (1982):191–220, in particular 196; Robert Evans, Jr., "The Economics of American Negro Slavery," in Universities National Bureau Committee for Economic Research, *Aspects of Labor Economics* (Princeton, N.J., 1962), p. 216.

36. Infra, p. 262. Phillip E. LeVeen, "The African Slave Supply Response," *African Studies Review,* 18 (1974):9–28; prices in excess of £20 per slave are indicated over a wide range of African coastal markets in the period 1800 to 1807. See Elizabeth Donnan, *Documents Illustrative of the History of the Slave Trade to America,* 4 vols. (New York, 1965), 4:535, 544, 551–567; Liverpool Public Library, Account books of the *Fortune, Lottery* and *Enterprise;* University of Liverpool Library, Account

Book of the *Lottery;* James Tobin's evidence in *Third Report of the Select Committee on the Slave Trade,* PP, 1847–48, 22:173, 175. For post-1807 prices, see R. Thorpe to Admiralty, Jan. 16, 1812, enc. R. Thorpe to Lord Liverpool, July 31, 1811, Adm. 1/4220; FO 308, vols. 1 and 2; and app. C.

37. Simonsen, *História econômica do Brasil,* p. 271; Angel Rosenblat, *La población indígena y el mestizaje en América,* 2 vols. (Buenos Aires, 1950), 1:36, gives 920,000 whites and 1.96 million slaves for 1825 out of a total population of 4.0 million. Cf. Oliver Onody, "Quelques traits caractéristiques de l'évolution historique de la population de Brésil," in Paul Deprez (ed.), *Population and Economics* (Winnipeg, 1970), pp. 339–40. S. J. Stein, *Vassouras,* 294, gives alternate figures for 1819 and 1823 which do not distinguish between white and nonwhite free populations.

38. Herbert S. Klein, "The Colored Freedmen in Brazilian Slave Society," *Journal of Social History,* 3 (1969):35–36; Bauss, "Rio de Janeiro," pp. 152, 157–58, 201. At the end of a century of mining activity, 76 percent of the population of Minas Gerais was black, the vast majority slaves. In the course of the first two decades of the nineteenth century, many slaves were shifted into cotton, and later into coffee, also products with a high value-to-weight ratio. Minas Gerais remained the most populous slave province until emancipation (Amilcar Martins Filho and Roberto B. Martins, "Slavery in a Nonexport Economy: Nineteenth-Century Minas Gerais Revisited," *Hispanic American Historical Review,* 63 [1983]:537–68).

39. For the mixture of slave and free labor in Bahia tobacco and cacao production and the provisioning zones of the larger cities, see Lugar, "Portuguese Tobacco Trade," 29–35, 53–54; Stuart Schwartz, "Free Labor in a Slave Economy: The 'Lavradores de Cana' of Colonial Bahia," in Alden, *Colonial Roots of Modern Brazil* (Berkeley, Calif., 1973), pp. 147–97; Colin M. MacLachlan, "African Slave Trade and Economic Development in Amazonia, 1700–1800," in Robert B. Toplin (ed.), *Slavery and Race Relations in Latin America* (Westport, Conn., 1974), pp. 121–26, 136–39; Amaral, *História geral da agricultura,* 1:291–300 and 2:119–29; Roberto Borges Martins, "Growing in Silence: The Slave Economy of Nineteenth-Century Minas Gerais, Brazil," *Journal of Economic History,* 42 (1982):222–23.

40. Johnson, "A Preliminary Inquiry into Money," p. 265; Bauss, "Rio de Janiero," pp. 242–44. José Jobson de Andrade Arruda, "O Brasil no comércio colonial (1796–1808)," Ph.D. diss., Universidad de São Paulo, 1972, p. 201, cited in Herbert S. Klein, *The Middle Passage* (Princeton, N.J., 1978), p. 63. The comment on real values is based on the conversion of Johnson's data for fourteen products to an unweighted price index for Rio de Janeiro.

41. App. F; Deerr, *History of Sugar,* 1:113, 131, 193–204, 2:377; Pezuela, *Diccionario . . . de la isla de Cuba,* 1:225; *Anuário estatístico do Brasil,* Ano V, pp. 1374, 1376. Comparisons of British and non-British sugar producers at this time have often been made on the basis of production trends in Cuba and Jamaica without regard to the output growth of Mauritius (in the Indian Ocean), Trinidad and British Guiana—prior, at least, to Stanley L. Engerman's work.

42. Figures on slave imports before 1780 are scarce. Information on ship destinations and slave exports for midcentury Angola suggest that imports into Rio de Janeiro in midcentury were at levels considerably in excess of the 7,000 arrivals per year in the early 1780s. Klein, *Middle Passage* (pp. 27, 32), found that 51 percent of slaves leaving Luanda in midcentury were destined for Rio de Janeiro. The equivalent proportion of Benguela exports was probably higher. Angolan exports in the 1750s and 1760s were in excess of 13,000 a year and Rio de Janeiro received some slaves in addition from other parts of Africa. Cf. Alden, "Late Colonial Brazil."

43. Arruda, *O Brasil no comércio colonial,* pp. 417–19, 627; Amaral, *História geral da*

*agricultura* 2:321–323; Taunay, *Pequena história do café,* pp. 33–50; Alden, "Late Colonial Brazil," pp. 643–46.

44. The sudden departure of the English and Americans from Angola and the Congo north region may well have reduced the African price of a slave substantially, but this is unlikely to have had a huge impact on the price in the Americas, given the size of the shipping-cost wedge. Even assuming a large impact, why should the response of the Rio de Janeiro slave purchaser have been so much stronger than that of his counterparts in other regions?

45. See Alan K. Manchester, "The Transfer of the Portuguese Court to Rio de Janeiro," in H. Keith and S. F. Edwards (eds.), *Conflict and Continuity in Brazilian Society* (Columbia, S.C., 1969), pp. 148–83.

46. *Anuário estatístico,* Ano V, p. 1374; J. H. Galloway, "The Sugar Industry of Pernambuco During the Nineteenth Century," *Annals of the Association of American Geographers,* 58 (1968):285–303.

47. Infra, pp. 52–55.

48. Estimates of total North Atlantic sugar imports in 1787 (Drescher, *Econocide,* p. 127) may be compared with world production estimates of cane sugar from the 1820s (Moreno Fraginals, *El ingenio, complejo económico social cubano del azúcar,* 3 vols. [Havana, 1978], 3:35).

49. For Cuban and Brazilian prices see app. C. For prices in Trinidad and the United States, see supra, pp. 296–97.

50. Supra, chap. 1.

51. The stream of indentured Asian labor used in most sugar-production areas did not become significant until after 1850. See Stanley L. Engerman, "Servants to Slaves to Servants: Contract Labor and European Expansion," in P. C. Emmer (ed.), *Colonialism and Migration: Indentured Labor before and after Slavery* (Dordrecht, 1986), pp. 263–94.

52. Pieter C. Emmer, "Surinam and the Decline of the Dutch Slave Trade," *Revue française d'histoire d'outre-mer,* 62 (1975):245–50.

### Chapter 4

1. For a broad survey of these supply side effects see H. A. Gemery and J. S. Hogendorn, "Technological Change, Slavery and the Slave Trade," in Clive Dewey and A. G. Hopkins (eds.), *The Imperial Impact: Studies in the Economic History of Africa and India* (London, 1978), pp. 246–59.

2. Richard B. Sheridan, "The Commercial and Financial Organization of the British Slave Trade, 1750–1807," *Economic History Review,* 11 (1958):249–50.

3. The eighteenth-century ratio is calculated from table 4 in Paul E. Lovejoy's "The Volume of the Atlantic Slave Trade: A Synthesis," *Journal of African History,* 23 (1982):473–501, on the assumption that the North American and Portuguese carriers were based in the Americas and all the rest were based in Europe. The nineteenth-century ratio is based on the region of origin breakdown provided infra, table 9, p. 147.

4. The major features of the late eighteenth- and early nineteenth-century southern Brazilian slave trade are outlined in Joseph C. Miller, "Some Aspects of the Commercial Organization of Slaving at Luanda, Angola—1760–1830," in H. A. Gemery and J. S. Hogendorn (eds.), *The Uncommon Market: Essays in the Economic History of the Atlantic Slave Trade* (New York, 1979), pp. 77–106; idem, "Legal Portuguese Slaving from Angola. Some Preliminary Indications of Volume and Direction, 1760–1830," *Revue française d'histoire d'outre-mer,* 62 (1975):135–76;

Rudolph W. Bauss, "Rio de Janeiro: The Rise of Late Colonial Brazil's Dominar.
Emporium, 1777–1808." Ph.D. diss., Tulane University, 1977, pp. 224–74; Herbert
S. Klein, *The Middle Passage* (Princeton, N.J., 1978), pp. 23–94; Mauricio Goulart,
*Escrivadão africana no Brasil (das origens à extinção do tráfico)* (São Paulo, 1950),
pp. 173–217.

5. Pierre Verger, *Flux et reflux de la traite des nègres entre le golfe de Bénin et Bahia
de Todos os Santos* (Paris, 1968), pp. 28–163; António Carreira, *As companhias
pombalinas de navegação comércio e tráfico de escravos entre a costa africana e o
nordeste brasileiro* (Porto, Portugal, 1969), pp. 388–90. For evidence of French
exports to Brazil, see Robert Stein, *The French Slave Trade in the Eighteenth Century* (Madison, Wis., 1979), p. 107.

6. Verger, *Flux et reflux,* pp. 64–65; Catherine Lugar, "The Portuguese Tobacco Trade
and Tobacco Growers of Bahia in the Late Colonial Period," in Dauril Alden and
Warren Dean (eds.), *Essays Concerning the Socioeconomic History of Brazil and
Portuguese India* (Gainesville, Fla., 1977), pp. 38–39, 46–49. Bauss, "Rio de
Janeiro," pp. 239–59, lists Angolan imports from Rio de Janeiro and attempts a
calculation of gold exports to Africa. See also José Honório Rodrigues, *Brazil and
Africa,* trans. Richard A. Mazzara and Sam Hileman (Berkeley, Calif., 1965), pp.
27–35.

7. Much of this paragraph is based on R. Stein, *French Slave Trade,* 25–47, Jean Tarrade, *Le Commerce colonial de la France à la fin de l'ancien régime: L'Evolution du
régime de "l'exclusif" de 1763 à 1789,* 2 vols. (Paris, 1972), 1:83–112; and *Report
of the Privy Council Committee on the Slave Trade,* pt. 6, France, in PP, 1789, 26
(646a).

8. A description of British slaver use of the French flag as well as a detailed explanation
of the methods employed to inflate the measured tonnage, and thereby the bounty,
may be found in Thomas Clarkson to Comte de Mirabeau, Nov. 17, 1789, CN 36,
Clarkson mss. See also Roger T. Anstey, *The Atlantic Slave Trade and British Abolition, 1760–1810* (London, 1975), pp. 11–12.

9. *Report of the Privy Council Committee on the Slave Trade,* pt. 6, Holland, in PP,
1789, 26(646a); Pieter C. Emmer, "Surinam and the Decline of the Dutch Slave
Trade," *Revue française d'histoire d'outre-mer,* 62 (1975):246–48.

10. See app. A.

11. Anstey, *Atlantic Slave Trade,* pp. 38–57; Svend E. Green-Pedersen, "The History of
the Danish Negro Slave Trade, 1733–1807: An Interim Survey Relating in Particular to Its Volume, Structure, Profitability and Abolition," *Revue française d'histoire d'outre-mer,* 62 (1975):209–11; Robert Stein, "The Profitability of the Nantes
Slave Trade, 1783–1792," *Journal of Economic History,* 35 (1975):779–93; Jay
Coughtry, *The Notorious Triangle: Rhode Island and the African Slave Trade, 1700–
1807* (Philadelphia, 1981), pp. 19–20; David Richardson, "Profits in the Liverpool
Slave Trade: The Accounts of William Davenport, 1757–1784," in Roger Anstey
and P. E. H. Hair (eds.), *Liverpool, the African Slave Trade, and Abolition: Essays
to Illustrate Current Knowledge and Research* (Liverpool, 1976), pp. 60–90; Joseph
E. Inikori, "Market Structure and the Profits of the British African Trade in the Late
Eighteenth Century," *Journal of Economic History,* 41 (1981):745–76. The last two
articles provide detailed accounts for 98 voyages (74 from Richardson, 24 from Inikori). Using Richardson's assumptions on insurance, discount rate on bills and
credit costs on goods advanced by the manufacturer (p. 74), the rate of return per
venture on the outset cost for all 98 voyages is 15.2 percent. As the average venture
in the Richardson sample lasted 18 months, this rate converts to an annual return
of 12.4 percent, again on the basis of Richardson's adjustments (p. 76). Inikori does

not provide preferred discount rates, and so on, but instead includes these items only when they are mentioned by the merchants involved and at the rates quoted in the accounts. The 27 percent return he cites on 24 ventures (p. 772) thus almost certainly does not take into account discounts on all bill remittances, insurance costs and credit costs, and it is certainly not an annualized rate, though the author does not make this last point explicit. On the evidence of these 98 voyages, Inikori and Richardson would presumably agree that profits in the British slave trade could not have much exceeded 15 percent a year, which would not seem to fall outside the range of normal profits, given the degree of risk involved.

12. Inikori, "British African Trade," argues that a high degree of concentration and considerable barriers to entry existed in the British slave trade. But in the industry as a whole, including all the nations involved, the competitive basis of transactions can scarcely be doubted. If each of the major national participants in the West African trade had only four major firms involved—say twelve to sixteen firms sharing two thirds of the market—concentration would have approached that in the current U.S. textile industry, scarcely an example of an oligopoly. Roger Anstey (*Atlantic Slave Trade,* pp. 6–10) has, moreover, calculated a somewhat lower ratio. But even supposing concentration ratios accurately indicate the ability to earn economic rent and even supposing that this rent was not passed along to suppliers of these firms, the monopoly profits for such merchants on the West African coast on a long-run basis must have been slim.

13. David Eltis, "Merchandise Exchanged for Slaves Entering the Transatlantic Slave Trade," unpublished paper, 1984.

14. Evidence given to the Privy Council Committee suggests that a better "sort" or mix of goods was possible in British ports, but the same sources indicate extensive trading on the coast before the exchange for slaves was made (*Report of the Privy Council Committee on the Slave Trade* in PP, 1789, 26 [646a]). For samples of trading cargoes see D. Rinchon, *Le Trafic négrier d'après les livres de commerce du capitaine Gantois Pierre-Ignace-Liévin van Alstein* (Paris, 1938), pp. 99–104; David Richardson, "West African Consumption Patterns and Their Influence on the Eighteenth-Century English Slave Trade," in Gemery and Hogendorn, *Uncommon Market,* pp. 312–15.

15. D. Richardson, "West African Consumption Patterns," pp. 323–24, 325–26.

16. See Klein, *Middle Passage,* chaps. 3, 7 and 8 for a comparison of these ratios for the three major eighteenth-century carriers, Britain, France and Portugal.

17. *Report of the Privy Council Committee on the Slave Trade* in PP, 1789, 26 (646a).

18. Coughtry, *Notorious Triangle,* pp. 73–78; Tommy Todd Hamm, "The American Slave Trade with Africa, 1620–1807." Ph.D. diss., University of Indiana, 1975, pp. 384–444.

19. See Virginia B. Platt, "'And Don't Forget the Guinea Voyage': The Slave Trade of Aaron Lopez of Newport," *William & Mary Quarterly,* 32 (1975):617.

20. On the importance and sources of credit, see Inikori, "British African Trade," pp. 756–57; and D. Richardson, "Profits in the Liverpool Slave Trade," pp. 71–72.

21. Sheridan, "Commercial and Financial Organization of the British Slave Trade," pp. 249–63, in particular pp. 261–62; S. G. Checkland, "Finance for the West Indies, 1780–1815," *Economic History Review,* 10 (1958):466–67; K. G. Davies, "The Origins of the Commission System in the West India Trade," *Transactions of the Royal Historical Society,* 5th ser., 2 (1952):91–94.

22. R. Stein, *French Slave Trade,* pp. 142–43.

23. *Report of the Privy Council Committee on the Slave Trade,* pt. 6, France, in PP, 1789, 26 (646a).

24. The disadvantage of the Rhode Island traders relative to their Liverpool counter-parts on the matter of bill remittances is discussed in Platt, "'And Don't Forget the Guinea Voyage,'" pp. 601–18. The author concludes, "Lack of established financial relations with the English planters in the West Indies resulted in slow payment for slave cargoes and protracted negotiations for the return cargoes of molasses and other products" (p. 617). Spanish and French merchants would presumably have been at an even greater disadvantage. Cf. George E. Brooks, Jr., *Yankee Traders, Old Coasters and African Middlemen. A History of American Legitimate Trade with West Africa in the Nineteenth Century* (Boston, 1970), p. 17.

25. Coughtry, *Notorious Triangle*, pp. 180–81, 197–98; Inikori, "British African Trade," p. 765. By the end of the period British slavers were returning with produce from Cuba (see Charles R. Hand, "The 'Kitty's Amelia,' The Last Liverpool Slaver," *Proceedings of the Historic Society of Lancashire and Cheshire*, 82 [1930]:70), but produce was not a substitute for credit instruments. This no doubt helps explain why so few of the *asientos* (including those granted to the British) were, in fact, filled. Inikori tends to recognize the advantages of cash transactions to the trade but not the drawbacks.

26. Petition of "the Town and Neighbourhood of Manchester," May 13, 1806, quoted in Seymour Drescher, "Capitalism and Abolition: Values and Forces in Britain, 1783–1814," in Anstey and Hair, *Liverpool, the African Slave Trade and Abolition*, p. 187; see also pp. 186–88.

27. There was, in fact, a steady stream of regulatory legislation from 1788 that tended to increase shipping costs: *Statutes at Large*, 28 Geo. 3. c. 54; 29 Geo. 3. c. 56; 35 Geo. 3. c. 90; 37 Geo. 3. c. 104; 37 Geo. 3. c. 118; 38 Geo. 3. c. 88; 39 Geo. 3. c. 80. For the passage of Dolben's Act, see James W. LoGerfo, "Sir William Dolben and 'The Cause of Humanity.' The Passage of the Slave Trade Regulation Act of 1788," *Eighteenth Century Studies*, 6 (1973):431–51; for the effectiveness of this legislation, see Seymour Drescher, *Econocide: British Slavery in the Era of Abolition* (Pittsburgh, 1977), pp. 210–13; Herbert S. Klein and Stanley L. Engerman, "Slave Mortality on British Ships, 1791–1797," in Anstey and Hair, *Liverpool, the African Slave Trade and Abolition*, pp. 119–21.

28. *Report of the Privy Council Committee on the Slave Trade*, pt. 6, Spain, in PP, 1789, 26 (646a). This source also reprints the 1789 cédula. See Hubert H. S. Aimes, *A History of Slavery in Cuba, 1511–1868* (New York, 1907), pp. 41–53. For the unsuccessful Spanish attempts to enter the traffic, see Bibiano Torres Ramirez, *La compañía gaditana de negros* (Seville, 1973), in particular pp. 111–18.

29. Klein, *Middle Passage*, pp. 215–19. For records of ships captured in the inter-island trade after 1796, see the returns of the Vice Admiralty courts in the Bahamas and Tortola in HC 49/97 and 101. For the years after 1807 these were printed in PP, 1813–14, 12:325–33.

30. One Liverpool merchant claimed that his entire capital was committed to eighteen ships supplying the Spanish colonies, an involvement with Britain's enemies to which James Stephen, the elder, referred in his *War in Disguise* and that stimulated the campaign for the abolition of the British trade to all foreign possessions. Averil MacKenzie-Grieve, *The Last Years of the English Slave Trade: Liverpool, 1750–1807* (London, 1941), p. 269; James Stephen, *War in Disguise or the Frauds of the Neutral Flags* (London, 1805); Anstey, *Atlantic Slave Trade*, pp. 350–56; Drescher, *Econocide*, p. 208. For Spanish involvement see Manuel Moreno Fraginals, *El ingenio, complejo económico social cubano del azúcar*, 3 vols. (Havana, 1978), 1:250–69.

31. Anstey, *Atlantic Slave Trade*, p. 376, n. 39, suggests 25 percent for the year ending

Oct. 10, 1805. Data on imports in tables A.5 and A.6 suggest about 40 percent for the years 1801–7, though this is biased upwards by perhaps 5 percentage points on account of the abolition of the British trade to foreign territories a year before the abolition of the complete trade.

32. Coughtry, *Notorious Triangle,* p. 176; David R. Murray, *Odious Commerce: Britain, Spain and the Abolition of the Cuban Slave Trade* (Cambridge, 1980), pp. 14–15; R. Stein, *The French Slave Trade,* p. 107; Svend E. Green-Pederson, "Colonial Trade under the Danish Flag: A Case Study of the Danish Slave Trade to Cuba, 1790–1807," *Scandinavian Journal of History,* 5 (1980):93–120, in particular 103.

33. Aimes, *History of Slavery in Cuba,* pp. 56, 94, 113. Moreno Fraginals implies significant Cuban involvement from the early 1800s but before 1815 much of this probably consisted of Cuban investment in American ventures or Cuban importing houses which accepted slaves on consignment (*El ingenio,* 1:262–69).

34. Klein, *Middle Passage,* p. 215.

35. "Minute Book of the British and Portuguese Mixed Commission," FO 308/1.

36. Sir William Scott (later Lord Stowell) to Admiralty, Aug. 1, 1814, Adm. 1/3902. This letter may also be found in Adm. 1/4233.

37. Commander Irby to Admiralty, Nov. 23, 1812, enc Lt. Pascoe, Nov. 7, 1812, Adm. 1/1997. Colonial Office to Admiralty, Apr. 10, 1813, enc. R. Thorpe, July 6, 1812, Adm. 1/4221. These reports are supported by the records of 444 slaving expeditions scattered in the correspondence of the British Foreign Office and Admiralty. These expeditions were to all parts of the Americas in the 1808–15 period and comprise perhaps one half of all voyages attempted in these years. A non-Iberian flag was flown in only six of these instances, and three of these involved the United States flag flown by Americans inadvertently delayed on the African coast until after formal abolition went into effect.

38. The seventeen slave ships under the Portuguese flag wrongfully detained by the British Navy between 1815 and 1817 (compensation for which was assessed by the Mixed Commission of 1819) were all owned by Portuguese residents in Brazilian ports. See Minute Book, FO 308/1. Cf. Verger, *Flux et reflux,* pp. 295–98, 637–38.

39. Moreno Fraginals, *El ingenio,* 1:263. Moreno describes his data as "expediciones . . . organizadas o contratadas por negreros hispanocriollos," a phrase which does not exclude the possibility of British and U.S. involvement.

40. The slave ship data set contains 51 ships with Cuban connections detained by British cruisers between 1808 and 1817. These comprise perhaps one eighth of all slaving voyages intending to land slaves in Cuba. The main sources for these ships are the Sierrra Leone Vice Admiralty Court bundles in HCA 49, boxes 97 and 101; the files on individual cases that were appealed to the High Court in HCA 37, boxes 1 to 6; and the Anglo-Portuguese mixed commission proceedings in FO 308/1 to 3. This sample is not as biased against real Spanish vessels as might at first appear. During wartime, belligerent rights assumed by the British allowed the Royal Navy to stop and search all ships and, for part of this period, Spanish ships were liable to capture as prizes of war. Even after Spain became an ally, there was a belief among naval officers, fostered by the African Institution (explored more fully later), that slave ships were liable to capture unless the slave trade was expressly permitted by the country to which the slave ship belonged (Zachary Macaulay to Admiralty, Aug. 3, 1810, Adm. 1/4982; Apr. 23, 1811, Adm. 1/4895). It was, in part, in compensation for wrongful captures arising from this conviction that Britain handed over large sums to Spain and Portugal after 1815. For Rhode Island ships, see Coughtry, *Notorious Triangle,* p. 235.

41. Zachary Macaulay to Admiralty, July 10, 1809, Adm. 1/4887. See also Z. Macaulay to W. Roscoe, Feb. 5, 1810, and W. Roscoe to Z. Macaulay, Feb. 10, 1812, Roscoe

Letters. For French- and Danish-owned slavers under Spanish flags, see the *Nueva Amable* and the *San José* (HCA 49/101) and the *San Juan Nepomuceno* (HCA 37/5). See also *American State Papers,* 5:102.

42. Derived by dividing estimated imports into Cuba (see app. A) by the mean cargo for 1815–19 (calculated from Klein, *Middle Passage,* p. 215) and by adding a small allowance for possible British and American ventures to other regions.

43. David M. Williams, "Abolition and the Re-deployment of the Slave Fleet, 1807–1811," *Journal of Transport History,* 11 (1973):103–15.

44. See, for example, the case of James Gill in Rio de Janeiro (*Intrepida* file, HCA 37/3), and the "English house in the Havana" to which the *Dolores* belonged (*American State Papers,* 5:104).

45. Established Liverpool and London firms such as S. Holland & Co. and Messrs. Clark & Co. cleared out authentic Portuguese slavers that subsequently landed slaves in the Brazils. Examples of such Portuguese ships were the *Paquete Volante, Ligeiro, Perula, Amizade, Urbano* and *Commercio de Rio.* See T. Clarkson to Z. Macaulay, Aug. 1809; Z. Macaulay to W. Roscoe, Nov. 10, 1809, and Feb. 5, 1810; Report of Z. Macaulay to the directors of the African Institution, Nov. 7, 1809; W. Roscoe to Duke of Gloucester, Mar. 17, 1810, Roscoe Letters. See also Z. Macaulay to Admiralty, July 10, 1809, Adm. 1/4887, and Captain Irby to Admiralty, Nov. 30, 1811, Adm. 1/1996.

46. Owners uncovered by the navy and the abolitionists included S. McDowal & Co., Leigh & Co., J. Bibby and Co., M. R. Dawson, and Messrs. Whitehead & Hebbert— all of Liverpool and most of them participants in the pre-1807 traffic. The McDowal Company was, in fact, the largest shipping firm in Liverpool. T. Clarkson to Z. Macaulay, Aug. 1809; Z. Macaulay to W. Roscoe, Feb. 5, 1810, Roscoe Letters; *Donna Marianna* folder, HCA 37/2; R. Craig and R. C. Jarvis, *Liverpool Registry of Merchant Ships* (Manchester, 1967), p. 195. Members of the D'Wolf and Smith families of Rhode Island, George Fowler Trenholm and John Kerr of New York, and Francis Depan and Broadfoot & Co. of Charleston, S.C., were also involved. (Coughtry, *Notorious Triangle,* pp. 234–35; Z. Macaulay to Admiralty, Oct. 15, 1811, Adm. 1/4897.)

47. For surveys of the practices of illegal British slave traders, see G. M. Gorthing, Doctors' Commons, to Admiralty, Aug. 8, 1810 (enc.), Adm. 1/3899; Z. Macaulay to Admiralty, Sept. 21, 1811, Adm. 1/4897; Col. Off. to Admiralty, Apr. 10, 1813, enc. R. Thorpe to Bathurst, July 6, 1812, Adm. 1/4221; *San Joaquim* folder, HCA 37/1; *Laberinto* folder, HCA 37/2; *Extracts from the Report of the Commissioners Appointed for Investigating the State of Settlements and Governments on the Coast of Africa,* PP, 1812, 10:278–79; E. I. Herrington, "British Measures for the Suppression of the Slave Trade off the West Coast of Africa, 1807–1833." M.A. thesis, University of London, 1923, chaps. 2, 3; Coughtry, *Notorious Triangle,* p. 235. The *Amelia* case was a particularly blatant example. "As you shall have to grant a bill of sale for the brig when she is apparently sold," wrote an owner to his captain and partner, "you must be very cautious to take a counter bill of sale; and again, as collateral security, a bottomry bond on the vessel for $10,000, with a power of attorney for the sham owner to you, to sell and dispose of her in any manner you shall think proper. I would wish you, besides, to take a very strong declaration in writing . . . that the sale made by you is merely fictitious; that the cargo and her earnings are bona fide your property." *Sixth Annual Report of the Committee of the African Institution* (London, 1812), pp. 37.

48. Captain Sneyd to Admiralty, Oct. 2, 1811, enc. "Memorandum . . . on the State of the Slave Trade," Adm. 1/2528.
*Extracts from the Report of the Commissioners . . . on the Coast of Africa,* p. 278. In

1812 the commander of HMS *Daring* wrote, "The slave trade between Cape St. Ann and De Verde is now confined entirely to small vessels . . . navigated by Americans (under Spanish colours)." (Captain Irby to Admiralty, Nov. 23, 1812, enc. Lt. Pascoe, Nov. 7, 1812, Adm. 1/1997.) Similar opinions were held by officials at Sierra Leone, the secretary of the Admiralty Board who read all naval despatches as well as members of the unofficial abolitionist committees that watched for infractions of the abolition laws in British ports. For the secretary of the Admiralty Board's opinion, see G. M. Gorthing to Admiralty, Aug. 8, 1810, enc. dated Aug. 2, 1810, Adm. 1/3899.

50. Even before 1807 large Liverpool firms such as McDowal & Co. and Leigh & Co. never specialized exclusively in the slave trade or indeed in shipping (see Craig and Jarvis, *Liverpool Registry,* p. 201), and the redeployment of most of the slaving fleet after 1807 must have meant that slave ventures formed a very small part of such firms' activities.

51. See, for example, "Prizes adjudicated at Sierra Leone from 26 March to 25 June, 1815," HCA 49/101, for the *General Silveira* case.

52. For the leading Cuban based traders in 1820, and for the continuing connections with a London firm of at least one of them see Moreno Fraginals *(El ingenio,* 1:264–69). For planter capital in the business, see Moreno Fraginals, ibid., and also Robert Jameson to Castlereagh, Sept. 1, 1821 (enc.), FO 84/13.

53. J. T. Williams to Canning, Mar. 20, 1826, FO 84/50; Captain G. R. Collier to Admiralty, Dec. 17, 1821, enc. "Final Report After Three Years on the West Coast of Africa," Adm. 1/1675; Canning to Frederick Lamb, Apr. 4, 1825 (sub enc.), FO 84/41. During James Kennedy's term of office at the Havana Mixed Court, 1837–51, U.S. ownership of slaving ventures was very rare (see *Report from the Select Committee on Slave Trade Treaties,* PP, 1852–53, 39:109). For privateers, see "Answers to queries," in *American State Papers,* 5:106–7.

54. Serge Daget, "Long cours et négriers nantais du trafic illégal, (1814–1833)," *Revue française d'histoire d'outre-mer,* 62 (1975):114; and personal communication from Serge Daget to the author. J. T. Kilbee and W. Macleay to Canning, Jan. 1, 1826, FO 84/51.

55. See app. A.

56. Slave ship data set. This change had probably already taken place by 1818. See *Twelfth Report of the Directors of the African Institution* (London, 1818), p. 166; and *American State Papers,* 5:106–7.

57. W. Macleay to Aberdeen, May 30, 1829, FO 84/91.

58. R. Stein, *French Slave Trade,* pp. 75–80; Coughtry, *Notorious Triangle,* pp.126–138. For a contemporary account of a factor's activities, see John Newton, *Journal of a Slave Trader,* ed. B. Martin and M. Spurrel (London, 1962). See also Margaret Priestley, *West African Trade and Coast Society: A Family Study* (London, 1969), pp. 55–90, 129–42.

59. Infra, pp. 169–70.

60. Captain J. Maxwell to Admiralty, Feb. 25, 1814, Adm. 1/2176; Bruce L. Mouser, "Women Slavers of Guinea-Conakry," in Claire C. Robertson and Martin A. Klein (eds.), *Woman and Slavery in Africa* (Madison, Wis., 1983), pp. 320–39.

61. *The Trials of the Slave Traders at Sierra Leone in April and June, 1812* (London, 1813); Herrington, "British Measures for the Suppression of the Slave Trade," pp. 59–70; Christopher Fyfe, *A History of Sierra Leone* (London, 1962), pp. 120–23.

62. Not all were as successful as Bailey Gomez Lightburn, the widow of an American factor. She had both the biggest slave factory and the biggest coffee plantation in the Pongo a quarter of a century after abolition. See Admiralty to Palmerston, Aug. 4 1841 (enc.), FO 84/384; E. Gregory and E. Fitzgerald to Canning, Apr. 29, 1823, F

84/21; J. Kennedy and C. Dalrymple, Feb. 26, 1841, FO 84/348; Mouser, "Women Slavers of Guinea-Conakry," pp. 331–33. For contemporary references to other British slave factors, see Colonial Office to Admiralty, Aug. 30, 1813 (enc.), Adm. 1/4226; Captain Ellis to Admiralty, Feb. 28, 1814 (enc.), Adm. 1/1771; Captain Brown to Admiralty, May 8, 1815, Adm. 1/1560.

63. *Report of the Select Committee on the West Coast of Africa*, PP, 1842, 9:419. *Sixth Annual Report of the Committee of the African Institution*, p. 153; J. F. Ade Ajayi, "Samuel Ajayi Crowther of Oyo," in Philip D. Curtin (ed.), *Africa Remembered: Narratives by West Africans from the Era of the Slave Trade* (Madison, Wis., 1967), pp. 21, 310.

64. *Trial of Pedro Zulueta, jun. on a charge of slave trading* ... (London, 1844), p. lxi. On British merchants supplying provisions and canoes, see Captain Sneyd to Admiralty, Oct. 2, 1811, enc. "Memorandum ... on the State of the Slave Trade," Adm. 1/2528; Captain Irby to Admiralty, Mar. 4, 1812 (enc.), May 16, 1812 (enc.), July 11, 1812 (enc.), Adm. 1/1996. Several of these dispatches were published in *Report from the Select Committee on Papers Relating to the African Forts*, PP, 1816 (506), 7:755–68. For the insuring of slave vessels in England see Rear Admiral Durham to Admiralty, July 19, 1814, Adm. 1/335, and the San José case listed in "Vessels ... proceeded against ... at Sierra Leone ... ," HCA 49/97. The *Gerona* and *Calypso*, condemned in 1811, were examples of ships previously employed in the British slave trade.

65. *Third Report of the Select Committee on the Slave Trade*, PP, 1847–48, 22:473.

66. Philip D. Curtin, *Economic Change in Precolonial Africa: Senegambia in the Era of the Slave Trade*, 2 vols. (Madison, Wis., 1975), 2:110; E. Phillip LeVeen, *British Slave Trade Suppression Policies, 1821–1865* (New York, 1977), pp. 118–21.

67. Neither the largest British firm trading to Cuba, John Dawson of Liverpool, nor its U.S. equivalent, owned by the D'Wolf family of Rhode Island, appear to have established any links with the island other than that of exchanging slaves for bullion or produce. For a list of merchants in the St. Thomas trade, see Green-Pedersen, "Colonial Trade under the Danish Flag," 120.

68. Emilia Viotti da Costa, "The Political Emancipation of Brazil," in A. J. R. Russell-Wood (ed.), *From Colony to Nation: Essays on the Independence of Brazil* (Baltimore, 1975), pp. 51–58; Alan K. Manchester, "The Transfer of the Portuguese Court to Rio de Janeiro," ibid., pp. 167–72. Richard Graham, "Commentary," in H. Keith and S. F. Edwards (eds.), *Conflict and Continuity in Brazilian Society* (Columbia, S.C., 1969), p. 185;

69. James Lang, *Portuguese Brazil, the King's Plantation* (New York, 1981), p. 198; Vitorino Magalhães Godinho, *Prix et monnaies au Portugal, 1750–1850* (Paris, 1955), p. 294.

70. Herbert Heaton, "A Merchant Adventurer in Brazil, 1808–1818," *Journal of Economic History*, 6 (1946):1–23; Alan K. Manchester, *British Preeminence in Brazil: Its Rise and Decline* (Chapel Hill, N.C., 1933), p. 76.

71. D. C. M. Platt, *Latin America and British Trade, 1806–1914* (London, 1972), p. 145.

72. None of the papers of any of the hundred-or-so British houses operating at Brazilian ports of entry in this period nor those of the Liverpool Brazilian Association have come to light. Two excellent studies of proxies exist, however: (1) Heaton's "A Merchant Adventurer in Brazil," and (2) John Killick's "Risk, Specialization and Profit in the Mercantile Sector of the Nineteenth-Century Cotton Trade: Alexander Brown and Sons, 1820–80," *Business History*, 16 (1974):1–16.

73. *Report from the Select Committee of the House of Lords ... for the African Slave Trade*, PP, 1850, 9:223.

74. These and the other data in the remainder of the paragraph are taken from Eltis,

"Merchandise Exchanged for Slaves." Values are in constant pounds sterling, 1821–25 = 100.
75. Supra, chap. 1.
76. Verger, *Flux et reflux,* pp. 197–98.

## Chapter 5

1. Paul E. Lovejoy, "The Volume of the Atlantic Slave Trade: A Synthesis," *Journal of African History,* 23 (1982):473–501. For the geographical limits of the regions discussed here see app. A.
2. The post-1810 export data on which this and the previous paragraph are based may be found in app. A. For the trade in the Bight of Biafra immediately after British abolition, see W. Roscoe to Macaulay, Aug. 18, 1811, Roscoe Letters, 2486. For pre-1811 trends in different regions see Lovejoy, "Volume of the Atlantic Slave Trade," p. 485; Philip D. Curtin, *Economic Change in Precolonial Africa: Senegambia in the Era of the Slave Trade,* 2 vols. (Madison, Wis., 1975), 1:153–96; Adam Jones and Marion Johnson, "Slaves from the Windward Coast," *Journal of African History,* 21 (1980):17–34; Patrick Manning, "The Slave Trade in the Bight of Benin, 1640–1890," in H. A. Gemery and J. S. Hogendorn (eds.), *The Uncommon Market: Essays in the Economic History of the Atlantic Slave Trade* (New York, 1979), pp. 107–25; Joseph C. Miller, "Legal Portuguese Slaving from Angola. Some Preliminary Indications of Volume and Direction, 1760–1830," *Revue française d'histoire d'outre-mer,* 62 (1975):135–76; Phyllis Martin, *The External Trade of the Loango Coast, 1576–1870* (Oxford, 1972), pp. 136–57; Edward E. Reynolds, *Trade and Economic Change on the Gold Coast, 1807–1874* (London, 1974), pp. 38–53.
3. The Malthusian position on Africa—that the slave trade had made no permanent impression on the African population—was not questioned until the proslavery camp began to use it as an argument in support of the slave trade (see B. W. Higman, "Slavery and the Development of Demographic Theory in the Age of the Industrial Revolution," in James Walvin [ed.], *Slavery and British Society, 1776–1846* [London, 1982], pp. 176–81). The Malthusian view of Africa is in T. R. Malthus, *An Essay on the Principle of Population,* (Holmwood, La., 1963; first published, 1803), pp. 69–79.
4. For one trader's comments see John Matthews, *A Voyage to the River Sierra Leone* (London, 1788), p. 145.
5. Kenneth F. Kiple and Virginia Himmelsteib King, *Another Dimension to the Black Diaspora: Diet, Disease and Racism* (London, 1981), pp. 4–23; Kenneth F. Kiple, *The Caribbean Slave: A Biological History* (Cambridge, 1984), pp. 7–50; Philip D. Curtin, "Slavery and Empire," *Annals of the New York Academy of Sciences,* 292 (1977):1–11; idem, *The Atlantic Slave Trade: A Census* (Madison, Wis., 1969), pp. 269–73; Alfred W. Crosby, *The Columbian Exchange: Biological and Cultural Consequences of 1492* (Westport, Conn., 1972), pp. 165–207; Marvin Miracle, *Maize in Tropical Africa* (Madison, Wis., 1966).
6. Data on the ninety-two hundred females on which the following discussion is based may be found in copies of the court registers located in FO 84/4, 9, 15, 21, 38, 63, 64, 76, 86, 87, 100, 101, 102, 116, 127, 166, 212.
7. A total of 264 mothers are listed in the registers with infants identified as their own. Of these, 234 can be identified as Yoruba on the basis of their port of embarkation (David Eltis, "Nutritional Trends in Africa and the Americas: Heights of Africans, 1819–1839," *Journal of Interdisciplinary History* 12, [1982]:459–60). Ages of both mother and children were recorded. The range of ages in the sample is 16.0 to 40.0,

with a mode at 25.0. The sample is part of 27,107 records of slaves taken from the Sierra Leone registers. In the full data set, there is no evidence of heaping at decadal or quinquennial values. There are other problems. The recorded ages must have been estimates. In addition, the downward truncation bias in the sample (i.e., the sample ignores the experience of younger women who might have given birth at a later date) more than offsets the upward bias arising from the exclusion of those women whose children died (for a discussion of this problem, see James Trussell and Richard Steckel, "The Age of Slaves at Menarche and Their First Birth," *Journal of Interdisciplinary History,* 8 [1978]:481). The age preference of slave traders, on the other hand, is unlikely to have caused bias. Price data suggest that the slave trader buying for the overseas market would have found ages between 17.0 and 25.0 equally acceptable. The sample is, therefore, probably broadly representative of the Yoruba mothers within these ranges. The data show that mothers 25.0 years old were ten times more common than their counterparts 18.0 years old, with only 8 percent less than 20.0 years of age at the birth of their infant. The question is how many of those in their middle 20s had previously given birth; there is no indication which of these children were, in fact, the first born. The distribution, however, is inconsistent with a mean age at first birth of less than 20.0. As the mean age of mothers was 25.6 and the child spacing interval (infra) was at least 3.0 years, births among teenagers must have been uncommon. The plausibility of this picture is increased by evidence on menarche among first-generation Creole slaves in Trinidad at this time. Estimates based on anthropometric data range from 15.5 to nearly 17.0 years (B. W. Higman, "Growth in Afro-Caribbean Slave Populations," *American Journal of Physical Anthropology,* 50 [1979]:382). Given relative growth patterns, menarche for most Africans was probably slightly later than this, as indeed data from several rural African areas also indicate. Because of the high incidence of anovulatory menstrual cycles at this stage of development, however, menarche is not synonymous with fecundity: A delay of 2.0 to 3.0 years commonly occurs between the two. Allowing for this and the period of pregnancy, it would seem, first, that a mean age at first birth of at least 20.0 was likely, and, second, that Yoruba women began to bear children close to the earliest possible age. At the very least, the delay between fecundity and first birth was shorter in Africa than the 2.6 to 4.1 years estimated for slave women in the U.S. South.
8. Hilary Page, "Fertility Levels: Patterns and Trends," in John C. Caldwell (ed.), *Population Growth and Socioeconomic Change in West Africa* (New York, 1975), pp. 51–54. On the Yoruba, in particular, see J. C. Caldwell and Pat Caldwell, "The Role of Marital Sexual Abstinence in Determining Fertility: A Study of the Yoruba in Nigeria," *Population Studies,* 31 (1977):196–203; P. O. Olusanya, "Modernization and the Level of Fertility in Western Nigeria," *Proceedings of the International Population Conference, London, 1969* (Liège, 1971), pp. 812–25, in particular fn. 7; P. A. Talbot, *The Peoples of Southern Nigeria,* 2 vols. (Oxford, 1926), 2:378–83.
9. P. C. Lloyd, "Osifekunde of Ijebu," in Philip D. Curtin (ed.), *Africa Remembered: Narratives by West Africans from the Era of the Slave Trade* (Madison, Wis., 1967), p. 255; Henry Meredith, *An Account of the Gold Coast of Africa* (London, 1812), p. 109. For the comments of eighteenth-century travelers on the prevalence of this practice among several different ethnic backgrounds, see the references cited in Herbert S. Klein and Stanley L. Engerman, "Fertility Differentials between Slaves in the United States and the British West Indies: A Note on Lactation Practices and Their Possible Implications," *William & Mary Quarterly,* 35 (1978):369, fn. 35. Of the 234 Yoruba mothers in the Sierra Leone sample, only a single mother had more than one child listed (other than a subject with a set of twins). As the mean age of

the children in the sample was 17.4 months and the median, 16.0 months, older infants were strongly represented in the sample. The data show considerable evidence of heaping with the 24.0-month age category containing the most observations. At the 12.0-month age level, this phenomenon should impart an upward bias, although a crude attempt has been made to compensate for this by assuming the age "1" (12-month category) refers to all infants in the 0.0 to 18.0 months' category and by assigning a value of 9.0 months to all in this category. On the other hand, given the high infant mortality rates of modern rural African, we might expect a pronounced downward bias from the absence of some ever-born children in the older infant age groups. Even ignoring this latter effect, the distribution of the sample and the absence of younger siblings for the 36 percent of the children registered in the 24-month to 60-month category is consistent with an interval of not less than 3 years between births.

10. Caldwell and Caldwell, "The Role of Marital Sexual Abstinence," pp. 196–98. In support of this we can once more call on the Sierra Leone data. Of the 103 Yoruba women registered between the ages of thirty-six and forty-five, only 7 had infant children. This proportion is not statistically different from the proportion of women with children in the age groups of prime fertility. On the other hand, an older woman with an attached infant would have been worth more to a slave dealer, and there were probably more of such women in the Sierra Leone group than in the population at large. There is, of course, the possibility of some observer bias against older women with children.

11. As the population was not stable, given the fact that both the transatlantic and trans-Saharan slave trades produced somewhat abnormal population pyramids, the crude birthrate may have been at the low end of this range.

12. Robert W. Fogel and Stanley L. Engerman, "Recent Findings in the Study of Slave Demography and Family Structure," *Sociology and Social Research,* 63 (1979):556–89. It might be noted, however, that infant mortality, which could in itself induce high fertility, was probably greater in Africa than in Europe.

13. Philip D. Curtin, "Epidemiology and the Slave Trade," *Political Science Quarterly,* 83 (1968):190–216; William H. McNeill, *Plagues and Peoples,* (Garden City, N.Y., 1977) pp. 176–207. For the sickle cell and other defense mechanisms, see Kiple, *Caribbean Slave,* pp. 12–22; Pierre Cantrelle, "Mortality: Levels, Patterns, and Trends," in Caldwell (ed.), *Population Growth, and Socioeconomic Change,* pp. 102, 114–17; H. J. Page and A. J. Coale, "Fertility and Child Mortality South of the Sahara," in S. H. Ominde and C. N. Ejiogu (eds.), *Population Growth and Economic Development in Africa,* (New York, 1972), pp. 51–66.

14. For secular trends in human stature see the special issue of *Social Science History,* 6 (1982), Robert W. Fogel and Stanley L. Engerman (eds.). For trends in Africa and a fuller statement of the argument in this paragraph see David Eltis, "Nutritional Trends in Africa and the Americas," 453–75; cf. Higman, "Growth in Afro-Caribbean Populations." It should be noted, however, that Phillip V. Tobias has raised the possibility of a declining secular trend among groups in southeast Africa (see most recently, "The Negative Secular Trend," *Journal of Human Evolution,* 14 (1985):347–65.

15. The argument that follows falls within the framework outlined by J. C. Caldwell, "The Social Repercussions of Colonial Rule: Demographic Aspects," in UNESCO, *General History of Africa,* 8 vols., edited by Adu Boahen (London, 1981–86), 7:458–86; and J. C. Caldwell "Major Questions in African Demographic History," in Christopher Fyfe and David McMaster (eds.), *African Historical Demography,* 1 (Edinburgh 1977):7–22. However, the author's emphasis in the former on "political

fragmentation" as a factor in reducing high population densities leaves open the possibility of a non-Malthusian interpretation. See also C. C. Wrigley, "Population in African History," *Journal of African History,* 20 (1979):127–31. That the Malthusian pattern was not confined to Africa is suggested by Karl F. Helleiner, "The Vital Revolution Reconsidered," *Canadian Journal of Economics and Political Science,* 23 (1957):1–9, and more recent E. A. Wrigley and R. S. Schofield, *The Population History of England, 1541–1871: A Reconstruction* (London, 1981), pp. 402–53, for England prior to 1800. For a non-Malthusian interpretation of African historical demography see J. E. Inikori, "Under-Population in Nineteenth-Century West Africa: The Role of the Export Slave Trade," in Fyfe and McMaster (eds.), *African Historical Demography,* 2 (Edinburgh 1981):283–313.

16. P. O. Olusanya, "Population Growth and its Components: The Nature and Direction of Population Change," in J. C. Caldwell (ed.), *Population Growth and Socioeconomic Change,* pp. 269–70; J. C. Caldwell, "The Social Repercussions of Colonial Rule," p. 463. Current rates for rural Nigeria are about 25 per thousand.

17. John Thornton, "An Eighteenth-Century Baptismal Register and the Demographic History of Manguenzo," in Fyfe and McMaster (eds.), *African Historical Demography,* 1:405–15; idem, "Demography and History in the Kingdom of the Kongo, 1550–1750," *Journal of African History,* 18 (1977):507–29. The former indicates the population of the Kongo kingdom had an age structure consistent with a growth rate of 7.5 per thousand but an actual growth rate of about 2.0 per thousand between 1700 and 1948.

18. For recent supporting evidence of this in west central Africa, see Jill R. Dias, "Famine and Disease in the History of Angola, c. 1830–1930," *Journal of African History* 22 (1981):349–78; and Joseph C. Miller, "The Significance of Drought, Disease and Famine in the Agriculturally Marginal Zones of West Central Africa," *Journal of African History,* 23 (1982):17–61.

19. Using a simulation model, data on slave exports and sex ratios as well as some reasonable assumptions, Patrick Manning has argued for a decrease in the population of the western half of the African continent for 1760 to 1850 ranging from 10 to 30 percent ("The Impact of Slave Exports on the Population of the Western Coast of Africa, 1700–1850." Paper presented at the Nantes International Colloquium on the Slave Trade, July 1985).

20. Patrick Manning, (ibid.) and John Fage ("The Effect of the Export Slave Trade on African Populations" in R. Moss and R. J. A. R. Rathbone [eds.], *The Population Factor in African Studies* [London, 1975], pp. 15–23; and idem, "Slavery and the Slave Trade in the Context of West African History," *Journal of African History,* 10 [1969]:393–404) have produced estimates of the West African population in the mid-nineteenth century by working backwards from data assembled in 1930 by, among others, R. R. Kuczynski, *Demographic Survey of the British Empire,* 2 vols. (Oxford, 1948). Unfortunately, the estimates vary widely (28.0 million for Fage and 11.0 to 16.3 million for Manning), partly, one suspects, because of differences over which parts of West Africa should be counted as being affected by the Atlantic slave trade. Small in this context would thus mean less than 12 million.

21. As Patrick Manning has pointed out ("Impact of Slave Exports"), African fertility was close to the maximum, in the sense that it is not clear which variables—child spacing, marriage patterns, age at first and last births—could have been changed if African women had somehow "responded" to the slave trade by adjusting their fertility pattern. Mortality changes, on the other hand, could have occurred in response to variations in food supply, itself a function of population pressure on available resources—the classic Malthusian case. In Manning's model the net intrinsic growth

rate of the raided populations is far more important than, say, the size and composition of slave raids in determining aggregate population trends. Those making a less severe assessment of the demographic impact of the slave trade include Fage (p. 319, fn. 20), and John Thornton, "The Slave Trade in Eighteenth-Century Angola: Effects on Demographic Structures," *Canadian Journal of African Studies,* 14 (1980):417–27. Roger T. Anstey argues for a small impact in western Africa and for a significant slave trade-induced population decline in west-central Africa (*The Atlantic Slave Trade and British Abolition* [London, 1975], pp. 79–82).

22. Patrick Manning's population estimates—the basis for rows (b) and (c) in pt. B of table 1—are probably more geographically restricted than John Fage's estimates. It is worth noting that if the population estimates for the British Isles, Portugal, Italy and India in pt. A of table 1 were similarly restricted to areas within these countries that supplied emigrants, the percentages for these countries in column 2 would also be greater.

23. This assessment is based on the population data for West Africa in Fage, "The Effect of the Export Slave Trade," p. 18; E. A. Wrigley and R. S. Schofield, *The Population History of England, 1541–1871: A Reconstruction* (Cambridge, Mass., pp. 209, 219. For the very high rates of Portuguese migration, see Vitorino Magalhães Godinho, "L'emigration portuguaise du XVe siècle à nos jours. Histoire d'une constante structurale," in *Conjoncture économique: structures sociales. Hommage à Ernest Labrousse* (Paris, 1974), pp. 254–55. For eighteenth-century England emigrants amounted to 10.2 percent of the population in 1700. For West Africa the equivalent figure was 13.8 percent. If Manning's population estimates are used in place of Fage's (Manning, "The Impact of Slave Exports," table 3) then the African ratio would be greater than 13.8 percent, but given the comment in n. 22 above, this would not be an appropriate procedure.

24. The case for a uniquely demographically devastating impact on Africa really hinges on the socially disruptive slave gathering activities induced by the traffic. Though the enclosures movement and the creation of a landless class in preindustrial Europe might be viewed by some as equally disruptive and coercive, generally, the non-African migrants in table 1 did not experience direct military action. On the other hand, warfare was not the only, or in many areas the major method of gathering slaves despite the large firearm imports into certain regions (Joseph E. Inikori, "The Import of Firearms into West Africa, 1750 to 1807: A Quantitative Analysis," *Journal of African History,* 18 [1977]:339–68; W. A. Richards, "The Import of Firearms into West Africa in the Eighteenth Century," *Journal of African History,* 21 [1980]:43–59). The Bight of Biafra, which attracted a disproportionately large share of gun imports among African slave-exporting zones also experienced one of the lowest incidences of warfare and state-organized slave raiding in the enslavement process. On this point, see David Northrup, *Trade Without Rulers: Pre-Colonial Economic Development in South-Eastern Nigeria,* (Oxford, 1978), pp. 65–80. In addition, the number of guns per person in Africa was probably always well below the same ratio on other continents—especially the Americas.

25. Joseph E. Inikori, "Introduction," in Inikori (ed.), *Forced Migration: The Impact of the Export Trade on African Societies* (London, 1982), pp. 19–51.

26. Eltis, "Free and Coerced Transatlantic Migrations." The figure of 3 million is an estimate of the number of Afro-Americans in the Americas in 1820 who were descended from West African antecedents. For a similar criticism of Joseph E. Inikori see Manning, "The Impact of Slave Exports."

27. Dias, "Famine and Disease" suggests that the ending of the slave trade possibly contributed to famine. Cf. Manning, "The Impact of Slave Exports."

28. Ester Boserup (*The Conditions of Agricultural Growth: The Economics of Agrarian Change Under Population Pressure* [London, 1965]), has argued that high population densities lead to changes in cultivation techniques rather than higher mortality rates. For a criticism of this in the African historical context, see Caldwell, "Social Repercussions of Colonial Rule," 464–65.

29. The five-year means of the male proportion of shipments from Upper Guinea and the bights of Benin and Biafra were regressed on the five-year annual means of export volumes from these regions. Dummy variables were added for each of these three regions. Export data are from app. A and male ratios were calculated from the age/sex data set, except for one observation from the Bight of Biafra taken from Herbert S. Klein, *The Middle Passage* (Princeton, N.J., 1978), p. 150. The regression equation is (standard error in first row of parentheses, *F* statistic in second):

$$MR = \quad 0.970 \; - \; 0.011X \; - \; 0.181Ben \; - \; 0.192\,Bia \; - \; 0.236\,UG$$
$$\phantom{MR =}\quad (0.093) \quad (0.003) \qquad (0.068) \qquad (0.061) \qquad (0.078)$$
$$\phantom{MR =}\quad (107.9) \quad (8.5) \qquad\;\; (7.1) \qquad\;\;\; (9.8) \qquad\;\;\; (9.2)$$

Where $MR$ = males/(males + females)
$X$ = exports ('000)
$Ben$ = Bight of Benin
$Bia$ = Bight of Biafra
$UG$ = Upper Guinea
n = 16
$r^2$ = 0.48

The quinquennial periods were all between 1811 and 1840 except for one Bight of Biafra observation taken from 1791 to 1798. Reliable price data are not available, but there are indications (discussed later) that prices on the African coast tended to vary directly with export volumes.

30. The male ratio of the all-time peak levels of transatlantic departures from the Bight of Biafra in the 1790s was 0.58, a figure probably lower than it had ever been before and certainly lower than that for any comparable period in the nineteenth century except perhaps for 1826–30 (Klein, *Middle Passage,* p. 150; app. B). In the Bight of Benin exports peaked in the 1780s and there is evidence that the male ratio dropped even lower to perhaps 0.54 (Seventeen shipments from the period 1784 to 1788 had a mean male ratio of 0.561 [Joseph E. Inikori, "Introduction," in idem (ed.), *Forced Migration: The Impact of the Export Slave Trade on African Societies* (London, 1982), p. 23]. A simple regression of five-year groupings of male ratios on five-year mean export volumes, using nineteenth-century data for the Bight of Benin only, predicts a ratio of 0.54 for the 1780s—using Lovejoy's estimate of Bight of Benin exports for that decade [Lovejoy, "Volume of the Atlantic Slave Trade," p. 485]). In the years immediately after abolition, when export volumes in these regions were 25 to 40 percent below eighteenth-century peaks, the equivalent ratios were 0.65 and 0.73 in the bights of Biafra and Benin, respectively. In west-central Africa, on the other hand, the ratio of males never fell below 0.65 in the nineteenth century and during the period of very high demand between 1836 and 1850 averaged 0.74. The difference between this figure and the mean ratios for each of the three main regions north of the equator for the whole period 1811–67 is statistically significant at the 5 percent level.

31. See app. B.

32. David W. Galenson ("The Atlantic Slave Trade and the Barbados Market, 1673–1723," *Journal of Economic History,* 42 [1982]:491–512) found that rising slave prices brought about an increase in the share of children in the traffic.

33. Male recaptives registered at Sierra Leone from the Bight of Biafra were, on average, five-years older than females from the same region, and girls made up 53 percent of the females embarked. In west-central Africa and southeast Africa, the equivalent percentages were even higher at 64 and 74 percent, respectively. Only in the Bight of Benin was the age differential between the sexes as little as one year and the girl proportion of females as low as one third. In regions other than the Bight of Benin where the data support analysis over time, higher demand may have increased the female ratio, but the females tended to be girls rather than women. These data are from two separate data sets. The ages are from the slave data set derived from the registers of the Sierra Leone Liberated African Department and the sex/child/adult breakdowns are taken from the set of slave-ship cargoes. Descriptions of both may be found in Sources. A regression of the proportion of adult women in slave cargoes on export volumes (five-year means, 1811–40 for both variables) and dummy variables for the Bight of Benin, Upper Guinea and the Bight of Biafra yielded an $r^2$ of 0.20. Only the Bight of Benin was significant (at the 1 percent level). The same procedure was followed using the ratio of girls to total embarked as the dependent variable. The $r^2$ was 0.59, but only the Bight of Biafra dummy variable was significant (at the 5 percent level).

34. Export volumes are in Lovejoy, "Volume of the Atlantic Slave Trade," 485; sex ratios from Inikori, "Introduction," p. 23; and Klein, *Middle Passage*, p. 150. A breakdown of 22,390 Sierra Leone recaptives (1819–39) from the bights into Manning's age categories yields the following ratios (rows sum to 1.0):

|  | Age 0–14 | Age 15–30 | Age 30 |
|---|---|---|---|
| A. Bight of Benin |  |  |  |
| male | 0.315 | 0.615 | 0.069 |
| female | 0.349 | 0.588 | 0.062 |
| B. Bight of Biafra |  |  |  |
| male | 0.312 | 0.594 | 0.094 |
| female | 0.513 | 0.469 | 0.018 |

Potential bias in these data are discussed later. For the Manning model, see "The Enslavement of Africans: A Demographic Model," *Canadian Journal of African Studies*, 15 (1981):504–09; and Patrick Manning and William S. Griffith, "Slave Exports and African Demography: A Recursive Simulation," unpublished paper, 1985.

35. In parts of west-central Africa departures in the 1780s and 1790s were probably high enough to induce decline even when male ratios were very high. Roger Anstey (*Atlantic Slave Trade*, pp. 88–92), Patrick Manning ("Local vs. Regional Impact of Slave Exports on Africa," in Joel Gregory and Denis Cordell [eds.], *African Demographic History* [forthcoming]), and J. C. Caldwell ("Social Repercussions of Colonial Rule," p. 467) all argue for a population decline in the Loango and Angola hinterlands at this time. The fact that the slave-trading supply routes were the longest on the continent, the male ratio of deportees among the highest and the high volumes of departures not maintained brings into question the length of the decline.

36. Patrick Manning has used his simulation model to estimate the effects of slave exports on regional and coastal (vs. interior) populations as well as Continental aggregates. In contrast to the findings here he hypothesizes population declines in every major export region for extended periods between 1700 and 1850 with the

Bight of Benin experiencing losses in every decade except the 1790s (Manning, "Local vs. Regional Impact of Slave Exports on Africa"). The severity of the impact suggested by Manning's work derives partly from the assumption of lower male ratios than actually occurred—in the nineteenth century at least. No major export region had male ratios as low as 63 percent after 1811. In addition, as noted above, the geographic and ethnic zones used by Manning may be more geographically restricted than other scholars have used on this issue. For lower assessments of the impact of slave exports on the Bight of Biafra see Northrup, *Trade Without Rulers*, pp. 80–84.

37. P. E. H. Hair, "Ethnolinguistic Continuity on the Guinea Coast," *Journal of African History*, 8 (1967):247–68.

38. Patrick Manning, *Slavery, Colonialism and Economic Growth in Dahomey, 1640–1960* (New York, 1982), pp. 10–12. For the Accra regions, see Marion Johnson, "Census, map and guesstimate: the past population of the Accra Region," in Fyfe and McMaster (eds.), *African Historical Demography*, 1:273–94.

39. For the strength and vibrancy of the domestic West African exchange economy before the mid-nineteenth century, see Lars Sundstrom, *The Exchange Economy of Pre-Colonial Tropical Africa* (London, 1974), in particular pp. 1–121; A. G. Hopkins, *An Economic History of West Africa* (New York, 1973), pp. 8–77. For major regional studies, see the collection of essays in Claude Meillassoux (ed.), *The Development of Indigenous Trade and Markets in West Africa* (London, 1971); Northrup, *Trade Without Rulers;* Manning, *Slavery, Colonialism and Economic Growth;* and Curtin, *Economic Change in Precolonial Africa.*

40. The import value is expressed in terms of invoice values at the ports of origin rather than cif. For West African slave prices in the 1780s see E. Phillip LeVeen, *British Slave Trade Suppression Policies, 1821–1865* (New York, 1977), pp. 113–15, 146. West-central Africa prices have been estimated at two-thirds of this figure. The calculations assume that all slaves were prime males, though this clearly cannot have been the case and biases the calculation upward. Cf. John Fage, *A History of West Africa* (Cambridge, 1969), pp. 91–92.

41. Henry A. Gemery and Jan S. Hogendorn, "The Economic Costs of West African Participation in the Atlantic Slave Trade: A Preliminary Sampling for the Eighteenth Century," in Gemery and Hogendorn (eds.), *The Uncommon Market*, p. 153.

42. Colin W. Newbury, "Trade and Authority in West Africa from 1850 to 1880," in L. H. Gann and P. Duignan (eds.), *The History and Politics of Colonialism, 1870–1914* (Cambridge, 1969), p. 67.

43. Patrick Manning, *Slavery, Colonialism and Economic Growth*, pp. 44–45.

44. Ibid., p. 45. For a realistic estimate of the king of Dahomey's income from the slave trade, see Capt. C. W. Riley to Admiralty, May 22, 1850, Adm. 123/173. See also the discussion in chap. 10 infra. For a similar assessment of the impact of the slave trade on the Gallinas, another important nineteenth-century slave exporting region, see Adam Jones, *From Slaves to Palm Kernels: A History of the Galinhas Country (West Africa), 1730–1890* (Wiesbaden, W. Ger. 1983), in particular pp. 86–88.

45. There remains the possibility that the price of a slave on the African coast did not reflect the value of his or her labor—that the private cost of capture, enslavement and deportation did not reflect the contribution the slave might have made to the African society (see Gemery and Hogendorn, "Economic Costs of West African Participation"). It seems unlikely, however, that those who exercised authority in Africa and who measured "wealth and power in men rather than in acres" (Hopkins, *An Economic History of West Africa*, p. 26), would consent to sell slaves for less than the present value of future labor and prestige that the slave might provide.

46. P. E. H. Hair, ("The Enslavement of Koelle's Informants," *Journal of African History,* 6 [1965]:196–200) estimated 34 percent of these slaves were taken in war, 30 percent kidnapped, 25 percent enslaved through judicial process, debt or sold by relatives. But see Northrup's refinement of these ratios (*Trade Without Rulers,* pp. 77–80). See also Victor C. Uchendu, "Slaves and Slavery in Igboland, Nigeria," in Suzanne Miers and Igor Kopytoff (eds.), *Slavery in Africa: Historical and Anthropological Perspectives* (Madison, Wis., 1977), pp. 125–27.

47. Walter Rodney, "African Slavery and Other Forms of Social Oppression on the Upper Guinea Coast in the Context of the Atlantic Slave Trade," *Journal of African History,* 7 (1966):431–43; Claude Meillassoux, "The Role of Slavery in the Economic and Social History of Sahelo-Sudanic Africa," in Inikori, *Forced Migration,* pp. 94–99.

48. Shipping data are from slave-ship data set. For Benin, see A. F. C. Ryder, *Benin and the Europeans, 1485–1897* (New York, 1969), pp. 20–21, 135–36, 198, 204–5, 227–32; and James D. Graham, "The Slave Trade, Depopulation and Human Sacrifice in Benin History," *Cahiers d'études africaines,* 18 (1965):317–34. That trade in the 1820s was at lower levels than earlier periods, however, is indicated in W. F. C. Owen, *Narrative of Voyages to Explore the Shores of Africa, Arabia and Madagascar,* 2 vols. (London, 1833), 1:357–59.

49. Ivor Wilks, "Asante Policy Towards the Hausa Trade in the Nineteenth Century," in Meillassoux, *Development of Indigenous Trade,* pp. 124–41.

50. Ivor Wilks, *Asante in the Nineteenth Century: The Structure and Evolution of a Political Order* (New York, 1975), pp. 82–90, 177–79, 679, 680, 701–20.

51. See Manning's estimate of state revenues for Dahomey (*Slavery, Colonialism and Economic Growth,* p. 43). Cf. Newbury, "Trade and Authority in West Africa," p. 74.

52. Reynolds, *Trade and Economic Change,* p. 47.

53. I. A. Akinjogbin, *Dahomey and Its Neighbours, 1708–1818* (Cambridge, 1967).

54. Robin Law, *The Oyo Empire c1600–c1836: A West African Imperialism in the Era of the Atlantic Slave Trade* (Oxford, 1977), pp. 299–312.

55. I. A. Akinjogbin, "Dahomey and Yoruba in the Nineteenth Century," in Joseph C. Anene and Godfrey N. Brown, *Africa in the Nineteenth and Twentieth Centuries* (Ibadan, Nigeria, 1966), pp. 263–66; Martin Lynn, "Consul and Kings: British Policy, 'the Man on the Spot,' and the Seizure of Lagos, 1851," *Journal of Imperial and Commonwealth History,* 10 (1982):150–67. There are records of fifteen slave voyages that embarked or intended to embark slaves at Ouidah in the last decade of the traffic (slave-ship data set). Ouidah was the last major point of embarkation in the Bight of Benin, and actual shipments greatly exceeded this number.

56. Law, *The Oyo Empire,* p. 255; Hugh Clapperton, *Journal of a Second Expedition into the Interior of Africa* (London, 1829), p. 102.

57. See A. J. H. Latham, *Old Calabar, 1600–1891: The Impact of the International Economy upon a Traditional Society* (Oxford, 1973), pp. 24–51; and for this process in the Bight of Biafra, see E. J. Alagoa, "The Development of Institutions in the States of the Eastern Niger Delta," *Journal of African History,* 12 (1971):269–78. For the Gold Coast see Kwame Y. Daaku, *Trade and Politics on the Gold Coast, 1600–1720: A Study of the African Reaction to European Trade* (Oxford, 1970), pp. 28–29.

58. Northrup, *Trade Without Rulers,* pp. 124–40; Jones, *From Slaves to Palm Kernels,* pp. 67–73.

59. P. Martin, *Loango Coast,* pp. 158–74. A similar process of political decentralization in the face of increasing slave demands has been noted for the interior of Angola.

Joseph Miller draws parallels between sixteenth century Kongo and eighteenth century Kasanje in "The Slave Trade of Congo and Angola," in Martin L. Kilson and Robert Rotberg (eds.), *The African Diaspora* (Cambridge, Mass., 1976), pp. 99–100.

60. All but a dozen of these disembarked or intended to disembark at Bahia. The significance of this is that 90 percent of these ships sailed in actuality from the Bight of Benin. Such ships gave Malemba as their point of embarkation merely to conform to the Anglo-Portuguese treaties under which slave trafficking north of the equator became illegal for Portuguese ships.

61. Of the 350 ships, only about 20 might be questioned on the basis of the treaty bias mentioned supra, n. 60.

62. Individual port data are from the slave–ship data set.

63. Mafouks who pleaded for the return of the French slave ships in 1805 and who charged European abolitionist governments with bringing ruin to this region were merely reflecting this fact ("Report of Admiral Linois on the Loango Coast." Dec. 1805, Archive Marine, Paris BB4/252. Cited in P. Martin, *Loango Coast,* p. 139; J. K. Tuckey, *Narrative of an Expedition to Explore the River Zaire* [London, 1818], pp. 61–62). Some of the traffic, of course, had been diverted through Angolan ports rather than stopped and a coastal trade continued between Loango and Cabinda.

64. P. Martin, *Loango Coast,* pp. 158–74.

65. See app. A; David Birmingham, *Trade and Conflict in Angola: The Mbundu and Their Neighbours Under the Influence of the Portuguese, 1483–1790* (Oxford, 1966), pp. 133–61.

66. Edward A. Alpers, *Ivory and Slaves in East Central Africa: Changing Patterns of International Trade to the Later Nineteenth Century* (Berkeley, Calif., 1975), pp. 185–91.

67. The takeover of Mauritius and the early years of British policy are described in R. W. Beachey, *The Slave Trade of Eastern Africa* (London, 1976), pp. 27–32; and in R. Coupland, *East Africa and Its Invaders* (Oxford, 1938), pp. 191–99. For a subtle review of the impact of that policy see Ralph A. Austen, "From the Atlantic to the Indian Ocean: European Abolition, the African Slave Trade, and Asian Economic Structures," in David Eltis and James Walvin (eds.), *The Abolition of the Atlantic Slave Trade* (Madison, Wis., 1981), pp. 117–39.

68. Alpers, *Ivory and Slaves,* pp. 194–200; Allen F. Isaacman, *Mozambique: The Africanization of a European Institution: The Zambezi Prazos, 1750–1902* (Madison, Wis., 1972), pp. 85–93.

69. Rodney, "African Slavery and Other Forms of Social Oppression," p. 443.

70. Fage, "Slavery and the Slave Trade," p. 402. See the discussion in Anstey, *Atlantic Slave Trade,* pp. 85–87.

## Chapter 6

1. The circular from S. Parker dated May 6, 1850, as well as the responses of the twenty-seven captains and one judge of the Sierra Leone Mixed Commission Court and a synopsis of these responses are all in Adm. 123/173. See, in particular, Capt. H. W. Gifford, May 9, 1850; Capt. C. J. Bosanquette, May 11, 1850; Capt. W. B. Monypenny, May 24, 1850; and Capt. G. Mansell, May 24, 1850, in this source. Aspects of this survey are discussed in Christopher Lloyd, *The Navy and the Slave Trade: The Suppression of the African Slave Trade in the Nineteenth Century* (London, 1968), pp. 122–24.

2. See Palmerston's evidence to the 1848 select committee on the slave trade PP, 1847–48, 22 (First Report):4. Returns to Parliament after 1840 on captured slave

ships usually included a column estimating the number of slaves saved from slavery in the Americas by the capture and destruction of empty ships.

3. *Statutes at Large*, 46 Geo. 3 c.52 s.6 and 9.
4. *Hansard*, 1st ser., 30:657–58, Apr. 18, 1815.
5. *Statutes at Large*, 5 Geo. 4 c.133 s.10.
6. *Statutes at Large*, 6 and 7 Vict. c.98.
7. These ships baffled naval officers and judges alike. The *George and James* was convicted in 1825 for aiding and abetting the slave trade after shipping goods from Bahia to the Bight of Benin (W. Pennel to Canning, Nov. 5, 1825, FO 84/42). The only other ship condemned was the *Guyana* in 1840 when the penalties exacted were returned to the owners by the Privy Council even though the case was almost identical to the *George and James* (see J. B. Moore's evidence in *Second Report from the Select Committee on Slave Trade*, PP, 1847–8, 22:156–62). There were many other ships similarly engaged but not prosecuted. For the *Liburnum* see J. Smith and H. W. Macaulay to Palmerston, Apr. 13, 1833, FO 84/133; for the *Creole* see J. Kennedy to Palmerston, Aug. 26, 1837, FO 84/217; for the *Robert Heddle*, "Memorandum . . . on British subjects or British capital engaged in the Slave Trade . . . from 1835 to 1845," Apr. 29, 1845, FO 84/616; for the *George Canning* and the *Maid of Islay*, see *Report from the Select Committee of the House of Lords . . . for the African Slave Trade*, PP, 1850, 9:419.
8. Christopher Fyfe, *A History of Sierra Leone*, (London, 1962), pp. 195–96. See also the evidence of Logan Hook, the Sierra Leone customs collector, *Report of the Select Committee on the West Coast of Africa*, PP, 1842, 11:528. For Foreign Office reaction see Findley and Smith to Palmerston, July 13, 1830, FO 84/102; James Stephen (the younger) to Palmerston, Apr. 29, 1837 (enc.), FO 84/227. For similar activities in Rio de Janeiro see H. Hamilton to Aberdeen, Dec. 14, 1844, enc. Henry A. Wise to H. Hamilton, Dec. 1, 1844, FO 84/525; "Memorandum . . . on British subjects . . . ," Apr. 29, 1845, FO 84/616; Treasury to Palmerston, July 8, 1848 (enc.), FO 84/742.
9. The British minister to the Brazilian court, Lord Ponsonby, described the "amount of British capital . . . indirectly employed in the slave trade" as "vast" and claimed that "there are few merchants here who do not annually receive large shipments of goods adopted for carrying on the same traffic . . . it is calculated that one third of all British maufactures imported into [Rio de Janeiro are] eventually used in the commerce with the coast of Africa" (Ponsonby to Aberdeen, June 27, 1829, FO 84/95; cf. C. Pennel to Palmerston, July 23, 1831, FO 84/122).
10. G. J. R. Gordon to Palmerston, Apr. 21, 1838, FO 84/252.
11. Ponsonby to Aberdeen, May 1829, FO 84/95; unsigned letter to Mark Phillips given by the latter to Palmerston, June 27, 1839, FO 84/305. For the withdrawal of credit see W. G. Ouseley to Palmerston, Sept. 17, 1839, FO 84/287. For Charles Tolmé's problems, see J. Kennedy to Palmerston, March 16, 1839, FO 84/274; See also D. Turnbull to Palmerston, August 16, 1839, FO 84/358.
12. See for example J. Backhouse to the Treasury, Dec. 27, 1836 enc. papers of the *Golondrina* case in which it had been clearly established that Messrs. Richard Wilson Parke and Singleton of Kingston, Jamaica, supplied the outbound cargo, FO 84/210.
13. Glenelg to Palmerston, Oct. 20, 1838, FO 84/265. Dodson, Campbell and Rolfe to Palmerston, Jan. 5, 1839, FO 83/2348.
14. Treasury to Palmerston, June 17, 1842, FO 84/431. For a similar case see T. Crawford to Aberdeen, Oct. 14, 1842, FO 84/401.
15. *Trial of Pedro de Zulueta jun. on a charge of slave trading* (London, 1844). See also

Zulueta's evidence to the committee that gave rise to the case, *Report of the Select Committee on the West Coast of Africa*, PP, 1842, 11:680–92.

16. For the select committee see *Report of the Select Committee on the West Coast of Africa*, PP, 1842, 11, 12. For the law officers' views of the action of a British merchant at Cape Coast Castle in selling goods to the captain of a slave ship see PP, 1842, 11:19–20. For Brougham's first bill on the subject, see *Bills, Public*, PP, 1843, 4:393; for its subsequent decimation, owing to both the form and content of the original, see *Hansard*, 3rd ser., 70:735, July 7, 1843; and 71:930–52, August 18, 1843.

17. Commodore Hayes to Admiralty, Jan. 20, 1831, Adm. 1/1.

18. Aberdeen to Brougham, Oct. 18, 1841, Brougham mss. 10205. See also the internal FO memo of Jan. 5, 1849, correcting Palmerston's view of the issue minuted on Admiralty to Palmerston; Dec. 29, 1848, FO 84/749; and the law officers' statement in J. Dodson to Palmerston, Oct. 2, 1841, FO 83/2349.

19. John Westlake, *International Law*, 4 vols. (Cambridge, 1904–13), 1:166–67; Robert Phillimore, *Commentaries upon International Law*, 4 vols. (London, 1879), 1:409–25; Hugo Fischer, "The Suppression of Slavery in International Law," *International Law Quarterly*, 3 (1950):28–51.

20. James Bandinel, "On the means to be taken by Great Britain for putting down the Slave Trade," Mar. 30, 1839, (confidential print) Additional manuscripts, British Library (henceforth referred to as Add. mss.), 43357.

21. Stephen Lushington, *Mirror of Parliament*, 1, 513, Mar. 5, 1828, for example. For a similar discussion, see David B. Davis, *Slavery and Human Progress* (New York, 1984), in particular pp. 231–39.

22. Palmerston to Lord John Russell, Oct. 5, 1864, Russell mss., 30/22/15C, fol. 160.

23. See Palmerston's evidence in *Report of the Select Committee on Sugar and Coffee Plantations*, PP, 1847–48, 23:pt. 1 pp.1–4. Full lists of slave trade treaties may be found in PP, 1850, 9:370–73; 1852–53 (920), 39:214. For those in force in 1858 with African powers, see Adm. 123/175. The texts of the latter are in Lewis Hertslet, *Hertslet's Commercial Treaties* (London, 1827–1925), vols. 7, 8 and 9 passim.

24. The operation of the mixed courts is described in Leslie Bethell, "The Mixed Commissions for the Suppression of the Transatlantic Slave Trade in the Nineteenth Century," *Journal of African History*, 7 (1966):79–93; and Pieter C. Emmer, "Abolition of the Abolished: The Illegal Dutch Slave Trade and the Mixed Courts," in David Eltis and James Walvin (eds.), *The Abolition of the Atlantic Slave Trade* (Madison, Wis., 1981), pp. 180–86.

25. Palmerston in PP, 1847–48, 23:pt. 1, p. 3.

26. Negotiations between Britain and most of the major slave-trading nations are well covered in existing works. For Anglo-U.S. exchanges, see Hugh G. Soulsby, *The Right of Search and the Slave Trade in Anglo-American Relations, 1814–1862* (Baltimore, 1933). For Anglo-Portuguese and Brazilian negotiations, see Leslie M. Bethell, *The Abolition of the Brazilian Slave Trade* (Cambridge, 1970). For Anglo-Spanish relations on the issue, see David R. Murray, *Odious Commerce: Britain, Spain and the Abolition of the Cuban Slave Trade* (Cambridge, 1980). There is no equivalent for Anglo-French exchanges, but see Lawrence C. Jennings, "France, Great Britain and the Repression of the Slave Trade, 1841–1845," *French Historical Studies*, 10 (1977):101–25 and Serge Daget, "France, Suppression of the Illegal Trade and England, 1817–1850," in Eltis and Walvin, *Abolition of the Atlantic Slave Trade*, pp. 193–217. For a survey of British slave-trade treaties with Latin America, see J. F. King, "The Latin American Republics and the Suppression of the Slave Trade," *Hispanic American Historical Review*, 24 (1944):387–411.

27. The Quintuple Alliance was an extension of the 1833 Anglo-French convention (see memo: "Negotiations for a treaty . . . " Sept. 1841 in FO 84/445).

28. Commodore Bullen to Admiralty, Nov. 26, 1826, PP, 1828, 26:264. The gradual disappearance of the flying of the French flag on slave ships in the early 1830s is documented in J. Smith and H. W. Macaulay to Palmerston, Jan. 5, 1833, FO 84/134; Jan. 6, 1834, FO 84/147.

29. The *Julius and Edward* and *Louise* were detained in February 1841, conducted to Bremen and Hamburg, respectively, and subsequently restored with damages paid by the British government. The *Sansone* and *Somariva* were taken to Genoa under similar circumstances in 1845, with identical consequences (see "Abstract showing state of business in S.T. dept. 1845–52," FO 97/430; PP, 1850, 9:360). For a statement of the law of the Hanseatic towns, see S. Canning to Admiralty, Oct. 16, 1841; and Adm. to Palmerston, Sept. 23, 1841 with enc., both in FO 84/385.

30. For a lucid discussion of the issues involved in the Anglo-French treaty of 1845, see "Memorandum," Stephen Lushington, July 29, 1845, Add. mss., 43125, fol. 319–39. For the background to the treaty, see Daget, "France, Suppression of the Illegal Trade"; and Jennings, "France, Great Britain and Repression." For the Anglo-American provision, see Howard Jones, *To the Webster-Ashburton Treaty: A Study in Anglo-American Relations, 1783–1843* (Chapel Hill, N.C., 1977), pp. 69–86, 142–45.

31. "Memorandum," Lushington, Add. mss., 43125, fol. 319–39; "Memorandum," unsigned, Oct. 3, 1851, FO 84/866; Daget, "France, Suppression of the Illegal Trade," pp. 208–9.

32. R. W. Beachey, *The Slave Trade of Eastern Africa* (London, 1976), pp. 43–52; K. Onwuka Dike, *Trade and Politics in the Niger Delta, 1830–1885* (Oxford, 1956), pp. 78–87; R. J. Gavin, "Palmerston's Policy Towards East and West Africa, 1830–1865." Ph.D. diss., Cambridge University, 1958, p. 128.

33. J. Backhouse to Admiralty, Apr. 14, 1838, FO 84/262. This letter and the confidential print can also be found in Buxton mss., 27, fol. 179–98.

34. "Draft of agreement with African chiefs," Apr. 14, 1840, FO 84/336.

35. The standard treaty is in PP, 1850, 9:371. For African objections to freer trade provisions in Porto-Novo and Dahomey, see Commander Edmonstone to Rear Admiral Walker, Sept. 22, 1861, enc. Mr. McCoskry, June 20, 1861, Adm. 123/183; and Admiralty to Malmesbury, Apr. 10, 1852, sub. enc. Commander T. G. Forbes, Jan. 18, 1852, FO 84/893.

36. "Memorandum on negotiations with the chiefs of the Bonny," Apr. 7, 1841, unsigned, FO 84/389. "Memo," n.d., attached to G. Brand to Palmerston, Dec. 20, 1849, FO 84/764; Duke of Somerset to Palmerston, Oct. 3, 1861 (private), Broadlands mss., GC/SO/62. Dike appears to be mistaken in claiming that an unratified slave-trade agreement existed in the Bonny as early as 1839. There had been discussions but no formal agreement. (Dike, *Trade and Politics*, p. 83).

37. Canning to Admiralty, Dec. 31, 1841, FO 84/385; Sept. 11, 1843, FO 84/497; Admiralty to Malmesbury, Apr. 10, 1852, enc. Commodore Bruce, Feb. 11, 1852, FO 84/893. See also Captain John Foote to Palmerston, July 25, 1846, Broadlands mss., SLT/34, in which the former argued that cash payments to African powers, however substantial, would be trifling compared to the cost of the squadron; and Capt. C. W. Riley to Admiralty, May 22, 1850, Adm. 123/173.

38. For naval action see Colonial Office to Aberdeen, Aug. 17, 1842, enc. Governor of Sierra Leone, May 6, 1842, FO 84/433; Admiralty to Palmerston, Apr. 8, 1850, FO 84/825.

39. A long Foreign Office review of Portuguese activities is in "Abstract of Facts as to Portuguese Slave Trade," Aug. 8, 1839, Broadlands, mss. SLT/14.

40. The act was *Statutes at Large,* 2 and 3 Vict., c. 73. For its genesis and passage into law see Bethell, *Abolition of the Brazilian Slave Trade,* pp. 155–66; idem, "Britain, Portugal, and the Suppression of the Brazilian Slave Trade: The Origins of Lord Palmerston's Act of 1839," *English Historical Review,* 80 (1965):761–84. For the objections of Wellington and other Tory peers, see *Hansard,* 3rd ser. 49:1063–73.

41. W. D. Jones, "The Origins and Passage of Lord Aberdeen's Act," *Hispanic American Historical Review,* 42 (1962):502–20; Bethell, *Abolition of the Brazilian Slave Trade,* pp. 242–66.

42. Canning to Admiralty, Dec. 23, 1841, FO 84/385; Bethell, *Abolition of the Brazilian Slave Trade,* pp. 167–77.

43. Stephen Lushington, "Memorandum on the right of Great Britain to treat Brazilian Slave Trade as Piracy," July 24, 1845, FO 97/430; J. Dodson, W. W. Follett and F. Thesiger to Aberdeen, May 30, 1845; and "Memorandum of Brazil Slave Trade Bill," July 3, 1845, both in Add. mss., 43125, fols. 147–48, 234–88.

44. Aberdeen to Peel, Oct. 18, 1844, Add. mss., 43044. The illegality of the act in international law was clearly spelled out in Sir Thomas Wylde's speech in *Hansard,* 3rd ser. 82:1059–60, July 24, 1845; and in "The Brazilian Slave Traders," *Law Magazine,* 25 (1846):251–63. According to Malmesbury, Aberdeen was never convinced that he had been right to recommend the 1845 act (Bethell, *Abolition of the Brazilian Slave Trade,* p. 266).

45. "The Brazilian Slave Traders," 251–63. For the *Felicidade* case, see *Regina* v. *Serva et al, English Reports,* vol. 169:169–91.

46. See Sir James Graham to Palmerston, Jan. 11, 1831, FO 84/124, penned a few weeks after he became first lord of the Admiralty. Graham wrote, "Wherein consists of the necessity of a squadron on this station [West Africa]? The prevention of the Slave Trade is its only employment; and does it effect its object? . . . it does not." See also, Palmerston to Lord John Russell, Aug. 13, 1862, quoted in A. E. M. Ashley, *Life and Correspondence of Henry John Temple, Viscount Palmerston, 1846–1865,* 2 vols. (London, 1876): 2:227. Palmerston wrote, "If there was a particularly old, slow going tub in the navy, she was sure to be sent to the coast of Africa to try to catch the fast sailing American clippers."

47. See, for example, "A Return of . . . vessels . . . furnished . . . with Slave Warrants . . . Dec. 1838 to Dec. 1844," PP, 1845, 49. Cf. infra, table 2.

48. Sir James Graham to Palmerston, Jan. 11, 1831, FO 84/124.

49. This percentage explains the discrepancy between Lloyd's figures (*Navy and the Slave Trade,* pp. 279–82) and those derived by Serge Daget from PP and the FO 84 series ("France, Suppression of the Illegal Trade," pp. 202–3, 211–12). Lloyd measures the effective strength of the squadron, whereas Daget counts all the ships that were assigned to Africa in a given year.

50. A full description of the type of ships used in the squadron may be found in Lloyd, *Navy and the Slave Trade,* pp. 279–84, and W. E. F. Ward, *The Royal Navy and the Slavers: The Suppression of the Atlantic Slave Trade* (London, 1969), pp. 22–37.

51. See, for example, PP (561), 44:5; 1850, 9:app., p. 147.

52. Depreciation is not, of course, an operating or variable cost, but the sum of other elements mentioned here divided by the number of ships in the squadron would yield something close to the marginal cost of (or the extra expense incurred in) sending a vessel to the African coast as opposed to holding it in reserve.

53. "Report of the Select Committee on the Slave Trade," Apr. 12, 1822, in *American State Papers,* 5:141; *The Federal Cases,* 30 vols. (St. Paul, 1894–97) Case no. 15,551; Lloyd, *Navy and the Slave Trade,* pp. 51–52; Hugh G. Soulsby, *The Right of Search and the Slave Trade in Anglo-American Relations, 1814–62* (Baltimore, 1933), pp. 22–23.

54. Alan R. Booth, "The United States African Squadron, 1843–61," in Jeffrey Butler (ed.), *Boston University Papers in African History,* 4 vols. (Boston, 1964), 1:82–87, 103–5, 115; Warren S. Howard, *American Slavers and the Federal Law, 1837–1862* (Berkeley, 1963), pp. 41–69, 239–40. U.S. Commodore Read wrote in 1846, "Nearly the whole time our vessels are on this station is consumed in going to the slave marts on the coast and returning to the Cape Verde for supplies. In consequence of this, it is found impossible to keep more than two vessels at the same time on the coast. At this moment, contrary to all my expectations and all my exertions, there is not a vessel of my command to the eastward of Cape Mesurado" (Commodore George C. Read to Secretary of Navy, Dec. 11, 1846, Letters to the Secretary of the Navy, National Archives, Washington [henceforth referred to as LSN], reel 103).

55. The USS *Constitution,* which contributed fifty-one of the seventy-five guns on the station, was of less use than an eight-gun brig (according to her commander) on account of her tall masts and provisioning difficulties (Commodore Isaac Mayo to Secretary of Navy, Nov. 10, 1853, LSN, reel 107). For the lack of U.S. authority over ships without colors, see the minute on E. Gabriel to Palmerston, Dec. 28, 1859, FO 84/1076; Howard, *American Slavers,* pp. 92–110, 155–210, 224–35.

56. Admiralty to Palmerston, Jan. 14, 1846, enc. Commodore (L. T.) Jones, Nov. 21, 1845, FO 84/657.

57. The equivalent to this on the east coast was a protocol signed Aug. 12, 1847, that formalized an earlier arrangement permitting English cruisers to pursue suppression within those Portuguese territorial waters where no Portuguese settlement existed. In other words, everywhere except Delagoa Bay, Inhambane, Sofala, Quelimane, Mozambique and Ibo (see Admiralty to Aberdeen, Oct. 8, 1845, sub enc. Commander Ricketts, May 8, 1845, FO 84/612; Admiralty to Palmerston, Jan. 31, 1849, enc. Vice Admiral Dacres, Dec. 1, 1848, FO 84/782). For Palmerston's attitude to Portuguese claims of sovereignty see a minute by Palmerston, July 31, 1849, FO 84/764.

58. G. Jackson and E. Gabriel to Palmerston, Feb. 14, 1848, FO 84/719; G. Jackson to Palmerston (private), Nov. 16, 1848, FO 84/720.

59. Admiralty to Palmerston, May 30, 1848, enc. Commodore Hotham, Mar. 14, 1848, FO 84/747. The Portuguese-Brazilian issue is discussed in Admiralty to Aberdeen, June 5, 1845, enc. Commander Daniels, Feb. 18, 1844, FO 84/610; G. Jackson and E. Gabriel to Palmerston, Aug. 22, 1848, and Palmerston to Jackson and Gabriel, Dec. 11, 1848, both in FO 84/720. For slave-trader influence over the government, see G. Jackson to Palmerston (private), Nov. 16, 1848, FO 84/720.

60. For a British report of Spanish naval activity in 1857–58, see Adm. to Malmesbury, July 3, 1858, sub enc. Commander Vesey, March 23, 1858, FO 84/1069. For a general survey of Spanish naval anti–slave-trade activities, see Murray, *Odious Commerce,* pp. 87–89, 250–51, 262–63, 309.

61. Bethell, *Abolition of the Brazilian Slave Trade,* pp. 77, 87, 138, 140, 367–68; Robert Conrad, "The Contraband Slave Trade to Brazil, 1831–1845," *Hispanic American Historical Review,* 49 (1969):622–23. An estimate of Brazilian naval strength is in Daniel P. Kidder, *Sketches of Residence and Travels in Brazil,* 2 vols. (London, 1845): 1:358.

62. Accepting an official position at one of these mixed commission courts was—like investing in the slave trade at this time—to partake in a lottery. Henry Hayne served eight years at his post of commissary judge in Rio de Janeiro out of the eleven years (1820–31) of his appointment. He adjudicated one ship in this period and, as the trade was largely legal, he had no difficulty in supplying the quarterly returns of slave imports into the region as required by the Foreign Office. He retired

in 1831 on a full pension. The first two commissioners at Luanda, on the other hand, were dead within weeks of their arrival; Sierra Leone commissioners lasted an average of less than thirty months between 1819 and 1845.

63. See the discussion supra, chap. 1, and E. Phillip LeVeen, *British Slave Trade Suppression Policies, 1821-1865* (New York, 1977).

64. PP, 1847 (653), 67:2-3. A detailed breakdown of net proceeds of ships condemned at the Sierra Leone Mixed Commission Court may be found in M. L. Melville and James Hook to Palmerston, Apr. 28, 1848 (enc.), FO 84/712. Between 1840 and 1848 these averaged £420 (in current pounds sterling) per ship (125 vessels) prior to division among parties to the commission. There remains some question on the disposition of captured specie. It is not clear how this was effected and not all of it is included here. The amounts involved however would scarcely disturb the general thrust of this discussion.

65. A tabulation of naval strength and costs, 1756-1859 is in PP, 1860 (168), 42:543.

66. Phyllis Deane and W. A. Cole (*British Economic Growth, 1688-1959: Trends and Structure,* 2nd ed. [Cambridge, 1969], p. 166), estimate National Product at £452 million in 1841. In 1821-25 prices this would be £462.6 million. Suppression costs in that year were £0.177 million.

67. Roger T. Anstey, *The Atlantic Slave Trade and British Abolition* (London, 1975), pp. 419-25.

68. Ibid., pp. 41-48; supra, chap. 4, n. 11; David Richardson, "Profits in the Liverpool Slave Trade: The Accounts of William Davenport, 1757-1784," in Roger Anstey and P. E. H. Hair (eds.), *Liverpool, the African Slave Trade, and Abolition: Essays to Illustrate Current Knowledge and Research* (Liverpool, 1976), pp. 60-90; Joseph E. Inikori, "Market Structure and the Profits of the British African Trade in the Late Eighteenth Century," *Journal of Economic History,* 41 (1981):745-76.

69. The calculation of this figure is:

| | Tonnage ('000) | Outset Cost per ton (Constant £s, 1821-25) | Profit Rate | Total Profits (£ millions) |
|---|---|---|---|---|
| 1761-70 | 153.0 | 76.9 | | 3.14 |
| 1771-80 | 120.7 | 69.0 | | 2.22 |
| 1781-90 | 191.1 | 62.3 | 0.267 | 3.18 |
| 1791-1800 | 320.0 | 40.3 | | 3.44 |
| 1801-7 | 264.0 | 26.2 | | 1.84 |
| Total: 1761-1807 | | | | 13.82 |

*Sources:* Anstey, *The Atlantic Slave Trade* p. 47; Seymour Drescher, *Econocide: British Slavery in the Era of Abolition* (Pittsburgh, 1977), p. 28; Inikori, "Market Structure and Profits of the British African Trade," p. 772. The outset costs have been adjusted to allow for the trade in African produce (Anstey, *Atlantic Slave Trade,* pp. 424-25) as well as the price indexes in B. R. Mitchell and Phyllis Deane, *Abstract of British Historical Statistics* (Cambridge, 1962), pp. 469-70. For an alternative method of calculating total profits, see Stanley L. Engerman, "The Slave Trade and British Capital Formation in the Eighteenth Century: A Comment on the Williams Thesis," *Business History Review,* 46 (1972):436-39.

70. Profits in the 1796-1801 period were 1.4 percent of National Income in 1801; costs in the 1816-1821 period were 0.65 percent of National Income in 1821 (supra, table n. 69; table 2; Deane and Cole, *British Economic Growth,* p. 166; Mitchell and Deane, *British Historical Statistics,* pp. 469-70). Reasonable adjustment for biases might well bring these ratios into equality.

71. There is an exception in that nine ships were restored after being divested of their slave cargoes. Data on captured ships are from the slave ship data set except for the French ships detained. That information, for the most part, has been kindly supplied by Serge Daget (personal communication). This total may be compared with the number of enemy ships captured by the British during the whole of the French Wars, 1793–1815. According to the *Colonial Magazine and Commercial Maritime Journal,* 1 (1840):374, these totaled 1,201.

72. Fifteen of the twenty-six slavers, however, embarked 5,256 slaves prior to capture and (allowing for the usual mortality) perhaps just under 5,000 disembarked. The remaining eleven ships probably disembarked a slightly smaller number of slaves. The distribution of these cargoes of unknown size by regions of embarkation and disembarkation is very similar to that of the known cargoes.

73. For an interesting treatment of parallel issues during the contemporary northern blockade of southern cotton ports in the American Civil War, see Stanley Lebergott, "Through the Blockade: The Profitability and Extent of Cotton Smuggling, 1861– 1865," *Journal of Economic History,* 41 (1981):867–88.

74. Captured ships without a known destination in the Americas amounted to 21 percent of all captured ships and are reflected in the column headed "Not Known" in table 3. These have been assigned a region of disembarkation for the purpose of calculating the ratios in figure 4. The basis of this assignment is simply the annual regional distribution of those ships that did have recorded destinations.

75. Of course, if the venture was insured, the loss to the individual would be confined to the insurance premium. As losses from captures and other hazards and total insurance premiums for each branch of the traffic would tend to be the same, we can ignore the insurance factor at the aggregate level.

76. All captured ships bound for Cuba before 1837 or in 1838 as well as those bound for Brazil before 1840 are assigned a weight of 1.0. After these dates a ship is assigned a weight of 1.0 only if it had slaves on board at the time of capture. One year was thus allowed for the slave traders to adjust to key British initiatives of 1836, 1838 and 1839; these are discussed more fully in chapter 8. For all other years, captured ships without slaves are given a weight of 0.33. A weight of 0.33 rather than 0.2 or lower is allocated because occasionally there were ships captured with bullion on board. In addition, naval attacks on shore-based establishments, particularly between 1840 and 1842 and after 1848, resulted in the destruction of trade goods.

## Chapter 7

1. For the general dilemma of liberalism in the aftermath of emancipation, see Thomas C. Holt, "'An Empire over the Mind': Emancipation, Race, and Ideology in the British West Indies and the American South," in J. Morgan Kousser and James M. McPherson (eds.), *Region Race and Reconstruction: Essays in Honor of C. Vann Woodward* (New York, 1982), pp. 283–313.

2. Roger T. Anstey, *The Atlantic Slave Trade and British Abolition* (London, 1975), pp. 157–73.

3. R. Coupland, *Wilberforce, a Narrative* (Oxford, 1923), pp. 405–46; Ford K. Brown, *Fathers of the Victorians* (Cambridge, 1961), pp. 83–88, 428–45; I. Bradley, *The Call to Seriousness: The Evangelical Impact on the Victorians* (London, 1976), pp. 94– 118. On the connection between the two societies, see M. J. D. Roberts, "The Society for the Suppression of Vice and Its Early Critics," *Historical Journal,* 26

(1983):159–76. For the quintessential Whig criticism of the activities of these societies, see Sydney Smith's article in the *Edinburgh Review,* 13 (1809):333–43. Some Evangelicals were also unhappy with the tactics of these societies. Zachary Macaulay opposed the Vice Society's use of spies and paid employees to collect evidence against Sabbath breakers and pornographers. Doing "evil that good may come" was against "Scriptural authority" he argued, and in this he was supported by Wilberforce and other Evangelical members of the Vice Society. It is perhaps significant, however, that these objections were rooted in the Scriptures rather than the concern for individual rights that motivated most of the Vice Society's critics (*British Press,* [Feb. 18, 1805], p. 3, col. 4, cited in M. J. D. Roberts, "Society for the Suppression of Vice," pp. 169–70; E. M. Howse, *Saints in Politics: The Clapham Sect and the Growth of Freedom* [Toronto, 1952], pp. 116–37).

4. C. Duncan Rice, "Controversies over Slavery in Eighteenth- and Nineteenth-Century Scotland," in Lewis Perry and Michael Fellman, (eds.), *Antislavery Reconsidered: New Perspectives on the Abolitionists* (Baton Rouge, La., 1979), pp. 36–37.

5. Ibid., pp. 40–43; C. Duncan Rice, "Enlightenment, Evangelism, and Economics: An Interpretation of the Drive Towards Emancipation in British West India," in Vera Rubin and Arthur Tuden (eds.), *Comparative Perspectives on Slavery in New World Plantation Societies* (New York, 1977), pp. 123–31. Howard Temperley, "Capitalism, Slavery and Ideology," *Past and Present,* 75 (1977):97–118; idem, "The Ideology of Antislavery," in David Eltis and James Walvin (eds.) *The Abolition of the Atlantic Slave Trade* (Madison, Wis., 1981), pp. 21–35.

6. Much of this paragraph is based on David Brion Davis, *Slavery and Human Progress* (New York, 1984), pp. 170–74.

7. J. Stephen (the elder) to Spencer Perceval, Nov. 13, 1807, Perceval Papers, British Library, Add. mss. 49183, fols. 11–14; cited in D. B. Davis, *Slavery and Human Progress,* p. 174.

8. Z. Macaulay to Thomas Ludlam, governor of Sierra Leone, Nov. 4, 1807, CO 267/25.

9. Christopher Fyfe, *A History of Sierra Leone,* (London, 1962), pp. 105–9; Register of Privy Council, Feb. 15, 1808, PC 2/175; Mar. 8, Mar. 12, and Mar. 16, 1808, PC 2/176; *Hansard,* 1st ser., 17:678.

10. E. I. Herrington, "British Measures for the Suppression of the Slave Trade off the West Coast of Africa, 1807–1833," M.A. thesis, University of London, 1923, p. 12.

11. Fyfe, *Sierra Leone,* 105–9; Z. Macaulay to the Admiralty, Apr. 23, 1811, Adm. 1/4895; *Sixth Annual Report of the Committee of the African Institution* (London, 1812), p. 9.

12. Zachary Macaulay did particularly well. A son and a nephew of his obtained lucrative appointments in the new Sierra Leone antislave-trade establishment. When a commission of inquiry was appointed in 1808 to investigate the British settlements on the west coast of Africa and the best methods of suppressing the slave trade, the Colonial Office asked Macaulay to draw up instructions for it and appointed two of his personal friends as its members. Even naval officers came within the commission's orbit: Captain Columbine, charged with taking the commission to the coast, was a director of the African Institution and for fifteen months, governor of Sierra Leone; Macaulay described Captain Irby, who commanded the squadron of five cruisers sent to the coast in 1811 as "a man of our choice." (Fyfe, *Sierra Leone,* 105; *Fourth Annual Report of the Committee of the African Institution* [London, 1810] pp. 4–5; Z. Macaulay to Roscoe, Oct. 6, 1811, Roscoe Papers; Z. Macaulay to Henr᷇ Brougham, Oct. 15, 1811, Brougham mss. 10527).

13. Z. Macaulay to Roscoe, Oct. 28, 1811, Roscoe Papers.
14. Z. Macaulay to Roscoe, July 8, Nov. 10, 1809, and Aug. 8, 1811; T. Clarkson to Roscoe, Aug. 20, 1810, Roscoe Papers.
15. Z. Macaulay to Brougham, Sept. 16, 1811, Brougham mss. 10524; Z. Macaulay to Roscoe, Nov. 10, 1809, Roscoe Papers.
16. David Eltis, "The British Trans-Atlantic Slave Trade After 1807," *Journal of Maritime History*, 4 (1974):7.
17. See the review of British legislation on the slave trade in "Summary Statement of Acts of Parliament . . . ," n.d. and unsigned, as well as the addendum, unsigned, June 28, 1819 in FO 84/8. For some of Charles Greville's acid comments on Brougham's reputation among lawyers, see Lytton Strachey and Roger Fulford (eds.), *The Greville Memoirs, 1814–1860*, 8 vols. (London, 1938), 2:426–27; 3:24; 5:76.
18. "Abstract of papers (selected for Lord Castlereagh in Aug. 1814) . . . ," nd, unsigned, FO 95, 9/2.
19. James Lang, *Portuguese Brazil, the King's Plantation* (New York, 1981), pp. 190–200; Alan K. Manchester, *British Preeminence in Brazil: Its Rise and Decline* (Chapel Hill, N.C., 1933).
20. Sir William Scott to Admiralty, Aug. 4, 1814, Adm. 1/3902.
21. Wilberforce to Brougham, Oct. 5, 1810, Brougham mss. 10954; *Fifth Annual Report of the Committee of the African Institution* (London, 1811), pp. 28–30. For the treaty, see *British and Foreign State Papers*, 1 (London, 1812):555–57.
22. David R. Murray, *Odious Commerce: Britain, Spain and the Abolition of the Cuban Slave Trade* (Cambridge, 1980), pp. 40–49. It should be pointed out, however, that *ex post facto* the High Court of Admiralty under Sir William Scott gave the abolitionists some support in the *Donna Marianna* case in June 1812. The judgment on this English-owned ship sailing under Portuguese colors, in effect, conceded that British cruisers had the right to enquire into the title of ships of any nation and to enforce British law if the foreign ownership was colorable only (see the report of this case in the *Sixth Annual Report of the Committee of the African Institution*, (London, 1812), pp. 167–70). It was in their wide interpretation of what should constitute evidence of these infractions that the abolitionists were mistaken.
23. D. B. Davis, *Slavery and Human Progress*, pp. 231–36.
24. Eltis, "British Trans-Atlantic Slave Trade," pp. 1–2.
25. Ibid., pp. 7–8; Fyfe, *Sierra Leone*, pp. 120–24; Anon., *The Trial of the Slave Traders at Sierra Leone in April and June, 1812* (London, 1813).
26. The *Amedie* and *Fortuna* cases are in *Fifth Annual Report of the Committee of the African Institution*, pp. 12–26. For other sources and a good discussion of this issue, see Murray, *Odious Commerce*, pp. 40–41.
27. A. W. Ward and G. P. Gooch (eds.), *The Cambridge History of British Foreign Policy, 1783–1919*, 3 vols. (Cambridge, 1923), 2:235; Herrington, "British Measures for the Suppression of the Slave Trade," pp. 76–77; Z. Macaulay to Admiralty, Apr. 23, 1811 (enc.), Adm 1/4895; *Sixth Annual Report of the Committee of the African Institution*, p. 9. For the African Institution's interpretation of the treaty see *Fifth Annual Report of the Committee of the African Institution*, pp. 28–30.
28. Count of ships captured taken from the slave ship data set. For an example of how naval commanders interpreted their instructions see Admiralty to Peel, May 8, 1812 (and enclosures) in CO 267/35. For the Portuguese response see Castlereagh to Admiralty, May 6, 1813, in Charles William Vane (ed.), *Correspondence, Dispatches and other Papers of Viscount Castlereagh*, 12 vols. (London 1853), 12:469–70, and "Abstract of Papers," FO 95, 9/2.

29. William Law Mathieson, *Great Britain and the Slave Trade, 1839–1865* (London, 1929), p. 11.

30. Herrington, "British Measures for the Suppression of the Slave Trade," p. 97. The treaty is in *British and Foreign State Papers,* 4 (London, 1816–17):348–55.

31. Mathieson, *Great Britain and the Slave Trade,* pp. 11–12. *San Juan Nepomuceno* folder in HCA 37/5. Folders on all other cases appealed to the High Court of Admiralty that involved wrongful detention may be found in HCA 37/1–6. See also *Hansard,* new ser., 1:1125–26, June 16, 1820.

32. Orders enclosed in Governor Maxwell to Liverpool, Dec. 10, 1811, FO 72/137, cited in Murray, *Odious Commerce,* p. 41. Count of captured ships is taken from the slave-ship data set.

33. Murray, *Odious Commerce,* pp. 40–49. Examples of authentic Spanish slave ships condemned at Sierra Leone were the *General Silveira* and *Dolores,* the former sailing under Portuguese colors. See "Prizes adjudicated at Sierra Leone from 26th March to 25 June, 1815," HCA 49/101. Others may be found in HCA 49/97, including the *Rayo,* which was restored because "her Spanish papers were deemed sufficient."

34. The minutes of the Anglo-Portuguese Commission are in FO 308/1. The treaties may be found in *British and Foreign State Papers,* 4: passim. For the *Louis* case, see J. Dodson, *Reports of Cases Argued and Determined in the High Court of Admiralty,* 2 vols. (London 1815–28), 2:210. A convenient summary of payments to Spain and Portugal is in *Report of the Select Committee on the Slave Trade Treaties,* PP, 1852–53, 29:215.

35. Murray, *Odious Commerce,* p. 69. One Spanish slave-ship owner received compensation of £21,180 in 1820 for a detention that had occurred in 1818, after the Anglo-Spanish treaty had been concluded (*Madrazo* v. *Willes, English Reports,* 106:692–94). This appears to have been an isolated case, though the grounds of the decision suggest that after the *Le Louis* case (1817) at least, English courts would compensate any wrongful arrest on this issue. However, see infra, n.80; *Buron* v. *Denman, Exchequer Reports,* 2 (1848–49):166–89.

36. *Hansard,* new ser., 1:1125.

37. *Hansard,* 1st ser., 17:663, June 15, 1810.

38. Ibid., pp. 679–82; (James Stephen, the elder), *The Slave Trade of Spain in Northern Africa* (London, 1816).

39. *Hansard,* new ser., 1:1126.

40. As well as official appointments for members of his family that gave the family advantages in their private business dealings at Sierra Leone, Macaulay himself acted as agent for numerous captors in London when the latter applied for prize money arising from capturing slaves and slave ships. Much of the Macaulay fortune, subsequently lost when Zachary turned over his business interests to his nephew, came from this source (Fyfe, *Sierra Leone,* pp. 116, 142, 166; and the numerous references to Z. Macaulay in the High Court of Admiralty records, HCA 37/1–12). See also the numerous pamphlets by Robert Thorpe, the major substance of which was contained in his first pamphlet, *A Letter to William Wilberforce, Esq. . . .* (London, 1815), pp. 1–69. It is curious that those interested in linking abolition to economic gains for the abolitionists (as opposed to gains to National Income) have focused on James Cropper rather than Zachary Macaulay.

41. See Betty Fladeland, "Abolitionist Pressures on the Concert of Europe, 1814–1822," *Journal of Modern History,* 38 (1966):355–73, for the mix of private abolitionist influence and the pressure of British public opinion.

42. Ibid., pp. 368–69.

43. "Memorandum on business of Slave Trade Dept.," unsigned, n.d., in FO 84/818; HMSO, *Records of the Foreign Office, 1782–1939* (London, 1969), pp. 13–16; Palmerston minute on Colonial Office to Palmerston, Dec. 8, 1838, FO 84/265; Memorandum, unsigned, Sept. 4, 1826, FO 84/61; Memorandum, unsigned, nd, on Spain no. 96, FO 84/193.

44. Leslie M. Bethell, *The Abolition of the Brazilian Slave Trade* (Cambridge, 1970), pp. 388–89.

45. For Lushington's public attacks on the Evangelicals see *Hansard,* new ser., 1:1125–26; 5:1117–18, 1490–91. The increasing association of the older generation of the Evangelicals with the Whigs and radicals on the slavery issue (despite Lushington's attacks) drove an increasing gulf between themselves and the main body of evangelicalism (see Ian S. Rennie, "Evangelicalism and English Public Life, 1823–1850." (Ph.D. thesis, University of Toronto, 1962, pp. 168–204).

46. D. B. Davis, *Slavery and Human Progress,* 231–79; David Eltis, "Abolitionist Perceptions of Society after Slavery," in James Walvin (ed.), *Slavery and British Society, 1776–1846* (London, 1982), p. 210.

47. Bethell, *Abolition of the Brazilian Slave Trade,* pp. 156, 263–64; Lushington, "Memorandum on the right of Great Britain to treat Brazilian Slave Trade as Piracy," July 24, 1845, FO 97/430; Aberdeen to Lushington, July 29, 1845, Add. mss., 40455.

48. J. Dodson to Aberdeen, July 5, 1843 and Aug. 8, 1843, FO 83/2351.

49. J. H. Tredgold, "Mission to the Brazils," n.d., but written in 1839 on instructions of British and Foreign Anti-Slavery Society Committee, file G79, Brit. Emp. mss., s.22. George Pilkington eventually published *An Address to the English Residents in the Brazilian Empire* (Rio de Janeiro, 1844).

50. Lord Minto to Palmerston, Sept. 10, 1839, Broadlands mss., GC/MI/402.

51. Napier to Joseph T. Crawford, June 11, 1858, FO 313/34; cf. Murray, *Odious Commerce,* pp. 264–65. The decoy proposal was approved by the Earl of Malmesbury (FO memo, June 1859, FO 84/1086), but the Admiralty went back to ideological first principles in objecting to it partly on grounds that it would be "unworthy to this country" and partly, and more practically, that the captain might become a double agent for the slave traders (Admiralty to Malmesbury, June 29, 1859, FO 84/1086).

52. Commander Grey Skipwith to Admiralty, n.d., but c1850, Adm. 123/173; Palmerston to Ouseley, Sept. 5, 1839, FO 84/287; E. Watts to Palmerston, Jan. 31, 1840, FO 84/326.

53. Russell to E. M. Archibald, Aug. 5, 1859, FO 84/1086; March 29, 1860, FO 84/1111.

54. Palmerston, memorandum, Aug. 24, 1851, FO 84/838; Crawford to Clarendon, May 30, 1853, FO 84/905.

55. The first two British representatives to the Anglo-Portuguese Luanda court of Mixed Commission died within five months of arriving in Africa. From June 6, 1844 to Apr. 23, 1845, the Portuguese judge and the Portuguese arbitrator, Eusébio Catella de Samos and Felix Antônio Dominguez, respectively, acted as Foreign Office correspondents and convinced the new British commissioner of their abhorrence of the traffic after his arrival. Both were important figures in the slave trade. See E. Gabriel to Aberdeen, Sept. 12, 1845; and Sept. 13, 1845, [both marked "private"] FO 84/569. The dismay in Aberdeen's minutes on these letters is palpable.

56. J. Hudson to Palmerston, Oct. 10, 1848, GC/HU/6, Broadlands mss.

57. Cited in Tony Smith, *Patterns of Imperialism: The United States, Great Britain and the Late Industrializing World Since 1815* (New York, 1981), p. 34.

58. Bethell, *Abolition of the Brazilian Slave Trade,* pp. 219, 221, 234, 272; quote from James Hudson to Palmerston, Feb. 21, 1850, GC/HU/21, Broadlands mss.

59. C. J. Hamilton to Aberdeen, Sept. 20, 1842 (private), Add. mss., 43124, fols. 1–4; James Hudson to Palmerston, Aug. 13, 1849, FO 84/767; Jan. 12, 1850, FO 84/801; July 27, 1850, FO 84/805 (all marked separate and secret). Hudson to Palmerston, Sept. 12, 1848 (private), GC/HU/5; Aug. 15, 1849, GC/HU/15; Aug. 3, 1850, GC/HU/25; all in Broadlands mss. For Palmerston's instructions to Hudson on this issue, see Palmerston, memorandum, Oct. 9, 1848, FO 84/726; Palmerston to Hudson, Mar. 31, 1850, GC/HUC/48, Broadlands mss.
60. James Hudson to Palmerston, Jan. 12, 1850, FO 84/801. It is worth noting that in Rio de Janeiro in the mid-1840s there was a total of only four daily newspapers and two "tri weeklies" (Daniel P. Kidder, *Sketches of Residence and Travels in Brazil,* 2 vols. [London, 1845] 1:116).
61. James Hudson to Palmerston, Jan. 17, 1850, FO 84/801; Palmerston's reply is dated Mar. 31, 1850, in GC/HU/48, Broadlands mss. For other informers—some kept on the payroll until the late 1850s, see James Hudson to Wylde, Aug. 22, 1859, FO 84/1095.
62. Palmerston to Clarke, Aug. 26, 1841, FO 84/360. This was at a time when the Baltimore clipper was widely used. For costs of obtaining information, see Thomas Ward, memorandum, Oct. 31, 1855, FO 84/959.
63. C. H. Haring, *The Spanish Empire in the Americas,* (New York, 1947), pp. 314–25; James F. King, "Evolution of the Free Trade Principle in Spanish Colonial Administration," *Hispanic American Historical Review,* 22 (1942):34–56; Manuel Moreno Fraginals, *The Sugarmill: The Socioeconomic Complex of Sugar in Cuba,* trans. Cedric Belfrage (New York, 1976), pp. 59–62; Robert L. Paquette, "The Conspiracy of *La Escalera:* Colonial Society and Politics in Cuba in the Age of Revolution." Ph.D. diss., University of Rochester, 1982, pp. 76–92; Drew Gilpin Faust (ed.), *The Ideology of Slavery: Proslavery Thought in the Antebellum South, 1830–1860* (Baton Rouge, La., 1981), pp. 1–136, 272–99.
64. "The Secretary's Report of His Recent Continental Visit," n.d., file G-77, Brit. Emp. mss., s22. See David Murray's discussion of Creole opposition to the slave trade in *Odious Commerce,* pp. 129–31; Moreno Fraginals, *Sugarmill,* pp. 133–34; and Paquette, "The Conspiracy of La Escalera," pp. 74–108. For del Monte, see Richard R. Madden, *The Island of Cuba* (London, 1849), pp. 114–56. For Arango y Parreño, see in addition W. W. Pierson, "Francisco de Arango y Parreño," *Hispanic American Historical Review,* 16 (1936):468–71.
65. For Kennedy's background see, U.S. Congress, Sen. Exec. Doc. no. 115, 26–2, p. 492. James Stephen, the younger, the permanent undersecretary, and Lord Glenelg, the secretary of state, were sons of James Stephen, the elder, and Charles Grant, respectively.
66. D. R. Murray, "Richard Robert Madden: His Career as a Slavery Abolitionist," *Studies,* 61 (1972):42–53; idem, *Odious Commerce,* pp. 127–32.
67. Paquette, "The Conspiracy of *La Escalera,*" 34–42; David Turnbull, *Travels in the West. Cuba: With Notices of Porto Rico and the Slave Trade* (London, 1840), pp. 340–60; Murray, *Odious Commerce,* pp. 133–39.
68. CO to Palmerston and accompanying memo by Palmerston, Dec. 8, 1838, FO 84/265; Murray, *Odious Commerce,* pp. 139–40.
69. F. Cocking to Palmerston, Oct. 1, 1846 and attached memoranda by Palmerston and John Bidwell, Nov. 1846, FO 72/709; see also Cocking's letters Apr. 10, 1844 and May 6, 1844 in FO 199/20. For accounts of the conspiracy, see Paquette, "The Conspiracy of *La Escalera,*" 193–203; and Murray, *Odious Commerce,* pp. 163–72.
70. J. Hudson to Palmerston, Oct. 10, 1848, GC/HU/6, Broadlands mss.
71. Thomas Fowell Buxton, *The African Slave Trade and Its Remedy,* 2nd ed. (London,

1840), p. 458; Philip D. Curtin, *The Image of Africa: British Ideas and Action, 1780–1850* (Madison, Wis., 1964), pp. 272–74.

72. *Ibid.,* pp. 274–75, 452–53; Fyfe, *Sierra Leone,* pp. 117–18; Thorpe, *Letter to William Wilberforce;* Eltis, "Abolitionist Perceptions of Society after Slavery," pp. 196–204.

73. Stephen, *Slave Trade of Spain,* pp. 18–23, 33–35.

74. Monsieur de Vattel, *The Law of Nations* (Philadelphia, 1849), p. 137. See also pp. lv–lvi and 80–81. For the position of James Stephen, the younger, see T. J. Barron, "James Stephen, the 'Black Race' and British Colonial Administration, 1813–47, *"Journal of Imperial and Commonwealth History,"* 5 (1977):134–35.

75. For early examples of naval attacks on the coast see W. E. F. Ward, *The Royal Navy and the Slavers* (London, 1969) pp. 65–68, 91–94; Commodore Mends to Admiralty, Apr. 18, 1823, Adm. 1/2190; Admiralty to Aberdeen, Apr. 19, 1845, sub enc. Col. E. Nicolls, Apr. 17, 1845 (recounting an incident in 1834), FO 84/609.

76. Admiralty to Palmerston, Feb. 18, 1841, enc. Commodore W. Tucker, Nov. 11, 1840 and sub enc., FO 84/383; Admiralty to Palmerston, Mar. 23, 1841, FO 84/383; Admiralty to Palmerston, July 14, 1841, enc. Capt. Joseph Denman, Apr. 30, 1841, FO 84/384; Lord Leveson to Admiralty, July 28, 1841, enc. Lt. Hill, n.d., FO 84/384; Admiralty to Palmerston, Aug. 4, 1841, enc. Capt. Nurse, May 4, 1841 and sub enc., FO 84/384; "Destruction of slave factories on the Coast of Africa," unsigned, Apr. 1, 1842, FO 84/445.

77. J. Backhouse to Admiralty, Apr. 6, 1841, FO 84/383. See also the letters of June 1 and June 17, 1841, and the First Lord's request for clarification, Minto to Palmerston, June 10, 1841 (private) FO 84/384.

78. Lord Leveson to Admiralty, July 28, 1841, FO 84/384.

79. Aberdeen to Admiralty; May 20, 1842 printed in PP, 1842, 12:516. For the law officer's opinion on which this letter was based, see J. Dodson to Aberdeen, Apr. 8, 1842, FO 83/2350. The FO 83 volumes for the 1840s are sprinkled with similar opinions on the part of the Crown's law officers. Initially the Foreign Office interpreted the law officers opinion as prohibiting the destruction of any European-owned goods found in the barracoons. In 1848 the prohibition was taken to cover only goods owned by European *legitimate* traders. See the exchange between Palmerston and Denman, Aug. 4 and Nov. 30, 1848, in FO 84/740, and the evidence of Denman before the 1848 Select Committee on Sugar and Coffee Plantations (PP, 1847–48, 23:pt. 1, pp. 151–61, 592).

80. Minto to Palmerston, June 10, 1841 (private), FO 84/384; J. Dodson to Aberdeen, Dec. 31, 1841, FO 83/2349. Compensation was, in fact, paid to René Valentin, a French merchant, whose trade goods were destroyed in Lightburn's factory in the Rio Pongo. Slave traders in Havana and Rio de Janeiro unsuccessfully sued naval officers in the British courts. The test case, *Buron* v. *Denman* (*Exchequer Reports,* 2 (1848–49):166–89), was decided in 1848 in favor of the navy on the grounds that the actions of the officers had been sanctioned by the Crown (see the discussion in Hugo Fischer, "The Suppression of Slavery in International Law," *International Law Quarterly,* 3 [1950]:38–39). The court in this case ignored the international law issue and based its decision on the fact that it was an English court and the actions had been approved by the English executive.

81. This well-known incident is discussed in most secondary authorities, and it is often described as delaying suppression (e.g., see Mathieson, *Great Britain and the Slave Trade,* pp. 59–66, 92–93). This conclusion is improbable. As long as Britain felt politically and legally inhibited from destroying the goods of American, French and other European merchants, however, it was not likely that the purpose for which the goods were intended (slave trade vs. legitimate trade) could have been of critical

importance. In 1848 the law officers stated that goods found in barracoons destined for the slave trade could be destroyed or handed over to the African ruler, but that still left open the difficulty of distinguishing intent and, of course, facing the hostile reactions of foreign "civilized" governments.

82. Adm. to Aberdeen, Mar. 29, 1845, enc. Comm. Jones, Feb. 5, 1845, FO 84/609; idem, May 5, 1845, enc. Jones, Feb. 18, 1845, FO 84/610. There were similar attacks on Cabinda led by Capt. Matson in 1842.

83. Palmerston minute, Apr. 12, 1850, on Admiralty to Palmerston, Apr. 8, 1850, FO 84/825; Francis Baring to Palmerston, Oct. 20, 1850, Aug. 31, 1851, Broadlands mss. GC/BA/290, GC/BA/303.

84. Palmerston to Baring, July 31, 1851, Broadlands mss., GC/BA/313.

85. Palmerston to Russell, Sept. 21, 1851, Broadlands mss., GC/RU/1087. See also, idem, June 12, 1851, ibid., GC/RU/1083.

86. "Memo on the State of Slave Trade Business in the Slave Trade Department," Jan. 3, 1852, FO 97/430. For some of the extensive discussions on invading Dahomey see Admiralty to Malmesbury, May 3, 1852, enc. Commodore Bruce, Apr. 1, 1852, FO 84/894; Admiralty to Clarendon, Feb. 9, 1858, enc. Commodore Wise, Dec. 21, 1857, and attached minute, FO 84/1068. The same logic explains the squadron's destruction of Old Town in the Old Calabar River in 1854 on account of repeated human sacrifices (Admiralty to Clarendon Feb. 3, 1855, FO 84/981).

87. See Curtin, *Image of Africa*, pp. 464–65, 467, for the broader setting of this process.

## Chapter 8

1. Thomas R. H. Thomson, *The Brazilian Slave Trade, and its Remedy* (London, 1850), chap. 1; W. R. Greg, *Past and Present Efforts for the Extinction of the African Slave Trade* (London, 1840), in particular pp. 3–4; "The Friends of the African", *Quarterly Review*, 82 (1847): pp. 153–75; Lord Howden to Palmerston, Feb. 9, 1848, FO 84/725. For naval opinion see, in addition to T. R. H. Thomson, the reports of naval officers and supporting documentation bound in Adm. 123/173.

2. Palmerston used these arguments in Parliament on several occasions but the clearest presentation of them and the source for these quotes is a draft reply to the Committee of the Anti-Slavery Society, Oct. 18, 1842, SLT/19, Broadlands mss.

3. In addition to the narratives of Ali Eisami Gazirmabe, Osifekunde, Samuel Ajayi Crowther and Joseph Wright (reprinted in Philip D. Curtin [ed], *Africa Remembered: Narratives by West Africans from the Era of the Slave Trade*, [Madison, Wis., 1967], pp. 193–333), see Samuel Moore, *Biography of Mahommah Gardo Baquaqua . . .* (Detroit, 1854); Thomas Pringle (ed.), *The History of Mary Prince . . . To Which Is Added the Narrative of Asa Asa, a Captured African* (London, 1831), pp. 42–44; John Warner Barber, *A History of the Amistad Captives* (New Haven, Conn., 1840); James McQueen, "Information Obtained from Thomas Wogga, an African," *Journal of the Royal Geographical Society*, 15 (1845): 374–76. See also the brief account given by Augustino to the 1849 House of Lords select committee on the slave trade, (PP, 1850, 9:162–63).

4. See, for example, William Law Mathieson, *Great Britain and the Slave Trade*, 1839–1865 (London, 1929), pp. 39–44, Christopher Lloyd, *The Navy and the Slave Trade: The Suppression of the African Slave Trade in the Nineteenth Century* (London, 1968), pp. 73–78, 93, 118.

5. Adm. to Aberdeen, Sept. 19, 1842, sub enc. "Proceedings of the trial of *Minerva*," FO 84/441; James Hook to Palmerston, Nov. 7, 1849, FO 84/752; Admiralty to Russell, Mar. 13, 1860, sub enc. Lt Simpson, Dec. 1, 1859, FO 84/1123; Comm.

Kellett to Buxton, July 22, 1840, 32/fol. 458–59; "Notes of a Conversation with Capt. Jones" (1838), 31/fol. 259, Buxton mss. For other examples of open boats with slaves making a transatlantic crossing, see E. Gabriel to Aberdeen, May 16, 1845, FO 84/570; and E. Porter to Palmerston, Mar. 31, 1848, FO 84/727. The latter recounts the appalling story of a twenty-four foot ship's longboat manned by three men that set out with fifty children to Bahia in 1848. The boat ran short of provisions and was supplied by a merchant vessel on the crossing, nevertheless, it disembarked only thirty-five survivors. Buxton's book was *The African Slave Trade and Its Remedy,* 2nd ed. (London, 1840).

6. Dolben's Act of 1788 restricted the number of slaves per ton that British ships could carry, and further legislation of 1799 regulated carrying capacity according to a vessel's physical dimensions. The first provision probably increased the size of the average slave ship by 44 percent (Herbert S. Klein and Stanley L. Engerman, "Slave Mortality on British Ships, 1791–1797," in Roger T. Anstey and P. E. H. Hair [eds], *Liverpool, the African Slave Trade, and Abolition: Essays to Illustrate Current Knowledge and Research* (Liverpool), 1976), pp. 120–21). For a discussion of the measured ton used here, see Christopher J. French, "Eighteenth-Century Shipping Tonnage Measurements," *Journal of Economic History,* 33 (1973):434–43; D. P. Lamb, "Volume and Tonnage of the Liverpool Slave Trade, 1772–1807," in Anstey and Hair, *Liverpool,* pp. 105–7. See also Roger T. Anstey, "The Volume and Profitability of the British Slave Trade, 1761–1807," in Stanley L. Engerman and Eugene D. Genovese (eds.), *Race and Slavery in the Western Hemisphere: Quantitative Studies* (Princeton, N.J., 1975), pp. 3–4; Seymour Drescher, *Econocide: British Slavery in the Era of Abolition* (Pittsburgh, 1977), pp. 205–12; Joseph Inikori, "Measuring the Atlantic Slave Trade: An Assessment of Curtin and Anstey," *Journal of African History,* 17 (1976):197–223.

7. Most of the West Africa-French Caribbean/Puerto Rico observations in table 5 set sail from the regions where they disembarked their cargoes.

8. Herbert S. Klein, *The Middle Passage* (Princeton, N.J., 1978), p. 159; for similar comments on the Nantes fleet, see p. 183.

9. E. Phillip LeVeen, *British Slave Trade Suppression Policies, 1821–1865* (New York, 1977), p. 91. For a discussion of changes in tonnage measurements, see Lamb, "Volume and Tonnage," pp. 105–6.

10. Douglass C. North, "Sources of Productivity Change in Ocean Shipping, 1600–1850," *Journal of Political Economy,* 76 (1968):962–63.

11. Regressions of voyage times on tonnage for various branches of the nineteenth-century traffic yielded a negative tonnage coefficient in all cases but, usually, low significance levels and $r^2$ below 0.15.

12. Robert Stein, *The French Slave Trade in the Eighteenth Century* (Madison, Wis., 1979), p. 132; Klein, *Middle Passage,* p. 143. The basic data on the eighteenth century French slave trade are in Jean Mettas, *Répertoire des expéditions négrières française au XVIIIe siècle,* 2 vols., édité par Serge et Michèle Daget (Paris, 1978–84).

13. Klein, *Middle Passage,* p. 157.

14. In 1864 the Commodore of the British African squadron wrote, "There is no doubt that slaves are to be procured in almost any numbers throughout the whole extent of the African Coast, and that the means of shipment alone are required" (Admiralty to Russell, Jan. 6, 1865, enc. Commodore Wilmot, Dec. 1, 1864, FO 84/1252).

15. Ibid. See also Admiralty to Russell, Jan. 23, 1863, enc. Commodore Edmonstone to R. Admiral Walker, Oct. 22, 1862, FO 84/1207.

16. There are some biases in these eighteenth-century figures, the net effect of which is unclear. Ratios for Jamaican ships are taken from the end of the middle passage after crew mortality had occurred, whereas the nineteenth-century data are a m'

ture of outset, African coast and American disembarkation ratios. The relationship, on the one hand, between the British ton of 1782–86 and the pre-revolutionary French and, on the other hand, the post-1786 British ton used for the nineteenth-century ratio is also uncertain (see supra n. 6). The French ton at least was substantially smaller than its pre-1786 British counterpart (R. Stein, *French Slave Trade*, pp. 70–71). The biases, however, are not likely to be big enough to disturb the basic point.

17. C. D. Tolmé to Palmerston, 4 Aug. 1838, FO 84/247. Ships in the general shipping business from Jamaica entering London in 1766 had a ton-per-crew ratio of 15.9 (Ralph Davis, *The Rise of the English Shipping Industry* [London, 1962], p. 71).

18. App. B.

19. For the incidents of rebellion see R. Hesketh and F. Grigg to Aberdeen, Mar. 21, 1845 (enc.), FO 84/563 (excerpts printed in Robert E. Conrad [ed.], *Children of God's Fire: A Documentary History of Black Slavery in Brazil* [Princeton, N.J., 1983], pp. 39–42); J. Crawford to Clarendon, Mar. 23, 1853, FO 84/905; *The Times* (London), June 18, 1858; J. V. Crawford to Russell, Sept. 5, 1859, FO 84/1080; R. Bunch to Russell, Oct. 4, 1865, FO 84/1241. All these incidents occurred after 1843. Perhaps the larger slave ships and smaller crews of this era made rebellion more of a threat. W. O. Blake, *The History of Slavery and the Slave Trade*, 2 vols. (New York, 1969), 1:337–39 also recounts a rebellion that I have not been able to verify.

20. Capt. Hastings commented, "No slave irons have been found on board and . . . they are articles . . . seldom used by the slave captains now" (Admiralty to Palmerston, July 7, 1850, sub enc. Apr. 26, 1850, FO 84/826). See also "Notes of a conversation with Capt. Jones," (1838), 31/fol. 259, Buxton mss.; and the *Colonist* (Barbados), Apr. 29, 1837.

21. See, for example, R. Hesketh and F. Grigg to Palmerston, Aug. 9, 1837, FO 84/219; Admiralty to Clarendon, Oct. 25, 1853, sub enc. Comm. Seymour, Dec.–May, 1852–53, FO 84/926.

22. Johannes Postma, ("Mortality in the Dutch Slave Trade 1675–1795," in H. A. Gemery and J. S. Hogendorn [eds.], *The Uncommon Market: Essays in the Economic History of the Atlantic Slave Trade* (New York, 1979), pp. 247–49), found evidence of twenty "serious slave rebellions" in the Dutch trade. The Postma data set contains records of twelve hundred voyages. Jay Coughtry (*The Notorious Triangle: Rhode Island and the African Slave Trade: 1700–1807* [Philadelphia, 1981], p. 151), suggests a ratio of one every fifty-five voyages in the Rhode Island traffic, 1730–1807. Richard H. Steckel and Richard A. Jensen have analyzed surgeons' logs from ninety-two English ships for 1792–96. Insurrections were a very minor cause of death, killing about as many slaves as did accidents. During loading they calculate a mortality from rebellions of 1.0 slaves per 1,000 per year, rising to 1.6 during the voyage itself. Deaths from all causes amounted to 45.7 and 115.7 per 1,000 per year during loading and voyage respectively (Steckel and Jensen, "New Evidence on the Causes of Slave and Crew Mortality in the Atlantic Slave Trade," *Journal of Economic History*, 46 (1986):60–62. Such evidence throws doubts on Robert Stein's assessment of the French eighteenth century trade that revolts were "so common in fact that they scarcely merited mentioning in the captains' reports" (*French Slave Trade*, p. 103).

23. R. Stein, *French Slave Trade*, p. 97; Coughtry, *Notorious Triangle*, pp. 158–59. Klein (*Middle Passage*, p. 192) shows mean passages of 101 days for Nantes slave ships sailing from the Gold Coast to St. Domingue, in the 1763–77 period.

24. Admiralty to Palmerston, May 30, 1848, enc. Commodore Hotham, Mar. 14, 1848, FO 84/747; G. Jackson and E. Gabriel to Palmerston, May 30, 1849 (enc.), FO 84/757.

25. W. Macleay to Aberdeen, 24 June 1829, FO 84/91.
26. Admiralty to Palmerston, May 30, 1848, enc. Commodore Hotham, March 14, 1848, FO 84/747. For steamers in the Brazil South traffic, see Admiralty to Aberdeen, Nov. 25, 1845, sub enc. Commodore Jones, Sept. 29, 1845, FO 84/612; W. Wilde to Palmerston, Apr. 10, 1850, FO 84/817; J. Hudson to Palmerston, Nov. 16, 1848, FO 84/726; Mar. 24, 1849, FO 84/765. For steamers in the Cuban trade, see Admiralty to Lord John Russell, Jan. 13, 1864, enc. Commodore Wilmot, Nov. 22, 1863, FO 84/1227; Admiralty to Lord John Russell, Jan. 12, 1866 enc. Commodore Wilmot, Dec. 19, 1865, FO 84/1267.
27. E. Porter to Palmerston, Jan. 28, 1848, FO 84/727. Differences in technology employed on the different routes were probably a function of environmental and political factors. In the Bight of Benin, the chief provenance zone for Bahian slavers, wind conditions guaranteed escape for specialized sailing vessels, even from steamers (Admiralty to Palmerston, May 30, 1848, enc. Commodore Hotham, Mar. 14, 1848, FO 84/747). Steam-powered slave ships cost several times the amount of sailing ships, and even joint stock companies found difficulty in absorbing the risk of capture. For this reason, they disappeared from the Brazil South branch when British pressure increased in 1850 (James Hudson to Palmerston July 27, 1850, FO 84/804). On the longer Cuban route steam-powered slave ships appeared to offer few advantages. Sailing vessels were used on the indentured labor traffic from Asia until the end of the nineteenth century.
28. Coughtry, *Notorious Triangle,* p. 77, 184; Roger T. Anstey, *The Atlantic Slave Trade and British Abolition* (London, 1975), p. 36; R. Stein, *French Slave Trade,* p. 117; Klein, *Middle Passage,* p. 157.
29. Of the 216 ships condemned at the Sierra Leone courts between 1821 and 1843 for which information is available, 183 freighted out their own trading cargo and 23 sailed with nominal cargo or in ballast, but the whole of the latter group sailed in the years 1839–43. At other British courts, in St. Helena and the Cape of Good Hope, trading cargoes rarely formed a part of the cruiser's prize after 1840.
30. Klein, *Middle Passage,* pp. 145–47, 183–86, 194–96, 234.
31. For plans of nineteenth-century slave ships, see *Model of a Spanish Slaver* (Salisbury, England 1840); also W. Norcott to Buxton, July 15, 1836 (enc.), 32/fol. 335, Buxton mss.; S. W. Blackwall to Russell, Sept. 17, 1864 (enc.) FO 84/1216; Robert Walsh, *Notices of Brazil in 1828 and 1829,* 2 vols. (London, 1829–30), 2:479; *London Illustrated News,* June 20, 1857. For eighteenth-century English slave ships it is possible to convert tonnage data into the inside dimensions of the ship. Regressions of mortality on this more precise estimate of space available for slaves, as with other measurements of density, yield no significant results. See Charles Garland and Herbert S. Klein, "The Allotment of Space for Slaves Aboard Eighteenth-Century British Slave Ships," *William & Mary Quarterly,* 42 (1985):238–48. It might be noted that nineteenth-century slave ships carried a larger proportion of children than their predecessors.
32. This estimate is based on a Foreign Office calculation for 1846–48 that was derived from data supplied by the Admiralty. See Palmerston's memo on Adm. to Palmerston, July 22, 1848, dated July 30, 1848, and the memorandum written in response, unsigned, Aug. 8, 1848, FO 84/748.
33. App. D; David Eltis, "Mortality and Voyage Length in the Middle Passage: New Evidence from the Nineteenth Century," *Journal of Economic History,* 44 (1984): 301–308. The best contemporary discussion of mortality is in the reports of officials at the recaptive slave depot in St. Helena in the 1840s. See Col. Off. to Palmerston November 27, 1849, enc. "Dr. Vowell's Report," and "Dr. C. H. Rawlins' Repor

FO 84/780. For the predominance of gastrointestinal deaths in the British trade in the 1790s see Steckel and Jensen, "New Evidence on the Causes of Slave and Crew Mortality," pp. 60–62. For diarrheal deaths among children in another shipboard environment, see Ralph Shlomowitz, "Infant-Mortality and Fiji's Indian Migrants, 1879–1919," *Indian Economic and Social History Review*, 23 (1986):296. Cohn and Jensen have revived the treatment argument (Raymond L. Cohn and Richard A. Jensen, "The Determinants of Slave Mortality Rates in the Middle Passage," *Explorations in Economic History*, 19 (1982):269–82). It might be noted, however, that the two data sets used in their analysis (derived by Herbert S. Klein and Philip D. Curtin, respectively) are not, as they imply, independent of each other. Of the Klein data for Rio de Janeiro in 1825–30, 80 percent are, in fact, included in the 1845 Parliamentary Paper from which Curtin created the second data set. In addition, the authors erroneously refer to the slave ships in the latter as English. Steckel and Jensen found a statistically significant relationship between crowding and slave deaths during loading of slaves in the British trade (in other words, on board ship but before the ship left the African coast), but not during the voyage itself (Steckel and Jensen, "New Evidence on the Causes of Slave and Crew Mortality," pp. 66–69).

34. Eltis, "Mortality and Voyage Length."
35. Before the last years of the Cuban trade, the major naval impact was on the insurance and profits components of shipping costs (see app. E). To derive estimates of this impact, it is first necessary to assess shipping costs in the absence of naval intervention. The relative abundance of nonslave trade-shipping costs for the nineteenth century as well as slave-trade data from the presuppression era provided a good historical basis for this procedure. The next step is to calculate the percentage decrease in costs that would have occurred in the absence of the navy. This figure may then be taken as the percentage shift in the supply of slaves to markets in the Americas. The effect of this on the quantity of slaves may be calculated from

$$\dot{Q} = \frac{\epsilon}{\gamma + \epsilon} \dot{S}$$

and on prices from

$$\dot{P} = \frac{\dot{S}}{\epsilon + \gamma}$$

Where:
$\dot{Q}$ = percentage change in quantity of slaves purchased.
$\epsilon$ = elasticity of demand for slaves in the Americas.
$\gamma$ = elasticity of supply of slaves in the Americas.
$\dot{S}$ = percentage change in supply.
$\dot{P}$ = percentage change in price.

A full exposition of these procedures and the data that they employ may be found in David Eltis, "The Impact of Abolition," unpublished paper, 1984. For the model itself as well as earlier estimates of the size of the impact see LeVeen, *British Slave Trade Suppression*, pp. 4–51; D. Eltis, "The British Contribution to the Nineteenth Century Transatlantic Slave Trade," *Economic History Review*, 32 (1979); 222–27; and idem, "The British Effort to Suppress the Slave Trade." Paper presented at the annual meeting of the African Studies Association, Baltimore, Nov. 1978. The estimates of the impact of the navy on the volume of the trade presented here are lower than those of LeVeen for two reasons. First, the data on slave prices, quantities and the financial parameters used here are from a different and larger sample. Second, the equation LeVeen used,

$$Q = \frac{\epsilon\gamma}{\epsilon + \gamma} \dot{S},$$

appears inappropriate and yields much higher quantities wherever the price elasticities of demand and supply exceed unity.

36. David R. Murray, *Odious Commerce: Britain, Spain and the Abolition of the Cuban Slave Trade* (Cambridge, 1980), p. 207.

37. Ibid., pp. 181–207; Arthur F. Corwin, *Spain and the Abolition of Slavery in Cuba, 1817–1886* (Austin, Tex. 1967), pp. 69–91.

38. Robert Conrad, "The Contraband Slave Trade to Brazil, 1831–1845, "*Hispanic American Historical Review,* 49 (1969):618–38; T. W. Palmer, "A Momentous Decade in Brazilian Administrative History, 1831–40," *Hispanic American Historical Review,* 30 (1950):209–17; Leslie M. Bethell, *The Abolition of the Brazilian Slave Trade,* (Cambridge, 1970), pp. 60–87, 214–41.

39. In the post–1850 period the changes in costs induced by suppression are too large to support a meaningful estimate of impact—at least with the present model.

40. The mean price of 17,323 newly imported slaves sold in Jamaica in the years 1793–99 was £48.05 or $230 in terms of 1821–25 prices. See supra, p. 298, n.8.

41. This paragraph is based on D. Eltis, "British Contribution," pp. 211–27. For British attitudes, see the *Report from the Select Committee on the West Coast of Africa,* PP, 1842, 11:3-21; and Aberdeen's reply to a deputation of Manchester merchants in "Proceedings of the Manchester Commercial Association," Aug. 5, 1845, Manchester Public Library.

42. Supra, pp. 108–9.

43. For the *Heroina* case, see J. Campbell and J. Reffel to Canning, Feb. 2, 1827, FO 84/65. Foreign Office approval based on the law officers' opinion is Dudley to Commissioners, Aug. 31, 1827, FO 84/66.

44. H. W. Macaulay to J. Bandinel, 20 May 1839, FO 84/266. For Macaulay's subsequent explanation of this point to the 1842 Select Committee on the West Coast of Africa, see PP, 1842, 11:285.

45. C. D. Tolmé to Palmerston, 15 Oct. 1836, FO 84/201.

46. Supra, chap. 6.

47. For a summary of these operations and the Aberdeen minute bringing them to an end, see "Destruction of slave factories on the Coast of Africa," Apr. 1, 1842, FO 84/445. For more detail on the activities of Foote and Matson, see Foote to Admiralty, May 31, 1842, Adm. 1/5517.

48. "Memorandum on . . . the final abolition of the Brazilian Slave Trade," unsigned, Sept. 2, 1828, FO 84/100. Approval of the capture of ships without slaves was based on the vaguely worded additional article signed Mar. 15, 1823 by Portugal and Britain (see Christopher Robinson to Viscount Dudley Ward, Aug. 17, 1827, Aberdeen papers, Add. mss., 43125, fols. 7–8). However, another law officer had major reservations on this (H. Jenner to Aberdeen, Sept. 22, 1828, Aberdeen papers, Add. mss., 43125, fols. 84–85).

## Chapter 9

1. Admiralty to Russell, June 11, 1863, enc. Commodore Eardley Wilmot, April 30, 1863, FO 84/1208; April 29, 1864, enc. Commodore Eardley Wilmot, Dec. 31, 1863, FO 84/1228. For other British steamers, see Consul Brackenbury to Russell, Feb. 10, 1864, FO 84/1218.

2. Supra, chap. 4.
3. Joseph E. Inikori, "Market Structure and the Profits of the British African Trade in the Late Eighteenth Century," *Journal of Economic History,* 41 (1981):746–53; B. L. Anderson and David Richardson, "Market Structure and Profits of the British African Trade in the Late Eighteenth Century: A Comment," *Journal of Economic History,* 43 (1983):713–21; J. E. Inikori, "A Rejoinder," *Journal of Economic History,* 43 (1983):723–28 and the literature cited in this debate.
4. Infra, app. E and chap. 11.
5. Supra, p. 115; infra, 216; For Muniz Barreto's activities, see James Hudson to Palmerston, July 10, 1849, GC/HU/14, Broadlands mss.
6. For two collections of this correspondence, one Spanish the other Brazilian, see PP, 1839, 48:49–67; and House of Lords Sessional Papers, 1852–53, 22:326–66.
7. See, for example, the evidence of José Cliffe to the select committee on sugar and coffee plantations, PP, 1847–48, 23:pt. 1, pp. 137–39.
8. For community action in support of slave dealers see Admiralty to Palmerston, July 8, 1846, enc. Commander C. B. Hamilton, Mar. 9, 1846, FO 84/659; Admiralty to Palmerston, Sept. 14, 1848, enc. Commander Eyncourt, n.d., FO 84/748; James Hudson to Palmerston, July 27, 1850, FO 84/804.
9. H. S. Fox to Palmerston, Nov. 8, 1835, enc. W. G. Ouseley, "Notes on the subject of the slave trade . . .," FO 84/179.
10. For eighteenth-century outset costs, see Roger T. Anstey, *The Atlantic Slave Trade and British Abolition* (London, 1975), pp. 419–21. The Anstey figures are pounds sterling per ton for ships sailing to the Caribbean; these may be converted to pounds per slave with Anstey's own data. The comparable data from the app. E. are dollars per slave for ships sailing to Cuba in the nineteenth century.
11. Manuel Moreno Fraginals, *El ingenio, complejo económico social cubano del azúcar,* 3 vols. (Havana, 1978), 1:265–68; J. T. Kilbee and W. Macleay to Canning, Jan. 1, 1826, FO 84/51; C. D. Tolmé to Wellington, May 9, 1835, FO 84/177. David Turnbull, *Travels in the West. Cuba: With Notices of Puerto Rico and the Slave Trade* (London, 1840), p. 143. See also Alexander von Humboldt, *The Island of Cuba* (New York, 1856), pp. 246–48.
12. W. Macleay to Aberdeen, July 21, 1829 (private) (enc.), FO 84/100; Admiralty to Aberdeen, July 9, 1829 (sub enc.), FO 84/98. All counts of slave-ship ownership are taken from the slave-ship data set.
13. H. W. Macaulay and R. Doherty to Palmerston, Dec. 15, 1838 (enc.), FO 84/234. See Adam Jones, *From Slaves to Palm Kernels: A History of the Galinhas Country (West Africa), 1730–1890* (Wiesbaden, W. Ger., 1983), pp. 42–44, for Blanco's early career.
14. G. Jackson and E. Gabriel to Palmerston, Feb. 5, 1850, FO 84/793; J. Crawford to Clarendon, March 24, 1857, FO 84/1016; Adm. to Russell, Aug. 11, 1859, enc. Lt. Pike, June 20, 1859, FO 84/1099. Manuel Moreno Fraginals refers to the Ximenes, Martínez and Lafitte as a New York slaving company (*El ingenio,* 1:280), but their stake in the industry must have been small at this time.
15. T. Denman to Bandinel, Dec. 3, 1842, FO 84/447; J. Kennedy and C. J. Dalrymple to Aberdeen, Sept. 8, 1845, FO 84/562; J. Kennedy to Palmerston, Jan. 1, 1850, FO 84/789. For the Forcade family, see Francisco Xavier de Santa Cruz y Mallén, *Historia de familias cubanas,* 5 vols. (Havana, 1940–50), 5:113–14. I am indebted to Robert Paquette for this reference.
16. J. Kennedy to Palmerston, May 25, 1848, FO 84/715: Evidence of J. Kennedy to select committee on slave trade treaties, PP, 1852–53, 39:92.
17. Admiralty to Clarendon, Nov. 18, 1857, enc. Commander Burgess, Aug. 12, 1857,

FO 84/1040; Admiralty to Malmesbury, Oct. 15, 1858, FO 84/1070; U.S. Congress H. Exec. Doc. no. 7, 36–2, p. 101.

18. Franklin W. Knight, "Origins of Wealth and the Sugar Revolution in Cuba, 1750–1850," *Hispanic American Historical Review,* 57 (1977): 250–51; Hugh Thomas, *Cuba: The Pursuit of Freedom* (London, 1971), pp. 136–39, M. L. Melville and J. Hook to Aberdeen, Oct. 17 (enc.), Nov. 12, 1844, FO 84/506; J. Crawford to Clarendon, July 9 and Oct. 10, 1853, FO 84/905–906; J. Crawford to Palmerston, Sept. 9, 1848, FO 84/722; E. M. Archibald to Malmesbury, May 3, 1859, enc. "Memorandum of the *Haidee* affair," and May 17, 1859, FO 84/1086; J. Crawford to Russell, Dec. 3, 1859, FO 84/1080; J. Crawford to Malmesbury, July 2, 1858, FO 84/1046; J. Crawford to Russell, Mar. 4 and May 10, 1864, FO 84/1218; David R. Murray, *Odious Commerce: Britain, Spain and the Abolition of the Cuban Slave Trade* (Cambridge, 1980), pp. 313–14.

19. E. M. Archibald to Russell, Oct. 10, 1859, FO 84/1086; J. Crawford to Russell, Dec. 12, 1863, FO 84/1203; J. Crawford to Clarendon, Feb. 5, 1854, FO 84/935; J. Crawford to Clarendon, Sept. 18, 1855, FO 84/965; J. Crawford to Russell, Aug. 6, 1864, FO 84/1218; Commodore Perry to Sec. of Navy, Oct. 12, 1844, enc. Lt. T. Craven, Oct. 16, 1844, Reel 101, LSN; J. Crawford to Clarendon, Feb. 4, 1857, FO 84/1012.

20. W. G. Ouseley to Palmerston, June 22, 1839, FO 84/286; R. Hesketh and F. Grigg to Palmerston, Dec. 19, 1836, FO 84/199; R. Hesketh and F. Grigg to Aberdeen, Apr. 20, 1842, FO 84/394.

21. These owners are listed in Pierre Verger, *Flux et reflux de la traite des nègres entre le golfe de Bénin et Bahia de Todos os Santos* (Paris, 1968), pp. 448–57, 638–46. For British ownership, see Anstey, *The Atlantic Slave Trade,* pp. 6–9.

22. Herbert S. Klein, *The Middle Passage* (Princeton, N.J. 1978), pp. 81–82. Ownership references to Bahian ships in the Sierra Leone court records are scattered throughout vols. 117, 127, 149, 169, 194, 214, 215, 235–37, 268–73, 307–10 of FO 84.

23. Verger, *Flux et reflux,* pp. 449–50, 453.

24. As large firms continued to hide behind nominal ownership into the 1840s and as it is not always possible to uncover this practice, it is possible that these ratios may understate the actual degree of concentration.

25. The bulk of this list is in J. Samo and F. Grigg to Aberdeen, July 17, 1843, FO 84/453, and was printed in PP, 1844, 48:222–27. Sources for the remainder of the list and for the other ownership data here are scattered throughout the FO 84 series and full citations would occupy many pages. For Bernadino da Sá's participation in the early years of the illegal trade, see José Honório Rodrigues, *Brazil and Africa,* trans. Richard A. Mazzara and Sam Hileman (Berkeley, Calif., 1965), p. 179.

26. Neither Manoel Pinto da Fonseca nor his brother Joaquim, reputed to be the biggest slave importers in Rio de Janeiro as early as 1840, appear on the Samo and Grigg list; this is probably because their company operated under another name. The British consul at Rio de Janeiro believed the custom house returns, on which the Samo and Grigg list is probably based, to be "misleading" as far as ownership was concerned (R. Hesketh to Palmerston, July 2, 1839, FO 84/289). He did not elaborate, but it might be noted that the list does contain individuals who are clearly identified in other sources as major traders as well as a few whose activities cannot be corroborated elsewhere. For additional information on the Fonsecas, da Sá, Guimaraes and, in Bahia, Marinho and Pedroso de Albuquerque, see Gervase Clarence-Smith, *The Third Portuguese Empire, 1825–1975: A Study in Economic*

*Imperialism* (Manchester, Eng. 1985), pp. 53–55; Mary Karasch, "The Brazilian Slavers and the Illegal Slave Trade, 1836–1851." M. A. thesis, University of Wisconsin, 1967, pp. 10–37.

27. R. Hesketh and F. Grigg to Aberdeen, Mar. 11, 1846, enc. "List of the Principal Slave-Dealers in Rio de Janeiro, 1845," FO 84/564.

28. PP, 1847–48, 23:pt. 1 p. 140.

29. H. Southern to Clarendon, Jan. 13, 1853, FO 84/911.

30. Rodrigues, *Brazil and Africa,* pp. 179–82; Henry Wise to H. Hamilton, July 31, 1846, U. S. Congress, Sen. Exec. Doc. no. 28, 30–1, p. 26; Lord Howden to Palmerston, Mar. 20, 1848, FO 84/725.

31. Verger, *Flux et reflux,* pp. 449–60. The fullest reference to Brazilian-based firms in this period is in the records of the British and Portuguese Mixed Commission established to settle claims against British captures between 1815 and 1817, FO 308. The resulting settlements, including the names of the firms involved, are printed in PP, 1822 (226), 22:653–657.

32. R. Jameson to Castlereagh, Sept. 1, 1821 (enc.), FO 84/13. Evidence of Admiral Fleming to the Select Committee on the Extinction of Slavery, PP (721), 1831–32, 20:205.

33. J. T. Kilbee to Canning, Jan. 1, 1825, FO 84/39; C. D. Tolmé to Palmerston, Sept. 16, 1839; W. S. Macleay to Aberdeen, Jan. 1, 1830, FO 84/107; C. D. Tolmé to Wellington, May 9, 1835 (enc.), FO 84/177.

34. See the batches of captured correspondence enclosed in Admiralty to Aberdeen, July 9, 1829, FO 84/98; and H. W. Macaulay and R. Doherty to Palmerston, Dec. 15, 1838, FO 84/234.

35. C. D. Tolmé to Wellington, May 9, 1835, FO 84/177. See also J. Kennedy and C. J. Dalrymple to Palmerston, Feb. 26, 1841, FO 84/348. The shareholders of the one slaver in which Yriate and Yrigoyen, a small Havana firm, had the major interest could not face the additional cost of fitting out a second ship to pick up the cargo of slaves left behind when the first was captured. Instead they told the factor to freight them to Cuba as best he could (W. W. Lewis and R. Doherty to Palmerston July 1, 1840 (enc.), FO 84/308B).

36. Admiralty to Palmerston, June 19, 1846, enc. Comm. Montgomery, Apr. 19, 1846, FO 84/658; Lt. J. P. Thurburn to Admiralty, May 17, 1850, Adm. 123/173. See also E. Porter to Palmerston, Dec. 31, 1847, FO 84/679.

37. E. Porter to Palmerston, Sept. 22, 1841 (enc.), FO 84/368; W. G. Ouseley to Palmerston May 19, 1836, FO 84/206; E. Porter to Aberdeen, July 30, 1843, FO 84/470; J. Campbell and W. W. Lewis to Palmerston, Feb. 25, 1837 (enc.), FO 84/214; H. W. Macaulay to Palmerston, May 20 and May 30, 1838; Admiralty to Palmerston, May 25, 1837 (enc.)—all in FO 84/228; J. Campbell and W. W. Lewis to Palmerston, Nov. 10, 1836, FO 84/194; Henry Wise to H. Hamilton, July 31, 1846, U.S. Congress, Sen. Exec. Doc., no. 28, 30–1, p. 26. For Bahian-based slave-trading companies, see also E. Porter to Palmerston, Dec. 31, 1847, FO 84/679; and Admiralty to Palmerston, June 14, 1847, enc. Comm. Moorman, Apr. 25, 1847, FO 84/704.

38. For the summary of a document establishing one such company in Nov. 1838, see M. L. Melville and J. Hook to Aberdeen, Feb. 18, 1845, enc. case of *El Cayman,* doc. 114, FO 84/619. For small-scale U.S. investment, see J. Crawford and W. P. Ryder to Russell, Dec. 5, 1859, FO 84/1073. U.S. direct investment in all aspects of the Cuban plantation economy was small in the slave trade era (Roland T. Ely, "The Old Cuba Trade: Highlights and Case Studies of Cuban-American Interdependence During the Nineteenth Century," *Business History Review,* 38

[1964]:456–78, in particular pp. 462–63). For the large companies of the 1850s see Comm. Crabbe to Sec. of Navy, Feb. 14, 1857, U.S. Congress, H. Exec. Doc., no. 7, 36–2, p. 520; Commodore Wise to Admiralty, Nov. 2, 1857, Adm. 123/175; Admiralty to Malmesbury, Oct. 15, 1858, enc. Wise to Adm. Grey, Aug. 6, 1858, FO 84/1070; J. Crawford to Russell, May 14, 1860, FO 84/1109.

39. For the efforts of a Pernambuco firm to establish a base in the River Benin, see H. W. Macaulay to Palmerston May 30, 1838 (enc.) FO 84/236. The extensive enclosures in this dispatch are reprinted in PP, 1839, 48:43–67, and were picked up from there by Turnbull, *Travels in the West,* pp. 203–06. A convenient source for the networks of the Rio de Janeiro dealers is Karasch, "Brazilian Slavers"; see also E. Gabriel to Aberdeen, Dec. 31, 1845, FO 84/572; Admiralty to Palmerston, July 6, 1850, enc. Comm. Parker, Dec. 31, 1849, FO 84/826; and H. W. Macaulay and R. Doherty to Palmerston, Dec. 15, 1838 (enc.), FO 84/234. For descriptions of barracoons at Gabon and Sangatanga, on the same coast, see K. David Patterson, *The Northern Gabon Coast to 1875* (Oxford, 1975), pp. 84–86.

40. Isidore Powell was a Matanzas slave merchant who managed his own factories in the Pongas and Nunez rivers and attracted the backing of a large New York house just before his death in 1834. Manoel António da Silva Brandao was a partner of the Pará firm of Brandao and da Silva who obtained cargoes for his own ships in the early 1820s. (For Powell, see W. Cole and H. W. Macaulay to Palmerston, Jan. 5, 1835 (enc.), FO 84/166; for Brandao, see E. Gregory and E. Fitzgerald to Castlereagh, Apr. 30, 1822, FO 84/16). Perhaps the most written about slave trader of the nineteenth century, Theophilus Conneau (Théodore Canot) never quite made it to the level of an independent transatlantic trader. He was at various times a slaver captain, a clerk and a factor who shipped some slaves on his own account. He was never, however, a major figure in the traffic compared to other individuals mentioned here, nor was he even involved in any of the most important African provenance zones. Although his autobiography is a valuable document, it is hard to find in it much sense of the critical organization trends of the nineteenth-century slaving business (see Conneau, *A Slaver's Log Book or 20 Years' Residence in Africa* [Englewood Cliffs, N.J., 1976]. Among the extensive literature on Conneau, see R. Pasquier, "A propos de Théodore Canot, negrière en Afrique," *Revue francaise d'histoire d'outre-mer,* 55 (1968):352–54; and Adam Jones, "Theophile Conneau at Galinhas and New Sestos, 1836–1841: A Comparison of the Sources, "*History in Africa,* 8 (1981): 89–106.

41. Admiralty to Palmerston, July 25, 1842, enc. Comm. Adams, May 7, 1842, FO 84/440. For other examples of partners performing the factor role, see H. W. Macaulay and R. Doherty to Palmerston, Nov. 12, 1838 (enc.), FO 84/233; and Dec. 15, 1838 (enc.), FO 84/234.

42. J. Hudson to Palmerston, July 14, 1851, enc. anon., June 26, 1851, FO 84/845; Admiralty to Palmerston, Apr. 6, 1850, sub enc. Comm. Schomberg, Jan. 15, 1850, FO 84/825.

43. For Francisco José de Campos, see M. Melville and J. Hook to Aberdeen, Aug. 12, 1845, FO 84/560. For the principals of Marcos, Nobre and Lima, see Adm. to Malmesbury, Apr. 10, 1852, sub enc. Comm. Wilmot, Feb. 11, 1852, FO 84/893; and J. Beecroft to Palmerston, Jan. 3, 1852, FO 84/886. For Emilio Martins, the principal of Gantois and Martins, and other examples, see Treasury to Aberdeen, Oct. 28, 1842 (enc.), FO 84/431; and the captured correspondence enclosed in Col. Off. to Palmerston, Dec. 1, 1840, FO 84/337.

44. W. W. Lewis and J. Campbell to Palmerston, Sept. 5, 1836, FO 84/192.

45. App. E. The regular surveys of the Congo, Cabinda and Ambriz slaving establishments by British naval officers after 1850 revealed little property owned by Cuban firms. The same was true of the southeast coast. In the Sherbro and Pongo rivers, however, shipments after 1850 were usually preceded by the establishment of a factory headed by a Spanish agent (Admiralty to Clarendon, Jan. 10, 1854, enc. "Extract of Journal . . .," FO 84/954; Admiralty to Clarendon, Mar. 1, 1853, enc. Rear Adm. Bruce, Jan. 24, 1853, FO 84/925). For the importance of the mail steamers, see Admiralty to Russell, Apr. 29, 1864, enc. Comm Wilmot, Dec. 31, 1863, FO 84/1228.

46. Elizabeth Donnan, *Documents Illustrative of the History of the Slave Trade to America*, 4 vols. (New York, 1965):4:584; *Abismo* folder in HCA 37/3.

47. Commander George Sprigg to Admiralty, May 17, 1850, Adm. 123/173.

48. For freighting arrangements to Brazil, see W. Cole and H. W. Macaulay to Palmerston, Jan. 5, 1835 (enc.), FO 84/166; R. Doherty and W. Cole to Palmerston, July 14, 1837; J. Campbell and W. W. Lewis to Palmerston, Feb. 25, 1837, enc. Laporite to Carvalho and Viale, Apr. 12, 1836, FO 84/214; Admiralty to Palmerston, May 26, 1841 (enc.), FO 84/384. See also the extensive collections of captured correspondence between Bahia and Bight of Benin dealers in Col. Off. to Palmerston, Dec. 1, 1840 (enc.), FO 84/337; PP (H. of Lords), 1852–53, 22:327–70; U.S. Congress, H. Exec. Doc. no. 148, 28–1, pp. 44–47. For Cuban examples see H. W. Macaulay and W. W. Lewis to Palmerston, Apr. 15, 1839, FO 84/269; J. Kennedy and C. Dalrymple to Palmerston, Feb. 26, 1841, FO 84/248.

49. In addition to app. E, see H. W. Macaulay and W. W. Lewis to Palmerston, Apr. 15, 1839, FO 84/269; W. S. Macleay to Bandinel, July 21, 1829, enc., FO 84/100; G. Frere and W. Surtees to Aberdeen Oct. 17, 1844, encs., FO 84/515; and the accounts in House of Lords Sessional Papers, 1852–53, 22:327–70. For the *Tartar*, see Donnan, *Documents Illustrative*, 4:584.

50. Commander George Sprigg to Adm., May 17, 1850, Adm. 123/173.

51. J. Hudson to Palmerston, Mar. 24, 1849, FO 84/765; July 27, 1850, FO 84/804; E. Porter to Palmerston, Apr. 25, 1848, FO 84/727.

52. H. Hamilton to David Tod, Jan. 16, 1849, U.S. Congress, Sen. Exec. Doc. no. 6, 31–2, p. 24.

53. R. Hesketh and F. Grigg to Aberdeen, Mar. 11, 1846; J. Hudson to Palmerston, Oct. 10, 1848, GC/HU/6, Broadlands mss. See also the discussion in Mary Karasch, "The Brazilian Slavers," pp. 27–34.

54. See app. E, tables E. 2(b) and E. 2(e).

55. R. Hesketh to Palmerston, Jan. 4, 1841, FO 84/368.

56. Supra, chap. 3; William Cobbett (ed.), *Parliamentary History of England*, 28:59; 29:297; David Richardson, "Profits in the Liverpool Slave Trade: The Accounts of William Davenport, 1757–1784," in Roger Anstey and P. E. H. Hair, *Liverpool, the African Slave Trade, and Abolition: Essays to Illustrate Current Knowledge and Research* (Liverpool, 1976), p. 72; G. Pilkington to J. Sturge, Mar. 25, 1840, Brit. Emp. mss., G79; *Report from the Select Committee of the House of Lords . . . for the African Slave Trade*, PP, 1850, 9:223; H. Hamilton to Aberdeen (enc.), Dec. 14, 1844, FO 84/525.

57. D. Turnbull to Palmerston, Aug. 2, 1841, FO 84/358; Treasury to Palmerston, June 17, 1842, FO 84/431; J. Crawford to Aberdeen, Oct. 14, 1842, FO 84/401; H. Wise to Gordon, Oct. 25, 1844, U.S. Congress, H. Doc. no. 148, 28–2, pp. 55–57.

58. *Report from the Select Committee of the House of Lords . . . for the African Slave Trade*, PP, 1850, 9:223; *British and Foreign Anti-Slavery Reporter* (London, 1840–

47), vols. 1–3 passim; "Petition of Directors of St. John del Rey Mining Co.," nd (c1843), FO 84/501. Turnbull, *Travels in the West,* pp. 191–92; *Hansard,* 1st ser. 30:657–58; D. Turnbull to Palmerston, Sept. 15, 1841, FO 84/358.

59. E. Watts to Palmerston, July 27, 1839, FO 84/289; W. Cullen to Palmerston, Mar. 31, 1838, FO 84/261; W. G. Ouseley to Palmerston, Dec. 15, 1838, FO 84/254.

60. W. G. Ouseley to Palmerston, Dec. 15, 1838 (enc.), FO 84/254; H. Hamilton to Aberdeen, Nov. 29, 1841, FO 84/367; Karasch, "Brazilian Slavers," p. 31; J. Crawford to Aberdeen, May 6, 1843, FO 84/463. For Gómez see James Kennedy's evidence to the Select Committee on the Slave Trade Treaties, PP, 1852–53, 39:103; Kennedy to Palmerston, Dec. 21, 1850, FO 84/789; H. T. Kilbee to Castlereagh, Dec. 19, 1820, FO 84/8; M. L. Melville and J. Hook to Aberdeen, Nov. 12, 1844 (enc.), FO 84/506; F. R. Cocking, Dec. 17, 1841 (enc.), Brit. Emp. mss., G77. Manuel Moreno Fraginals lists Gómez as the eighth largest importer before 1821 and one of the three most important in the first decade of the illicit traffic. It has not, however, been possible to trace the ownership of a single venture to this individual (*El Ingenio,* 1:267–68).

61. W. S. Macleay and R. Mackenzie to Palmerston, Feb. 28, 1833, FO 84/136; J. Campbell and W. W. Lewis to Palmerston, Nov. 10, 1836 (enc.), Dec. 24, 1836, FO 84/194.

62. The first Brazilian slaver arrived in 1831 (W. S. Macleay to Palmerston, Jan. 19, 1831, FO 84/119). Later André Pinto da Silveira, the Bahia agent of the de Souzas, was heavily involved in this traffic on his own account (J. Parkinson to Palmerston, Dec. 10, 1834, FO 84/157). For other references, see R. Whateley to Palmerston, Oct. 24, 1839, FO 84/289; W. Smith and H. W. Macaulay to Palmerston, Jan. 6, 1834, FO 84/147; J. Campbell and W. W. Lewis to Palmerston, Mar. 30, 1837, FO 84/214; H. S. Fox to Palmerston, Nov. 8, 1835 (enc.), FO 84/179. See also Gervase Clarence-Smith, "The Portuguese Contribution to the Cuban Slave and Coolie Trades in the Nineteenth Century," *Slavery & Abolition,* 5 (1984):27–28.

63. Col. Off. to Palmerston, Dec. 31, 1840, sub enc. José Henrique Ferreira to José de Brito Lund, Jan. 17, 1840, as well as sub enc., "Judgement in the case of the 'Guiana'," FO 84/337. Verger, *Flux et reflux,* p. 540.

64. M. L. Melville and J. Hook to Aberdeen, Nov. 12, 1844, FO 84/506; J. Kennedy and C. J. Dalrymple to Aberdeen, June 10, 1845, FO 84/561. Three of the nine Cuban slavers captured off Africa in 1845 were planning to carry slaves to the Brazils (M. L. Melville and J. Hook to Aberdeen, Dec. 31, 1845, FO 84/560). At least two Cuban ships made the voyage in the mid-1830s (J. Parkinson to Palmerston Apr. 11, 1834, enc. "deposition," FO 84/157; John H. Robilliard to Palmerston, July 28, 1835, FO 84/180).

65. App. C. An analogous situation had existed for a time during the French wars beginning in 1793. British cruisers restricted the traffic to Cuba more than that to the Brazils, thus widening the price differential between the regions. In 1810 the captain of the *Amelia* was ordered to buy his Cuban-bound slaves in Bahia rather than in Africa. (*Sixth Annual Report of the Committee of the African Institution* [London, 1812], p. 37).

66. J. Kennedy to Palmerston, June 23, and Dec. 26, 1849, FO 84/754; Jan. 1, 1850, and Feb. 26, 1850, FO 84/789; Jan. 1, 1851, FO 84/832; G. Jackson and E. Gabriel to Palmerston Feb. 5, 1850, FO 84/835. See also Karasch, "Brazilian Slavers," p. 17.

67. Col. Off. to Palmerston, Nov. 27, 1850, FO 84/822.

68. J. Kennedy and C. J. Dalrymple to Palmerston, Feb. 26, 1841, FO 84/348; R. Hesketh and F. Grigg, Mar. 11, 1846 (enc.), FO 84/622; H. F. Howard to Clarendon, Feb. 11, 1854 (sub enc.), FO 84/942; Dec. 12, 1854, enc. Limpo de Abreo to Howard, Jan. 23, 1854, FO 84/943.

69. H. F. Howard to Clarendon, Feb. 11, 1854 (sub enc.), FO 84/942; J. Hudson to Palmerston, July 14, 1851, enc. anon., June 26, 1851, FO 84/845; G. Jackson and E. Gabriel to Clarendon, Mar. 28, 1854, FO 84/932; Admiralty to Palmerston, Apr. 7, 1851, sub. enc. T. Lysaght, Jan. 1, 1851, FO 84/865.

70. E. Gabriel to Clarendon, Feb. 11, 1857, FO 84/1013; Admiralty to Russell Oct. 21, 1859, sub enc. Commodore Wise to Adm. Grey, July 20, 1859, FO 84/1100; E. Gabriel to Clarendon, Jan. 22, 1856, FO 84/985; J. Crawford to Clarendon, April 12, 1856, FO 84/988; and March 13, 1857 (enc.) FO 84/1016; J. Saville Lumley to Clarendon, July 22, 1856 (enc.), Dec. 6, 1856 (enc.), FO 84/999; Gervase Clarence-Smith, "The Portuguese Contribution to the Cuban Slave and Coolie Trades in the Nineteenth Century," p. 29; idem, *Third Portuguese Empire*, p. 71.

71. Admiralty to Malmesbury, Oct. 20, 1858, sub. enc. Lt. Pike, Aug. 16, 1858, FO 84/1070; E. M. Archibald to Malmesbury, Mar. 8, 1859; Russell to Archibald, Aug. 5, 1859, FO 84/1086.

72. J. Crawford and F. Lousada to Clarendon, Oct. 30, 1856, FO 84/984.

73. Sánchez y Dolz's reports suggest that about 40 percent of the slavers that left New York in 1859 were dispatched by the Portuguese group. See the enclosures in Archibald's dispatches during 1859 in FO 84/1086.

74. The British consul at Lagos wrote in 1857 that the Cuban dealers since 1854 "have rendered the most unsatisfactory returns to the shippers here of their consignments; . . . a vessel sent out by the usual parties from Havana, fully equipped to receive consignments from the slave merchants . . . six months since, was sent away without slaves; and that none will be shipped on freight and consignment from hence unless the vessel is sent by some firm in the Havana on whom every reliance can be placed for fair dealing," B. Campbell to Clarendon, May 11, 1857, FO 84/1031.

75. J. Parkinson to Palmerston, Apr. 11, and Dec. 10, 1834, FO 84/157; G. Jackson and E. Gabriel, May 30, 1849, enc. "Seizor's claim" and "Report of the Case of the *Galianna*", FO 84/758.

76. Col. Off. to Palmerston, Dec. 31, 1840, sub enc. José Joaquim Guims to Martins, Jan. 26, 1840, FO 84/337; David A. Ross "The Career of Domingo Martinez in the Bight of Benin, 1833–64," *Journal of African History*, 6 (1965): 79–90; Verger, *Flux et reflux*, pp. 452, 648–49.

77. Comm. N. Harris to Palmerston, Sept. 16, 1846, FO 84/663.

78. W. Cole and H. W. Macaulay to Palmerston, Jan. 5, 1835, (enc.) FO 84/166; Admiralty to Aberdeen, July 23, 1842, (enc.) FO 84/440; Findlay and Smith to Palmerston, Oct. 12, 1831 (enc.) FO 84/117; António Carreira, *O Tráfico de Escravos nos Rios de Guiné e Ilhas de Cabo Verde (1810–1850)* (Lisbon, 1981), pp. 31–34.

79. Joseph Miller has suggested that dealers in Luanda and Benguela were successful in asserting their independence from merchants in Brazil before 1830 ("Some Aspects of the Commercial Organization of Slaving at Luanda—1760–1830," in H. A. Gemery and J. S. Hogendorn [eds.], *The Uncommon Market: Essays in the Economic History of the Atlantic Slave Trade* [New York, 1979], p. 87). Anne Stamm also stresses the power and status of the Luanda dealers, including Donna Anna Joaquina ("La Société créole à Saint Paul de Loanda dans les années 1838–1848," *Revue française d'histoire d'outre-mer*, 59 [1972], pp. 595–97, 599–600).

But only 1 of the 117 vessels bound for Pernambuco, Bahia and Rio de Janeiro that were captured by the Royal Navy between 1821 and 1843 can be clearly assigned to Angolan ownership; of the thirty-two ships in the Luanda roadstead in Aug. 1835, almost all were owned by merchants in Brazil and Cuba (E. Gregory and E. Fitzgerald to Canning, Apr. 22, 1823 [enc.], FO 83/22; Admiralty to Palmerston, Jan. 29, 1836, sub. enc. Lt. Mercer, Sept. 6, 1835, FO 84/208). Angolan merchants no doubt continued to consign batches of their slaves to Brazilian merchants in the fashion described by Joseph Miller and, for an earlier period Herbert Klein (*Middle Passage*, pp. 37–41). Some lent their names to the fictitious sales of Havana-owned ships in the 1840s (Capt. Foote to Admiralty, Sept. 10, 1842, Adm. 1/5517), but there was probably no one who could carry on a transatlantic business on the scale of de Souza.

80. Admiralty to Palmerston, Nov. 12, 1850, sub enc. G. Brand, Aug. 31, 1850, FO 84/828; Admiralty to Palmerston, June 26, 1851, enc. Comm. Fanshawe, Apr. 24, 1851, FO 84/865. In addition to Donna Anna, Arsénio Pompilio Pompeu do Carpo, another Angola dealer, is reported as owning two ships (António Carreira, *O tráfico português de escravos na costa oriental africana nos começos do século XIX* [Lisbon, 1979], pp. 52–55; G. Tams, *Visit to the Portuguese Possessions in South Western Africa,* 2 vols. [London, 1845], 1:224). I am indebted to Gervase Clarence-Smith for these references. For Henry Tucker's activities, see Admiralty to Aberdeen, Jan. 11, 1845, sub enc. Comm. Buckle, Nov. 5, 1844; Mar. 31, 1845, enc. Comm. Jones, Feb. 7, 1845, FO 84/608.

81. J. Morgan to Clarendon, Mar. 19, 1853, FO 84/912; J. Murray to Clarendon, Oct. 9, 1855, FO 84/964; B. Campbell to Clarendon, Aug. 12, 1854, FO 84/950. One of the shipments, of 420 slaves, was in an unseaworthy brig that a group of Ouidah dealers purchased from a French merchant (B. Campbell to Clarendon, Dec. 1, 1854, FO 84/950).

82. B. Campbell to Clarendon, May 11, 1857, FO 84/1031; Admiralty to Russell, Apr. 29, 1864, enc. Comm. Wilmot, Dec. 1, 1864, FO 84/1228.

83. G. Jackson and E. Gabriel to Clarendon, Sept. 27, 1854, sub enc. Nath. Solmon, Dec. 14, 1854. Other major local dealers in Angola included Arsénio do Carpo (prior to his bankruptcy) and Augusto Guedes Coutinho Garrido. Cf. the discussion in Clarence-Smith, *Third Portuguese Empire,* pp. 49–50.

84. E. Gabriel to Clarendon, Oct. 16, 1856, and Nov. 4, 1856, FO 84/985; J. Morgan to Clarendon, Mar. 8, 1856, enc. "Manifest and cargo of barque 'Dolores',"FO 84/995. See also the ownership of the slaves of the *Haydee* (Admiralty to Russell, Apr. 29, 1864. enc. Comm. Wilmot, Dec. 31, 1863, FO 84/1228).

85. This paragraph is based on the work of Serge Daget. See "Long cours et négriers nantais du traffic illégal, 1814–1833," *Revue française d'histoire d'outre mer,* 62 (1975):90–134; idem. "L'abolition de la traite des noirs en France de 1814 à 1831," *Cahiers d'études africaines,* 11 (1971):14–58. Professor Daget's thèse d'état, "Les Croisières françaises de répression de la traite des noirs sur les côtes occidentales de l'Afrique, 1817–1867," will be the definitive work on the French nineteenth-century slave trade.

86. Daget, "Long cours et négrier nantais," pp. 129–30.

87. Ibid.; Daget, "British Repression of the Illegal French Slave Trade: Some Considerations," in Gemery and Hogendorn, *Uncommon Market,* pp. 425–40; idem, "France, Suppression of the Illegal Trade and England, 1817–1850" in David Eltis and James Walvin (eds.), *The Abolition of the Atlantic Slave Trade* (Madison, Wis., 1981), pp. 193–217; "Some intelligence about the Slave Trade at Senegal," Clarkson mss., CN 132; Sir Charles McCarthy to T. Clarkson, Nov. 14, 1820 (enc.),

Clarkson mss., CN 125; C. Findley and W. Smith to Aberdeen, Dec. 30, 1830 (enc.), FO 84/102; W. Macleay to Aberdeen, Dec. 8, 1828, FO 84/81; Commodore Bullen to Admiralty, Sept. 12, 1825, Adm. 1/1572.

88. H. Wise to Gordon, Oct. 25, 1844, U.S. Congress, H. Doc. no. 148, 28-2, p. 55; Felix Walker to Clarendon, May 1, 1854, FO 84/951. For Zulueta see Robert L. Paquette, "The Conspiracy of *La Escalera:* Colonial Society and Politics in the Age of Revolution." Ph.D. diss., University of Rochester, 1982, p. 22.

89. W. S. Macleay to Aberdeen, Jan. 1, 1830, FO 84/107; J. Kennedy to Palmerston, Jan. 1, 1850, FO 84/789.

90. J. Kennedy to Palmerston, May 25, 1848, FO 84/715; Jan. 1, 1850, FO 84/789; E. M. Archibald to Lord John Russell, Dec. 29, 1859, enc. (Sánchez y Dolz) Dec. 24, 1859, FO 84/1086.

91. J. Hudson to Palmerston, Oct. 10, 1849 (private), Broadlands mss., GC/HU/17; R. Hesketh to Palmerston, Mar. 3, 1851, FO 84/848; J. Hudson to Palmerston, Nov. 11, 1850 (private) and enc., FO 84/801; J. Hudson to Palmerson, July 14, 1851 (secret) and enc., FO 84/845. Thomas Ewbank was told at Rio de Janeiro in 1846 that "the great slave-merchants do not flourish long, and never prosper to the last," (*Life in Brazil; Or a Journal of a Visit to the Land of the Cocoa and the Palm* [New York, 1856], p. 127). This and other impressionistic comments by contemporaries are of dubious value in establishing the case for high risks in the slave-trading business. It is, however, worth citing them as a counterweight to the picture of high and apparently certain profits for slave traders that has been built in the past on the basis of similar evidence.

92. E. Gabriel to Malmesbury, May 5, 1859 (private), FO 84/1075; Admiralty to Palmerston, June 26, 1851, enc. Commodore Fanshawe, Apr. 29, 1851; FO 84/865; G. Jackson and E. Gabriel to Clarendon, Feb. 25, 1855, FO 84/960; W. Vredenburg to Russell, Oct. 31, 1863 (enc.), FO 84/1195; Karasch, "Brazilian Slavers," pp. 24-25; Clarence-Smith, *Third Portuguese Empire,* p. 49.

93. John Duncan to Palmerston, Sept. 22, 1849, FO 84/775; Admiralty to Palmerston, May 6, 1850, enc. Lt. Forbes, Apr. 2, 1850, FO 84/826. Other major failures were the Dennis firm in Nantes (Daget, "Long cours et négriers nantais," p. 131) and Charles Edward Gantois in Bahia in 1837 (R. Hesketh to Aberdeen, Oct. 24, 1844 [enc.], FO 84/526). Examples in Havana include the Busto and Inclan firm (W. S. Macleay to Aberdeen Dec. 2, 1829, FO 84/107) and the Quevedo bankruptcy (J. Kennedy to Palmerston, Mar. 16, 1839, FO 84/274).

94. Hugh Thomas, *Cuba: The Pursuit of Freedom* (London, 1971), pp. 136-39; J. Kennedy and C. J. Dalrymple to Palmerston, Mar. 10, 1841, FO 84/348; J. Kennedy to Palmerston, Jan. 1, 1849, FO 84/753; G. C. Backhouse to Clarendon, July 9, and Oct. 10, 1853, FO 84/899; J. Crawford to Russell, Dec. 3, 1859, FO 84/1080; May 10, 1864 (and enc.), FO 84/1218. For Aguirre, see J. Kennedy to Palmerston Dec. 21, 1850, FO 84/789.

95. For a description of Manoel Pinto da Fonseca's large coffee estates, see J. Hudson to Palmerston, Apr. 6, 1851, FO 84/844.

96. Adm. to Palmerston, Feb. 4, 1851, enc. B. Campbell, Oct. 28, 1850, FO 84/864; David A. Ross "Career of Domingo Martinez"; George E. Brooks, "A Nhara of the Guinea-Bissau Region: Mãe Aurélia Correia," in Claire C. Robertson and Martin A. Klein, (eds.), *Women and Slavery in Africa* (Madison, Wis., 1983), pp. 301-3; Carreira, *O Tráfico Escravos,* p. 34.

97. After fourteen years spent observing the Havana slave traffic James Kennedy told a parliamentary select committee that with one exception none of the landed proprietors in Cuba were engaged in the foreign slave trade (PP, 1852-53, 39:102). See

Franklin W. Knight, *Slave Society in Cuba During the Nineteenth Century* (Madison, Wis., 1970), p. 56; and Manuel Moreno Fraginals *The Sugarmill: The Socioeconomic Complex of Sugar in Cuba,* trans. Cedric Belfrage (New York, 1976), p. 132, for a different view of this issue.

98. Simon Perez de Terán, a peninsula Spaniard, probably became a planter after prospering first as a slave trader (R. Doherty and J. Hook to Palmerston, Mar. 12, 1840, FO 84/308A; Thomas, *Cuba,* p. 139).

99. Of the fifty-five largest plantations in Cuba in 1860, ten were owned by individuals who had acquired wealth early in their careers in the slave trade. For the list of plantations, see Thomas, *Cuba,* pp. 138–39. In Brazil, Joaquim José de Sousa Breves was one large coffee planter who set up slave-importing establishments at Marambaia, west of Rio de Janeiro, and took into his own estates perhaps the last successful transatlantic slave shipment in Brazil South in 1852 (Karasch, "Brazilian Slavers," p. 19; Leslie M. Bethell, *The Abolition of the Brazilian Slave Trade,* [Cambridge, 1970], p. 370).

100. For the metamorphosis of the old nobility into the new plantocracy, see Franklin W. Knight, "Origins of Wealth and the Sugar Revolution in Cuba, 1750–1850," 250–51. Moreno Fraginals has shown the links of some of these old families, the Alfonsos, Poeys and Aldamas, for example, with the early slave trade (*El ingenio,* 1:265–69), but many of these links appear to have been formed after the slave-trading side of the partnership had been successfully established and could be interpreted as part of a shift of slave-trading capital into plantations rather than the reverse, particularly when the trade became illegal. References to planter involvement in the traffic by British observers are very rare in the generation after 1820.

101. A lower price for slaves, in the absence of suppression, would no doubt have greatly increased the nonplantation use of slaves, and therefore the slave trade.

## Chapter 10

1. App. A; Paul E. Lovejoy, "The Volume of the Atlantic Slave Trade: A Synthesis," *Journal of African History,* 23 (1982):485; David Eltis, "Free and Coerced Transatlantic Migrations: Some Comparisons," *American Historical Review,* 88 (1983):255–6.

2. App. A.

3. *Sierra Leone Gazette,* Sept. 21, 1822; Comm. Foote to Admiralty Feb. 2, 1842, enc. Capt. Denman, Nov. 1, 1841, Adm. 1/5517; Capt. Kellet to Macaulay, Apr. 23, 1841, FO 84/389; J. Hook to Palmerston, Nov. 7, 1849, FO 84/752; Adam Jones, *From Slaves to Palm Kernels: A History of the Galinhas Country (West Africa), 1730–1890* (Wiesbaden, W. Ger., 1983), pp. 37–38. The *Venus,* a Cuban slave ship, was turned away from Bissau in late 1843 or early 1844. This is the first evidence of effective official action against the trade (C. Clarke to Aberdeen, May 12, 1844, FO 84/520).

4. Admiralty to Palmerston, Aug. 4, 1841 (enc.), FO 83/384; Admiralty to Malmesbury, Dec. 8, 1858, sub enc. Comm. Close, Sept. 13, 1858, FO 84/1070; Admiralty to Russell, June 17, 1861, enc. Comm. Edmonstone, May 7, 1861, FO 84/1149.

5. *Sierra Leone Gazette,* Sept. 21, 1822; W. Cole and H. W. Macaulay to Palmerston, Jan. 5, 1835, enc. B. Campbell, Jan. 5, 1835, FO 84/166; Admiralty to Palmerston, Nov. 2, 1839, enc. Lt. Hill, Apr. 5, 1839, FO 84/303. Col. Off. to Palmerston, Apr. 5, 1841, sub enc. Comm. Tucker, Feb. 1, 1841, FO 84/380.

6. George E. Brooks, "Peanuts and Colonialism: Consequences of the Commerciali-

zation of Peanuts in West Africa, 1830–70," *Journal of African History*, 16 (1975):29–54.

7. A. Jones, *From Slaves to Palm Kernels,* pp. 95–99. The money to purchase the Gallinas was actually raised by private subscription and came mainly from abolitionists though the British government gave to the Liberians an armed schooner as well as additional assistance for specific operations. See A. H. Foote, *Africa and the American Flag* (New York, 1854), pp. 184–85; Comm. Fanshawe to Admiralty, Apr. 4, 1849, Adm.1/5596; memo attached to Col. Off. to Palmerston, Sept. 28, 1850, FO 84/822; Admiralty to Palmerston, Oct. 30, 1850, enc. Comm. Fanshawe, Aug. 12, 1850, FO 84/827.

8. George E. Brooks, Jr. *Yankee Traders, Old Coasters and African Middlemen. A History of American Legitimate Trade with West Africa in the Nineteenth Century* (Boston, 1970), pp. 198–205.

9. J. Hook to Palmerston, Jan. 21, 1850, FO 84/788. See also Admiralty to Palmerston, Apr. 17, 1849, sub enc. Comm. Murray, Feb. 5, 1849, FO 84/783. There was, however, a thriving coastal trade as well as trade with the interior. See Admiralty to Aberdeen, Oct. 15, 1844, sub enc. Gov. Ferguson of Sierra Leone, July 31, 1844, FO 84/551; A. Jones, *From Slaves to Palm Kernels,* pp. 40–41, 104–5.

10. For slave exports and prices see app. A and C. For trade trends in the Pongo and neighboring rivers see PP, 1842, 11:491; 12:185, 190–91; W. Melville and J. Hook to Palmerston, Dec. 31, 1847, FO 84/666; Admiralty to Palmerston enc. Comm. Fanshawe, Apr. 29, 1851, FO 84/865; Admiralty to Russell, Apr. 19, 1860, enc. Comm. Edmonstone Mar. 17, 1860, FO 84/1123.

11. In the Pongo River in 1850 the Afro-European factor Paul Faber "called in a large number of his slaves from the ground nut fields, a course which necessarily deprived him of their labour and which he would certainly not have adopted as it was then the ground nut season had he not made other and more remunerative arrangements." The latter, of course, was the sale of 240 of his slaves to a Brazilian trader for $15,000, perhaps double the going rate for ground nut labor. The slave ship that took them had managed to avoid the naval patrol (Admiralty to Palmerston, Oct. 1, 1850, enc. B. Campbell Aug. 13, 1850, FO 84/828; and Col. Off. to Palmerston, Dec. 24, 1850, sub. enc. Campbell, Aug. 31, 1850, FO 84/822). Faber performed a similar operation in 1858 (Admiralty to Malmesbury, Jan. 11, 1859, sub enc. Comm. Close, Nov. 8, 1858, FO 84/1097). For other rivers, see PP, 1842, 11:412, 474; Admiralty to Clarendon, Jan. 10, 1854 enc. "Extract of Journal of Comm. Need," nd, FO 84/954; Comm. Edmonstone to Rear Adm. Walker, July 20, 1861, Irish University Press series of British Parliamentary Papers (henceforth referred to as I.U.P.), *Slave Trade,* vol. 47: pt. B, p. 93. Comm. Edmonstone to Rear Adm. Walker, Oct. 10, 1862, Admiralty 123/180; Admiralty to Malmesbury, May 8, 1852, sub enc. "Journal kept by Edward S. Sotheby," 1851–52, FO 84/894.

12. App. A and E; Lovejoy, "Volume of the Atlantic Slave Trade," p. 485; Richard N. Bean, *The British Trans-Atlantic Slave Trade, 1650–1775* (New York, 1975), pp. 158–59.

13. Of the 259 recaptives, 216 were assigned ethnic labels that can be identified. Regions less than one hundred miles from the coast account for 151, or 70 percent, of these. Bambarra (Bambara), Mandingo, Foulah, Kissry (Kissi) and "Footajalla" (Fulbe) account for the remaining 30 percent. The Sierra Leone registers are in FO 84/9 and 15. The ethnic and language groupings among British West Indian slaves from one hundred miles or less inland account for 44 percent of Higman's sample for Senegambia, Sierra Leone and the Windward Coast combined (listed in Barry Higman, *Slave Populations of the British Caribbean, 1807–1824* [Baltimore, 1984],

pp. 442–57). The samples for the French Antilles tabulated by Philip D. Curtin (*The Atlantic Slave Trade: A Census* [Madison, Wis., 1969], pp. 192–98) are not sufficiently numerous or detailed for similar comparisons.

14. Curtin, *Atlantic Slave Trade,* pp. 289–98.

15. W. Cole and H. W. Macaulay to Palmerston, Jan. 5, 1835, enc. B. Campbell Jan. 5, 1835, FO 84/166.

16. E. Gregory and E. Fitzgerald to Canning, Apr. 29, 1823, FO 84/21; Capt. Kellet to Macaulay, Apr. 23, 1841, FO 84/389; Admiralty to Palmerston, Dec. 26, 1849, sub enc. Lt. Dunlop. Oct. 12, 1849, FO 84/785; Admiralty to Palmerston, Apr. 17, 1849, sub enc., Journal of William A. Parker, Feb. 4, 1849, FO 84/783; Admiralty to Malmesbury, Oct. 15, 1858, enc. Rear Adm. Grey, Aug. 6, 1858, FO 84/1070; Christopher Fyfe, *A History of Sierra Leone* (London, 1962), pp. 183–84; John Warner Barber, *A History of the Amistad Captives* (New Haven, Conn., 1840), pp. 9–15; A. Jones, *From Slaves to Palm Kernels,* pp. 34–36, 47–54.

17. One anomaly in the Upper Guinea region should be noted. In Senegambia, alone of all African provenance zones, slave prices rose toward the end of the transatlantic trade (in this case from 1780 on) and remained high thereafter. A decrease in supply appears likely though whether or not this was a manifestation of some competing activity such as trans-Saharan demand or increased production for domestic purposes is unclear. European demand for Senegambian produce cannot have been responsible. Gum production for export grew rapidly only from the 1820s, not the 1780s, and it was not in any event as labor intensive as, say, peanut and palm oil cultivation. Though we should expect any flow of slaves to have been toward the higher-priced north, some slaves continued to be sold directly into the Atlantic trade from Gorée in the 1840s as well as brought overland to the Casamance, Cacheu and Geba rivers. The 1840 coastal trade from Gorée is described in Rendall to Palmerston, May 11, 1841 (enc.) FO 84/363. For slave price and quantities and the gum trade in Senegambia see Philip D. Curtin, *Economic Change in Precolonial Africa: Senegambia in the Era of the Slave Trade,* 2 vols. (Madison, Wis., 1975), 1:156–68, 187–96, 215–18, though Curtin's "negative supply elasticity" is the result of the difficulty in identifying and isolating demand and supply curves. For the nineteenth century slave trade see also Daget, "L'Abolition de la traite," p. 31; and "Quelque notes sur le Senegal, Juillet 1823" in the Clarkson mss; CN 207. See app. A for slave departures.

18. Adam Jones and Marion Johnson, "Slaves from the Windward Coast," *Journal of African History,* 21 (1980):17–34.

19. See the exchange of correspondence in FO 84/110, in particular Bagot to Aberdeen, Aug. 21, 1830, enc. Comm. Collier to Gov. of Elmina, June 15, 1829. See also Admiralty to Dudley, July 28, 1827, enc. Comm. Bullen, Apr. 4, 1827, FO 84/74; and app. A. For the supply of slaves to Keta see, C. W. Newbury, *The Western Slave Coast and Its Rulers* (Oxford, 1961), pp. 39–41; Edward E. Reynolds, *Trade and Economic Change on the Gold Coast,* (London, 1974), pp. 141–42; D. E. K. Amenumey, "Geraldo de Lima: A Reappraisal," *Transactions of the Historical Society of Ghana,* 9 (1968):65–68; For the *Ulysses's* slaves, see Rev. T. E. Ward to Rev. Whitehorne, n.d., 30/104, Buxton mss.

20. Paul E. Lovejoy, *Caravans of Kola: The Hausa Kola Trade, 1700–1900* (Zaria, Nigeria, 1980), in particular pp. 11–27; Ivor Wilks, *Asante in the Nineteenth Century* (New York, 1975), pp. 176–78. Exports from the Gold Coast, 1853–62, averaged £123,000 per year in current prices (PP, 1867, 72:102–3). Dutch exports were certainly lower than this. Slave exports from the Gold Coast in the 1780s averaged about 9,400 a year (Lovejoy, "Volume of the Atlantic Slave Trade," p. 485) and a

price of £25 a slave might be assumed (E. Phillip LeVeen, *British Slave Trade Suppression Policies, 1821–1865* [New York, 1977], p. 146, gives a price of £27 for prime males in West Africa at this time). Conversion to fob values would not change this assessment.

21. App. A.
22. A description of this strategy is in William Hutton to Palmerston, July 19, 1847, FO 84/710. Hutton later writes to Palmerston (Mar. 6, 1848, FO 84/739), "The heavy surf of the sea . . . on that part of the coast will not admit ship's boats being used, nor are European seamen sufficiently expert"; see also Newbury, *Western Slave Coast,* pp. 2–4.
23. Admiralty to Malmesbury, May 3, 1852, enc. Comm. Bruce Apr. 1, 1852, FO 83/894. The best review of the strategic problems is in Admiralty to Malmesbury, Feb. 9, 1858 and enc. Comm. Wise, Dec. 21, 1857, FO 84/1068. As late as 1861 the head of the Admiralty was stressing the magnitude of the task (Duke of Somerset to Palmerston, Oct. 3, 1861, GC/SO/62, Broadlands mss.).
24. Admiralty to Stanley, Jan. 9, 1868, enc. Comm. Hornby, June 7, 1867, FO 84/1294.
25. J. F. Ade Ajayi and R. S. Smith, *Yoruba Warfare in the Nineteenth Century* (Cambridge, 1964), pp. 9–39; Robin Law, *The Oyo Empire c. 1600–c. 1836: A West African Imperialism in the Era of the Atlantic Slave Trade* (Oxford, 1977), pp. 278–312; S. O. Biobaku, *The Egba and their Neighbours, 1842–1872* (Oxford, 1957), pp. 12–13, 16–24, 33–34, 38–52; Babatunde Agiri, "Slavery in Yoruba Society in the Nineteenth Century," in Paul Lovejoy (ed.), *The Ideology of Slavery in Africa* (Beverley Hills, Calif. 1981), pp. 123–48. For memoirs of Africans caught up in these struggles see Philip D. Curtin (ed.), *Africa Remembered: Narratives by West Africans from the Era of the Slave Trade* (Madison, Wis., 1967), pp. 193–333. P. E. H. Hair's analysis of the enslavement of Koelle's informants indicates 48 percent were war captives ("The Enslavement of Koelle's Informants," *Journal of African History,* 6 (1965):196–197). Half of the 436 slaves on board de Souza's ship, *Don Francisco* which left Ouidah in 1836 were war captives. The rest were natives of Mahi, a Dahomey province (*Colonist* [Barbados], Apr. 29, 1837).
26. Robin Law, "Royal Monopoly and Private Enterprise in the Atlantic Trade: The Case of Dahomey," *Journal of African History,* 18 (1977):559–71; Arthur E. Wilmot to Wylde, Feb. 4, 1854, FO 84/951; Frederick E. Forbes, *Dahomey and the Dahomans,* 2 vols. (London, 1851), 1:111, 111–15; Adm. to Palmerston, July 6, 1850, sub enc. Lt. Forbes, Apr. 2, 1850, FO 84/826.
27. B. Campbell to Clarendon, Dec. 7, 1854, FO 84/950. Some of the recaptive Yoruba who returned to their homeland from Sierra Leone after 1838 proved no more immune to proslave-trade social pressures than did their British merchant counterparts in Havana and Rio de Janeiro. Many of the Africans who made up the cargo of the *Abbot Devereux* in 1857 were purchased from individuals near Ouidah who had themselves been released from the hold of a transatlantic slaver (S. Hill to Clarendon, Sept. 2, 1857, FO 84/1011. See also Jean Herskovits Kopytoff, *A Preface to Modern Nigeria: The "Sierra Leonians" in Yoruba, 1830–1890* [Madison, Wis., 1965], pp. 108–9).
28. Law, "Royal Monopoly and Private Enterprise," pp. 560–61; "Memorandum for the use of Deputation of the C.M.S.," Dec. 4, 1849, FO 84/777, fol. 281–89; Capt. C. W. Riley to Admiralty, May 22, 1850, Adm. 123/173. Geraldo de Lima of Keta was still buying slaves from the Volta for the transatlantic trade in the early 1860s (see Admiralty to Russell, Apr. 29, 1864, enc. Comm. Wilmot, Dec. 31, 1863, FO 84/1228; Comm. Edmonstone to Rear Adm. Walker, Oct. 22, 1862, Adm. 123/

180). Dealers at Lagos wrote in 1844, "I was obliged to pay [the king] 14 doubloons: and every person that comes here has to do the same, according to the cargo"; "For each slave that is put on board 2 pieces of cloth are to be given to the king"; and "I paid the king 14 doubloons, besides anchorage, discharging, conveyance from the beach to the town, canoes, etc." These may be found in the enc. in H. Wise to Calhoun, Nov. 1, 1844, U.S. Congress, H. Exec. Doc. no. 148, 28–2, pp. 44–47. On Ouidah's position after 1851 see B. Campbell to Clarendon, July 27, 1857; Aug. 31, 1857, FO 84/1031; and S. Hill to Clarendon, Sept. 2, 1857, enc. T. G. Lawson, Aug. 29, 1857, FO 84/1011.

29. Curtin, *Atlantic Slave Trade*, pp. 251–60. As Cuban demand picked up, slaves escaping to Lagos from Ouidah in 1858 were "most of them . . . from the interior Houssa and Nuffee in particular" (B. Campbell to Clarendon, Mar. 27, 1858, FO 84/1061). The ethnic origins of 406 slaves acquired as part of four separate slaving expeditions in the Bight of Benin during 1821–22 are available from the Sierra Leone slave registers (in FO 84/9 and 15). All but 10 slaves were embarked at Lagos and Badagry (Badagri). Unfortunately only 177 can be identified—probably because for the Yoruba the name of the village or town was used under the heading, "Country of Origin." Of these 177 slaves, 3 were from the Cross River (Ibibio), 78 from the lower Niger (Igbo), 41 may be tentatively identified as Nupe, 34 were Hausa, 12 were from the Gold Coast hinterland (Coromontee, Apam), 8 were Yoruba and 1 was Fulani.

30. Macgregor Laird to Malmesbury, Mar. 14, 1859, enc. "Extracts from Mr. Lyall's Journal . . . ," FO 84/1095. For slave-trade routes from the north to Lagos, Badagry and Ouidah, see Mahdi Adamu, "The Delivery of Slaves from the Central Sudan to the Bight of Benin in the Eighteenth and Nineteenth Centuries," in H. A. Gemery and J. S. Hogendorn (eds.), *The Uncommon Market: Essays in the Economic History of the Atlantic Slave Trade* (New York, 1979), pp. 172–78.

31. See app. B and chap. 5. The adult male ratios of the Yoruba and Nupe slaves in the 1821–2 Sierra Leone sample are exceptionally high: for Yoruba the ratio was 0.61, (263 observations); for Nupe 0.58 (45 obs.), all embarked at Bight of Benin ports. This compares to 0.43 for Igbo (786 obs.) and 0.36 for Ibibio (253 obs.) from Bight of Biafra ports. For the Bight of Benin as a whole in the years 1811–67, the ratio was 0.46 (see table B.1). It is tempting to link these high ratios with the Ijebu conquest of Owu in 1821 and the Fulbe conquest of Nupe. It might be assumed that the immediate impact of a military campaign would be to increase the number of adult male captives sold.

32. Patrick Manning, *Slavery, Colonialism and Economic Growth in Dahomey, 1640–1960* (Cambridge, 1982), pp. 51–53, and the literature cited there. Palm oil prices are in A. J. H. Latham, *Old Calabar, 1600–1891: The Impact of the International Economy up on a Traditional Society* (Oxford, 1973), pp. 69–71; idem, "Price Fluctuations in the Early Palm Oil Trade," *Journal of African History*, 19 (1978):213–18.

33. Catherine Coquery-Vidrovitch, "De la traite des esclaves à l'exportation de l'huile de palme et des palmistes au Dahomey: XIXe siècle," in Claude Meillassoux (ed.), *The Development of Indigenous Trade and Markets in West Africa* (London, 1971), pp. 107–23; Law, "Royal Monopoly and Private Enterprise," pp. 571–76; Honorat Aguessy, "Le Dan-Homê du XIXe siècle était-il une société esclavagiste?" *Revue française d'études politiques africaines*, 50 (1970):71–91. One possible explanation for the contrary trends in oil output and prices is that the African price of palm oil diverged somewhat from its Liverpool counterpart as a result of declines in freight rates or bulking costs. Another possibility is the active promotion of the technology of production that several European merchants undertook in these years (see

PP, 1842, 11:108; and Manning, *Slavery, Colonialism and Economic Growth*, p. 53).

34. Commodity trade estimates (overseas) for the Bight of Benin are in Admiralty to Malmesbury, Oct. 15, 1858, enc. Comm. Wise, Aug, 6, 1858, FO 84/1070; and B. Campbell to Clarendon, Feb. 2, 1858; FO 84/1061. For slave-trade values, see apps. A and C.

35. Apps. C and E.

36. Evidence of W. M. Hutton to the Select Committee on the West Coast of Africa, PP, 1842, 11:607–8; Hutton to Palmerston, July 19, 1847, enc. Thomas Hutton, Mar. 17, 1847, FO 84/1622.

37. Admiralty to Malmesbury, Aug. 6, 1852, sub enc. Comm. Bruce, Jan. 17, 1852, FO 84/895; B. Campbell to Clarendon, Dec. 1, 1854, FO 84/950; Admiralty to Clarendon, Sept. 14, 1857, enc. Comm. Hope, May 23, 1857, FO 84/1040.

38. Admiralty to Malmesbury, Apr. 10, 1852, enc. Comm. Bruce, Feb. 11, 1852, and sub encs., FO 84/893.

39. David Northrup (*Trade Without Rulers: Pre-Colonial Economic Development in South Eastern Nigeria* [Oxford, 1978], 58–65, 231) has presented breakdowns of the Igbo and Ibibio slaves in the Sierra Leone registers who were recaptured by the British after being shipped from Bonny and Calabar, though he did not include those shipped from Bight of Benin ports. On the basis of this and other evidence, he concludes that the Igbo made up 60 percent, the Ibibio and northwest Bantu about 16.5 percent each and the Hausa and others the remainder. However Bonny and Calabar, the ports where Igbo and Ibibio predominated, claimed a larger share of the Bight of Biafra's slave trade than has been realized (app. A). In addition, few Hausa or other Upper Niger peoples entered the trade through Niger ports for reasons discussed earlier, whereas Igbo and Ibibio left from Lagos and Badagry. It would thus appear that Northrup's ratios for Igbo and Ibibio peoples should be increased.

40. Ibid. for Northrup's careful identification of provenance regions. For slave prices see app. C. The sex ratios as well as the mean ages within the groupings headed "Men," "Women," "Boy" and "Girl" are very similar for the Igbo and Ibibio captives. The major difference between the two peoples is the proportion of children taken. For the Igbo, who were generally located further away from the point of embarkation the ratio was 0.34. For the Ibibio, 0.45. A chi square test indicates that differences are significant at the 0.01 percent level. Similarly the group of Igbo embarked at Lagos and Badagry were older than those embarked at Bight of Biafra ports. Mean age: Lagos and Badagry = 19.4; Bonny and Calabar = 18.0. Differences significant at the 5 percent level.

41. App. A.

42. R. F. Stevenson, *Population and Political Systems in Tropical Africa* (New York, 1968), pp. 195–212. See the discussion on this in Northrup, *Trade Without Rulers*, pp. 114–19.

43. The regression equation is (standard errors in first set of parentheses, $F$ statistic in second):

$$X_t = 43.3 - .03\, L_t - 1$$
$$(6.4)\,(0.03)$$
$$(45.8)\,(1.1)$$
$$n = 20$$
$$r^2 = 0.06$$

Where $X_t$ = Annual slave departures in year $t$

$L_t - 1$ = slave ships lost/total slave ships ventured in $t - 1$.

Exports from the Bight of Biafra continued into the 1850s, chiefly from Sangatanga near Cape Lopez; but the traffic was finished from the major embarkation ports in the palm oil rivers by the early 1840s.

44. David Northrup, "The Compatibility of the Slave and Palm Oil Trades in the Bight of Biafra," *Journal of African History,* 17 (1976):353–64. Between 1833 and 1837, 77,800 slaves left the Bight of Biafra (app. A). If the average value of a slave is taken at £7.6 (prime male slave prices from app. C × 0.8, expressed in fob values), then the total value of the slave trade was £886,920. Palm oil exports may be conservatively estimated at 8,000 tons a year or 40,000 tons for five years (Customs 4, vols. 28–32 gives total United Kingdom oil imports of 64,500 tons between 1833–37; for Latham's estimate of exports, see *Old Calabar,* p. 66). Palm oil prices at Calabar and Bonny may be taken at £15 per ton, which is half the Liverpool price (Latham, "Price Fluctuations," p. 214, coupled with an adjustment for his estimate of a 100 percent markup between Calabar and Liverpool; see *Old Calabar,* pp. 69–72). This yields a total value for oil exports of £600,000. The net income of any one trading state would, of course, be a small fraction of this. King Pepple of Bonny, for example, required goods to the value of $6,000 per annum (or £1,333) to give up the slave trade (Adm. to Palmerston, Feb. 18, 1841, enc. Comm. Tucker Nov. 8, 1840, FO 84/383) and eventually settled for $2,000 (£444), which was not, in fact, paid. Some further idea of the income of the trading states from slaves may be obtained from their reaction to Commander Tucker's undertaking in 1841 to pay $10,000 (£2,222) a year to Bonny (also rejected by the Foreign Office). Tucker reported that within weeks "the information . . . spread over the whole coast and all the native Kings and Chiefs are eager to enter into Treaties to suppress the Slave Trade" (Adm. to Aberdeen, May 23, 1842, enc. Tucker, Jan. 28, 1842, FO 84/439). Mean net annual income from the slave trade for most individual oil states was probably below £1,000 per annum.

45. Supra, chap. 6. For British prevarication over subsidies, see "Memorandum on negotiations with the Chiefs of Bonny," Apr. 7, 1841, FO 84/389. For the list of treaties, see PP, 1850, 9:372–73.

46. Macgregor Laird to Clarendon, May 14, 1857, FO 84/1034; Admiralty to Palmerston, Feb. 19, 1841 enc. Comm. Tucker, Nov. 8, 1840, FO 84/383; Admiralty to Palmerston, July 30, 1841, enc. Comm. Tucker, May 25, 1841, FO 84/384; Admiralty to Aberdeen, Nov. 25, 1841, sub enc. Christopher Jackson, Aug. 21, 1841, FO 84/385; Admiralty to Palmerston, Aug. 31, 1846, sub. enc. Comm. Young, July 1, 1846, FO 84/659.

47. Admiralty to Palmerston, Jan. 4, 1851, enc. Comm. Fanshawe, Oct. 15, 1850, FO 84/864; Admiralty to Palmerston, June 26, 1851 enc., Comm. Fanshawe, Apr. 29, 1851, FO 84/865; Admiralty to Palmerston, Aug. 30, 1841, sub enc. John Lilley May 12, 1841, FO 84/384; Admiralty to Malmesbury, Aug. 6, 1852, enc. Comm. Bruce June 18, 1852, FO 84/895; Admiralty to Palmerston, July 7, 1846, enc. Comm. Bosanquet, July 4, 1846, FO 84/659; Capt. Trottier to Russell, Feb. 19, 1853 (enc.), FO 84/921. Treaties with African rulers of Sangatanga and Cape Lopez were signed on Feb. 1, 1853. For French intervention and the deteriorating position of the Mpongwe and Orungu states, see K. David Patterson, *The Northern Gabon Coast to 1875* (Oxford, 1975), pp. 68–113, 131–43; Elikia M'Bokolo, *Noirs et blancs en afrique équatoriale: les sociétés côtiéres et la pénétration française* (Paris, 1981), pp. 29–127.

48. App. A.

49. The governor general of Angola, Bernado Vidal, at first refused to enforce the Portuguese decree; he was not recalled until 1838 (Manuel Pinheiro Chagas, *As colon-*

*ias portuguezas no seculo XIX (1811 a 1890)* [Lisbon, 1890], pp. 76–77). For subsequent Anglo-Portuguese joint action and an assessment of the impact of the Portuguese occupation of Ambriz, see Admiralty to Aberdeen, Jan. 10, 1845, enc. Comm. Jones, Nov. 18, 1844, FO 84/608; Comm. Wise to R. Adm. Grey, Aug. 6, 1858, Adm. 123/175. In Oct. 1845 the British commodore wrote that since Apr. 1844 the British had taken eighty-one vessels, the Portuguese fifteen. "It was finally settled between us that the Portuguese squadron should undertake to watch the coast between Ambriz and Cape Ledo, while we should cruise northward and southward of those limits" (Admiralty to Aberdeen, Nov. 25, 1845 [enc.], FO 84/612). Portuguese colonial officials continued to be bribed by slave traders throughout the 1840s, however.

50. Capt. Foote to Admiralty, Aug. 25, 1842, Adm. 1/5517; Admiralty to Aberdeen, Nov. 18, 1842 (enc.), and Nov. 21, 1842 (enc.), FO 84/442; E. Gabriel to Aberdeen, Dec. 31, 1845, FO 84/577; G. Jackson and E. Gabriel to Palmerston, Feb. 18, 1847, FO 84/671. For the increasing pressure on Luanda slave traders exerted by the Portuguese civil authorities see Anne Stamm, "La société creole à Saint Paul de Loanda dans les années, 1838–1848," *Revue française d'histoire d'outre-mer,* 59 (1972):599–601.

51. This shift from Luanda to Ambriz as well as the broader concentration of the traffic on the Congo River does not show up in the tables in app. A because both Luanda and Ambriz are included in the Angola category. It might also be noted that Ambriz refers here to the Ambriz region. Most slaves were embarked to the north of the settlement after the early 1840s. For the importance of Ambriz after 1836, see Capt. R. S. Tinkler to Admiralty, Oct. 4, 1839, Adm. 1/3336. Also see the captured slave-trader correspondence in H. W. Macaulay and W. Lewis to Palmerston, July 20, 1839 (enc.), FO 84/270.

52. Comm. Perry, Nov. 25, 1844, enc. Abbott, Nov. 6, 1844, LSN, reel 101; Adm. to Palmerston, Jan. 29, 1836, sub enc. Lt. Mercer, Sept. 6, 1835, FO 84/208; Admiralty to Aberdeen, Nov. 24, 1842, sub enc. Bishop, July 29, 1842, FO 84/442; H. W. Macaulay and W. W. Lewis to Palmerston, July 20, 1839 (enc.), FO 84/270.

53. Curtin, *Atlantic Slave Trade,* pp. 260–62; Roger T. Anstey, *The Atlantic Slave Trade and British Abolition* (London, 1975), pp. 60–69; J. Vansina, "Long Distance Trade Routes in Central Africa," *Journal of African History,* 3 (1962):379–82; Joseph C. Miller, "The Slave Trade of Congo and Angola," in Martin L. Kilson and Robert Rotberg (eds.), *The African Diaspora* (Cambridge, Mass., 1976), pp. 75–113; Phyllis Martin, *The External Trade of the Loango Coast, 1576–1870* (Oxford, 1972), pp. 86–87, 124–29; Robert Harms, *River of Wealth, River of Sorrow* (New Haven, Conn., 1981), pp. 24–39, 126–33. For the Mussorongo's role, see J. Hudson to Palmerston, Aug. 14, 1851, FO 84/842. In the last years of the Atlantic trade, there were still slaves embarked who had travelled from the lakes that form the eastern headwaters of the Congo (R. Burton to Lord John Russell, Dec. 1863, enc., "Conclusion of Report on Ascent of Congo," FO 84/1203).

54. App. A; Lovejoy, "Volume of the Atlantic Slave Trade," p. 485.

55. Joseph C. Miller, "Cokwe Trade and Conquest in the Nineteenth Century," in Richard Gray and David Birmingham (eds.), *Pre-Colonial African Trade: Essays on Trade in Central and Eastern Africa before 1900* (London, 1970), pp. 175–201.

56. Herbert S. Klein's Luanda data from the mid-eighteenth century indicate much lower child ratios than those from west-central Africa a century later (*The Middle Passage* [Princeton, N.J., 1978], pp. 28, 35–37; infra, app. B).

57. Admiralty to Palmerston, June 4, 1850, sub enc. Capt. Hastings, Mar. 4, 1850, FO 84/826; E. Gabriel to Russell, Sept. 20, and Dec. 20, 1859, FO 84/1076.

58. E. Gabriel to Aberdeen, Dec. 31, 1845, FO 84/577; Admiralty to Russell, Jan. 21, 1853, sub enc. Comm. Seymour, Nov. 1, 1852, FO 84/925; Admiralty to Malmesbury, May 8, 1852, sub enc. Comm. Foote, Feb. 22, 1852, FO 84/894; J. Hudson to Palmerston, Aug. 14, 1851, FO 84/842; Admiralty to Clarendon, Mar. 29, 1855, enc. Lt. Bedingfield, July 3, 1854, FO 84/981.

59. Capt. Foote to Admiralty May 31, 1842, Adm. 1/5517; Admiralty to Aberdeen, Sept. 15, 1842, sub enc. Kenyon, June 7, 1842, FO 84/441; Admiralty to Aberdeen, Aug. 12, 1842, enc. Capt. Foote, May 24, 1842, FO 84/440.

60. The three British agreements were with Cabinda, Feb. 11, 1853, Ambrizete, Sept. 17, 1855 and Kinsembo, July 13, 1857.

61. Admiralty to Aberdeen, Apr. 5, 1843, enc. Capt. Brundy, Jan. 27, 1843, FO 84/495; Admiralty to Aberdeen, Aug. 5, 1843, enc. Capt. Foote, May 11, 1843, FO 84/497; Admiralty to Russell, Jan. 21, 1853, sub enc. Comm. Seymour, Nov. 11, 1852, FO 84/925; Admiralty to Lord John Russell, Feb. 18, 1864, sub enc. Comm. Perry, Oct. 27, 1863, FO 84/1227.

62. Commander Henry Need to Comm. Adams, Jan. 30, 1855, IUP, *Slave Trade,* 42:128; Admiralty to Russell, Jan. 21, 1853, sub enc. Comm. Seymour, Nov. 11, 1852, FO 84/925; P. Martin, *External Trade of the Loango Coast,* pp. 146–48; P. Martin, "Cabinda and the Cabindans: Some Aspects of an African Maritime Society," in Jeffrey C. Stone (ed.), *Africa and the Sea* (Aberdeen, Scot., 1985), p. 89.

63. Admiralty to Malmesbury, May 8, 1852, sub enc. Comm. Foote, Feb. 22, 1852, FO 84/894; E. Gabriel to Malmesbury, Apr. 15, 1859, FO 84/1075. Gabriel's assessment of the Congo palm oil trade probably does not include the Ambriz traffic. In 1863 the British commodore reported, "Everything is quiet in the Congo . . . there is very little legitimate trade and scarcely any Slave Trade" (Comm. Wilmot to R. Adm. Walker, July 1, 1863, Adm. 123/180).

64. Pinheiro Chagas, *As colonias portuguezas,* p. 89.

65. Capt. Foote to Admiralty Aug. 25, 1842, Adm. 1/5517; Admiralty to Aberdeen, Nov. 21, 1842, sub enc. Capt. Foote, June 24, 1842, FO 84/442; E. Gabriel to Aberdeen Dec. 31, 1845, FO 84/572; G. Jackson and E. Gabriel to Palmerston, Feb. 14, 1848, FO 84/719; G. Jackson and E. Gabriel to Clarendon, Feb. 23, 1855, FO 84/960; Joseph C. Miller, "Some Aspects of the Commercial Organization of Slaving at Luanda, Angola—1760–1830," in Gemery and Hogendorn, *Uncommon Market,* pp. 84–85.

66. The reconstruction of Angolan trade figures for the 1850s is not easy. The British consul provided a detailed breakdown of prices and quantities of exports for 1857, though it might be noted that the former appear suspiciously high and may be official values (E. Gabriel to Clarendon, Feb. 25, 1858, FO 84/1043). Comments on trends may be found in G. Brand to Clarendon, Mar. 16, 1853, FO 84/909; G. Jackson and E. Gabriel to Clarendon, Feb. 25, 1855, FO 84/960; and Feb. 16, 1856, FO 84/985; W. Vrendenburg to Russell, Oct. 31, 1863 (enc.), FO 84/1195. Allen Isaacman has assembled fragmentary figures for Luanda exports for a few of these years ("An Economic History of Angola, 1835–1867." M.A. thesis, University of Wisconsin, 1966, pp. 95–96). For 1857 his data are roughly consistent with Gabriel's, which means that official values may have been used here also. If this is the case, then the estimates derived in the present text may be too high by as much as 50 percent. For trade at Ambriz, see E. Gabriel to Palmerston, Aug. 5, 1850, FO 84/792, and Bibbens and Blagden to Clarendon, Dec. 4, 1855, FO 84/977: Both are discussed in Roger Anstey, *Britain and the Congo in the Nineteenth Century* (Oxford, 1962), p. 23. For U.S. trade at Ambriz, see Brooks, *Yankee Traders,* pp 287–88. For trade at Benguela and Mossâmedes (Moçamedes), we have on

impressions summarized in Isaacman ("An Economic History of Angola," pp. 24–26, 60–61). For comments on the expansion of both slave and commodity trades in the late 1850s, see E. Gabriel to Clarendon, Feb. 25, 1858, FO 84/1043.

67. G. Jackson and E. Gabriel to Palmerston, Feb. 5, 1850, FO 84/793; Admiralty to Russell, Feb. 18, 1864, sub enc. Comm. Wilmot, Dec. 31, 1863, FO 84/1227.

68. G. Macdonald and J. Hook to Aberdeen, Jan. 1, 1844, FO 84/505; E. Gabriel to Russell, Nov. 25, 1859, FO 84/1076; Lt. Sprigg to Aberdeen, July 11, 1844, FO 84/555; Admiralty to Palmerston, June 18, 1850, enc. Comm. Fanshawe, Apr. 10, 1850, FO 84/826; Comm. Wise to Grey, Oct. 17, 1857, Adm. 123/173.

69. Admiralty to Palmerston, Mar. 29, 1849, enc. Comm. Hotham, Dec. 5, 1848, FO 84/782.

70. In the 1850s slave and produce exports combined cannot have totaled more than $5 million per year. The population of Africa south of the equator, west of the great lakes and north of the Zambezi watershed would have had to have been only 5 million strong for the inhabitants to have received even $1 a year in mean per capita export revenue. Even the lowest estimates of the central African population are in excess of this.

71. Ralph A. Austen, "From the Atlantic to the Indian Ocean: European Abolition, the African Slave Trade, and Asian Economic Structures," in David Eltis and James Walvin (eds.), *The Abolition of the Atlantic Slave Trade* (Madison, Wis., 1981), pp. 117–39. For the volume of the Islamic traffic, see idem, "The Islamic Slave Trade out of Africa (Red Sea and Indian Ocean): An Effort at Quantification," unpublished paper, 1977, pp. 27–30; R. W. Beachey, "Some Observations on the Volume of the Slave Trade of Eastern Africa in the 19th Century," *African Historical Demography,* 1 (1977):365–72.

72. Alpers, *Ivory and Slaves in East Central Africa* (Berkeley, Calif., 1975), pp. 185–203; A. F. Isaacman, *Mozambique: The Africanization of a European Institution: The Zambezi Prazos, 1750–1902* (Madison, Wis., 1972), pp. 79–93, 95–110; app. A. The British commissioners at the Cape talked to the various Portuguese officials who touched there. See, in particular, their report to Palmerston, Mar. 30, 1849, FO 84/755, printed in part in IUP, *Slave Trade,* 37:77.

73. Admiralty to Palmerston, July 9, 1847, sub enc. Capt. Cornwallis Ricketts, Apr. 29, 1847, FO 84/705; Admiralty to Aberdeen, May 1, 1845, sub enc. Lt. Barnard, Oct. 26, 1844, FO 84/610; G. Frere and F. R. Surtees to Palmerston Jan. 2, 1851, FO 84/833; Thomas Bellott to Buxton, Nov. 1, 1836, 29/294, Buxton mss.; Admiralty to Palmerston, Dec. 1, 1837, sub enc. Lt. Bosanquet, Sept. 29, 1837, FO 84/229A.

74. Admiralty to Palmerston, Feb. 11, 1841, enc. Lt. J. Adams, Sept. 19, 1840, FO 84/383; G. Frere and F. R. Surtees to Aberdeen, Apr. 25, 1844, FO 84/515; Admiralty to Palmerston, Sept. 22, 1838, sub enc. Lt. Bosanquet, Apr. 9, 1838, FO 84/264; Admiralty to Palmerston, Mar. 17, 1847, sub enc. Lt. Barnard, Aug. 15, 1846, FO 84/703. This last document is an indispensable source for the southeast African slave trade. It may be found also in Adm. 1/5575 and a long extract was published in PP, 1847–48, 64:274–76.

75. Lieutenant–Governor Abreu de Madeira of Quelimane began this practice in 1843. The Portuguese government withheld approval, but Governor General Abreu de Lima granted further informal authorization in 1844 (G. Frere and F. R. Surtees to Palmerston, Nov. 25, 1846, enc. Lt. Barnard, Nov. 21, 1846, FO 84/623). Written authority followed in 1845 (Admiralty to Aberdeen, Oct. 8, 1845, sub enc. Comm. Ricketts, May 8, 1845, FO 84/612). This was withdrawn in July 1846 but reinstated for three years more formally through a protocol of a conference held in

London in 1847. It was renewed again in 1850 (G. Frere and F. R. Surtees to Palmerston, Jan. 2, 1851, FO 84/833, conveniently summarizes the story). An incomplete account may be found in G. S. Graham, *Great Britain in the Indian Ocean, 1810–1850* (Oxford, 1967), p. 127.

76. The small Portuguese squadron under Captain do Valle based at Mozambique captured several slave ships and raided barracoons independently of the British. British historians have tended to give more prominence to activities such as those of the lieutenant–governor of Quillemane, Major Teixera, who after abetting the traffic absconded on a slave ship to Rio de Janeiro. R. W. Beachey (*Slave Trade of Eastern Africa* [London, 1976], p. 16) erroneously cites the principal in this incident as the governor of Mozambique.

77. G. Frere and F. R. Surtees to Aberdeen, Oct. 15, 1845, FO 84/567; April 6, 1846, FO 84/623; G. Frere and F. R. Surtees to Palmerston, Jan. 2, 1851, FO 84/833; Admiralty to Palmerston, Sept. 18, 1849, sub enc. Capt. Watson, July 11, 1849, FO 84/784.

78. G. Frere and F. R. Surtees to Palmerston, Sept. 17, 1846, FO 84/623. The Sultan of Angoche was actually of Persian origin.

79. Admiralty to Malmesbury, Nov. 16, 1852, enc. Capt. Wyvill, Oct. 4, 1852, FO 84/895.

80. Admiralty to Palmerston, Nov. 27, 1850, enc. Capt. Wyvill, July 26, 1850, FO 84/828; G. Frere and F. R. Surtees to Palmerston, Jan. 2, 1851, FO 84/833. Angoche did not come under Portuguese control until 1861. For the joint attack on Pemba Bay, see Admiralty to Palmerston, Mar. 28, 1846, sub enc. Comm. Crawford, Nov. 25, 1845, FO 84/657.

81. See, for example, G. Frere and F. R. Surtees to Palmerston, Jan. 2, 1851, FO 84/833; Admiralty to Palmerston, Jan. 1, 1851, enc. Comm. Bunce, June 8, 1850, FO 84/863. For the treaties see Beachey, *Slave Trade of Eastern Africa,* pp. 51–54; and R. Coupland, *East Africa and Its Invaders* (Oxford, 1938), pp. 503–23.

82. G. Frere and F. R. Surtees to Russell, Sept. 18, 1862, FO 84/1169.

83. Alpers, *Ivory and Slaves,* in particular, chaps. 6 and 7.

84. The large slave exports of the late 1840s, for example, were reported to have ruined agriculture in the Sena area (Admiralty to Palmerston, Jan. 31, 1849, enc. Admiral Dacres, Dec. 1, 1848, FO 84/782). For clove production, see Frederick Cooper, *Plantation Slavery on the East Coast of Africa* (New Haven, Conn., 1977), pp. 47–67, 130–36.

85. Captain Browne to Admiralty, May 8, 1815 (enc.), Adm. 1/1560; F. Hopkins to Lord Arden, June 26, 1816 (enc.), HCA 49/101; Captain G. R. Collier to Admiralty, March 15, 1819, Adm. 1/1673.

86. There is a suggestion of this system being used north of the line in 1812 when, as a result of war, the British had an almost free hand at capturing slave ships. See Captain Irby to Admiralty Nov. 23, 1812, enc. Lt. Pascoe, Nov. 7, 1812, Adm. 1/1997.

87. "After a passage of fifty days . . . I stopped at River Shebar . . . to obtain information on what business was doing on the Coast of Africa," wrote the master of a French ship in words that could have been written at any point in the seventeenth and eighteenth centuries. "Leave nothing in the country; but . . . bring back, in produce, the value of the overplus," instructed the owner of another ship (J. Reffel and D. M. Hamilton to Canning, Apr 10, 1825 (enc.), FO 84/38).

88. Captain Owen to Admiralty, Feb. 21, 1828, enc. "Report on Old Calabar River," and July 14, 1828, Adm. 1/2273; Admiralty to Palmerston, July 30, 1841, FO 84/384; Admiralty to Aberdeen, Nov. 18, 1842 (sub enc.), FO 84/442; Miller, "Commercial Organization of Slaving at Luanda," pp. 97–98.

89. A. Jones, *From Slaves to Palm Kernels,* pp. 42–44. W. Macleay to Aberdeen, July 21, 1829 (enc.), FO 84/100; Admiralty to Palmerston, May 14, 1841, sub enc. Lt. Norcock, Jan. 26, 1841, FO 84/384; H. W. Macaulay and R. Doherty to Palmerston, Nov. 30, 1838, FO 84/23. Emilio Martins, the head of the Lagos factory was also a partner of Gantois and Martins of Bahia, (Admiralty to Palmerston, July 30, 1841 [enc.], FO 84/384).

90. Admiralty to Palmerston, Feb. 18, 1841 (enc.), FO 84/383; Adm. to Aberdeen, July 25, 1842 (enc.), FO 84/440; W. W. Lewis and J. Campbell to Palmerston, Sept. 5, 1836 (enc.), FO 84/192; Capt. Rodney Mundy to Capt. R. Fitzroy, Jan. 18, 1843, FO 84/501.

91. Admiralty to Malmesbury, May 8, 1852, sub enc. Lt. Drew, Feb. 20, 1852, FO 84/894; Admiralty to Russell, Jan. 24, 1853, sub enc. Comm. Wilmot, Sept. 29, 1852, FO 84/925.

92. The contract between Angel Ximenes of the Martínez firm and one of the Gallinas headmen in 1839 reads in part, "I Lusini Rogers, Chief and Proprietor in the Gallinas river do grant, sell and dispose to Angel Ximenes for the sum of $5000.00 to me . . . the peninsular of Drumbocarro, its lands appurtenances . . . granting him also the free use of the [illegible] River and fishing grounds." (Admiralty to Aberdeen, Mar. 29, 1845, enc. Comm. Jones, Feb. 5, 1845, FO 84/609).

93. For a Spanish network covering the Congo, Cabinda, Black Point (Pointe Noire) and Loango see Admiralty to Aberdeen, July 25, 1842, enc. Comm. Adams, May 7, 1842, FO 84/440. For others in Angola, see Admiralty to Palmerston, Aug. 1, 1840, enc. Rear Adm. Elliot, April 29, 1840, FO 84/340. See also Admiralty to Palmerston, May 26, 1847, enc. Comm. Hotham, Apr. 7, 1847, FO 84/704. For the Bight of Benin, see H. Foote to Russell, Feb. 9, 1861, FO 84/1141. After the publication of Lord Aberdeen's letter of 1842, the trading goods were thought to be secure from British attack and warehouses for them were maintained close to the shore itself. In the Congo River, the island of Puerto de Lenha became the great depository of goods for slaves embarked many miles away north and south of the river mouth (J. Hudson to Palmerston, July 14, 1851, enc. anon., June 26, 1851, FO 84/845).

94. Admiralty to Malmesbury, Oct. 16, 1858, enc. Comm. Wise, Aug. 12, 1858, FO 84/1070; A. Jones, *From Slaves to Palm Kernels,* p. 62.

95. Consul Freeman to Lord John Russell, May 9, and July 1, 1862, FO 84/1175. For slave traders' advice to African rulers on the legality of British initiatives, see Admiralty to Aberdeen, Mar. 19, 1845, enc. Comm. Jones, Feb. 5, 1845, FO 84/609. At Ambriz in 1852 a visit from the squadron was the occasion of a major increase in rent for the slave dealers as compensation for the refusal of the Ambriz chiefs to sign as antislave-trade treaty (G. Jackson and E. Gabriel to Malmesbury, Jan. 25, 1853, FO 84/902).

96. Admiralty to Malmesbury, May 3, 1852, sub enc. Comm. Sotheby, FO 84/894.

97. The 1835 Anglo-Spanish treaty, the 1839 and 1845 acts and the 1842 Anglo-Portuguese treaties provided for the breaking up of the condemned ships. Prior to this, condemned ships were sold to the highest bidder. Ships condemned at the Portuguese prize court in Luanda continued to be auctioned until the decree of Sept. 14, 1846 (G. Jackson and E. Gabriel to Palmerston, Nov. 19, 1846, FO 84/671).

98. Admiralty to Palmerston, Apr. 17, 1849, sub enc. Capt. Jones, Feb. 6, 1849, FO 84/783; Admiralty to Aberdeen, July 25, 1842, enc. Comm. Adams, May 7, 1842, FO 84/440.

99. In 1844 Conneau was building a vessel of about 150 tons at his factory (Comm. Perry, Oct. 21, 1844, enc. extract of Lt. Craven. Oct. 16, 1844, LSN, reel 101). This may have been the same vessel that was rowed out to sea in 1846. (J. Hook and

N. Macdonald to Palmerston, Jan. 27, 1847, FO 84/665). These incidents are not mentioned in Conneau's autobiography (*A Slaver's Log Book or 20 Years' Residence in Africa* [Englewood Cliffs, N.J., 1976]. Most transatlantic vessels built in Africa were constructed in the Congo River in the early 1850s and early 1860s at the end of the Brazilian and Cuban trades, respectively. Commodore H. Bruce pointed out that he had no power to destroy these ships prior to launching (Admiralty to Palmerston, Aug. 21, 1851, sub enc. Comm. Chamberlain, June 8, 1851, FO 84/865; Admiralty to Granville, Jan. 7, 1852, enc. Comm. Bruce, Oct. 17, 1851, FO 84/892; Admiralty to Malmesbury, Mar. 26, 1852, enc. Comm. Bruce, Jan. 23, 1852, FO 84/893; G. Jackson and E. Gabriel to Palmerston, Dec. 23, 1846, FO 84/672; E. Gabriel to Russell, Aug. 8, 1862, FO 84/1167; Admiralty to Clarendon, Jan. 12, 1866, enc. Comm. Wilmot, Dec. 19, 1865, FO 84/1267.) For evidence of manufacturing in the Congo River, see, Admiralty to Malmesbury, July 10, 1852, sub enc. Lt. Wise, Apr. 9, 1852, FO 84/895. For Cabindan shipbuilding activity and its possible connection with transatlantic ventures, see Martin, "Cabinda and the Cabindans," pp. 89–91. Two Cabindan launches made the voyage to Brazil with slaves in 1847 (G. Jackson and E. Gabriel to Palmerston, Apr. 2, 1847, FO 84/671). I wish to thank Phyllis Martin for this reference.

100. In 1852 Havana dealers sent out ships without first establishing a shore-based factory, perhaps expecting to use the remnants of the Brazilian network. The difficulties they encountered are described in G. Jackson and E. Gabriel to Russell, Jan. 25, 1853, FO 84/902, and captured slave merchants' correspondence in H. Howard to Clarendon, Feb. 11, 1854 (enc.), FO 84/942. At the very end of the traffic, there is some evidence that slave traders were abandoning these elaborate factories and going back to the supercargo system. The supercargo would arrive at some region where domestic slavery was extensive and use specie to assemble a small or medium-sized cargo quickly. The essence of this was mobility and speed. There were instances of this in the Rio Pongo area (Admiralty to Russell, Nov. 18, 1864, sub enc. E. King to Mr. Nicol, Sept. 19, 1864, FO 84/1229) and on the southeast coast where extensive networks of slaves for the supply of other regions existed, usually controlled by Banians. For the activities of one supercargo, Buona Ventura Mas, see Col. Rigby to Russell, July 12, 1861, FO 84/1120. There is no evidence of this system in the Bight of Benin.

101. Infra, n. 104.

102. Northrup, "Compatibility of the Slave and Palm Oil Trades," pp. 353–64; idem, "Nineteenth-Century Patterns of Slavery and Economic Growth in Southeastern Nigeria," *International Journal of African Historical Studies,* 12 (1979):1–16.

103. A. G. Hopkins, *An Economic History of West Africa* (New York, 1973), pp. 125–34, reviews the evidence. Paul E. Lovejoy (*Transformations in Slavery* [Cambridge, 1983], pp. 159–83), finesses the question by arguing that the external slave trade created slave-based societies in Africa that in turn eased the transition to a commodity exporting economy. The commodities were produced by slaves. For a fuller discussion of Lovejoy's position see chap. 13.

104. This conclusion is supported by regression analysis. Annual time series for the period 1811–65 are available for palm oil imports into the United Kingdom, for the ratio of slave ventures lost through naval action to the total of all ventures launched and for slave departures from Africa. In addition a quinquennial series of slave prices in Africa is possible for the years 1821–65. Palm oil imports may be taken as a proxy for alternative uses of labor in Africa. Britain was not the only customer for palm oil, but she was by far the largest. The trend in the British figures may be taken to reflect the growth of demand in all European centers, including

Marseilles and Hamburg. The data themselves were collected from Customs 4, vols. 5–53. The data were not, unfortunately, recorded by African region of provenance. Some of the data appear in the Parliamentary Papers and in Latham, *Old Calabar*, pp. 56–57. A multiple regression of quinquennial transatlantic slave departures from all Africa on slave prices, and palm oil imports into the United Kingdom explained 87 percent of the variations in slave exports between 1821 and 1865. Slave exports varied directly with slave prices and inversely with palm oil imports, and the coefficients were highly significant. The price coefficient suggests that a dollar increase in the price of slaves was consistent with an increase of 1,149 slaves per year leaving Africa. Using mean values of price and slave departures, this means a 10 percent rise in the former generated slightly more than a 9 percent rise in quantities of slaves sold. A regression was also run on annual, as opposed to quinquennial data. In this case the slave price data are not good enough to include, but palm oil imports and loss ratios explain 56 percent of the annual fluctuation in slave exports between 1816 and 1865. Slave exports varied inversely with both the independent variables. The loss ratio coefficient, however, was not significant at the 20 percent level and explained less than 1 percent of the export fluctuations.

The two equations are (standard errors in first row of parentheses, $F$ statistic in second):

$$(1) \quad X = 272.3 + 1.149P - 0.085OM$$
$$\qquad\quad (223.3) \quad (0.4) \qquad (0.016)$$
$$\qquad\quad\; (1.5) \quad (9.5) \qquad (28.9)$$

$$n = 9$$
$$r^2 = 0.87$$

$$(2) \quad X = 832.5 - 0.079OM - 0.176L$$
$$\qquad\quad (56.5) \quad (0.013) \qquad (0.37)$$
$$\qquad\quad (216.9) \, (33.4) \qquad\;\; (0.23)$$

$$n = 50$$
$$r^2 = 0.56$$

Where $X$ = five-year mean annual slave exports from Africa ('000).

$P$ = five-year mean slave prices in constant dollars (1821–25 = 100).

$OM$ = palm oil imports into the United Kingdom ('000 cwt).

$L$ = five-year mean annual slave ships lost/total number of slave-ships ventured.

Remembering that the loss ratio reflects only naval activity and not the response of the Brazilian and Cuban governments to British pressure, these results are entirely in accord with the discussion in the text.

## Chapter 11

1. The actual ratio of British cotton imports from the U.S. to the total United States' crop was 56 percent in 1820 and 49 percent in 1850 (calculated from J. A. Mann, *The Cotton Trade of Great Britain* [Manchester, Eng., 1860], table 12; and James L. Watkins, *Production and the Price of Cotton for One Hundred Years* [U.S. Dept. of Agriculture, Misc. Bulletin, no. 9, 1895], pp. 5, 8). Foreign-grown sugar accounted for 14.3 percent of British imports, 1846–50 (see Roberta M. Delson, "Sugar Production for the Nineteenth Century British Market: Rethinking the Roles of Brazil and the British West Indies," in Bill Albert and Adrian Graves [eds.], *Crisis and*

*Change in the International Sugar Economy, 1860-1914* [Norwich, 1984], p. 78). The equivalent coffee ratio was 15.8 percent (PP, 1856, 55:278-79, 292-93).

2. For the direction of Brazilian exports in 1844 and 1845, see the *Rio Mercantile Journal*, Oct. 24, 1846 enc. in H. Hamilton to Palmerston, Nov. 4, 1846, FO 84/634. For Cuban data, see J. Kennedy to Palmerston (enc.), Mar. 20, 1848, FO 84/714; Francisco Pérez de la Riva y Pons, *El café: historia de su cultivo y explotación en Cuba* (Havana, 1944), p. 73. Manuel Moreno Fraginals, *El ingenio, complejo económico social cubano del azúcar,* 3 vols. (Havana, 1978):3:69-70 provides a slightly different breakdown for Cuba.

3. For the response of British colonies to abolition in a comparative perspective, see Stanley L. Engerman, "Economic Adjustments to Emancipation in the United States and the British West Indies," *Journal of Interdisciplinary History,* 13 (1982):191-205. For British Guiana markets from the 1850s, see Alan H. Adamson, *Sugar Without Slaves: The Political Economy of British Guiana, 1838-1904* (New Haven, Conn., 1972), pp. 214-35.

4. In addition to the sources in table 8, see Mann, *Cotton Trade,* pp. 95-96; Noel Deerr, *The History of Sugar,* 2 vols. (London, 1949-50), 2:530-31; John J. McCusker, "The Rum Trade and the Balance of Payments of the Thirteen Continental Colonies, 1650-1775." Ph.D. diss., University of Pittsburgh, 1970, pp. 1143-48; PP, 1856, 55:588-89.

5. Slave prices among the British West Indies possessions (not shown in figure 8) developed very large differentials in the quarter century after the abolition of the slave trade. Prices in British Guiana and Trinidad were only a little below those in the United States in the 1820s and were greatly in excess of those anywhere else in the Americas (supra, p. 296, n. 19; Engerman, "Economic Adjustments to Emancipation," p. 142; Laurence J. Kotlikoff, "The Structure of Slave Prices in New Orleans, 1804 to 1862," *Economic Inquiry,* 17 (1979):496-517.

6. Ulrich Bonnell Phillips, "The Economic Cost of Slaveholding in the Cotton Belt," *Political Science Quarterly,* 20 (1905):257-75; Ulrich Bonnell Phillips, *American Negro Slavery: A Survey of the Supply Employment and Control of Negro Labor as Determined by the Plantation Regime* (New York, 1918), pp. 359-401; Robert W. Fogel and Stanley L. Engerman, *Time on the Cross: The Economics of American Negro Slavery,* 2 vols. (Boston, 1979), 1:59-106; 2:54-87.

7. William N. Parker and Judith L. V. Klein estimated that in the case of wheat the shift westward between 1840-60 and 1900-10 increased output per acre by 18 percent compared to 299 percent improvements attributable to other factors ("Productivity Growth in Grain Production in the United States: 1850-1910," in National Bureau of Economic Research Studies in Income and Wealth, Vol. 30, *Output, Employment and Productivity in the United States after 1800* [New York, 1966], p. 533).

8. Norman S. Buck, *The Development of the Organization of Anglo-American Trade, 1800-1850* (New Haven, Conn., 1925), in particular chaps. 3 and 4; John Killick, "Risk, Specialization and Profit in the Mercantile Sector of the Nineteenth-Century Cotton Trade: Alexander Brown and Sons, 1800-80," *Business History,* 16 (1974):1-16; Douglass C. North, "Sources of Productivity Change in Ocean Shipping," *Journal of Political Economy,* 76 (1968):953-70; Charles K. Harley, "The Shift from Sailing Ships to Steamships, 1850-1890: A Study in Technological Change and Its Diffusion," in Donald N. McCloskey (ed.), *Essays on a Mature Economy: Britain After 1840* (Princeton, N.J., 1971), pp. 215-34.

9. Did change over time in any of these variables result in overstatement of the productivity measurement? On the crop-mix issue, for example, planters could have

shifted resources from food production into main-crop activities and thus inflated productivity measurements based on main-crop output alone (Cf. Robert W. Fogel and Stanley L. Engerman, "Explaining the Relative Efficiency of Slave Agriculture in the Antebellum South," *American Economic Review*, 67 (1977):288–90). At the time of first measurement of productivity, however, there was already considerable specialization within the main-crop plantations and major bias from this source is unlikely. For the age structure (labor-force), variable, the bias is toward understating productivity. In the British West Indies approximately 70 percent of the slave population was over the age of fourteen in 1817. Age profiles of the population for that and adjacent years suggest that the over-fourteen ratio was higher than this in 1810 and probably much lower in 1830 (Barry Higman, *Slave Populations of the British Carribean 1807-1824*, [Baltimore, 1984], pp. 137, 462–68). In Cuba the ratio of the slave population over fifteen (actually males over fifteen and females over twelve) dropped from 82 percent in 1827 to 72 percent in 1861 (Cuba, *Cuadro estadístico de la siempre fiel isla de Cuba correspondiente al año de 1827* [Havana, 1829], p. 90 [foldout]; Cuba, *Noticias estadísticas de la Isla de Cuba en 1862* [Havana, 1864] unpaginated). For *ingenio* records that show similar trends, see Moreno Fraginals, *El ingenio*, 2:83–90. There are no reliable census data for Brazil in the immediate aftermath of suppression, but the experience of other plantation societies and the known age patterns of African arrivals suggest that, in the generation after the ending of trade in 1852, the number of effective workers must have fallen here, also. In the coffee-growing region of Vassouras, for example, there was a steady decline in the ratio of slaves in the fifteen to forty age group from the 1840s to the 1880s (Stanley J. Stein, *Vassouras, a Brazilian Coffee County, 1850-1900* [Cambridge, Mass., 1957], p. 79). On the hours-worked issue we might assume that slaves were already being worked the maximum number of hours per week consistent with profit maximization at the beginning of the periods covered in table 11. In the British West Indies work hours were reduced somewhat in the early nineteenth century owing largely to ameliorative legislation (Higman, *Slave Populations*, pp. 181–88).

10. Between 1800 and 1840 in the United States, man-hours required to produce 100 bushels of wheat fell by 38 percent, for the same amount of corn by 20 percent and for a bale of cotton by 27 percent (Stanley Lebergott, *The Americans: An Economic Record* (New York, 1984), p. 301). For trends in the second half of the century see Parker and Judith Klein, "Productivity Growth in Grain Production in the United States, 1840-60 to 1900-10," pp. 523–82; and William N. Parker, "Labour Productivity in Cotton Farming: The History of a Research," *Agricultural History*, 53 (1979): pp. 228–44.

11. Declared values of exports were taken from Ralph Davis, *The Industrial Revolution and British Overseas Trade* (Leicester, 1979), p. 15. These values are divided by the total occupied British population less workers in the public service and the domestic and personal service categories, which are taken from Phyllis Deane and W. A. Cole, *British Economic Growth, 1688-1959*, 2nd ed. (Cambridge, 1969), p. 143. Productivity trends in the British cotton industry are calculated from M. Blaug, "The Productivity of Capital in the Lancashire Cotton Industry During the Nineteenth Century," *Economic History Review*, 13 (1961):366.

12. The share of the U.S. slave population living on cotton farms grew from approximately 12 percent in the first decade of the nineteenth century (U.S. Congress, H. Doc., no. 146, 24–1, p. 16) to 73 percent in 1850, though not all of these were actually growing cotton (Fogel and Engerman, *Time on the Cross*, 1:41–42).

13. For sugar and coffee trends see, app. F. For copper exports see the British consular reports from Santiago de Cuba in the FO/72 series, in particular Wright to Palmer-

ston, Jan. 15, 1841 (enc.) FO 72/587. See also, J. Kennedy to Palmerston, Mar. 20, 1848, FO 84/714. Trends in tobacco production are taken from Ramon de la Sagra, *Cuba en 1860: selección de articulos sobre agricultura cubana* (Havana, 1963) ed. Manuel Moreno Fraginals, pp. 174–78; and José García de Arboleya, *Manuel de la isla de Cuba . . .* (Havana, 1859), cited in Franklin W. Knight, *Slave Society in Cuba During the Nineteenth Century* (Madison, Wis., 1970), p. 65.

14. For the distribution of coffee output by department in 1846 and 1862, see Cuban Economic Research Project, *A Study on Cuba: The Colonial and Republican Periods* (Coral Gables, Fla. 1965), p. 75.

15. A regression of coffee exports on slave prices and slave imports supports this conclusion (standard errors in first set of parenthesis, F statistic in second):

$$CCoffX = 1674.4 - 1.9SLVP + 39.7CUBAM$$
$$(312) \quad (0.39) \quad (14.6)$$
$$(28.2)(24.0) \quad (7.4)$$
$$n = 11$$
$$r^2 = 0.77$$

where $CCoffX$ = Cuban coffee exports in tons.

$CUBAM$ = slave arrivals from Africa in thousands.

$SLVP$ = price of typical bozales debarked in Cuba, in constant dollars $(1821-25 = 100)$.

All data are annual. Note that adequate data on slave prices were available for only eleven years between 1821 and 1865.For data see app. C and F. The slave-price coefficient was significant at the 1 percent level and by itself explained 56 percent of variations in coffee exports. Francisco Pérez de la Riva, among others, has cited rising slave prices as one of several factors in the decline of coffee (*El café*, pp. 68–75).

16. For the 1827 ratio see the discussion in Hugh Thomas, *Cuba: The Pursuit of Freedom* (London, 1971), pp. 169–69. Ratios for 1841, 1846 and 1861 are derived from estimates of the number of slaves and indentured laborers resident in ingenios and cafetales (see app. F) divided by the total population of slaves, Asians and Yucatán Indians in Cuba. For 1861 cf. Knight, *Slave Society in Cuba,* p. 67.

17. J. Kennedy and W. Dalrymple to Palmerston, Jan. 1, 1847, FO 84/667. See also, idem, Jan. 1, 1846, FO 84/620; and Jan. 1, 1844, FO 84/561.

18. J. Kennedy to Palmerston, Jan. 1, 1849, FO 84/753.

19. Fernando Ortiz Fernandez, *Cuban Counterpoint: Tobacco and Sugar,* trans. Harriet de Onis (New York, 1947). For a corrective view, see Jean Stubbs, *Tobacco on the Periphery: A Case Study in Cuban Labor History, 1860-1958* (Cambridge, 1985). Higman, (*Slave Populations,* pp. 46–50) shows that tradesmen and supervisors were almost as numerous as domestic servants in the British Caribbean. Fogel and Engerman (*Time on the Cross,* 1:38–43), show that on a sample of sugar estates in Louisiana, 19 percent of male agricultural workers were supervisors or tradesmen.

20. Spanish colonial restrictions and, in the case of Bahia, proximity to Africa were responsible for this situation before 1789. After this date, war and British attempts to suppress the trade continued to keep Cuban slave prices relatively high. For slave use in mid century Cuba see Stubbs, *Tobacco on the Periphery,* p. 69.

21. The crude rate of decrease is discussed in Manuel Moreno Fraginals, *The Sugarmill: The Socioeconomic Complex of Sugar in Cuba,* trans. Cedric Belfrage (New York, 1976), p. 142. For unresolved issues on the factors determining this trend see Jack Ericson Eblen, "On the Natural Increase of Slave Populations: The Example of the Cuban Black Population, 1775–1900," in Stanley L. Engerman and Eugene D. Ger

ovese (eds.), *Race and Slavery in the Western Hemisphere: Quantitative Studies* (Princeton, N.J., 1975), pp. 211–47. For new evidence on the importance of infant mortality in the Caribbean, see Higman, *Slave Populations,* pp. 25–33, 303–78. For the age and sex imbalances see Manuel Moreno Fraginals, Herbert S. Klein and Stanley L. Engerman, "The Level and Structure of Slave Prices on Cuban Plantations in the Mid-Nineteenth Century: Some Comparative Perspectives," *American Historical Review,* 88 (1983):1203–4; and Kenneth F. Kiple, *Blacks in Colonial Cuba, 1774–1899* (Gainesville, Fla., 1976), pp. 45, 61.

22. Moreno Fraginals et al., "The Level and Structure of Slave Prices," p. 1204; cf. Francisco A. Scarano, *Sugar and Slavery in Puerto Rico: The Plantation Economy of Ponce, 1800–1850* (Madison, Wis.), pp. 137–43, for Puerto Rican trends.

23. A regression of annual slave imports into Cuba on sugar exports, the price of sugar in New York and coffee exports for forty-five years (1821–65), yielded the following result (standard errors in first set of parentheses, $F$ statistics in second):

$$CUBAM = 10.63 + 0.023CSugX + 124.0NYSugP + 0.007CCoffX$$
$$\phantom{CUBAM =} (8.3) \quad (0.01) \qquad\quad (78.8) \qquad\quad (0.002)$$
$$\phantom{CUBAM =} (1.7) \quad (4.8) \qquad\qquad\quad (2.5) \qquad\quad (10.7)$$
$$n = 45$$
$$r^2 = 0.23$$

For key to symbols, see supra, n. 15. In addition:

$CSugX$    = Cuban sugar production in metric tons
$NYSugP$ = Wholesale price of sugar in New York, cents per pound.

The coffee exports and sugar exports variables were significant at the 5 percent level. Other variables, such as the ratio of Cuban slave ventures lost as a result of naval activity and the New York price of coffee, were added to the equation but proved nonsignificant and added little to the $r^2$. For data, see app. A and F. This result is modest, but given the strong increases in output per slave taken up in the text, it is not unexpected.

24. A regression of sugar exports on slave prices yielded the following results (standard errors in first row of parentheses, $F$ statistic in second):

$$CSugX = 3.6 + 0.42SLVP$$
$$\phantom{CSugX =} (45.8) \quad (0.06)$$
$$\phantom{CSugX =} (0.01) \ (43.7)$$
$$n = 11$$
$$r^2 = 0.83$$

For key to symbols, see supra, nn. 15 and 23. For data see app. A and F. The slave-price variable was significant at the 0.1 percent level. Several other variables were included in the equation but none proved significant or increased the $r^2$.

The best interpretation of this result is that major labor-productivity improvements were underway, which only the slave prices in this group of variables captured. If slave productivity had remained constant, we would have expected slave arrivals to have explained a large share of the fluctuations in sugar exports.

25. For values of Cuban sugar and coffee exports, and for slaves and indentured laborers resident on sugar and coffee estates, see app. F. For all three years (1827, 1846 and 1861) the values of exports used were five-year averages centered on 1827, 1846 and 1861. It should be noted that these values incorporate the New York wholesale prices of produce, which would be much greater than their Havana counterparts. The values, therefore, cannot be taken to represent the revenue realized by the slave owner. The trend in the values, however, would approximate the trend in the rev-

enues generated per slave/indentured worker. These estimates are, of course, sensitive to long-run changes in produce prices and the age structure of the population. The former was subject to a relatively mild secular decline. The ratio of slaves over fifteen also declined somewhat (supra, n. 9). Both these trends would bias the above productivity ratios downward. For a counterargument (based on plantation records) that output per worker declined, at least in the later period, see Moreno Fraginals, *El ingenio,* 2:28–29.

26. Rebecca J. Scott, *Slave Emancipation in Cuba: The Transition to Free Labor, 1860–1899* (Princeton, N.J., 1985), pp. 26–35, 90–91, 97–98.

27. Kiple, *Blacks in Colonial Cuba,* pp. 47, 63: Moreno Fraginals, *Sugarmill,* pp. 81–127; Knight, *Slave Society in Cuba,* pp. 30–41. By 1850, 20 percent of the sugar estates had converted to steam-powered grinding mills (J. Kennedy to Palmerston, Jan. 1, 1850, FO 84/789).

28. J. Kennedy to Palmerston, Mar. 20, 1848, FO 84/714.

29. The British commissioners and consul as well as the U.S. consul at Havana commented extensively on the indentured labor business. See, in particular, J. Crawford to Palmerston, Aug. 4, 1847, FO 84/674; J. Crawford to Clarendon, Aug. 7, 1855, FO 84/965; J. Crawford to Russell, Feb. 5, 1861, FO 84/1135; R. Bunch to Russell, Mar. 30, 1865, FO 84/1241. One of the most informative letters, however, was written by the British commissioners at the Cape Colony, another area experiencing labor shortages, on the occasion of the arrival of a shipload of indentured Chinese en route to Cuba (G. Frere and F. Surtees to Clarendon, Apr. 21, 1853, FO 84/901). Note that prices to the plantation owner would be higher than those paid to the shipper. Note also that the trend in prices of contracts is roughly consistent with the trend in slave prices (see app. C); cf. Moreno Fraginals, *Sugarmill,* pp. 140–41, and Scott, *Slave Emancipation in Cuba,* pp. 28–35.

30. For arrivals in the British West Indies, see K. O. Laurence, *Immigration into the West Indies in the 19th Century* (St. Lawrence, Barbados, 1971), pp. 13–39; Dwaka Nath, *A History of Indians in British Guiana* (London, 1950), pp. 179–80; Engerman, "Economic Change and Contract Labour," pp. 141–45 and the literature cited there.

31. Instituto brasileiro de geografia e estatística, *Anuário estatístico do Brazil,* Ano V, pp. 1374–6.

32. Statement of Mr. Freese, "who is engaged in the Brazil Trade," PP, 1830–31, 9:511. See also, Robert Walsh, *Notices of Brazil in 1828 and 1829,* 2 vols. (London, 1829–30), 1:451; 2:535–36.

33. J. Hudson to Palmerston, Oct. 10, 1848, GC/HU/6, Broadlands mss.

34. App. F.

35. B. Newcomen to Aberdeen, Feb. 3, 1845, FO 84/584. For developments in the cotton sector, see Luís Amaral, *História geral da agricultura brasileira,* 2 vols. (São Paulo, 1958), 2:3–47.

36. Catherine Lugar, "The Portuguese Tobacco Trade and Tobacco Growers of Bahia in the Late Colonial Period," in Dauril Alden and Warren Dean (eds.), *Essays Concerning the Socioeconomic History of Brazil and Portuguese India* (Gainesville, Fla.,) pp. 53–57. For re-exports of slaves from Bahia, see E. Porter to Palmerston, Dec. 31, 1846, FO 84/632.

37. See Claudia Dale Goldin, *Urban Slavery in the American South, 1820–1860: A Quantitative History* (Chicago, 1976).

38. Sugar exports from Rio de Janeiro were valued at two-thirds of coffee exports in 1828, but by 1845 the ratio had fallen to only 12.5 percent and during the coffee boom in the late 1840s fell further to 7 percent. Absolute volumes of sugar export

also declined substantially (Walsh, *Notices of Brazil* 2:536; R. Hesketh and F. Grigg to Aberdeen, Mar. 11, 1846, FO 84/622; Thomas Westwood to Palmerston, Feb. 17, 1848, FO 84/727; Feb. 28, 1849, FO 84/767; R. Hesketh to Palmerston, Mar. 14, 1850, FO 84/808; Mar. 3, 1851, FO 84/848. See also T. Nelson, *Remarks on the Slavery and Slave Trade of the Brazils* [London, 1846], p. 83). Sugar production in Rio Claro, north of Santos, also declined after 1836 (Warren Dean, *Rio Claro: A Brazilian Plantation System, 1820–1920* [Stanford, Calif., 1976], p. 26) and political unrest and a prolonged drought hampered expansion in the Pernambuco region in the 1840s (see H. Augustus Cowper to Palmerston, Mar. 2, 1846, FO 84/632). The expansion of Brazilian sugar exports shown in table 13 must therefore have been concentrated in Bahia. For Bahian slave imports, see app. A. Some re-exports of slaves to Pernambuco and Rio de Janeiro occurred in this period, but the vast majority of arrivals were absorbed into the Bahian sugar sector.

39. Regressions were run with several variables, including ship losses and coffee exports and prices, though not, unfortunately, slave prices where the data are inadequate. The best result was (standard errors in first row of parentheses, *F* statistic in second):

$$BAHIAM = -8.27 + 0.065\ BRSugX + 0.447\ BRSugP$$
$$(3.7)\quad (0.02)\qquad\quad (0.12)$$
$$(5.1)\quad (9.0)\qquad\quad (13.8)$$
$$n = 30$$
$$r^2 = 0.36$$

Where

$BAHIAM$ = slave imports into Bahia in thousands.
$BRSugX$ = sugar exports from Brazil in metric tons.
$BRSugP$ = average value of sugar exported in constant dollars per ton.

All data are annual for the years 1821 to 1850.
All coefficients significant at the one percent level. For data see app. A and F. Again the modesty of this result is explained in part by rising output per worker during the period covered by the data.

40. See, for example, Peter Eisenberg, *The Sugar Industry in Pernambuco: Modernization Without Change, 1840–1910* (Berkeley, Calif., 1974), pp. 36–39; the chapter on sugar in Amaral, *História geral da agricultura brasileira,* 1:326–407; J. H. Galloway, "The Sugar Industry of Pernambuco during the Nineteenth Century," *Annals of the Association of American Geographers* 58 (1968):285–303. On the impact of diamond discoveries, see Admiralty to Palmerston, June 19, 1846, enc. Comm. Montgomery, Apr. 9, 1846, FO 84/658; H. Augustus Cowper to Palmerston, Mar. 2, 1846, FO 84/632.

41. See the letters from the Pilkingtons in G79, Brit. Emp. mss., in particular, Charlotte Pilkington to Tredgold, Feb. 24, 1840; see also "Correspondent," Pernambuco, May 30, 1843, in 44/76, Buxton mss. For an analysis of urban slavery stressing the wide range of slave occupations see Mary Karasch, "From Porterage to Proprietorship: African Occupations in Rio de Janeiro, 1808–50," in Engerman and Genovese, *Race and Slavery,* pp. 369–93; and in Buenos Aires, George Reid Andrews, *The Afro-Argentinians of Buenos Aires, 1800–1900* (Madison, Wis., 1980), pp. 29–41.

42. Amilcar Martins Filho and Roberto B. Martins, "Slavery in a Nonexport Economy: Nineteenth-Century Minas Gerais Revisited," *Hispanic American Historial Review,* 63 (1983):537–68; Stuart B. Schwartz, "Patterns of Slaveholding in the Americas: New Evidence from Brazil," *American Historical Review,* 87 (1982):55–86.

43. A productivity ratio of a half-ton-of-coffee-per-slave exported seems reasonable for

the 1850s (see app. F, table 9). Applying this to Brazilian coffee exports for 1851–55 (ibid., table 4) suggests the 311,000 figure. This argument also suggests that the Martins and Martins projection backward of a productivity ratio for the 1880s is an inappropriate procedure. In the early 1850s slave prices and probably productivity were lower, and the slave labor force necessary to produce a given amount of coffee higher than in the 1880s. ("Slavery in a Nonexport Economy," pp. 547–48.) Thus the Martins and Martins estimates of slaves in coffee should be revised upward. The estimate of 24 percent of the slave population in coffee is derived from the 311,000 calculated above, divided by a projection backward of Robert W. Slenes's computations from the 1872 census. A rate of natural decrease of 7.5 per thousand is assumed—the midpoint of Slenes's range ("The Demography and Economics of Brazilian Slavery: 1850–1888." Ph.D. diss., Stanford University, 1976, pp. 57, 369).

44. Total values of slave imports for each of the decades 1821–30, 1831–40 and 1841–50 are calculated from app. A and C. Export values are taken from *Anuário estatístico* Ano V, p. 1358. The actual ratios are 1821–30, 0.38; 1831–40, 0.25; 1841–50, 0.34.

45. Regressions of slave imports were run on a number of different independent variables, including coffee and sugar exports as well as coffee and sugar prices, all in annual values. The best result was (standard errors in first row of parentheses, $F$ statistic in second):

$$RIOM = 22.6 - 57.4SHLOSS + 0.011BRCoffX$$
$$(4.8) \quad (40.3) \quad (0.005)$$
$$(22.5) \quad (2.0) \quad (3.8)$$
$$n = 30$$
$$r^2 = 0.12$$

Where
   $RIOM$ = slave imports into Brazil south of Bahia in thousands.
   $SHLOSS$ = ships lost through naval action divided by the total number of slave ventures launched.
   $BRCoffX$ = coffee exports from Brazil in metric tons.

All data are annual for the years 1821 to 1850. For data see app. A and F. The coefficients were significant at the 20 percent level. As noted above for the regressions of slave imports into Bahia and Cuba, the modesty of this result is explained in part by rising output per slave. For the Brazil south equation there is however the additional fact that the abolition-induced drop in slave imports in the early 1830s coincided with the rapid growth of coffee exports. Furthermore a number of crops other than coffee and sugar were absorbing slaves in the 1820s.

46. Emília Viotti da Costa, *Da senzala à colônia* (São Paulo, 1966), pp. 177–86; Stein, *Vassouras*, pp. 47, 91; Nathaniel H. Leff, "Economic Retardation in Nineteenth-Century Brazil," *Economic History Review*, 25 (1972):491.

47. See sources supra, pp. 372–73, n. 38.

48. The actual ratios were: coffee, 42.6 percent; sugar, 26.2 percent (*Anuário estatístico* Ano V, p. 1379).

49. For prices see app. C. Cf. the doubling in the share of planter assets comprising slaves in Vassouras. See Pedro Carvalho de Mello, "The Economics of Labor in Brazilian Coffee Plantations, 1850–88." Ph.D. diss., University of Chicago, 1977, p. 21. For the internal slave trade see Slenes "The Demography and Economics of Brazilian Slavery," pp. 120–233, in particular p. 145. As William L. Miller has pointed out in the case of the U.S. South, the internal shift of slaves does not indicate that slavery as an institution was dying in the source areas but merely that

slaves were more productive in the receiving zones ("A Note on the Importance of the Interstate Slave Trade of the Antebellum South," *Journal of Political Economy*, 73 [1965]:181–87; cf. Laurence J. Kotlikoff and Sebastian E. Pinera, "The Old South's Stake in the Inter-Regional Movement of Slaves, 1850–1860," *Journal of Economic History*, 37 [1977]:434–50).

50. Herbert S. Klein, *The Middle Passage* (Princeton, N.J., 1978), pp. 95–120; Martins and Martins, "Slavery in a Non-export Economy," pp. 552–56; and Robert W. Slenes, "Comment on 'Slavery in a Non-export Economy,'" *Hispanic American Historical Review*, 63 (1983):576–79.

51. Martins and Martins, "Slavery in a Non-export Economy," p. 547; C. F. Van Delden Laërne, *Brazil and Java. Report on Coffee Culture in America, Asia and Africa* (London, 1885), pp. 125–52.

52. Space constraints prevent discussion of the French Caribbean. It should be noted, however, that in Guadaloupe in the fifteen or so years between the ending of the slave trade and the ending of slavery itself, the same pattern of a shift to monoculture emerged. Although sugar output declined somewhat, the secondary crops of coffee, cotton and cocoa declined by much more (Christian Schnakenbourg, *Histoire de l'industrie sucrière en Guadaloupe aux XIXe et XXe siècles*. Tome 1: *La Crise du système esclavagiste (1835–1847)* (Paris, 1980), pp. 137–46.

53. J. Kennedy and C. J. Dalrymple to Palmerston, Jan. 1, 1841; FO 84/348; Admiralty to Palmerston, July 17, 1841, sub enc. Lt. Fitzgerald, Sept. 1840, FO 84/384; W. Macleay to Aberdeen, Apr. 1, 1829, FO 84/91; C. D. Tolmé to Palmerston, Dec. 12, 1836, FO 84/201; J. J. Gurney, *A Winter in the West Indies* (London, 1840), pp. 209–11: David R. Murray, *Odious Commerce: Britain, Spain and the Abolition of the Cuban Slave Trade* (Cambridge, 1980), pp. 87–91. For bribes, see app. E.

54. R. Jameson to Castlereagh, Sep. 1, 1821 (enc.), FO 84/13; H. T. Kilbee to Canning, Oct. 25, 1823, FO 84/23; and Nov. 15, 1824, FO 84/29; W. S. Macleay to Palmerston, Nov. 2, 1829, FO 84/92; Jackson to Aberdeen, Jan. 27, 1829 (enc.), FO 84/89 (see also the cases of the *Jules, La Jeune Eugenie* and *L'Hirondelle* in the same source); Admiral Cockburn to Admiralty, Apr. 30, 1834 (enc.), Adm. 1/292; Admiralty to Aberdeen, Dec. 8, 1829 (enc.), FO 84/99; Col. Off. to Palmerston, Apr. 7, 1837 (enc.), FO 84/229; Murray, *Odious Commerce*, pp. 72–91.

55. Pieter C. Emmer, "Abolition of the Abolished: The Illegal Dutch Slave Trade and the Mixed Courts," in David Eltis and James Walvin (eds.), *The Abolition of the Atlantic Slave Trade* (Madison, Wis., 1981), pp. 177–92; Governor Sir Neill Campbell wrote, "French papers with the regular seal of office are obtained without difficulty by stealth and breach of trust from subordinate persons in the Departments of the Marines [at Martinque and Guadaloupe]" (Col. Off. to Canning, Feb. 14, 1827 [enc.], FO 84/73). These papers were frequently delivered at Danish St. Thomas. Those for the *Musquito* in 1828 cost only $150 (Bannister to Dudley, Aug. 8, 1828, FO 84/78; PP, 1831, 19, pt. B:171). In the 1820s most non-Brazilian slave ships trading north of the equator carried a set of French papers (Comm. Bullen to Adm. Nov. 26, 1826 enc., in Adm. to Canning, Feb. 1827, FO 84/73). The details of ownership transfers at this time between U.S. and Cuban owners on the coast of Africa may be found in the report of the *United States* v *The Catherine*, no. 14,755, in *The Federal Cases*, 30 vols. (St. Paul, Minn., 1894–97). For purchases of Portuguese papers at the Cape Verde Islands, see W. G. Merrill to Palmerston, Apr. 20, 1836, FO 84/202.

56. Supra, chap. 8; A. Aston to Aberdeen, Mar. 27, 1830 (enc.), FO 84/111.

57. H. S. Fox to Palmerston, Nov. 8, 1835, enc. W. G. Ouseley, Sept. 1835, FO 84/179; H. Hamilton to Aberdeen, Nov. 29, 1841, FO 84/367; E. Porter to Palmerston, Dec.

31, 1847, FO 84/679; and Dec. 31, 1849, FO 84/767; M. L. Melville and J. Hook to Aberdeen, Aug. 29, 1845, FO 84/560; Col. Nichol to Aberdeen, Apr. 4, 1846 (enc.), FO 84/663; Admiralty to Palmerston, Feb. 15, 1840, enc. Comm. Matson, Oct. 9, 1839, FO 84/338. The ship-loss-ratio variable was not significant at the 20 percent level and added nothing to the explanatory power of the regression equation for slave imports into Bahia. See p. 373, n. 39, supra.

58. The quote is from E. Porter to Palmerston, Oct. 18, 1847, FO 84/679. See also J. Hudson to Palmerston, Nov. 11, 1850, enc. Comm. Schomberg, Oct. 10, 1850, FO 84/807; and Feb. 11, 1851, FO 84/843; E. Porter to Palmerston, Dec. 31, 1849, FO 84/767. For bribes see J. Parkinson to Wellington, Dec. 10, 1834, FO 84/157.

59. This discussion is based on W. G. Ouseley to Palmerston, Dec. 15, 1838 (enc.), FO 84/254; R. Hesketh to Palmerston, Feb. 19, 1847, FO 84/679; Lord Howden to Palmerston, Mar. 20, 1848, FO 84/725. A description of the Vallongo market in the 1820s is in Robert Walsh, *Notices of Brazil in 1828 and 1829,* 2 vols. (London, 1829–30), 2:323–28. For Brazilian policy, see Robert E. Conrad, "The Struggle for the Abolition of the Brazilian Slave Trade: 1808–1853." Ph.D. diss., Columbia University, 1967, pp. 228–51; for diplomatic exchanges between Britain and Brazil see Leslie M. Bethell, *Abolition of the Brazilian Slave Trade* (Cambridge, 1970), pp. 72–87.

60. G. Jackson and F. Grigg to Palmerston, Jan. 15, 1834, enc. "Extract from an Ultra Periodical of Rio de Janeiro," FO 84/152; idem, Sept. 30, 1836, FO 84/199; H. Hamilton to Palmerston, Nov. 11, 1836, enc. no. 12, FO 84/204; Mr. Stevenson to Buxton, Jan. 1, 1837, 29/111–12, Buxton mss.; W. G. Ouseley to Palmerston, Dec. 15, 1838 (enc.), FO 84/254; Conrad, "Abolition of the Brazilian Slave Trade," p. 236.

61. From 1833, duties on goods re-exported were 2 percent instead of the normal consumption rate of 15 percent, but even this low rate could be avoided at the smaller ports (G. Jackson and F. Grigg to Palmerston, Sept. 30, 1836, and enc. Inspector of Customs to Minister of Finance, Dec. 4, 1835; idem, Nov. 2, 1836, FO 84/199; W. G. Ouseley to Palmerston, Mar. 20, 1840, confidential, FO 84/323). Re-exportation at Montevideo was free and some slave ships preferred to call there (T. Hood to Aberdeen, Mar. 28, 1842, FO 84/447).

62. The ship-loss ratio varied inversely with slave arrivals and was significant at the 20 percent level. However, as in all branches of the nineteenth-century trade for which data exist, this variable explained little of the annual variation in the arrival of slaves. See the equation supra p. 374, n. 45.

63. W. G. Ouseley to Palmerston, Apr. 13, 1840, confidential, FO 84/324; Mar. 13, 1841, confidential, FO 84/364; H. Hamilton to Aberdeen, Nov. 29, 1841, FO 84/367; R. Hesketh to Aberdeen, Jan. 3, 1843, FO 84/470; R. Hesketh to Palmerston, Feb. 19, 1847, FO 84/679; T. Westwood to Palmerston, Oct. 10, 1848, FO 84/727; Admiralty to Palmerston, May 23, 1850, sub enc. Lt. Croften, Jan. 15, 1850, FO 84/825. For descriptions of these establishments, see J. Hudson to Palmerston, Feb. 20, 1850 (enc.), FO 84/802; Apr. 11, 1851 (enc.), FO 84/844.

64. See Carvalho de Mello, "The Economics of Labour," pp. 75–79, for population data by counties. The British minister listed fifteen separate bases at the end of the trade (J. Hudson to Palmerston, Jan. 11, 1851, enc. Hudson to Paulino, Jan. 11, 1851, FO 84/843). For the southward shift in the trade, see G. Stephen to Aberdeen, June 17, 1843 (enc.), FO 84/501; H. Hamilton, Jan. 27, 1844 (enc.), FO 84/523; J. Hudson to Palmerston, Dec. 16, 1848, FO 84/726; June 9, 1849, FO 84/765; July 27, 1850, enc., "Extract of Customs Report," and enc. Comm. Schomberg, July 3, 1850, FO 84/804.

65. Adm. to Palmerston, Apr. 10, 1849, sub enc. Comm. Skipwith, Dec. 23, 1848, FO 84/783; Conrad, "Abolition of the Brazilian Slave Trade," p. 234. For at least one item slave-trading costs were lower after 1830 than before. The Rio de Janeiro newspaper *Aurora Fluminense* pointed out that the re-exportation duty of 2 percent introduced in 1833 was substantially lower than the 15 percent consumption duty previously levied on these goods (G. Jackson and F. Grigg to Palmerston, Dec. 16, 1835 (enc.), FO 84/175).

66. Murray, *Odious Commerce*, p. 187; J. Rendall to Aberdeen, Dec. 27, 1842, enc. Declaration of Jeremiah Macarthy, FO 84/405; J. Crawford to Aberdeen, Feb. 20, 1843; and Dec. 11, 1843, FO 84/463; Admiralty to Aberdeen, May 28, 1842, sub enc. Comm. Murray, Mar. 28, 1842, FO 84/439. Bahía Honda was popular as was Guanimar and Batabanó because of the railway connection with Havana (J. Kennedy and C. Dalrymple to Aberdeen, Apr. 8, 1845, FO 84/561; W. L. Melville and J. Hook to Aberdeen, June 18, 1845 [enc.], FO 84/559. See also J. Kennedy to Palmerston, Jan. 1, 1850, FO 84/789).

67. The British commissioners wrote in 1844, "The slave traders have been desired to fit out their vessels in some of the neighbouring keys where the equipment can be taken out to them and the authorities here be enabled all positively to assert that no such proceedings take place under their observations" (J. Kennedy and C. J. Dalrymple to Aberdeen, July 8, 1844, FO 84/509). See also J. Crawford to Palmerston, Aug. 5, 1848 (enc.) FO 84/722.

68. The Commander of the *Romney* commented when the Spanish Navy brought in one such ship, "This, Sir, is indeed an event in the annals of Slave Trading in Cuba, that a Slave Ship is fearful of entering her ports" (Admiralty to Aberdeen, Dec. 9, 1845, enc. Lt. Clare, Oct. 6, 1845, FO 84/612). See also J. Crawford to Palmerston, Aug. 5, 1848, FO 84/722; J. Kennedy to Palmerston, Apr. 4, 1849, FO 84/754; J. Kennedy and C. J. Dalrymple to Aberdeen, Aug. 21, 1843, FO 84/452.

69. J. Kennedy and C. J. Dalrymple to Aberdeen, Jan 2, 1843, FO 84/448; Jan. 1, 1844, FO 84/508; app. A.

70. For the details of and background to the penal law, see Murray, *Odious Commerce*, pp. 191–207.

71. For the involvement of Cuban officials and Queen Christina as investors, see J. Kennedy and C. J. Dalrymple to Aberdeen, Apr. 8, 1845, FO 84/620; Thomas, *Cuba*, pp. 154, 156.

72. Looking back over fourteen years of personal monitoring of efforts to suppress the slave trade in Cuba, James Kennedy assigned the crucial role in suppression to the attitude of the governor general (*Report from the Select Committee on the Slave Trade Treaties*, PP, 1852–53, 39:95). John Crawford, another long-time observer had the same opinion (J. Crawford to Malmesbury, Sept. 25, 1852, FO 84/874). See also John Glanville Taylor (*The United States and Cuba: Eight Years of Change and Travel* [London, 1851], p. 194) on the perceived impact of the new law.

73. J. Kennedy and C. J. Dalrymple to Palmerston, Mar. 24, 1849, FO 84/753; app. A. Only 571 Chinese arrived in Cuba before 1853, all in 1847 (Thomas, *Cuba*, p. 1541).

74. J. Kennedy to Palmerston, Jan. 1, 1849, FO 84/753; Aug. 8, 1849, FO 84/754; Jan. 1, 1850, FO 84/789. Price observations based on annual mean for 1836–40 compared to 1846–50 (app. C and F; supra, p. 368, n. 5).

75. Comm. Hickley to Vice Admiral Milne, June 5, 1862, I.U.P., *Slave Trade*, 48:pt A, pp. 191–92; J. V. Crawford to Russell, July 2, 1862, FO 84/1174; Sept. 30, 1863, FO 84/1197; E. Gabriel to Malmesbury, May 26, 1859 (enc.), FO 84/1075; J. Crawford to Malmesbury, Oct. 9, 1852, FO 84/870; J. Crawford to Clarendon, Oct. 11, 1854 (enc.), FO 84/935. See in particular the *Venus* case. The latter left Havana to ren-

dezvous at Cayo Blanco with three separate ships carrying equipment. HMS *Vestal* shadowed the *Venus* from Havana (J. Crawford to Malmesbury, Dec. 28, 1852, and enc., FO 84/874).

76. J. Crawford to Palmerston, Jan. 1, 1852, FO 84/870; to Clarendon, Mar. 2, and Nov. 1, 1856, FO 84/988; Feb. 6, 1857, FO 84/1016; Admiralty to Malmesbury, July 3, 1858, enc. Comm. Vesey, Mar. 23, 1858, FO 84/1069.

77. J. Crawford to Malmesbury, Sept. 25, 1852, FO 84/874; J. Crawford to Russell, Dec. 3, 1859, FO 84/1080. Exceptionally, the 560 slaves from the *Orion* were sold on the beach as they landed for the full price of $1,000 each. As there was no official interference, the authorities had presumably been bought off in advance (J. Crawford to Russell, May 12, 1860, FO 84/1109). During the years when the slave registration system was in effect, 1855–59, it was usual for *bozal* slaves to be offered "at one price without their *cédulas,* and at another price with them" (J. Crawford and F. Lousada to Clarendon, Sept. 29, 1857, FO 84/1012).

78. See app. E. For the lieutenant-governor of Trinidad's bribe, see J. V. Crawford to Russell, July 18, 1860, FO 84/1109. For references to other cases see the sources to table E.2.

79. The British vice consul at Trinidad de Cuba reported the departure of two recently arrived slavers because no one was prepared to take on the risk of accepting the slaves despite the very low prices offered by one of them. A total of seven full slavers were turned away in the second half of 1855 (S. Smith to Clarendon, Sept. 25, and Dec. 31, 1855, FO 84/964). Similar incidents were reported at Batabanó and Puerto Príncipe the following year (J. Crawford to Clarendon, May 7, 1856, FO 84/988).

80. G. C. Backhouse to Clarendon, July 9, and Oct. 10, 1853, FO 84/899; Murray *Odious Commerce,* 249–53. G. C. Backhouse estimated slaves seized by the Cuban government at 3,299 in 1854 (to Clarendon, Jan. 1, 1855, FO 84/959), whereas Consul Crawford put the number taken during Pezuela's term at 2,699 (J. Crawford to Clarendon, Sept. 27, 1854, FO 84/937). See also J. Crawford to Clarendon, Feb. 23, 1854, FO 84/936; Admiralty to Malmesbury, July 3, 1858, enc. Comm. Vesey Mar. 23, 1858, FO 84/1069.

81. J. Crawford to Granville, Mar. 13, 1852, FO 84/874; J. Crawford to Clarendon, Apr. 13, 1856, FO 84/988; and J. Crawford to Clarendon Feb. 2, and Aug. 9, 1857, FO 84/1016; J. Crawford to Russell, Nov. 5, 1859, FO 84/1080; J. V. Crawford to Russell July 7, and Sept. 30, 1863, FO 84/1203; T. Savage, June 29, and July 25, 1858, U.S. Congress, H. Exec. Doc., no. 7, 36–2, pp. 111, 145. For a detailed list of criminal proceedings in 1857, see J. Crawford to Malmesbury July 8, 1858, enc. "Statement of the Criminal Cases . . . ," FO 84/1046. For the Argüelles case, see Murray, *Odious Commerce,* pp. 313–14.

82. J. Crawford to Clarendon, Dec. 22, 1854 (enc.), FO 84/937; G. Jackson and E. Gabriel to Clarendon, Oct. 16, 1856, FO 84/985. British reports in the 1850s convey a strong sense that native Cubans, in the rural areas, at least looked upon any *bozal* as fair game for appropriation. The goal of such activity was not, needless to say, freedom for the African. See J. Crawford to Clarendon, Mar. 10, 1853, FO 84/905; Feb. 5, 1854, FO 84/936; Oct. 2, 1855, FO 84/965; Admiralty to Malmesbury, July 3, 1858, enc. Comm Vesey, Mar. 23, 1858, FO 84/1069.

83. J. Kennedy to Palmerston, Dec. 1, 1849, FO 84/761; J. Crawford to Clarendon, May 30, 1853, FO 84/899; Feb. 28, 1856, FO 84/988.

84. J. Crawford to Russell, Mar. 8, 1862, FO 84/1174.

85. See the discussion in Bethell, *Abolition of the Brazilian Slave Trade,* pp. 67–69; Conrad, "Abolition of the Brazilian Slave Trade," pp. 220–21.

86. App. C. For exchange rate and adjustments to constant dollars, see app. F.

## Chapter 12

1. Donald L. Robinson, *Slavery in the Structure of American Politics, 1765–1820* (New York, 1971), p. 339. For divisions in the U.S. South on the slave-trade issue, ibid., pp 232–33, 295–346.
2. David B. Davis, *Slavery and Human Progress* (New York, 1984), p. 241; Gavin Wright, *The Political Economy of the Cotton South: Households, Markets and Wealth in the Nineteenth Century* (New York, 1978), pp 150–54. See also Ronald T. Takaki, *A Pro-Slavery Crusade: The Agitation to Reopen the African Slave Trade* (New York, 1971).
3. Michael Craton, *Sinews of Empire: A Short History of British Slavery* (New York, 1974), pp. 263–64.
4. R. W. Beachey, *The Slave Trade of Eastern Africa* (London, 1976), pp. 20–21, assigns the yellow fever epidemic of 1849–50 a key role in Brazilian suppression. The speedier voyages of the nineteenth century did indeed increase the likelihood of American epidemics. There was certainly widespread public concern in the first half of 1850 at an epidemic that originated with a slave ship, but this was scarcely a major factor. The contribution of disease to suppression was probably limited to removing Bernardo Pereira de Vasconcelos from the scene at the critical point in 1850. The latter, a staunch supporter of the slave trade on the Brazilian Council of State, died of yellow fever (Leslie M. Bethell, *The Abolition of the Brazilian Slave Trade* [Cambridge, 1970], p. 334).
5. See the contemporary comparison of Brazil and the United States on the issue of slavery and immigration in C. F. Van Delden Laërne, *Brazil and Java, Report on Coffee Culture in America, Asia and Africa* (London, 1885), pp. 89–90.
6. H. Southern to Malmesbury, June 11, 1852, enc. extracts of Paulino Soares de Souza's speech of May 29, 1852, FO 848–78.
7. Bethell, *Abolition of the Brazilian Slave Trade*, p. 333; Takaki, *A Pro-Slavery Crusade*, pp. 231–33.
8. Tappan's letter is in *Anti-Slavery Reporter*, 3rd ser., vol. 1, (1853). For Henry Wise, the American minister, see H. Hamilton to Aberdeen, Dec. 14, 1844, enc. H. Wise, Dec. 1, 1844, FO 84/525; H. Hamilton to Palmerston, Nov. 4, 1846, sub enc. H. Wise, July 31, 1846, FO 84/634.
9. Russell to Lord Auckland, Aug. 26, 1848, cited in Spencer Walpole, *Life of Lord John Russell,* 2 vols. (London, 1889), 2:29.
10. David R. Murray, *Odious Commerce: Britain, Spain and the Abolition of the Cuban Slave Trade* (Cambridge, 1980), pp. 208–70; Arthur F. Corwin, *Spain and the Abolition of Slavery in Cuba* (Austin, Tex., 1967), pp. 101–28; Basil Rauch, *American Interest in Cuba: 1848–1855* (New York, 1948), pp. 48–100; Robert L. Paquette, "The Conspiracy of *La Escalera:* Colonial Society and Politics in Cuba and the Age of Revolution," Ph.D. diss., University of Rochester, 1982, pp. 215–55.
11. Murray, *Odious Commerce,* pp. 262–65; Hugh G. Soulsby, *The Right of Search and the Slave Trade in Anglo-American Relations, 1814–1862* (Baltimore, Md., 1933), pp. 138–63.
12. Roger T. Anstey, "The Pattern of British Abolitionism in the Eighteenth and Nineteenth Centuries," p. 18. (This reference is to an earlier and unpublished version of the essay that appeared in Christine Bolt and Seymour Drescher [eds.], *Anti-Slavery, Religion and Reform* (Folkestone, Eng., 1980), pp. 19–42.)
13. Bethell, *Abolition of the Brazilian Slave Trade,* pp. 254–66; supra, chap. 6.
14. Palmerston's proposal to extend the Aberdeen Act to Brazilian subjects as well as property is in Palmerston to Admiralty Aug. 5, 1848, FO 84/745. The Brazilian for-

eign minister's objection to the Aberdeen Act—that the right Britain claimed under the 1826 treaty could not have been given without a "clear and positive delegation of this power" by Brazil—was echoed in the British House of Commons by an ex-attorney general, Sir Thomas Wilde (H. Hamilton to Aberdeen, No. 11, 1845, enc. Limpo de Abreu, Oct. 22, 1845, FO 84/582; Bethell, *Abolition of the Brazilian Slave Trade,* pp. 263–64). The British law officers "remained silent" when asked for their opinion of the legality of the Aberdeen Act in the light of Brazilian protests against it (ibid., p. 275). On the issue of blockades, see Palmerston's comments in *Hansard,* 3rd ser., 76:945, July 16, 1842; Palmerston to Hudson, Aug. 4, 1848, GC/HU/45, Broadlands mss. For Russell's views, see Russell to Palmerston, Nov. 18, 1848 GC/RU/230; Nov. 24, 1849, GC/RU/306; and Mar. 19, 1851, GC/RU/406, Broadlands mss.

15. Earl Grey to Russell, Dec. 16 and 19, 1845, 30/22/4E, fol. 219–21, Russell mss., cited in Anstey, "Pattern of British Abolitionism" (unpublished version).

16. Earl Grey to Russell, Sept. 1, 1846, 30/22/5C, Russell mss.; Lord Denman to Brougham, Aug. 17, 1848?, 10911, Brougham mss; Russell to Palmerston Nov. 18, 1848, GC/RU/230; and Nov. 24, 1849, GC/RU/306, Broadlands mss. Anstey, "Pattern of British Abolitionism" (published version), pp. 32–34. D. C. M. Platt, *Latin America and British Trade, 1806–1914* (London, 1972), p. 316; John Prest, *Lord John Russell* (London, 1972), pp. 223–31.

17. Anstey, "Pattern of British Abolitionism" (published version); p. 34; *Hansard,* 3rd ser., 109:1093–1186; Bethell, *Abolition of the Brazilian Slave Trade,* pp. 321–26. Bethell argues that "even so prominent an abolitionist as Stephen Lushington had come out against the West African squadron" (p. 321). In fact, neither Lushington nor any of the old-line abolitionists changed sides on the coercion issue. Bethell's reference may be to Charles Lushington, Stephen's brother, who opposed the squadron in 1848 (*Hansard,* 3rd ser. 97:1006) and abstained at the crucial March 19, 1850 division. Stephen Lushington left the Commons permanently in 1841.

18. Russell to Palmerston, Nov. 24, 1849, GC/RU/306, Broadlands mss.

19. Admiralty to Palmerston, May 21, 1849 (enc.), FO 84/767; Sir Francis Baring to Palmerston, Sept. 9, 1849, GC/BA/14/5 Broadlands mss.; John F. Cady, *Foreign Intervention in the Río de la Plata, 1838–50* (Pittsburgh, 1929), pp. 244–71.

20. For the law officers' opinion, see J. Dodson to Aberdeen, Sept. 29, 1843, FO 83/2351; May 9, 1844, FO 83/2351. The 1839 act also allowed the detention of vessels without a declared nationality, and this part of the act continued in force after the 1842 Anglo-Portuguese convention. The issue in 1844 was thus whether British cruisers could detain vessels of no declared nationality within Brazilian territorial waters (H. Hamilton to Aberdeen, Feb. 14, and Feb. 27, 1844, FO 84/523). The law officers' denial of this underlines the questionable nature of Palmerston's position six years later. See Aberdeen to Hamilton, July 2, 1844, FO 84/524; cf. Bethell's discussion of this issue (*Abolition of the Brazilian Slave Trade,* pp. 210–13).

21. Commander Layton of the HMS *Cygnet* was one of several commanders replaced as a consequence of wrongful detention of U.S. merchant ships, which in most cases were merely disguised slave ships using the U.S. flag (see Admiralty to Palmerston, Feb. 14, 1846, FO 84/657). There is no record of any officer being relieved of his command for similar actions against shipping within Brazilian territorial waters—prima facie a much more serious offence and one counter to the Sec. 1, Art. 5, and Sec. 2, Art. 6 of the general instructions to naval officers. Commander Hamilton maintained a virtual blockade of Macaé in 1846 and destroyed three fishing feluccas being used as couriers by the slave traders (Admiralty to Palmerston, July 8, 1846, enc. Comm. Hamilton, Mar. 9, 1846, FO 84/659).

22. Palmerston memo, Apr. 12, 1850, attached to Admiralty to Palmerston, Apr. 6, 1850, FO 84/825.
23. The fullest account of these events is in Bethell, *Abolition of the Brazilian Slave Trade*, pp. 327–63.
24. Russell to Palmerston, Mar. 19, 1851, GC/RU/406, Broadlands mss.
25. Hudson wrote in 1851, "Of what use is the Anti Slave Trade society? [*sic*] They appear to muddle away their time and money in a most unaccountable way." Beside the first question, Palmerston scribbled "None whatever" (Hudson to Palmerston, Sept. 13, 1851, FO 84/842.
26. Hudson was cooperating with Rosas's minister in Rio de Janeiro. The latter informed Hudson, "I am about to press the Brazilians in Rio Grande, if you will do as much by cruizing, the day is ours." Hudson told Palmerston, "There is nothing you cannot do at this moment" (Feb. 21, 1850, [private], FO 84/801). For the Praieros's offer, see J. Hudson to Palmerston, Jan. 17, 1850, GC/HU/20, Broadlands mss.
27. G. Jackson and F. Grigg to Palmerston, Dec. 18, 1834, enc. Juiz de Direito to President of the Province of Rio de Janeiro, nd, FO 84/153.
28. J. Hudson to Palmerston, Sept. 2, 1850, FO 84/806.
29. These incidents are reported in J. Hudson to Palmerston, Mar. 15, 1851, FO 84/844; Admiralty to Palmerston, Nov. 15, 1850, enc. Comm. Tatham, Sept. 9, 1851, FO 84/866; J.Hudson to Palmerston, July 14, 1851, enc. Lt. Curtis, June 24, 1851, FO 84/845. Extracts of the Justice Ministry report are in Hudson to Palmerston, June 11, 1850, FO 84/845; Bethell, *Abolition of the Brazilian Slave Trade*, pp. 340–41, 353.
30. Supra, pp. 172–74; Mary Karasch, "From Porterage to Proprietorship: African Occupations in Rio de Janeiro, 1808–50," in Stanley L. Engerman and Eugene D. Genovese (eds.), *Race and Slavery in the Western Hemisphere* (Princeton, 1975).
31. "Grounds for Expecting the Extinction of Brazilian Slavery," nd (c1849), in G79, Brit. Emp. mss., s.22. For Leopoldo da Câmara's position, see J. Hudson to Palmerston, Sept. 12, 1848, GC/HU/5, Broadlands mss. For the position of the Porgutuese in Brazil, see Alan K. Manchester, "The Growth of Bureaucracy in Brazil, 1808–1821," *Journal of Latin American Studies*, 4 (1972): 77–83: and Emília Viotti da Costa, "The Political Emancipation of Brazil," in A. J. R. Russell-Wood (ed.), *From Colony to Nation: Essays on the Independence of Brazil* (Baltimore, 1975), pp. 43–83. The British minister had extensive discussions with the opposition party, the Santa Luzias or "native Brazilian party," in 1849. As a result of these, he reported that "the Brazilian born of the lower class will allow us to do anything against the slavers provided that the Portuguese are the chief sufferers" (J. Hudson to Palmerston, July 10, 1849, GC/HU/14, Broadlands mss). See also Consul Newcomen to Palmerston, Sept. 5, 1850, FO 84/809, "Many opposed to the Portuguese here (Paraíba) have adopted an antislave-trade stance as a means of discrediting their enemies." See also J. Hudson to Palmerston, Sept. 12, 1848, GC/HU/5, Broadlands mss., for a review of the role of anti-Portuguese feeling in the politics of mid–nineteenth-century Brazil.
32. Russell's comment is in Russell to Palmerston, Sept. 24, 1850, GC/RU/363, Broadlands mss. For Hudson's concern about the direction of the popular response to British actions and the importance of avoiding a clash with the Brazilians as opposed to the Portuguese slave trader, see his letter to Adm. Reynolds, Feb. 3, 1850. This is enclosed in Hudson to Palmerston, Feb. 21, 1850, which may be found in both FO 84/801 and GC/HU/21, Broadlands mss. See also idem., July 27, 1850, FO 84/805; and March 15, 1851, GC/HU/34, Broadlands mss. as well as H. Augus-

tus Cowper to Palmerston, Sept. 24, 1850, FO 84/819. For the impact of naval action, see Robert Conrad, "The Struggle for the Abolition of the Brazilian Slave Trade: 1808–1853." Ph.D. diss., Columbia University, 1967, pp. 323–27.

33. S. Jerningham to Clarendon, June 12, 1856, and enc., FO 84/994; J. Morgan to Clarendon, Aug. 11, 1856 (enc.), FO 84/995.

34. App. C; R. Hesketh to Palmerston, Mar. 14, 1850, FO 84/808; Robert W. Slenes, "The Demography and Economics of Brazilian Slavery, 1850–1888." Ph.D. diss., Stanford University, 1976, pp. 120–78. For the position of coffee planters and slave traders, see the report of comments made by Paulino in H. Southern to Malmesbury, May 10, 1852, FO 84/878.

35. Bethell, *Abolition of the Brazilian Slave Trade,* pp. 359–63; Conrad, "Struggle for the Abolition of the Brazilian Slave Trade," pp. 317–18, 326–29. The key document is J. Hudson to Palmerston, June 11, 1851, FO 84/845, which counterposes the origin and passage of the Law of September 4 with the claims of Paulino in his speech to the Brazilian Senate on May 29, 1852.

36. J. Hudson to Palmerston, June 11, 1851, FO 84/845; Bethell, *Abolition of the Brazilian Slave Trade,* pp. 341–43.

37. Luiz-Felipe de Alencastro, "La Traite négrière et l'unité nationale bresilienne," *Revue française d'histoire d'outre-mer,* 66 (1979):415; Nathaniel H. Leff, "Economic Retardation in Nineteenth-Century Brazil," *Economic History Review,* 25 (1972):500.

38. The British commissioners normally reported the number of *bozales* taken by the Cuban government each year together with their report of the slave trade itself. These summaries were normally sent at the beginning of January each year (September 30 after 1858) and may be found in the appropriate volumes of the FO 84 series and PP.

39. J. V. Crawford to Russell, May 5, and July 7, 1863, FO 84/1203; Sept. 30, 1863, FO 84/1197; Apr. 29, 1864, FO 84/1215. See also supra, chap. 11. For Malmesbury's decision, see Soulsby, *Right of Search and the Slave Trade,* pp. 163–66.

40. PP, 1863, 67:299; PP, 1878–79, 13:417.

41. App. C; Corwin, *Spain and the Abolition of Slavery in Cuba,* pp. 154–214; Consul Crawford reported the "greatest alarm here" as a result of Lincoln's declaration of freedom for slaves (J. V. Crawford to Russell, Sept. 30, 1862, FO 84/1174). For a similar response in Puerto Rico, see José Curet, "About Slavery and the Order of Things: Puerto Rico, 1845–1873," in Manuel Moreno Fraginals, Frank Moya Pons and Stanley L. Engerman (eds.), *Between Slavery and Free Labor: The Spanish-Speaking Caribbean in the Nineteenth Century* (Baltimore, Md., 1985), pp. 127–28.

42. Corwin, *Spain and the Abolition of Slavery in Cuba,* pp. 173–84; Murray, *Odious Commerce,* pp. 317–24.

43. Soulsby, *Right of Search and the Slave Trade,* pp. 173–76, and Warren S. Howard, *American Slavers and the Federal Law, 1837–1862* (Berkeley, Calif., 1963), pp. 62–64, among others, give a central position to this treaty in their accounts of the ending of the traffic though the latter provides an accurate assessment of the operation of the courts. Robert William Love, Jr., "The End of the Atlantic Slave Trade to Cuba," *Caribbean Quarterly,* 22 (1976): 51–57, offers an account that is consistent with that given here.

44. For the *Volador,* see J. Kennedy and C. J. Dalrymple to Aberdeen, Aug. 13, 1842, FO 84/395. The British consul reported a total of eight hundred to nine hundred slaves for the period 1841–43, including a cargo of 330 in late 1843, which was probably the last numerically significant group to arrive (John Lindegren to Aberdeen, Sept. 11, and Sept. 26, 1844, FO 84/520; June 11, 1845, FO 84/578. See also

J. Clarke to Aberdeen, Oct. 8, 1842, FO 84/402). The *Triumfo,* which intended to carry slaves to Puerto Rico, was condemned at St. Helena in 1845, and another ship (without a name) supposedly had the same intention in 1862.

45. For prices before 1840, see Francisco A. Scarano, *Sugar and Slavery in Puerto Rico: The Plantation Economy of Ponce, 1800–1850* (Madison, Wis., 1984), p. 134; Col. Off. to Palmerston, Apr. 7, 1837, enc. Fuller, Dec. 31, 1836, FO 84/227. For prices after 1844, see Curet, "About Slavery and the Order of Things," pp. 124–25. For Cuban prices see app. C.

46. Scarano, *Sugar and Slavery in Puerto Rico,* pp. 5–8, 132–34. There were also shipments of slaves from Curaçao, St. Eustatius and St. Martin to Puerto Rico in 1847 and possibly 1846 (J. Lindegren to Palmerston, Mar. 27, May 25, and June 10, 1847, FO 84/674; Admiralty to Palmerston, Aug. 14, 1847 (enc.), FO 84/705). The general interpretation here—that of suppression imposed on Puerto Rico by outside pressures—is consistent with the mainly diplomatic study of Arturo Morales Carrión, *Auge y decadencia de la trata negrera en Puerto Rico (1820–1860)* (San Juan, 1978).

47. Corwin, *Spain and the Abolition of Slavery in Cuba,* 185–214.

48. Hubert H. S. Aimes, *A History of Slavery in Cuba, 1511 to 1868* (New York, 1907), p. 209; Hugh Thomas, "Cuba from the Middle of the Eighteenth Century to c. 1870," in Leslie Bethell (ed) *The Cambridge History of Latin America,* 5 vols. (Cambridge, 1985), 3:294; Scott, *Slave Emancipation in Cuba,* pp. 39–40, 111–24.

49. J. V. Crawford to Stanley, Sept. 30, 1867, FO 84/1287.

50. Joaquim Nabuco, *Abolitionism: The Brazilian Antislavery Struggle,* trans. Robert Conrad (Urbana, Ill., 1977), pp. 41–45; Robert Conrad, "Struggle for the Abolition of the Brazilian Slave Trade," pp. 150–59.

51. Nabuco's, *O Abolicionismo* was first published in 1883; J. E. Cairnes, *The Slave Power: Its Character, Career and Probable Designs* (London, 1862).

## Chapter 13

1. Supra, chap. 5, but see in particular Philip D. Curtin, *Image of Africa: British Ideas and Action; 1780–1850* (Madison, Wis., 1964), pp. 123–286.

2. See the breakdown of American populations in David Eltis, "Free and Coerced Transatlantic Migrations: Some Comparisons," *American Historical Review,* 88 (1983):278. It is unlikely that more than a quarter of the inhabitants of the Americas in 1820 were living in societies in which the raison d'être was earnings from trade with Europe.

3. Patrick O'Brien, "European Economic Development: The Contribution of the Periphery," *Economic History Review,* 35 (1982):1–18.

4. For estimates of aggregate exports, see Colin W. Newbury, "Trade and Authority in West Africa from 1850 to 1880," in L. H. Gann and P. Duignan (eds.), *The History and Politics of Colonialism, 1870-1914,* pp. 76–79; A. G. Hopkins, *An Economic History of West Africa* (New York, 1973), p. 128. For an estimate of the West African population c. 1810, see Fage, "The Effect of the Export Slave Trade on African Populations," in R. P. Moss and R. J. A. R. Rathbone (eds.), *The Population Factor in African Studies* (London, 1975), p. 16. For Dahomey exports, see Patrick Manning, *Slavery, Colonialism and Economic Growth in Dahomey, 1640–1960* (Cambridge, 1982), p. 3. Philip D. Curtin, calculates a lower exports per capita figure for Senegambia in 1800, but his table 8.9 implies a very rapid growth in the ratio in the early nineteenth century (*Economic Change in Precolonial Africa: Senegambia in the Era of the Slave Trade,* 2 vols. [Madison, Wis., 1975] 1:333–34).

5. Paul E. Lovejoy, *Transformations in Slavery: A History of Slavery in Africa* (Cam-

bridge, 1983), in particular, pp. 8–12, 183, 239–45, 269–82; idem, "Indigenous African Slavery," *Historical Reflections*, 6 (1979):25–27, 56–71. Cf. Gerald M. McSheffrey, "Slavery, Indentured Servitude, Legitimate Trade and the Impact of Abolition in the Gold Coast, 1874–1901: A Reappraisal," *Journal of African History*, 24 (1983):364–67. Influential examples of earlier statements of the importance of external influences are Walter Rodney, "African Slavery and Other Forms of Social Oppression on the Upper Guinea Coast in the Context of the Atlantic Slave Trade," *Journal of African History*, 7 (1966):431–43; and Basil Davidson, "Slaves or Captives? Some Notes on Fantasy and Fact," in Nathan I. Huggins, Martin Kilson and Daniel M. Fox (eds.), *Key Issues in the Afro-American Experience* (New York, 1971), pp. 57–73.

6. Stephen Baier and Paul E. Lovejoy, "The Tuareg of the Central Sudan: Graduations in Servility at the Desert Edge," in Suzanne Miers and Igor Kopytoff (eds.), *Slavery in Africa: Historical and Anthopological Perspectives* (Madison, Wis., 1977), pp. 393–94.

7. David Northrup, "Nineteenth-Century Patterns of Slavery and Economic Growth in Southeastern Nigeria," *International Journal of African Historical Studies*, 12 (1979):5–16.

8. Ibid.; David Northrup, "The Ideological Context of Slavery in Southeastern Nigeria in the 19th Century," in Paul E. Lovejoy (ed.), *The Ideology of Slavery in Africa* (Beverly Hills, Calif., 1981), pp. 100–122. On the delta states, cf. E. J. Alagoa, "Long Distance Trade and States in the Niger Delta," *Journal of African History*, 11 (1970):319–29.

9. Much of the foregoing has been influenced by Hopkins, *Economic History of West Africa*, in particular chap. 4; and Lars Sundstrom, *The Exchange Economy of Pre-Colonial Tropical Africa* (London, 1974). For a recent discussion of the slave mode of production, see Lovejoy, *Transformations in Slavery*, pp. 269–73.

10. Supra, chap. 10. A naval officer who visited the peanut-growing regions north of Sierra Leone commented that the price of a slave ($35) was such that transatlantic slave trading would not be profitable (Admiralty to Russell, Feb. 18, 1864, sub enc. Comm. Cochrane, Jan. 9, 1864, FO 84/1227). This however is an isolated reference and coincided with both the end of the transatlantic traffic, when slave prices were low in the Americas, and a period of very high prices for slave grown peanuts.

11. Estimated from George E. Brooks, "Peanuts and Colonialism: Consequences of the Commercialization of Peanuts in West Africa, 1830–70," *Journal of African History*, 16 (1975):29–54; "Les Membres de la Commission . . . au Gouverneur, Aug. 23, 1863," in Jacques Charpy, *La Fondation de Dakar* (Paris, 1958), pp. 416–17; J. M. Gray, *A History of the Gambia* (Cambridge, 1940), pp. 380–82; Comm. Ruxton, "Report on Slave Trade . . . ," Apr. 15, 1865, fols. 204–10, FO 84/1253. One ton is assumed to equal 114 bushels. Some data for midcentury may be found in Eugene Saulnier, *La Compagnie de Gabam au Sénégal* (Paris, 1921), pp. 173–74, 187.

12. Brooks, "Peanuts and Colonialism," pp. 43–44; N. Macdonald to Palmerston, Nov. 4, 1850, FO 84/788; J. Hook to Palmerston, Dec. 31, 1849, FO 84/752; S. J. Hill to Clarendon, Jan. 10, 1857, FO 84/1011; Admiralty to Palmerston, June 18, 1850, enc. Comm. Fanshawe, Apr. 10, 1850, FO 84/826.

13. J. Hook to Palmerston, Dec. 31, 1849, FO 84/752; A. W. Hanson to Clarendon, Dec. 31, 1853, FO 84/920; A. W. Hanson to Clarendon, June 23, 1855, FO 84/976; A. W. Hanson to Russell, Jan. 4, 1860, FO 84/1117; T. C. Weston to Clarendon, Jan. 13, 1855, FO 84/958; Admiralty to Malmesbury, May 8, 1852, sub enc., "Journal kept by Edward S. Sotheby . . . Sept. 1, 1851 to Feb. 1, 1852," FO 84/894; Admiralty to Russell, June 17, 1861, enc. Comm. Edmonstone, May 7, 1861, FO 84/1149;

Comm. Ruxton, "Report on Slave Trade . . . ," Apr. 15, 1865, fols. 204–10, 1253.
Rice cultivation for the Sierra Leone market and small-scale coffee production had
been continuous in the Pongo River from at least the early 1820s (E. Gregory and
E. Fitzgerald to Canning, Apr. 29, 1823, [enc.], FO 84/21).

14. Col. Off. to Palmerston, Dec. 24, 1850, sub enc. B. Campbell, Aug. 31, 1850, FO 84/
822; Admiralty to Malmesbury, May 8, 1852, sub enc. "Journal kept by Edward S.
Sotheby . . . Sept. 1, 1851 to Feb. 1, 1852," FO 84/894; T. C. Weston to Clarendon,
Jan. 13, 1855, FO 84/958; Comm. Edmonstone to Rear Adm. Walker, July 20, 1861,
and Oct. 22, 1862, Adm. 123/180; Admiralty to Russell, Feb. 18, 1864, sub enc.
Comm. Cochrane, Jan. 9, 1864, FO 84/1127. For relative prices see app. C; J. Hook
to Palmerston, Dec. 31, 1849, FO 84/752; T. C. Weston to Clarendon, Jan. 13, 1855,
FO 84/958.

15. Curtin, *Economic Change in Precolonial Africa,* 1:217–18; 2:64–65, 74–77.

16. The $4 million figure is actually the mean value of annual oil imports into the
United Kingdom from all of Africa for 1857–59. The assumption is made here that
the quantity of oil exported from the bights of Benin and Biafra to all destinations
approximated the amounts imported into the United Kingdom from all of Africa.
This is reasonable, first, because the amount of oil produced by areas outside the
bights at this period was very small, second, because the United Kingdom took 70
percent of all the exports from the Bight of Benin and almost all the Bight of Biafra's
output (B. Campbell to Malmesbury, Feb. 2, 1858, FO 84/1061). The United Kingdom import figures are readily available from Customs 4; PP 1857–8, 54:80; and
1863, 65:33. These are converted into values with the aid of A. J. H. Latham's price
series (*Old Calabar, 1600–1891; The Impact of the International Economy upon a
Traditional Society* [Oxford, 1973], pp. 70–72. For volumes and prices of French
imports of palm oil at this time, see Bernard Schnapper, *La Politique et la commerce
française dans le golfe de Guinée de 1838 à 1871* [Paris, 1961], p. 140). Given the
rough order of the calculation conversion into real values appears superfluous. The
estimate of the relative importance of palm oil in the bights trade is also based on
the Campbell letter cited above. The 1871–75 values of palm-product imports into
the United Kingdom may be found in PP, 1876, 72:14

17. Manning, *Slavery, Colonialism and Economic Growth,* p. 52. The percentage breakdown of exports by port: Lagos, 22.9; Porto Novo, Appi Vista and adjacent areas,
20.8; Palma, 15.1; Benin River, 12.3; Ouidah and Agoué, 11.6 each; and Badagry
5.8. The distribution for 1856 was very similar (B. Campbell to Malmesbury, Feb.
2, 1858 (enc.), FO 84/1061. Campbell's estimates of total output for 1856 and 1857
in the region came to just under half of the gross imports into the United Kingdom
in those years (PP, 1857, 35:427; 1857–8, 54:80). For the rise of Lagos, see Latham,
*Old Calabar,* p. 67.

18. Manning, *Slavery, Colonialism and Economic Growth,* pp. 50–56; Frederick E.
Forbes, *Dahomey and the Dahomans,* 2 vols. (London, 1851), 1:114, 115, 123;
Robin Law, "Royal Monopoly and Private Enterprise in the Atlantic Trade: The
Case of Dahomey," *Journal of African History,* 18 (1977): 571–76; John Duncan to
Palmerston, Aug. 17, 1849, FO 84/775. The king of Dahomey taxed produce much
as he taxed slaves. Forbes reported, "In Whydah are six agents or traders for His
Majesty. The Charchar has the advantage of trading with these or other traders without paying the king's duty: all trade, whether in slaves or oil must be first submitted
to the Charchar" (Admiralty to Palmerston, May 6, 1850, enc. Lt. Forbes, Apr. 2,
1850, FO 84/826). This suggests something less that a trading monopoly. Ouidah in
any event exported less than one eighth of the region's oil. By 1863, however, even
at Ouidah the king had ordered that "all the produce of his country may be freely

offered to the merchants" (Comm. Wilmot to Rear Adm. Walker, Dec. 31, 1863, Adm. 123/180).

19. Hopkins, *Economic History of West Africa*, pp. 124–125; Manning, *Slavery, Colonialism and Economic Growth*, p. 54; Lovejoy, *Transformations in Slavery*, p. 183; Law "Royal Monopoly and Private Enterprise." Catherine Coquery-Vidrovitch stresses the continuity of social structures between the slave-trade and agricultural-export eras for Dahomey at least ("De la traite des esclaves à l'exportation de l'huile de palme et des palmistes au Dahomey: XIXe siècle," in Claude Meillassoux [ed.], *The Development of Indigenous Trade and Markets in West Africa* [London, 1971]). For the emergence and destruction of an African merchant class, see Schnapper, *La Politique et le commerce française;* Edward Reynolds, "The Rise and Fall of an African Merchant Class," *Cahiers d'études africaines,* 54 (1974): 253–74; Christopher Chamberlin, "Bulk Exports, Trade Tiers, Regulation and Development: An Economic Approach to the Study of West Africa's Legitimate Trade," *Journal of Economic History,* 39 (1979): 419–38.

20. Manning, *Slavery, Colonialism and Economic Growth*, p. 3; Newbury estimated West African exports at £8 million in the 1880s ("Trade and Authority in West Africa," p. 77). For a discussion of per capita domestic product see chap. 5.

21. Manning, *Slavery, Colonialism and Economic Growth*, pp. 57–84.

22. Northrup, "The Ideological Context of Slavery in Southeastern Nigeria," pp. 111–17; Latham, *Old Calabar*, pp. 113–45.

23. [George Stephen], *Analysis of the Evidence Given Before the Select Committee upon the Slave Trade* (London, 1850), pp. 84–86. Discussion of several British initiatives may be found in Curtin, *Image of Africa,* pp. 438–56. For modestly successful African attempts at larger scale commercial agriculture on the Gold Coast, see Edward E. Reynolds, "Abolition and Economic Change on the Gold Coast," in David Eltis and James Walvin (eds.), *The Abolition of the Atlantic Slave Trade* (Madison, Wis., 1981), pp. 141–51.

24. Allen Isaacman, "An Economic History of Angola, 1835–1867." M.A. thesis, University of Wisconsin, pp. 55–68; David Birmingham, "The Coffee Barons of Cazengo," *Journal of African History,* 19 (1978): 523–38; James Duffy, *A Question of Slavery* (Oxford, 1967) pp. 5–39; E. Gabriel to Russell, Feb. 25, 1860, FO 84/1104.

25. Comm. Edmonstone to Rear Adm. Walker, Nov. 18, 1861, Adm. 123/180.

26. The British captured at least a dozen small ships bound for either Ile Príncipe or São Tomé between 1819 and 1850. Details may be found in the correspondence between the Foreign Office and Sierra Leone commissioners. These have not been entered in the slave-ship data set as these ships were not involved in the transatlantic trade.

27. Birmingham "Coffee Barons," p. 535; Duffy, *Question of Slavery,* pp. 5–39: During 1861, a year when the British commissioners commented on the large differential in the price of labor between Angola and São Tomé (E. Gabriel and H. V. Huntley to Russell, Oct. 10, 1861, FO 84/1133), nine-hundred slaves were shipped (idem., Jan. 8, 1862, FO 84/1166). In 1864, however, the British commodore believed the traffic to have ended completely (Comm. Wilmot, Dec. 1, 1864, Adm. 123/184). For the numbers of *libertos* carried after 1875, see Duffy, *Question of Slavery,* p. 98.

28. Frederick Cooper, *Plantation Slavery on the East Coast of Africa* (New Haven, Conn., 1977), pp. 47–60. In contrast to west-central and West Africa, slave prices on the east coast may not have decreased very much in the 1820–65 era (app. C).

29. Cooper, *Plantation Slavery,* pp. 60–67; app. C.

30. Admiralty to Russell, Nov. 5, 1863, sub enc. extract from Journal of Comm. Wildman, Oct. 1862, FO 84/1209.

31. Curtin, *Image of Africa*, pp. 453–56; Grey's well-known dispatch on tropical lab written to Viscount Torrington, July 19, 1848, was circulated among the West Indian governors. For this and the background to the dispatch, see Earl Grey, *The Colonial Policy of Lord John Russell's Administration*, 2 vols. (London, 1853), 1:81, and K. M. de Silva, *Letters on Ceylon 1846–50: the Administration of Viscount Torrington and the Rebellion of 1848* (Kandy, Sri Lanka, 1965), pp. 7–10, 78–79; W. Kloosterboer, *Involuntary Labour Since the Abolition of Slavery* (Leiden, 1960), pp. 21–25, 144–46. McSheffrey, "Slavery, Indentured Servitude, Legitimate Trade," p. 367. For the poll tax in the Gold Coast, see Edward E. Reynolds, *Trade and Economic Change on the Gold Coast* (London, 1974), pp. 124–31. For Grey's position on slave emancipation, see David Brion Davis, *Slavery and Human Progress* (New York, 1984), pp. 189–90, 216–18, 308–9.

32. The key statistic in this issue is the rate of intrinsic natural population change. "Crude rates are ... derived from raw population data, natural rates are those calculated for a closed population, and intrinsic rates are ones reflecting the characteristics of a closed population with a stable age structure." These terms are defined in Jack Eblen's "On the Natural Increase of Slave Populations: The Example of the Cuban Black Population, 1775–1900," in Stanley L. Engerman and Eugene D. Genovese [eds.], *Race and Slavery in the Western Hemisphere* (Princeton, N.J., 1975), p. 214.

33. See the discussion and literature cited in Robert W. Fogel and Stanley L. Engerman, "Recent Findings in the Study of Slave Demography and Family Structure," *Sociology and Social Research*, 63 (1979):556–89.

34. The discussion is based on Barry Higman's *Slave Populations of the British Caribbean, 1807–1824* (Baltimore, Md., 1984), pp. 100–157, 303–78. Higman does not attempt to derive an intrinsic rate as defined by Eblen (supra, n. 32), but there seems little doubt on the basis of the natural rates he calculates that such an intrinsic rate would be positive.

35. The crude rate of population change for slaves steadily improved from 1817 to 1827, 1827 to 1846 and 1846 to 1861 until it averaged −0.6 percent per annum in the last period. (Rates are calculated using the formula in Henry A. Gemery, "Emigration from the British Isles to the New World, 1630–1700: Inferences from Colonial Populations," *Research in Economic History*, 51 (1980): 183–85. Data are taken from app. A and the population estimates in Kenneth Kiple, *Blacks in Colonial Cuba, 1774–1899* [Gainesville, Fla., 1976]). As the slave trade increased, the proportion of the slave population in the older age categories no doubt increased also and the crude mortality rates would have been high. Intrinsic rates (as defined supra, n. 32) were likely positive. Cf. Eblen, "On the Natural Increase of Slave Populations."

36. Svend E. Green-Pederson, "Slave Demography in the Danish West Indies and the Abolition of the Danish Slave Trade," in Eltis and Walvin, *Abolition of the Atlantic Slave Trade*, pp. 231–57; Hans Chr. Johansen, "Slave Demography of the Danish West Indian Islands," *Scandanavian Economic History Review*, 29 (1981): pp. 16–20; Alexander Moreau de Jonnès, *Recherches statistiques sur l'esclavage colonial et sur les moyens de la supprimer* (Paris, 1842), pp. 16–22.

37. Higman, *Slave Populations of the British Caribbean*, 325–29; Slenes, "The Demography and Economics of Brazilian Slavery," 363–65. Slenes has calculated a negative intrinsic rate for Brazil as a whole for the early 1870s. As he does not attempt regional estimates of intrinsic rates, the possibility remains of an average for the country as a whole made up of a strongly negative rate for the sugar-growing regions and a positive rate for the coffee-growing areas.

38. Some rough calculations of the ratio of slave imports over the highest volume

twenty-five-year period to the slave population at the end of the period (chosen because of data availability) yielded the following results ('000):

| | Imports | Population at End of Period | Imports/Population |
|---|---|---|---|
| Brazil, 1826–50 | 962.9 | 1,800.0[a] | 0.5 |
| Cuba, 1816–40 | 392.4 | 436.5[b] | 0.9 |
| | | 350.0[c] | 1.1 |
| St. Domingue, 1767–91 | 434.2 | 480.0 | 0.9 |
| British West Indies, 1783–1807 | 380.0 | 776.0 | 0.5 |

*Notes:* [a]Projected backward from 1872 census, assuming 1 percent per annum decline in the population 1850–72. [b]1841. [c]Derived from 1846 census.

*Sources:* App. A; Philip D. Curtin, *The African Slave Trade: A Census* (Madison, Wis., 1969), pp. 78–79; Barry Higman, *Slave Populations in the British Caribbean, 1807–1824* (Baltimore, 1984), p. 74; Robert W. Slenes, "The Demography and Economics of Brazilian Slavery, 1850–1888." Ph.D. diss., Stanford University, 1976, p. 57.

39. Eltis, "Free and Coerced Transatlantic Migrations."
40. Supra, chap. 11. For the failure of free African migration, see Monica Schuler, *Alas, Alas, Kongo: A Social History of Indentured African Immigration into Jamaica 1841–1865* (Baltimore, 1980), pp. 18–29. In the 1830s the Duke of Buckingham subsidized free English migrants to the Hope plantation in Jamaica (see the correspondence in the Stowe mss., Hope and Middleton plantations, Henry E. Huntington Library, San Marino, Calif.) For the modest flow of white Cuban immigration prior to emancipation see Duvon C. Corbett, "Immigration in Cuba," *Hispanic American Historical Review*, 22 (1942): 280–308.
41. Stanley L. Engerman, "Economic Change and Contract Labor in the British Caribbean: The End of Slavery and the Adjustment to Emancipation," *Explorations in Economic History*, 21 (1984):133–50; idem, "Servants to Slaves to Servants: Contract Labor and European Expansion," in P. C. Emmer (ed.), *Colonialism and Migration; Indentured Labour before and after Slavery* (Dordrecht, 1986), p. 272.
42. Slenes, Demography and Economics of Brazilian Slavery," pp. 366–68; Robert Conrad, *The Destruction of Brazilian Slavery* (Berkeley, Calif., 1972), in particular chap. 16; Luiz Aranha Correa do Lago, "The Transition from Slave to Free Labour in Agriculture in the Southern and Coffee Regions of Brazil: A Global and Theoretical Approach and Regional Case Studies." Ph.D. diss., Harvard University, 1978; Thomas H. Holloway, *Immigrants on the Land: Coffee and Society in São Paulo, 1886–1934* (Chapel Hill, N.C., 1980), pp. 35–69. For earlier and unsuccessful attempts to use immigrant labor see C. F. Van Delden Laërne, *Brazil and Java. Report on Coffee Culture in America, Asia and Africa* (London, 1885), pp. 127–52; and Warren Dean, *Rio Claro: A Brazilian Plantation System, 1820–1920* (Stanford, Calif., 1976), pp. 88–123. For the later arrivals, see Dean, *Rio Claro*, pp. 156–61.
43. App. A and C.; George Reid Andrews, *The Afro-Argentinians of Buenos Aires, 1800–1900* (Madison, Wis., 1980), pp. 47–53, 178–208; Herbert S. Klein, "The Integration of Italian Immigrants into the United States and Argentina: A Comparative Analysis," *American Historical Review*, 88 (1983):308.
44. The $350 price is the average for Cuban prime male *bozales* in the 1820s and 1830s. There seems little doubt that an open transatlantic slave trade would have seen a

similar price established in New Orleans (though some adjustment it might be nc͡ is required for seasoning). The $700 price is for Creole slaves.

45. Arthur Zilversmit, *The First Emancipation: The Abolition of Slavery in the North* (Chicago, 1967), pp. 137–200; Leon F. Litwack, *North of Slavery: The Negro in the Free States, 1790–1860* (Chicago, 1961), pp. 3–5.

46. Ramon de la Sagra, *Historia económico-politíca y estadística de la isla de Cuba* (Havana, 1831), p. 336; Higman, *Slave Populations of the British Caribbean,* p. 77; Ralph Davis, *The Industrial Revolution and British Overseas Trade* (Leicester, 1979), pp. 119, 121: Instituto brasileiro de geografia estatística, *Anuário estatístico,* Ano V, 1939–40, p. 1358; Stanley J. Stein, *Vassouras, a Brazilian Coffee County, 1850–1900* (Cambridge, Mass., 1957), p. 294; Manning, *Slavery, Colonialism and Economic Growth,* p. 333. All ratios calculated in constant prices (1821–25 = 100)

47. Juan Pérez de la Riva, "Aspectos demográficos y su importancia en el proceso revolucionario del siglo XIX," in *Union de periodistas de Cuba* (Havana, 1968), p. 46, cited by Francisco Lopez Segrera, "Cuba: Dependence, Plantation Economy, and Social Classes, 1762–1902," in Manuel Moreno Fraginals, Frank Moya Pons, and Stanley L. Engerman (eds.), *Between Slavery and Free Labour (Baltimore, Md., 1985),* p. 85. British per capita income calculated from Phyllis Deane and W. A. Cole, *British Economic Growth, 1688–1959,* 2nd ed. (Cambridge, 1969), pp. 8, 166. U.S. data from Robert E. Gallman, "Gross National Product in the United States, 1834–1900," in Conference on Research in Income and Wealth, *Output, Employment and Productivity in the United States after 1800* (New York, 1966), p. 26.

48. Supra, fig. 7 shows the divergence between slave and produce prices; also see the accompanying discussion.

49. Stanley L. Engerman, "Contract Labor, Sugar and Technology in the Nineteenth-Century," *Journal of Economic History,* 43 (1983):635–59; idem, "Economic Adjustments to Emancipation in the United States and the British West Indies," *Journal of Interdisciplinary History,* 13 (1982):191–205.

50. Taking the Brazilian population at 4 million in 1823 and 8 million in 1850 (Stein, *Vassouras,* p. 294) and using the five-year mean of exports in pounds sterling centered on these years (*Anuário estatístico,* Ano. V, p. 1358)—adjusted for price changes (Rostow, Gayer, and Schwarz, and Rousseaux index)—yields a per capita export figure of £1.06 for 1823 and £1.21 for 1850. Celso Furtado has argued for a decline in per capita income levels in the first half of the nineteenth century on the basis of substantially the same population and export data used here, except for the conversion to real terms. He argues that prices of Brazilian imports (British exports are used as a proxy) remained constant while Brazilian export prices declined by 40 percent (*The Economic Growth of Brazil: A Survey from Colonial to Modern Times* [Berkeley, Calif., 1971], pp. 114–18). In fact British export prices declined by even more that 40 percent (A. H. Imlah, *Economic Element ·in the Pax Britannica* [Cambridge, Mass., 1958], p. 99) which would suggest that the above ratios understate the growth in purchasing power of Brazilian exports. More recently Nathanial Leff using money-supply data and a range of assumptions on the velocity of circulation has calculated a small annual average increase in income between 1822 and 1869 ("A Technique for Estimating Income Trends from Currency Data and an Application to Nineteenth-Century Brazil," *Review of Income and Wealth,* 18 (1972): 363–64. The explanation here is closer to the Leff that the Furtado interpretation although money-supply data imperfectly reflect trends in the subsistence economy.

51. Furtado, *Economic Growth of Brazil,* pp. 119–34; Nathaniel H. Leff, *Underdevelopment and Development in Brazil,* 2 vols. (London, 1982), 1:15–22.

App. C.

3. German immigrants to Rio Grande do Sul in the 1820s and again at midcentury gravitated toward subsistence agriculture despite support for the settlement from the imperial government (Furtado, *Economic Growth of Brazil*, p. 136). Only a small proportion of the German and Swiss indentured immigrants in Rio Claro in the 1850s eventually bought land in the area (Dean, *Rio Claro*, pp. 120–22). For the shift to the land by immigrants to São Paulo in the later period, see Holloway, *Immigrants on the Land*, pp. 139–66. In the late 1850s Englishman James A. Mann commented, "If Brazil could command the needful labour there is no question but that she would become a large supplier of our [raw cotton] wants" (*The Cotton Trade of Great Britain* [Manchester, Eng., 1860], p. 86).

54. Cuban rates calculated from Rebecca J. Scott, *Slave Emancipation in Cuba: The Transition to Free Labor* (Princeton, N.J., 1985), p. 217, and Kiple, *Blacks in Colonial Cuba*, pp. 98–99. Brazilian rates from Walter F. Wilcox and Imre Ferenczi, *International Migrations*, 2 vols. (New York, 1929–31), 1:209.

55. Scott, *Slave Emancipation in Cuba*, pp. 63–226.

56. For the continued high prices for slaves into the last years of slavery, see Scott, *Slave Emancipation*, pp. 96–97.

57. Engerman, "Contract Labour, Sugar and Technology," pp. 656–57, and the essays in Bill Albert and Adrian Graves (eds.), *Crisis and Change in the International Sugar Economy, 1860–1914* (Norwich, Eng., 1984).

58. Supra, chap. 11; Susan Schroeder, *Cuba: A Handbook of Historical Statistics* (Boston, 1982); pp. 41, 401.

59. Coffee exports grew at an average annual rate of over 8 percent between 1821–25 and 1851–55 and at 2.5 percent from 1851–55 to 1881–85. The equivalent rates for sugar were 3.8 and 2.1 percent, respectively (calculated from *Anuário estatístico*, Ano V, pp. 1358–59). For estimates of profits from slaveholding see Pedro Carvalho de Mello, "The Economics of Labor in Brazilian Coffee Plantations, 1850–1888." Ph.D. diss., University of Chicago, pp. 170 ff. For Brazilian shares of world output see Hans Scherrer, *Die Kaffeevalorisation und Valorisationsversuche in anderen Artikeln des Welthandels* (Jena, 1919), p. 5.

60. Higman, *Slave Populations of the British Caribbean*, pp. 188–99.

61. G. W. Roberts ("Immigration of Africans into the British Caribbean," *Population Studies*, 7 [1954]: 3) lists 39,332 between 1834 and 1867, but most of these had been recently removed from slave ships by the British Navy and the extent to which they exercised choice over their destination is debatable.

62. Michael Craton, *Testing the Chains: Resistance to Slavery in the British West Indies* (Ithaca, N.Y., 1982), pp. 241–53; Schuler, *Alas, Alas, Kongo*, pp. 30–44; Sidney W. Mintz, "Slavery and the Rise of Peasantries," *Historical Reflections*, 6 (1979): 213–42; Richard Graham, "Slave Families on a Rural Estate in Colonial Brazil," *Journal of Social History*, 9 (1976): 382–402. See also the essays in Margaret E. Crahan and Franklin W. Knight (eds.), *Africa and the Caribbean: The Legacies of a Link* (Baltimore, Md., 1979).

63. Mintz, "Slavery and the Rise of Peasantries," pp. 214–15.

64. Christopher Hill, "Pottage for Freeborn Englishmen: Attitudes to Wage Labour in the Sixteenth and Seventeenth Centuries," in H. Feinstein (ed.), *Socialism, Capitalism and Economic Growth: Essays Presented to Maurice Dobb* (Cambridge, 1967), pp. 338–50; Eric Foner, *Free Soil, Free Labor, Free Men: The Ideology of the Republican Party before the Civil War* (New York, 1970); and Mintz, "Slavery and the Rise of Peasantries," may be read as establishing the similarities in the aspirations of working people widely separated in time and space.

65. Robert W. Fogel et al., "Secular Changes in American and British Stature and Nu tion," in Robert I. Rotberg and Theodore K. Rabb (eds.), *Hunger and History: T Impact of Changing Food Production and Consumption Patterns on Society* (Cambridge, 1985) pp. 247–83; B. W. Higman, "Growth in Afro-Caribbean Slave Populations," *American Journal of Physical Anthropology*, 50 (1979), 378–85; David Eltis, "Nutritional Trends in Africa and the Americas: Heights of Africans, 1819–1839," *Journal of Interdisciplinary History*, 12 (1982):247–83; Robert A. Margo and Richard H. Steckel, "Heights of American Slaves: New Evidence on Slave Nutrition and Health," *Social Science History*, 6 (1982):516–38. See also the other essays in this special issue. That a similar African/Creole differential emerged in St. Domingue is suggested by trends in stature in Haiti, see Jean Fouchard, *The Haitian Maroons: Liberty or Death*, trans. A. Faulkner Watts (New York, 1981), p. 177; see also the discussion in supra, chap. 5.

66. The periodic food shortages experienced by the British Caribbean in the late eighteenth century were not typical of American or even Caribbean societies. Such shortages may be attributed in the main to the interruption of food supplies to the British islands following the independence of the United States and a series of severe hurricanes. Higman's evidence (*Slave Populations in the British Caribbean*, pp. 280–92) suggests that nutritional gains relative to Africans in Africa were clearly established in the early nineteenth-century British Caribbean.

67. Ralph A. Austen, "From the Atlantic to the Indian Ocean: European Abolition, the African Slave Trade, and Asian Economic Structures," in D. Eltis and J. Walvin, *The Abolition of the Atlantic Slave Trade*, p. 132.

## Appendix A

1. The Colby paper was subsequently published in two parts: David Eltis, "The Export of Slaves from Africa, 1821–1843," *Journal of Economic History*, 37 (1977): 409–33; idem, "The Direction and Fluctuation of the Transatlantic Slave Trade, 1821–43: A Revision of the 1845 Parliamentary Paper," in H. A. Gemery and J. S. Hogendorn (eds.), *The Uncommon Market: Essays in the Economic History of the Atlantic Slave Trade* (New York, 1979), pp. 273–301. The later period was taken up in idem, "The Direction and Fluctuation of the Transatlantic Slave Trade, 1844–1867," paper presented at the African Studies Association meetings, Bloomington, Ind., 1981. The series presented in these papers have been revised and extended in idem, "The Nineteenth-Century Transatlantic Slave Trade: An Annual Time Series of Imports into the Americas Broken Down by Region," *Hispanic American Historical Review* (forthcoming); idem, "The Volume of the Transatlantic Slave Trade, 1781–1867," unpublished paper, 1983.

2. Philip D. Curtin, *The Atlantic Slave Trade: A Census* (Madison, Wis., 1969), p. 268; Paul E. Lovejoy, "The Volume of the Atlantic Slave Trade: A Synthesis," *Journal of African History*, 23 (1982): 483, 497.

3. As slave voyages could last three or more months, the conversion of annual import into export data raises a problem of dating. Three quarters of the voyages in the slave ship data set were recorded as they arrived in the Americas. For about three quarters of these ships no precise date of departure from Africa is available. For the remainder a voyage length in days was recorded from which a departure date may be readily calculated. However, for all major branches of the slave trade, it is possible to calculate a mean voyage length (see chap. 8) which is taken as the inferred time at sea whenever the actual data are missing. For a full explanation of the derivation process see David Eltis, "The Volume of the Transatlantic Slave Trade, 1781–1867."

## Appendix B

1. For a regession-based analysis of variance of these ratios between major regions of export and import, see David Eltis, "Fluctuations in the Age and Sex Ratios of Slaves in the Nineteenth-Century Transatlantic Slave Traffic," *Slavery & Abolition: A Journal of Comparative Studies,* 7 (1986):45–60.

## Appendix C

1. Richard N. Bean, *The British Trans-Atlantic Slave Trade, 1650–1775* (New York, 1975), pp. 133–212; Philip D. Curtin, *Economic Change in Precolonial Africa: Senegambia in the Era of the Slave Trade,* 2 vols. (Madison, Wis., 1975), 2:45–53.
2. See Bean, *British Slave Trade,* pp. 123–24, 133–34, for a discussion.
3. The data are from the following sources: Anti-Slavery Papers, Rhodes House Library, Oxford, files G-77, G-78; African Institution, *Report of the Committee of the African Institution,* annually from 1807 to 1821; *British and Foreign Anti-Slavery Reporter;* I. U. P. *Slave Trade,* various volumes. Buxton mss., various volumes; Thomas Fowell Buxton, *The African Slave Trade and Its Remedy* (London, 1840); T. Conneau, *A Slaver's Log Book;* Frederick Cooper, *Plantation Slavery on the East Coast of Africa* (New Haven, Conn., 1977); Pedro Carvalho de Mello, "The Economics of Labour in Brazilian Coffee Plantations, 1850–1888." Ph.D. diss., University of Chicago, 1977; Warren Dean, *Rio Claro: A Brazilian Plantation System, 1820–1920* (Stanford, Calif., 1976); Ramirez Guerra y Sánchez et al., *Historia de la nación cubana,* (Havana, 1952), pp. 301–2; FO 84, various volumes; FO 72, various volumes; Admiralty 1, various volumes; High Court of Admiralty records; FO 308, vol. 1; Robert F. Jameson, *Letters from Havana During the Year 1820* (London, 1821), p. 32: Parliamentary Papers, Great Britain, House of Lords, 1852, 22:346–86; Manuel Moreno Fraginals, Herbert S. Klein, Stanley L. Engerman, "The Level and Structure of Slave Prices on Cuban Plantations in the Mid-Nineteenth Century: Some Comparative Perspectives," *American Historical Review,* 88 (1983):1201–18; Stanley J. Stein, *Vassouras, a Brazilian Coffee County, 1850–1900* (Cambridge, Mass., 1957).
4. The series may be found in PP, 1847–48, 22: app. to *Third Report from Select Committee on the Slave Trade,* p. 232. The letter discrediting Cliffe's evidence is W. J. Henwood to M. M. Pendaroes, March 9, 1850, FO 84/818.
5. David Eltis, "Price Trends in the Atlantic Slave Trade after 1810," unpublished paper, 1984.

## Appendix D

1. David Eltis, "Mortality and Voyage Length in the Middle Passage: New Evidence from the Nineteenth Century,"*Journal of Economic History,* 44 (1984): 301–8.
2. For three of the African regions discussed in table D.1, it is possible to carry out the monthly analysis on the basis of daily mortality rates calculated with actual rather than inferred voyage lengths—in other words, using the small rather than the enlarged data set. The three are the Bight of Benin, Congo North and Luanda regions. The results for all three were almost indentical to those produced by carrying out the same procedures with the enlarged data set.
3. For a fuller exploration of these points, see David Eltis, "Mortality in the Nineteenth Century Transatlantic Slave Trade," Unpublished paper, 1984.

## Appendix E

1. The discussion of costs has been subsumed in the debate over profitability. See Kenneth G. Davies, *The Royal African Company* (London, 1957), chap. 2; Roger T. Anstey, *The Atlantic Slave Trade and British Abolition* (London, 1975), chap. 2; Stanley Dumbell, "The Profits of the Guinea Trade," *Economic Journal*, 2 (1931):254–57; F. E. Hyde, B. B. Parkinson and Sheila Marriner, "The Nature and Profitability of the Liverpool Slave Trade," *Economic History Review*, 5 (1952–53):368–77; David Richardson, "Profits in the Liverpool Slave Trade: The Accounts of William Davenport, 1757–1784," in Roger Anstey and P. E. H. Hair (eds.), *Liverpool, the African Slave Trade and Abolition: Essays to Illustrate Current Knowledge and Research* (Liverpool, Eng., 1976), pp. 60–90; Joseph E. Inikori, "Market Structure and the Profits of the British African Trade in the Late Eighteenth Century," *Journal of Economic History*, 41 (1981):745–76; William A. Darity, "The Numbers Game and the Profitability of the British Trade in Slaves," *Journal of Economic History*, 45 (1985):693–703.

2. David Turnbull, *Travels in the West. Cuba: With Notices of Porto Rico and the Slave Trade* (London, 1840), pp. 403–6; E. Phillip LeVeen, *British Slave Trade Suppression Policies, 1821–1865,* (New York, 1977), pp. 9–34, 164.

3. Philip D. Curtin, "The Abolition of the Slave Trade in Senegambia," in David Eltis and James Walvin (eds.), *The Abolition of the Atlantic Slave Trade* (Madison, Wis., 1981), pp. 89–91.

4. For Curtin's discussion of costs, see *Economic Change in Precolonial Africa: Senegambia in the Era of the Slave Trade*, 2 vols. (Madison, Wis., 1975), 1:156–57, 168–69, 173–77; 2:45–53.

5. Captain Owen to Admiralty, Feb. 21, 1828, enc. "Report on the Old Calabar River," Adm. 1/2273.

6. W. Rothery to Palmerston, Jan. 23, 1841 (enc.), FO 84/379.

7. T. Conneau, *A Slaver's Log Book* (Englewood Cliffs, N.J., 1976), pp. 64–65, 76–77.

8. W. Macleay to Aberdeen, July 21, 1829 (enc.), FO 84/100.

9. LeVeen, *British Slave Trade Suppression,* pp. 11, 115.

10. Curtin, *Economic Change in Precolonial Africa,* 1:174.

11. G. Jackson and E. Gabriel to Palmerston, Feb. 18, 1847, FO 84/671; Consul Foote to Russell, Feb. 9, 1861, FO 84/1141. For a general assessment of factor operations in the 1840s, see Adm. to Palmerston, May 30, 1848, enc. Commodore Hotham, Mar. 14, 1848, FO 84/747.

12. For prices, see app. C. The increase in factor cost relative to African cost was even larger than it appears. At the end of the traffic, the total quantity of slaves shipped fell. The drop in African cost was thus partly a function of lower prices paid to the African supplier and the resultant drop in quantity supplied. Factor costs, too, should have fallen in this period as quantities declined.

13. McTavish to Palmerston, Jan. 30, 1840, FO 84/332.

14. F. R. Cocking to Tredgold, Dec. 17, 1841, Brit. Emp. mss., s.22. G 77; Joseph Crawford to Clarendon, Jan. 14, 1856, FO 84/984.

15. J. Jones to Palmerston, Aug. 8, 1849, FO 84/764. As inspection of ships' papers was a major part of the naval policing function, there are many references to purchase prices in the naval and court correspondence. As the age of the ship was only occasionally recorded, however, the pricing information on its own is of limited use. Nevertheless, it is worth noting that ships costing more than $12,000 became common only in the later years of the illicit trade, when average ship size increased significantly and when steamers began to be used. Converted to real terms, this cost-

per-ton-figure is at the lower end of the range of $35 to $45 per ton, which was the cost of a two hundred-ton ship in England in the late eighteenth century (Ralph Davis, *The Rise of the English Shipping Industry,* [London, 1962], p. 375).

16. For the *Serpente,* see Hudson to Palmerston, Mar. 24, 1849, FO 84/765; July 27, 1850, FO 84/804. For the *Ciceron,* see Admiralty to Russell, Jan. 13, 1864 sub enc. Commander Leveson Wildman, Oct. 24, 1863, FO 84/1227; J. Brackenbury to Russell, Feb. 10, 1864, FO 84/1218; Adm. to Palmerston, Nov. 25, 1845, enc. Commodore Jones, Sept. 29, 1845, FO 84/612; Hudson to Palmerston, Nov. 16, 1848, FO 84/726; and July 27, 1850, FO 84/804.

17. Porter to Palmerston, Jan. 1, 1848, FO 84/727.

18. Adm. to Clarendon, Jan. 12, 1866 enc. Commodore Wilmot, Dec. 19, 1865, FO 84/1267. Apart from cost, a key deterrent to the use of steam seems to have been the widespread use of steam vessels in the British suppressive squadron from the 1840s on. It is also worth noting that sail predominated on many long-distance routes until the early twentieth century, in particular on the Far Eastern/Caribbean indentured labor traffic and that the major reductions in transportation costs in the general cargo business took place before the widespread introduction of steam ships at midcentury.

19. See the discussion in LeVeen, *British Slave Trade Suppression,* pp. 94–95; cf. David Richardson, "Profits in the Liverpool Slave Trade," pp. 70–71. For comments on the speed versus durability issue, see G. Jackson and E. Gabriel to Palmerston, May 30, 1849, enc. "Seizor's claim," FO 84/758; and Adm. to Aberdeen, Apr. 19, 1845, enc. Col. E. Nicolls, Apr. 17, 1845, FO 84/609. For examples of increased wear and tear induced by suppression, see Lt. Forbes, *Six Months Service in the African Blockade* (London, 1849), pp. 86–87.

20. LeVeen, *British Slave Trade Suppression,* p. 94.

21. H. W. Macaulay to Palmerston, Nov. 18, 1836 (enc.), FO 84/168. For payrolls, see W. Macleay to Palmerston, July 21, 1829 (enc.), FO 84/100; Jan. 1, 1829 (enc.), FO 84/91; H. W. Macaulay and W. W. Lewis to Palmerston, Apr. 15, 1839, FO 84/269; W. Cole and H. W. Macaulay to Wellington, June 5, 1835 (enc.), FO 84/166; Gregory and Fitzgerald to Canning, July 24, 1822, FO 84/16. For court evidence, see *Federal Cases,* 30 vols. (St. Paul, Minn., 1894–97), case No. 14,454; Gregory and Hamilton to Canning, Sept. 10, 1823, FO 84/22. For higher wages in the 1840s, see Crawford to Palmerston, Nov. 4, 1849, FO 84/761; and Kennedy to Palmerston, Jan. 1, 1850, FO 84/797. For wages in the last decade, see Admiralty to Clarendon Mar. 29, 1855, sub enc. John McLaughlin, FO 84/981; U.S. Congress, Sen. Exec. Doc., 34–1, 99:69; H. Exec. Doc. 36–2, 7:115–18; Admiralty to Russell, Mar. 13, 1863, enc. Commander Beamish, Dec. 31, 1862, FO 84/1207; Consul Dunlop to Russell, Oct. 7, 1864, FO 84/1218. For the Gordon case, see Warren S. Howard, *American Slavers and the Federal Law, 1837–1862* (Berkeley, Calif., 1963), pp. 199–202. References to wages in the Bahia and Rio de Janeiro traffic may be found in I.U.P., *Slave Trade,* 27:369; 29:208, 224, 233, 247–365, passim.

22. For commission rates in the nineteenth-century, in addition to supra, n. 13, see M. L. Melville and J. Hook to Aberdeen, Apr. 14, 1845 (enc.) FO 84/558; George Jackson to Palmerston, June 17, 1850, FO 84/794; and Sept. 18, 1850, FO 84/795; C. O. to Palmerston, Dec. 31, 1840 (sub enc.), FO 84/337.

23. This assessment is based on the list of cargo contents of sixty-four slave ships and adjudicated before the mixed commission courts and the Vice Admiralty courts after 1840.

24. PP, 1830, 10:136. The rate was actually 3 pence per diem for adults and 1.5 pence for children.

25. M. L. Melville, J. Hook to Aberdeen, Dec. 24, 1844, enc. "Opinion of British Co missory Judge," FO 84/507; Cole and Macaulay to Palmerston, Nov. 21, 1834 (enc. FO 84/148; *Federal Cases,* case No. 14,918; Adm. to Malmesbury, Oct. 20, 1858, sub enc. Lt. Pike, Aug. 16, 1858, FO 84/1070.
26. W. S. Macleay and E. Schenley to Palmerston, Aug. 31, 1835, FO 84/172, refers to a "normal" rate of 22 percent for the Cuban traffic. See also J. Brackenbury to Canning, Feb. 27, 1826 (enc.), FO 84/54; Jose Gardé to Admiralty, Apr. 11, 1835, Adm. 1/4670. For the post-1835 period, see E. Schenley to Palmerston, Jan. 31, 1837, FO 84/216; W. Macleay to Palmerston, October 15, 1835, FO 84/170; H. Hamilton to Palmerston, Nov. 11, 1836, FO 84/204; *Third Report of the House of Commons Select Committee on the Slave Trade,* PP, 1847–48, 22:76.
27. W. G. Ouseley to Palmerston, May 19, 1836, FO 84/204; Henry S. P. Eyre to Thomas Fowell Buxton, July 6, 1836, 29/100, Bx mss.; "Minute Book" of Anglo-Portuguese Mixed Commission, fols. 103–4, FO 308/1; W. G. Ouseley to Palmerston, July 7, 1841, FO 84/365; C. D. Tolmé to Palmerston, Sept. 17, 1839, FO 84/280; Turnbull *Travels,* p. 142. See also the references to insurance in Robert Conrad, "The Contraband Slave Trade to Brazil, 1831–1845," *Hispanic American Historical Review,* 49 (1969): 623, 629, 635.
28. For bribes to Portuguese Angolan officials, see Adm. to Aberdeen, Nov. 24, 1842, enc. Bishop to Capt. Foote, July 29, 1842, FO 84/442.
29. For fraudulent registers, see W. Macleay to Backhouse, July 21, 1829 (enc.), FO 84/100; H. W. Macaulay to Palmerston, Apr. 26, 1837 (enc.), FO 84/211; J. Campbell and W. W. Lewis to Palmerston, Jan. 6, 1837, FO 84/212; H. Hamilton, Nov. 24, 1842 (sub enc.), FO 84/442. See also Conneau, *Slaver's Log Book,* pp. 78–79 and passim. For estimates of freight costs see Admiralty to Palmerston, Sept. 23, 1841 (enc.), FO 84/385; W. G. Ouseley to Palmerston, Mar. 13, 1841, FO 84/364; H. W. Macaulay and R. Doherty to Palmerston, Dec. 15, 1838 (enc.), FO 84/237; Adm. to Palmerston, June 8, 1841 (enc.), FO 84/384. The master of the *Mary E. Smith* received $8,000 for taking that ship to the coast in 1856 (J. Morgan to Clarendon, Aug. 11, 1856 [enc.], FO 84/995). Captain Watson of the *Lydia Gibbs* was to receive $6,000 for a similar trip in 1859 (Admiralty to Russell, Feb., 1859 enc. Commander Close to Admiralty Dec. 22, 1859, FO 84/1097).
30. Several different houses in Bahia charged King Kosoko 5 percent on eleven different slave consignments between 1848 and 1850 (PP, H. of Lords, 1852–53, 22:328–66). For British Caribbean rates, see Anstey, *Atlantic Slave Trade,* p. 417; and LeVeen, *British Slave Trade,* pp. 32–33. For descriptions of the sale of newly imported Africans in Cuba and Rio de Janeiro, see W. Macleay and W. Schenley to Palmerston, Dec. 1, 1835, FO 84/172; H. Hamilton to Palmerston, November 11, 1836, FO 84/204; W. G. Ouseley to Palmerston, Dec. 15, 1838, FO 84/254; George Stephen to Aberdeen, June 17, 1843 (enc.), FO 84/501; G. Canning to Frederick Lamb, Apr. 4, 1825 (enc.), FO 84/41.
31. John Parkinson to Palmerston, Dec. 10, 1834, FO 84/157.
32. For Cuba, see W. Macleay to Palmerston, Jan. 1, 1831, FO 84/119; J. Crawford to Palmerston, Sept. 27, 1842, FO 84/401. For Brazil, see G. Jackson and F. Grigg to Palmerston, Dec. 18, 1834, enc. "Juiz de direito to President of the Province of Rio de Janeiro," FO 84/204; H. S. Fox to Palmerston, Nov. 8, 1835 (enc.), FO 84/179; W. G. Ouseley to Palmerston, Jan. 31, 1836, FO 84/204.
33. For increasing bribes in the 1840s in addition to the sources cited in table E.2, see J. Kennedy and C. J. Dalrymple to Palmerston, Mar. 5, 1846, FO 84/620; J. Kennedy to Palmerston, Dec. 28, 1847, FO 84/674.
34. PP, H. of Lords, 1852–53, 22:328–66.

This assessment is based on the annual reports of the British commissioners in Havana to the Foreign Office, Jan. 1, 1857, FO 84/1012; Jan. 28, 1858, FO 84/1042; Jan. 25, 1859, FO 84/1073; Sept. 30, 1860, FO 84/1106; Sept. 30, 1862, FO 84/1174; Sept. 30, 1863, FO 84/1197; Sept. 30, 1865, FO 84/1236.

36. W. T. Kilbee to Canning, Jan. 1, 1825, FO 84/39; Colonial Office to Palmerston, July 27, 1840, enc. R. R. Madden, July 1, 1839, FO 84/336. An English clerk in a Havana merchant's office also estimated the total cost figure at $40,000. See "Conversations with D. R. Clarke, June 6, 1838, 31/250–51, Buxton mss.

37. LeVeen, *British Slave Trade Suppression*, pp. 10, 21–24.

38. W. Macleay to Aberdeen, July 21, 1829, enc. P. Blanco to Martinez, Feb. 23, 1829, FO 84/100; H. W. Macaulay and R. Doherty to Palmerston, Dec. 15, 1838, enc. Messrs. Blanco and Carballo to Mariano Dias, Sept. 26, 1838, FO 84/237; G. Jackson to Palmerston, Dec. 27, 1833 (enc.), FO 84/138; H. W. Macaulay and W. Cole to Palmerston, June 5, 1835 (enc.) FO 84/166; Admiralty to Palmerston, Feb. 24, 1848, enc. Comm. Sprigg, Dec. 27, 1847, FO 84/746.

39. Buxton, *African Slave Trade*, pp. 221–25. For criticisms see W. G. Ouseley to Palmerston, July 18, 1839, FO 84/287, in particular the discussion of the variance of profits in the trade.

40. Roger Anstey, "The Profitability of the Slave Trade in the 1840s," in Vera Rubin and Arthur Tuden (eds.), *Comparative Perspectives on Slavery in New World Plantation Societies* (New York, 1977), pp. 84–93; LeVeen, *British Slave Trade Suppression*, p. 22.

41. Colonial Office to Aberdeen, July 27, 1840 (enc.), FO 84/336.

42. W. Macleay to Aberdeen, July 31, 1829, FO 84/92. For comments on the losses of slave traders, see Colonial Office to Aberdeen, June 30, 1842, FO 84/433; C. D. Tolmé to Palmerston, Sept. 16, 1839, FO 84/280; W. G. Ouseley to Palmerston, Sept. 16, 1839, FO 84/287.

## Appendix F

1. D. C. M. Platt, "Problems in the Interpretation of Foreign Trade Statistics Before 1914," *Journal of Latin American Studies,* 3 (1971):119–30.

2. James Kennedy estimated that Cuban trade statistics underreported actual sugar exports by about one fifth (to Palmerston, Mar. 20, 1848, FO 84/714).

3. For comments on official valuations, see Consul Clarke to Aberdeen, Dec. 28, 1841, FO 72/587.

4. Manuel Moreno Fraginals, *El ingenio, complejo económico social cubano del azúcar,* 3 vols. (Havana, 1978), 3:35–37. For Noel Deerr's data, see *The History of Sugar,* 2 vols. (London, 1949–50), 1:131. See also PP, 1878–79, 13:403 and, for 1853–78 only the report prepared by an Amsterdam sugar importing firm (ibid., p. 409).

5. The equations are (standard errors in first set of parentheses, F statistics in second):

$$NYSug = -0.00157 + (0.852\ PHSug)$$
$$(0.0035) \quad (0.04)$$
$$(0.2) \quad (439.8)$$
$$n = 37$$
$$r^2 = 0.93$$

$$NYSug = 0.00057 + (0.0024\ LSug)$$
$$(0.007) \quad (0.0003)$$
$$(0.06) \quad (85.2)$$
$$n = 37$$
$$r^2 = 0.71$$

Where *NYSug, PHSug* and *LSug,* are the wholesale prices of sugar in New Y̶
Philadelphia and London, respectively in cents per pound.

A convenient source for the two U.S. series is Francisco A. Scarano, *Sugar anₐ*
*Slavery in Puerto Rico: The Plantation Economy of Ponce, 1800–1850* (Madison,
Wis., 1984), pp. 184–85. The London series is in PP, 1856, 55:2–3; 1863, 67:3, 1878–
79, 13:402.

6. José Curet, "About Slavery and the Order of Things: Puerto Rico, 1845–1873," in
   Manuel Moreno Fraginals, Frank Moya Pons, and Stanley L. Engerman (eds.),
   *Between Slavery and Free Labor: The Spanish Speaking Caribbean in the Nine-*
   *teenth Century* (Baltimore, Md., 1985), p. 126.

7. Jacobo de la Pezuela y Lobo, *Diccionario, geográfico, estadístico, histórico de la isla*
   *de Cuba,* 4 vols. (Madrid, 1863–66), 1:225; Ramón de la Sagra, *Historia económico*
   *- politíca y estadística de la isla de Cuba* (Havana, 1831), pp. 174, 211.

8. In 1827 exports from Havana accounted for 50 percent of the total crop harvested
   and 72 percent of all coffee exports from the island (Cuba, Comision de estadística,
   *Cuadro estadístico de la siempre fiel isla de Cuba correspondiente al año de 1827*
   [Havana, 1829], p. 30).

9. The equations are (standard errors in first set of parentheses, F statistic in
   second):

$$NYcof = 0.0548 + (0.0393 \ BRcof)$$
$$(0.015) \quad (0.008)$$
$$(13.3) \quad (25.0)$$
$$n = 37$$
$$r^2 = 0.42$$

Where *NYcof* = wholesale price of coffee in New York in cents per pound.

*BRcof* = average value of 60 kilograms of coffee exported from Rio de
Janeiro in pounds sterling.

The sources are Scarano, *Sugar and Slavery in Puerto Rico,* pp. 184–85; Instituto
brasileiro de geografia e estatística, *Anuário estatístico do brasil,* Ano V, 1939–40,
p. 1379.

10. Roberto C. Simonsen, *História econômica do Brasil (1500-1820),* 6th ed. (São
    Paulo, 1969), p. 375; PP, 1878–79, 13:409; Lúis Amaral, *História geral da agricul-*
    *tura brasileira,* 2 vols. (São Paulo, 1958), 2:304.

11. See Nathaniel H. Leff, *Underdevelopment and Development in Brazil,* 2 vols. (Lon-
    don, 1982), 1:122–24 for the formal presentation of this point.

### Appendix G

1. For the pound/milreis exchange rate, see the British consular reports in the FO 84
   series and Instituto brasileiro de geografia e estatística, *Anúario estatístico do Brasil,*
   Ano V, 1939–40, p. 855. For conversion of pounds into dollars, see Edwin J. Perkins,
   "Foreign Interest Rates in American Financial Markets: A Revised Series of Dollar
   Sterling Exchange Rates: 1835-1900," *Journal of Economic History,* 38 (1978):392–
   417, and Lawrence H. Officer, "Dollar Sterling Mint Parity and Exchange Rates,
   1791-1834," *Journal of Economic History,* 43 (1983):579–616.

2. Arthur Gayer, W. W. Rostow, and Anna J. Schwartz, *The Growth and Fluctuation of*
   *the British Economy, 1790-1850,* 2 vols. (London, 1953), 2:468–69; Paul Rousseaux,
   *Les Mouvements de fond de l'économie anglaise, 1800-1913* (Louvain, 1938), pp.
   266–67.

3. See Nathaniel H. Leff, *Underdevelopment and Development in Brazil,* 2 vols. (New
   York, 1982), 1:122–24, for a formal presentation of this point.

# Sources

## 1. DATA

Six separate data sets have been developed or expanded for this study.

*(a) Slave-Ship Data Set.*
In the 1960s Philip Curtin put the 2,313 records of slave-ship voyages listed in the 1845 Parliamentary Papers into machine readable form (Curtin, *The Atlantic Slave Trade: A Census* [Madison, Wis., 1969], pp. 233–43. The original return is PP, 1845, 49:593–633.) This set, comprising fifteen different fields of information, has since been available from the University of Wisconsin data center. This list of ships was originally prepared for Parliament by the British Foreign Office, and it has been possible to consult the internal correspondence that the Foreign Office clerks used to create the list. Examination of the original sources has allowed the improvement and expansion of the 1845 list in three respects. First, missing data have been added to the fifteen fields requested by the House of Commons. Second, nine categories of information beyond the original request have been added. Third, additional records have been uncovered both for the 1817 to 1843 period covered by the 1845 paper and, more important, for the years before and after this period. In addition twenty-one voyages were deleted from the 1845 listing on the basis of double counting or other errors. The original sources for this data are letters to the British Foreign Office and Admiralty from diplomatic representatives, naval officers, and judges as well as from merchants and other individuals of several nationalities located around the Atlantic littoral. These are deposited in the British Public Record Office and may be found mainly in the FO 84 series. Almost all the manuscript and printed sources in the following list have, however, contributed something to the data set. In addition, for the 1850s and 1860s, Warren S. Howard, *American Slavers and the Federal Law* (Berkeley, Calif., 1963), pp. 213–62 has proved a useful source. The final data set used in the present study spanned the years 1811–67 and included 5,378 ships and twenty-four different fields of information. The two major additions to the 1845 list were ships that completed the voyage to the Americas after 1843 (about 1,000 in number) and ships that set sail throughout the years 1811–67 but were diverted from a successful outcome by cruiser action (approximately 1,600 in number). Most of the latter

...processed by the mixed commission courts and Vice Admiralty courts and infor-
...tion about them is thus relatively abundant in the extracts of court records that were
...eturned to the Foreign Office and frequently published in the parliamentary papers. In
addition, Joseph C. Miller and Herbert S. Klein kindly made available data not included
in either of the above categories. Miller's data, from the FO 63 series, comprising 388
records, were for branches of the Brazilian traffic in the years 1811–19. (These data are
presented in Miller's "Sources and Knowledge of the Slave Trade in the Southern Atlantic," unpublished paper, 1977, and will be incorporated into his forthcoming book, *Way
of Death: Merchant Capitalism and the Angolan Slave Trade, 1730–1830*). Klein's data,
taken from the Rio de Janeiro newspaper reports of ship arrivals at that port, covered
the years 1825 to 1830, though only 88 of these ships during the years 1826 and 1828
were not already included in the 1845 Parliamentary Paper (Klein's data formed the
basis of chapter 4 of his *The Middle Passage* [Princeton, N.J., 1978]). Many ships in
both the Miller and Klein sets which were included in the original 1845 list provided a
useful base for checking and correcting copying errors and omissions.

*(b) Slave Data Set.*
Between 1819 and 1845 British cruisers landed almost 60,000 African slaves at Sierra
Leone, most of whom had been recaptured while en route to the Americas or to islands
off the African coast. The age, height, name, distinguishing body marks, and, in a few
cases, the country of origin of 56,935 of these Africans were officially registered by the
courts. Because the slaves were registered by the ship on which they were found, the
official trial reports for each ship make it possible to determine the date, the port of
embarkation, and the port of intended disembarkation (British Public Record Office,
Foreign Office: Series 84, vols. 4, 9, 15, 21, 38, 63, 64, 76, 86, 87, 100, 101, 102, 116,
166, 212). The data are made up of 27,107 records. They include entries for the first
26,046 Africans the courts liberated between 1819 and 1832; an additional 1,061 records
from the later 1830s were added because they document slaves taken from regions of
Africa not represented in the earlier period. Not all points of embarkation, much less all
regions of origin, are present in the data. Because of treaty restrictions on naval activity,
Angola is represented by only three young females, and there are only 481 records of
embarkation points from the Congo River north to Cape Lopez and 577 records for the
whole of southeast Africa. Because the slave trade had virtually stopped by 1821 in Senegambia and the Ivory and Gold coasts, these areas are also seriously underrepresented.
Thus the great bulk of the slaves recorded embarked from Upper Guinea and the bights
of Benin and Biafra, or from the coast between Cape Lopez and the Casamance River.
Within these limits, we may treat the Sierra Leone recaptives as a representative sample
of those slaves taken to the Americas in the 1820s and 1830s.

*(c) Slave-Price Data Set.*
This set comprises 412 observations of slave prices on both sides of the Atlantic. Most
of these observations are for large groups of slaves, often cargoes or part cargoes. A number of prices already published in secondary sources such as those developed by Stanley
J. Stein, Pedro Carvalho de Mello and Warren Dean for Brazil as well as Manuel Moreno Fraginals, Herbert S. Klein and Stanley L. Engerman for Cuba have been incorporated into the present data. A fuller description of the set may be found in appendix C.

*(d) Age/Sex Data Set.*
For 435 of the slave cargoes embarked in the nineteenth-century traffic, data on sex and
adult/child status are available. Most of this information again comes from copies of
the Sierra Leone court records in the Public Record Office, London. The age/sex categories in the records are broad: "men," "women," "girls" and "boys"—occasionally just
"children" and even "males" and "females," with no further elaboration. There will

likely be some bias on account of the earlier maturation of females and no attemp~~t has~~ been made to correct for this. In almost all cases it is possible to locate place of emb~~ar~~kation, details of the ship carrying the slaves, and in many cases the intended (or actua~~l)~~ port of disembarkation in the Americas. Cross reference to the slave-ship data set is usually possible. There are 114,225 slaves in this data set.

*(e) Slave-Ship-Dimensions Data Set.*
When a British cruiser captured a slave ship that it could not conduct to court, the captain would normally take the length, breadth and depth of hold of the slaver before setting the prize on fire or using it as target practice. The measurements were then submitted to the courts together with equipment from the captured vessel as proof of capture. The dimensions of 127 slave ships have survived in the court records and once more cross reference to the main slave-ship data set is usually possible. Unfortunately in most cases tonnage measurements are not available for these ships.

*(f) Plantation Output Data Set.*
Annual output and average prices for the major plantation crops in the Americas have been collected into one data set together with mean annual slave prices, where available, and average slave imports for each major importing region. The derivation and sources of this data are taken up more fully in appendix F.

The slave-ship, slave and age/sex data sets are on deposit at the Government of Canada archives, Ottawa.

# 2. MANUSCRIPT SOURCES

## Great Britain

### (a) Public Record Office, London

Admiralty 1 (Letters to the Secretary's Department of the Admiralty): 102 volumes consulted, covering the years 1809 to 1839. Access to these naval despatches is via the annual indexes and digests contained in Admiralty 12, 4898–12164. Increasingly from the 1820s on copies of naval dispatches on the slave trade were transmitted to the Foreign Office where they were filed in the FO 84 series described later. By the 1840s it is likely that the FO 84 series contains duplicates of almost all the slave-trade material in Admiralty 1.

Admiralty 7: 605, 606.

Admiralty 123 (Station Records, Africa): vols. 173–185.

Colonial Office 267 (Sierra Leone): vols. 25, 31, 36, 51. From the mid-1820s on, copies of slave-trade material from Sierra Leone were routinely sent to the Foreign Office and deposited in FO 84.

Customs 4: vol. 5–53.

Customs 8: vol. 10–74.

Foreign Office 13 (Brazil): vols. 40, 141.

Foreign Office 63 (Portugal): vol. 223, 230.

Foreign Office 72 (Spain): vols. 297, 372, 384, 415,431,449,468,489,513, 538, 559, 560A, 584–587, 608–610, 634.

Foreign Office 83 (Law Officers): vols. 2348–2351.

Foreign Office 84 (Correspondence of the Slave Trade Department): vols. 2, 3, 4, 7–24, 26–30, 34–42, 44–108, 110–122, 124–130, 134–138, 140–141, 144–153, 155, 157, 161–180, 183–184, 186, 188–199, 201–204, 208–219, 221–223, 227–230, 232–242, 244–255, 261–277, 280, 284–289, 299–305, 207–216, 319–320, 322–326, 335–351, 356–360, 363–368, 379–385, 389–398, 401–402, 405–409, 411, 428, 431–443, 445–

, 457–461, 463, 466–470, 489–491, 494–511, 514–518, 520, 523–526, 542, 545–
51, 555–564, 566–573, 578, 581–582, 584, 608–612, 618, 620–634, 651, 657–660,
663–668, 672, 678–679, 696, 703–706, 709–716, 719–722, 725–727, 738–740, 746–
749, 752–755, 757–761, 764–767, 775–785, 788–795, 801–819, 816–818, 821–828,
831–835, 838, 841–848, 858–859, 864–866, 869–872, 874, 880, 886–887, 892–902,
905–907, 912, 920–921, 925–926, 928–932, 936–937, 950–951, 954–961, 964–965,
975–977, 980–981, 983–986, 988, 1001–1003, 1008–1009, 1011–1014, 1016, 1030–
1032, 1037–1038, 1040–1044, 1046, 1059, 1061–1062, 1068–1078, 1080, 1086–1088,
1097–1100, 1102–1107, 1109, 1111, 1115, 1117, 1123–1124, 1132–1136, 1138, 1140,
1148–1150, 1166–1170, 1172, 1174, 1183–1186, 1194–1195, 1197–1198, 1203, 1207–
1209, 1214–1216, 1218, 1227–1229, 1234–1238, 1241, 1252–1253, 1263, 1265, 1267–
1268, 1270–1272, 1274, 1281–1282, 1286.

Foreign Office 95: vol. 9/2.

Foreign Office 97: vols. 430, 432.

Foreign Office 308: (British and Portuguese Commission, 1819–24): vols. 1–3.

Foreign Office 313 (Havana Mixed Commission): vols. 7, 18, 32–36, 49. Much of the material in this series is duplicated in the FO 84 series.

Foreign Office 315 (Sierra Leone Mixed Commissions): vols. 41, 69. Much of the material in this series is duplicated in FO 84. Here and in the records of other mixed commission courts there are many bundles of papers taken from ships condemned in the courts. Only a few of these have been sampled for the present study.

Foreign Office 541 (Confidential Print, Slave Trade): vols. 1–11. Most of this material, covering the years 1858 to 1867, appeared in the Parliamentary Papers.

High Court of Admiralty 37 (Slave Trade, Treasury Papers): vols. 1–6.

High Court of Admiralty 49 (Vice Admiralty Court Records): vols. 97, 101.

Privy Council 2: vols. 175–176, 183, 196–199.

Public Record Office. 30/22 (Russell Papers).

*(b)  Rhodes House Library, Oxford*

Mss. Brit. Emp. s.22 (Anti-Slavery Papers): files G77–80.

Mss. Brit. Emp. s.444 (Papers of Sir Thomas Fowell Buxton): vols. 17, 23–24, 26–34, 38–46.

*(c)  National Register of Archives, London*

Palmerston Papers (Broadlands Mss.): General correspondence with James Hudson, Lord John Russell, William Gore Ouseley, Sir Francis Baring, Lord Minto, the Duke of Somerset; Slave-trade Memoranda.

*(d)  British Library, London (British Museum)*

Aberdeen Papers (Additional Mss.): vols. 43064–43065, 43123–43125, 43242–43246, 433357.

Peel Papers (Additional Mss.): vols. 40453–40455.

*(e)  University College Library, University of London*

Brougham Papers.

*(f)  University of Liverpool Library*

"Memorandum of African Trade, 1830–1840" for W. A. and G. Maxwell and Co. Account Book of *Lottery*.

*(g)  Liverpool Public Library*

920 ROS (Letters of William Roscoe): fols. 354–3069.

*Sources*

387 MD (Account Books of Ships of Thomas Leyland and Co.: *Enterprise, For* *Lottery, Earl of Liverpool*): vols. 40–44.

*(h) Chamber of Commerce, Manchester*

Proceedings of the Chamber of Commerce and Manufacturers of Manchester Annual Reports of Chambers of Commerce, 1821–1850.

*(i) Manchester Public Library*

Proceedings of the Manchester Commercial Association.

*(j) Chamber of Commerce, Glasgow*

Minute Books, 1821–1839.

**United States**

*(a) National Archives, Washington*

NA 89 (Letters to the Secretary of the Navy from the African Squadron, 1843–1861): vols. 82, 105–115.

*(b) Henry E. Huntington Library, San Marino, California*

Clarkson Papers.
Macaulay Papers.


## 3. PRINTED SOURCES

A comprehensive catalog of printed material on the slave trade and its suppression is Peter C. Hogg, *The African Slave Trade and Its Suppression: A Classified and Annotated Bibliography of Books, Pamphlets and Periodical Articles* (London, 1973). There seems little purpose in reproducing what would essentially be excerpts of that volume as a bibliography here. The following published sources, mainly official, are not included in the Hogg volume:

**Brazil**

Instituto brasileiro de geografia e estatística, Conselho nacional de estatística, *Anuário estatístico do Brasil,* ano III–1937; idem, *Anuário estatístico do Brasil,* ano V 1939/ 1940

**Cuba**

*Balanza general del commercio de la isla de Cuba en al año de 1826* (Havana, 1827).
*Balanza general del commercio de la isla de Cuba en al año de 1840* (Havana, 1840).
*Balanza mercantil de la Habana correspondiente al año de 1828* (Havana, 1829).
*Balanza mercantil de la Habana correspondiente al año de 1836* (Havana, 1837).
*Cuadro estadístico de la siempre fiel isla de cuba correspondiente al año de 1827* (Havana, 1829).
*Cuadro estadístico de la siempre fiel isla de Cuba correspondiente al año de 1846* (Havana, 1847).
*Noticias estadísticas de la isla de Cuba en 1862* (Havana, 1864).

**Great Britain**

Parliamentary Papers, Irish University Press series:
(a) *Slave Trade:* vols. 1–51, 61–68, 75, 77, 80, 81, 87–91.

*Colonies, Africa:* vols. 1–3, 5, 50, 52.
) *Colonies, West Indies:* vols. 1, 2.

...hese volumes include most of the slave-trade material published annually in the Parliamentary Papers as well as the reports of the select committees of both the House of Commons and the House of Lords on the slave trade, Africa and the West Indies. The following papers used in the present study are not included in the above volumes:

1789 (646a) 26: *Report of the Privy Council Committee on the Slave Trade.*

1830–1831 (120) 9: *Statement, Calculations and Explanations Submitted to the Board of Trade Relating to the ... British West India Colonies.*

1847–1848 (123, 137, 167, 184, 206, 230, 245, 361, 409, 518) 23: *Report from the Select Committee on Sugar and Coffee Planting* (eight reports).

1852–1853 (House of Lords Sessional Papers) 22: 327–72, *Slave Trade Correspondence.*

1856 (209) 55: 587–91, *Return of the Quantities of Sugar Imported into the United Kingdom from 1800 to 1855 Inclusive.*

1856 (2055) 55:271–306, *Statistical Abstract for the United Kingdom in Each of the Last Fifteen Years.*

1857–58 (2422) 54: *Annual Statement of the Trade and Navigation of the United Kingdom in 1857.*

1860 (168) 42: *Tabular Statement of the Number of Seamen ... also the Number of Ships ... and the Amount of Money Voted ... for the Service ... from 1756 ... to the Present Time.*

1863 (3218) 65: *Annual Statement of the Trade and Navigation of the United Kingdom for 1862.*

1863 (272) 67: *Quantities of Sugar Imported ... 1844 to 1862.*

1867–68 (167) 65: *Number of HM Ships ... on the Different Stations on 1st March of Each Year from 1847 to 1867. ...*

1876 (c1570–11) 72: *Navigation and Shipping, Part III, Comparative Tables for the Years 1870 to 1875.*

1878–79 (321) 13: *Report from the Select Committee on the Sugar Industries.*

## United States

*American State Papers,* 2nd ser, vols. 3, 5.
*The Federal Cases,* 30 vols. (St. Paul, Minn. 1894–97), case nos. 8,985; 9,194; 10,575; 11,284; 14,477; 14,656; 14,755; 14,869; 14,918; 15,352; 15,447; 15,449; 15,597; 15,858; 15,914; 16,320; 16,668; 17,139.

## U.S. Congress

Senate Executive Documents: 28–1, 217; 28–2, 150; 30–1, 28; 31–2, 6; 47; 33–1, 386; 34–1, 99; 35–1, 49; 37–2, 40; 37–2, 53; 43–1, 23.
House Report: 27–3, 283.
House Miscellaneous Document: 33–1, 14.
House Documents: 24–1, 146; 27–3, 283; 28–2, 148; 30–1, 28.
House Executive Documents: 15–2, 107; 20–1, 262; 26–2, 115; 27–1, 34; 28–1, 148; 30–2, 61; 31–1, 73; 35–2, 104; 36–2, 7.

# Index

**Awarded Honorable Mention for the 1988 John Ben Snow Foundation Prize in History and the Social Sciences**

Praise for
*Economic Growth and the Ending
of the Atlantic Slave Trade*

"A work of prodigious and meticulous scholarship, Eltis's book will be studied and debated well into the next century . . . . Eltis's provocative arguments will require historians to reconsider the entire Anglo-American antislavery movement as well as the place of coerced labor in an emerging industrial and free market Atlantic world."

David Brion Davis, *The New York Review of Books*

"Eltis has produced a landmark study in the history of Atlantic slave trade. He combines a mastery of the sources with a critical and encyclopedic grasp of the extensive historiography on the subject."

Seymour Drescher, *University of Pittsburgh*

"For light on slavery and the slave-trade—the latest, strongest light—it is necessary to turn to the formidable treatise by David Eltis."

*Times Literary Supplement*

"A major book and an important contribution to the literature on slavery. It will become the standard work on the impact of slave-trade abolition in the Americas, [and] the operation of the trade during the abolition era . . . . There is much that is new and exciting." *Albion*

In this revisionist study of the consequences of the abolition of the Atlantic slave trade, economic historian David Eltis contends that the move did not bolster the Atlantic economy; rather, it vastly hindered economic expansion, just as the earlier great reliance on slave labor had played a role in the development of that economy.

David Eltis is Associate Professor at Queen's College, Kingston, Canada.

9 780195 045635

ISBN 0-19-50456